SELF CATERING ACCOMMODATION

ii Welcome to Scotland

iii-iv Using this Book

v-xiii Signs you need to Know

xiv Français

xv Deutsch

xvi-xvii Travellers' Tips

xix-xxiv Maps

2–40 A South of Scotland

41–60 B Edinburgh and Lothians

61–70 C Greater Glasgow and Clyde Valley

71–126 D West Highlands and Islands, Loch Lomond, Stirling and Trossachs

127–174 E Perthshire, Angus and Dundee and the Kingdom of Fife

175–205 F Grampian Highlands, Aberdeen and the North East Coast

206–302 G The Highlands and Skye

303–316 H Outer Islands

317 Hostel Accommodation

320 Accommodation providing facilities for visitors with disabilities

324 **Index–Alphabetical list of locations**

330 Display Advertisements

331 Books to help you

332 Publication Order Form

SCOTLAND IS SPLIT INTO EIGHT TOURIST AREAS. YOU WILL FIND ACCOMMODATION LISTED ALPHABETICALLY BY LOCATION WITHIN EACH OF THESE AREAS. THERE IS AN INDEX AT THE BACK OF THIS BOOK WHICH MAY ALSO HELP YOU.

Welcome
to Scotland

For flexibility and independence there's nothing quite like a self catering holiday. And in Scotland, self catering comes in all shapes and sizes.

There are cottage retreats, university residences, pine lodges, caravan holiday homes, flats and houses, luxurious mansion suites; some in cities, some in secluded countryside, some in chalet parks where it's easy – and safe – for the children to wander and make new friends.

In fact, self catering is ideal for families. There's no timetable to follow – mealtimes can come and go, and you'll eat when you want to. You'll enjoy a lie-in one day, set off for the hills at dawn the next – it's your holiday!

And while Scotland offers a host of things to do – hillwalking, historic houses, castles, museums, fishing and golf, to name but a few! - when you're self catering, just a trip to the local shops is an outing. Buying fish fresh from the pier, trying different breads and cakes from the bakery, sampling Scottish cheeses, prime meats and soft fruits – it all makes a treat to enjoy in the comfort of your "own" holiday home!

Enjoy your holiday the way you want to – try self catering in Scotland.

Using this book

Where to Stay...?

Over 1100 answers to the age-old question!

Revised annually, this is the most comprehensive guide to self catering properties in Scotland.

Every property in the guide has been graded and classified by Scottish Tourist Board inspectors. See page vi for details of this reliable quality assessment scheme.

How to find accommodation

This book split into eight areas of Scotland:

ACCOMMODATION

2-40	A	South of Scotland
41-60	B	Edinburgh and Lothians
61-70	C	Greater Glasgow and Clyde Valley
71-126	D	West Highlands and Islands, Loch Lomond, Stirling and Trossachs
127-174	E	Perthshire, Angus and Dundee and the Kingdom of Fife
175-205	F	Grampian Highlands, Aberdeen and the North East Coast
206-302	G	The Highlands and Skye
303-316	H	Outer Islands

The map on page xix shows these areas. Within each area section you will find accommodation listed alphabetically by location.

Alternatively there is an **index** at the back of this book listing alphabetically all accommodation locations in Scotland.

Using this book

Learn to use the symbols in each entry – they contain a mine of information! **There is a key to symbols on the back flap.** Naturally, it is always advisable to confirm with the establishment that a particular facility is still available. Prices in the guide are quoted per unit and represent the minimum and maximum rentals expected to be charged for one week's let in the low and high season. They include VAT at the appropriate rate and service charges where applicable. Unless otherwise stated, minimum let is one week.

The prices of accommodation, services and facilities are supplied to us by the operators and were, to the best of our knowledge, correct at the time of going to press. However, prices can change at any time during the lifetime of the publication, and you should check again when you book.

Bookings can be made direct to the establishment, through a travel agent, or through a local Tourist Information Centre.

Self catering in Scotland is very popular, and it is wise to book as early as possible, particularly for the high season months of July and August.

Remember, when you accept accommodation by telephone or in writing, you are entering a legally binding contract which must be fulfilled on both sides. Should you fail to take up accommodation, you may not only forfeit any deposit already paid, but may also have to compensate the establishment if the accommodation cannot be re-let.

Signs you need to know

Accommodation

Follow the stars and you won't be disappointed when you get to the inn.

The new Scottish Tourist Board Star System is a world-first. Quality is what determines our star awards, not a checklist of facilities. We've made your priorities our priorities.

Quality makes or breaks a visit. This is why it is the most important aspects of your stay; the cleanliness of the property, the condition of the furnishing, fitments, decor and equipment, the welcome touches and the overall ambience which earn Scottish Tourist Board Stars, not the size of the accommodation or the range of available facilities.

This easy to understand system tells you at a glance the quality standard of all types and sizes of accommodation from the smallest B&B and self catering cottage to the largest countryside and city centre hotels.

Look out for this distinctive sign of Quality Assured Accommodation

The standards you can expect.

★★★★★ **Exceptional, world-class**
★★★★ **Excellent**
★★★ **Very Good**
★★ **Good**
★ **Fair and Acceptable**

A trained Scottish Tourist Board inspector grades each property every year to give you the reassurance that you can choose accommodation of the quality standard you want.

To help you further in your choice the Scottish Tourist Board System also tells you the type of accommodation and the range of facilities and services available.

Please turn over for details.

For further information call into any Tourist Information Centre, or contact the Scottish Tourist Board.

More details available from:
Quality Assurance Department
Scottish Tourist Board
Thistle House
Beechwood Park North
INVERNESS
IV2 3ED

Tel: 01463 716996
Fax: 01463 717244

Signs you need to know

Accommodation

Accommodation Types

Self Catering

A house, cottage, apartment, chalet or similar accommodation which is let normally on a weekly basis to individuals where facilities are provided to cater for yourselves.

Serviced Apartments

Serviced apartments are essentially self catering apartments where services such as a cleaning service is available and meals and drinks may be available. Meals and drinks would normally be provided to each apartment or in a restaurant and/or bar which is on site.

Guest House

A Guest House is usually a commercial business and will normally have a minimum of 4 letting bedrooms, of which some will have ensuite or private facilities. Breakfast will be available and evening meals may be provided.

B&B

Accommodation offering bed and breakfast, usually in a private house. B&B's will normally accommodate no more than 6 guests, and may or may not serve an evening meal.

Hotel

A Hotel will normally have a minimum of 6 letting bedrooms, of which at least half must have ensuite or private bathroom facilities. A hotel will normally have a drinks licence (may be a restricted licence) and will serve breakfast and dinner.

International Resort Hotel

A Hotel achieving a 5 Star quality award which owns and offers a range of leisure and sporting facilities including an 18 hole golf course, swimming and leisure centre and country pursuits.

Lodge

Primarily purpose-built overnight accommodation, often situated close to a major road or in a city centre. Reception hours may be restricted and payment may be required on check in. There may be associated restaurant facilities. A car parking space will normally be provided for each bedroom.

Inn

Bed and breakfast accommodation provided within a traditional inn or pub environment. A restaurant and bar will be open to non-residents and will provide restaurant or bar food at lunchtime and in the evening.

Restaurant with Rooms

In a Restaurant with Rooms, the restaurant is the most significant part of the business. It is usually open to non-residents. Accommodation is available, and breakfast is usually provided.

Campus Accommodation

Campus accommodation is provided by colleges and universities for their students and is made available-with meals-for individuals, families or groups at certain times of the year. These typically include the main Summer holiday period as well as Easter and Christmas.

For Self Catering Accommodation Facility and Service Symbols

- TV in self catering unit
- Satellite/cable TV
- Payphone provided
- Ensuite bath and/or shower room(s) in self catering unit
- No TV
- Washing machine
- Tumble dryer
- Laundry facilities on site
- Bed linen provided
- Towels provided
- Microwave
- Telephone in unit
- Hi-fi
- Dishwasher
- Domestic help
- Freezer
- Video

Additional Serviced Apartments Symbols

- Restaurant
- Evening meal available
- Full alcohol drinks licence
- Restricted alcohol drinks licence
- Room service

Signs you need to know

for a quality destination

You want to be sure of the standard of accommodation you choose to stay in whichever type it may be, and you want to be sure you make the most of your time.

The Scottish Tourist Board inspects every type of accommodation every year, and a wide range of visitor attractions every second year to grade the quality standards provided for visitors.

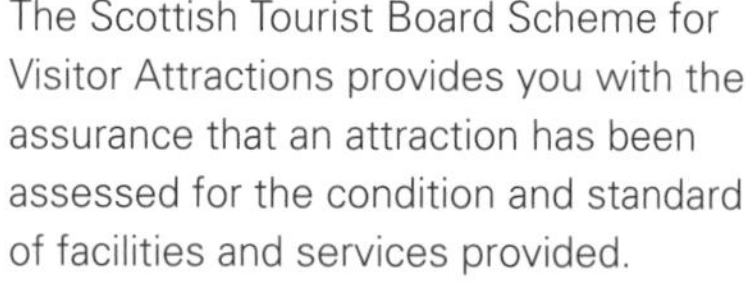
The Scottish Tourist Board Scheme for Visitor Attractions provides you with the assurance that an attraction has been assessed for the condition and standard of facilities and services provided.

Highly Commended	VERY GOOD quality standard
Commended	GOOD quality standard
Approved	ACCEPTABLE quality standard

Look out for the signs of Scottish Tourist Board Quality Assurance that tell you we have visited on your behalf to give you an indication of the quality standards to expect.

Signs you need to know

Holiday Park Grading

Holiday Park Grading

Every park in this guide has been visited by Scottish Tourist Board inspectors and graded for quality under the British Graded Holiday Parks Scheme.

All aspects of the park have been assessed for quality, and particular emphasis has been placed on the level of cleanliness of facilities.

Each entry in this guide, carries a square grid, which is easily decoded to give useful information about the park.

The top line – the "ticks" – shows the park's overall quality grading. Ticks are awarded on a rising scale of excellence.

✓ – Park facilities are maintained, decorated, furnished and equipped to an **acceptable** standard throughout.

✓✓ – Park facilities are maintained, decorated, furnished and equipped to a **fair** standard throughout.

✓✓✓ – Park provides a good level of comfort and service; and facilities are maintained, decorated, furnished and equipped to a good standard throughout.

✓✓✓✓ – Park provides a very good level of comfort and service; and facilities are maintained, decorated, furnished and equipped to a **very good** standard throughout.

✓✓✓✓✓ – Park provides an excellent level of comfort and service; and facilities are maintained, decorated, furnished and equipped to an **excellent** standard throughout.

Look out for the quality symbol

The remaining symbols in the grid show you if caravan holiday homes are available for hire, which types of caravans are accepted at the park and whether tents are accepted. The total number of pitches are shown which gives a good indication of the overall size of the park.

- Pitches for touring caravans
- Caravan holiday-homes on the park
- Caravan holiday-homes for hire
- 12 Total number of pitches
- Tents welcome
- Motor caravans welcome

Signs you need to know

Mobility Needs

Visitors with particular mobility needs must be able to be secure in the knowledge that suitable accommodation is available to match these requirements. Advance knowledge of accessible entrances, bedrooms and facilities is important to enable visitors to enjoy their stay.

Along with the quality awards which apply to all the establishments in this, and every Scottish Tourist Board guide, we operate a national accessibility scheme. By inspecting establishments to set criteria, we can identify and promote places that meet the requirements of visitors with mobility needs.

The three categories of accessibility – drawn up in close consultation with specialist organisations are:

Unassisted wheelchair access for residents

Assisted wheelchair access for residents

Access for residents with mobility difficulties

Look out for these symbols in establishments, in advertising and brochures. They assure you that entrances, ramps, passageways, doors, restaurant facilities, bathrooms and toilets, as well as kitchens in self catering properties, have been inspected with reference to the needs of wheelchair users, and those with mobility difficulties. Write or telephone for details of the standards in each category – address on page v.

For more information about travel, specialist organisations who can provide information and a list of all the Scottish accommodation which has had the access inspection write (or ask at a Tourist Information Centre) for the Scottish Tourist Board booklet "Accessibility Scotland".

Useful advice and information can also be obtained from:-

Disability Scotland
Information Department
Princes House
5 Shandwick Place
Edinburgh EH2 4RG
Tel: 0131 229 8632
Fax: 0131 229 5168

Holiday Care Service
2nd Floor
Imperial Buildings
Victoria Road
Horley, Surrey RH6 7PZ
Tel: 01293 774535
Fax: 01293 784647

Welcome Host

You can be sure of a warm welcome where you see the Welcome Host sign displayed.

Welcome Host is one of the most exciting and far reaching customer programmes ever developed for the tourism industry. The aim of Welcome Host is to raise the standards of hospitality offered to you during your stay. You will see the Welcome Host badge being worn by a wide variety of people in Scotland (people who have taken part in STB's Welcome Host training programme and have given a personal commitment to providing quality service during your stay). In many organisations you will also see the Welcome Host certificate, displaying an organisation's commitment to the provision of this quality service.

Welcome Hosts are everywhere, from Shetland to Coldstream and from Peterhead to Stornoway and all places in between.

Scotland is famous for its warm welcome and Welcome Hosts will ensure you receive first class service throughout your stay. Look out for the Welcome sign.

Signs you need to know

Taste of Scotland

From Scotland's natural larder comes a wealth of fine flavours.

The sea yields crab and lobster, mussels and oysters, haddock and herring to be eaten fresh or smoked. From the lochs and rivers come salmon and trout.

Scotch beef and lamb, venison and game are of prime quality, often adventurously combined with local vegetables or with wild fruits such as redcurrants and brambles. Raspberries and strawberries are cultivated to add their sweetness to trifles and shortcakes, and to the home-made jams that are an essential part of Scottish afternoon tea.

The Scots have a sweet tooth, and love all kinds of baking – rich, crisp shortbread, scones, fruit cakes and gingerbreads. Crumbly oatcakes make the ideal partner for Scottish cheeses, which continue to develop from their ancient farming origins into new – and very successful – styles.

And in over a hundred distilleries, barley, yeast and pure spring water come together miraculously to create malt whisky – the water of life.

Many Scottish hotels and restaurants pride themselves on the use they make of these superb natural ingredients – around 400 are members of the Taste of Scotland Scheme which encourages the highest culinary standards, use of Scottish produce and a warm welcome to visitors. Look for the Stockpot symbol at establishments, or write to Taste of Scotland for a copy of their guide.

In Shops		£7.99
By Post:	UK	£8.50
	Europe	£9.50
	US	£11.00

Taste of Scotland Scheme
33 Melville Street
EDINBURGH
EH3 7JF
Tel: 0131 220 1900
Fax: 0131 220 6102
e-mail: enquiry@taste-of-scotland.com
www.taste-of-scotland.com

THE TASTE OF SCOTLAND

Signs you need to know

The Natural Cooking of Scotland

Scotland has some of the finest food products in the world.

Our seafood, beef, lamb, venison, vegetables and soft fruit are renowned for their high quality. These fine indigenous raw materials and a wide assortment of international food products are skilfully combined by cooks and chefs into the vast range of cuisine available in Scotland.

As you travel throughout the country you will find an excellent standard of cooking in all sorts of establishments from restaurants with imaginative menus to tea rooms with simple wholesome home-baking.

You will find some of these culinary gems by reading of their reputation in newspapers and magazines, from advice given by Tourist Information Centre staff, by looking for the Taste of Scotland logo, or by using your own instinct to discover them yourself.

The Scottish Tourist Board has recognised that it would be helpful to you, the visitor, to have some assurance of the standards of food available in every different type of eating establishment; and indeed to be able to find a consistent standard of food in every place you choose to eat.

We launched The Natural Cooking of Scotland as a long-term initiative to encourage eating places to follow the lead of those who are best in their field in proving a consistently high standard of catering.

We have harnessed the skills of chefs, the experience of restaurateurs and the expertise of catering trainers to introduce a series of cooking skills courses which will encourage the use of fresh, local produce, cooked in a simple and satisfying way. We are providing advice and guidance to eating places throughout Scotland on high quality catering and the skills involved in efficient food service and customer care. Many more initiatives are being planned to support this enhancement of Scottish cooking standards and a high dependency on the food available on our own doorsteps.

Whilst you will appreciate the food experiences you will find in eating your way around Scotland this year, the Natural Cooking of Scotland will ensure that the profile of fine Scottish cooking is even greater in future years.

Français

Où séjourner?

Plus de 1100 réponses à cette vieille question.

Ceci est le guide le plus complet des locations en Ecosse, revu chaque année.

Chaque location dans ce guide a fait l'objet d'une notation et d'un classement par les inspecteurs de l'Office de tourisme écossais. Voir page v pour plus de détails sur le nouveau système d'assurance de la qualité.

ASSURANCE QUALITE

Le nouveau système de notation par étoiles de l'Office de tourisme écossais est le premier du monde à indiquer la qualité de l'hébergement en utilisant 1 à 5 étoiles. Plus les étoiles sont nombreuses, plus le niveau de qualité est élevé. Ce système aisément compréhensible vous indique d'un seul coup d'œil le niveau de qualité des modes d'hébergement de tous types et de toutes tailles, du plus petit des B&B ou cottages à louer aux plus grands hôtels ruraux ou de centre-ville.

***** Exceptionnel, première qualité
**** Excellent
*** Très bon
** Bon
* Assez bon et acceptable

Un inspecteur de l'Office de tourisme formé à cet effet note annuellement chaque propriété pour vous offrir la garantie de pouvoir choisir la formule d'hébergement du niveau de qualité que vous souhaitez. Une simple description comme "B&B", "auberge", "location", ou "restaurant avec chambres", accompagne la notation par étoiles et une série de symboles faciles à comprendre vous indique les aménagements et services disponibles.

Pour de plus amples informations sur les formules d'hébergement, contactez le bureau de la British Tourist Authority le plus proche de chez vous et demandez votre liste gratuite des formules d'hébergement de qualité assurée.

Vous pouvez aussi obtenir de plus amples détails sur le système de notation par étoiles auprès de la British Tourist Authority ou dans les Tourist Information Centres.

Pour de plus amples informations contacter:

Central Information Department
Scottish Tourist Board
23 Ravelston Terrace
Edinburgh
EH4 3EU

Scottish Tourist Board
19 Cockspur Street
London
SW1Y 5BL

Britain Visitor Centre
1-3 Regent Street
London
SW1

Deutsch

Wo kann man unterkommen?

Mehr als 1100 Antworten auf die alte Frage.

Dieser Leitfaden wird jedes Jahr aktualisiert und ist das ausführlichste Verzeichnis von Unterkünften für Selbstversorger in Schottland.

Jede Unterkunft im Verzeichnis wurde von den Inspektoren des Scottish Tourist Board inspiziert und eingestuft. Einzelheiten zum neuen Qualitätssicherungssystem finden Sie auf Seite v.

QUALITÄTSBEWERTUNG

Das neue Bewertungssystem des Scottish Tourist Board mit einem oder mehreren Sternen macht als erstes Qualitätsbewertungssystem der Welt Angaben über die Qualität der Unterkunft mit einem bis fünf Sternen. Dieses System ist leicht zu verstehen und teilt Ihnen auf einen Blick mit, mit welchem Standard Sie bei einer Unterkunft in allen erwähnten Kategorien rechnen können, angefangen vom kleinsten B&B und Cottage für Selbstversorger bis hin zum größten Landhotel oder Hotel im Zentrum einer Großstadt.

*****	Hervorragend, Weltklasse
****	Ausgezeichnet
***	Sehr gut
**	Gut
*	Angemessen, akzeptabel

Jedes Jahr reisen die eigens ausgebildeten Prüfer des Scottish Tourist Board durch Schottland und überprüfen die Qualität aller Unterkünfte, damit Sie sicher sein können, daß Sie den gewünschten Standard antreffen. Zur Angabe über die Kategorie, z.B. B&B, Gasthaus, Unterkunft für Selbstversorger oder Restaurant mit Gastzimmern kommen ein oder mehrere Sterne, die Angaben zur Qualität machen, sowie eine Reihe von leicht verständlichen Symbolen, die Ihnen Informationen über die vorhandenen Einrichtungen und erhältlichen Leistungen geben.

Weitere Informationen über Unterkunftsmöglichkeiten erhalten Sie von Ihrem nächstgelegenen Büro der British Tourist Authority – verlangen Sie auch die Gratisbroschüre über nach Qualität bewertete Unterkunftsmöglichkeiten. Nähere Einzelheiten zu unserem neuen Sternsystem sind ebenfalls von der British Tourist Authority sowie bei den Tourist Information Centres erhältlich.

Weitere Informationen von:

Central Information Department
Scottish Tourist Board
23 Ravelston Terrace
Edinburgh
EH4 3EU

Scottish Tourist Board
19 Cockspur Street
London
SW1Y 5BL

Britain Visitor Centre
1-3 Regent Street
London
SW1

Travellers' tips

Getting around

Scotland is a small country and travel is easy. There are direct air links with UK cities, with Europe and North America. There is also an internal air network bringing the islands of the North and West within easy reach.

Scotland's rail network not only includes excellent cross-border InterCity services but also a good internal network. All major towns are linked by rail and there are also links to the western seaboard at Mallaig and Kyle of Lochalsh (for ferry connections to Skye and the Western Isles) and to Inverness, Thurso and Wick for ferries to Orkney and Shetland.

All the usual discount cards are valid but there are also ScotRail Rovers (multi journey tickets allowing you to save on rail fares) and the Freedom of Scotland Travelpass, a combined rail and ferry pass allowing unlimited travel on ferry services to the islands and all of the rail network. In addition Travelpass also offers discounts on bus services and some air services.

InterCity services are available from all major centres, for example: Birmingham, Carlisle, Crewe, Manchester, Newcastle, Penzance, Peterborough, Preston, Plymouth, York and many others.

There are frequent InterCity departures from Kings Cross and Euston stations to Edinburgh and Glasgow. The journey time from Kings Cross to Edinburgh is around 4 hours and from Euston to Glasgow around 5 hours.

Coach connections include express services to Scotland from all over the UK; local bus companies in Scotland offer explorer tickets and discount cards. Postbuses (normally minibuses) take passengers on over 130 rural routes throughout Scotland.

Ferries to and around the islands are regular and reliable, most ferries carry vehicles, although some travelling to smaller islands convey only passengers.

Contact the Information Department, Scottish Tourist Board, PO Box 705, Edinburgh EH4 3EU, or any Tourist Information Centre, for details of travel and transport.

Many visitors choose to see Scotland by road – distances are short and driving on the quiet roads of the Highlands is a new and different experience. In remoter areas, some roads are still single track, and passing places must be used. When vehicles approach from different directions, the car nearest to a passing place must stop in or opposite it. Please do not use passing places to park in!

Speed limits on Scottish roads: Dual carriageways 70mph/112kph; single carriageways 60mph/96kph; built-up areas 30mph/48kph.

The driver and front-seat passenger in a car must wear seatbelts; rear seatbelts, if fitted, must be used. Small children and babies must at all times be restrained in a child seat or carrier.

Opening times

Public holidays: Christmas and New Year's Day are holidays in Scotland, taken by almost everyone. Scottish banks, and many offices, will close in 1999 on 1 January, 2 and 5 April, 3 and 31 May, 30 August, 27 and 28 December. Scottish towns also take Spring and Autumn holidays which may vary from place to place, but are usually on a Monday.

Banking hours: In general, banks open Monday to Friday, 0930 to 1600, with some closing later on a Thursday. Banks in cities, particularly in or near the main shopping centres, may be open at weekends. Cash machines in hundreds of branches allow you to withdraw cash outside banking hours, using the appropriate cards.

Pubs and restaurants: Pubs and restaurants are allowed to serve alcoholic drinks between 1100 hours and 2300 hours Monday through to Saturday; Sundays 1230 hours until 1430 hours then again from 1830 hours until 2300 hours.

Residents in hotels may have drinks served at any time, subject to the properietors discretion.

Extended licensing hours are subject to local council applications.

Telephone codes

If you are calling from abroad, first dial your own country's international access code (usually 00, but do please check). Next, dial the UK code, 44, then the area code except for the first 0, then the remainder of the number as normal.

Quarantine regulations

If you are coming to Scotland from overseas, please do not attempt to bring your pet on holiday with you. British quarantine regulations are stringently enforced, and anyone attempting to contravene them will incur severe penalties as well as the loss of the animal.

Maps

Scotlands Tourist areas

ACCOMMODATION

2–40	**A**	South of Scotland
41–60	**B**	Edinburgh and Lothians
61–70	**C**	Greater Glasgow and Clyde Valley
71–126	**D**	West Highlands and Islands, Loch Lomond, Stirling and Trossachs
127–174	**E**	Perthshire, Angus and Dundee and the Kingdom of Fife
175–205	**F**	Grampian Highlands, Aberdeen and the North East Coast
206–302	**G**	The Highlands and Skye
303–316	**H**	Outer Islands

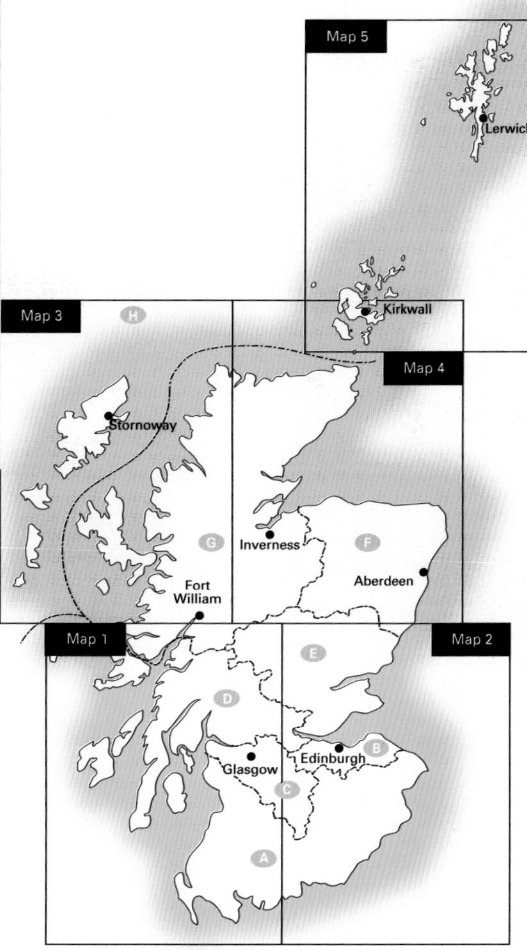

MAP 1

Car ferries and terminals:
Brodick
Rothesay
Scale 1:1 300 000
0 10 20 miles
© Bartholomew Ltd 1998
These maps are for "Self Catering" locations only. For route planning and touring please use a current road atlas.
ATLANTIC OCEAN
MULL
ISLAY
JURA
ARRAN
BUTE
KINTYRE
COLONSAY
TIREE
COLL
IONA
Tobermory
Oban
Campbeltown
Stranraer
Larne
BELFAST
Ayr
Troon
Largs
Dunoon
Rothesay
Brodick
Inveraray
Lochgilphead
Tarbert
Girvan
Newton Stewart
Port Ellen
Bowmore
Summer only
To Douglas, Isle of Man
To Liverpool

MAP 2

A B C D E F G H

1 2 3 4 5 6 7 8 9 10 11 12

Pitlochry
Bridge of Cally
Kirriemuir
Burnside
Guthrie
Forfar
Aberfeldy
Alyth
Kenmore
Blairgowrie
Glamis
Meigle
Arbroath
Dunkeld
Coupar Angus
Carnoustie
Bankfoot
Dundee
E
Tayport
Methven
Scone
Newport-on-Tay
Firth of Tay
Inchyra
Wormit
Perth
Leuchars
Crieff
Forgandenny
Bridge of Earn
St Andrews
Dunning
Auchtermuchty
Cupar
Craigrothie
Kingsbarns
Auchterarder
Dunshalt
Glenfarg
Crail
Anstruther
Muckhart
Pittenweem
Kinross
Dunblane
St Monans
Elie
Bridge of Allan
Firth of Forth
Kelty
Cowdenbeath
Stirling
North Berwick
Aberdour
Aberlady
Dunbar
North Queensferry
Falkirk
Linlithgow
South Queensferry
Innerwick
Maddiston
Haddington
Cockburnspath
EDINBURGH
B
Coldingham
Dalkeith
Humbie
Abbey St Bathans
West Calder
Mordington
Longformacus
Foulden
Berwick-upon-Tweed
Paxton
Hamilton
West Linton
Westruther
Romanno Bridge
Swinton
Dolphinton
Lanark
Peebles
Coldstream
New Lanark
Galashiels
Carmichael
Melrose
Clovenfords
Kelso
Wiston
Bowden
Selkirk
Yetholm
Ettrick Valley
Minto
Jedburgh
Ashkirk
Hawick
Moffat
A
Moniaive
Ae
Lochmaben
Lockerbie
Dumfries
Crocketford
Gretna
Newcastle upon Tyne
Sunderland
Dalbeattie
Sandyhills
Carlisle
Kippford
Rockcliffe
Southerness
Kirkcudbright
Solway Firth
Middlesbrough

NORTH SEA

MAP 3

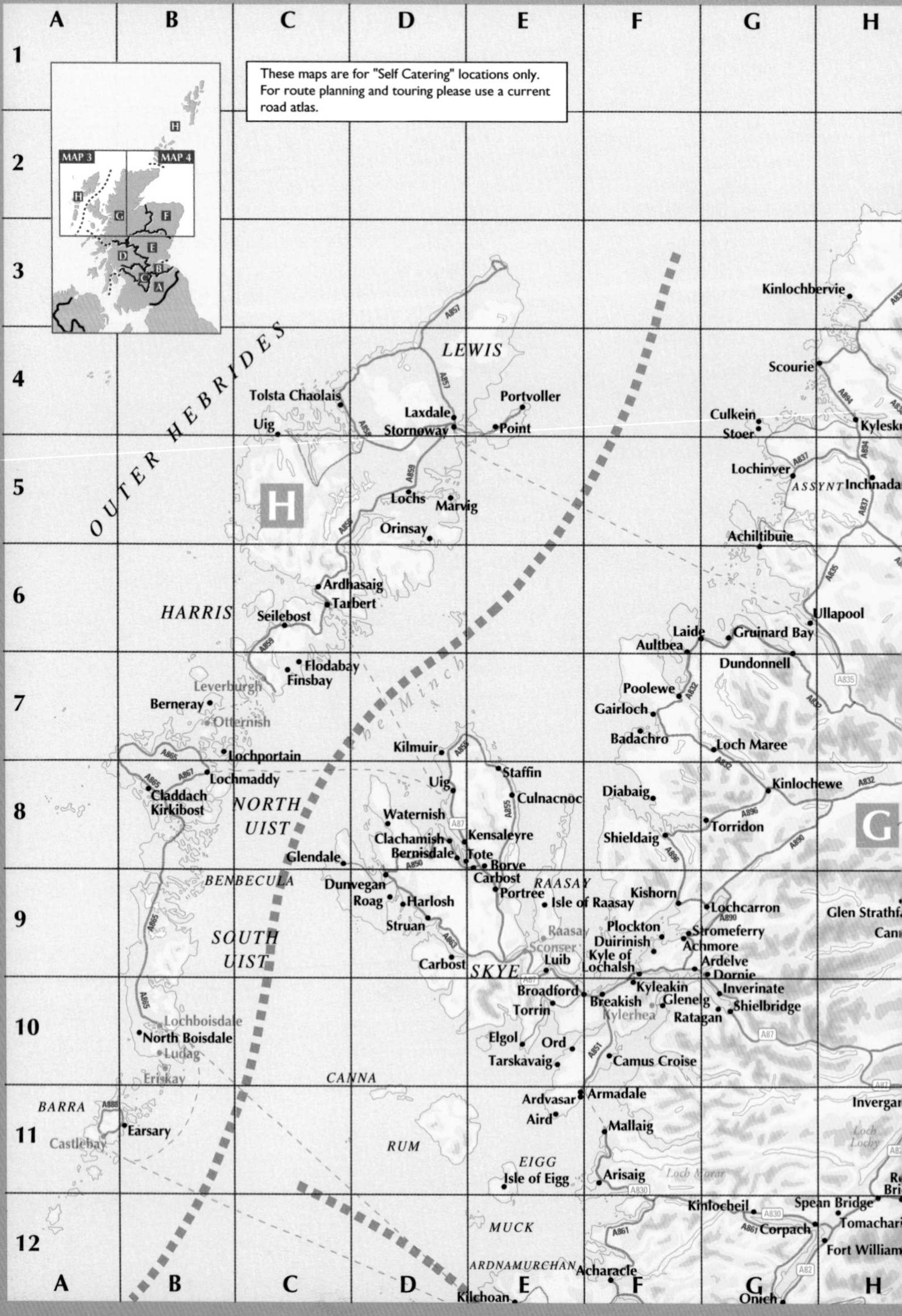

A B C D E F G H
1 2 3 4 5 6 7 8 9 10 11 12
These maps are for "Self Catering" locations only. For route planning and touring please use a current road atlas.
MAP 3
MAP 4
H G F E D C B A
OUTER HEBRIDES
LEWIS
Tolsta Chaolais
Uig
Laxdale
Stornoway
Portvoller
Point
Lochs
Marvig
Orinsay
H
Ardhasaig
Tarbert
HARRIS
Seilebost
Flodabay
Finsbay
Leverburgh
Berneray
Otternish
Lochportain
Lochmaddy
Claddach Kirkibost
NORTH UIST
BENBECULA
SOUTH UIST
Lochboisdale
North Boisdale
Ludag
Eriskay
BARRA
Earsary
Castlebay
CANNA
RUM
EIGG
Isle of Eigg
MUCK
ARDNAMURCHAN
Kilchoan
Acharacle
The Minch
Kilmuir
Uig
Staffin
Culnacnoc
Waternish
Clachamish
Kensaleyre
Bernisdale
Tote
Borve
Glendale
Dunvegan
Carbost
Portree
Roag
Harlosh
Struan
Carbost
SKYE
RAASAY
Isle of Raasay
Raasay
Sconser
Luib
Broadford
Torrin
Elgol
Ord
Tarskavaig
Ardvasar
Armadale
Aird
Mallaig
Arisaig
Loch Morar
Kinlocheil
Corpach
Spean Bridge
Tomachar
Fort William
Onich
Kishorn
Plockton
Duirinish
Kyle of Lochalsh
Kyleakin
Breakish
Kylerhea
Glenelg
Ratagan
Camus Croise
Lochcarron
Stromeferry
Achmore
Ardelve
Dornie
Inverinate
Shielbridge
Diabaig
Shieldaig
Torridon
Kinlochewe
G
Loch Maree
Badachro
Gairloch
Poolewe
Aultbea
Laide
Gruinard Bay
Dundonnell
Ullapool
Achiltibuie
Lochinver
ASSYNT
Inchnada
Culkein
Stoer
Kylesku
Scourie
Kinlochbervie
Glen Strathf
Invergar
Loch Lochy
A857 A858 A859 A865 A867 A888 A87 A850 A855 A863 A851 A830 A861 A82 A832 A835 A837 A894 A890 A896

MAP 4

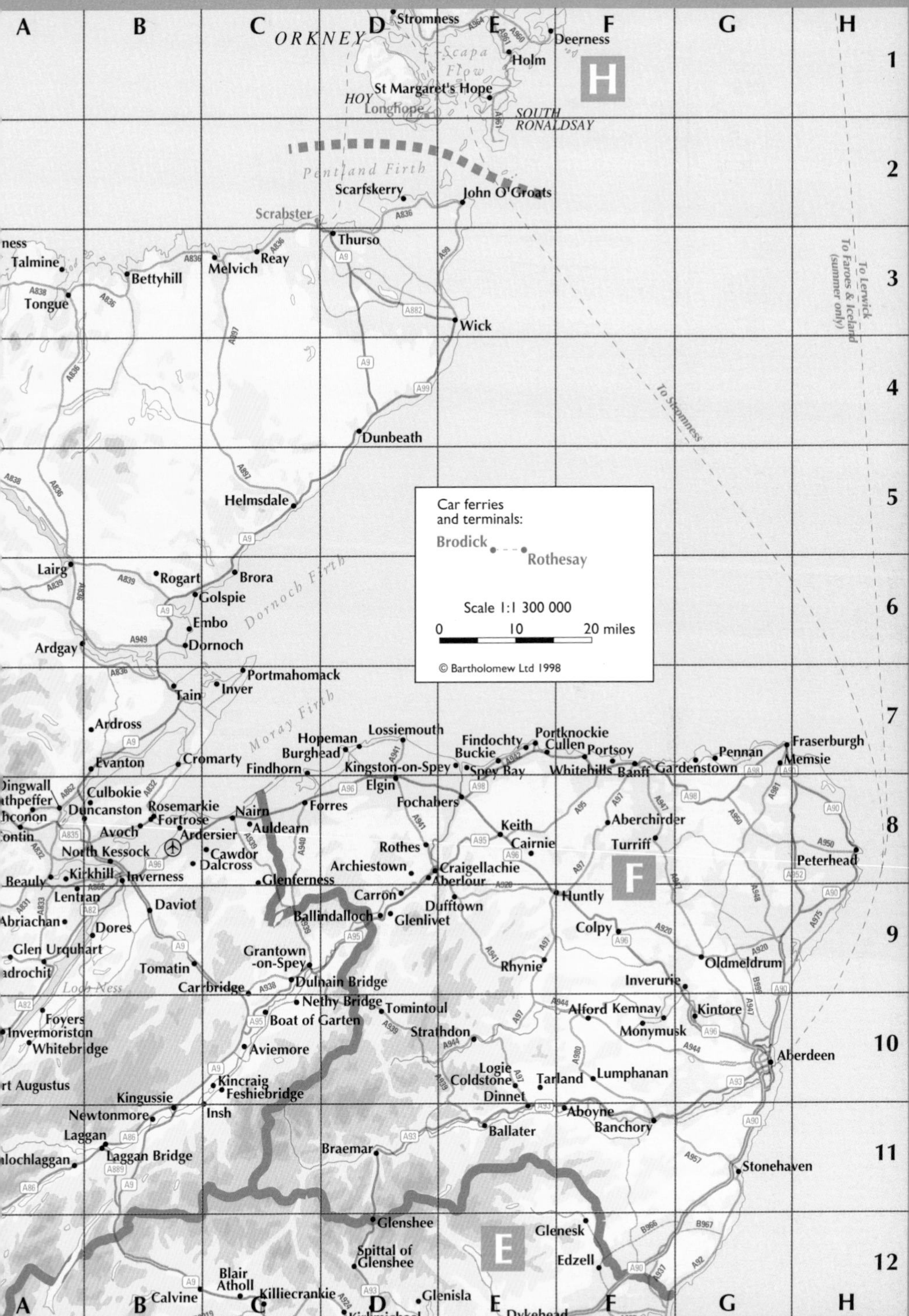

A
B
C
D
E
F
G
H
1
2
3
4
5
6
7
8
9
10
11
12
ORKNEY
Stromness
Deerness
Holm
Scapa Flow
H
HOY
St Margaret's Hope
Longhope
SOUTH RONALDSAY
Pentland Firth
Scarfskerry
John O'Groats
Scrabster
Thurso
Talmine
Bettyhill
Melvich
Reay
Tongue
Wick
To Lerwick
To Faroes & Iceland (summer only)
To Stromness
Dunbeath
Helmsdale
Car ferries and terminals:
Brodick
Rothesay
Scale 1:1 300 000
0
10
20 miles
© Bartholomew Ltd 1998
Lairg
Rogart
Brora
Golspie
Dornoch Firth
Embo
Dornoch
Ardgay
Portmahomack
Inver
Tain
Moray Firth
Ardross
Evanton
Cromarty
Hopeman
Lossiemouth
Burghead
Findhorn
Kingston-on-Spey
Findochty
Buckie
Portknockie
Cullen
Portsoy
Spey Bay
Whitehills
Banff
Gardenstown
Pennan
Fraserburgh
Memsie
Dingwall
Culbokie
Duncanston
Rosemarkie
Fortrose
Avoch
Ardersier
Nairn
Auldearn
Forres
Elgin
Fochabers
Keith
Cairnie
Aberchirder
Turriff
Peterhead
North Kessock
Cawdor
Dalcross
Kirkhill
Inverness
Beauly
Lentran
Glenferness
Archiestown
Rothes
Craigellachie
Aberlour
Carron
Huntly
F
Daviot
Abriachan
Dores
Ballindalloch
Glenlivet
Dufftown
Colpy
Glen Urquhart
Tomatin
Grantown-on-Spey
Dulnain Bridge
Rhynie
Oldmeldrum
Inverurie
Carrbridge
Loch Ness
Nethy Bridge
Tomintoul
Alford
Kemnay
Kintore
Foyers
Invermoriston
Whitebridge
Boat of Garten
Strathdon
Monymusk
Aviemore
Aberdeen
Logie Coldstone
Tarland
Lumphanan
Kincraig
Feshiebridge
Kingussie
Dinnet
Newtonmore
Insh
Aboyne
Banchory
Ballater
Laggan
Laggan Bridge
Braemar
Stonehaven
Glenshee
Glenesk
Spittal of Glenshee
E
Edzell
Blair Atholl
Calvine
Killiecrankie
Glenisla
Kirkmichael
Dykehead

MAP 5

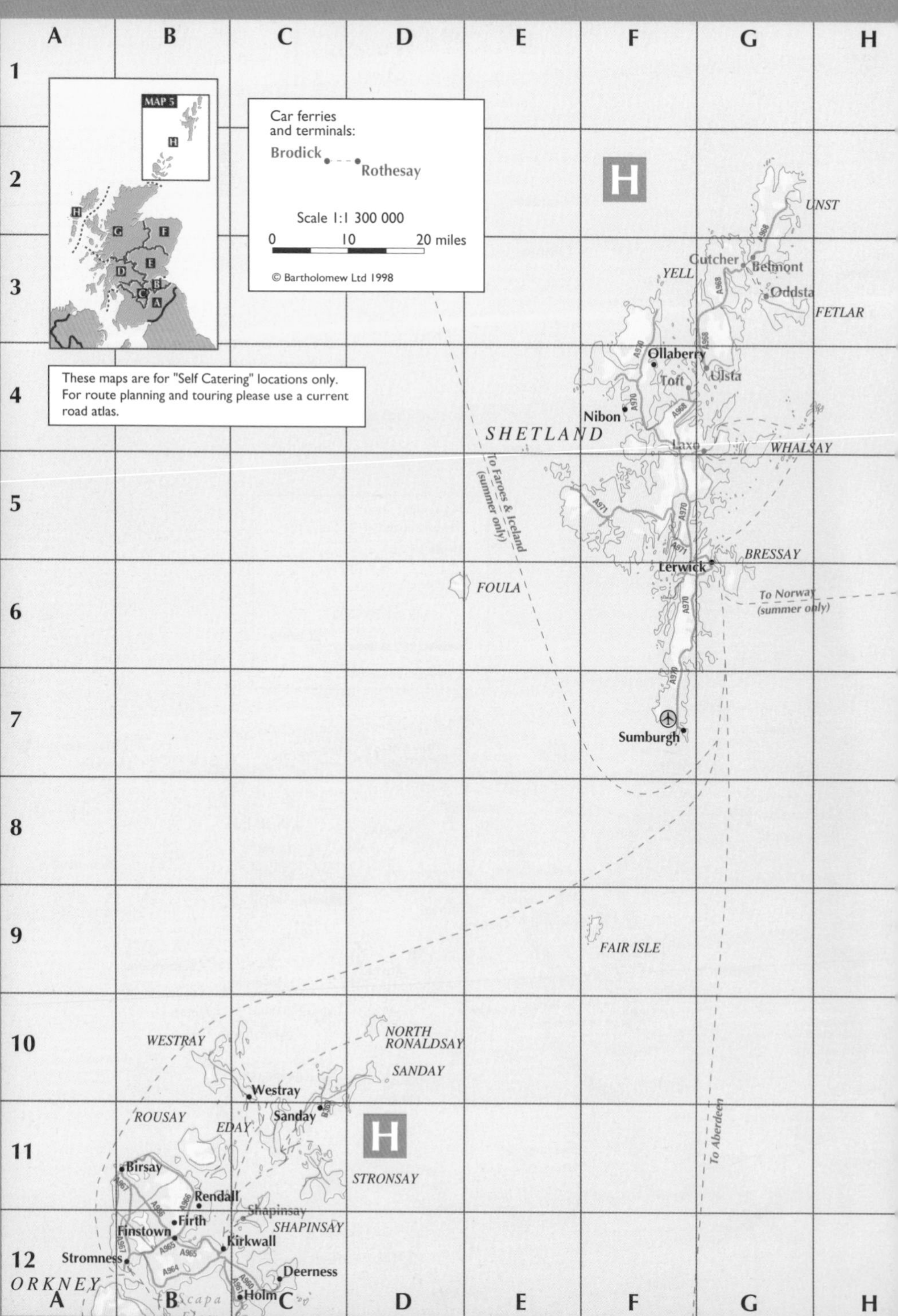

A B C D E F G H
1 2 3 4 5 6 7 8 9 10 11 12
MAP 5
Car ferries and terminals:
Brodick
Rothesay
Scale 1:1 300 000
0 10 20 miles
© Bartholomew Ltd 1998
These maps are for "Self Catering" locations only. For route planning and touring please use a current road atlas.
H
UNST
Gutcher
Belmont
Oddsta
YELL
FETLAR
Ollaberry
Toft
Ulsta
Nibon
SHETLAND
Laxo
WHALSAY
To Faroes & Iceland (summer only)
BRESSAY
Lerwick
FOULA
To Norway (summer only)
Sumburgh
FAIR ISLE
WESTRAY
NORTH RONALDSAY
SANDAY
Westray
Sanday
ROUSAY
EDAY
H
STRONSAY
To Aberdeen
Birsay
Rendall
Shapinsay
Firth
SHAPINSAY
Finstown
Kirkwall
Stromness
Deerness
ORKNEY
Holm

Where to stay
Self Catering '99

Welcome to...

The South of Scotland

The South of Scotland is the first part of Scotland you encounter by road or rail after you cross the Border. Right away, it has all the subtle characteristics which make Scotland different from the rest of the UK, from different names for beer to Scottish banknotes!

First impressions can be of a surprisingly wild area, though the river valleys of the Scottish Borders with their woodlands and farms soon give a softer appearance. However, if it is ruggedness you want, then head west for Galloway, where, at places like the Galloway Forest Park there is quintessentially 'Scottish' scenery of lochs and steep-sided hills. Or head for the island of Arran, often called Scotland in miniature because it too has these characteristics of rocky hillslopes as well as a softer and gentler side.

South of Scotland towns are very distinctive. The typical Galloway townscape of wide streets and pastel painted frontages is highly attractive (Kirkcudbright, for example, has a long tradition of attracting artists).

In the Scottish Borders, places like Melrose or Kelso are full of personality and they also offer plenty to do: visiting abbeys or stately homes or museums will take up lots of time. Another distinct feature is the wealth of attractions in Ayrshire, along the Clyde coast. This makes a superb family holiday destination, with places like the Magnum Leisure Centre at Irvine, Loudoun Castle Park (featuring Scotland's largest carousel!) near Galston, Kelburn Country Park near Largs, Wonderwest World at Ayr and lots more places all great for children. Also consider the options of the ferry connections to the Cumbraes (excellent for cycling) or to Arran, with its wealth of walking, cycling and other outdoor pursuits.

The thriving town of Peebles on the River Tweed. Ancient royal burgh and site of a hunting lodge of the early Scottish Kings.

Other highlights and 'must sees' of the area include the Border abbeys, for example, Dryburgh in its beautifully secluded setting or Jedburgh, where a visitor centre tells the story of the part played by the great abbeys in Borders life. The abbeys are open to visitors all year. There is a great choice of stately homes and castles: for example, Brodick Castle on Arran (superb gardens, too), Culzean Castle near Ayr (magnificent country park) or Floors Castle (the largest inhabited house in Scotland) – though these are just the start of a long list.

Out of the ordinary visitor attractions include the Scottish Museum of Lead Mining at Wanlockhead, Mill on the Fleet at Gatehouse-of-Fleet and the Scottish Maritime Museum at Irvine. All these provide entertainment and an insight into other facets of Scottish life.

You can walk the Southern Upland Way from west to east, all 212 miles if time permits, go mountain biking in the forests, go angling in our rivers – there are activities galore here.

You can enjoy this area at any time of year – it is easy to reach and there is plenty going on from the Common Ridings in the Borders in summer, to the spectacular winter flights of wild geese at places like Caerlaverock National Nature Reserve near Dumfries. For town or country breaks this area is ideal at any time of year.

Events
South of Scotland

Dec 30-Jan 2

The Land, The Light, The Locals
Folk music sessions, afternoon and evenings, various venues in the Scottish Borders.
Tel: 01835 863668.

Mar 26-28

Gatehouse-of-Fleet Festival of Music, Arts and Crafts
Gatehouse-of-Fleet, Dumfriesshire.
Contact: George McCulloch.
Tel: 01557 814030.

May 28-June 6

Dumfries & Galloway Arts Festival
20th anniversary of this festival, celebrates the best in arts and entertainment, various venues.
Contact: Sheena Widdal.
Tel: 01387 260447.

June 7-13

Isle of Arran Folk Festival
Various venues around the Isle of Arran.
Contact: Nici McLellan.
Tel: 01770 302311.

July 24 – 31

International Celtic Watersports Festival
5th festival with participants from Scotland, Ireland, Wales, Cornwall, Isle of Man, Galicia and Austrias, includes various cultural activities.
Contact: Jim Wilson, Sail Scotland.
Tel: 01309 676737.

Aug 28 – Sep 12

Peebles Arts Festival
Festival covering performing and visual arts including music, exhibitions and outdoor events. Various venues in Peebles.
Contact: Peebles Tourist Information Centre.
Tel: 01721 720138.

Sep 10 – 12

Borders Festival of Jazz and Blues
Weekend of jazz entertainment around the border town of Hawick.
Contact: Tel: 01450 377278

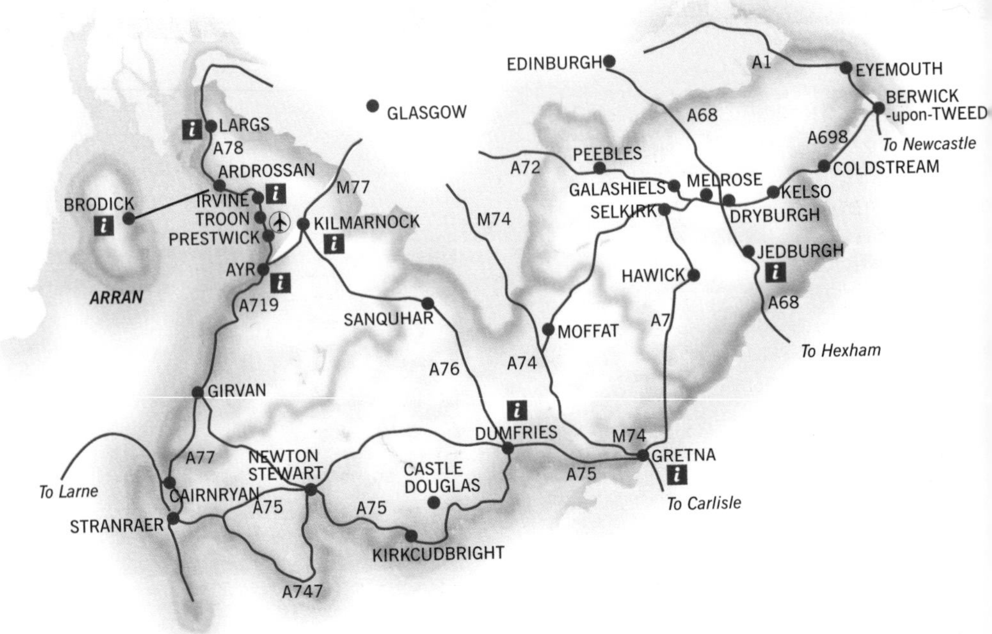

Area Tourist Board Addresses

1 Ayrshire and Arran Tourist Board
Burns House
Burns Statue Square
AYR
KA7 1UP
Tel: 01292 288688/ 262555
Fax: 01292 288686/ 269555
e.mail:
ayr@ayrshire-arran.com
website:
www.ayrshire-arran.com

2 Dumfries and Galloway Tourist Board
64 Whitesands
DUMFRIES
DG1 2RS
Tel: 01387 245550/ 253862
Fax: 01387 245551/ 245555
e.mail:
info@agtb.demon.co.uk
website:
www.galloway.co.uk

3 Scottish Borders Tourist Board
Tourist Information Centre
Murray's Green
JEDBURGH
TD8 6BE
Tel: 01835 863435/ 863688
Fax: 01835 864099
e.mail:
info@scot-borders.co.uk

Tourist Information Centres in Scotland

AYRSHIRE & ARRAN TOURIST BOARD

AYR ✉
Burns House
Burns Statue Square
Tel: (01292) 288688
Jan-Dec

BRODICK ♿ ✉
The Pier
Isle of Arran
KA27 8AU
Tel: (01770) 302140/302401
Jan-Dec

GIRVAN
Bridge Street
Tel: (01465) 714950
April-Oct

IRVINE
New Street
Tel: (01294) 313886
Jan-Dec

KILMARNOCK ♿ ✉
62 Bank Street
KA1 1ER
Tel: (01563) 539090
Jan-Dec

LARGS ✉
Promenade, KA30 8BG
Tel: (01475) 673765
Jan-Dec

MILLPORT ♿
28 Stuart Street
Isle of Cumbrae
Tel: (01475) 530753
Easter-Oct

TROON
Municipal Buildings
South Beach
Tel: (01292) 317696
Easter-Sept

DUMFRIES & GALLOWAY TOURIST BOARD

CASTLE DOUGLAS
Markethill Car Park
Tel: (01556) 502611
Easter-Oct

DUMFRIES ✉
Whitesands
DG1 4TH
Tel: (01387) 253862
Jan-Dec

GATEHOUSE OF FLEET
Car Park
Tel: (01557) 814212
Easter-Oct

GRETNA GREEN
Old Blacksmith's Shop
Tel: (01461) 337834
Easter-Oct

KIRKCUDBRIGHT ♿
Harbour Square
Tel: (01557) 330494
Easter-Oct

LANGHOLM
High Street
Tel: (01387) 380976
Easter-Sept

MOFFAT
Churchgate
Tel: (01683) 220620
Easter-Oct

NEWTON STEWART
Dashwood Square
Tel: (01671) 402431
Easter-Oct

SANQUHAR ♿
Tolbooth, High Street
Tel: (01659) 50185
Easter-early Oct

STRANRAER
Burns House
28 Harbour Street
Tel: (01776) 702595
Easter-Oct

SCOTTISH BORDERS TOURIST BOARD

COLDSTREAM ♿
High Street
Tel: (01890) 882607
April-Oct

EYEMOUTH ♿
Auld Kirk
Manse Road
Tel: (018907) 50678
April-Oct

GALASHIELS ♿
St Johns Street
Tel: (01896) 755551
April-Oct

HAWICK ♿
Drumlanrig's Tower
Tel: (01450) 372547
April-Oct

JEDBURGH ♿ ✉
Murray's Green
TD8 6BE
Tel: (01835) 863435/863688
Jan-Dec

KELSO
Town House
The Square
Tel: (01573) 223464
April-Oct

MELROSE ♿
Abbey House
Tel: (01896) 822555
April-Oct

PEEBLES ♿
High Street
Tel: (01721) 720138
Jan-Dec

SELKIRK ♿
Halliwell's House
Tel: (01750) 20054
April-Oct

 Accept written enquiries
♿ Disabled access

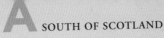

Abbey St Bathans, by Duns, Berwickshire

Map Ref: 2E5

★★★ SELF CATERING

Self contained wing of beautifully situated mansion house in secluded river valley. Lovely views of river and woods. Plenty of wildlife and walks.

1 wing of mansion house, 4 pub rms, 6 bedrms (grd flr avail), sleeps 9-13, £400.00-£1000.00, Jan-Dec, bus 5 mls

Mrs Charlotte Dobie
Weirburn House, Abbey St Bathans, Duns, Berwickshire
Tel: (Abbey St Bathans) 01361 840251 Fax: 01361 840248

Ae, Dumfriesshire

Map Ref: 2B9

★★ SELF CATERING

Renovated former shepherd's flat situated in a traditional square stone building on a pastural farm in a secluded valley beside the Forest of Ae. Ideal location for those who enjoy walking and peaceful countryside.

2 flats, 1 pub rm, 2 bedrms, sleeps 4-5, total sleeping capacity 9, £120.00-£230.00, Jan-Dec, bus 1 1/2 mls, rail 11 mls

D & G Stewart
Gubhill Farm, Ae, Dumfriesshire, DG1 1RL
Tel: (Dumfries) 01387 860648 Fax: 01387 860648

Alloway, Ayrshire

Map Ref: 1G7

★★★★ SELF CATERING

Former stable converted into a cosy modern cottage. Ideal for a couple. 2 minutes from Alloway with Burns Cottage. 20 minutes from Culzean Castle.

1 cottage, 1 pub rm, 1 bedrm (grd flr avail), sleeps 2-4, £200.00-£240.00, Apr-Oct

Mr Miller
Whiteleys Farm, Alloway, Ayr, KA7 4EG
Tel: (Alloway) 01292 443968 Fax: 01292 442876
Email: wbm@millerint.co.uk

Annbank, Ayrshire

Map Ref: 1G7

★★★★ SELF CATERING

Gadgirth Estate welcome you to its beautiful 28 acres of ground with a selection of converted stables and courtyard cottages, boasting many features including exposed beams and open fire places. This picturesque setting, only 10 minutes by car from Ayr has lovely picnic areas, wooded riverside walks and estate fishing.

6 log cabins, 6 cottages, 1-2 pub rms, 1-3 bedrms (grd flr avail), sleeps 4-6, total sleeping capacity 26, min let weekend, £120.00-£500.00, Jan-Dec, bus 1 ml, rail 5 mls, ferry 6 mls, airport 5 mls

Mr & Mrs I Hendry
Gadgirth Estate, Gadgirth Mains, by Ayr, Ayrshire, KA6 5AJ
Tel: (Ayr) 01292 520721 Fax: 01292 520721

Brodick, Isle of Arran

Map Ref: 1F7

★★ SELF CATERING

Two flats right on the sea front overlooking Brodick Bay and Goatfell. Close to ferry and local bus stop. Central for all attractions. Private off-street parking.

1 flat, 1 pub rm, 3 bedrms, sleeps 5, min let weekend, £150.00-£295.00, Jan-Dec, bus nearby, ferry 1/4 ml

Mrs S Currie
Castleview, Invercloy, Brodick, Isle of Arran, KA27 8AJ
Tel: (Brodick) 01770 302268/302315

Important: Prices stated are estimates and may be subject to amendments

Brodick, Isle of Arran

Map Ref: 1F7

SELF CATERING

This period mansion has been tastefully extended and refurbished to include all the facilities expected of a luxury hotel. Bedrooms are bright and well-appointed . Excellent leisure facilities include a 20 metre pool, sauna, steam room, gym, snooker, salon and aromatherapy. There is a choice of award-winning Garden Restaurant (AA 2 Rosettes) and Brambles Bistro serving Taste of Scotland dishes using fresh local produce. Close to Golf Course.

8 lodges, 1 pub rm, 2-3 bedrms (grd flr avail), sleeps 4-8, total sleeping capacity 40, £250.00-£595.00, Jan-Dec, bus 400 yds, ferry 1 ml

Auchrannie Country Club
Brodick, Isle of Arran, KA27 8BZ
Tel: (Brodick) 01770 302020/302234 (eve) Fax: 01770 302812

SELF CATERING

A variety of cottages within walking distance of Brodick town centre. Ideal for the golf course, Brodick Castle and the museum. Private parking.

1 house, 2 cottages, 1-2 pub rms, 1-4 bedrms (grd flr avail), sleeps 2-8, total sleeping capacity 16, £200.00-£700.00, Jan-Dec

Orwin Holiday Cottage's
Glen Croy Road, Brodick, Isle of Arran, KA27 8DW
Tel: 01770 302009 Fax: 01770 302868

SELF CATERING

A modern 3 bedroom bungalow and a converted stable with BBQ, situated in the grounds of Carrick Lodge with extensive and interesting garden. On elevated position with open views across the bay to Goatfell.

1 cottage, 1 bungalow, 1-2 pub rms, 2-3 bedrms (grd flr avail), sleeps 4-7, total sleeping capacity 11, min let 3 nights (low season), £200.00-£450.00, Jan-Dec, bus 300 yds, ferry 300 yds

Mairi M Thompson
Carrick Lodge, Brodick, Isle of Arran, KA27 8BH
Tel: (Brodick) 01770 302550 Fax: 01770 302550

Corrie, Isle of Arran

Map Ref: 1F6

SELF CATERING

Traditional semi-detached cottage on elevated position overlooking the Firth of Clyde. In a quiet conservation village just 100 yards from the shore. Secluded garden. Ideal for families.

1 cottage, 2 pub rms, 3 bedrms, sleeps 8, £220.00-£320.00, Jan-Dec, bus 500 yds, ferry 6 mls

Mr G Davidson
Prospect, Corrie, Isle of Arran, KA27 8JB
Tel: (Corrie) 01770 810213

VAT is shown at 17.5%: changes in this rate may affect prices.

Key to symbols is on back flap.

Corrie, Isle of Arran

Map Ref: 1F6

SELF CATERING

Traditional whitewashed cottage in small hamlet, set in the hills with superb views over both the sea and mountains, with lovely walks on the doorstep.

1 cottage, 1 pub rm, 2 bedrms, sleeps 4, £150.00-£325.00, Jan-Dec, bus 1/2 ml

Mrs E Harvey
Winterseeds, Haggs Lane, Cartmel, Grange-over-Sands, Cumbria, LA11 6HD
Tel: (Cartmel) 015395 36322 Fax: 015395 36322

SELF CATERING

Extensively refurbished red sandstone cottages, enclosed rose garden. All rooms have views over Firth of Clyde.

2 cottages, 1 pub rm, 3 bedrms (grd flr avail), sleeps 6, £175.00-£345.00, Jan-Dec, bus nearby, ferry 6 mls

Mr J Lees
Cir Mhor, Sannox, Isle of Arran, KA27 8JD
Tel: (Corrie) 01770 810248/810661 Fax: 01770 810248

SELF CATERING

Small cottage adjoining owner's house in elevated position with panoramic views over Firth of Clyde. Private garden available. Off road parking. Non smoking house.

1 cottage, sleeps 2, £180.00-£280.00, Jan-Dec, bus nearby, ferry 5 mls

Mr & Mrs Thorburn
Tigh-na-Achaidh, Corrie, Isle of Arran
Tel: (Corrie) 01770 810208 Fax: 01770 810208

Lamlash, Isle of Arran

Map Ref: 1F7

SELF CATERING

Converted farm steading set in 2 1/2 acres with easy access to shore. Owner resident on site. All weather tennis court and kids play area.

4 houses, 2 flats, 1 pub rm, 2 bedrms (grd flr avail), sleeps 4-5, total sleeping capacity 28, £90.00-£300.00, Jan-Dec, bus 3/4 ml, ferry 4 mls

Mr & Mrs Muirhead
Oakbank Farm, Lamlash, Isle of Arran, KA27 8LH
Tel: (Lamlash) 01770 600404

SELF CATERING

Semi-detached cottage with its own patio. Situated on the south side of the village with views to the hills. Close to all village amenities such as tennis, bowling green and shops. The Lamlash Golf Club is one mile away. B&B also available.

1 cottage, 2 pub rms, 2 bedrms, sleeps 4, £200.00-£300.00, Feb-Nov, bus nearby, rail 18 mls, ferry 4 mls, airport 39 mls

Miss E Sloan
Westfield, Lamlash, Isle of Arran, KA27 8NN
Tel: (Lamlash) 01770 600428

'irnmill, Isle of Arran

Map Ref: 1E6

SELF CATERING

Log cabin situated by a small stream on the outskirts of the peaceful village of Pirnmill. Sheltered by natural mature woodland the property boasts a fine westward view over Kilbrennan Sound to Kintyre with splendid sunsets.

1 log cabin, 1 pub rm, 2 bedrms (grd flr avail), sleeps 4, from £199.00, Jan-Dec, bus nearby, ferry 15 mls

Mrs A Dale
The Learig, Pirnmill, by Brodick, Isle of Arran, KA27 8HP
Tel: (Pirnmill) 01770 850228

hiskine, Isle of Arran

Map Ref: 1E7

SELF CATERING

1950's brick built bungalow, recently refurbished reflecting a Swedish influence. Set in the picturesque Shiskine Valley with extensive views over the Kilbrennan Sound to the Mull of Kintyre.

1 bungalow, 1 pub rm, 2 bedrms, sleeps 4, from £250.00, Jan-Dec, bus nearby, ferry 2 mls

Mr J Henderson
Croftlea, Shiskine, Isle of Arran, KA27 8EW
Tel: (Shiskine) 01770 860259

'hiting Bay, Isle of Arran

Map Ref: 1F7

SELF CATERING

Timber clad chalets, in elevated position, on a small quiet site overlooking the Bay. Many interesting walks in local area.

4 chalets, 1 pub rm, 3 bedrms, sleeps 6, total sleeping capacity 24, £150.00-£320.00, Mar-Oct, bus nearby, ferry 8 mls

Mr Brian Francis
Heatherhill, Middle Road, Whiting Bay, Isle of Arran, KA27 8PS
Tel: (Whiting Bay) 01770 700355

shkirk, Selkirkshire

Map Ref: 2D7

SELF CATERING

Recently renovated semi-detached cottages situated to one side of farm steading. Peaceful setting, yet central for all Borders attractions, including golf, fishing, riding and an ideal situation for touring the Borders. One cottage suitable for guests with mobility difficulties.

2 cottages, 1 pub rm, 3 bedrms (grd flr avail), sleeps 6, total sleeping capacity 12, £140.00-£300.00, Jan-Dec, bus 1/4 ml, rail 44 mls, airport 45 mls

Mr & Mrs Christopher Davies
The Davies Partnership, Synton Mains Farm, Ashkirk, nr Selkirk, TD7 4PA
Tel: (Ashkirk) 01750 32388 Fax: 01750 32388

★★★ UP TO ★★★★

SELF CATERING

Three traditional, and very well equipped stone terraced cottages on working farm with enclosed garden. Also spacious modern bungalow with own garden, equally well equipped in rural setting close by. Halfway between Selkirk and Hawick. Own fishing loch plus riding and golf nearby. Bicycle hire and stabling available by prior arrangement.

3 cottages, 1 bungalow, 1-2 pub rms, 2-3 bedrms (grd flr avail), sleeps 4-7, total sleeping capacity 22, £120.00-£411.00, Jan-Dec, bus 3/4 ml, rail 44 mls, airport 45 mls

Mrs Hunter
Headshaw Farm, Ashkirk,by Selkirk, Selkirkshire
Tel: (Ashkirk) 01750 32233 Fax: 07071 781891

VAT is shown at 17.5%: changes in this rate may affect prices.

Key to symbols is on back flap.

Ayr **Map Ref: 1G7**

Semi-detached cottage in rural surroundings. Ideally situated for touring Burns Country, Dumfries and Galloway. Bed linen and towels available on request.

1 house, 1 pub rm, 3 bedrms, sleeps 6, £200.00-£300.00, Jan-Dec, bus nearby

Mrs J Cochrane
2 Garrock Hill Cottages, Coalhall, Ayr, Ayrshire, KA6 6NA
Tel: (Ayr) 01292 591321

Bothy Cottage is ideal for two, situated five miles south of Ayr at the coastal village of Dunure on a working farm, overlooking the Firth of Clyde to Arran. It has a lounge, kitchen, 2 double bedrooms one of which is ensuite. Ideal for Culzean Castle, Burns Heritage, Galloway Forest Farm Park and many more activities. A peaceful retreat for those wishing to capture a country coastal farm atmosphere at its best.

1 cottage, 1 pub rm, 2 bedrms (grd flr avail), sleeps 4, £180.00-£250.00, Jan-Dec, bus 1 ml, rail 6 mls

Agnes Y Gemmell
Dunduff Farm, Dunure, Ayr, Ayrshire, KA7 4LH
Tel: (Dunure) 01292 500225 Fax: 01292 500222

The accommodation consists of two large rooms and a bedroom comprising the upper floor of a detached house. Access is reached by a communal entrance. The house is situated in a quiet area close to the town centre.

1 part of house, 1 pub rm, 1 bedrm, sleeps 1-5, £150.00-£200.00, Jan-Dec, bus 1/4 ml, rail 1/4 ml, airport 5 mls

K Handley
2 Gordon Terrace, Ayr, KA8 0EF
Tel: (Ayr) 01292 261213

Cottage with all accommodation on the one level, situated in quiet residential area, yet convenient for the railway station and the town centre with all its amenities. Conservatory at the rear of the cottage overlooking a colourful private garden.

1 cottage, 2 bedrms (grd flr avail), sleeps 4-6, £120.00-£350.00, Jan-Dec, bus nearby, rail nearby, airport 2 mls

Mrs Hardie
Woodcroft, 23 Midton Road, Ayr, KA7 2SF
Tel: (Ayr) 01292 264383

★★★ SELF CATERING

Tastefully renovated cottage within traditional farm steading, dating back to the 18th century. The situation enjoys panoramic views of the surrounding countryside. Ayr 4 miles.

1 cottage, 1 pub rm, 1 bedrm, sleeps 2, £180.00-£190.00, Apr-Nov, bus 1 ml, rail 4 mls, airport 11 mls

Mrs M MacNicol
Newarkhill, Newark, Ayr, KA7 4ED
Tel: (Alloway) 01292 441606

Important: Prices stated are estimates and may be subject to amendments

yr

Map Ref: 1G7

Sundrum Castle Holiday Park

by Ayr, Ayrshire, KA6 5JH Tel: (Ayr) 01292 570057 Fax: 01292 570065

Booking Enquiries: Haven Holidays Ltd 1 Park Lane, Hemel Hempstead, Herts, HP2 4GL

Tel: 01442 233111 Fax: 01442 239126

23 acres, mixed, Apr-Oct, prior booking in peak periods, latest time of arrival 2400, overnight holding area. Extra charge for electricity, awnings.

52 tourers or 52 motors or 52 tents. Total Touring Pitches 52. Charges on application.

103 Holiday Caravans to let, sleep 2-8, total sleeping capacity 624, min let 2 nights.

Leisure facilities: 

Take A70 from Ayr for approx. 3 mls. Park signposted on road. Or A70 Cumnock to Ayr 1/2 ml W of Coylton.

allantrae, Ayrshire

Map Ref: 1F9

★★ SELF CATERING

Balnowlart Lodge is a tastefully furnished cottage offering 'home for home' comforts with superb views. Located in the peaceful Stinchar Valley with panoramic scenery, the cottage is ideal to enjoy beautiful Galloway and Ayrshire Burn's Country. Many golf courses nearby - 2 miles from shops, beach, hotels. Many country walks.

1 cottage, 1 pub rm, 3 bedrms (grd flr avail), sleeps 6, min let weekend, £130.00-£250.00, Jan-Dec, bus 2 mls, rail 15 mls, ferry 12 mls, airport 35 mls

Mrs M Drummond

Ardstinchar Cottage, Ballantrae, Ayrshire, KA26 0NA

Tel: (Ballantrae) 01465 831343

★★ SELF CATERING

The cottage on our working dairy farm offers comfortable accomodation with open fire in the living room. Situated in quiet unspoilt area, 1 mile from Ballantrae and the coast. Ideal for walking with abundant wildlife and birdwatching.

1 cottage, 1 pub rm, 3 bedrms (grd flr avail), sleeps 8, £120.00-£240.00, Mar-Nov, bus 3/4 ml, rail 12 mls, ferry 11 mls, airport 60 mls

Mrs R McKinley

Laggan Dairy, Ballantrae, Ayrshire, KA26 0JZ

Tel: (Ballantrae) 01465 831426

arr, by Girvan, Ayrshire

Map Ref: 1F8

★★ UP TO ★★★★ SELF CATERING

Detached renovated period farmhouse and self catering cottage adjoining Glengennet farmhouse situated in a rural location in peaceful Stinchar Valley. Conservation village with hotel and shops nearby. Ideal for walking in the Galloway Forest and Glen Trool. Good base for visiting Culzean Castle, golfing touring or just relaxing in unspoilt south west Scotland.

1 cottage, 1 house, 1 pub rm, 3 bedrms (grd flr avail), sleeps 2-8, min let 2 nights, £150.00-£320.00, Jan-Dec, bus 2 mls, rail 9 mls

Mrs V Dunlop

Glengennet Farm, Barr,by Girvan, Ayrshire, KA26 9TY

Tel: (Barr) 01465 861220 Fax: 01465 861220

owden, by Melrose, Roxburghshire

Map Ref: 2D6

★★ SELF CATERING

Comfortable cottage on the green, in a tranquil Borders village at the foot of the Eildon Hills.

1 cottage, 1 pub rm, 2 bedrms (grd flr avail), sleeps 3, £70.00-£190.00, Jan-Dec, bus 4 mls, rail 40 mls, airport 40 mls

Mrs Alison Speirs

Bowden Knowe, Bowden, Melrose, TD6 0ST

Tel: (St Boswells) 01835 823768

VAT is shown at 17.5%: changes in this rate may affect prices.

Key to symbols is on back flap.

Cairnryan, Wigtownshire

Map Ref: 1F10

✓✓✓✓ 110

Cairnryan Caravan Park

Cairnryan, Wigtownshire, DG9 8QX Tel: 01581 200231 Fax: 01581 200207

7 1/2 acres, grassy, level, sheltered, Mar-Oct, latest time of arrival 2200. Extra charge for electricity, showers.

15 tourers £8.00-8.50 or 15 motors £8.00-8.50 or 10 tents £4.00-4.50. Total Touring Pitches 15.

5 Holiday Caravans to let, sleep 4 £100.00-245.00, total sleeping capacity 20, min let 1 night.

Leisure facilities:

5 mls N of Stranraer on A77 opposite P&O Ferry Terminal, Cairnryan.

Carsphairn, Kirkcudbrightshire

Map Ref: 2A9

★ SELF CATERING

Former gate lodge and farm workers cottage modernised to create simple but cosy accommodation. Situated on 100 acre estate which has private fishing. Ideal for bird watching.

2 cottages, 2 pub rms, 1-2 bedrms (grd flr avail), sleeps 2-4, total sleeping capacity 6, £90.00-£160.00, Jan-Dec, bus nearby, rail 27 mls, airport 30 mls

Mrs Agnes Holden
Dalshangan, Carsphairn, Kirkcudbrightshire, DG7 3SZ
Tel: (Carsphairn) 01644 460651

Castle Douglas, Kirkcudbrightshire

Map Ref: 2A10

★ UP TO ★★★ SELF CATERING

Selection of properties on working farm in peaceful country setting just off A75. Castle Douglas 4 miles (6kms).

9 flats, 3 cottages, 3 bungalows, 1-2 pub rms, 1-4 bedrms (grd flr avail), sleeps 2-9, total sleeping capacity 68, min let 1 night, £90.00-£500.00, Jan-Dec, bus 1/2 ml, rail 23 mls, ferry 55 mls, airport 86 mls

Mrs E A Ball
Barncrosh Farm, Castle Douglas, Kirkcudbrightshire, DG7 1TX
Tel: (Bridge of Dee) 01556 680216 Fax: 01556 680 442
Email: @barncros.demon.co.uk

★★ SELF CATERING

Former farm workers cottage situated between Castle Douglas and Kirkcudbright, one mile from the A75, and ideally placed for touring the Solway Coast and the Galloway Hills.

1 cottage, 2 pub rms, 3 bedrms, sleeps 7, £150.00-£250.00, Apr-Oct, bus 1 ml, rail 23 mls, airport 48 mls

Mrs Bendall
Dalvadie, Meikle Knox Farm, Castle Douglas, DG7 1NS,
Tel: (Castle Douglas) 01556 503336

★★ SELF CATERING

This comfortable and compact chalet with magnificent views over the Galloway countryside is ideally placed for exploring South West Scotland. Equidistant from Kirkcudbright, Castle Douglas and Gatehouse of Fleet.

1 chalet, sleeps 2, £70.00-£135.00, Jan-Dec, bus 1 ml

Mrs Helen Hutton
The Bungalow, Crumquhill, Ringford, Castle Douglas, DG7 2AF
Tel: 01557 820269

Important: Prices stated are estimates and may be subject to amendments

Castle Douglas, Kirkcudbrightshire

Map Ref: 2A10

★★ SELF CATERING

Ideal for medium to very large parties. Two wings sleep 14 and 12. Total 26. Some disability access - please enquire. Dogs welcome. 40 acres informal wooded grounds, free game fishing. Unspoilt, historic area - coast, hills, wildlife, castles, gardens and golf, riding, cycling and walking. Good shopping, restaurant, pubs 3 miles. Contact Neil and Penny McMillan, tel. 01387 254647.

2 separate wings of country house, 2-3 pub rms, 3-5 bedrms (grd flr avail), sleeps 12, total sleeping capacity 24, £325.00-£500.00, Apr-Oct, Xmas/New Year, bus 1 ml, rail 18 mls, ferry 40 mls, airport 70 mls

Mr & Mrs N McMillan
Old Stakeford, College Road, Dumfries
Tel: (Dumfries) 01387 254647
Email: neil@nandp.demon.co.uk

★★ SELF CATERING

Traditional farm cottage set amidst the beautiful Galloway countryside steeped in history and surrounded by castles, abbeys, gardens, nature trails and sandy beaches, yet only a quarter of a mile from the A75 with the nearest town of Castle Douglas and Kirkcudbright only 5 miles away.

1 cottage, 1 pub rm, 3 bedrms (grd flr avail), sleeps 2-6, £180.00-£320.00, Jan-Dec, bus 1/4 ml, rail 24 mls, ferry 50 mls, airport 60 mls

Mrs E Millar
Balannan Farm, Ringford, Castle Douglas, Kirkcudbrightshire, DG7 2AF
Tel: (Ringford) 01557 820283

★★★ SELF CATERING

Comfortable semi-detached farm cottage on one level, with own walled patio garden in rural surroundings. Free trout and salmon fishing on River Urr.

1 cottage, 1 pub rm, 2 bedrms, sleeps 5, £180.00-£280.00, Mar-Nov, bus 1 ml, rail 16 mls, ferry 55 mls, airport 95 mls

Mrs A Muir
Milton Park Farm, Castle Douglas, Kirkcudbrightshire, DG7 3JJ
Tel: (Haugh of Urr) 01556 660212

★★★★ SELF CATERING

Tastefully converted farm steading. 3 bedrooms all ensuite with bath and shower. All decorated to a different theme – choose from the African, Florintine or Scottish bedroom. French windows from sitting room into courtyard. Full central heating and luxury fitted kitchen. Catch a trout on our loch for breakfast. Dinner available in the farmhouse.

1 converted farm steading, 1 pub rm, 3 bedrms (grd flr avail), sleeps 6, £300.00-£350.00, Jan-Dec

Celia Pickup
Craigadam, Castle Douglas, DG7 3HU
Tel: 01556 650233 Fax: 01556 650233

Catrine, Ayrshire

Map Ref: 1H7

★ SELF CATERING

The bungalow is peacefully situated in the heart of Ayrshire, on a working dairy farm with excellent access to all attractions within Ayrshire. Enclosed garden, ideal for children. Pet donkeys who love visitors. Ample parking. Bed linen and towels provided.

1 bungalow, 1 pub rm, 2 bedrms (grd flr avail), sleeps 6, £258.50, May-Sep, bus 1/4 ml, rail 2 1/2 mls, airport 15 mls

Mrs Forrest
Bogend Farm, Catrine, Mauchline, Ayrshire, KA5 6NJ
Tel: (Mauchline) 01290 551325

VAT is shown at 17.5%: changes in this rate may affect prices.

Key to symbols is on back flap.

Clovenfords, by Galashiels, Selkirkshire

Map Ref: 2D6

In a secluded rural location set back from A72 and overlooking the River Tweed. Self contained two bedroom ground level flat adjoining owner's cottage. The non smoking and no pets policy and natural fibre futon mattresses and bedding means the property is particularly suitable for people seeking an allergy free environment.

1 flat, 1 pub rm, 2 bedrms (grd flr avail), sleeps 4, £120.00-£240.00, Jan-Dec, bus nearby (100yds)

Mrs V J Nordmann
Thornielee Vale, by Clovenfords, nr Galashiels, TD1 3LN
Tel: 01896 850634

Cockburnspath, Berwickshire

Map Ref: 2E5

Terraced farm cottages on working farm, set high up overlooking the sea. Sandy beaches near by. Only 38 miles (61kms) from Edinburgh.

2 cottages, 1 pub rm, 2 bedrms, sleeps 4-6, total sleeping capacity 10, from £200.00, Apr-Dec, bus 1 1/2 mls, rail 9 mls, airport 50 mls

Mrs B M Russell
Townhead Farm, Cockburnspath, TD13 5YR
Tel: (Cockburnspath) 01368 830 465

Coldingham, Berwickshire

Map Ref: 2F5

Recently refurbished cottage of individual character, adjoining large house, overlooking Coldingham village green.

1 house, 1 pub rm, 1 bedrm, sleeps 2, £100.00-£160.00, Jan-Dec, bus nearby, rail 11 mls, airport 50 mls

Dr & Mrs Laidlaw
Courtburn House, Coldingham, Berwickshire
Tel: (Coldingham) 018907 71266

Fully refurbished apartments within this historic 17th century castle, also secluded pine lodges set in 22 acres of mature wood and parkland. Ideal for golf, fishing, walking etc. Sandy beaches and shops 3 miles.

6 flats, 1 cottage, 6 pine lodges, 1-2 pub rms, 1-3 bedrms (grd flr avail), sleeps 2-8, total sleeping capacity 58, £142.00-£489.00, Jan-Dec, bus 2 mls, rail 11 mls, ferry 80 mls, airport 45 mls

Mr R Penaluna
Press Castle Complex, Coldingham, Eyemouth, Berwickshire, TD14 5TS
Tel: (Coldingham) 018907 71257 Fax: 018907 71729

Secluded cottages and chalets, centred on private trout loch in wooded country estate close to sea. Ideal for anglers, naturalists and walkers. An ideal and peaceful base for touring the Borders, Edinburgh and Northumberland.

6 chalets, 3 cottages, 1-2 pub rms, 1-3 bedrms (grd flr avail), sleeps 2-6, total sleeping capacity 42, min let weekend, £160.00-£325.00, Mar-Nov, bus 2 mls, rail 14 mls, airport 50 mls

Dr & Mrs E J Wise
West Loch Holidays, West Loch House, Coldingham, Berwickshire, TD14 5QE
Tel: (Coldingham) 018907 71270

Important: Prices stated are estimates and may be subject to amendments

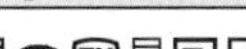

ldstream, Berwickshire

Map Ref: 2E6

★★★

SELF ATERING

Stone built, single storey terraced cottages, recently refurbished. Quietly situated with open country views.

3 cottages, 1 pub rm, 2-3 bedrms (grd flr avail), sleeps 4-7, total sleeping capacity 17, min let weekend, £190.00-£350.00, Jan-Dec, bus 1/2 ml, rail 15 mls, airport 60 mls

Mrs O Brewis
Little Swinton, Coldstream, Berwickshire, TD12 4HH
Tel: (Swinton) 01890 860280 Fax: 01890 860280

★★★

SELF ATERING

Single storey, semi-detached farm cottage, with own garden area, in peaceful rural setting, with uninterrupted views of the Cheviot Hills.

1 cottage, 1 pub rm, 3 bedrms (grd flr avail), sleeps 5, from £130.00, Jan-Dec, bus 8 mls, rail 20 mls, airport 52 mls

Mrs S Walker
Springwells, Greenlaw, Duns, Berwickshire
Tel: (Leitholm) 01890 840216 Fax: 01890 840216

lmonell, by Girvan, Ayrshire

Map Ref: 1G9

★★★ UP ★★★★

SELF ATERING

Ground floor flat in peaceful country village and traditional stone semi-detached cottage in rural hamlet, both with beautiful views of the River Stinchar and surrounding hills. Sandy beach and Galloway Forest Park within easy reach. Ideal base for touring Ayrshire coast and Galloway.

1 flat, 1 pub rm, 1 bedrm (grd flr avail), sleeps 2, min let weekend, £100.00-£200.00, Jan-Dec, bus nearby, rail 10 mls, ferry 25 mls, airport 40 mls

Mrs Anne Shankland
19 Main Street, Colmonell, Girvan
Tel: 01465 881265/881220

etown, Wigtownshire

Map Ref: 1H10

★

SELF ATERING

Adjoining stone built terraced houses in residential side street, within easy reach of village centre.

2 houses, 1-3 pub rms, 2-3 bedrms, sleeps 4-6, total sleeping capacity 10, £260.00-£360.00, Apr-Oct, bus nearby, rail 40 mls, ferry 40 mls, airport 50 mls

Mrs Dawson
70 Coach Road, Brotton, Saltburn-by-Sea, Cleveland
Tel: (Guisborough) 01287 676991

Crocketford, Kirkcudbrightshire

Map Ref: 2B10

PARK OF BRANDEDLEYS

CROCKETFORD, DUMFRIES DG2 8RG
Tel: 01556 690250 Fax: 01556 690681

Quiet exclusive accommodation set in parkland with magnificent views over Auchenreoch Loch to the Galloway Hills. The two cottages and three chalets form part of a small holiday park with a very full range of amenities. Sightseeing, birdwatching, golfing, walking, shopping and many other pursuits are possible in the surrounding area.

SELF CATERING

Choice of cottages or pine chalets with views of Auchenreoch Loch and Galloway Hills. Ideal for touring.

3 chalets, 2 cottages, 1-2 pub rms, 1-2 bedrms, sleeps 2-6, total sleeping capacity 30, £260.00-£500.00, Feb-Dec, bus nearby, rail 9 mls

Linda Purdie
Park of Brandedleys, Crocketford, by Dumfries, DG2 8RG
Tel: (Crocketford) 01556 690250 Fax: 01556 690681

Millport, Isle of Cumbrae

Map Ref: 1F6

SELF CATERING

Semi detached pine lodges situated in quiet residential area close to the sea front and a short walk from the sandy beaches of Kames Bay and the town centre.

2 log cabins, 1 pub rm, 2 bedrms, sleeps 4, total sleeping capacity 4, £256.00-£335.00, Jan-Dec

Mr A Caldwell
Millport Holiday Lodges Ltd, 1 Ninian Street, Millport, Isle of Cumbrae, KA28 0EB
Tel: (Millport) 01475 530128

SELF CATERING

The apartments are situated in the centre of Millport adjacent to the pier area. All the flats at Quayhead have sea views and ready access to sandy beaches. Linen can be provided if required. Some flats have bed setees and bunk beds only.

8 flats, 1-2 pub rms, 1-2 bedrms (grd flr avail), sleeps 2-6, total sleeping capacity 34, £80.00-£260.00, Jan-Dec, bus nearby, ferry 3 mls

Cumbrae Holiday Apartments Ltd
Mrs S Murden, 32 Stuart Street, Millport, KA28 0AJ,
Tel: (Millport) 01475 530094

SELF CATERING

Three small ground floor flats with entrance off a communal stair. One with sea view the other two centrally situated. Ideal for couples.

3 flats, 1 pub rm, 1 bedrm (grd flr avail), sleeps 2-4, total sleeping capacity 8, £85.00-£220.00, Jan-Dec, bus 200 yds, ferry 4 mls

Mrs A Mapes
13 Bute Terrace, Millport, Isle of Cumbrae, KA28 0BA
Tel: (Millport) 01475 530445

Important: Prices stated are estimates and may be subject to amendments

illport, Isle of Cumbrae

Map Ref: 1F6

★ UP TO ★★★★ SELF CATERING

Properties that have been in the family since the 18th century with prime position over Millport Bay. All now renovated but individual style and character retained. Many fun features added.

1 house, 4 flats, 1-2 pub rms, 1-3 bedrms (grd flr avail), sleeps 4-10, total sleeping capacity 32, £110.00-£465.00, Jan-Dec, bus nearby, rail 5 mls, ferry 4 mls, airport 20 mls

Mrs B McLuckie
Muirhall Farm, Larbert, Stirlingshire, FK5 4EW
Tel: (Larbert) 01324 551570 Fax: 01324 551223

ailly, Ayrshire

Map Ref: 1G8

★★★★ SELF CATERING

This new development offers lodge bungalows on a landscaped site with panoramic views of the Girvan Valley. There are a wide range of activities/attractions in the area or you can relax at the leisure centre with its indoor heated swimming pool, children's pool, and sauna as well as the lounge/bar serving meals from breakfast till dinner. Adjacent to the holiday resort is the Brunston Castle Golf Course with its 6800 yds Burns Championship course.

75 bungalows, 1 pub rm, 2-4 bedrms (grd flr avail), sleeps 4-8, min let weekend, £150.00-£395.00, Jan-Dec, bus 1/4 ml, rail 5 mls, ferry 35 mls, airport 25 mls

Brunston Castle Holiday Resort
Dailly, Ayrshire, KA26 9RH
Tel: 01465 811589 Fax: 01465 811411

lbeattie, Kirkcudbrightshire

Map Ref: 2A10

★★★★ SELF CATERING

Completely renovated, traditional stone-built cottage. Ideally situated for walking, touring or just relaxing.

1 cottage, 1 pub rm, 2 bedrms (grd flr avail), sleeps 4, £130.00-£280.00, Jan-Dec, bus 2 mls, rail 12 mls, ferry 50 mls, airport 80 mls

Mr G Cook
Haywood Property Management Ltd, Barclosh, Dalbeattie, Kirkcudbrightshire, DG5 4PL
Tel: (Dalbeattie) 01556 610380 Fax: 01556 610364

★★★ UP TO ★★★★ SELF CATERING

Recent conversion of former stable and barn on site of Maidenholm Forge Mill. Quiet location on banks of Dalbeattie Burn. 10 minutes walk to town.

2 flats, 1 cottage, 2-4 pub rms, 4 bedrms (grd flr avail), sleeps 2-3, total sleeping capacity 7, £175.00-£390.00, Jan-Dec, bus 1/2 ml, rail 14 mls

Mr & Mrs G C Elkins
Maidenholm Forge Mill, Dalbeattie, Dumfries & Galloway, DG5 4HT
Tel: 01556 611552 Fax: 01556 611552

lry, by Castle Douglas, Kirkcudbrightshire

Map Ref: 1H9

★★★ SELF CATERING

Two charming semi-detached cottages set in farmland midway between the villages of Dalry and New Galloway. There are magnificent views of the river, hills and rolling countryside. Free trout fishing on the river Ken and pets welcome.

2 cottages, 1 pub rm, 1 bedrm, sleeps 2, total sleeping capacity 4, £150.00-£210.00, Mar-Nov, bus 2 mls, rail 28 mls, airport 45 mls

Mr R Agnew
Glenlee Holiday Houses, New Galloway, Castle Douglas, Kirkcudbrightshire, DG7 3SF
Tel: (Dalry) 01644 430212 Fax: 01644 430340

VAT is shown at 17.5%: changes in this rate may affect prices.

Key to symbols is on back flap.

Dalry, by Castle Douglas, Kirkcudbrightshire

Map Ref: 1H9

SELF CATERING

Former gardener's cottage to the rear of Grennan House, overlooking restored watermill.

1 cottage, 1 pub rm, 2 bedrms (grd flr avail), sleeps 4, £180.00-£300.00, May-Oct, bus 3 mls, rail 23 mls, ferry 60 mls, airport 90 mls

Miss S Harrison
Grennan Mill, St John's Town of Dalry, Kirkcudbrightshire
Tel: (Dalry) 01644 430297

Dolphinton, West Linton, Peeblesshire

Map Ref: 2B6

SELF CATERING

Fully-modernised cottage on a working upland farm. Secluded, yet not isolated, in beautiful countryside. Children and well-behaved pets welcome. Ideal for bird watching. Come and relax in the garden, or fish on the private pond, or take a gentle stroll along the quiet country roads.

1 cottage, 2 pub rms, 2 bedrms (grd flr avail), sleeps 4-6, Jan-Dec, bus 1 ml, rail 20 mls, airport 20 mls

Mrs A Hutchison
Roberton Mains, Dolphinton, West Lothian
Tel: (Dolphinton) 01968 682256 Fax: 01968 682256

Dumfries

Map Ref: 2B9

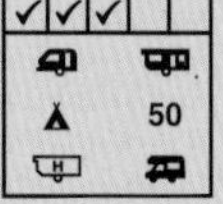

50

Barnsoul Farm

Irongray, Shawhead, Dumfries, DG2 9SQ Tel: 01387 730249 Fax: 01387 730249 Email: barnsouldg@aol.com Web: barnsouldg@aol.com

10 acres, mixed, Apr-Oct, latest time of arrival 2350, overnight holding area. Extra charge for electricity, showers.

20 tourers £5.00-8.00 or 20 motors £5.00-8.00 or 20 tents £5.00-8.00. Total Touring Pitches 20.

3 Holiday Caravans to let, sleep 4-6 £150.00-250.00, total sleeping capacity 14, min let 4 days.

Leisure facilities:

Dunure, by Ayr, Ayrshire

Map Ref: 1G7

SELF CATERING

Semi-detached cottage with enclosed garden on working dairy farm, overlooking Firth of Clyde with views westwards to Isle of Arran. Convenient for golfing, fishing and touring the area, with Culzean Castle and Country Park 6 miles.

1 cottage, 1 pub rm, 3 bedrms (grd flr avail), sleeps 4-6, £100.00-£285.00, Jan-Dec, bus 1 ml, rail 6 mls, airport 10 mls

Mrs C Montgomerie
Millhouse, Dunure Mains, Dunure, Ayr, Ayrshire, KA7 4LY
Tel: (Dunure) 01292 500348 Fax: 01292 500348

SELF CATERING

Modern bungalow with private lawned garden set on a traditional working farm with lovely coastal views to the Isle of Arran and surrounding farmland. Ideal base for touring Burns Country with many activities including golfing, fishing and walking. 5 miles from Ayr and convenient for Prestwick airport.

1 bungalow, 2 pub rms, 3 bedrms (grd flr avail), sleeps 6, £150.00-£320.00, Jan-Dec, bus nearby, rail nearby, airport 8 mls

Mrs L Wilcox
Fisherton Farm, Dunure, Ayrshire, KA7 4LF
Tel: (Dunure) 01292 500223 Fax: 01282 500223

Ettrick Valley, Selkirkshire

Map Ref: 2C7

✓✓✓ 30

Honey Cottage Caravan Park

Hopehouse, Ettrick Valley, Selkirkshire, TD7 5HU Tel: (Ettrick Valley) 01750 62246/015395 31291

7 acres, grassy, hard-standing, level, sheltered, Jan-Dec, latest time of arrival 2200, overnight holding area. Extra charge for electricity, showers.

30 tourers £5.50-7.50 or 30 motors £5.50-7.50 or 30 tents £5.50-6.50. Total Touring Pitches 30.

Holiday Caravan to let, sleeps 6 £185.00, min let week.

Leisure facilities:

Honey Cottage is 1 ml from Tushielaw Inn on the B709. From Selkirk B7009 15mls. From Hawick B711 15mls. From Lockerbie B723 28mls.

✓✓✓✓ 49

Messrs P G & K A Newton

Angecroft Caravan Park, Ettrick Valley, Selkirkshire, TD7 5HY Tel: (Ettrick Valley) 01750 62251/01721 730657 Fax: 01721 730627 Email:

5 acres, mixed, 5 Feb-15 Jan, prior booking in peak periods, latest time of arrival 2200, overnight holding area. Extra charge for electricity, awnings.

6 tourers £7.50-9.00 or 6 motors £7.50-9.00 or 6 tents £5.00-7.50. Total Touring Pitches 6.

4 Holiday Caravans to let, sleep 6 £100.00-295.00, total sleeping capacity 24, min let weekend.

Leisure facilities:

From A74 at Lockerbie, Site only 24 mls. From A7 at Langholm take B709 to park (24 mls). From A7 at Hawick take B711. Park 4 mls W of Tushielaw on B709.

SELF CATERING

At the edge of the caravan park with its own private garden and parking space, the cottage overlooks Tima water and wooded hills.

1 cottage, 2 holiday lodges, 1 pub rm, 3-4 bedrms, sleeps 6, total sleeping capacity 18, £125.00-£300.00, Jan-Dec, bus 18 mls, rail 24 mls, airport 50 mls

Messrs P G & K A Newton

Angecroft Caravan Park, Ettrick Valley, Selkirk, Selkirkshire
Tel: (Selkirk) 01750 62251/01721 730657 Fax: 01721 730627
Email: kevinnewton@compuserve.com

Fairlie, Ayrshire

Map Ref: 1G6

★★★

SELF CATERING

Modern ground floor seafront apartment with balcony right on the beach. Views to the Cumbraes, Arran and Isle of Bute. Ideal situation for just sitting out on the balcony.

1 flat, 1 pub rm, 1 bedrm (grd flr avail), sleeps 2-3, £200.00-£300.00, Jan-Dec, bus nearby (100yds), rail 1/2 ml

Mrs Carol Dunn

32 Greenholm Avenue, Clarkston, Glasgow, G76 7AH
Tel: 0141 571 7417

Foulden, Berwickshire

Map Ref: 2G5

SELF CATERING

Sympathetically converted school in the picturesque conservation village of Foulden. Drumoyne enjoys panoramic views across the Tweed Valley to the Cheviot Hills. 1.5 miles from England/Scotland border and 56 miles from Edinburgh.

1 house, 1 pub rm, 3 bedrms (grd flr avail), sleeps 4-6, min let 3 days, £200.00-£280.00, Jan-Dec, bus nearby, rail 5 mls

Mrs I B Williams

Old Schoolhouse, Foulden, By Berwick on Tweed, TD15 1UH
Tel: (Paxton) 01289 386332
Email: jwfoulden@aol.com.uk

Galashiels, Selkirkshire **Map Ref: 2D6**

SELF CATERING

Modern and fully equipped flats on College Campus. Ideally situated for touring the Borders. Groups especially welcome.

12 flats, 1 pub rm, 6 bedrms (grd flr avail), sleeps 6, total sleeping capacity 72, £230.00-£270.00, Easter, Jul-Sep, bus nearby, rail 34-38 mls, airport 42 mls

Scot Conference & Holiday Centre
Halls of Residence, Tweed Road, Galashiels, Selkirkshire, TD1 3EY
Tel: (Galashiels) 01896 753474 Fax: 01896 755884

SELF CATERING

Delightful cottage in very quiet position close to the River Tweed, yet only 1.5 miles from Galashiels.

1 cottage, 2 pub rms, 2 bedrms, sleeps 4, £260.00-£295.00, May-Oct, bus 400 yds, rail 40 mls, airport 40 mls

D Scott
Netherbarns Farm, Galashiels, TD1 3NW
Tel: (Galashiels) 01896 755568 Fax: 01896 752806

Garlieston, Dumfriesshire **Map Ref: 1H11**

★★ UP TO ★★★

SELF CATERING

Semi detached cottages in quiet location set in large lawned area on 530 acre working farm, 2 miles from the picturesque village of Garlieston. Ideal location for golfers, fishers, walkers and of particular interest to birdwatchers. The cottages are also ideal for two families wishing to holiday together.

2 cottages, 2 pub rms, 3 bedrms (grd flr avail), sleeps 6, total sleeping capacity 12, £200.00-£250.00, Jan-Dec, bus 1 ml, rail 36 mls, ferry 36 mls, airport 60 mls

Mrs M Simpson
Culscadden, Garlieston, Newton Stewart, DG8 8AD
Tel: 01988 600208

Gatehouse of Fleet, Kirkcudbrightshire **Map Ref: 1H10**

66

Anwoth Holiday Park

Gatehouse of Fleet, Kirkcudbrightshire, DG7 2JU Tel: (Gatehouse) 01557 814333

Booking Enquiries: Mr & Mrs Swalwell Auchenlarie Holiday Farm, Gatehouse of Fleet, Kirkcudbrightshire, CA22 2UD

Tel: 01557 840251 Fax: 01557 840333

4 acres, grassy, level, sheltered, Mar-Oct, prior booking in peak periods, latest time of arrival 2000. Extra charge for electricity, awnings.

28 tourers £5.00-9.00 or 28 motors £5.00-9.00. Total Touring Pitches 28. No tents.

4 Holiday Caravans to let, sleep 6 £100.00-300.00, total sleeping capacity 24, min let 2 nights.

Proceed W through High Street in Gatehouse to the bridge over River Fleet, and past the Anwoth Hotel on the right. First turning right after Anwoth Hotel, and site entrance is 100yds.

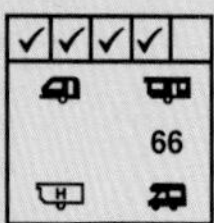

287

Auchenlarie Holiday Park

Gatehouse of Fleet, Kirkcudbrightshire, DG7 2EX Tel: (Mossyard) 01557 840251 Fax: 01557 840333

20 acres, mixed, Mar-Oct, prior booking in peak periods, latest time of arrival 2000, overnight holding area. Extra charge for electricity, awnings, showers.

49 tourers £5.50-10.00 or 49 motors £5.50-10.00 or 26 tents £5.50-10.00. Total Touring Pitches 75.

45 Holiday Caravans to let, sleep 4-6 £90.00-390.00, total sleeping capacity 270, min let weekend.

Leisure facilities:

A75 5 mls W of Gatehouse-of-Fleet.

Important: Prices stated are estimates and may be subject to amendments

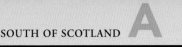

Gatehouse of Fleet, Kirkcudbrightshire

Map Ref: 1H10

★★
SELF CATERING

Lovely old farmhouse with beautiful views, also woodland cottages. Use of tennis court. Loch and river fishing with tuition given.

1 house, 2 bungalows, 1-3 pub rms, 2-5 bedrms (grd flr avail), sleeps 4-10, total sleeping capacity 18, min let weekend, £150.00-£600.00, Jan-Dec, bus 2 mls, rail 35 mls, ferry 45 mls, airport 90 mls

Mrs B Gilbey
Rusko, Gatehouse of Fleet, Castle Douglas, Kirkcudbrightshire, DG7 2BS
Tel: (Gatehouse) 01557 814215 Fax: 01557 814679

★★★
SELF CATERING

Self contained half of owner's house. Peace and quiet, lovely outlook to village and hills beyond. Ideal touring centre.

1 house, 1 pub rm, 3 bedrms, sleeps 6, to £320.00, Jan-Dec, bus 1/2 ml, rail 34 mls, ferry 39 mls, airport 87 mls

Major & Mrs I A D Gordon
Brownhill, Planetree Park, Gatehouse of Fleet, Kirkcudbrightshire, DG7 2EQ
Tel: (Gatehouse) 01557 814401

★★★
SELF CATERING

This two bedroomed terraced cottage with large rear garden and patio area is a Listed building of special architectural and historic interest. Located in the conservation area of Gatehouse, a small country town on the Solway Firth, it is only 5 minutes drive to sandy beaches.

1 cottage, 3 pub rms, 2 bedrms, sleeps 4-5, £160.00-£270.00, Jan-Dec, bus nearby, rail 22 mls, ferry 60 mls, airport 62 mls

Mr M P Mullan
4 Woodhouse Close, Woodhouse Road, Hove, East Sussex, BN3 5LS
Tel: (Brighton) 01273 413655

Girvan, Ayrshire

Map Ref: 1F8

First floor flat situated above shops in main street of town centre. Easy access to local facilities including beach, swimming pool, golf course and bowling green.

1 flat, 1 pub rm, 2 bedrms, sleeps 5, £95.00-£290.00, Jan-Dec, bus nearby, rail 1/2 ml

Mrs Moyra M Hay
50 Dalrymple Street, Girvan, Ayrshire, KA26 9BT
Tel: (Girvan) 01465 714421 Fax: 01465 714421

Gretna, Dumfriesshire — **Map Ref: 2C10**

SELF CATERING

Modernised, traditional sandstone fisherman's cottages with own secluded gardens. In quiet location on seashore of Solway Estuary.

3 cottages, 3-4 pub rms, 1-2 bedrms (grd flr avail), sleeps 2-4, total sleeping capacity 12, £170.00-£330.00, Jan-Dec, bus 1 ml, rail 3 mls

Mr & Mrs Read
7 Brow Houses, Eastriggs, Annan, DG12 6TG
Tel: (East Riggs) 01461 40873 Fax: 01461 40740
Email: mike_read@compuserve.com

Hawick, Roxburghshire — **Map Ref: 2D7**

SELF CATERING

Second floor flat furnished to high standard, overlooking the river and park, with beautiful garden for tennant's use. Right in the town centre yet with ample free parking.

1 flat, 1 pub rm, 3 bedrms, sleeps 5, £200.00-£350.00, Jan-Dec, bus nearby, rail 50 mls, airport 50 mls

Mr W Combe
6 Teviot Crescent, Hawick, Roxburghshire, TD9 9RE
Tel: (Hawick) 01450 374258/373237

SELF CATERING

Comfortable detached cottage on a working farm. Ideal base for touring the Borders. Close to Hawick and all amenities. Attractive gardens front and rear.

1 cottage, 1 pub rm, 3 bedrms (grd flr avail), sleeps 6, £145.00-£200.00, Apr-Oct, bus 1 ml, rail 50 mls, airport 50 mls

Mrs M Scott
Overhall Farm, Hawick, Roxburghshire, TD9 7LJ
Tel: (Hawick) 01450 375045

SELF CATERING

Semi-detached farm cottage beside a stream on mixed working hill farm, offering tranquility without isolation.

1 cottage, 1 pub rm, 3 bedrms (grd flr avail), sleeps 4-5, £100.00-£250.00, Jan-Dec, bus 2 mls, rail 42 mls, airport 50 mls

Sheila Shell
Wiltonburn Farm, Hawick, Roxburghshire, TD9 7LL
Tel: (Hawick) 01450 372414

Important: Prices stated are estimates and may be subject to amendments

Jedburgh, Roxburghshire — **Map Ref: 2E7**

MILLHOUSE & LETTER BOX COTTAGE

OVERWELLS, JEDBURGH, ROXBURGHSHIRE TD8 6LT
Tel: 01835 863020   Fax: 01835 864334

Two quality cottages, each sleeping four, on working farm, three miles from Jedburgh. **Millhouse** – detached house stylishly converted with spectacular views. **Letter Box Cottage** – semi-detached newly modernised in quiet location. Both ideal centres for exploring the Borders, sporting holidays or just to "get away from it all".

★★★★

SELF CATERING

2 recently renovated properties on a working farm. Only 3 miles from Jedburgh yet quiet, peaceful location. Ideal for walking, golf and exploring the Borders country.

2 cottages, 2 pub rms, 2 bedrms (grd flr avail), sleeps 4, total sleeping capacity 8, £200.00-£320.00, Jan-Dec, bus 3 mls, airport 54 mls

Mrs A Fraser
Overwells, Jedburgh, Roxburghshire, TD8 6LT
Tel: (Jedburgh) 01835 863020 Fax: 01835 864334

★★★★

SELF CATERING

Set in large pleasant garden lying just off main A68 2 miles south of Jedburgh. Two pine cabins, well equipped and with ample parking.

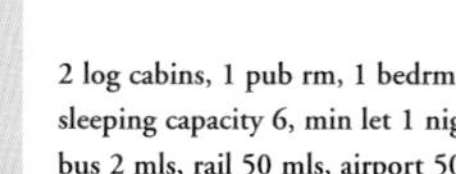

2 log cabins, 1 pub rm, 1 bedrm (grd flr avail), sleeps 3, total sleeping capacity 6, min let 1 night, £200.00-£250.00, Jan-Dec, bus 2 mls, rail 50 mls, airport 50 mls

Mrs S Fry
The Spinney, Langlee, Jedburgh, Roxburghshire, TD8 6PB
Tel: (Jedburgh) 01835 863525 Fax: 01835 864883

★★★

SELF CATERING

Recently refurbished and tastefully furnished, near to golf range and country restaurant, ideal for touring or sporting holidays. Linen included.

1 cottage, 1 pub rm, 2 bedrms (grd flr avail), sleeps 4, £145.00-£295.00, Jan-Dec, bus 50 yds, rail 40 mls, airport 45 mls

Ms Alyson Minto
Hooly Cottage, Mounthooly Farm, Crailing, Jedburgh, TD8 6TJ
Tel: 01835 850787

Kelso, Roxburghshire — **Map Ref: 2E6**

★★★

SELF CATERING

Traditional, beautifully refurbished stone built semi-detached cottage with open fire, on working farm beside River Tweed. Farm walks, fishing, fine views. Ideally situated for touring.

1 cottage, 1 pub rm, 3 bedrms, sleeps 2-6, min let 2 nights, £200.00-£350.00, Jan-Dec, bus 1/2 ml, rail 20 mls, airport 50 mls

Mrs J Aitchison
Karingal, Lochton, Coldstream, Berwickshire
Tel: (Birgham) 01890 830205 Fax: 01890 830210
Email: lochton@btinternet.com.uk

VAT is shown at 17.5%: changes in this rate may affect prices.

Key to symbols is on back flap.

Kelso, Roxburghshire | **Map Ref: 2E6**

Comfy and peaceful. The cottages stand at the end of their own lane, between the Tweed and Eden Water, completely surrounded by open farmland.

3 cottages, 1 pub rm, 2 bedrms, sleeps 4-5, total sleeping capacity 16, £100.00-£280.00, Jan-Dec, bus 1/2 ml, rail 20 mls, airport 50 mls

Mrs Sue Beck
Hendersyde Farm, Holiday Cottages, Kelso, Roxburghshire, TD5 7QA
Tel: (Kelso) 01573 223495 Fax: 01573 223495

★★

SELF CATERING

Traditional terraced farm cottages on working farm. 3 miles (5kms) from Kelso. Ideal for touring Scottish Borders, Northumbria and Edinburgh.

2 cottages, 1-2 pub rms, 2-3 bedrms, sleeps 5-7, total sleeping capacity 12, £110.00-£320.00, Jan-Dec, bus 3 mls, rail 27 mls, ferry 60 mls, airport 60 mls

Mrs M Clark
Kerchesters, Kelso, Roxburghshire, TD5 8HR
Tel: (Kelso) 01573 224321 Fax: 01573 226609

★★★ UP TO ★★★★

SELF CATERING

Individual character cottages on 250 acre arable farm, 3 miles from Kelso. Indoor heated pool, sauna, games room, tennis court, fitness suite, children's play park, target golf, mountain bike hire and petanque.

5 cottages, 1-2 pub rms, 1-3 bedrms (grd flr avail), sleeps 2-8, total sleeping capacity 28, £100.00-£510.00, Jan-Dec, bus nearby, rail 20 mls, airport 58 mls

Peter & Jacqui Hottinger
Houndridge, Ednam, Kelso, Roxburghshire, TD5 7QN
Tel: (Stichill) 01573 470 604 Fax: 01573470 604

Comfortable well appointed, semi-detached house on working farm. Within easy reach of all Borders centres and facilities. Fishing can be arranged. Suitable for all ages.

1 cottage, 1 pub rm, 3 bedrms (grd flr avail), sleeps 6, £180.00-£250.00, Jan-Dec, bus 1 ml, rail 25 mls, airport 40 mls

J Mauchlen
Spotsmains, Kelso, Roxburghshire, TD5 7RT
Tel: (Smailholm) 01573 460226 Fax: 01573 460226

Semi-detached shepherd's cottage fully equipped and with oil fired central heating. Situated in open farm land on a working livestock farm, the cottage gives the impression of seclusion, yet only 2 1/2 miles from the village of Yetholm. Ideal for birdwatching and wildlife, walking and exploring the Borders and Northumberland.

1 cottage, 1 pub rm, 3 bedrms, sleeps 6, min let weekend, £120.00-£280.00, May-Dec, bus 2 1/2 mls, rail 20 mls, airport 60 mls

Mrs A Robson
Venchen,by Yetholm, Roxburghshire
Tel: (Yetholm) 01573 420207 Fax: 01573 420233

Important: Prices stated are estimates and may be subject to amendments

Kelso, Roxburghshire

Map Ref: 2E6

SELF CATERING

Recently refurbished detached stone cottage dating from 1851. On a working farm in attractive rural location yet only 3 miles from Kelso. Golf and fishing available locally. Centrally located for walking and the many attractions of the Borders.

1 cottage, 1 pub rm, 2 bedrms, sleeps 5, min let 2 nights, £200.00-£280.00, Jan-Dec, bus 1/4 ml, rail 28 mls, airport 47 mls

Louise Stewart
Steading Cottage, Sunlawshill, Kelso, Roxburghshire TD5 8LB
Tel: (Kelso) 01573 450272 Fax: 01573 450270

SELF CATERING

Two attractive, well equipped, semi-detached cottages. Centrally heated with appealing views. Set in the heart of the Borders countryside.

2 cottages, 1 pub rm, 1-3 bedrms (grd flr avail), sleeps 2-6, total sleeping capacity 10, £120.00-£300.00, Jan-Dec, bus 5 mls, rail 30 mls, airport 45 mls

P Twemlow
Roxburgh Newtown Farm, Kelso, Roxburghshire, TD5 8NN
Tel: (Roxburgh) 01573 450250 Fax: 01573 450250
Email: pauline.twemlow@which.net
Web: http//:homepages.which.net/~pauline.twemlow/

Kilmarnock, Ayrshire

Map Ref: 1G6

No 2 Old Rome Mews Cottage

Old Rome Farmhouse, Gatehead, by Kilmarnock KA2 9AJ
Tel: 01563 850265

Superb barn conversion in courtyard off the A759, 5 miles from Troon. Accommodation consists of 2 twin bedded rooms, 1 double bedded room, 2 bathrooms, showers, large lounge, colour TV, video, fully fitted kitchen, oil central heating. Bed linen included, excellent location for touring Ayrshire or golfing. Licensed restaurant serving excellent home-cooked food on site.

SELF CATERING

Converted byre with full central heating set in a small village midway between Irvine and Kilmarnock. Adjacent restaurant.

1 cottage, 1 pub rm, 3 bedrms (grd flr avail), sleeps 6, min let 3 days, £250.00-£450.00, Jan-Dec, bus 350 yds, rail 2 1/2 mls, airport 5 mls

Mrs R Elliot
Old Rome Farmhouse Hotel, No 2 Old Rome Mews Cottage, Gatehead, Kilmarnock, Ayrshire, KA2 9AJ
Tel: 01563 850265

SELF CATERING

Fully equipped detached farm cottage and farmhouse with lovely views, situated in open quiet countryside on working dairy farm, 1 mile east of Kilmarnock. Safe parking. Storage heaters and open fire. Ideal location for touring west of Scotland and Glasgow.

1 house, 1 bungalow, 1 pub rm, 3 bedrms, sleeps 6-9, total sleeping capacity 15, £140.00-£340.00, Jan-Dec, bus 1 ml, rail 2 mls, airport 20 mls

Mrs Mary Howie
Hillhouse Farm, Grassyards Road, Kilmarnock, Ayrshire, KA3 6HG
Tel: (Kilmarnock) 01563 523370

VAT is shown at 17.5%: changes in this rate may affect prices.

Key to symbols is on back flap.

Kippford, by Dalbeattie, Kirkcudbrightshire — **Map Ref: 2A10**

Kippford Caravan Park

Kippford, by Dalbeattie
Kirkcudbrightshire DG5 4LF
Telephone: 01556 620636 Fax: 01556 620636

Thistle award family owned park in undulating part of wooded setting, rocky outcrops planted with trees and flowering shrubs. Top quality caravan and bungalows for sale or hire, fully serviced with colour TV and fridge. Launderette, public phone. Tents and tourers, electric hook-ups. Free hot showers and covered washing-up areas. Adventure and junior play areas, small shop adjoining 9-hole golf course across road. Fishing, sailing, birdwatching etc, all very local.

✓ ✓ ✓ ✓ ✓

★★ SELF CATERING

Set in award-winning beautifully landscaped caravan park. Ideal centre for touring or for a relaxing holiday.

6 chalets, 1 pub rm, 3 bedrms, sleeps 4-6, total sleeping capacity 32, £85.00-£325.00, Mar-Oct, bus nearby, rail 17 mls, airport 60 mls

C M Aston
Kippford Caravan Park, by Dalbeattie, Kirkcudbrightshire, DG5 4LF
Tel: (Kippford) 01556 620636 Fax: 01556 620636

Kirkcudbright — **Map Ref: 2A10**

★ SELF CATERING

Self-contained flat adjoining farmhouse. On working dairy farm surrounded by open countryside.

1 flat, 1 pub rm, 1 bedrm, sleeps 5, £135.00-£160.00, Apr-Oct, bus ½ ml, rail 27 mls, airport 75 mls

Mrs Jean W Clark
Glencairn, Tarff, Kirkcudbright, DG6 4NQ
Tel: (Ringford) 015572 820343

★★ SELF CATERING

Traditional stone built cottages, recently modernised, double glazed and all electric. On farm in elevated position, 1 mile (2kms) from town.

2 cottages, 1 pub rm, 3-5 bedrms (grd flr avail), sleeps 2-10, total sleeping capacity 16, £180.00-£500.00, Jan-Dec, bus 1 ml, rail 30 mls, airport 90 mls

Mrs Dunlop
Cannee, Kirkcudbright, DG6 4XD
Tel: (Kirkcudbright) 01557 330684

Important: Prices stated are estimates and may be subject to amendments

Kirkcudbright

Map Ref: 2A10

★★★ SELF CATERING

Two non self-contained flats on first and second floors of large stonebuilt house standing in it's own 4.5 acres of garden, lawns and woodland. It is an ideal place for those who prefer a quiet holiday. Lawn tennis and croquet. 2.5 miles from Kirkcudbright.

2 flats, 2-4 pub rms, 2 bedrms, sleeps 4-6, total sleeping capacity 10, £115.00-£230.00, Jan-Dec, bus 2 1/2 mls, rail 30 mls, airport 100 mls

D M Henry
The Grange, Kirkcudbright, DG6 4XG
Tel: (Kirkcudbright) 01557 330519

★★ SELF CATERING

Maisonette attached to farmhouse in peaceful rural location, 4 miles from picturesque fishing town of Kirkcudbright. This well equipped property with ensuite bathroom makes this a comfortable base for a couple or a family of four. Available weekly or on a daily basis.

1 flat, 1 cottage, 1 pub rm, 1-3 bedrms (grd flr avail), sleeps 2-6, total sleeping capacity 10, £140.00-£175.00, Jun-Oct, bus 4 mls, rail 30 mls

Mrs E Wannop
Castle Creavie, Kirkcudbright, DG6 1QE
Tel: (Kirkcudbright) 01557 500238

Kirkoswald, Ayrshire

Map Ref: 1G8

★★ SELF CATERING

Spacious detailed house with extensive enclosed woodland gardens with river boundary on the edge of the village. Ideal for those interested in outdoor pursuits.

1 cottage, 2 pub rms, 3 bedrms (grd flr avail), sleeps 6, £180.00-£200.00, Jan-Dec, bus nearby, rail 7 mls

Mrs P Guthrie
The Manse, Kirkoswald, by Maybole, Ayrshire, KA19 8JA
Tel: (Kirkoswald) 01655 760210

Largs, Ayrshire

Map Ref: 1F5

★★ SELF CATERING

Flat in almost two acres of secluded surroundings of lawns, gardens and mature woodlands. 10 minute walk from Largs.

2 flats, 1 pub rm, 2-3 bedrms (grd flr avail), sleeps 4-6, total sleeping capacity 12, £100.00-£350.00, Apr-Oct, bus 50 yds, rail 1 ml, ferry 1 ml, airport 25 mls

Haus Saron Apartments
106 Greenock Road, Largs, Ayrshire, KA30 8PG
Tel: (Largs) 01475 673162 Fax: 01475 686244
Email: haussaraon@aol.com

★ SELF CATERING

2nd floor flat in 19th century villa with views over the Clyde to the islands. Access via main house. Ideal touring base even without a car.

1 flat, 1 pub rm, 3 bedrms, sleeps 5, £200.00-£300.00, Jan-Dec, bus 1/2 ml, rail 1/2 ml, ferry 1/2 ml, airport 30 mls

Mrs Seona Mills
6 Buchanan Street, Largs
Tel: (Largs) 01475 674290

VAT is shown at 17.5%: changes in this rate may affect prices.

Key to symbols is on back flap.

Lendalfoot, by Girvan, Ayrshire

Map Ref: 1F9

SELF CATERING

Modernised cottage on shore line with fine views to Ailsa Craig and Firth of Clyde. Own steps to beach and rocky shore. Peaceful setting.

1 cottage, 1 pub rm, 2 bedrms, sleeps 5, £95.00-£290.00, Jan-Dec, bus 1/2 ml, rail 9 mls

Mrs Moyra M Hay
50 Dalrymple Street, Girvan, Ayrshire, KA26 9BT
Tel: (Girvan) 01465 714421 Fax: 01465 714421

Lochmaben, Dumfriesshire

Map Ref: 2B9

SELF CATERING

Whitewashed cottage in peaceful rural setting 1.5 miles (2kms) from Lochmaben. Convenient base for touring Dumfries and Galloway and the Borders.

1 cottage, 1 pub rm, 3 bedrms, sleeps 2-6, £200.00-£220.00, Apr-Oct, bus 1 1/2 mls, rail 4 mls

Mrs J A Forsyth
60 Nunholm Road, Dumfries
Tel: (Dumfries) 01387 254212

SELF CATERING

Set on a commanding hillside giving spectacular views over the rolling South West Scotland countryside, Creagan Cottage, a detached traditional single storey cottage, will appeal to those seeking a peaceful holiday.

1 cottage, 3 pub rms, 4 bedrms (grd flr avail), sleeps 6-7, £180.00-£395.00, Jan-Dec, bus 1 ml, rail 8 mls, airport 75 mls

Mr & Mrs S Smith
Bank Top, Millers Dale, Derbyshire, SK17 8SN
Tel: (Millers Dale) 01298 872546/872165 Fax: 01298 872545

Lockerbie, Dumfriesshire

Map Ref: 2C9

SELF CATERING

This first floor flat with own private entrance has been tastefully converted from an old farmhouse. It is situated close to the pottery where you can take the opportunity to make your own pots. Safe enclosed play area for children.

1 flat, 1 pub rm, 2 bedrms, sleeps 4-6, up to £250.00, Jan-Dec, bus nearby, rail 5 mls, ferry 80 mls, airport 80 mls

Mr & Mrs Finch
Dalton Pottery, Meikle Dyke, Dalton, nr Lockerbie
Tel: (Carrutherstown) 01387 840236

Longformacus, Berwickshire

Map Ref: 2E5

SELF CATERING

Cottage of real character peacefully set in a row overlooking the river. Unspoilt village: fine centre for touring the Borders. Edinburgh 1 hour over the hammemuirs.

Mrs Jean Durbin
4 Inverleith Row, Edinburgh, EH3 5LP
Tel: (Edinburgh) 0131 5565398

Important: Prices stated are estimates and may be subject to amendments

Maybole, Ayrshire

Map Ref: 1G8

SELF CATERING

Recently renovated traditional cottage 10 miles (16kms) south of Ayr en route to Turnberry, by the Electric Brae.

1 cottage, 2 pub rms, 2 bedrms (grd flr avail), sleeps 2-4, £120.00-£220.00, Mar-Oct, bus 2 mls, rail 4 mls, ferry 20 mls, airport 12 mls

Mrs Margaret Johnstone Duncan
4 Arrol Drive, Ayr, Ayrshire, KA7 4AF
Tel: (Ayr) 01292 264022

SELF CATERING

Two cottages approx. 6 miles South of Ayr, each with their own private enclosed garden and parking. Tastefully decorated and furnished with many extras for all year comfort. Shops restaurants within walking distance. An ideal location within short travelling distance to many places of interest, coastal, country leisure and historic. In the heart of Burns Country and world famous golf courses. Glasgow 40 miles.

2 cottages, 1 pub rm, 2 bedrms (grd flr avail), sleeps 2-5, total sleeping capacity 8-10, from £140.00, Jan-Dec, bus nearby, rail 1/4 ml, ferry 40 mls, airport 12 mls

Mrs L Wallace
Lyonston, Maybole, Ayrshire, KA19 7HS
Tel: (Maybole) 01655 883176 Fax: 01655 883176

Melrose, Roxburghshire

Map Ref: 2D6

SELF CATERING

Modern detached cottage on 200 acre mixed sheep and arable farm near Melrose, with views to surrounding hills.

1 bungalow, 1 pub rm, sleeps 5-6, £120.00-£300.00, Apr-Oct

Mrs Cameron
Dimpleknowe, Lilliesleaf, Melrose, TD6 9JU
Tel: 01835870 333 Fax: 01835870 333

SELF CATERING

Award winning farm steading conversion. Small adjoining golf course, just 1/2 mile from Melrose and 40 miles from Edinburgh. Views over Tweed Valley. Five cottages are fully equipped for disabled visitors, two with welcome host.

1 flat, 5 cottages, 1 pub rm, 1-3 bedrms (grd flr avail), sleeps 1-6, total sleeping capacity 25, £240.00-£520.00, Jan-Dec, bus 1/2 ml, rail 35 mls, airport 42 mls

Mrs Jill Hart
Eildon Holiday Cottages, Dingleton Mains, Melrose, Roxburghshire, TD6 9HS
Tel: (Melrose) 01896 823258 Fax: 01896 823258

SELF CATERING

Attractive, compact Edwardian cottage, peacefully hidden behind Abbey, yet within 4 minutes of shops, hotels and restaurants.

1 house, 1 pub rm, 3 bedrms, sleeps 4, £206.00-£360.00, Apr-Nov, bus nearby, rail 40 mls, airport 40 mls

Mrs E Rodger
BRAIP Ltd, Abbey Place, Cloisters Road, Melrose, TD6 9LQ
Tel: (Melrose) 01896 822595

Minto, Roxburghshire

Map Ref: 2D7

Charming semi-detached country farm cottage nestling in the peaceful and fascinating Scottish Borders. South facing view to Minto Hill.

1 cottage, 1 pub rm, 2 bedrms (grd flr avail), sleeps 5, £150.00-£200.00, Apr-Oct, bus 4 mls, rail 50 mls, airport 50 mls

Mrs Susan Manners
Deanfoot Farm, Denholm,by Hawick, Roxburghshire, TD9 8SH
Tel: (Denholm) 01450 870229

Moffat, Dumfriesshire

Map Ref: 2B8

Mid 19th century terraced cottage on the outskirts of the town, recently modernised and upgraded. No children. No smoking.

1 cottage, 1 pub rm, 2 bedrms, sleeps 3, min let 3 nights, £140.00-£200.00, Jan-Dec, bus nearby, rail 15 mls

Mr & Mrs D A Armstrong
Boleskine, 4 Well Road, Moffat, Dumfriesshire, DG10 9AS
Tel: (Moffat) 01683 220601

Traditional stone built coachouse, fully renovated and set in courtyard off Waterside House, sharing 12 acres of woodland garden and river. Located in the lovely Moffat Water Valley. 3 miles from Moffat. Fishing, golf, birdwatching and walking. No-smoking. Brochure available.

1 cottage, 1 pub rm, 3 bedrms (grd flr avail), sleeps 6, £200.00-£400.00, Jan-Dec, bus 3 mls, rail 16 mls, airport 55 mls

Mrs Elizabeth Edwards
Waterside Coach House, Moffat, Dumfriesshire, DG10 9LF
Tel: (Moffat) 01683 220092

Self-contained lodges in a peaceful, rural wooded setting by a stream. Only 1 mile (2kms) from town centre.

4 bungalows, 2 pub rms, 3 bedrms (grd flr avail), sleeps 6, total sleeping capacity 24, £170.00-£360.00, Jan-Dec, bus 3/4 ml, rail 15 mls

Mr B Larmour
Heatheryhaugh, Moffat, Dumfriesshire, DG10 9LD
Tel: (Moffat) 01683 220107 Fax: 01683 220832

Two comfortably appointed apartments in a central position overlooking the town square and convenient for all amenities. Make this your base for exploring the beautiful countryside or enjoying your favourite pursuits. Golfing, fishing, bird watching and sightseeing.

2 flats, 2 pub rms, 2-4 bedrms, sleeps 6-8, total sleeping capacity 14, £210.00-£575.00, Jan-Dec, bus 100yds, rail 16 mls, airport 55 mls

Mrs A Wishart
3 Bath Place, Moffat, Dumfries and Galloway, DG10 9HS
Tel: (Moffat) 01683 220026

Important: Prices stated are estimates and may be subject to amendments

oniaive, Dumfriesshire

Map Ref: 2A9

★★ UP TO ★★★ SELF CATERING

Four well-equipped cottages set around a shared courtyard in the grounds of a large country house half a mile from the village of Moniaive. Convenient for walking the Southern Upland way or visiting Drumraurig Castle and the marbles of Durisdeer Church.

4 cottages, 1 pub rm, 1-4 bedrms (grd flr avail), sleeps 2-6, total sleeping capacity 14, £120.00-£340.00, Jan-Dec, bus 1/2 ml, rail 20 mls

Sue Grant
Glenluiart House, Moniaive, Dumfriesshire, DG3 4JA
Tel: 01848 200331 Fax: 01848 200675

ordington, Berwickshire

Map Ref: 2F5

★★ SELF CATERING

Stone built lodge to Mordington House, set in 70 acres of woodland. Excellent views over surrounding countryside. 4 miles (6kms) from Berwick.

1 bungalow, 2 pub rms, 2 bedrms, sleeps 4, £150.00-£210.00, Mar-Dec, bus 1/2 ml, rail 4 mls, airport 60 mls

Mrs J Trotter
Mordington House, Berwick-upon-Tweed, Northumberland, TD15 1XA
Tel: (Berwick-upon-Tweed) 01289 386470 Fax: 01289 386470
Email: j.trotter@btinternet.com

w Galloway, Kirkcudbrightshire

Map Ref: 1H9

★★★ SELF CATERING

Five charming cottages around a central courtyard, converted from the former home farm of Glenlee Estate, 2 miles (3km) from New Galloway and Delny in a peaceful woodland setting. Each spacious cottage has it's own character. Magnificent walks around a wooded glen. Free trout fishing. Pets welcome.

5 cottages, 1-2 pub rms, 2-3 bedrms, sleeps 4-7, total sleeping capacity 28, £190.00-£350.00, Mar-Nov, bus 2 mls, rail 28 mls, airport 45 mls

Mrs R Agnew
Glenlee Holiday Houses, New Galloway, Castle Douglas, Kirkcudbrightshire, DG7 3SF
Tel: (Dalry) 01644 430212 Fax: 01644 430340

wmilns, Ayrshire

Map Ref: 1H6

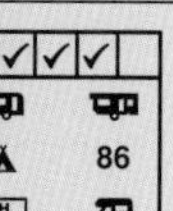

★★★ SELF CATERING

Loudon Mains is a converted farm steading situated in a commanding position on the hills overlooking the Irvine valley. The surrounding countryside is rich in wildlife and country walks abound. Ideal for touring Burns Country and easy access to Ayrshire's many golf courses. Loudon Theme Park is nearby for a fun day out.

7 cottages, 1 pub rm, 1-2 bedrms, sleeps 2-6, total sleeping capacity 30, £145.00-£360.00, Jan-Dec, bus 1 1/2 mls, rail 8 mls, airport 14 mls

Mrs M K Hodge
Loudoun Mains, Newmilns, Ayrshire, KA16 9LG
Tel: (Darvel) 01560 321246 Fax: 01560 320657
Email: loudounmains@btinternet.com

wton Stewart, Wigtownshire

Map Ref: 1G10

✓✓✓ 86

Creebridge Caravan Park
Newton Stewart, Wigtownshire, DG8 6AJ Tel: (Newton Stewart) 01671 412324 Fax: 01671 402324
Booking Enquiries: Creebridge Caravan Park Newton Stuart, DG8 6AJ

Tel: 01671 402324 Fax: 01671 402324

4 1/2 acres, mixed, Mar-Oct, prior booking in peak periods, latest time of arrival 2000, overnight holding area. Extra charge for electricity, awnings, showers.

25 tourers £8.00 and 5 motors £7.70 and 10 tents £7.20. Total Touring Pitches 40.

5 Holiday Caravans to let, sleep 6 £160.00-245.00, total sleeping capacity 30, min let 1 night.

Leisure facilities:

1/4 ml E of Newton Stewart off A75, or through centre of Newton Stewart over bridge to Minnigaff, 300 mtrs on right.

VAT is shown at 17.5%: changes in this rate may affect prices.

Key to symbols is on back flap.

Parton, by Castle Douglas, Dumfriesshire Map Ref: 2A9

✓✓✓✓✓ 80

Loch Ken Holiday Park

Parton, Castle Douglas, Kirkcudbrightshire, DG7 3NE Tel: (Parton) 01644 470282 Fax: 01644 470297

7 acres, grassy, level, sheltered, late March-early Nov, prior booking in peak periods, latest time of arrival 2000. Extra charge for electricity, awnings, showers.

55 tourers from £8.00 or 30 motors from £8.00 or 30 tents from £7.00. Total Touring Pitches 55.

14 Holiday Caravans to let, sleep 4-6 from £150.00, total sleeping capacity 78, min let 2 nights.

Leisure facilities:

from A75 Castle Douglas bypass follow A713 for 7 mls. From A77 Ayr bypass follow A713 for 44 mls. Park entrance is off A713.

Peebles Map Ref: 2C6

★★★ SELF CATERING

Deceptively spacious dormer bungalow on A703 on outskirts of Peebles. Double glazing and full central heating.

1 bungalow, 2 pub rms, 3 bedrms (grd flr avail), sleeps 5, £185.00-£250.00, Jan-Dec, bus nearby, rail 23 mls, airport 23 mls

Mrs Loraine Chisholm
Ferndene, 93 Edinburgh Road, Peebles, Tweeddale, EH45 8ED
Tel: (Peebles) 01721 720501 Fax: 01721 720501

✓✓✓✓✓ 130

Crossburn Caravan Park

Edinburgh Road, Peebles, EH45 8ED
Tel: (Peebles) 01721 720501 Fax: 01721 720501
Email: xburncaravans@matrex.co.uk
Web: www.martex.co.uk/nec/xburn

6 acres, mixed, Apr-Oct, prior booking in peak periods, latest time of arrival 2300, overnight holding area. Extra charge for electricity, awnings.

35 tourers £9.00-10.00 or 35 motors £8.50-9.50 or 35 tents £8.00-10.00. Total Touring Pitches 35.

4 Holiday Caravans to let, sleep 3-5 £225.00-325.00, total sleeping capacity 18, min let 3 nights.

Leisure facilities:

1/2 ml N of Peebles on A703.

★★★ SELF CATERING

The original byre of Winkston Farm has been carefully converted to form two charming semi-detached cottages which retain the original character of the rhine-stone building, with its natural wood interior and pine floors. Open plan design and tastefully decorated with spiral staircase to upper sleeping area.

2 cottages, 1 pub rm, 2 bedrms, sleeps 4, total sleeping capacity 8, min let weekend, £165.00-£295.00, Jan-Dec, bus 100yds

Mrs Janice Haydock
Winkston Farmhouse, Peebles, Tweeddale, EH45 8PH
Tel: (Peebles) 01721 721264

★★★★ SELF CATERING

Original coach house c1750 with views of Glentress Forest. Fully modernised, peaceful courtyard setting with own walled garden and stream yet less than a mile to the centre of historic Peebles.

1 coach house, 1 pub rm, 2 bedrms (grd flr avail), sleeps 4, £250.00-£350.00, Apr-Oct, bus nearby, rail 23 mls, airport 24 mls

Mrs Holmes
Kerfield Cottage, Innerleithen Road, Peebles, EH45 8BG
Tel: (Peebles) 01721 720264

Important: Prices stated are estimates and may be subject to amendments

eebles — Map Ref: 2C6

★★★
SELF CATERING

Cosy cottage style upper flat over looking the "Cuddy Burn" in the centre of this historic town. Walking distance to all amenities and restaurants.

1 flat, from £180.00, Jan-Dec, bus ¼ ml

Miss Evelyn Inglis
46 Edinburgh Road, Peebles, EH45 8EB
Tel: (Peebles) 01721 720226

★★
SELF CATERING

Cottage on 1300 acre farm, in area of scenic beauty. Ideal base for touring and walking. 4 miles (6 kms) from Peebles. 23 miles from Edinburgh.

1 cottage, 1 pub rm, 4 bedrms (grd flr avail), sleeps 8, £200.00-£375.00, Jan-Dec, bus 4 mls, rail 23 mls, airport 24 mls

Mrs Arran Waddell
Lyne Farmhouse, by Lyne Station, Peebles, EH45 8NR
Tel: (Kirkton Manor) 01721 740255

★★
SELF CATERING

Whinstone built lower flat in residential area of Peebles, also centrally located flat with sunny rear garden. Ideal touring base. Varied local amenities.

2 flats, 1 pub rm, 4 bedrms, sleeps 6, total sleeping capacity 12, £200.00-£325.00, Apr-Sep, bus ¼ ml, rail 24 mls, airport 24 mls

Mr & Mrs R K Walkinshaw
The Glack Farm, Manor, Peebles, EH45 9JL
Tel: (Kirkton Manor) 01721 740277

rtpatrick, Wigtownshire — Map Ref: 1F10

★★★★
SELF CATERING

Cosy garden flat centrally situated in picturesque coastal village, 100 yards from the harbour. Enclosed private garden.

1 flat, 2 pub rms, 1 bedrm (grd flr avail), sleeps 2, min let weekend, £70.00-£140.00, Jan-Dec, bus nearby, rail 8 mls, ferry 8 mls, airport 70 mls

Mr P Benney
Sowberry Cottage, Moulsford, Oxon, OX10 9JG
Tel: (Cholsey) 01491 651346

✓✓✓

90

Sunnymeade Caravan Park

Portpatrick, Wigtownshire, DG9 8LN Tel: (Portpatrick) 01776 810293
Fax: 01776 810293

8 acres, grassy, hard-standing, level, Mar-Oct, prior booking in peak periods. Extra charge for electricity, showers.

15 tourers £7.00-9.00 or 15 motors £7.00-9.00 or 15 tents £7.00-9.00. Total Touring Pitches 15.

5 Holiday Caravans to let, sleep 6 £140.00-300.00, total sleeping capacity 30, min let 2 nights.

Leisure facilities:

Take A77 to Portpatrick, on entering the village turn left. Park ¼ ml on left.

Port William, Wigtownshire

Map Ref: 1G11

★★ SELF CATERING

Comfortable cottages from Lermay close to the shore with views over Luce Bay to the Mull of Galloway.

1 flat, 2 cottages, 1 pub rm, 2 bedrms (grd flr avail), sleeps 4-5, total sleeping capacity 13, £150.00-£400.00, Jan-Dec, bus nearby, rail 17 mls, ferry 17 mls, airport 100 mls

Hon Mrs Andrew Agnew
Sweethaws Farm, Crowborough, Sussex, TN6 3SS
Tel: (Crowborough) 01892 655045

★★★ SELF CATERING

In an elevated position in the village, this comfortable first floor apartment with large enclosed garden has the benefit of lovely sea views out over the village looking towards the harbour. Ideal base for which to discover the beautiful coasts and countryside this corner of Scotland has to offer, with sandy beaches, sea fishing, golf, pleasant walks and birdwatching all at hand.

1 flat, 2 pub rms, 3 bedrms (grd flr avail), sleeps 5, £90.00-£200.00, Jan-Dec, bus nearby, rail 25 mls, ferry 25 mls, airport 70 mls

Mrs J Kinnear
Glen Maree, Monreith, Newton Stewart, DG8 9LW
Tel: (Port William) 01988 700356

Prestwick, Ayrshire

Map Ref: 1G7

★★ SELF CATERING

Self-contained cottage all on ground floor in gardens of hotel with private parking. Short distance from town centre, railway station, golf course and beaches. Close to airport.

1 cottage, 1 pub rm, 1 bedrm (grd flr avail), sleeps 4, £150.00-£200.00, Jan-Dec, bus nearby, rail 1/4 ml, airport 1 ml

The Fairways
19 Links Road, Prestwick, Ayrshire, KA9 1QG
Tel: (Prestwick) 01292 470396 Fax: 01292 470396

Ringford, Kirkcudbrightshire

Map Ref: 2A10

★★★ SELF CATERING

At Queenshill we offer holidays to suit all tastes. Our visitors can enjoy either a quiet relaxing " get away from it all" holiday or one with more activity. Available to our visitors on site are: farm tours, bicycles for hire, pony trekking, fishing, clay pidgeon shooting, tennis and nature trails.

6 chalets, 1 flat, 3 cottages, 1 10 bed dormitory, 2 bedrms (grd flr avail), sleeps 2-4, total sleeping capacity 50, £150.00-£380.00, Jan-Dec, bus 1 ml, rail 30 mls

Queenshill Country Cottages
Fellend, Ringford, Castle Douglas, DG7 2AT
Tel: (Ringford) 01557 820227 Fax: 01557 820227

Rockcliffe, by Dalbeattie, Kirkcudbrightshire

Map Ref: 2A10

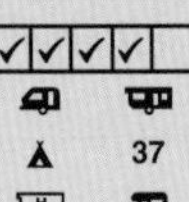

Castle Point Caravan Site
Rockcliffe, by Dalbeattie, Kirkcudbrightshire, DG5 4QL Tel: (Rockcliffe) 01556 630248

3 acres, grassy, level, sloping, Mar-Oct, prior booking in peak periods. Extra charge for electricity, awnings.

E W D

29 tourers £7.75-10.20 or 29 motors £7.75-10.20 or 29 tents £7.75-10.20. Total Touring Pitches 29.

6 Holiday Caravans to let, sleep 6 £150.00-280.00, total sleeping capacity 36, min let 1 night.

E

From Dalbeattie take A710 SW for 5 mls, turn right to Rockcliffe, then after 1 ml turn left down signposted road to Site.

Important: Prices stated are estimates and may be subject to amendments

ockcliffe, by Dalbeattie, Kirkcudbrightshire

Map Ref: 2A10

SELF CATERING

Individual farm properties on the edge of a small village within easy reach of the beach. Kirkland Farmhouse has an open fire and a large, private garden.

1 house, 1 cottage, 1 , 1-3 pub rms, 2-4 bedrms (grd flr avail), sleeps 2-9, total sleeping capacity 10, min let weekend, £95.00-£490.00, Jan-Dec, bus nearby, rail 18 mls, airport 70 mls.

Mrs S Sinclair
Mount of Glenluffin, Rockcliffe, Dalbeattie, Kirkcudbrightshire
Tel: (Rockcliffe) 01556 630205

omanno Bridge, Peeblesshire

Map Ref: 2C6

SELF CATERING

Traditional semi-detached stone cottage accessed up a flight of steps on small holding. 3 miles (5kms) from West Linton on A701. An excellent golf course at West Linton and fishing on our private stretch of River Lynne. Ideal base for exploring Borders and Edinburgh area.

1 cottage, 2 pub rms, 1 bedrm (grd flr avail), sleeps 2, £140.00-£180.00, May-Sep, bus 3 1/2 mls, rail 17 mls, airport 20 mls

Dr Margaret Habeshaw
Damside, Romanno Bridge, West Linton, Peeblesshire, EH46 7BY
Tel: (West Linton) 01968 660887 Fax: 01968 660887

ltcoats, Ayrshire

Map Ref: 1G6

SELF CATERING

Spacious family house on dairy farm, with open views over the Firth of Clyde towards Arran. Large sun porch and separate dining room add to the large public areas.

1 house, 3 pub rms, 3 bedrms, sleeps 7, £150.00-£300.00, Apr-Oct, bus 1 ml, rail 2 mls, ferry 3 mls, airport 20 mls

Mrs A Hogarth
Knockrivoch Farm, Saltcoats, Ayrshire, KA21 6NH
Tel: (Saltcoats) 01294 463052

ndhead, Wigtownshire

Map Ref: 1F11

SELF CATERING

Comfortable, cosy cottage with garden and lovely views. Ideally situated for enjoying the peace and tranquility of the Galloway Hills and Solway Firth. 3 golf courses within easy reach, including the Links at Portpatrick.

1 cottage, 3 pub rms, 2 bedrms (grd flr avail), sleeps 4, £195.00-£370.00, Mar-Dec, bus 1 1/2 mls, rail 8 mls, ferry 8 mls, airport 80 mls

Peter J Benney
Sowberry Cottage, Moulsford, Oxon OX10 9JG
Tel: (Cholsey) 01491 651346

60

Sands of Luce Caravan Park
Sandhead,by Stranraer, Wigtownshire, DG9 9JR Tel: (Sandhead) 01776 830456 Fax: 01776 830456

12 acres, mixed, mid Mar-Oct, prior booking in peak periods, latest time of arrival 2200, overnight holding area. Extra charge for electricity, awnings.

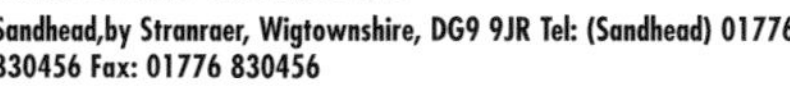

36 tourers £7.00-9.00 or 36 motors £6.50-8.50 or 10 tents £7.00-9.00. Total Touring Pitches 36.

6 Holiday Caravans to let, sleep 4-6 £140.00-285.00, total sleeping capacity 30, min let 2 days.

Leisure facilities:

From Stranraer take A77/A716 S for 7 mls. Entrance at junction of A716/B7084 approx. 1 ml N of Sandhead.

VAT is shown at 17.5%: changes in this rate may affect prices.

Key to symbols is on back flap.

Sandyhills, by Dalbeattie, Kirkcudbrightshire

Map Ref: 2B10

SELF CATERING

Log houses of varied character & design with B.H.S. Approved Riding School & Trekking centre. Sandy beach 400 yds. Indoor pool. A la carte restaurant and bar meals.

27 log cabins, 1-2 pub rms, 2-3 bedrms, sleeps 5-10, total sleeping capacity 236, £160.00-£530.00, Jan-Dec, bus nearby, rail 18 mls, airport 100 mls

Barend Properties Ltd
Sandyhills, Dalbeattie, Kirkcudbrightshire, DG5 4NU
Tel: (Southwick) 01387 780663 Fax: 01387 780283

Seamill, Ayrshire

Map Ref: 1F6

SELF CATERING

First floor apartment with own private entrance within large country house, set in 2 acres of garden with magnificent views over West Kilbride, Golf course, Firth of Clyde and the picturesque Isle of Arran.

1 flat, 1 pub rm, 1 bedrm, sleeps 2, £150.00-£220.00, Jan-Dec, bus 1/4 ml, rail 1 ml, ferry 5 mls, airport 30 mls

Mrs A Wilson
Ardchattan, Summerlea Road, Seamill, West Kilbride, KA23 9HP
Tel: (West Kilbride) 01294 822238

Skelmorlie, Ayrshire

Map Ref: 1F5

SELF CATERING

Converted apartment adjoining castle retaining many original features, with panoramic views. Excellent base for touring. Near marinas. South wing in maincastle. Also available with outstanding views.

1 house, 1 flat, 1-2 pub rms, 3 bedrms, sleeps 5-6, total sleeping capacity 11, £100.00-£450.00, Jan-Dec, bus 1 1/2 mls, rail 1 1/2 mls, ferry 1 1/2 mls

Mrs V Wilson
Skelmorlie Castle, Skelmorlie, Ayrshire, PA17 5EY
Tel: (Wemyss Bay) 01475 521127/521616 Fax: 01475 521616

Southerness, Dumfriesshire

Map Ref: 2B10

SELF CATERING

Terraced cottage situated on the seashore of the Solway coast with excellent sea views. Ideal for golfers, walkers and for touring the area.

1 cottage, 2 pub rms, 3 bedrms, sleeps 6, £250.00-£260.00, Jan-Dec, bus nearby, rail 15 mls, airport 70 mls

Miss M E Brown
Wendy Cottage, Auchenlarie, Gatehouse of Fleet, Kirkcudbrightshire, DG7 2EU
Tel: (Mossyard) 01557 840261/01725 518418

Straiton, by Maybole, Ayrshire

Map Ref: 1G8

SELF CATERING

Blairquhan is surrounded by a country estate in the beautiful wooded valley of the Water of Girvan. The Dower House and 7 holiday cottages are available all year round. Our guests can enjoy walks and picnics anywhere on the 2,000 acre estate or fish in the river lochs. Ayrshire is a world centre for golf. Local places of interest include Crossraguel Abbey, Culzean Castle and its country park, Loch Doon and the seaside resorts of Ayr and Girvan.

5 houses, 1 flat, 2 cottages, 1-4 pub rms, 1-10 bedrms (grd flr avail), sleeps 5-18, total sleeping capacity 60, £123.00-£136.00, Jan-Dec, bus 4 mls, rail 7 mls, airport 20 mls

Mrs A Hay
Blairquhan Estate Office, Maybole, Ayrshire, KA19 7LZ
Tel: (Straiton) 01655 770239 Fax: 01655 770278

Important: Prices stated are estimates and may be subject to amendments

Stranraer, Wigtownshire

Map Ref: 1F10

SELF CATERING

Superb sea views from two uniquely located cottages, adjacent to 18c lighthouse. North Channel Cottage has a large conservatory/sitting room with 300 degrees sea view.

2 cottages, 1-2 pub rms, 1-2 bedrms (grd flr avail), sleeps 2-4, total sleeping capacity 6, min let 1 night, £400.00-£1400.00, Jan-Dec, bus 4 mls, rail 11 mls, ferry 11 mls, airport 50 mls

Corsewall Lighthouse Hotel
Stranraer
Tel: 01776 853220 Fax: 01776 854231

SELF CATERING

Three recently renovated cottages in courtyard setting, large garden suitable for relaxing or barbecuing. Walking, golf and country sports available locally.

3 cottages, 1-2 pub rms, 2 bedrms (grd flr avail), sleeps 4-6, total sleeping capacity 14, £125.00-£350.00, Jan-Dec, bus 2 mls, rail 2 mls, ferry 2 mls, airport 60 mls

H G Walker
Bridgend, Old Port Road, Stranraer, DG9 8JA
Tel: (Stranraer) 01776 705529 Fax: 01776 705529

SELF CATERING

Set amidst open countryside on a small holding. These 2 cosy cottages are close to the start of the Southern Upland Way and are perfect for those enjoying walking and cycling. Locally there is a leisure centre, golf course and plenty of attractive gardens to visit.

2 flats, 2 bedrms (grd flr avail), sleeps 4, total sleeping capacity 8, £140.00-£240.00, Jan-Dec, bus nearby, rail 1 1/2 mls, ferry 1 1/2 mls, airport 55 mls

Mrs Anne Wilson
Spoutwells House, Stranraer, Wigtownshire, DG9 8LX
Tel: (Stranraer) 01776 704086

Troon, Ayrshire

Map Ref: 1G7

SELF CATERING

Two first floor flats situated in town centre, convenient for local shops. Close to local beaches and golf courses. Both flats have telephones which receive incoming calls only.

2 flats, 1 pub rm, 2 bedrms, sleeps 4-5, total sleeping capacity 10, £130.00-£250.00, Jan-Dec, bus nearby, rail 1/2 ml, airport 5 mls

Marion I Gibson
16 Harling Drive, Troon, Ayrshire, KA10 6NF
Tel: (Troon) 01292 312555

SELF CATERING

Second floor top flat on seafront with magnificent views over beach and sea. Near shops and transport. On street parking.

1 flat, 1 pub rm, 2 bedrms, sleeps 2-6, £160.00-£320.00, Jan-Dec, bus nearby, rail 1/2 ml, airport 3 mls

Mrs M Tweedie
50 Ottoline Drive, Troon, Ayrshire, KA10 7AW
Tel: (Troon) 01292 313312 Fax: 01292 319007
Email: andrew@scotsec.demon.co.uk

VAT is shown at 17.5%: changes in this rate may affect prices.

Key to symbols is on back flap.

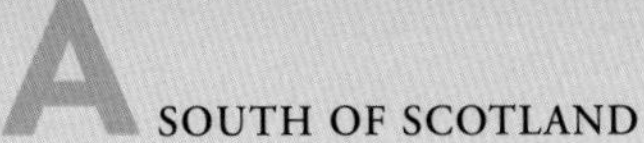

West Linton, Peeblesshire

Map Ref: 2B6

★★★ SELF CATERING

Attractive individual cottages one of which is attached to owner's house, set in 100 acres of woodlands overlooking stocked private fishing loch.

2 cottages, 1 pub rm, 2-3 bedrms (grd flr avail), sleeps 4-6, total sleeping capacity 10, from £310.00, Jan-Dec, bus nearby, rail 18 mls, airport 24 mls

Mrs C M Kilpatrick
Slipperfield House, West Linton, Peeblesshire, EH46 7AA
Tel: (West Linton) 01968 660401 Fax: 01968 660401
Email: hols@kilpat.demon.co.uk
Web: http://www.kilpat.demon.co.uk

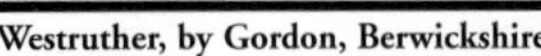

Westruther, by Gordon, Berwickshire

Map Ref: 2E6

★★ SELF CATERING

Modern semi-detached single storey cottage on large mixed farm. Superb view of surrounding countryside. Westruther 1.5mls (3kms), Edin 40mls (64kms).

1 cottage, 1 pub rm, 3 bedrms (grd flr avail), sleeps 5, £180.00-£230.00, May-Nov, bus 6 mls, rail 25 mls, airport 40 mls

Mrs M MacFarlane
Flass, Westruther, Gordon, Berwickshire, TD3 6NJ
Tel: (Westruther) 01578 740215 Fax: 01578 740215

Yetholm, by Kelso, Roxburghshire

Map Ref: 2E7

★ SELF CATERING

Homely terraced cottages on a typical Borders sheep farm in the Cheviot Hills commanding excellent views. Ideal hillwalking/touring base.

2 cottages, 1 pub rm, 2-3 bedrms (grd flr avail), sleeps 5-7, total sleeping capacity 12, min let weekend (low season), £80.00-£200.00, Jan-Dec, bus 2 1/2 mls, rail 20 mls, airport 50 mls

Mrs A Freeland-Cook
Cliftoncote Farm, Yetholm, Kelso, Roxburghshire, TD5 8PU
Tel: (Yetholm) 01573 420241

Important: Prices stated are estimates and may be subject to amendments

Edinburgh and Lothians

Who could ever tire of Edinburgh and the hills, beaches, castles and golf courses in the Lothian countryside around it?? With a city skyline every bit as spectacular as the postcards suggest, Scotland's capital is simply outstanding.

Though it reaches near capacity during the annual Edinburgh International Festival in late August, when the great accommodation choice outside the city is at its most valuable, Edinburgh remains the liveliest of places all year round.

Its castle is one of the most famous symbols of Scotland. Though there is much to see here it is only one of a whole range of historic attractions stretching down the Royal Mile, the heart of the Old Town of Edinburgh. Between the castle and the Palace of Holyroodhouse are museums such as Huntly House or the unique Museum of Childhood, historic properties such as John Knox House or Gladstone's Land and attractions such as the Scotch Whisky Heritage Centre. There is also a whole range of historic details to be explored – and excellent shopping and plenty of places to eat as well. The same is true of the towns of the Lothians: attractive Georgian architecture in places like Haddington, or superb giftwares such as crystal glassware from Penicuik.

As a major cultural centre, Edinburgh is well supplied with galleries and important collections: the National Gallery of Scotland is simply unmissable for any art lover, while the Fruitmarket Gallery and the City Art Centre ring the changes with their stimulating exhibition programme. The Gallery of Modern Art extends the cultural options further, as do a range of smaller commercial galleries.

The fine Georgian streets of Edinburgh's New Town, with their cobbles and grand facades, add much to the city ambience.

The fine Georgian streets of Edinburgh's New Town, with their cobbles and grand facades, add much to the city ambience. The period settings of the National Trust for Scotland's Georgian House in Charlotte Square re-create life the New Town in the time of its first occupants. Only a little further afield, the city's Royal Botanic Garden features the largest rhododendron collection in the world, and many other horticultural delights besides – worth a visit at any season.

As a relaxing green space in the bustling city, 'the Botanics' also offer fine views south, over the city rooftops to the Pentland Hills. These rolling hills are a reminder that an essential part of the Edinburgh experience is really outside the city, in the attractive Lothians countryside which surrounds it.

You can get to grips with the Lothians countryside at high-level places like the Pentland Hills, or sea-level sites like the John Muir Country Park, near the handsome little resort of Dunbar.

However, there is plenty more to see: Tantallon Castle on its dramatic coastal headland setting, Linlithgow Palace, birthplace of Mary, Queen of Scots, Hopetoun House for sheer opulence and style. Explore the attractive red-roofed villages out in the wooded countryside below the Lammermuir Hills, discover Scotland's finest mediaeval stone carving at Rosslyn Chapel by the village of Roslin, or experience a day in the life of a miner at the Scottish Mining Museum at Newtongrange. Remember, too, that the coastline and countryside of the Lothians is all so easy to reach from the city. Combine city and countryside for the total experience.

Events

Edinburgh - City, Coast & Countryside

Mar 22 – Apr 17

Puppet Animation Festival
Annual festival of the best of film and television from Scotland, Ireland, Wales, Cornwall and Brittany.
Netherbow Arts Centre, Edinburgh.
Contact: Simon Hart.
Tel: 0131 556 6579.

Apr 1 – 4

Edinburgh Folk Festival
One of Britain's premier folk festivals. Various venues in Edinburgh.
Contact: David Francis.
Tel: 0131 556 3092/0585.

Apr 3 – 18

Edinburgh International Science Festival
The World's largest event devoted to the celebration of science.
Contact: Dr Simon Gage.
Tel: 0131 220 3977.

June 24 – 27

Royal Highland Show
Scotland's national agricultural show,
Ingliston, Edinburgh.
Tel: 0131 333 2444.

Aug 6 – 28

Edinburgh Military Tattoo
The Castle Esplanade, Edinburgh Castle.
Contact: The Box Office.
Tel: 0131 225 1188.

Aug 15 – Sep 4

Edinburgh International Festival
One of the world's most prestigious arts festivals. Various venues in Edinburgh.
Contact: Festival Office.
Tel: 0131 473 2001 Fax: 0131 473 2002/3.

Aug 16 – 30

Edinburgh International Film Festival
Edinburgh Filmhouse Theatre,
Lothian Road, Edinburgh.
Tel: 0131 228 4051.
e.mail: info@edifilfest.org.uk

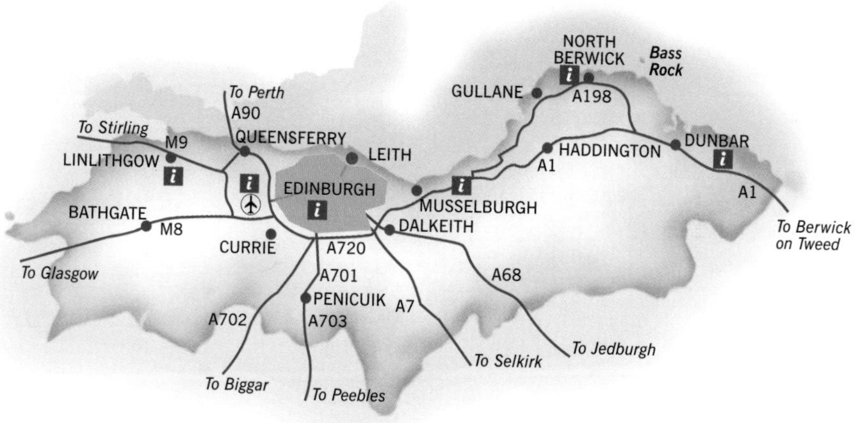

Area Tourist Board Addresses

Edinburgh and Lothians Tourist Board
Edinburgh and Scotland Information Centre
3 Princes Street
EDINBURGH
EH2 2QP
Tel: 0131 473 3800
Fax: 0131 473 3881
e.mail:
esic@eltb.org
website:
www.edinburgh.org

Edinburgh and Lothians

Tourist Information Centres in Scotland

EDINBURGH & LOTHIANS TOURIST BOARD

DUNBAR ♿
143 High Street
Tel: (01368) 863353
Jan-Dec

EDINBURGH ♿ ✉
Edinburgh & Scotland
Information Centre
3 Princes Street, EH2 2QP
Tel: (0131) 473 3800
Jan-Dec

EDINBURGH AIRPORT ♿
Tourist Information Desk
Tel: (0131) 333 2167
Jan-Dec

LINLITHGOW ♿ ✉
Burgh Halls
The Cross, EH49 7EJ
Tel: (01506) 844600
Jan-Dec

NEWTONGRANGE
Scottish Mining Museum
Lady Victoria Colliery
Tel: (0131) 663 4262
Apr-Oct

NORTH BERWICK
Quality Street
Tel: (01620) 892197
Jan-Dec

OLDCRAIGHALL ♿
Granada Service Area (A1)
Musselburgh
Tel: (0131) 653 6172
Jan-Dec

PENICUIK
Edinburgh Crystal
Visitor Centre
Eastfield
Tel: (01968) 673846
May-Oct

✉ Accept written enquiries
♿ Disabled access

erlady, East Lothian
Map Ref: 2D4

Aberlady Station Caravan Park
Haddington Road, Aberlady, East Lothian, EH32 0PZ Tel: 01875 870666

15 tourers £8.50 or 15 motors £8.50 or 20 tents £6.50. Total Touring Pitches 15.

4.5 acres, grassy, hard-standing, Mar-Oct. Extra charge for electricity.

SELF CATERING

Traditional stone upstairs flat attached to owners house. Situated in an attractive conservation village. There are 7 golf courses within 5 miles. An ideal location for coastal walks, bird watching, yet only 17 miles from Edinburgh city.

1 flat, 1 pub rm, 1 bedrm, sleeps 2, £125.00-£250.00, Jan-Dec, bus nearby, rail 3 mls, airport 25 mls

Mrs J McCallum
Seafield, Main Street, Aberlady, East Lothian, EH32 0RB
Tel: (Aberlady) 01875 870736

alkeith, Midlothian
Map Ref: 2C5

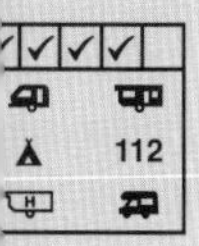

SELF CATERING

2 self catering apartments one in up market residential area of Edinburgh and the other in the conservation area of Eskbank. Ideal for the capital experience and country touring.

2 flats, 2 pub rms, 2-3 bedrms (grd flr avail), sleeps 4-5, total sleeping capacity 10-11, £220.00-£650.00, Jan-Dec, bus nearby, rail 7 mls, airport 8 mls

Mr E D H MacRae & Mrs I B H MacRae
45 Eskbank Road, Dalkeith, Midlothian, EH22 3BH
Tel: 0131 663 3291 Fax: 0131 663 3291
Email: ewan.a2362540@infotrade.co.uk

unbar, East Lothian
Map Ref: 2E4

112

Belhaven Bay Caravan Park
Belhaven Bay, Dunbar, East Lothian, EH42 1TU Tel: (North Berwick) 01620 893348 Fax: 01620 895623
Booking Enquiries: Tantallon Caravan Park Dunbar Road, North Berwick

Tel: 01620 893348 Fax: 01620 895623

8 acres, grassy, hard-standing, sheltered, mid Mar-Oct, prior booking in peak periods, overnight holding area. Extra charge for electricity, awnings.

60 tourers from £6.00 or 60 motors £5.75-9.50 or 60 tents £5.00-7.50. Total Touring Pitches 60.

5 Holiday Caravans to let, sleep 6 £130.00-350.00, total sleeping capacity 30, min let 1 night.

From S or N follow A1 to r/bout west of Dunbar.

SELF CATERING

Modernised flat with balcony, close to traditional fishing harbour. Within easy walking distance of town centre and leisure pool. Ideal base for golfers and families.

1 house, 2 pub rms, 3 bedrms (grd flr avail), min let 4 days, to £285.00, Jan-Dec, rail 1 ml

Mrs P Dawson
Walnut Tree House, Village Road, Coleshill, Amersham, Bucks, HP7 0LG
Tel: (Amersham) 01494 433036

VAT is shown at 17.5%: changes in this rate may affect prices.

Key to symbols is on back flap.

Dunbar, East Lothian

Map Ref: 2E4

SELF CATERING

Two cottages and East wing of 19c mansion. In extensive grounds with walled garden, quiet and peaceful. Two paddocks with interesting animals.

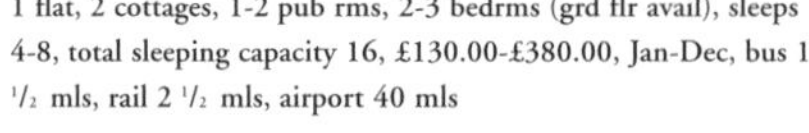

1 flat, 2 cottages, 1-2 pub rms, 2-3 bedrms (grd flr avail), sleeps 4-8, total sleeping capacity 16, £130.00-£380.00, Jan-Dec, bus 1 1/2 mls, rail 2 1/2 mls, airport 40 mls

Mrs Moira Marrian
Bowerhouse, Dunbar, East Lothian, EH42 1RE
Tel: (Dunbar) 01368 862293

SELF CATERING

Recently restored two-storey, pan tiled cottage. Pleasantly situated with rural outlook and adjacent to babbling trout stream. 25 miles from Edinburgh. Ideal base for beaches, golfing and Lammermuir Hills. Strictly no-smoking.

1 cottage, 1 pub rm, 1 bedrm, sleeps 2, £125.00-£250.00, Jan-Dec, bus 1 1/2 mls, rail 5 mls, airport 30 mls

June Wilson
The Lint Mill, Stenton,by Dunbar, East Lothian, EH42 1TD
Tel: (Dunbar) 01368 850354

Edinburgh

Map Ref: 2C5

SELF CATERING

Refurbished cottage semi-detached to owner's house with rear patio and garden. Easy access to local amenities and on main bus route to city centre.

1 cottage, 1 pub rm, 2 bedrms, sleeps 4, £250.00-£400.00, Apr-Sep, bus nearby, rail 4 mls, airport 14 mls

Mr Aitken
St Margarets Cottage, 32 Duddingston Park, Edinburgh, EH15 1JU
Tel: 0131 6698327

SELF CATERING

Third floor flat in apartment block with lift. Centrally situated near Princes Street, Conference Centre and Theatres. Private leisure facilities include pool, sauna and gym. Superb view of Edinburgh Castle.

1 flat, 1 pub rm, 1 bedrm, sleeps 4, min let 3 nights, £430.00-£565.00, Jan-Dec, bus nearby, rail 1/2 ml, airport 7 1/2 mls

Mr Lloyd Ballantyne
Lothian House Building Manager, Apt 38 Lothian House, 124 Lothian Road, Edinburgh, EH3 9DD
Tel: 0131 221 1888 Fax: 0131 229 2295
Email: lothian39@hotmail.com
Web: www.aboutscotland.co.uk/edin/lothian.html

SELF CATERING

Spacious first floor flat, close to main bus route (city centre 15 mins).

1 flat, 1 pub rm, 1 bedrm, sleeps 2, £350.00-£450.00, Jun-Sep, bus nearby, rail 1 ml, airport 7 mls

Mrs M Ballentyne
4 Hampton Terrace, Edinburgh, EH12 5JD
Tel: 0131 337 1210 Fax: 0131 337 1210
Email: georgeb@netcomuk.co.uk
Web: www.netcomuk/~georgeb/ballentyne.html

Important: Prices stated are estimates and may be subject to amendments

inburgh **Map Ref: 2C5**

SELF ATERING

Compact self-contained flat in large house, with excellent coastal views. Excellent bus service to city centre (15 minutes). Off street parking. 5 - 10 minutes walk to Joppa Beach, and within easy access of East Lothian.

1 flat, 1 pub rm, 1 bedrm, sleeps 4, £180.00-£280.00, Jan-Dec, bus nearby, rail 3 1/2 mls, airport 10 mls

Baronscourt
7 Milton Road East, Edinburgh, EH15 2ND
Tel: 0131 669 6900

SELF ATERING

Traditional farm cottage on sheep farm in the Pentlands. Hillwalking from the doorstep yet only 12 miles (19kms) from Edinburgh and 5 miles to motorway.

1 cottage, 2 pub rms, 2 bedrms (grd flr avail), sleeps 5, £245.00-£405.00, Jan-Dec, bus 4 mls, rail 12 mls, airport 8 mls

Bavelaw Estate
Wester Bavelaw, Balerno, Edinburgh, EH14 7JS
Tel: 0131 449 5515

SELF ATERING

Well furnished flats. Quiet central location. Private parking. Overlooking Arthurs Seat. Convenient for central amenities.

4 flats, 1 pub rm, 1-2 bedrms (grd flr avail), sleeps 2-4, total sleeping capacity 14, £212.00-£503.00, Jan-Dec, bus nearby, rail 1 ml, airport 8 mls

Mrs I A Birt
Beechwood, Woodhead, Fyvie, Turriff, Aberdeenshire, AB53 8LT
Tel: (Fyvie) 01651 891341 Fax: 01651 891341

★★★★

SELF ATERING

Beneath the castle in the heart of the Old Town this non smoking apartment is the ideal pied-a-terre for couples with its stylish rooms containing many thoughtful extras. The lounge overlooks the lively cosmopolitan Grassmarket, while the bedroom is quietly situated to the rear. Within 10 minutes walk are the Castle, Royal Mile, Princes Street and many Festival venues. The area teems with restaurants, characterful old inns and intriguing shop

1 flat, 1 pub rm, 1 bedrm, sleeps 2, min let 3 nights, £300.00-£500.00, Dec-Oct, bus nearby, rail 1/2 ml, airport 6 mls

Mrs L Burge
Heathbank, Boat of Garten, Inverness-shire, PH24 3BD
Tel: 0411 317401

★

SELF ATERING

Studio flat with own entrance from communal stair, close to all City Centre amenities. Views of Scott Monument and Princes Street.

1 flat, 1 pub rm, sleeps 1-4, £220.00-£420.00, May-Sep

Mr A Cameron
51/2 Cockburn Street, Edinburgh, EH1 1BS
Tel: 0131 225 4772

VAT is shown at 17.5%: changes in this rate may affect prices.

Key to symbols is on back flap.

Edinburgh **Map Ref: 2C5**

Impressive first floor Georgian flat with many period features. Peaceful location in a prestigious area just 10 minutes' walk from Princes St and Royal Mile.

1 house, 2 pub rms, 2 bedrms, sleeps 1-4, £280.00-£650.00, Jan-Dec, bus nearby, rail nearby, airport 8 mls

John Crooks
Dunstaffnage, 12 Regent Terrace, Edinburgh, EH7 5BN
Tel: 0131 556 8309

Attractive 2-storey mews cottage in the heart of the Georgian new town. 5 minutes walk from Princes Street. Ideal location to explore Edinburgh on foot.

1 cottage, 1 pub rm, 3 bedrms, sleeps 5, min let 4 days, £250.00-£600.00, Jan-Dec, bus 1/4 ml, rail 1/4 ml, airport 10 mls

Mrs Mary Curran
8 East Bay, North Queensferry, Fife, KY11 1JX
Tel: (Inverkeithing) 01383 413242

Modern top floor flat with partial views of Holyrood Park. Close to Festival Theatre, Royal Commonwealth Pool and wide range of restaurants and shops. Private parking. Edinburgh University close by.

1 flat, 2 pub rms, 2 bedrms, sleeps 3, min let 1 night, £450.00-£560.00, Jan-Dec, bus nearby, rail 1 ml, ferry 100 mls, airport 4 mls

James Davidson & Miss J M G Inglis
28 Braid Crescent, Edinburgh, , EH10 6AU
Tel: 0131 446 9393 Fax: 0131 446 9393
Email: 101322.3565@compuserve.com

Single storey cottage adjoining busy bakery, with house next door. In centre of Corstorphine, close to zoo. Convenient for city centre.

1 house, 1 cottage, 1 pub rm, 2-3 bedrms, sleeps 5-6, total sleeping capacity 11, £380.00-£420.00, Jan-Dec, bus nearby, rail 5 mls, airport 5 mls

Mrs Donachie, P & S Donachie
64 St John's Road, Edinburgh, EH12 8AT
Tel: 0131 334 2860

★★ SELF CATERING

First floor flat in residential area, with local bus routes to city centre. Good restaurants, cinemas and theatres all in walking distance. Unrestricted on-street parking.

1 flat, 2 pub rms, 3 bedrms, sleeps 5, £300.00-£485.00, Jan-Dec, bus 500 yds, rail 1 ml, airport 4 mls

Mr J Donaldson
Invermark, 60 Polwarth Terrace, Edinburgh, EH11 1NJ
Tel: 0131 337 1066

Important: Prices stated are estimates and may be subject to amendments

Edinburgh | Map Ref: 2C5

★★ UP TO ★★★★ SELF CATERING

Garden and main door flats, centrally situated in Edinburgh New Town, close to city centre and major bus routes. Variety of restaurants nearby.

2 flats, 1 pub rm, 1 bedrm, sleeps 2, £290.00-£340.00, Jan-Dec, bus 200 yds, rail 1 ml, airport 5 mls

Mrs Elizabeth Epps
3d Scotland Street, Edinburgh, EH3 6PP
Tel: 0131 556 9797

★★★ SELF CATERING

Modernised apartment close to Queen's Park, Royal Commonwealth Pool and Edinburgh University residences. Easy access to city centre.

2 flats, 2 pub rms, 2 bedrms (grd flr avail), sleeps 6, total sleeping capacity 12, £190.00-£700.00, Jan-Dec, bus nearby

Fairnington Apartments
152 Dalkeith Road, Edinburgh, EH16 5DX
Tel: 0131 667 7161/0421 853940

★★ SELF CATERING

Garden flat in prestigious Georgian Terrace skirting Calton Hill. Five minutes walk to Princes Street. Access to extensive Calton Hill Gardens.

1 flat, 1 pub rm, 2 bedrms (grd flr avail), sleeps 5-6, min let 2 nights, £325.00-£625.00, Jan-Dec, bus 150 yds, rail 3/4 ml

Sally le Bert - Francis
4 Regent Terrace, Edinburgh, EH7 5BN
Tel: 0131 558 9536

★ SELF CATERING

First floor flat situated close to castle and a few minutes walk to Princes St. Leisure facilities and laundry available.

1 flat, 1 pub rm, 1 bedrm, sleeps 4, min let weekend, £200.00-£480.00, Jan-Dec, bus nearby, rail nearby

Aileen Gilchrist
7/8 St Clair Avenue, Edinburgh
Tel: 0131 553 6239

★★★★ SELF CATERING

Modern luxury penthouse flat near historic Dean Village in west end of city centre. Fully equipped and serviced. All bedding and towels supplied. Continental breakfast on first morning. Lounge with balcony. Private garage.

1 flat, 2 pub rms, 1 bedrm, sleeps 2-4, min let 3 nights, £300.00-£550.00, Jan-Dec, bus 1/4 ml, rail 1 ml, airport 3 mls

Mr Alan Gray
1 Kew Terrace, Edinburgh, Lothian, EH12 5JE
Tel: (Edinburgh) 0131 313 0700 Fax: 0131 313 0747

VAT is shown at 17.5%: changes in this rate may affect prices.

Key to symbols is on back flap.

Edinburgh **Map Ref: 2C5**

Very spacious second and third floor flats with four bedrooms. Centrally situated in London Street. 10 minutes walk to Princes Street.

2 flats, 1 pub rm, 4 bedrms, sleeps 6, total sleeping capacity 12, min let 3 nights, £250.00-£700.00, Jan-Dec, bus nearby, rail 1/2 ml, airport 6 mls

Mr Stephen Harrison
48 London Street, Edinburgh, EH3 6LX
Tel: 0131 556 1979

Self contained luxury furnished one bedroom city centre flat. Just minutes from Princes Street.

1 flat, 1 pub rm, 1 bedrm, sleeps 2-4, £420.00-£560.00, Jan-Dec, bus nearby, rail nearby, airport 5 mls

A J Hewlett
6 Haymarket Terrace, Edinburgh, EH12 5JZ
Tel: 0131 346 7752 Fax: 0131 539 8425

Attractive, comfortable ground floor flat with small park opposite. Short stroll to main bus routes and local shops. Unrestricted street parking.

1 flat, 1 pub rm, 1 bedrm (grd flr avail), sleeps 3, min let 3 nights, £200.00-£350.00, Jan-Dec, bus nearby, rail 1 ml, airport 4 mls

Mrs Pam Jamieson
32 Polton Cottages, Lasswade, Midlothian, EH18 1JT
Tel: 0131 663 6741

Cottage style apartment in central location. Close to Kings Theatre and Conference Centre, within walking distance of Princes Street and the Castle. Private parking. Majority of property on ground level.

1 cottage style apartment, 2 pub rms, 2 bedrms (grd flr avail), sleeps 4, min let 3 nights, £250.00-£500.00, Please contact the establishment, bus nearby, rail 1 ml, airport 8 mls

Karen & Gerry Johnstone
Adam Drysdale Apartment, , 42 Gilmore Place, Edinburgh, EH3 9NQ
Tel: 0131 228 8952 Fax: 0131 228 8952

★ SELF CATERING

Selection of serviced flats and apartments, 1 mile (2kms) south-west of centre. Convenient bus routes to city. Resident caretaker. Entryphone system.

39 flats, 5 bedsit complex, 1 pub rm, 1-3 bedrms (grd flr avail), sleeps 1-7, total sleeping capacity 173, min let 1 day, £90.00-£575.00, Jan-Dec, bus nearby, rail 1 ml, airport 5 mls

Linton Court Apartments
Linton Court, Murieston Road, Edinburgh, EH11 2JJ
Tel: 0131 337 4040 Fax: 0131 337 8547
Email: lintoncourt@enterprise.net

Important: Prices stated are estimates and may be subject to amendments

Edinburgh Map Ref: 2C5

★★★ SELF CATERING

Lower ground floor flat with own garden, convenient for Haymarket Station and all city centre amenities. Non-smoking apartment.

1 flat, 1 pub rm, 3 bedrms, sleeps 2-6, min let 3 days, £300.00-£700.00, Jan-Dec, bus nearby, rail nearby, airport 2 mls

R L & E K MacDonald
11 Coates Gardens, Edinburgh, EH12 5LG
Tel: 0131 337 1050 Fax: 0131 346 2167
Email: gardeneh12@aol.com

★★★ SELF CATERING

Compact apartments, ideal location in the heart of Edinburgh's historic Grassmarket. Minutes walk from Princes Street and the castle.

3 flats, 1 pub rm, 1 bedrm, sleeps 2-4, total sleeping capacity 10, £175.00-£350.00, Jan-Dec, rail 1/2 ml

Mrs M MacDougall
63 Langside Drive, Newlands, Glasgow, G43 2QX
Tel: 0141 637 0448/0421 338549 (mobile) Fax: 0141 637 0448

★★★ SELF CATERING

Recently refurbished ground floor terraced flat just off Queensferry Rd. Main bus route nearby gives easy access to city centre. Local shops within a short walking distance. Private parking at doorway.

1 cottage, 1 pub rm, 1 bedrm (grd flr avail), sleeps 2-4, min let 3 nights, £170.00-£290.00, Jan-Dec, bus nearby, rail 2 mls

Ms E McElliott
12 Keith Row, Edinburgh, Midlothian, EH4 3NL
Tel: 0131 343 1508

★★★★ SELF CATERING

Spacious and attractively furnished new town apartment. Ideally situated for all city centre amenities.

1 main door flat, 2 pub rms, 3 bedrms (grd flr avail), sleeps 6, min let 4 days, £450.00-£800.00, Jan-Dec, bus nearby, rail 1/2 ml, airport 5 mls

Mr L E MacIntosh
42 Inverleith Row, Edinburgh, EH3 5PY
Tel: (Pilton) 0131 552 2954

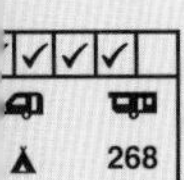

268

Mortonhall Park
38 Mortonhall Gate, Frogston Rd East, Edinburgh, EH16 6TJ
Tel: 0131 664 1533 Fax: 0131 664 5387
Email: meadowhed@aol.com

22 acres, mixed, end Mar-end Oct, prior booking in peak periods, latest time of arrival 2100, overnight holding area. Extra charge for electricity, awnings.

250 tourers from £8.25 or 250 motors £8.25-£12.75 or 250 tents £8.25-£12.75. Total Touring Pitches 250.

17 Holiday Caravans to let, sleep 6 £170.00-£425.00, total sleeping capacity 96, min let 2 days.

Leisure facilities:

From N or S leave city bypass at Straiton junction and follow signs for Mortonhall. From city take main road S from E or W end of Princes Street.

Edinburgh **Map Ref: 2C5**

★★★ UP TO ★★★★

SELF CATERING

Newly refurbished detatched houses in garden grounds with ample private parking. Quiet residential area. Approx 1 mile to city centre and 5 mins walk to Royal Botanical Gardens.

2 houses, 2 pub rms, 3 bedrms (grd flr avail), sleeps 5-6, total sleeping capacity 11, min let 2 nights, £450.00-£790.00, Jan-Dec, bus 1 1/2 mls, rail 1 1/2 mls, airport 7 mls

Mrs Shirley Mowat
c/o Dunstane House Hotel, 4 West Coates, Edinburgh, EH12 5JQ
Tel: 0131 337 6169 Fax: 0131 337 6169
Email: smowat@compuserve.com
Web: http://members.edinburgh.org/mowat

★

SELF CATERING

Self-contained university flats in central area with nearby bus routes, restaurants, cinema and the Kings Theatre.

81 flats, 1 pub rm, 3-5 bedrms (grd flr avail), sleeps 3-5, total sleeping capacity 382, min let 3 nights, £280.00-£430.00, early Jul-3rd.wk Sep, bus nearby, rail 1 ml, airport 5 mls

Napier University
219 Colinton Road, Edinburgh, EH14 1DJ
Tel: 0131 455 4331 Fax: 0131 455 4411

★

SELF CATERING

Victorian terraced villas in quiet location close to town centre.

3 houses, 1-2 pub rms, 7-9 bedrms (grd flr avail), sleeps 13-15, total sleeping capacity 38, £105.00-£170.00, Jul-Sep, bus nearby, rail 2 mls, airport 5 mls

Napier University
St Andrews Hall, 219 Colinton Road, Edinburgh, EH14 1DJ
Tel: 0131 455 4291 Fax: 0131 455 4411

★★★★

SELF CATERING

An upmarket conversion of a former bonded warehouse into stylish modern apartments close to the Waterfront of Leith. An old port makes this a fascinating destination for both business and leisure trips.

3 flats, 1 pub rm, 1 bedrm (grd flr avail), sleeps 2-4, total sleeping capacity 12, min let 3 days, £280.00-£497.00, Jan-Dec, bus nearby, rail 2 mls, airport 5 mls

Premier Vacations
Dalfaber Road, Aviemore, PH22 1PX,
Tel: 07000 200099/ Fax: 07000 846363
Email: reservations@premiervacations.net
Web: www.premiervacations.net

Important: Prices stated are estimates and may be subject to amendments

Edinburgh

Map Ref: 2C5

CANON COURT

20 CANONMILLS, EDINBURGH EH3 5LH
Tel: 0131-474 7000 Fax: 0131-474 7001
e.mail: canon.court@dial.pipex.com

A modern complex of 43 apartments in an ideal city centre location, offering flexible and secure quality accommodation. Purpose built in 1997, the apartments are bright and comfortable with 1 or 2 bedrooms, lounge/dining room, bathroom and fitted kitchen. Close to the Royal Botanic Gardens and excellent local amenities. Lift. On-site parking.

★★★★

SERVICED APARTMENTS

Modern complex of apartments in City centre location. Facilities include reception on site, complimentary parking, security entry phone and 24hr laundry service available. Other limited services available at extra cost.

43 flats, 1-2 pub rms, 1-2 bedrms (grd flr avail), sleeps 1-4, total sleeping capacity 60, min let 1 night, £413.00-£1260.00, Jan-Dec, bus nearby, rail 1 ml, airport 8 mls

N Paul
Canon Court Apartments, 20 Canonmills, Edinburgh, EH3 5LH
Tel: 0131 474 7000 Fax: 0131 474 7001
Email: canon.court@dial.pipex.com
Web: www.canoncourt.co.uk

Pollock Halls

Holyrood Park Road, Edinburgh EH16 5AY
Tel: 0131-667 1971 Fax: 0131-662 9479
e.mail: Hotel.Service@ed.ac.uk

Well-equipped self-catering flats and houses for 3 to 5 persons in convenient city locations at great value for money prices. Weekly terms (Saturday to Saturday) from £280 fully inclusive.

★★

SELF CATERING

A range of 58 flats accommodating 3-5 persons, converted from a former school and overlooking the Meadows and Bruntsfield Links. Some flats have views of Edinburgh Castle. Convenient for the city centre with good public transport links. Restaurants, cafes, delicatessens and theatres nearby. Putting, tennis, swimming in the close vicinity. 10 minutes Edinburgh cycle way, cycle hire locally.

38 flats, 1 pub rm, 3-5 bedrms (grd flr avail), sleeps 3-5, total sleeping capacity 140, £280.00-£420.00, Jul-Sep, bus nearby, rail 2 mls, airport 6 mls

Pollock Halls
Holyrood Park Road, Edinburgh, EH16 5AY
Tel: 0131 667 1971 Fax: 0131 662 9479
Email: Hotel.Service@ed.ac.uk

★★

SELF CATERING

Holiday flats in a secluded campus with an 18c flower garden. 20 minutes from city centre. On site leisure facilities.

37 flats, 3-4 bedrms (grd flr avail), sleeps 3-4, total sleeping capacity 138, £380.00-£485.00, Jun-Sep, bus nearby, rail 3 mls, airport 3 mls

Queen Margaret College
Clerwood Terrace, Edinburgh, EH12 8TS
Tel: 0131 317 3310 Fax: 0131 317 3169

VAT is shown at 17.5%: changes in this rate may affect prices.

Key to symbols is on back flap.

Edinburgh **Map Ref: 2C5**

SELF CATERING

Small, luxuriously furnished one bedroom city centre flat situated on 2nd floor of house 48 metres off Princes Street. Convenient for all the amenities that the city has to offer.

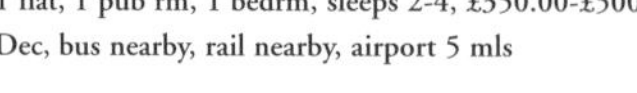

1 flat, 1 pub rm, 1 bedrm, sleeps 2-4, £350.00-£500.00, Jan-Dec, bus nearby, rail nearby, airport 5 mls

Robinson Lettings
1 Young Street, Edinburgh, EH2 4HU
Tel: 0131 225 2365 Fax: 0131 225 2846

SELF CATERING

Good quality, budget priced self catering offering a range of single, double and twin bedded units. Each unit is fully equipped. Some have ensuite bathrooms, others share four public bath/shower rooms. Some off-road parking, also unrestricted street parking. Frequent buses to city centre and well kept beach 200 metres distance.

2 flats, 5 studio apartments, 1 pub rm, 1 bedrm, sleeps 1-3, total sleeping capacity 18, £60.00-£350.00, Jan-Dec, bus nearby, rail 4 mls, airport 6 mls

Self Catering Apartments
No5, 3 Abercorn Terr, Portobello, Edinburgh, EH15 2DD
Tel: 0131 669 1044

SELF CATERING

Newly refurbished, ground and basement luxury flat in Edinburgh New Town. In the centre of the city but in quiet area. Princes Street 7 minutes walk.

1 flat, 1 pub rm, 4 bedrms (grd flr avail), sleeps 5, min let 4 days, £380.00-£700.00, Jan-Dec, bus 1/2 ml, rail 1/2 ml, airport 8 mls

Mr & Mrs Sibbett
Sibbet House, 26 Northumberland Street, Edinburgh, EH3 6LS
Tel: 0131 556 1078 Fax: 0131 557 9445
Email: sibbet.house@zetnet.co.uk
Web: www.sibbet-house.co.uk

SELF CATERING

New housing development 1 mile south of Princes Street, adjacent to Holyrood Park. Central yet peaceful location. Private Parking.

1 flat, 1 pub rm, 1 bedrm (grd flr avail), sleeps 4, £160.00-£400.00, Jan-Dec, bus 200 yds, rail 1 ml

Mrs Simpson
97 Market Street, Musselburgh, EH21 6PY
Tel: 0131 665 7140

Edinburgh Map Ref: 2C5

★★★ SELF CATERING

Central spacious third floor apartment situated in Marchmont area of the city, 1 1/2 miles south of the city centre with fine views of Blackford Hill and Edinburgh Castle. Princes Street and city amenities including theatres and restaurants all within walking distance. Unrestricted street parking.

1 flat, 1 pub rm, 4 bedrms, sleeps 7, min let 3 days, £400.00-£700.00, bus nearby, rail 1 ½ mls, airport 10 mls

Mrs Simpson
Rosebank, Greenside, Peebles
Tel: 01721 722255 Fax: 01968 661303
Email: glenrath.farms@glenrathfarms
Web: ndirect.co.uk

★★★ SELF CATERING

Lower ground flat with traditional character in listed Georgian villa. On main bus route, adjacent to the Botanic gardens in this prestigious area.

1 house, 2 flats, 1 pub rm, 2 bedrms, sleeps 4, total sleeping capacity 8, £361.00-£682.00, Jan-Dec, bus nearby, rail 1 ml, airport 10 mls

Mrs F Speight
5 Inverleith Row, Edinburgh, EH3 5LP
Tel: 0131 558 1653 Fax: 0131 624 0015

★★★★ SELF CATERING

Very comfortable spacious second floor flat in a substantial stone built gracious Georgian crescent. Ideally located for all amenities including theatres, excellent shopping and transport facilities. A short walk to the conference centre, Edinburgh Castle and Princes Street.

1 flat, 2 pub rms, 2 bedrms, sleeps 6, min let 2 nights, £504.00-£630.00, Jan-Dec, bus nearby, rail ½ ml, airport 8 mls

Gillian Stephens
23 Dublin Street, Edinburgh, EH1 3PG
Tel: 0131 225 1101 Fax: 0131 623 7123
Email: edinburgh.accommodation@cableinet.co.uk
Web: http://wkweb4.cableinet.co.uk/edinburgh_accommodation

★★★ SELF CATERING

Spacious Mews cottage with ensuite bedrooms in quiet location in city centre. Very close to Princes Street and within walking distance of both the old and new towns of Edinburgh, as well as city centre shops, theatres and main line station. There is instant access to all amenities you would expect of a capital city.

1 cottage, 1 pub rm, 2 bedrms, sleeps 4, £115.00-£450.00, Jan-Dec, bus nearby, rail 1 mile, airport 12 mls

Mrs A Stewart
24 Craigleith Hill Crescent, Edinburgh, EH4 2JZ
Tel: 0131 332 4422 Fax: 0131 332 0993

★★★ SELF CATERING

Self contained flat adjoining owners house with access to garden, in quiet residential area on South side of Edinburgh. Private parking.

1 flat, 3 pub rms, 1 bedrm (grd flr avail), sleeps 2-4, min let 2 nights, £240.00-£280.00, Jan-Dec, bus ½ ml, rail 3 mls, airport 5 mls

Mrs S Tully
Dunalton, 43 Braid Farm Road, Edinburgh, EH10 6LE
Tel: 0131 447 3065/0370 482945 (mobile) Fax: 0131 452 8497
Web: www.edinhire.demon.co.uk

VAT is shown at 17.5%: changes in this rate may affect prices.

Key to symbols is on back flap.

Edinburgh

Map Ref: 2C5

SELF CATERING

First floor flat in picturesque old town of Edinburgh. Formerly an 18th century coaching inn, restored by a conservation trust. Kitchen window overlooks ancient Greyfriars Church and Kirkyard.

1 flat, 1 pub rm, 1 bedrm, sleeps 2-4, £235.00-£509.00, Jan-Dec, bus nearby, rail ½ ml, airport 5 mls

Dr Julie Watt
630 Lanark Road, Edinburgh, EH14 5EW
Tel: (Edinburgh) 0131 538 0352 Fax: 0131 453 4088

SELF CATERING

Apartments and studio apartments situated in elegant Victorian terraced house, close to West End and city centre. Unrestricted parking close by and frequent bus services.

5 flats, 1 pub rm, 1-2 bedrms, sleeps 2-5, total sleeping capacity 13, min let 2 nights, £200.00-£800.00, Jan-Dec, bus nearby, rail 1 ml, airport 7 mls

West End Apartments
2 Learmonth Terrace, Edinburgh, EH4 1PQ
Tel: 0131 332 0717/226 6512 Fax: 0131 226 6513
Email: brian@sias.co.uk

Haddington, East Lothian

Map Ref: 2D4

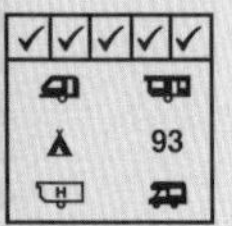

SELF CATERING

Beautiful, secluded cottage and interesting garden with stunning views over East Lothian countryside. 40 minutes by car to Edinburgh city centre and with easy access onto A1. Ideal for outdoor enthusiasts - a variety of walks in the area and golf courses.

1 cottage, 1 pub rm, 4 bedrms (grd flr avail), sleeps 6, £250.00-£500.00, Jan-Dec, bus 1 ml, rail 7 mls, airport 30 mls

M Duricacz
31 Carlton Mews, Edinburgh, EH7 5DA
Tel: 0131 556 7934

✓✓✓✓✓ 93

The Monks' Muir
Haddington, East Lothian, EH41 3SB
Tel: (Haddington) 01620 860340 Fax: 01620 861770

7 acres, grassy, level, sheltered, Jan-Dec, prior booking in peak periods, latest time of arrival 2400. Extra charge for electricity, awnings.

67 tourers £12.00 or 67 motors £12.00 or 67 tents £9.50. Total Touring Pitches 67.

8 Holiday Caravans to let, sleep 2-6 £120.00-420.00, total sleeping capacity 40, min let 1 night.

On A1 midway between Haddington and East Linton, signposted on A1 in advance.

Humbie, East Lothian

Map Ref: 2D5

SELF CATERING

Former gate lodge, 15 miles (24kms) from Edinburgh, in quiet countryside offering peace and tranquility. Ideal for hillwalking, golfing and outdoor pursuits.

1 cottage, 2 pub rms, 2 bedrms (grd flr avail), sleeps 5, £130.00-£290.00, Jan-Dec, bus 2 mls, rail 17 mls, airport 20 mls

Fiona Lewis
10 Kippithill, Humbie, East Lothian, EH36 5PP
Tel: (Humbie) 01875 833323

Important: Prices stated are estimates and may be subject to amendments

Humbie, East Lothian

Map Ref: 2D5

A semi-detached cottage in the small village of Humbie with uninterrupted views of the Lammermuir Hills. 30 minutes drive to Edinburgh, also within easy reach of East Lothian and Scottish Borders.

1 cottage, 2 pub rms, 3 bedrms (grd flr avail), sleeps 5, min let weekend, £140.00-£285.00, Jan-Dec, bus 300 yds, rail 10 mls, airport 24 mls

Mrs Anne Phillips
Hillview Cottage, Upper Keith, Humbie, East Lothian, EH36 5PJ
Tel: (Humbie) 01875 833307

Linlithgow, West Lothian

Map Ref: 2B4

Nine chalets on a wooded hillside, on the outskirts of historic Linlithgow with extensive views over the Forth Valley. Convenient access to Glasgow and Edinburgh. Children's play area.

9 chalets, 1 pub rm, 2 bedrms, sleeps 4-5, total sleeping capacity 43, from £151.00, Jan-Dec, bus 1 ml, rail 1 1/2 mls, airport 14 mls

Mr & Mrs Howie
Craigs Lodges, Williamscraigs, Linlithgow, West Lothian, EH49 6QF
Tel: (Linlithgow) 01506 845025 Fax: 01506 845025

Innerwick, by Dunbar, East Lothian

Map Ref: 2E4

Traditional Scottish home in sheltered walled garden with garden furniture and private parking. It has immediate access on to the golf course (18th green) and nearby sandy beach. Convenient for rail station and local amenities in town.

1 house, 1 pub rm, 3 bedrms (grd flr avail), sleeps 6, £125.00-£425.00, Jan-Dec, bus nearby, rail nearby, airport 30 mls

Mrs E M MacDonald
Blake Holt, Browsea View Avenue, Lilliput, Poole, Dorset, BH14 8LQ
Tel: (Canford Cliffs) 01202 707894

North Berwick, East Lothian

Map Ref: 2D4

Self contained south facing comfortable garden studio situated within our garden with its own patio, furnished to a high standard. Close to beach and nearby golf courses. Private parking. Only 2 minutes walk from the shops and restaurants.

1 studio apartment, 1 pub rm, 1 bedrm (grd flr avail), sleeps 2, £160.00-£220.00, Jan-Dec, bus 50 yds, rail 1/2 ml, airport 26 mls

Mrs M Stamp
10 Westgate, North Berwick, East Lothian, EH39 4AF
Tel: (North Berwick) 01620 893785 Fax: 01620 893785

✓✓✓✓✓ 207

Tantallon Caravan Park

Dunbar Road, North Berwick, East Lothian, EH39 5NJ Tel: (North Berwick) 01620 893348 Fax: 01620 895623 Email: meadowhed@aol.com

20 acres, mixed, end Mar-end Oct, prior booking in peak periods, latest time of arrival 2000, overnight holding area. Extra charge for electricity, awnings.

147 tourers or 147 motors £7.00-£11.00 or 147 tents £7.00-£11.00. Total Touring Pitches 147.

10 Holiday Caravans to let, sleep 6 from £130.00, total sleeping capacity 60, min let 2 nights.

Leisure facilities:

Located on E side of North Berwick between town and Tantallon Castle and just off A198 Dunbar road.

VAT is shown at 17.5%: changes in this rate may affect prices.

Key to symbols is on back flap.

South Queensferry, West Lothian

Map Ref: 2B4

SELF CATERING

Modernised ground floor flat in a seventeenth century listed building in the heart of historic South Queensferry. Shops and supermarket, take away and variety of restaurants within walking distance. It is an ideal holiday base for Edinburgh and for touring Fife, Central and Southern Scotland.

1 flat, 1 pub rm, 2 bedrms (grd flr avail), sleeps 5, £225.00-£360.00, Jan-Dec, bus 1/2 ml, rail 1 1/2 mls, airport 7 mls

Black Castle Enterprises
The Old School, Flichity, Inverness-shire, IV1 2XD
Tel: (Farr) 01808 521288 Fax: 01808 521464
Email: magbrin@btinternet.com

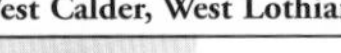

West Calder, West Lothian

Map Ref: 2B5

SELF CATERING

Enviable location on Pentland Hills, 1/2's hr's drive from the heart of Edinburgh. Within an hour's drive of Glasgow, Rob Roy, Braveheart and Border country, this is the perfect place to relax. Our 1700 acre sheep farm offers 3 very special 200 year old properties: two imaginatively designed cottages (one isolated) and a farmhouse "wing", cosy peat/coal fires, C.H. Thoughtfuly equipped, three bedrooms each. Car essential. Photographic brochure.

2 cottages, 1 apartment, 1-2 pub rms, 2-3 bedrms (grd flr avail), sleeps 5-6, total sleeping capacity 17, £230.00-£460.00, Jan-Dec, bus 6 mls, rail 6 mls, airport 16 mls

Mrs Geraldine Hamilton
Crosswoodhill Farm, West Calder, West Lothian, EH55 8LP
Tel: (Auchengray) 01501 785205 Fax: 01501 785308

Important: Prices stated are estimates and may be subject to amendments

Greater Glasgow and Clyde Valley

For sheer excitement, Glasgow is one of the top UK destinations. For shopping choice, entertainment and culture, it should not be missed.

The legendary Glasgow friendliness is a bonus but first time visitors will be struck by the sheer panache of 'downtown' Glasgow. The magnificent Victorian architecture of the city centre further adds to the vibrancy. In short, Glasgow is where things happen, whatever time of year you visit.

For example, in 1996, Glasgow opened its new Gallery of Modern Art, right in the heart of the city in the former Stirling's Library, a handsome neoclassical building.

Charles Rennie Mackintosh's 'House for an Art Lover', designed for a competition in 1901, was also completed, as a further addition to the several locations in the city where Mackintosh, its most famous architect, can be encountered. Other places include his peerless School of Art and also the Mackintosh House at the Hunterian Art Gallery. On the subject of art collections, one of Britain's finest civic collections can be viewed at the Art Gallery and Museum at Kelvingrove. Then you can nip across the road to the Museum of Transport. East of the city-centre, close to the old heart of Glasgow around its magnificent cathedral, you will also find the unique St Mungo Museum taking its wide ranging foray through the world's religions (lots of artefacts and paintings). Another excursion which is a must is to see the magnificent Burrell Collection, the lifetime's hobby of a shipping magnate, now in the care of the city and housed in an inspiring sylvan setting in Pollok Park. With so much to see indoors, Glasgow is an especially good winter break destination.

Glasgow in the nineties is a city with a style all its own with a range of shops that ranks it one of the top three shopping cities in the U.K.

If all this cultural gallivanting sounds tiring, then take a break in one of the city's many pubs and eating places. You will certainly need to if you have been shopping along one of the many pedestrianised streets, such as Buchanan Street, or sampling the upmarket wares at Princes Square or the chic Italian Centre. Remember, though, that the city itself has no monopoly on cultural centres of excellence. For example, take a look at the Paisley Museum and Art Galleries, not only for the story of the renowned Paisley shawl with its distinct pattern, but for a major painting collection.

Similarly, on no account overlook what the Clyde Valley can offer.

The River Clyde winds out of the grassy rounded hills then enters a rocky wooded gorge with such force that it this beautiful setting became the site for a textile mill village. New Lanark became a bold experiment in social welfare and worker care and its fame went round the world. Today it is a nominated World Heritage Site – but, even more importantly, a great day out for visitors with lots to see and do. Its sheltered location make it a particularly good late season place to visit (and its visitor centre opens all year round). In addition, the town of Biggar is also within easy reach, with a further choice of museums and places of interest. Between them, Glasgow and Clyde Valley offer an unrivalled range of things to see and do.

Events

Greater Glasgow & Clyde Valley

Throughout 1999

GLASGOW 1999 – UK CITY OF ARCHITECTURE AND DESIGN

A programme of events, exhibitions, conferences, festivals and displays which will position Glasgow as a major European city of ideas, promoting an awareness of the cultural and economic importance of design.
Tel: 0141 287 1999 Fax: 0141 248 8754.
e.mail: info@glasgow1999.co.uk

Jan 13 – 31

CELTIC CONNECTIONS

Glasgow's annual celebration of music from the Celtic world. Glasgow Royal Concert Hall, Glasgow and other city venues.
Contact: Colin Hynd.
Tel: 0141 332 6633.

June 4 – 6

SCOTLAND'S NATIONAL GARDENING SHOW

Strathclyde Country Park, near Glasgow.
Tel: 01698 252565.

June 12 – 27

WEST END FESTIVAL

Music, theatre, exhibitions, free events, food and drink and the Midsummer Carnival Parade in the West End of Glasgow.
Tel: 0141 341 0844.

June 14 – July 3

THE SHOT

Renfrewshire's annual festival including music, choral, arts and drama.
Contact: Paul Hogan.
Tel: 0141 887 1010.

July 30 – Aug 2

CUTTY SARK TALL SHIPS RACE

Geenock.
Contact: The Tall Ships Office.
Tel: 01475 551256.

Aug 15

WORLD PIPE BAND CHAMPIONSHIPS

The world's top pipe bands, Glasgow Green, Glasgow.
Contact: The Royal Scottish Pipe Band Association.
Tel: 0141 221 5414.

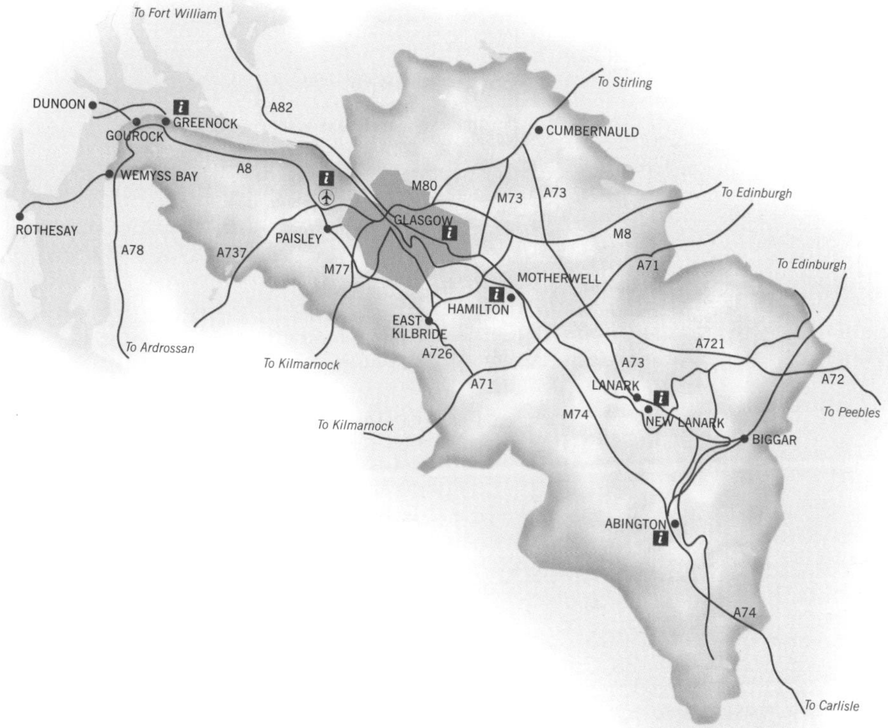

Area Tourist Board Addresses

Greater Glasgow and Clyde Valley Tourist Board
11 George Square
GLASGOW
G2 1DY
Tel: 0141 204 4400
Fax: 0141 221 3524
e.mail:
TourismGlasgow@ggcvtb.org.uk

Greater Glasgow and Clyde Valley

Tourist Information Centres in Scotland

GREATER GLASGOW & CLYDE VALLEY TOURIST BOARD

ABINGTON ♿
Welcome Break
Service Area
Junction 13, M74
Tel: (01864) 502436
Jan-Dec

BIGGAR
155 High Street
Tel: (01899) 221066
April-end Oct

GLASGOW ✉
11 George Square
G2 1DY
Tel: (0141) 204 4400
Jan-Dec

GLASGOW AIRPORT
Tourist Information Desk
Tel: (0141) 848 4440
Jan-Dec

GREENOCK
7A Clyde Square
Tel: (01475) 722007
Jan-Dec

HAMILTON ♿
Road Chef Services
(M74 Northbound)
Tel: (01698) 285590
Jan-Dec

LANARK ♿ ✉
Horsemarket
Ladyacre Road, ML11 7LQ
Tel: (01555) 661661
Jan-Dec

✉ Accept written enquiries
♿ Disabled access

earsden

Map Ref: 1H5

★★★ SELF CATERING

Modern terraced cottages in residential area 6 miles (10 kms) from Glasgow city centre. On main bus route. Close to railway station.

3 cottages, 1 pub rm, 1-2 bedrms (grd flr avail), sleeps 2-6, total sleeping capacity 12, £220.00-£400.00, Jan-Dec, bus nearby, rail 500 yds, airport 9 mls

Kilmardinny Estate
Milngavie Road, Bearsden, Glasgow, G61 3DH
Tel: 0141 943 1310

ambuslang, Lanarkshire

Map Ref: 1H5

★★★★ SELF CATERING

Unique apartments within 18c building. Relaxed setting yet offering close proximity to shops, restaurants and sports facilities, situated in green belt area. 5 miles from Glasgow, Edinburgh, Burns Country and Loch Lomond within easy reach.

2 self-contained apartments, 1 pub rm, 1-2 bedrms, sleeps 2-4, total sleeping capacity 6, min let 3 nights (low season), £150.00-£355.00, Jan-Dec, bus 300 yds, rail 1 1/2 mls, airport 12 mls

Mrs Anne M Leggat
Greenleeshill Farm, Cambuslang, Glasgow, G72 8YL
Tel: 0141 641 3239 Fax: 0141 641 3239
Email: reservations@greenleeshill.prestel.co.uk

armichael, Lanarkshire

Map Ref: 2B6

★★ UP TO ★★★★ SELF CATERING

Attractive 18c stone cottages on historic wooded estate. Ideal touring base. Farm visitor centre, shop, restaurant and wax museum. Tennis, fishing, pony trekking, and off-road buggy racing all available. Some no-smoking cottages.

15 cottages, 1 farmhouse apartment, 1-2 pub rms, 1-3 bedrms (grd flr avail), sleeps 2-7, total sleeping capacity 65, min let 2 nights, £180.00-£500.00, Jan-Dec, bus 1/2 ml, rail 5 mls, ferry 90 mls, airport 30 mls

Mr Richard Carmichael of Carmichael
Carmichael Estate Office, West Mains, Carmichael, by Biggar, Lanarkshire, ML12 6PG
Tel: (Tinto) 01899 308336 Fax: 01899 308481
Email: chiefcarm@aol.com Web: www.carmichael.co.uk/cottages

lasgow

Map Ref: 1H5

★★★ SELF CATERING

Studio flat in 1920's bungalow. Easy access and off-street parking. Ideal for touring and city centre. B & B also available.

1 flat, 1 pub rm, 1 bedrm (grd flr avail), sleeps 2-3, £195.00, Jan-Dec, bus nearby, rail 3 mls, airport 12 mls

Mr H Bain & Mr A E Mole
32 Riddrie Knowes, Glasgow, G33 2QH
Tel: 0141 770 5213 Fax: 0141 770 0955
Email: AlanMole@compuserve.com

Glasgow | **Map Ref: 1H5**

★ SELF CATERING

Modern, purpose built hall of residence, ideally situated for S.E.C.C., Kelvingrove Park and museum.

156 self catering rooms, 1 pub rm, 1 bedrm (grd flr avail), sleeps 1-2, total sleeping capacity 242, to £75.00, Jul-Sep, bus nearby, rail 3 mls, airport 9 mls

Conference & Vacation Office
University of Glasgow, 81 Great George Street, Glasgow, G12 8RR
Tel: 0141 330 5385 Fax: 0141 334 5465
Email: imd4m@udcf.gla.ac.uk

★ SELF CATERING

Flat in the Merchant City, with security entrance. Convenient for all amenities. Ideal base for non car visitors as a short stroll to museums and galleries.

1 flat, 1 pub rm, 1 bedrm, sleeps 2-4, £175.00-£275.00, Jan-Dec, bus nearby, rail nearby, airport 5 mls

Executive Properties-Scotland
Mr John Kelly, 29 Lanark Road, Carluke, Lanarkshire, ML8 4HA
Tel: (Carluke) 01555 750078 Fax: 01555 750078

★★★ SELF CATERING

Victorian house in old Cathcart, Glasgow southside. 15 minutes city centre. This attractive house with period features offers spacious accommodation. Own garden front and back.

1 house, 2 pub rms, 3 bedrms, sleeps 6, £275.00-£400.00, Jan-Dec, bus 1/4 ml, rail 1/4 ml

Mrs J Gibson
33 Kirkwell Road, Cathcart, Glasgow, G44 5UN
Tel: 0141 637 7217

★ UP TO ★★ SELF CATERING

Top & ground floor flats with security access to communal stairway centrally situated in Glasgows West End. Convenient for the subway. Walking distance to Kelvingrove Art Gallery, the Glasgow University Campus, Botanic Gardens and BBC.

2 flats, 2 pub rms, 3-5 bedrms (grd flr avail), sleeps 6, total sleeping capacity 12, £300.00-£400.00, Jul-Sep, bus nearby, rail nearby, airport 10 mls

Mrs Helen A McAdam
Comrie Farm, Keltheyburn, Aberfeldy
Tel: (Kenmore) 01887 830261 Fax: 01887 830261

★ SELF CATERING

Purpose built modern flats within hall of residence on campus. Centrally situated for all amenities.

20 flats, 1 pub rm, 4-6 bedrms, sleeps 4-6, total sleeping capacity 104, min let 3 nights, £250.00-£310.00, Jun-Sep, bus nearby, rail 1/2 ml, airport 8 mls

University of Strathclyde
Residence & Catering Services, 50 Richmond Street, Glasgow, G91 1XP
Tel: 0141 553 4148 Fax: 0141 553 4149
Email: rescal@mis.strath.ac.uk

Important: Prices stated are estimates and may be subject to amendments

reenock, Renfrewshire — Map Ref: 1G5

★★ SELF CATERING

Modern purpose-built campus accommodation on waterfront.

7 flats, 7 pub rms, 7 bedrms (grd flr avail), sleeps 7, total sleeping capacity 49, £90.00-£100.00, Jan-Dec, bus nearby, rail 200 yds, ferry 2 mls, airport 14 mls

Angela Hurrell
James Watt College, Roseath Hall, Waterfront Campus, Customhouse Way, Greenock, PA15 1EN, PA15 1EN
Tel: (Greenock) 01475 731360

amilton, Lanarkshire — Map Ref: 2A6

SELF CATERING

One bedroomed ground floor flat centrally situated in residential area, within easy walking distance of shopping centre and local amenities. 17miles south of Glasgow and within easy reach of all major routes.

1 flat, 1 pub rm, 1 bedrm (grd flr avail), sleeps 4, min let 2 nights, £175.00-£250.00, Jan-Dec, bus 1/2 ml, rail 1/2 ml

Paula Connell
5 Parkburn Industrial Estate, Burnbank, Hamilton, ML3 0QQ
Tel: (Hamilton) 01698 825169/0385 512271 Fax: 01698 824265

nark — Map Ref: 2A6

✓✓✓✓ 45

Newhouse Caravan & Camping Park
Ravenstruther, Lanark, ML11 8NP Tel: (Carstairs) 01555 870228 Fax: 01555 870228

8 acres, mixed, mid Mar-mid Oct, latest time of arrival 2200, overnight holding area. Extra charge for electricity, awnings, showers.

25 tourers from £6.50 or 25 motors from £6.50 or 25 tents from £6.50. Total Touring Pitches 45.

4 Holiday Caravans to let, sleep 2-6 from £160.00, total sleeping capacity 20, min let 3 days.

Leisure facilities:

Site on A70, 1/2 ml W of Carstairs village, 3 mls E of Lanark.

chwinnoch, Renfrewshire — Map Ref: 1G5

SELF CATERING

A courtyard of cottages and a studio overlooking Loch Barr and the Renfrewshire countryside. Set in two acres of gardens and ideally positioned for the Ayrshire coast, Burns country, Glasgow and Loch Lomond.

3 cottages, 1 pub rm, 1-3 bedrms (grd flr avail), sleeps 2-6, total sleeping capacity 10, £160.00-£500.00, Jan-Dec, bus 1 ml, rail 1 ml, airport 7 mls

Mrs J Anderson
East Lochhead Farm, Largs Road, Lochwinnoch, PA12 4DX
Tel: (Lochwinnoch) 01505 842610 Fax: 01505 814610
Email: winnoch@aol.com

SELF CATERING

Two converted byres attached to former farmhouse. In idyllic location with fine views, yet only half an hour's drive from Glasgow. Close to Muirshiel Country Park; North Ayrshire, Burn Country and Loch Lomond.

2 flats, 1 pub rm, 1 bedrm (grd flr avail), sleeps 4, total sleeping capacity 8, £95.00-£205.00, Jan-Dec, bus 1 ml, rail 3 mls, ferry 15 mls, airport 10 mls

Mrs Janet MacGregor
Barrs of Cloak, Calderside Road, by Lochwinnoch, PA12 4LB
Tel: 01505 842252 Fax: 01505 843001

VAT is shown at 17.5%: changes in this rate may affect prices.

Key to symbols is on back flap.

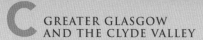

New Lanark, by Lanark, Lanarkshire — Map Ref: 2A6

The Waterhouses at New Lanark

Mill One, New Lanark ML11 9DB
Telephone: 01555 667200
Fax: 01555 667222

On the banks of the River Clyde in the heart of the 200-year-old village of New Lanark, The Waterhouses offer a unique opportunity to experience beauty, history and peace. The views from the cottages over the river are unrivalled and the facilities of the New Lanark Mill Hotel are only a few steps away. Less than an hour from Glasgow, Edinburgh and the Borders. A unique experience.

★★★★ SELF CATERING

Recently renovated row of millhouses situated on the banks of the River Clyde on the lane behind the New Lanark Mill Hotel.

8 houses, 1-2 pub rms, 1-2 bedrms, sleeps 4-6, total sleeping capacity 28, £250.00-£700.00, Jan-Dec, bus 1/2 ml, rail 1 ml, airport 40 mls

Mr Stephen Owen
New Lanark Mill Hotel, New Lanark, Lanark, ML11 9DB
Tel: (Lanark) 01555 667200 Fax: 01555 667222

Old Kilpatrick, Dunbartonshire — Map Ref: 1H5

★★ SELF CATERING

Two adjoining cottages beautifully situated overlooking the Clyde Estuary. Totally rural, yet only 20 minutes from Glasgow city centre.

2 houses, 1 pub rm, 2-4 bedrms, sleeps 4-8, total sleeping capacity 12, min let weekend, £100.00-£320.00, Jan-Dec, bus 1 ml, rail 1 ml, airport 5 mls

Mrs S Fleming
Gavinburn Farm, Old Kilpatrick, Glasgow, G60 5NH
Tel: 01389 873058/0831 383084

Wiston, Lanarkshire — Map Ref: 2B7

★★★ SELF CATERING

Tastefully modernised, converted barn and dairy premises adjoining 17c farmhouse. Set in a green picturesque valley with extensive views to Tinto Hill.

3 cottages, 2 pub rms, 1-2 bedrms (grd flr avail), sleeps 4-6, total sleeping capacity 16, £120.00-£260.00, Jan-Dec, bus 1 ml, rail 12 mls, airport 30 mls

Mrs G McCaskie
Wiston Place, Wiston, by Abington, Lanarkshire, ML12 6HT
Tel: (Biggar) 01899 850235

West Highlands and Islands, Loch Lomond, Stirling and Trossachs

From the islands of Coll and Tiree, lying low out in the Hebridean sea to the west, to the green slopes of the Ochil Hills east of Stirling, this is a large chunk of Scotland straddling Highland and Lowland.

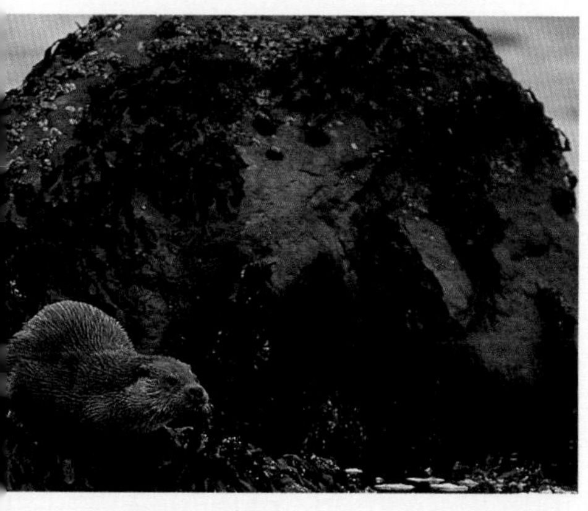

In the early days of tourism, the location of Loch Lomond and the Trossachs, a highly scenic area just beyond the Highland line, made them easy to reach. Visitors have been admiring the 'bonny banks' and the beauties of the Trossachs at all seasons since the dawning of the romantic age, two centuries ago. Today, these areas are still an excellent choice, particularly for off-peak holidays. Similarly, the west has its own old established resorts, at places like Oban, a railhead on the western seaboard and gateway to the islands. Visitors come to the West Highlands at least partly for the scenic attractions: for the wildness of Breadalbane around Crianlarich; for the interplay of land and sea-loch that adds so much interest to the western seaboard; for the glorious views of islands from Knapdale or Kintyre. However, the area offers much more than simply scenery. As well as Oban, there are other towns with plenty to see and do. Inveraray on Loch Fyne offers a good range of attractions in and around it, including Inveraray Castle and Inveraray Jail. Dunoon, so easily accessible across the Clyde, is the gateway to the richly forested lands of Cowal.

Situated west of Gloom Hill and beside Burn of Sorrow and the Burn of Care, Castle Campbell was once known as Castle Gloom. However 'Castle Gloom' is a wholly inappropriate name when you see the spectacular views of the Dollar Glen and Pentland Hills.

As a gateway and an important route centre leading on to the Highlands, Stirling played a leading role in Scotland's story. Today its castle is just one of many attractions which range from the National Wallace Monument – find out the real story of Braveheart – to the Old Town Jail. Falkirk is another major town where, within easy reach, the Bo'ness and Kinneil Railway is the re-creation of a typical Scottish branch line in the days of steam.

There are plenty of surprises in store as well. East of Stirling, you will find Scotland's second largest textile area, around the Hillfoots towns below the Ochil Hills – worth following up if you want to combine a late season break with some Christmas shopping. Follow the Mill Trail to look for the best of the wool and tweed bargains.

In the west, the mild climate grows some great gardens at places like Crarae on Loch Fyne or Arduaine south of Oban. A late spring trip here is a gardener's delight. Or discover a grand Gothic mansion, with breathtaking interiors of marble and stained glass, at Mount Stuart on the island in Bute.

Mull, with its spectacular scenery and tiny Iona, Cradle of Scottish Christianity, close by;

As well as Bute, whose main town Rothesay, has been a popular destination for generations, there is a great choice. Mull, with its spectacular scenery and tiny Iona, Cradle of Scottish Christianity, close by; Islay and Jura as two contrasting places, one busy with distilling and farming, the other comparatively empty and wild. Lots more to choose from – just head for Oban and make your choice. Or go cruising on the Firth of Clyde or even on inland waters such as Loch Lomond, Loch Katrine or, to the west, Loch Awe.

Finally, however you choose, transport links are excellent, with motorways within minutes of Stirling Castle or simply one of the most scenic train journeys in Scotland taking you to Oban.

Events

West Highlands & Islands, Loch Lomond, Stirling and Trossachs

Apr 29 – May 3

Isle of Bute Jazz Festival
Various venues throughout Bute.
Contact: Rothesay Tourist Information Centre.
Tel: 01700 502151.

Apr 30 – May 2

The Highlands and Islands Dance Festival
Oban
Contact: Neil Sinclair.
Tel: 01631 710201.

July 7 – 10

Standard Life Loch Lomond Golf Invitational
One of the PGA European tour's main tournaments with the world's top golfers. Loch Lomond Golf Club, Luss.
Tel: 0990 661661.

July 23 – Aug 1

Trossachs Festival
Open air entertainment – concerts, folk music and dance.
Contact: Ian Milligan.
Tel: 01877 330396.

July 30 – Aug 6

West Highland Yachting Week
Sailing regatta – Crinan, Oban and Tobermory.
Contact: Julia Heep.
Tel: 01631 563309.

Aug 27 – 28

Cowal Highland Games
Dunoon.
Contact: Stuart Donald.
Tel: 01369 703206.

Sep 17 – 19

Tarbert Music Festival
Music festival with open-air concerts and music in local hotels. Tarbert, Loch Fyne.
Contact: Les Oman.
Tel: 01880 820001.

Oct 9 – 11

Tour of Mull Rally
Car rally attracting entrants from all over the UK competing around the island roads.
Contact: Eddie O'Donnel.
Tel: 01688 302133.

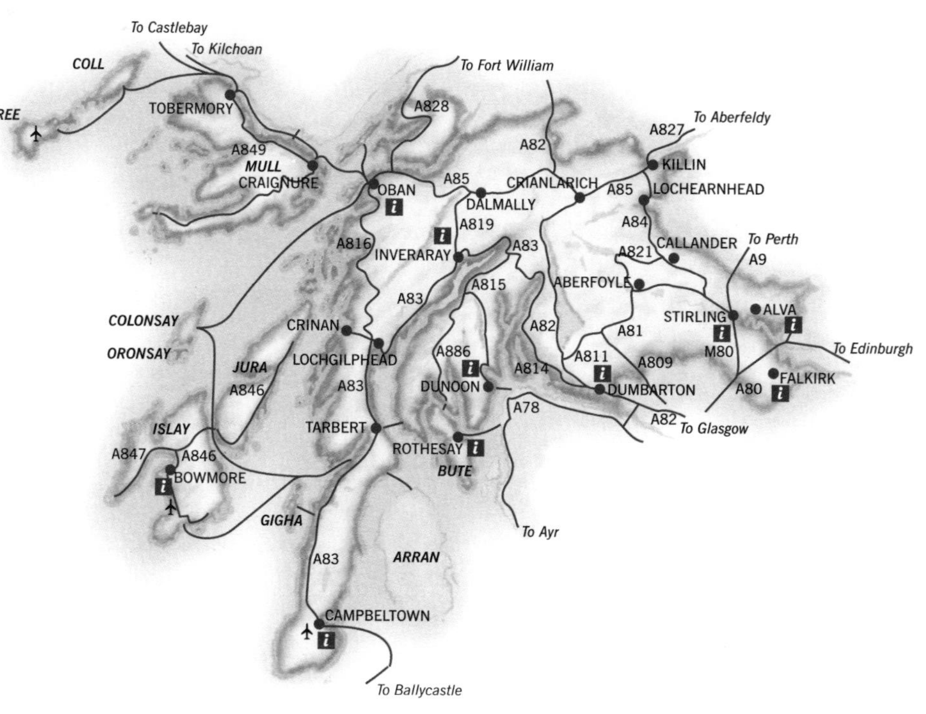

Area Tourist Board Addresses

Argyll, The Isles, Loch Lomond, Stirling and Trossachs Tourist Board
Dept SUK
7 Alexandra Place
DUNOON
Argyll
PA23 8AB
Tel: 01369 701000
Fax: 01369 706085
e.mail:
information@scottish.heartlands.org

West Highlands and Islands, Loch Lomond, Stirling and Trossachs

Tourist Information Centres in Scotland

ARGYLL, THE ISLES, LOCH LOMOND, STIRLING & TROSSACHS TOURIST BOARD

ABERFOYLE ♿
Main Street
Tel: (01877) 382352
April-Oct

ALVA ♿
Mill Trail Visitor Centre
Tel: (01259) 769696
Jan-Dec

ARDGARTAN ♿
Arrochar
Tel: (01301) 702432
April-Oct

BALLOCH ♿
Balloch Road
Tel: (01389) 753533
April-Oct

BO'NESS
Seaview Car Park
Tel: (01506) 826626
April-Sept

BOWMORE
Isle of Islay
Tel: (01496) 810254
Jan-Dec

CALLANDER ♿
Rob Roy & Trossachs Visitor Centre
Ancaster Square
Tel: (01877) 330342
Jan-Dec

CAMPBELTOWN ✉
Mackinnon House
The Pier
ARGYLL, PA28 6EF
Tel: (01586) 552056
Jan-Dec

CRAIGNURE
Isle of Mull
Tel: (01680) 812377
April-Oct

DRYMEN
Drymen Library
The Square
Tel: (01360) 660068
May-Sept

DUMBARTON
Milton
A82 Northbound
Tel: (01389) 742306
Jan-Dec

DUNBLANE ♿
Stirling Road
Tel: (01786) 824428
May-Sept

DUNOON ✉
7 Alexandra Parade
Argyll, PA23 8AB
Tel: (01369) 703785
Jan-Dec

FALKIRK ♿ ✉
2-4 Glebe Street
Tel: (01324) 620244
Jan-Dec

HELENSBURGH ♿
The Clock Tower
Tel: (01436) 672642
April-Oct

INVERARAY
Front Street
Argyll
Tel: (01499) 302063
Jan-Dec

KILCHOAN ♿
Ardnamurchan
Argyll
Tel: (01972) 510222
April-Oct

KILLIN ♿
Breadalbane Folklore Centre
Tel: (01567) 820254
March-Dec

KINCARDINE BRIDGE
Airth, by Falkirk
Tel: (01324) 831422
Easter-Sept

LOCHGILPHEAD
Lochnell Street, Argyll
Tel: (01546) 602344
April-Oct

OBAN ♿ ✉
Argyll Square
Argyll, PA34 4AR
Tel: (01631) 563122
Jan-Dec

ROTHESAY ✉
15 Victoria Street
Isle of Bute, PA20 0AJ
Tel: (01700) 502151
Jan-Dec

STIRLING ♿ ✉
Dumbarton Road, FK8 2L
Tel: (01786) 475019
Jan-Dec
Royal Burgh of Stirling Vis
Centre
Tel: (01786) 479901
Jan-Dec
Pirnhall Motorway Service Area
Junction 9 (M9)
Tel: (01786) 814111
April-Oct

TARBERT
Harbour Street, Argyll
Tel: (01880) 820429
April-Oct

TARBET-LOCH LOMON
Main Street
Tel: (01301) 702260
April-Oct

TOBERMORY
Isle of Mull
Tel: (01688) 302182
Jan-Dec

TYNDRUM ♿
Main Street
Tel: (01838) 400246
April-Oct

✉ Accept written enquiries
♿ Disabled access

Aberfoyle, Perthshire

Map Ref: 1H3

SELF CATERING

Newly renovated cottages with log burning stoves. Set beside the River Chon, in the scenic foothills of the Trossachs, at the head of Loch Ard.

2 cottages, 1 pub rm, 1-2 bedrms (grd flr avail), sleeps 4-6, total sleeping capacity 10, £175.00-£375.00, Jan-Dec, bus 1/4 ml, rail 25 mls, airport 30 mls

Ingrid Anderson
Lochside Cottages, Kinlochard, by Aberfoyle
Tel: (Kinlochard) 01877 387212 Fax: 01877 387212

SELF CATERING

Totally refurbished former mill in secluded 35 acre site. 1.5 miles from Gartmore. Near Aberfoyle and Rob Roy country.

1 converted barn, 1 pub rm, 3 bedrms (grd flr avail), sleeps 8, £195.00-£475.00, Jan-Dec, bus 1 ml, rail 15 mls, airport 26 mls

David & Melanie McNeil
Blarnaboard Farm, Gartmore, Aberfoyle, Stirlingshire, FK8 3SE
Tel: (Aberfoyle) 01877 382374

SELF CATERING

Reconstructed traditional coach house c1900 in own grounds, 1 mile from the village. Pets by arrangement.

1 cottage, 1 pub rm, 2 bedrms (grd flr avail), sleeps 4, £275.00-£375.00, Jan-Dec, bus nearby

Oak Royal Guest House
Aberfoyle, Perthshire, FK8 3UX
Tel: 01877 382633 Fax: 01877 382633
Email: tartan.time@virgin.net

Appin, Argyll

Map Ref: 1E1

SELF CATERING

Timber bungalows with excellent views over Loch Creran to the hills beyond. Free fishing, boat hire and access to safe beach.

10 chalets, 1-2 pub rms, 1-2 bedrms (grd flr avail), sleeps 2-5, total sleeping capacity 40, £155.00-£345.00, Jan-Dec exc Nov, bus nearby, rail 16 mls

Appin Holiday Homes
Argyll, PA38 4BQ
Tel: (Appin) 01631 730287

VAT is shown at 17.5%: changes in this rate may affect prices.

Key to symbols is on back flap.

Appin, Argyll

Map Ref: 1E1

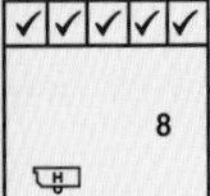

Appin Lochside Caravan Park

Appin, Argyll, PA38 4BQ Tel: (Appin) 01631 730287 Web: www.oban.org.uk

2 acres, Apr-Oct.

5 Holiday Caravans to let, sleep 2-5 from £135.00, total sleeping capacity 20, min let weekend (low season), Apr-Oct.

Leisure facilities:

15 mls N of Connel Bridge. 15 mls S of Ballachulish Bridge, on A828.

Beautifully situated in its own grounds in Strath of Appin overlooking Loch Linnhe, midway between Oban and Fort William.

4 flats, 1 cottage, 1 pub rm, 1-2 bedrms, sleeps 2-5, total sleeping capacity 17, £126.00-£375.00, Jan-Dec, bus nearby, rail 18 mls

Mr & Mrs D E Hutchison
Kinlochlaich House, Appin, Argyll, PA38 4BD
Tel: (Appin) 01631 730342 Fax: 01631 730482
Email: 101602.3101@compuserve.com
Web: www.robbins-associates.co.uk/kinlochlaich

Apartments of individual character and design adjoining historic country house and two lodges in large garden with superb views. Barbecue.

2 chalets, 2 flats, 4 apartments, 1-2 pub rms, 1-3 bedrms, sleeps 2-6, total sleeping capacity 28, min let 3 nights, £130.00-£390.00, Dec-Oct, bus nearby, rail 20 mls, ferry 5 mls, airport 100 mls

Mrs Mathieson
Appin House, Appin, Argyll, PA38 4BN
Tel: (Appin) 01631 730207 Fax: 01631 730567

Arden, Argyll & Bute

Map Ref: 1G4

Totally renovated Victorian walled garden cottages in peaceful rural setting. Close to Loch Lomond and Clyde coast.

3 cottages, 1 pub rm, 1-2 bedrms (grd flr avail), sleeps 2-6, total sleeping capacity 10, min let 3 days, £160.00-£463.00, Jan-Dec, bus nearby, rail 3 mls, airport 15 mls

Mr Andrew MacLeod
The Gardeners Cottages, Arden House, Arden, Dunbartonshire, G83 8RD
Tel: (Arden) 01389 850601 Fax: 01389 850601
Email: andymacleod@sol.co.uk
Web: www.vacations-scotland.co.uk/gardeners.html

dentinny, by Dunoon, Argyll

Map Ref: 1F4

★★ SELF ATERING

Modern cottages, built in traditional style, on working hill farm. Magnificent views over Loch Long.

4 cottages, 1 pub rm, 3 bedrms (grd flr avail), sleeps 5-7, total sleeping capacity 23, £160.00-£424.00, Mar-Feb, bus 1/4 ml, rail 12 mls, ferry 9 mls, airport 29 mls

Mrs Marshall
Stronchullin Holiday Cottages, Ardentinny, by Dunoon, Argyll, PA23 8TP
Tel: (Ardentinny) 01369 810246

dfern, Argyll

Map Ref: 1E3

★★ SELF ATERING

Bungalows set in secluded gardens by the lochside.

1 bungalow, 3 pub rms, 2 bedrms, sleeps 5, £300.00-£375.00, May-Sep, bus 1 ml, rail 26 mls

Mrs A Gill
Rowancraig, Ardfern, Argyll, PA31 8QN
Tel: (Barbreck) 01852 500257
Email: tgill@alystra.win-uk.net

Loch Craignish Cottages

ARDFERN, by LOCHGILPHEAD, ARGYLL PA31 8QN
Telephone/Fax: 01852 500671

Eight beautifully appointed cottages in private grounds beside the sea, offering all-year-round comfort. Superb scenery for many outdoor (and indoor) activities, pets welcome. Excellent shop(s), restaurant and PO in village. A wonderful holiday experience. Linen, towels, high chairs and cots included in rent. Mastercard and Visa. *Colour brochure.* **Prices: £180 min - £510 max per week.**

★★★★ SELF ATERING

White washed cottages overlooking Loch Craignish on 3.5 acre private site in the village of Ardfern.

8 cottages, 1 pub rm, 1-3 bedrms, sleeps 2-6, total sleeping capacity 32, £180.00-£510.00, Jan-Dec, bus 2 mls, rail 25 mls, ferry 25 mls, airport 98 mls

Mrs Joan Wylie
Loch Craignish Holiday Cottages, Ardfern, by Lochgilphead, Argyll, PA31 8QN
Tel: (Barbreck) 01852 500671 Fax: 01852 500671

drishaig, by Lochgilphead, Argyll

Map Ref: 1E4

★ UP TO ★★★★ SELF ATERING

Modern terraced cottages built in 1993 and chalet on traditional croft with open views over Loch Fyne. Luxury pine lodge on beach.

3 cottages, 1 pub rm, 3 bedrms (grd flr avail), sleeps 6, total sleeping capacity 18, to £420.00, Jan-Dec, bus nearby

Mrs MacDonald
Brenfield Croft, Ardrishaig, Argyll
Tel: (Lochgilphead) 01546 603284

VAT is shown at 17.5%: changes in this rate may affect prices.

Key to symbols is on back flap.

Arduaine, Argyll Map Ref: 1E3

ARDUAINE COTTAGES

Arduaine, Kilmelford, by Oban, Argyll PA34 4XA
Telephone: 01852 200331 Fax: 01852 200337

Three warm, well-equipped cottages, sleeping 2-8. Each with garden and breathtaking panoramic views of Islands of Jura, Scarba, Shuna. Moorings, dinghy launching. Excellent seafood restaurants, gardens, sailing school, riding, hillwalking, loch fishing nearby. Oban and Lochgilphead 20 miles.

Owned and carefully managed by John and Jane Rentoul and family.

★★ UP TO ★★★

SELF CATERING

Two cottages and one chalet of individual character and design, each with own garden. Breathtaking views towards isles of Shuna, Scarba and Jura.

1 chalet, 1 house, 1 cottage, 1-2 pub rms, 1-4 bedrms (grd flr avail), sleeps 2-8, total sleeping capacity 20, min let 2/3 nights, £110.00-£800.00, Jan-Dec, bus nearby, rail 20 mls, ferry 20 mls, airport 100 mls

Mrs Rentoul
Arduaine Cottages, Arduaine, Argyll, PA34 4XA
Tel: (Kilmelford) 01852 200331 Fax: 01852 200337

Arnprior, by Kippen, Stirlingshire Map Ref: 1H4

★★★

SELF CATERING

Tastefully converted barn with stunning rural views. Centrally situated for touring. Variety of leisure activities in the area.

1 converted barn, 1 pub rm, 3 bedrms, sleeps 6-7, £200.00-£475.00, Jan-Dec, bus 1/2 ml, rail 11 mls

Mrs Carol Seymour
Thorntree, Arnprior, Stirlingshire, FK8 3EY
Tel: (Kippen) 01786 870710 Fax: 01786 870710
Email: cms@seymour.telme.com

Balloch, Dunbartonshire Map Ref: 1G4

★★

SELF CATERING

Original railway cottage in the heart of the village. Newly converted to form a small, well-appointed holiday home.

1 cottage, 1 pub rm, 1 bedrm (grd flr avail), sleeps 2-6, £150.00-£350.00, Jan-Dec, bus nearby, rail nearby

Mr & Mrs McAteer
Station Cottages, Balloch Road, Balloch, G83 8SS
Tel: (Alexandria) 01389 750759/07050 354793 (mobile)
Fax: 01389 750759

✓✓✓✓✓

200

Tullichewan Holiday Park
Old Luss Road, Balloch, Loch Lomond, Dunbartonshire Tel: 01389 759475
Fax: 01389 755563

13 acres, mixed, Dec-Oct, prior booking in peak periods, latest time of arrival 2200, overnight holding area. Extra charge for electricity, awnings.

110 tourers £8.50-12.50 or 110 motors £8.50-12.50 or 30 tents £8.50-12.50. Total Touring Pitches 140.

6 Holiday Caravans to let, sleep 4-8 £175.00-£410.00, total sleeping capacity 40, min let 3 nights.

Leisure facilities:

Turn right off A82 Glasgow-Fort William road onto A811 at r/about. Follow international caravan/camping signs for 1/4 ml.

Important: Prices stated are estimates and may be subject to amendments

lloch, Dunbartonshire **Map Ref: 1G4**

★★★★ SELF CATERING

Pine lodges with high level of insulation and feature pine decoration situated in family holiday park by Loch Lomond. Leisure suite and games room available.

6 pine lodges, 1 pub rm, 3 bedrms (grd flr avail), sleeps 4-6, total sleeping capacity 36, min let 3 nights, £180.00-£510.00, Jan-Dec, bus 1/4 ml, rail 1/4 ml, airport 15 mls

Tullichewan Holiday Park
Old Luss Road, Balloch, Loch Lomond, Dunbartonshire, G83 8QP
Tel: (Alexandria) 01389 759475 Fax: 01389 755563

lquhidder, Perthshire **Map Ref: 1H2**

★★★ SELF CATERING

Flat in former Alehouse dated back to Rob Roy's time. Peacefully situated in the famous Braes of Balquhidder.

1 flat, 1 pub rm, 1 bedrm, sleeps 2, £140.00-£220.00, Jan-Dec, bus 2 mls, rail 30 mls, airport 70 mls

Mrs P L M Barber
Keepers Cottage, Balquhidder, Lochearnhead, Perthshire, FK19 8PA
Tel: (Strathyre) 01877 384301 Fax: 01877 384301

★★★★ SELF CATERING

Tastefully renovated secluded cottage situated in the delightful Braes of Balquhidder. Ideal for touring, walking and water sports.

1 cottage, 2 pub rms, 3 bedrms, sleeps 6, min let weekend, £140.00-£420.00, Jan-Dec, bus nearby, rail 28 mls, airport 60 mls

Mrs Sandra Carter
Craigruie House, Balquhidder, by Lochearnhead, FK19 8PQ
Tel: (Strathyre) 01877 384240 Fax: 01877 384240

★★★ SELF CATERING

Semi detached cottage surrounded by woods, in the heart of Rob Roy country. Centrally located for both outdoor activities and touring.

1 cottage, 1 pub rm, 2 bedrms (grd flr avail), sleeps 4, £180.00-£310.00, Jan-Dec, bus nearby, rail 24 mls, airport 40 mls

Mr K P Horsley
Rob Roy Workshop, Balquhidder, Lochearnhead, Perthshire, FK19 8NX
Tel: (Callander) 01877 384274/330780 (after 6.30pm)
Fax: 01877 384252

Balquhidder, Perthshire

Map Ref: 1H2

SELF CATERING

Two self contained units in a courtyard development with adjoining Taste of Scotland restaurant.

3 cottages, 2-3 pub rms, 2-3 bedrms, sleeps 4-6, total sleeping capacity 10, £225.00-£700.00, Jan-Dec, bus 6 mls, rail 35 mls, airport 65 mls

Mr R Lewis
Monachyle Mhor, Balquhidder, Lochearnhead, Perthshire, FK19 8PQ
Tel: (Strathyre) 01877 384622 Fax: 01877 384305

Balvicar, Argyll

Map Ref: 1E3

SELF CATERING

Modern semi-detached house located in the quiet village of Balvicar, overlooking Balvicar Bay. Oban and ferries to islands 15 miles (24km), via the Bridge over the Atlantic. Good base for exploring Seil Island and for enjoying walking, fishing and golfing on the 9 hole golf course nearby. The village of Ellenabeich, with its disused slate quarries is 4 miles away, ferry to Easdale Island. Three hotels for eating out on Seil Island.

1 apartment, 1 pub rm, 2 bedrms, sleeps 4, £150.00-£250.00, Jan-Dec, bus 1/4 ml, rail 15 mls, airport 100 mls

J Robertson
Barchailein, Balvicar, Seil, by Oban
Tel: 01852 300441

Benderloch, by Oban, Argyll

Map Ref: 1E2

SELF CATERING

Sixteen lodges in woodland setting with views to Tralee Beach. Part of Tralee Holiday Park with full access to all its facilities.

16 log cabins, 1 pub rm, 2-3 bedrms, sleeps 4-6, total sleeping capacity 96, min let 2 days, £225.00-£525.00, Feb-Dec, bus 1 ml, rail 3 mls, ferry 5 mls, airport 2 mls

Tralee Bay Holidays
Benderloch, by Oban, Argyll
Tel: (Ledaig) 01631 720255 Fax: 01631 720545

Bridge of Allan, Stirlingshire

Map Ref: 2A3

SELF CATERING

Modern ground floor flat in quiet residential area, close to Stirling University Campus. Centrally situated for touring.

1 flat, 2 pub rms, 2 bedrms (grd flr avail), sleeps 4, £200.00-£350.00, Jan-Dec, bus nearby, rail 1 ml, airport 30 mls

Isobel Johns
3 Wolsey Close, Kingston upon Thames, Surrey, KT2 7ER
Tel: 0181 942 7203 Fax: 0181 942 7203
Email: 106362.1201@compuserve.com

Buchlyvie, Stirlingshire

Map Ref: 1H4

SELF CATERING

Most attractive detached cottage in its own garden with accommodation all on one level. About 10 minutes walk to village. Ideal base for touring central Scotland and walking parts of the West Highland Way.

1 cottage, 1 pub rm, 1 bedrm (grd flr avail), sleeps 4, £110.00-£250.00, Jan-Dec, bus 1/4 ml, rail 14 mls, airport 27 mls

Mrs Rosemary Rollinson
Ballamenoch, Buchlyvie, Stirlingshire, FK8 3NX
Tel: (Buchlyvie) 01360 850577 Fax: 01360 850535

t Bannatyne, Isle of Bute Map Ref: 1F5

★★★ SELF ATERING

Traditional stone built cottages comfortably furnished. Perfect for family holidays. Tranquil setting in grounds of 14c Kames Castle. Ideal for walking, cycling and birdwatching. Pets welcome.

6 cottages, 1-2 pub rms, 2-4 bedrms (grd flr avail), sleeps 2-9, total sleeping capacity 33, min let 2 nights, £225.00-£590.00, Jan-Dec, bus nearby, ferry 3 mls, airport 35 mls

Mrs J Hardy
Kames Castle, Port Bannatyne, Isle of Bute, PA20 0QP
Tel: (Rothesay) 01700 504500
Email: kames-castle@easynet.co.uk
Web: http://www.kames-castle.co.uk

hesay, Isle of Bute Map Ref: 1F5

★ UP TO ★★★★ SELF ATERING

Built in 1829 this Palladian style mansion, now converted into luxury apartments, enjoys superb views over the Firth of Clyde. Set within 9 acres of mature garden and woodland we also offer comfortable detached chalet accommodation. Ideal base for touring and enjoying outdoor activities.

7 chalets, 5 Apartments, 1 pub rm, 1-2 bedrms, sleeps 2-6, total sleeping capacity 64, £145.00-£430.00, Jan-Dec, bus 400 yds, ferry 1 1/2 mls

Mr & Mrs Torrens
Ardencraig Self Catering Holidays, Rothesay, Isle of Bute, PA20 9EP
Tel: (Rothesay) 01700 504550

★★★ SELF ATERING

Two individual complexes in conservation area, one with cottage on the sea front with its own garden and private parking; the other in town centre overlooking Loch Striven and the Cowal hills. Within easy walking distance of golf course.

5 flats, 1 cottage, 1 pub rm, 1-2 bedrms (grd flr avail), sleeps 2-5, total sleeping capacity 18, min let 3 days, £189.00-£359.00, Jan-Dec, bus nearby, ferry 1 ml

Mrs G Shaw
Morningside, Mount Pleasant Road, Rothesay, Isle of Bute, PA20 9HQ
Tel: (Rothesay) 01700 503526 Fax: 01700 503526

rndow, Argyll Map Ref: 1F3

★★★ SELF ATERING

Two individual cottages in beautiful position on privately owned Highland estate at head of Loch Fyne. Good walking country, with abundant wildlife.

2 cottages, 1-2 pub rms, 2-3 bedrms (grd flr avail), sleeps 4-6, total sleeping capacity 10, £215.00-£510.00, Jan-Dec, bus 200 yds, rail 11 mls, airport 50 mls

Achadunan Estate
c/o Mrs Delap, Little Armsworth, Alresford, Hampshire, SO24 9RH
Tel: (Alresford) 01962 732004 Fax: 01962 732004

lander, Perthshire Map Ref: 1H3

★★★ SELF ATERING

Charming two-storey stonebuilt cottage on small livestock farm, in peaceful setting with superb views.

1 cottage, 2 pub rms, 3 bedrms (grd flr avail), sleeps 6, £220.00-£450.00, Jan-Dec, bus 3 mls, rail 12 mls, airport 40 mls

Mr & Mrs B Barker
Mid Torrie Farm, Callander, Perthshire, FK17 8JL
Tel: (Callander) 01877 330 203 Fax: 01877 330203

Callander, Perthshire **Map Ref: 1H3**

Invertrossachs Country Hous

Nr CALLANDER, PERTHSHIRE FK17 8H
Telephone: 01877 331126 Fax: 01877 33122
e-mail: iain_aitchison@compuserve.com

This elegant lochside Edwardian Mansion offers superior, spac apartments amidst 33 acres of outstanding natural beauty and privately managed grounds. Cottage available. All units have d washer, laundry, microwave, TV/video, CD/cassette, telephone plus the 1st class facilities you would expect in this prestigious country house. Classified 4 Stars – Serviced Apartments. Enjo memorable views and an ideal touring base. Loch/woodland walks, fishing, cycling on site. Nearby golf and other activities offered. Enjoy the original flair, hospitality and personal attentic of resident proprietors and staff dedicated to your comfort and privacy. Exquisite country house bedrooms and suites for B&B also available.

Contact Iain H. Aitchison, BA. Ref. ESC.

Website: www.invertrossachs.co.uk

As featured in BBC "Summer Holiday" TV Programme

SERVICED APARTMENTS

Separate cottage and spacious self-contained mansion apartments within a former Edwardian Hunting Lodge; enjoying a secluded lochside position in the midst of an area of breathtaking natural beauty.

1 log cabin, 4 flats, 1 cottage, 1-2 pub rms, 1-3 bedrms (grd flr avail), sleeps 2-8, total sleeping capacity 31, min let 2 nights, £195.00-£1350.00, Jan-Dec, bus 4 mls, rail 20 mls, airport 40 mls

Mr Iain Aitchison B.A.
Invertrossachs Country House, Invertrossachs, by Callander, Perthshire, FK17 8HG
Tel: (Callander) 01877 331126 Fax: 01877 331229
Email: iain_aitchison@compuserve.com
Web: www.invertrossachs.co.uk

SELF CATERING

Modern bungalow on a farm, situated on the outskirts of Callander, with magnificent views to Ben Ledi.

1 bungalow, 2 pub rms, 4 bedrms, sleeps 7, £200.00-£360.00, Jan-Dec, bus 1/4 ml, rail 16 mls, airport 45 mls

Mrs J Donald
Trean Farm, Callander, Perthshire, FK17 8AS
Tel: (Callander) 01877 331160 Fax: 01877 331160

SELF CATERING

Modern semi-detached bungalow in quiet residential area yet only minutes walk from the town centre.

1 bungalow, 1 pub rm, 2 bedrms (grd flr avail), sleeps 3, £190.00-£230.00, Jan-Dec, bus nearby, rail 12 mls, airport 40 mls

Mr & Mrs J Greenfield
Annfield, North Church Street, Callander, Perthshire, FK17 8EG
Tel: (Callander) 01877 330204

Important: Prices stated are estimates and may be subject to amendments

llander, Perthshire **Map Ref: 1H3**

Leny Estate Lodges

Leny House, Callander, Perthshire FK17 8HA
Tel: 01877 331078 Fax: 01877 331335
e.mail: res@lenyestate.demon.co.uk – see our own web site on: www.lenyestate.demon.co.uk

Six new solid spruce lodges set in parkland on the Leny Estate near Callander. The private Leny Glen, in which visitors may walk, and where deer safely graze, contains much wildlife. Within the grounds of Leny House itself, which dates from 1513, there is a small goat herd and horses. Every luxury including washing/drying machine, dishwasher, colour TV and telephone. The ONLY self-catering accommodation in Scotland awarded Four to Five Stars – Self Catering and recommended by the television travel programme "Wish You Were Here". Own picnic area and barbecue. Perfect centre for touring. Open all year, weekends available. Colour brochure.

Winner of Antartex "Best Self-Catering" award.
★★★★ TO ★★★★★ SELF CATERING

SELF CATERING

Spruce lodges and stone cottages on a small peaceful site set in acres of parkland on Leny Estate, with superb views to the Trossachs. Our own private, unspoilt glen to enjoy walks amongst the plentiful wildlife. Paddocks with angora goats. Tranquil estate but only 2 miles from Callander, the gateway to the Highlands. Beautiful at any time of the year. Central location with good access to both Scottish coasts.

6 log cabins, 2 cottages, 2 pub rms, 2 bedrms (grd flr avail), sleeps 4-6, total sleeping capacity 48, min let 2 nights, £333.00-£610.00, Jan-Dec, bus 1 ml, rail 15 mls, airport 36 mls

Mrs Roebuck & Mr Roebuck
Leny House, Leny Estate, Callander, Perthshire, FK17 8HA
Tel: (Callander) 01877 331078 Fax: 01877 331335
Email: res@lenyestate.demon.co.uk
Web: www.lenyestate.demon.co.uk

mpbeltown, Argyll **Map Ref: 1D7**

SELF CATERING

Friendly welcome, comfortable, all electric cottage accommodation in castle grounds. Campbeltown amenities and beaches within short distance. Bed linen included.

6 cottages, 1 pub rm, 1-2 bedrms (grd flr avail), sleeps 2-6, total sleeping capacity 22, £135.00-£299.00, Apr-Oct, bus 600 yds, airport 3 mls

Col & Mrs W T C Angus
Kilchrist Castle, Campbeltown, Argyll, PA28 6PH
Tel: (Campbeltown) 01586 553210 Fax: 01586 553210
Email: william.t.c.angus@btinternet.com
Web: www.oas.co.uk/ukcottages/kilchrist/index.htm

rradale, Argyll **Map Ref: 1E6**

SELF CATERING

Commanding views over Carradale Bay to Arran and Ailsa Craig from a secluded, elevated position. Abundance of birds and wildlife. Area rich in archaeology.

1 house, 1 pub rm, 4 bedrms (grd flr avail), sleeps 8, from £175.00, Jan-Dec, bus nearby, ferry 16 mls, airport 14 mls

Mrs Campbell
Gorton House, Gorton Wood, Carradale, Argyll
Tel: (Carradale) 01583 431641

Carradale, Argyll

Map Ref: 1E6

A varied selection of properties on beautiful, peaceful estate halfway down the Mull of Kintyre. Own sandy bay and rowing boat. All cottages set in individual location in natural woodland with many rhododendrums.

2 houses, 3 flats, 3 cottages, 1-3 pub rms, 1-5 bedrms (grd flr avail), sleeps 2-10, total sleeping capacity 42, min let 3 nights, £120.00-£410.00, Jan-Dec (flat), Apr-Oct (cottages), bus 800 yds, ferry 16 mls, airport 13 mls

Mrs M MacAlister Hall
Torrisdale Castle, Carradale,by Campbeltown, Argyll, PA28 6QT
Tel: (Carradale) 01583 431233 Fax: 01583 431233

Very attractive and comfortable studio cottages recently converted from former steading. Traditional box bedroom off living area. Very fully equipped to high standards. Ideal for romantic breaks, single occupancy lets available.

2 studio cottages, 1-2 pub rms, sleeps 2, total sleeping capacity 4, min let 2 nights, £90.00-£250.00, Jan-Dec, bus nearby, airport 15 mls

Mr M Hurst
The Steading, Carradale, Argyll, PA28 6QG
Tel: (Carradale) 01583 431683

Detached bungalow and converted byre peacefully situated in Carradale Glen yet only 1.5 miles (2.5kms) from village. Fishing and golfing available locally. Pony Trekking. Children welcome, pets corner and adventure play area.

2 cottages, 1 pub rm, 3-4 bedrms (grd flr avail), sleeps 6-8, total sleeping capacity 14, £250.00-£620.00, Jan-Dec, bus 2 mls, ferry 10 mls, airport 15 mls

David & Phyllis Washington
Lag Kilmichael, Carradale, Argyll, PA28 6QJ
Tel: (Carradale) 01583 431626

Pine lodges in quiet area of caravan park, with own safe sandy beach. Canoeing instruction. Trout and salmon fishing available. Forest walks, abundance of wildlife and 9-hole golf course all nearby.

3 log cabins, 1 pub rm, 2 bedrms (grd flr avail), sleeps 5, total sleeping capacity 15, min let 3 nights, £120.00-£325.00, Apr-Oct, bus 1/2 Mile, rail 60 Miles, ferry 15 Miles, airport 25 Miles

Ruth Watson
Carradale Chalets, Carradale Bay Caravan Park, Carradale, Argyll, PA28 6QG
Tel: (Carradale) 01583 431665

Clynder, Argyll & Bute

Map Ref: 1G4

Bungalow centrally located for touring, sea-fishing and walking. Lovely views of the Gare Loch. Non-smoking property.

1 bungalow, 1 pub rm, 1 bedrm, sleeps 4, £150.00-£250.00, Jan-Dec, bus nearby, rail 11 mls, ferry 3 mls, airport 42 mls

Mrs Lulu Staahl
Bella Vista, Annachmor Road, Clynder, G84 0QD
Tel: (Clynder) 01436 831312 Fax: 01436 831312

Important: Prices stated are estimates and may be subject to amendments

olonsay, Isle of, Argyll Map Ref: 1C4

A former byre, this charming cottage has been refurbished in character, with comfort and warmth foremost. Small studio adjoins. Enjoy the peace and tranquility of this unique island, sandy beaches, woodland gardens, moorland, cliffs and lochs. This varied scenery gives you the opportunity to enjoy walking, cycling, golf, bird watching or just relaxing in unspoilt surroundings.

1 cottage, 1 studio flat, 1-3 pub rms, 1-3 bedrms (grd flr avail), sleeps 2-5, total sleeping capacity 8, £95.00-£450.00, Jan-Dec, ferry 3 1/2 mls

Mr and Mrs W Lawson
Seaview, Isle of Colonsay, Argyll, PA61 7YR
Tel: (Colonsay) 01951 200315

Traditional houses, cottages and flats on island of outstanding natural beauty. Famous for sunshine, sandy beaches, woodland gardens and wildlife.

7 houses, 6 flats, 8 cottages, 3 bungalows, 2-3 pub rms, 1-5 bedrms (grd flr avail), sleeps 2-12, total sleeping capacity 156, min let 2 nights, £180.00-£850.00, Mar-Nov, Xmas/New Year, ferry 3 1/2 mls

Mrs E McNeill
Machrins Farm, Isle of Colonsay, Argyll
PA61 7YR
Tel: (Colonsay) 01951 200312 Fax: 01951 200312

raobh Haven, by Lochgilphead, Argyll Map Ref: 1E3

Traditionally built with open fires and timber beams, the cottages combine the warmth and comfort of home with wonderful, unspoilt views of the islands. Right beside the sea and a short stroll from the village, they make a cosy and well equipped base for walking, touring or just relaxing. Website - http://www.craobh.demon.co.uk

2 cottages, 1 pub rm, 2-3 bedrms, sleeps 4-6, total sleeping capacity 10, £320.00-£520.00, Jan-Dec, bus 1/4 ml, rail 20 mls, ferry 20 mls, airport 100 mls

Ms Alison Hampton
Craobh Haven Cottages, 17 Brunton Terrace, Edinburgh, EH7 5EH
Tel: 0131 661 2783 Fax: 0131 478 0566
Email: cottages@craobh.demon.co.uk
Web: www.craobh.demon.co.uk

Craobh Haven, by Lochgilphead, Argyll **Map Ref: 1E3**

★

SELF CATERING

18c mansion house on 3000 acre private coastal estate. Two flats and two adjacent cottages. Superb views over Sound of Jura and Firth of Lorne.

1 house, 2 flats, 2 cottages, 1-2 pub rms, 1-3 bedrms, sleeps 2-8, total sleeping capacity 20, min let 3 days, £96.50-£415.00, Jan-Dec, bus 2 mls, rail 20 mls, airport 90 mls

Mr C Lindsay MacDougall
Lunga, Ardfern, Argyll, PA31 8QR
Tel: (Barbreck) 01852 500237 Fax: 01852 500639
Email: colin@lunga.demon.co.uk

Crianlarich, Perthshire **Map Ref: 1G2**

★ UP TO ★★

SELF CATERING

Former shooting lodge and courtyard cottage situated back from the main road, 0.25 miles (0.5km) from village. Superb mountain views. Satellite television.

1 house, 1 cottage, 1-3 pub rms, 2-4 bedrms (grd flr avail), sleeps 4-8, total sleeping capacity 12, £220.00-£360.00, Jan-Dec, bus nearby, rail 1 ml, ferry 45 mls, airport 50 mls

Mr W J C & Mrs J Christie
Inverardran, Crianlarich, Perthshire, FK20 8RS
Tel: (Crianlarich) 01838 300240/0468 496374 mobile
Fax: 01838 300240

★★★★ UP TO ★★★★★

SELF CATERING

Well spaced lodges with spectacular Highland views on private estate overlooking Glen Dochart. Free fishing. Boats and canoes available.

16 chalets, 2 cottages, 1-2 pub rms, 1-3 bedrms (grd flr avail), sleeps 2-8, total sleeping capacity 82, min let 1 day, £195.00-£1095.00, Jan-Dec, bus nearby, rail 1 1/2 mls, airport 45 mls

Portnellan Lodges
Crianlarich, Perthshire, FK20 8QS
Tel: (Crianlarich) 01838 300284 Fax: 01838 300332
Email: lodges@portnellan.demon.co.uk
Web: www.portnellan.demon.co.uk

Important: Prices stated are estimates and may be subject to amendments

y Lochgilphead, Argyll Map Ref: 1E4

★★ SELF CATERING

Modernised stone built cottage on isolated peninsula, surrounded by sandy beaches. Ideal for quiet holiday, bird watching, fishing and walking.

1 cottage, 3 pub rms, 3 bedrms, sleeps 6, £230.00-£475.00, Jan-Dec, bus 8 mls, rail 30 mls

Mrs Walker
The Change House, Crinan Ferry,by Lochgilphead, Argyll, PA31 8QH
Tel: (Kilmartin) 01546 510232 Fax: 01546 510249

rinan, by Lochgilphead, Argyll Map Ref: 1E4

★★ SELF CATERING

Apartments of individual character and style, converted from farm steading. Peaceful location under 1/2 mile (1km) from Crinan.

3 flats, 1-2 pub rms, 1-2 bedrms, sleeps 2-6, total sleeping capacity 14, £100.00-£400.00, Jan-Dec, bus nearby, rail 35 mls, airport 80 mls

Daphne Murray
Kilmahumaig, Crinan, by Lochgilphead, Argyll, PA31 8SW
Tel: (Crinan) 01546 830238 Fax: 01546 830238

rossapol, Argyll Map Ref: 1A2

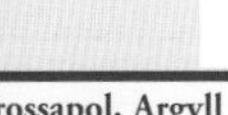

★ SELF CATERING

Annexe to owner's house, close to airfield and local shop. Open views across the countryside. 4 miles (7 kms) from ferry and in centre of island.

1 house, 1 pub rm, 2 bedrms, sleeps 5, £130.00-£150.00, Jan-Dec, ferry 3 1/2 mls, airport 1/2 ml

Mrs M Davies
Viewfield, Crossapol, Isle of Tiree, Argyll
Tel: (Scarinish) 01879 220458

almally, Argyll Map Ref: 1F2

★★★ SELF CATERING

Delightful stone cottage on the banks of the River Orchy. Perfect for fishing, hillwalking and family activities. Ideal for Western and Central Highlands.

1 cottage, 2 pub rms, 2 bedrms, sleeps 4, £230.00-£325.00, Jan-Dec, bus 1/2 ml, rail 1/2 ml

Ms Irene Chapman
Troughwood, Kippen, Stirlingshire, FK8 3HU
Tel: (Kippen) 01786 870778

Dalmally, Argyll

Map Ref: 1F2

SELF CATERING

On private 4000 acre estate overlooking Loch Awe. 11 miles (17.5 kms) from Inveraray, 28 miles (45 kms) from Oban.

3 cottages, 2 pub rms, 2-4 bedrms, sleeps 4-8, total sleeping capacity 16, £150.00-£480.00, Apr-Nov, bus 1/4 ml, rail 5 mls, ferry 28 mls, airport 70 mls

Mrs D Fellowes
Inistrynich, Lochaweside, by Dalmally, Argyll, PA33 1BQ
Tel: (Dalmally) 01838 200256 Fax: 01838 200253

Dunblane, Perthshire

Map Ref: 2A3

SELF CATERING

Luxurious, pretty cottage with spectacular views south to Gargunock Hills in central rural location at the Gateway to the Highlands. Ideal base for Trossachs, Loch Lomond, Perth, Glasgow, Edinburgh and Stirling. Hill and mountain walking, historic sights. Own garden. Open fire. Ensuite bathrooms. Easy reach of airports. Available all year for short or long lets.

1 cottage, 1 pub rm, 2 bedrms (grd flr avail), sleeps 4, min let weekend, £150.00-£425.00, Jan-Dec, bus 2 mls, rail 5 mls, airport 40 mls

Mrs Fiona & Mr Colin Graham
Mackeanston House, Doune, Perthshire, FK16 6AX
Tel: (Thornhill) 01786 850213 Fax: 01786 850414

SELF CATERING

Completely renovated historic cottages with individual charm, close to town centre and amenities. Ideal touring centre. Personal supervision.

4 cottages, 2 pub rms, 1-2 bedrms (grd flr avail), sleeps 2-4, total sleeping capacity 14, £150.00-£360.00, Jan-Dec, bus 200 yds

Mrs Kate Dalgleish
Ryland Lodge, Dunblane, Perthshire, FK15 0HY
Tel: (Dunblane) 01786 823351

SELF CATERING

In grounds of large country house with magnificent open views. Peaceful, yet only 2 miles (3kms) from Doune. Easy access to M9, A9 and airports.

1 cottage, 1 pub rm, 2 bedrms, sleeps 4-5, £210.00-£250.00, Jan-Dec exc Xmas/New Year, bus 2 mls, rail 7 mls, airport 30 mls

Mrs Wordie
The Row, Dunblane, Perthshire, FK15 9WZ
Tel: (Doune) 01786 841200/841575

Dunoon, Argyll

Map Ref: 1F5

SELF CATERING

Located on the outskirts of Dunoon adjacent to the 18-hole Cowal golf course and bowling club. On the door step of this lovely home are mountains, fells, hills, forests to walk, cycle, climb and enjoy. There are many roads, lochs and vistas to view with pleasure. This is an area of outstanding natural beauty.

1 house, 2 pub rms, 2 bedrms, sleeps 4-6, £150.00-£250.00, Apr-Oct, bus nearby, rail 6 mls, ferry 2 mls, airport 20 mls

Mr Lawson
The Close, Mill Lane, Cloughton, nr Scarborough, N. Yorkshire, YO13 0AB
Tel: (Cloughton) 01723 870455 Fax: 01723 870349

Important: Prices stated are estimates and may be subject to amendments

Dunoon, Argyll — Map Ref: 1F5

★ SELF CATERING

Holiday flats and chalets situated on the sea front between Hunter's Quay and Dunoon Pier.

5 flats, 1 pub rm, 1-2 bedrms (grd flr avail), sleeps 2-5, total sleeping capacity 22, min let weekend (low season), £90.00-£240.00, Jan-Dec, bus nearby, ferry 1 ml, airport 12 mls

Mr John Quirk
Dunmore Holiday Flats, Alexandra Parade, Kirn, Dunoon, Argyll, PA23 8DX
Tel: (Dunoon) 01369 704205

By Dunoon, Argyll — Map Ref: 1F5

★★ SELF CATERING

Spacious house recently built in traditional style and set back from coastal road overlooking Loch Long. Eight bedrooms and four bathrooms make this property ideal for large groups or several families holidaying together. Sauna, jacuzzi and pool table.

1 house, 4 pub rms, 8 bedrms (grd flr avail), sleeps 16, £795.00-£1550.00, Jan-Dec, bus nearby, rail 10 mls, ferry 10 mls, airport 30 mls

Mrs G Cox
Blairmore Holidays Ltd, 22 Victoria Park Gardens North, Glasgow, G11 7EJ
Tel: 0141 337 6669 Fax: 07070 604089

Easdale, by Oban, Argyll — Map Ref: 1D3

★ SELF CATERING

150 year-old cottage, modernised yet retaining original character, in peaceful village with views of the Atlantic Ocean and Inner Hebrides.

1 cottage, 1 pub rm, 2 bedrms, sleeps 5, £220.00-£240.00, Jan-Dec, bus 500 yds, rail 16 mls

Mrs J Forster
Kilchurn, Killin, Perthshire, FK21 8TN
Tel: (Killin) 01567 820298

Falkirk, Stirlingshire — Map Ref: 2A4

★★ UP TO ★★★ SELF CATERING

Two flats in converted detached house and one detached bungalow in quiet residential street within walking distance of Falkirk town centre, railway station and all amenities. Private parking. Centrally situated for Edinburgh, Glasgow and Stirling.

1 house, 2 flats, 1 pub rm, 2-3 bedrms (grd flr avail), sleeps 3-5, total sleeping capacity 14, min let weekend, £100.00-£450.00, Jan-Dec, bus 400 yds, rail 400 yds, airport 17 mls

The Georgian Finance Co Ltd
11 Hillcrest Road, Falkirk, FK1 5NH
Tel: 01324 623287

★★★ SELF CATERING

Semi-detached house with garden, in quiet residential area, within easy access to M9 3 miles from Falkirk town centre. Good base for touring central Scotland - an ideal base for business or pleasure.

1 cottage, 2 pub rms, 3 bedrms (grd flr avail), sleeps 7, £185.00-£380.00, Jan-Dec, bus nearby, rail 1 ½ mls, airport 30 mls

Mrs J Maitland
7/9 Wallacestone Brae, Reddingmuirhead, by Falkirk, FK2 0DQ
Tel: (Polmont) 01324 715597 Fax: 01324 715597

Falkirk, Stirlingshire

Map Ref: 2A4

SELF CATERING

Newly built detached villa in quiet residential area with private garage and garden. Adjacent to railway line. Ideal base for touring - equal distance from Glasgow, Edinburgh & Stirling.

1 villa, 1 pub rm, 3 bedrms (grd flr avail), sleeps 6, £250.00-£350.00, Jan-Dec

Mrs Williamson
Polmont Park West, Polmont, FK2 0XT
Tel: 01324 717081

Fintry, Stirlingshire

Map Ref: 1H4

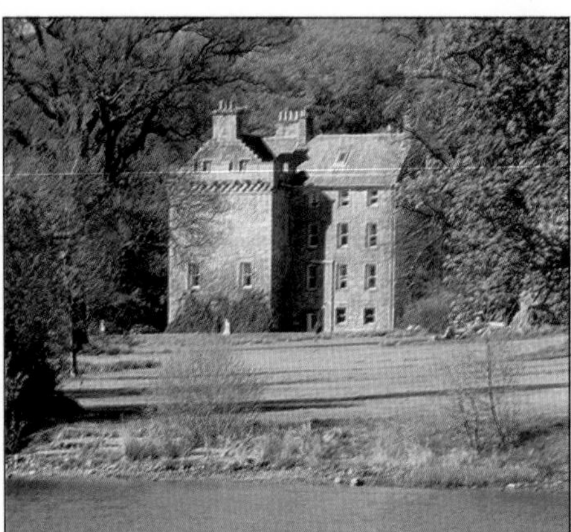

SELF CATERING

Lodges on elevated site with impressive views over 1600 acre parkland.

8 lodges, 1 pub rm, 2-3 bedrms (grd flr avail), sleeps 4-6, total sleeping capacity 40, £169.00-£429.00, Jan-Dec, bus 1 ml, rail 17 mls, airport 30 mls

Laird of Culcreuch, Culcreuch Castle Lodges
Culcreuch Castle & Country Park, Fintry, Stirling, G63 0LW
Tel: (Fintry) 01360 860228/860555 Fax: 01360 860556

Ford, by Lochgilphead, Argyll

Map Ref: 1E3

SELF CATERING

Three comfortable and warm traditional stonebuilt highland cottages, all recently refurbished and equipped, situated in various locations on extensive working estate. An abundance of wildlife, different habitats, ancient chaple, burial site and castle all to be explored on the estate.

3 cottages, 1 pub rm, 1-4 bedrms, sleeps 2-7, total sleeping capacity 16, £150.00-£355.00, Jan-Dec, bus 1 ml, ferry 20 mls

Mrs W Cairns
Finchairn, Ford, by Lochgilphead, Argyll, PA31 8RJ
Tel: (Ford) 01546 810 223

Gartocharn, Dunbartonshire

Map Ref: 1G4

SELF CATERING

Farmhouse cottage in rural setting of 6 acres, with panoramic country views.

1 cottage, 1 pub rm, 1 bedrm, sleeps 2-4, £180.00-£300.00, Jan-Dec, bus 3 mls, rail 5 mls, ferry 25 mls, airport 20 mls

Mrs Sarah Thomson
Greystonelea, Gartocharn, G83 8SD
Tel: 01389 830419 Fax: 01389 830419

Glendaruel, Argyll

Map Ref: 1F4

SELF CATERING

Traditional farm-house, with enclosed south-facing garden, in peaceful glen. Ideal base for touring West coast. Shop and hotel 1 mile.

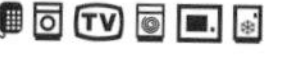

1 farmhouse, 2 pub rms, 5 bedrms (grd flr avail), sleeps 9, from £180.00, May-Sep, bus 1 ml, rail 40 mls, ferry 8 mls, airport 60 mls

Mrs S MacKellar
Ardacheranmor, Glendaruel, Argyll, PA22 3AE
Tel: (Glendaruel) 01369 820209

Inchmurrin, Island of, Loch Lomond, Dunbartonshire

Map Ref: 1G4

SELF CATERING

Flats attached to Hotel on small quiet island in Loch Lomond. Ferry service to mainland available. Water skiing. Wind surfing.

2 flats, 1 pub rm, 2 bedrms, sleeps 4-6, total sleeping capacity 12, £200.00-£400.00, Apr-Oct

Mrs D Scott
Inchmurrin Hotel, Island of Inchmurrin, Loch Lomond, Dunbartonshire, G63 0JY
Tel: (Arden) 01389 850245 Fax: 01389 850232

Inveraray, Argyll

Map Ref: 1F3

SELF CATERING

19c stone building tastefully converted into two houses and 2- person studio, peacefully situated with views to the Cowal Hills. Ideal for touring Argyll.

3 houses, 2 pub rms, 1-2 bedrms (grd flr avail), sleeps 2-5, total sleeping capacity 11, £150.00-£350.00, Jan-Dec, bus 1/2 ml, rail 23 mls, airport 70 mls

Mrs Crawford
Brenchoille Farm, Inveraray, Argyll, PA32 8XN
Tel: (Furnace) 01499 500662 Fax: 01499 500662

VAT is shown at 17.5%: changes in this rate may affect prices.

Key to symbols is on back flap.

LOCH LOMOND
INVERBEG HOLIDAY PARK

• 01436 860 267 •

CARAVANS & CHALETS FOR HIRE

Most with loch view (most chalets are beach front). The park is located on a promontary which stretches into the loch, and has the River Douglas flowing down one side of it. The position and the view across the loch to Ben Lomond (3198ft) is fabulous. Stirling and much of the West Coast can be reached by car in under an hour.

- ★ FISHING FROM SHORE
- ★ HARBOUR & SLIPWAY
- ★ CYCLE HIRE

COMMENDATION AWARD

All our chalets, Gold, Silver & Bronze Caravans surpass the "Thistle"

Loch Lomond (from the South)

- ★ PRIVATE BEACH
- ★ LAUNDRETTE
- ★ FAMILY RESTAURANT (200 YARDS)
- ★ FERRY (200 YARDS), BOAT TRIPS (4 MILES)
- ★ TRAIN (6 MILES), CITYLINK BUSES (AT GATE)

Looking across the harbour

A Lochside Chalet

INVERBEG HOLIDAY PARK
Inverbeg, Luss,
Dumbartonshire G83 8PD.

01436 860 267

Brochure will be sent by return.

Inverbeg, Dunbartonshire Map Ref: 1G4

✓✓✓✓ 181

Inverbeg Holiday Park

Inverbeg,by Luss, Dunbartonshire, G83 8PD Tel: (Luss) 01436 860267 Fax: 01436 860266

15 acres, hard-standing, level, sheltered, Mar-Nov, prior booking in peak periods, latest time of arrival 2300, overnight holding area. Extra charge for electricity, awnings.

30 tourers £9.50-10.75 and 10 motors £9.50-10.75. Total Touring Pitches 40. No tents.

12 Holiday Caravans to let, sleep 4-8 £140.00-485.00, total sleeping capacity 72, min let 3 nights.

Leisure facilities:

Take M8 through Glasgow. Go over Erskine Bridge, take A82 for Crianlarich. Park is 4 mls N of Luss on right hand side. beside Loch Lomond.

Inveruglas, Argyll & Bute Map Ref: 1G3

★★★★ SELF CATERING

Chalets, luxury lodges and a cottage; situated on the lochside in this peaceful 13 acre park, with superb open views.

4 chalets, 1 cottage, 9 luxury lodges, 1 pub rm, 2-3 bedrms, sleeps 4-6, total sleeping capacity 52, £180.00-£625.00, Jan-Dec, exc Nov/Feb, bus 1/4 ml, rail 4 mls, airport 35 mls

Loch Lomond Holiday Park

Inveruglas, by Tarbet, Argyll & Bute, G83 7DW
Tel: (Inveruglas) 01301 704224 Fax: 01301 704206

Ballygrant, Isle of Islay, Argyll Map Ref: 1C5

★★ SELF CATERING

Three flats in stonebuilt house situated in the centre of a small village. An ideal base for walkers and nature lovers. Short lets available.

3 flats, 1 pub rm, 1-4 bedrms (grd flr avail), sleeps 3-8, total sleeping capacity 17, £120.00-£250.00, Jan-Dec, bus nearby, ferry 3 mls, airport 11 mls

Mrs C Bell

Knocklearach, Ballygrant, Isle of Islay, Argyll, PA45 7QL
Tel: (Port Askaig) 01496 840209/656 Fax: 01496 840209

Bowmore, Isle of Islay, Argyll Map Ref: 1C6

★★ SELF CATERING

Four modernised flats overlooking the bay in the centre of the village.

4 flats, 1 pub rm, 1-2 bedrms, sleeps 4-6, total sleeping capacity 22, £120.00-£265.00, Jan-Dec, bus nearby, ferry 10 mls, airport 6 mls

Islay Rhind, c/o Mrs F McNeill

19 Elder Crescent, Bowmore, Isle of Islay, Argyll, PA43 7HU
Tel: (Bowmore) 01496 810532

★★ SELF CATERING

Traditional island welcome awaits you in our spacious, family home centrally situated in Bowmore. Stones throw from the harbour, shops, restaurants, swimming pool, tourist information centre and distillery all within 5 minutes walking distance. Ideal centre for touring island. Parking available on street in front of house. Fully double glazed and centrally heated.

1 house, 1 pub rm, 3 bedrms, sleeps 7, £100.00-£250.00, Jan-Dec, bus nearby, ferry 10 mls, airport 6 mls

Mr & Mrs L MacLean

Distillery House, School Street, Bowmore, Islay, PA43 7JS
Tel: 01496 810630

Bowmore, Isle of Islay, Argyll

Map Ref: 1C6

UP TO ★★

SELF CATERING

These well-equipped cottages are situated one and a quarter miles from Bowmore the islands capital, in open countryside and are ideally placed for shopping and exploring all quarters of Islay. Children and pets are especially welcome.

2 cottages, 1 pub rm, 1-2 bedrms, sleeps 4-6, total sleeping capacity 10, £85.00-£260.00, Jan-Dec, bus nearby, rail 100 mls, ferry 8 mls, airport 4 mls

W Murray
Clachan, Bowmore, Isle of Islay, Argyll, PA43 7JF
Tel: (Bowmore) 01496 810440

Bridgend, Isle of Islay, Argyll

Map Ref: 1C5

★★★★

SELF CATERING

Modern cottage, 2 miles from Bridgend in peaceful, rural setting with panoramic views of the surrounding countryside. Real fire.

1 cottage, 1 pub rm, 3 bedrms (grd flr avail), sleeps 6, £220.00-£390.00, Jan-Dec, bus 2 mls, ferry 10 mls, airport 6 mls

Mrs E C Cuninghame
Neriby Farm , Bridgend, Isle of Islay, Argyll, PA44 7PZ
Tel: (Bridgend) 01496 810274

★

SELF CATERING

Owners own holiday home. Spacious, comfortable accommodaion. Set in its own grounds. Ideal for two families. View of the sea. Three quarters of a mile from Bridgend village, with shops and hotel. Sleeps twelve. Centrally heated and carpeted throughout.

1 house, 6 bedrms (grd flr avail), sleeps 12, £475.00-£530.00, Jan-Dec, bus 1 ml, ferry 10 mls, airport 7 mls

Mrs M Dunne
Chadshunt, Kineton, Warwicks, CV35 0EQ
Tel: (Kineton) 01926 640215/583

Bruichladdich, Isle of Islay, Argyll

Map Ref: 1B5

★★

SELF CATERING

Cottages individual in character and location on 6000 acre private estate. Fishing on trout loch, boat available. Pony-trekking.

3 bungalows, 1-2 pub rms, 2-3 bedrms (grd flr avail), sleeps 4-6, total sleeping capacity 16, £220.00-£300.00, Jan-Dec, bus 1 3/4 mls, ferry 20 mls, airport 18 mls

Mrs D H Doyle
Foreland Estate, Bruichladdich, Isle of Islay, Argyll, PA49 7UU
Tel: (Port Charlotte) 01496 850211 Fax: 01496 850337

★★★

SELF CATERING

A comfortable traditional style cottage in a quiet village location with uninterrupted views of Loch Indaal. The cottage is attached to our main house but is completely self contained in every aspect. Ample off-road car parking. Conservatory and secure garden. The cottage has 2 main bedrooms, a spacious kitchen with dining for 6, bathroom and a comfortable lounge with open fire. An additional bedroom on the 1st floor is available if required.

1 cottage, 2 pub rms, 3 bedrms (grd flr avail), sleeps 1-6, £200.00-£325.00, Jan-Dec, bus nearby, ferry 20 mls, airport 15 mls

Mr R E R Falconer
Rose Cottage, Odiham Woods, Odiham, Hants, RG29 1JQ
Tel: (Basingstoke) 01256 704178 Fax: 01256 704178

Important: Prices stated are estimates and may be subject to amendments

ruichladdich, Isle of Islay, Argyll

Map Ref: 1B6

★★★

SELF CATERING

Modern cottage and spacious apartment with wonderful views on busy working farm on the west coast. 5 minutes from sandy beach. Non-smokers preferred.

1 flat, 1 cottage, 1 pub rm, 1-2 bedrms, sleeps 2-6, total sleeping capacity 8, £175.00-£290.00, Jan-Dec, bus 8 mls, ferry 20 mls, airport 20 mls

Mrs Pat Jones
Coull Farm, Kilchoman, Bruichladdich, Isle of Islay, Argyll, PA49 7UT
Tel: (Bruichladdich) 01496 850317 Fax: 01496 850317

ruinart, Bridgend, Isle of Islay, Argyll

Map Ref: 1B5

★★★

SELF CATERING

Modern detached cottage with garden in quiet location close to RSPB Reserve on north side of island.

1 cottage, 2 pub rms, 3 bedrms, sleeps 6, £230.00-£326.00, Jan-Dec, bus 3 mls, ferry 16 mls, airport 12 mls

Mr & Mrs J Adamson
Newton House, Bridgend, Isle of Islay, Argyll, PA44 7PD
Tel: (Bowmore) 01496 810293

★★

SELF CATERING

Detached cottage with large enclosed gardens, overlooking Loch Gruinart and the RSPB Reserve.

1 bungalow, 2 pub rms, 3 bedrms, sleeps 6, £199.75-£293.75, Jan-Dec, bus 3 mls, ferry 17 mls, airport 15 mls

Mr & Mrs G Archibald
Tigh-na-Speur, Bowmore, Isle of Islay, Argyll, PA43 7LL
Tel: (Bowmore) 01496 810592 Fax: 01496 850256

lchoman, Isle of Islay, Argyll

Map Ref: 1B6

★★ UP TO ★★★★

SELF CATERING

Overlooked by magnificient crags that run down to a mile long dune-fringed sandy Atlantic beach, Kilochoman House with its Five self-catering cottages and Restaurant with rooms, offers a truly peaceful location, but only 15 minutes from nearby villages. Choughs for birdwatchers, trout for fishermen, hills for walkers, safety for children. Adjacent pony trekking. Open fires. Short breaks offered September to May.

5 cottages, 1-2 pub rms, 2-3 bedrms (grd flr avail), sleeps 2-6, total sleeping capacity 22, £200.00-£450.00, Jan-Dec, ferry 19 mls, airport 15 mls

Stuart & Lesley Taylor
Kilchoman House Cottages, Bruichladdich, Isle of Islay, Argyll, PA49 7UY
Tel: (Port Charlotte) 01496 850382 Fax: 01496 850277
Email: kilchoman@aol.com

rt Charlotte, Isle of Islay, Argyll

Map Ref: 1B6

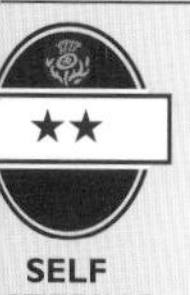

★★

SELF CATERING

Large family house facing small safe beach. Ideal base for water sports, bird watching and sightseeing of island.

1 house, 2 pub rms, 3 bedrms, sleeps 8, £100.00-£350.00, Jan-Dec, bus nearby, ferry 20 mls, airport 20 mls

Braehead Properties
5 Barnton Avenue West, Edinburgh, EH4 6DF
Tel: 0131 312 8010

VAT is shown at 17.5%: changes in this rate may affect prices.

Key to symbols is on back flap.

Port Charlotte, Isle of Islay, Argyll Map Ref: 1B6

SELF CATERING

Carefully renovated 19c house situated in picturesque conservation village. Sandy beach, fishing pier, well stocked shop, post office and 2 hotels all within 100 yards. Centrally heated sunny patio area to rear. Parking/garage beside property available. Pets by arrangement ideal centre for touring island and bird watching.

1 house, 2 pub rms, 4 bedrms, sleeps 6, £150.00-£350.00, Jan-Dec, bus nearby, ferry 15 mls, airport 13 mls

J M Bricknell
The Corran, School Street, Port Charlotte, Islay, Argyll, PA48 7TW
Tel: (Port Charlotte) 01496 850434 Fax: 01496 850434

SELF CATERING

A renovated traditional cottage close to Octomore, a working farm overlooking Loch Indaal, a large sea loch in the south west of the island. There are nesting owls and chuffs in nearby farm buildings and the adjacent field is home to migrating geese during the winter months.

1 cottage, 1 pub rm, 3 bedrms (grd flr avail), sleeps 6, £200.00-£350.00, Jan-Dec, bus 1/4 ml, ferry 20 mls, airport 15 mls

James & Sheila Brown
Octomore Farm, Port Charlotte, Isle of Islay, PA48 7UD
Tel: 01496 850235

SELF CATERING

Spacious, semi-detached house in the Rhinns of Islay, with superb views over Loch Indaal to Bowmore and the hills beyond.

1 house, 2 pub rms, 4 bedrms, sleeps 8, £160.00-£325.00, Jan-Dec, bus nearby, ferry 18 mls, airport 18 mls

Mrs C A Clark
Craigfad Farm, Port Charlotte, Isle of Islay, Argyll, PA48 7UE
Tel: (Port Charlotte) 01496 850244

SELF CATERING

Seafront cottage and traditional family home in centre of village. Ideally situated for relaxing or exploring the Island.

1 house, 2 pub rms, 3 bedrms, sleeps 5, £260.00-£320.00, Mar-Dec, ferry 16 mls, airport 12 mls

Mrs S Daniel
Flat2, 3 Earlham Street, London, WC2H 9LL
Tel: 0171 836 3232

SELF CATERING

Comfortable family house in recently modernised cottage in charming coastal village. 1 minute walk from safe sandy beach.

1 house, 1 flat, 1-3 pub rms, 1-4 bedrms, sleeps 2-8, total sleeping capacity 10, £100.00-£350.00, Jan-Dec, bus nearby, ferry 16 mls, airport 18 mls

Mr & Mrs MacLellan
11 Main Street, Port Charlotte, Isle of Islay, Argyll, PA48 7TX
Tel: 01496 850404 Fax: 01496 850404

Important: Prices stated are estimates and may be subject to amendments

rt Charlotte, Isle of Islay, Argyll

Map Ref: 1B6

★★★ SELF ATERING

Split level studio accommodation adjacent to owners home situated in attractive courtyard development in picturesque conservation village. Sun trap cultivated garden to rear with easy access to sandy beach. Restaurants close by.

1 cottage, 2 pub rms, 1 bedrm, sleeps 2-4, £120.00-£280.00, Jan-Dec, bus nearby, ferry 15 mls, airport 15 mls

Mrs G Roy
Sgioba House, Port Charlotte, Isle of Islay, Argyll
Tel: (Port Charlotte) 01496 850334

★★ UP TO ★★★★ SELF ATERING

Semi-detached cottages of individual character in picturesque setting with direct access to safe sandy beach. Superb views across the loch.

5 cottages, 1 pub rm, 1-2 bedrms (grd flr avail), sleeps 2-6, total sleeping capacity 22, £105.00-£365.00, Jan-Dec, bus nearby, ferry 20 mls, airport 18 mls

Mrs S Roy
Lorgba House, Port Charlotte, Isle of Islay, Argyll, PA48 7UD
Tel: (Port Charlotte) 01496 850208 Fax: 01496 850208

★★ SELF ATERING

Flats in centre of Port Charlotte, close to seafront and local sandy beach.

2 flats, 1 pub rm, 2 bedrms, sleeps 4, total sleeping capacity 8, £185.00-£250.00, Jan-Dec, bus nearby, ferry 20 mls, airport 16 mls

Mrs M Shaw
10 An-Creagan Place, Port Charlotte, Isle of Islay
Tel: (Bowmore) 01496 850355

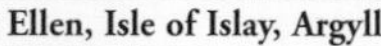

t Ellen, Isle of Islay, Argyll

Map Ref: 1C6

UP TO ★★ SELF ATERING

3 individual stone built cottages situated in grounds to rear of Tighcargamon House. Two overlook the bay with magnificent views to Ireland. Garden cottage is compact; sleeping 2 only.

3 cottages, 1-2 pub rms, 1-2 bedrms (grd flr avail), sleeps 2-4, total sleeping capacity 10, £100.00-£275.00, Jan-Dec, bus nearby, ferry 1/2 ml, airport 4 mls

Pat & John Kent
Tighcargaman, Port Ellen, Isle of Islay, Argyll, PA42 7BX
Tel: (Port Ellen) 01496 302345 Fax: 01496 302345

★ SELF ATERING

Apartments in converted farm buildings on 250 acre stock farm. Pony-trekking centre, bird-watching, golf and diving within easy access.

3 apartments, 1 pub rm, 1-2 bedrms, sleeps 2-6, total sleeping capacity 8, min let weekend (low season), £90.00-£215.00, Jan-Dec, bus 2 mls, ferry 2 mls, airport 5 mls

Mrs H Roxburgh
Ballivicar Farm, Port Ellen, Isle of Islay, Argyll, PA42 7AW
Tel: (Port Ellen) 01496 302251 Fax: 01496 302251

VAT is shown at 17.5%: changes in this rate may affect prices.

Key to symbols is on back flap.

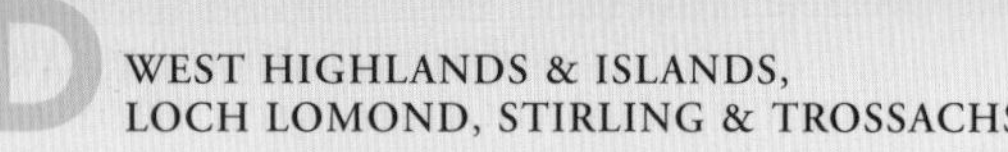

Port Ellen, Isle of Islay, Argyll

Map Ref: 1C6

Spacious and very comfortable quiet cul-de-sac. Private garden, driveway, patio. Village 2 mins. Beach 150 yds. Tennis, putting, bowling adjacent. Golf 4 miles.

1 bungalow, 2 pub rms, 2 bedrms (grd flr avail), sleeps 4, £170.00-£350.00, Jan-Dec, bus 500 yds, ferry 3/4 ml, airport 5 mls

Mr J & Mrs A Toland
133 Lathro Park, Kinross, Perthshire, KY13 7RU
Tel: (Kinross) 01577 863658

Mr & Mrs Whyte

Booking Enquiries: Mr & Mrs Whyte, GLenmachrie Farm, Port Ellen, Isle of Islay, Argyll, PA42 7AW
Tel: (Port Ellen) 01496 302560 Fax: 01496 302560

Holiday Caravan to let, sleeps 6, £180.00-200.00, min let Day, Jan-Dec

Midway between Bowmore and Port Ellen on A846

Isle of Seil, Argyll

Map Ref: 1D3

Renovated traditional cottage situated in peaceful surroundings, with excellent facilities including open fire, parking and garden with views to the sea.

1 cottage, 2 pub rms, 2 bedrms, sleeps 4, £260.00-£350.00, Jan-Dec, bus 1/2 ml, rail 14 mls, ferry 14 mls, airport 100 mls

Mr Donald J MacDougall
Oban Seil Croft, Isle of Seil, Argyll, PA34 4TN
Tel: (Balvicar) 01852 300457 Fax: 01852 300457

Killin, Perthshire

Map Ref: 1H2

Modern detached bungalow situated in its own grounds. Panoramic views of river and surrounding hills. Ideal for fishing and walking. Private fishing available.

1 bungalow, 2 pub rms, 2 bedrms, sleeps 4, min let weekend, £220.00-£300.00, Jan-Dec, bus nearby, rail 14 mls, airport 75 mls

Mrs C A Campbell
Ledcharrie Farm, Luib, by Crianlarich, Perthshire, FK20 8QT
Tel: (Killin) 01567 820532

✓✓✓ 74

Cruachan Farm Caravan & Camping Park
Cruachan, Killin, Perthshire, FK21 8TY Tel: (Killin) 01567 820302

Booking Enquiries: J Campbell Cruachan, Morenish, Killin, Perthshire, FK21 8TY

10 acres, mixed, mid Mar-Oct, latest time of arrival 2200, overnight holding area. Extra charge for electricity, awnings, showers.

14 tourers from £6.50 and 20 motors from £6.00 and 40 tents from £5.00. Total Touring Pitches 74.

8 Holiday Caravans to let, sleep 6, £195.00-220.00, total sleeping capacity 48, min let 1 night.

Leisure facilities:

From Kirkwall take A961 for abt 11mls to Killin-Aberfeldy road, 3 1/2 mls along on right. Travelling E from Killin. Site is on A827 Killin - Aberfeldy road, 3.5 mls along on right.

Important: Prices stated are estimates and may be subject to amendments

lin, Perthshire

Map Ref: 1H2

★★ SELF ATERING

Listed traditional stone and harl building which forms part of one side of steading. Own fishing available, river and hill walks.

1 cottage, 1 pub rm, 1 bedrm, sleeps 4-6, £120.00-£280.00, Jan-Dec, bus $^1/_2$ ml, rail 14 mls, airport 65 mls

Mrs K Dowling
Gardeners Cottage, Kinnell Estate, Killin, Perthshire, FK21 8SR
Tel: (Killin) 01567 820814/820590 Fax: 01567 820590

★★ UP TO ★★★★ SELF ATERING

Houses, both with all rooms on the one level, centrally situated in Killin. Enclosed garden with swings and barbecue.

2 houses, 2 pub rms, 3 bedrms (grd flr avail), sleeps 4-7, total sleeping capacity 11, £150.00-£350.00, Jan-Dec, bus nearby, rail 13 mls, ferry 60 mls, airport 60 mls

Mrs Dani Grant
Breadalbane House, Main Street, Killin, Perthshire
Tel: (Killin) 01567 820386 Fax: 01567 820386

★★★ SELF ATERING

Traditional country cottage on 200 acre estate surrounded by spectacular Highland scenery at the head of Loch Tay. Fishing available, with golf, watersports and hill walking close by.

1 cottage, 2 pub rms, 2 bedrms, sleeps 6, £275.00-£375.00, Jan-Dec, bus $^1/_2$ ml, rail 15 mls

J D Howe
Finlarig, Killin, Perthshire, FK21 8TN
Tel: 01567 820259

★★ SELF ATERING

Traditional stone cottage with enclosed garden situated close to the Falls of Dochart. Short walk to village centre.

1 cottage, 1 pub rm, 3 bedrms (grd flr avail), sleeps 6, £140.00-£230.00, Jan-Dec, bus nearby, rail 13 mls

Mr & Mrs D K Mardon
Fagus, Manse Road, Killin, Perthshire, FK21 8UY
Tel: (Killin) 01567 820248

★★ UP TO ★★★ SELF ATERING

Log chalets in woodland setting overlooking the rolling hills at the west end of Loch Tay.

8 chalets, 1 bungalow, 1 pub rm, 2-4 bedrms (grd flr avail), sleeps 4-8, total sleeping capacity 40, min let 2 nights, £150.00-£550.00, Jan-Dec, bus 1 ml, rail 14 mls, airport 50 mls

Mr A Whitehead
Shieling Accommodation, Killin, Perthshire, FK21 8TX
Tel: (Killin) 01567 820334 Fax: 01567 820334

VAT is shown at 17.5%: changes in this rate may affect prices.

Key to symbols is on back flap.

– OPEN ALL YEAR –

Forty luxury pine lodges set in a beautiful, well-maintained, 160-acre private estate on the shore of Loch Tay. The lodges have 2 or 3 bedrooms sleeping 4 to 6 people (New for 1999 superior waterside bunkhouse – sleeps 8). All lodges are warm, comfortable and fully-equipped (some with en-suite, dishwasher, microwave and pay phone) for an enjoyable trouble-free holiday.

Loch Tay is in the heart of Scotland, ideal for touring or relaxing. There is a private harbour with boats for hire, salmon and trout fishing are available on the loch.

On the estate is the Equestrian Centre with new, purpose-built olympic size indoor riding school for all year round riding. (All-inclusive riding/fishing short breaks available low season.) Novice and experienced riders welcome, guests may bring own horse. Pony trekking, expert tuition and children's pony rides are available.

Other on-site facilities include a putting green, clay pigeon shooting and private 4 mile hill-track for walking, riding and mountain-biking. Golf, watersports, swimming and ski-ing are available nearby.

Prices for 1999 £224-£764. (Millenium week on application.) We have 40 log cabins, total sleeping capacity 180.

Also for sale: 2 and 3 bedroom Pine Lodges as a whole, 1/2 or 1/4 share (Freehold – not Time-share). Management Letting/Cleaning Service available.

Contact below for further details.

★★★★ SELF CATERING

For full details and colour brochure, please contact: Mr and Mrs J. C. Booth

Loch Tay
Highland Lodges

Milton Morenish Estate, Killin, Perthshire FK21 8TY
Tel: 01567 820323 Fax: 01567 820581

By Killin, Perthshire

Map Ref: 1H2

SELF CATERING

Timber lodges on the shores of Loch Tay. Trout and salmon fishing, boat hire, horse riding and other activities available.

35 log cabins, 1 house, 1 cottage, 1 pub rm, 2-3 bedrms (grd flr avail), sleeps 4-6, total sleeping capacity 168, £196.00-£670.00, Jan-Dec, bus 3 mls, rail 8 mls, airport 80 mls

Loch Tay Highland Lodges
Milton Morenish, by Killin, Perthshire, FK21 8TY
Tel: 01567 820323 Fax: 01567 820581

Kilmartin, by Lochgilphead, Argyll

Map Ref: 1E4

SELF CATERING

Very comfortably and tastefully renovated stable buildings on 100 acre working sheep farm in historic Kilmartin Glen. Sandy beaches and Crinan Canal nearby. Very quiet rural location, ideal base for walking, nature watching or simple relaxing holidays.

1 cottage, 1 wing of large house, 1 pub rm, 2-3 bedrms (grd flr avail), sleeps 4-6, total sleeping capacity 10, £190.00-£380.00, Jan-Dec, bus 1 ml, rail 30 mls, airport 85 mls

Sandy Gordon
Ri Cruin West, Kilmartin, by Lochgilphead, Argyll, PA31 8QF
Tel: (Kilmartin) 01546 510316

SELF CATERING

Individually sited stone built cottages and honeymoon bothy on 5000 acre estate with 6 miles (10 kms) of coastline. Country pursuits and fishing. Area rich in pre-history. Excellent restaurants and hotels within a short driving distance.

6 cottages, 1-2 pub rms, 1-3 bedrms (grd flr avail), sleeps 2-5, total sleeping capacity 26, £200.00-£350.00, Mar-Nov, bus 8 mls, rail 32 mls, airport 85 mls

Mrs Malcolm
Duntrune Castle, Kilmartin, Argyll, PA31 8QQ
Tel: (Kilmartin) 01546 510283

Kilmelford, by Oban, Argyll

Map Ref: 1E3

SELF CATERING

Comfortably converted stable cottage within a small farm courtyard, built c1780. Set in a peaceful and beautiful remote glen, close to Loch Alrich, it is the perfect base for those with interests in the great outdoors. Rich in bird and wildlife, fishing by permit locally. Watersports can be arranged in the village of Kilmelford 4 miles (6 km).

1 cottage, 1 pub rm, 2 bedrms, sleeps 4, min let 3 days, £220.00-£346.00, Apr-Oct, bus 4 mls, rail 18 mls, ferry 18 mls, airport 100 mls

Mrs G H Dalton
Maolachy, Lochavich, Taynuilt, Argyll, PA35 1HJ
Tel: (Lochavich) 01866 844212 Fax: 01866 844295

Kilmelford, by Oban, Argyll **Map Ref: 1E3**

★★ UP TO ★★★★

SELF CATERING

Stone built cottages/houses in natural setting on 150 acre estate with views over Loch Melfort to the hills beyond.

4 houses, 4 cottages, 1-2 pub rms, 1-4 bedrms (grd flr avail), sleeps 2-10, total sleeping capacity 36, £110.00-£620.00, Jan-Dec, bus 3 mls, rail 21 mls, ferry 18 mls, airport 21 mls

Mrs Atkinson
Woodside Park Estates Ltd, Park Avenue, Hartlepool, TS26 0EA
Tel: (Hartlepool) 01429 267266 Fax: 01429 267266

★★★★★

SELF CATERING

Private fully ensuite harbour houses, at the waters edge, each with saunas and spa baths. Views across Loch Melfort.

10 houses, 1-3 pub rms, 1-3 bedrms (grd flr avail), sleeps 2-6, total sleeping capacity 44, min let 2 nights, £75.00-£165.00 per house/night, Jan-Dec, bus 1 1/2 mls, rail 16 mls, ferry 16 mls, airport 100 mls

Melfort Pier & Harbour
Kilmelford, by Oban, Argyll, PA34 4XD
Tel: (Kilmelford) 01852 200333 Fax: 01852 200329

★★

SELF CATERING

Widely spaced Norwegian chalets set in magnificent scenery in secluded private glen 12 miles south of Oban. Close to Loch Tralaig, with free trout fishing and boating. Children and pets welcome. Parking by each chalet. Walking and birdwatching. Pony-trekking, sailing, golf and other sports can be arranged locally. Evening entertainment locally and in Oban - open March to October. Prices include electricity. Brochure from resident owners.

7 chalets, 1 pub rm, 2-3 bedrms (grd flr avail), sleeps 4-6, total sleeping capacity 40, £195.00-£445.00, Mar-Oct, bus 1/2 ml, rail 12 mls, ferry 12 mls, airport 100 mls

Mr & Mrs A A W Stevens
Eleraig Highland Chalets, Kilninver, by Oban, Argyll, PA34 4UX
Tel: (Kilmelford) 01852 200225 Fax: 01852 200225

Important: Prices stated are estimates and may be subject to amendments

nelford, by Oban, Argyll Map Ref: 1E3

Melfort Village

Kilmelford, by Oban, Argyll PA34 4XD
Telephone: 01852 200257
Fax: 01852 200321

Luxury 19th century Gunpowder Village at the head of Loch Melfort amidst beautiful walking and touring scenery. Carefully restored cottages providing luxury accommodation with dishwashers, microwaves, colour television, video recorders, central heating. Linen and towels provided. On-site facilities include indoor swimming pool, sauna, solarium, games rooms, children's playground and horse riding.
Our restaurant and bar, **The Shower of Herring Inn**, offers excellent, reasonably priced meals with entertainment a regular feature throughout the year.
Water sports and boat trips nearby.
Ideal for families. Pets most welcome.

★★ UP TO ★★★
SELF ATERING

Comfortable, spacious, 19th century cottages set amidst beautiful walking and touring scenery. Peaceful setting. Cottages have dishwasher, microwave, colour TV and video, central heating, linen, on-site indoor swimming pool, sauna, solarium, tennis, games rooms, horse riding, restaurant, bar. Pets welcome.

10 houses, 5 flats, 17 cottages, 1-2 pub rms, 1-3 bedrms, sleeps 2-8, total sleeping capacity 146, £270.00-£825.00, Jan-Dec, bus 1 1/2 mls, rail 16 mls, ferry 16 mls, airport 100 mls

Melfort Village
Kilmelford, by Oban, Argyll, PA34 4XD
Tel: (Kilmelford) 01852 200257 Fax: 01852 200321

nichael Glen, by Lochgilphead, Argyll Map Ref: 1E4

★ UP TO ★★★
SELF ATERING

Two cottages in the grounds of former Victorian shooting lodge. Peaceful location in a scenic glen south of Loch Awe. Salmon and trout fishing available by permit.

2 cottages, 1-3 pub rms, 1-3 bedrms, sleeps 2-6, total sleeping capacity 8, £180.00-£475.00, Jan-Dec, bus 2 mls, rail 32 mls, airport 90 mls

Mrs Breakell
Kirnan Country House, Kilmichael Glen, by Lochgilphead, Argyll, PA31 8QL
Tel: (Dunadd) 01546 605217

nun, by Dunoon, Argyll Map Ref: 1F4

★
SELF ATERING

South facing Victorian villa overlooking the peaceful and beautiful Holy Loch, set in spacious grounds laid out mostly in lawns, with private parking. It is situated on the edge of the Kilmun Forest, within the small lochside village of Kilmun.

1 house, 4 pub rms, 5 bedrms (grd flr avail), sleeps 10, £250.00-£450.00, Easter-Oct, Xmas/New Year, bus 100 yds, rail 6 mls, ferry 4 mls, airport 10 mls

Derek J Barclay
16 Marlborough Avenue, Glasgow, G11 7BW
Tel: 0141 339 5141

VAT is shown at 17.5%: changes in this rate may affect prices.

Key to symbols is on back flap.

Kilninver, by Oban, Argyll

Map Ref: 1E2

Apartments in Victorian shooting lodge, situated at head of Loch Scammadale, amongst mountains and overlooking the Loch. Excellent walking & wildlife country.

3 flats, 1 pub rm, 2-3 bedrms, sleeps 4-9, total sleeping capacity 19, £130.00-£320.00, Jan-Dec, bus 5 mls, rail 15 mls, ferry 15 mls

Mrs J Handley
Bragleenbeg, Kilninver,by Oban, Argyll, PA34 4UU
Tel: (Kilninver) 01852 316283

Traditional spacious stone cottage, with open fire. In own fenced and extensive grounds overlooking trout stream. 12 miles (19 kms) south of Oban. 2 bathrooms. An excellent location for exploring this beautiful part of Scotland with easy access to the islands of Giha, Jura, Mull and Iona.

1 house, 2 pub rms, 3 bedrms (grd flr avail), sleeps 6, £295.00-£575.00, Apr-Oct, Xmas, N/Year, bus nearby, rail 12 mls, ferry 12 mls

Mrs D A Macdonald
21 Lindisfarne Road, Newcastle-upon-Tyne, NE2 2HE
Tel: (Tyneside) 0191 281 1695 Fax: 0191 281 1253
Email: dacmac@btinternet.com
Web: www.stilwell.co.uk

Lerags, by Oban, Argyll

Map Ref: 1E2

Period flat in converted Georgian stables. Secluded setting by Loch Feochan . 5 miles (8kms) south of Oban.

1 cottage, 2 pub rms, 4 bedrms, sleeps 2-6, £150.00-£350.00, Mar-Nov, bus 5 mls, rail 5 mls

Miss E Lees Whittick
Lerags Beg, by Oban, Argyll, PA34 4SE
Tel: (Oban) 01631 562450

Lochawe, Argyll

Map Ref: 1F2

Second and third floor apartments in this six storey granite tower house. Magnificent views over Loch Awe.

3 flats, 2-4 bedrms, sleeps 2-4, total sleeping capacity 7, £170.00-£310.00, Jan-Dec, bus 1/4 ml, rail 1/4 ml

Sheena Anderson
St Conan's Tower, Loch Awe, Argyll, PA33 1AH
Tel: 01838 200342 Fax: 01838 200342

West Highland country house apartments dating from the 17th century and sleeping 2-12 in a spectacular lochside location. On site licensed bar serving meals, games room, tennis and laundry. Record breaking loch fishing with boat hire. Detached cottages also available.

8 flats, 5 cottages, 3 pub rms, 1-5 bedrms (grd flr avail), sleeps 2-12, total sleeping capacity 77, min let weekend, £175.00-£840.00, Jan-Dec, bus 6 mls, rail 6 mls, ferry 30 mls, airport 65

Ardbrecknish House
South Lochaweside, by Dalmally, Argyll, PA33 1BH
Tel: 01866 833223 Fax: 01866 833223

Important: Prices stated are estimates and may be subject to amendments

ıearnhead, Perthshire

Map Ref: 1H2

★★★ SELF ATERING

Modern Danish pine cottages in elevated position overlooking Loch Earn, alongside hotel. Mooring and jetty facilities included and water sports centre. Ideal centre for golfing, touring, fishing and cycling.

8 log cabins, 1 pub rm, 2-3 bedrms, sleeps 4-6, total sleeping capacity 36, £130.00-£470.00, Jan-Dec, bus nearby, rail 16 mls, airport 60 mls

Hoseasons Holidays
Sunway House, Lowestoft, Suffolk, NR32 3LT
Tel: (Lowestoft) 01502 500500

★★★ SELF ATERING

Spacious modern home with commanding views over Loch Earn. Ideal base for watersports, golf and hillwalking.

1 bungalow, 2 pub rms, 4 bedrms (grd flr avail), sleeps 8, £300.00-£600.00, Jan-Dec

Mr & Mrs K A Logan
1 Corbiehill Park, Edinburgh, EH4 5EQ
Tel: 0131 336 2290

ıgilphead, Argyll

Map Ref: 1E4

★★★ SELF ATERING

Private home situated within the quiet hamlet of Port Ann located close to the A83 road, having beautiful views toward the Cowal and Arran hills. Beach within 10 minutes walk. Shrub garden provides parking, picnic and barbecue areas. Ideal central touring location.

1 house, 1 pub rm, 3 bedrms, sleeps 6, £175.00-£325.00, Apr-Sep, bus nearby, rail 40 mls, ferry 40 mls, airport 83 mls

Cnoc-na-Coille
6 Port Ann, by Lochgilphead
Tel: (Lochgilphead) 01546 603640

ıgoilhead, Argyll

Map Ref: 1F3

★ SELF ATERING

Spacious Victorian lochside house with 5 bedrooms, sleeping 12. Large grounds with superb west facing views. 1/2 mile to village. Golf, water sports and walking locally. Coal, electricity and linen included. Cot available. Pets by arrangement.

1 house, 2 pub rms, 5 bedrms, sleeps 12, £220.00-£580.00, Jan-Dec, bus 1/2 ml, rail 7 mls, airport 30 mls

Mr G E F Johnston
Upper Dunard, Station Road, Rhu, Dunbartonshire, G84 8LW
Tel: (Rhu) 01436 820563

ı, Argyll & Bute

Map Ref: 1G4

★★ SELF ATERING

Traditional stone cottage on hill sheep farm. Superb views over Loch Lomond. Ideal for touring, hill walking and water sports.

1 cottage, 1 pub rm, 2 bedrms (grd flr avail), sleeps 6, min let weekend, £150.00-£350.00, Jan-Dec, bus 1/2 ml, rail 6 mls, airport 20 mls

Mrs A Lennox
Shantron Farm, Luss, by Alexandria, Dunbartonshire, G83 8RH
Tel: (Arden) 01389 850231 Fax: 01389 850231
Email: rjlennox@shantron.u-net.com

VAT is shown at 17.5%: changes in this rate may affect prices.

Key to symbols is on back flap.

Luss, Argyll & Bute

Map Ref: 1G4

SELF CATERING

Newly converted courtyard cottages in quiet rural situation. Within walking distance of Loch Lomond Golf Course.

2 cottages, 1 pub rm, 1-2 bedrms (grd flr avail), sleeps 2-5, total sleeping capacity 7, £200.00-£450.00, Jan-Dec, bus 1/4 ml, rail 5 mls, airport 20 mls

Mrs C Wishart
Shegarton Farm, Luss, Loch Lomond, G83 8RH
Tel: 01389 850269 Fax: 01389 850269

Machrihanish, Argyll

Map Ref: 1D7

SELF CATERING

Victorian stone built house with own garden overlooking Machrihanish Bay, sandy beach and local golf links. Ideal for walkers and birdwatchers.

1 house, 2 pub rms, 4 bedrms, sleeps 5-6, £292.00-£344.00, mid Mar-mid Oct, bus nearby, ferry nearby, airport 5 mls

Mrs M Craig
The Garth, Tynron, Thornhill, Dumfriesshire, DG3 4JY
Tel: (Thornhill) 01848 200364

Maddiston, Stirlingshire

Map Ref: 2B4

SELF CATERING

Newly built pine chalets situated in forty acres of beautiful surroundings, overlooking the River Avon. Kids play park. Free fishing on the River Avon. An ideal base for touring Scotland, with easy access to all major routes.

3 chalets, 2 bedrms, sleeps 6, total sleeping capacity 6, min let weekend, £185.00-£375.00, Jan-Dec, bus 1 ml, rail 4 mls, airport 15 mls

Dorothy Seaton
Avon Glen Chalets, Melons Place, Maddiston, FK2 0BT
Tel: 01324 621341/861242

Minard, by Inveraray, Argyll

Map Ref: 1E4

SELF CATERING

Two courtyard flats and modern bungalow situated in the private grounds of Minard Castle. Salmon fishing in season. 13 miles (20km) from Inveraray.

2 flats, 1 bungalow, 1 pub rm, 2 bedrms (grd flr avail), sleeps 4-6, total sleeping capacity 16, min let weekend, £95.00-£340.00, Jan-Dec, bus 3/4 ml, rail 75 mls, airport 75 mls

R Gayre
Minard Castle, Minard, Argyll, PA32 8YB
Tel: (Minard) 01546 886272 Fax: 01546 886272

SELF CATERING

Modernised former crofter's cottage, situated above village of Minard with excellent views over loch and hills.

1 cottage, 2 pub rms, 2 bedrms, sleeps 6, £180.00-£250.00, Jan-Dec, bus 1/4 ml

Mrs H D McNab
Park House, Montacute, Somerset, TA15 6UN
Tel: (Martock) 01935 822949

Important: Prices stated are estimates and may be subject to amendments

ckhart, Clackmannanshire — **Map Ref: 2B3**

★★
SELF
ATERING

Private self catering accommodation in the heart of Scotland. Ideally suited as a base for walking, fishing and golfing holidays. Studio type accomodation.

1 cottage, 1 pub rm, sleeps 2, £125.00-£140.00, Jan-Dec, bus nearby, rail 17 mls, airport 28 mls

H Maak
The Old Schoolhouse, Pool of Muckhart, Nr Dollar, Clackmannanshire, FK14 7JN

Tel: 01259 781527

s, Isle of Mull, Argyll — **Map Ref: 1D1**

★★
SELF
ATERING

Three individual units in secluded rural positions on family farm, with outstanding views of the sea and mountains. Centrally located for touring.

1 log cabin, 1 flat, 2 cottages, sleeps 2-8, total sleeping capacity 20, £100.00-£500.00, bus 1/4 ml, ferry 11 mls

G Forster
Kentallen Farm, Aros, Isle of Mull, PA72 6JS
Tel: 01680 300427 Fax: 01680 300489

★
SELF
ATERING

Estate cottages, close to A849, each of individual character and centrally placed on the island.

1 house, 4 cottages, 2 pub rms, 2-4 bedrms (grd flr avail), sleeps 4-7, total sleeping capacity 26, £210.00-£350.00, Jan-Dec, bus 500 yds, ferry 12 mls

Mr & Mrs C B Scott
Kilmore House, Kilmore, by Oban, Argyll, PA34 4XT
Tel: (Kilmore) 01631 770369 Fax: 01631 770329

★★
SELF
ATERING

Peacefully located traditional stone built cottage on shore of Loch na Keal, 6 miles (10km) from Salen. The garden and bedrooms are south facing. Magnificent view over loch to Ben More. Summerhouse in garden.

1 cottage, 2 pub rms, 3 bedrms (grd flr avail), sleeps 5, £150.00-£380.00, Jan-Dec, bus 6 mls, ferry 15 mls

Mrs J O Williams
Halthorpe, Sandy Lane, Coopers Green, Uckfield, Sussex, TN22 3AE
Tel: (Buxted) 01825 732637

essan, Isle of Mull, Argyll — **Map Ref: 1C3**

★★★
SELF
ATERING

Ground floor apartment attached to hotel with magnificent view towards Colonsay, Jura and Islay. 7 miles (11 km) from Iona ferry 2 miles (4 km) from Bunessan and local shops.

1 flat, 1 pub rm, 1 bedrm (grd flr avail), sleeps 3, £200.00-£250.00, Apr-Sep, bus 2 mls, ferry 32 mls

Ardachy House Hotel
Uisken, by Bunessan, Isle of Mull, Argyll, PA67 6DS
Tel: 01681 700505 Fax: 01681 700505

Bunessan, Isle of Mull, Argyll

Map Ref: 1C3

Two traditional granite farmhouses located on scenic Ross of Mull. Secluded location with views over surrounding hills . Convenient for boat trips to Staffa and Treshnish Isles. 10 minute drive to Iona Ferry.

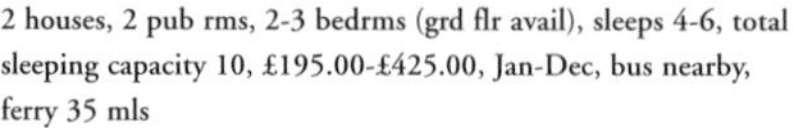

2 houses, 2 pub rms, 2-3 bedrms (grd flr avail), sleeps 4-6, total sleeping capacity 10, £195.00-£425.00, Jan-Dec, bus nearby, ferry 35 mls

Ardfenaig Farmhouses
Tiraghoil, Bunessan, Isle of Mull, Argyll, PA67 6DU
Tel: (Iona) 01681 700260 Fax: 01681 700260

In the grounds of Ardfenaig House Hotel but quite separate. Completely rebuilt to highest standards in 1994 and with extensive views over sea loch and moorland. Ardfenaig is close to the boats to Iona and Staffa and there are many walks across deserted moors to hidden white sandy beaches. Hotel facilities and restaurant are all available to Coach House guests.

1 house, 1 pub rm, 2 bedrms, sleeps 4-6, £370.00-£535.00, Jan-Dec, bus Nearby, rail 40 mls, ferry 35 mls, airport 100 mls

Mr and Mrs Davidson
Ardfenaig House, By Bunessan, Isle of Mull, Argyll, PA67 6DX
Tel: (Fionnphort) 01681 700210 Fax: 01681 700210

Calgary, Isle of Mull, Argyll

Map Ref: 1C1

Traditional modernised Highland cottage in 0.5 acre garden with magnificent views over the white sands of Calgary Beach. 0.5 mile to local hotel for evening meals.

1 cottage, 2 pub rms, 3 bedrms (grd flr avail), sleeps 6, £200.00-£395.00, Jan-Dec, bus nearby, rail 45 mls, ferry 28 mls, airport 20 mls

J E G Bartholomew
Calgary, Isle of Mull, PA75 6QT
Tel: (Dervaig) 01688 400240 Fax: 01688 400240

Secluded family house, in large natural grounds, set back from road. 1.5 miles (2.5kms) from Calgary Bay, 3.5 miles (6km) from Dervaig.

1 house, 2 pub rms, 4 bedrms (grd flr avail), sleeps 6, £300.00-£430.00, Jan-Dec, bus nearby, ferry 30 mls

Dr Morgan
Tigh-na-Drochaid, Salen, Aros, Isle of Mull, Argyll, PA72 6JB
Tel: (Aros) 01680 300536 Fax: 01680 300536

Dervaig, Isle of Mull, Argyll

Map Ref: 1C1

Refurbished traditional cottage in centre of conservation village and within walking distance of all amenities.

1 cottage, 2 pub rms, 2 bedrms, sleeps 4, £120.00-£325.00, Jan-Dec, bus nearby, ferry 22 mls

Mr Sid Austin
Brow Top Farm House, Bothel, Carlisle, CA5 2HS
Tel: 016973 22843 Fax: 016973 22843

Important: Prices stated are estimates and may be subject to amendments

vaig, Isle of Mull, Argyll

Map Ref: 1C1

★★★ SELF ATERING

Traditional stone built croft house over 300 years old right on the harbour at the road end, with spectacular views to Outer Isles. 500m to owner's nearest sandy bay. In-tune piano in lounge for guests' use.

1 house, 2 pub rms, 3 bedrms (grd flr avail), sleeps 6, £100.00-£330.00, Jan-Dec, bus 1 ml, ferry 26 mls

Mrs Galbraith
Croig, Dervaig, Isle of Mull, Argyll, PA75 6QS
Tel: (Dervaig) 01688 400219

★★★★ SELF ATERING

Recently converted stone farmhouse, centrally heated. Situated 4 miles (6 Kms) from Dervaig in tranquil Glen Bellart. Courtesy mountain bikes available.

1 house, 1 pub rm, 3 bedrms, sleeps 6, £250.00-£365.00, Feb-Nov, bus 4 mls, ferry 12 mls

Mrs Smith
Achnacraig, Dervaig, Isle of Mull, Argyll, PA75 6QW
Tel: (Dervaig) 01688 400309

★★ SELF ATERING

Modern bungalow in elevated position with fine views towards the sea.

1 bungalow, 3 pub rms, 3 bedrms (grd flr avail), sleeps 6, £275.00-£370.00, Apr-Oct, bus 1/2 ml, ferry 26 mls

P J C Sumner
Buttercliff, Winscombe Hill, Winscombe, Somerset, BS25 1DQ
Tel: (Winscombe) 01934 842219

nnphort, Isle of Mull, Argyll

Map Ref: 1B2

★★ SELF ATERING

Superb views to Iona across the Sound with direct access to the sandy beach. Secluded, yet village nearby.

1 bungalow, 1 pub rm, 3 bedrms, sleeps 6, £198.00-£380.00, Jan-Dec, bus nearby, rail 45 mls, ferry 500 yds, airport 140 mls

Ms A Rimell
Dungrianach, Fionnphort, Isle of Mull, Argyll, PA66 6BL
Tel: (Fionnphort) 01681700 417

line, Isle of Mull, Argyll

Map Ref: 1D2

★★ SELF ATERING

Stone built 19c converted farm buildings in courtyard setting situated in 5 acres of pasture and garden grounds. Located in centre of island - Ideal for touring.

2 cottages, 1 pub rm, 2 bedrms (grd flr avail), sleeps 4, total sleeping capacity 8, £170.00-£280.00, Jan-Dec, bus 3 mls, rail 12 mls, ferry 14 mls, airport 10 mls

Mrs G M Atkinson & Mrs A L Boocock
Gruline Home Farm, Gruline, Isle of Mull, Argyll, PA71 6HR
Tel: (Aros) 01680 300437 Fax: 01680 300581
Email: gruline@aol.com.uk

Gruline, Isle of Mull, Argyll

Map Ref: 1D2

SELF CATERING

Centrally situated on our working croft,our 2 log cabins, 2 stone cottages and old fashioned tearoom are surrounded by beautiful scenery and unusual animals such as Kune Kune pigs and llamas.

2 log cabins, 2 cottages, 1 pub rm, 1-2 bedrms (grd flr avail), sleeps 2-4, total sleeping capacity 14, £205.00-£295.00, Jan-Dec, bus 2 mls, ferry 13 mls

Diana McFarlane
Torlochan, Gruline, Isle of Mull, Argyll, PA71 6HR
Tel: (Aros) 01680 300380 Fax: 01680300 380

Killiechronan, Isle of Mull, Argyll

Map Ref: 1D2

KILLIECHRONAN
Isle of Mull

With spectacular views over Loch Na Keal – this former farmhouse and steading have been tastefully converted to provide seven cottages and one house. Centrally situated on the island, Killiechronan can offer fishing, pony trekking and hill walking and has active farming and forestry enterprises.

Highland Holidays, 1 Springkerse Road, Stirling FK7 7SN.
Tel: 01786 462519 Fax: 01786 471872

SELF CATERING

Comfortable cottages centrally situated on a mixed agricultural estate overlooking Loch Na Keal. Pony trekking available on site. 12 miles (19 km) from Craignure ferry.

1 house, 7 cottages, 1-2 pub rms, 1-3 bedrms, sleeps 2-6, total sleeping capacity 32, min let 2 nights (low season), £120.00-£410.00, Mar-Nov, ferry 12 mls, airport 5 mls

Killiechronan
1 Springkerse Road, Stirling, FK7 7SN
Tel: (Stirling) 01786 462519 Fax: 01786 471872

Kinlochspelve, Isle of Mull, Argyll

Map Ref: 1D2

SELF CATERING

Former farmhouse of character, dating from 1600, situated at the head of Loch Spelve. Excellent scenery and interesting wildlife.

1 house, 4 pub rms, 4 bedrms, sleeps 8, £200.00-£750.00, Jan-Dec, bus 4 mls, ferry 11 mls, airport 80 mls

Mrs G M Railton-Edwards
The Barn, Barrachandroman, Kinlochspelve, Lochbuie, Isle of Mull, Argyll, PA62 6AA
Tel: (Kinlochspelve) 01680 814220 Fax: 01680 814247
Email: spelve@aol.com

Lochdon, Isle of Mull, Argyll

Map Ref: 1D2

SELF CATERING

Modern bungalow near the shore of Lochdon with its own garden and uninterrupted views over the water. 3 miles (5kms) from ferry at Craignure.

1 bungalow, 2 pub rms, 2 bedrms (grd flr avail), sleeps 4, £150.00-£400.00, Jan-Dec, bus 300 yds, ferry 3 mls

Mrs G M Railton-Edwards
Kinlochspelve, Isle of Mull, PA62 6AA
Tel: (Kinlochspelve) 01680 814220

nyghael, Isle of Mull, Argyll

Map Ref: 1C2

★ SELF ATERING

In small village en-route to Iona. Enclosed garden overlooking shores of Loch Scridain.

1 cottage, 1 pub rm, 4 bedrms (grd flr avail), sleeps 6, £150.00-£300.00, Apr-Oct, bus 10-20 mls, ferry 20 mls

Mrs Fiona Love
2 Quarry Road, Oban, Argyll
Tel: (Oban) 01631 563212 (eve)

★★ SELF ATERING

Semi-detached cottages with uninterrupted view across Loch Scridain from Ben More down to Iona. Third cottage adjacent.

3 cottages, 1 pub rm, 2-3 bedrms (grd flr avail), sleeps 4-6, total sleeping capacity 14, £200.00-£400.00, Jan-Dec, ferry 20 mls

Pennyghael Hotel & Cottages
Pennyghael, Isle of Mull, Argyll, PA70 6HB
Tel: (Pennyghael) 01681 704288 Fax: 01681 704205

en, Aros, Isle of Mull, Argyll

Map Ref: 1D1

★★★ SELF ATERING

Former School now converted into a two bedroom cottage situated on a quiet road, in the centre of the Island, 2 miles (4km) from Salen. Ideal base for touring, nature lovers and walkers (Ben More, 5 miles).

1 cottage, 2 pub rms, 2 bedrms (grd flr avail), sleeps 4, total sleeping capacity 4, £150.00-£360.00, Jan-Dec, bus 2 1/2 mls, rail 20 mls, ferry 8 mls, airport 3 mls

Mrs A L Boocock
Gruline Home Farm, Gruline, By Salen, Isle of Mull, PA71 6HR
Tel: 01680 300581 Fax: 01680 300573
Email: gruline@ukonline.co.uk

★★★ SELF ATERING

This cottage with all rooms on the ground floor has views over the Sound of Mull and is a mere 100yds, (100 m) from the beach. Around 1 mile to Salen and shop.

1 cottage, 2 pub rms, 3 bedrms (grd flr avail), sleeps 8, from £150.00, Jan-Dec, bus nearby, ferry 8 mls

Mrs MacPhail
Callachally Farm, Glenforsa, Salen, Isle of Mull, Argyll, PA72 6JN
Tel: (Aros) 01680 300424 Fax: 01680 300424

★★★ SELF ATERING

Delightful single storey cottage, comfortably refurbished, with lovely private gardens running down to the burn.

1 cottage, 3 pub rms, 2 bedrms (grd flr avail), sleeps 4, £160.00-£260.00, Jan-Dec, bus nearby, ferry 11 mls

Mrs Moisey
7 Combe Park, Bath, Avon, BA1 3NP
Tel: (Bath) 01225 332996

Salen, Aros, Isle of Mull, Argyll

Map Ref: 1D1

SELF CATERING

19th century former Inn and Stables refurbished to provide studio or cottage accommodation. Restaurant serving food all day (limited service off season). Non smoking throughout. Open all year.

2 cottages, 2 studio apartments, 1-2 pub rms, 1-2 bedrms, sleeps 2-6, total sleeping capacity 12, £150.00-£315.00, Jan-Dec, bus nearby, ferry 10 mls

Steve and Alison Willis
Argyll House, Salen, Isle of Mull, Argyll, PA72 6JJ
Tel: (Aros) 01680 300555 Fax: 01680 300555
Web: www.zynet.co.uk/mull/members/argyll.html

Tobermory, Isle of Mull, Argyll

Map Ref: 1C1

SELF CATERING

Refurbished wings of 17th Century former shooting lodge set in 8 acres. 5 miles (8 km) from Tobermory and 2 miles (3 km) from Dervaig. Local base for fishing, walking and exploring Mull.

1 chalet, 1 house, 1-2 pub rms, 1-3 bedrms (grd flr avail), sleeps 2-6, total sleeping capacity 8, £200.00-£500.00, Feb-Nov, bus nearby, rail 30 mls, ferry 20 mls, airport 90 mls

Achnadrish House
Isle of Mull, PA75 6QF
Tel: 01688 400388
Email: 100243.56@compuserve.com

SELF CATERING

Self-contained, ground floor granny flat, of modern house with large south facing garden, and with fine views over the Sound of Mull and Morven Hills.

1 flat, 1 pub rm, 1 bedrm (grd flr avail), sleeps 2, £160.00-£190.00, Jan-Dec, bus 1/2 ml, ferry 1/2 ml, airport 12 mls

Mrs Gallagher
Raraig House, Tobermory, Isle of Mull, Argyll
Tel: (Tobermory) 01688 302390 Fax: 01688 302390
Email: paul@scotshop.demon.co.uk

SELF CATERING

Waterfront property right in the centre of the picturesque fishing village of Tobermory, which is also the capital of the Island of Mull. The property is a first floor flat overlooking the fisherman's pier. Ideal centre for those wanting the convenience of facilities on their doorstep, while being only a few minutes drive into the hills to explore all the beauty of scenery that Mull has to offer.

1 flat, 1 pub rm, 3 bedrms, sleeps 6, min let 2 nights, £250.00-£350.00, Jan-Dec, bus nearby, ferry 20 mls

Mr & Mrs J Matthew
Ardrioch, Dervaig, Isle of Mull, Argyll, PA75 6QR
Tel: (Dervaig) 01688 400264 Fax: 01688 400264

SELF CATERING

Castle c1860 and cottages on 5000 acre farming estate, 4 miles (6km) from Tobermory. Fishing, walking and wildlife in abundance. Garden produce and plants available for sale from June each year. Views to small outer isles.

3 flats, 6 cottages, 1-2 pub rms, 2-4 bedrms (grd flr avail), sleeps 4-8, total sleeping capacity 42, £115.00-£435.00, Mar-Nov, bus 4 mls, ferry 25 mls

Mrs Janet Nelson
Glengorm Castle, by Tobermory, Isle of Mull, Argyll, PA75 6QE
Tel: (Tobermory) 01688 302321

Important: Prices stated are estimates and may be subject to amendments

rth Connel, Argyll

Map Ref: 1E2

SELF ATERING

Delightful comfortable house with half acre secluded garden and glorious views over Loch Etive and surrounding hills. Non-Smoking.

1 house, 2 pub rms, 3 bedrms (grd flr avail), sleeps 6, £195.00-£480.00, Jan-Dec, rail 2 mls

Mrs Aileen Binner
Ailand, North Connel, Argyll, PA37 1QX
Tel: (Connel) 01631 710264

SELF ATERING

Modernised croft with superb views of Loch Etive and Ben Cruachan. Ideal base for touring Highlands and Islands. Oban 5 miles (8 km).

1 cottage, 1 bungalow, 1 pub rm, 3 bedrms, sleeps 6, total sleeping capacity 12, £110.00-£320.00, Jan-Dec, bus 2 mls, rail 3 mls

Mrs D Campbell
Achnacree Bay, North Connel, Argyll, PA37 1QZ
Tel: (Connel) 01631 710288 Fax: 01631 710799

SELF ATERING

Modern bungalows, beautifully situated overlooking Loch Etive. Ideal base for touring and visiting the islands.

2 bungalows, 1 pub rm, 3 bedrms, sleeps 6, total sleeping capacity 12, £110.00-£320.00, Jan-Dec, bus 1 ml, rail 2 mls, airport 1 ml

Mrs Isobel Campbell
Druimbhan, North Connel, Argyll, PA37 1RA
Tel: (Connel) 01631 710424

an, Argyll

Map Ref: 1E2

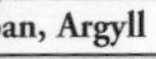

SELF ATERING

End terraced house in residential area within walking distance of swimming pool and tennis courts. 10 minutes walk from town centre shops.

1 house, 1 pub rm, 2 bedrms, sleeps 5, £180.00-£290.00, Apr-Oct

Mrs Adams
Westmount, Dalriach Road, Oban, Argyll
Tel: (Oban) 01631 562884

SELF ATERING

Modern 4th floor apartment within an attractive development adjacent to the seafront and close to the town centre and all amenities. Excellent views across Oban Bay and towards McCaigs Tower. Lift access, secure entry, private parking. Non-smoking.

1 flat, 1 pub rm, 1 bedrm, sleeps 2, £220.00-£260.00, Jan-Dec, rail nearby, ferry nearby, airport 90 mls

Mrs Dorothy Bingham
Glenara, Rockfield Road, Oban, Argyll, PA34 5DQ
Tel: (Oban) 01631 563172

Oban, Argyll **Map Ref: 1E2**

SELF CATERING

Timber lodges nestling in 7 acres of scenic wooded glen overlooking Loch Feochan only 3.5 miles (6 kms) from the picturesque harbour town of Oban "Gateway to the Isles."

17 lodges, 1 pub rm, 1-3 bedrms (grd flr avail), sleeps 2-6, total sleeping capacity 78, min let 2 nights, £135.00-£485.00, Jan-Dec, bus 1 1/2 mls, rail 3 1/2 mls, ferry 3 1/2 mls

Colin Mossman
Lagnakeil Highland Lodges, Lerags, Oban, Argyll, PA34 4SE
Tel: (Oban) 01631 562746 Fax: 01631 570225

SELF CATERING

Discover the secret world of Lerags Glen. Chalets, farmyard animals, country pub and restaurant, fishing, walking, peace and tranquility only minutes from Oban's bustling centre.

19 bungalows, 1-2 pub rms, 1-3 bedrms (grd flr avail), sleeps 2-6, total sleeping capacity 96, min let 1 day, £140.00-£425.00, chalets to sleep up to 6 people from £140 to £390 per week, Jan-Dec, bus 1 ml, rail 3 mls, ferry 3 mls, airport 90 mls

Cologin Farm Holiday Chalets
Lerags Glen, by Oban, Argyll, PA34 4SE
Tel: (Oban) 01631 564501 Fax: 01631 566925
Email: cologin@oban.org.uk

an, Argyll | Map Ref: 1E2

SELF CATERING

Purpose built self-catering unit in owners garden, quiet location on outskirts of Oban, with south facing sun terrace and private parking. Ideal location for visiting historic sights, with scenic walks and numerous castles and gardens within the Oban Lochaber area.

1 flat, 1 pub rm, 2 bedrms, sleeps 2-3, min let 3 days, £120.00-£250.00, Jan-Dec, bus 300 yds, rail 1 ml, ferry 1 ml

Mr & Mrs Eccleston
Braeside, Soroba Road, Oban, Argyll, PA34 4SA
Tel: (Oban) 01631 563303

SELF CATERING

Central, modern purpose built block with superb views of sea and islands. Elevator to all floors. Walking distance to all transport terminals. Private parking for all units. Ideal base for enjoying Oban and all surrounding areas.

28 flats, 1 pub rm, 1-3 bedrms, sleeps 1-4, total sleeping capacity 82, £220.00-£400.00, Apr-Nov, bus 1/4 ml, rail 1/4 ml, ferry 1/4 ml

Esplanade Court Apartments
The Esplanade, Oban, Argyll, PA34 5PW
Tel: (Oban) 01631 562067 Fax: 01631 562067

SELF CATERING

Ground floor flat with seaview, convenient for ferry, railway and town centre.

1 flat, 2 pub rms, 2 bedrms (grd flr avail), sleeps 4-6, £150.00-£300.00, Jan-Dec, bus nearby, rail nearby, ferry nearby

Mrs D McDougall
Harbour View, Shore Street, Oban, Argyll
Tel: (Oban) 01631 563462

★★

SELF CATERING

Each flat has direct views over harbour and the neighbouring Islands. In central shopping area close to ferry, bus and railway station. Lift access.

5 flats, 1 pub rm, 2-3 bedrms, sleeps 4, total sleeping capacity 20, £120.00-£350.00, Jan-Dec, bus nearby, rail 500 yds, ferry 500 yds, airport 96 mls

McDougalls of Oban Ltd
32 Combie Street, Oban, Argyll, PA34 4HT
Tel: (Oban) 01631 562304 Fax: 01631 564408

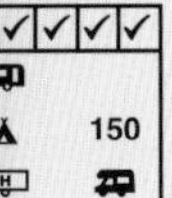

150

Oban Caravan & Camping Park

Gallanachmore Farm, Gallanach Road, Oban, Argyll, PA34 4QH Tel: (Oban) 01631 562425 Fax: 01631 566624

15 acres, grassy, hard-standing, level, Apr-mid Oct, latest time of arrival 2300, overnight holding area. Extra charge for electricity, awnings.

50 tourers £7.00-8.00 or 150 motors £7.00-8.00 or 150 tents £7.00-8.00. Total Touring Pitches 50.

10 Holiday Caravans to let, sleep 6-8 £160.00-350.00, total sleeping capacity 64, min let weekend (low season).

Leisure facilities:

2 mls S of Oban on coast road from town centre. Follow signs to Gallanach.

VAT is shown at 17.5%: changes in this rate may affect prices.

Key to symbols is on back flap.

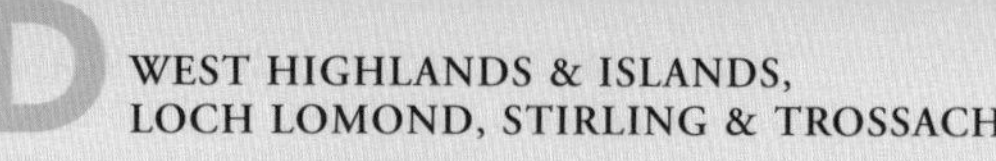

Oban, Argyll **Map Ref: 1E2**

SELF CATERING

Flat attached to owners house, located in an elevated position in a modern residential estate on the south side of Oban 1 mile from the town centre and all amenities. Hotel and limited local public transport nearby.

1 flat, sleeps 2, £190.00-£230.00, May-Oct, bus nearby

Mr & Mrs Leslie Reid
Eileraig, 17 Coe Gardens, Oban, PA34 4JT
Tel: 01631 562272

SELF CATERING

Two modern chalets, on shores of Loch Feochan, 5 miles (8kms) south of Oban. Ardoran Marine is also a farm, breeding pedigree Highland Cattle. Launch slipway and moorings adjacent to chalets, launch facilities free of charge to guests.

2 chalets, 1 pub rm, 2-3 bedrms (grd flr avail), sleeps 5-6, total sleeping capacity 11, min let weekend, £200.00-£350.00, Jan-Dec, bus 2 1/2 mls, rail 5 mls, ferry 5 mls, airport 8 mls

Mrs A Robertson
Ardoran, Lerags, Oban, PA34 4SE
Tel: (Oban) 01631 566123 Fax: 01631 566611

SELF CATERING

Self-contained apartment in an elevated position, close to Oban town centre (2 minutes walk). Fine views across Oban Bay to the islands of Mull and Kerrera. Private parking.

1 flat, 3 bedrms, sleeps 5, £200.00-£350.00, Jan-Dec, bus 1 ml, rail 1 ml, ferry 1 ml

Sgeir-Mhaol Guest House
Soroba Road, Oban, PA34 4JF
Tel: (Oban) 01631 562650 Fax: 01631 562650

SELF CATERING

Well appointed modern apartment close to all public transport links and within a short walk from Oban town centre. Restaurants, hotels and leisure facilities nearby.

1 flat, 1 pub rm, 1 bedrm, sleeps 2, £150.00-£350.00, Jan-Dec, bus 1/4 ml, rail 1/4 ml, ferry 1/4 ml

G Strachan
Glenburnie, Esplanade, Oban, PA34 5AQ
Tel: 01631 562089 Fax: 01631 562089

SELF CATERING

Modernised, traditional country cottage in a pleasant, secluded glen within 3 miles (5 kms) of Oban. Birdwatching, fishing, walking in the immediate vicinity. Popular country pub/restaurant close by. Come along and enjoy the peace and tranquility of this beautiful part of Argyll.

1 house, 1 pub rm, 2 bedrms, sleeps 8, £130.00-£280.00, Jan-Dec, bus 3 mls, rail 3 mls, ferry 3 mls

Mrs M R Whitton
Kilbride Farm, Lerags,by Oban, Argyll
Tel: (Oban) 01631 562878

Important: Prices stated are estimates and may be subject to amendments

ter Ferry, Argyll Map Ref: 1E4

Individually owned cedar chalets and a traditional farmhouse anexe forming part of a family run estate on the east shore of Loch Fyne. South west facing with superb views and sunsets. Slipway and moorings available. Ideal base for sea and loch fishing, scuba diving, hill walking, cycling and water sports. Boat hire and fishing trips available on site. Shop on site, pub and restaurant nearby. Tighnabruaich 25 mins and Dunoon 45 mins by car.

7 chalets, 1 farmhouse annexe, 1 pub rm, 2-3 bedrms (grd flr avail), sleeps 4-6, total sleeping capacity 34, min let 3 nights, £165.00-£330.00, Jan-Dec, bus 18 mls, rail 26 mls, ferry 20 mls, airport 90 mls

Largiemore Holiday Estate
Otter Ferry, Loch Fyne, by Tighnabruaich, Argyll, PA21 2DH
Tel: (Kilfinnan) 01700 821235 Fax: 01700 821235

rtavadie, Argyll Map Ref: 1E5

Idyllic setting overlooking Loch Fyne. Spectacular sea views minutes from the beach. Good local walking, birdwatching, fishing, golf and watersports. Ideal base.

1 chalet, 2 pub rms, 2 bedrms (grd flr avail), sleeps 4-6, £100.00-£250.00, Mar-Oct, bus nearby, ferry 1/2 ml

Pat Currie
Ashcliffe, Tighnabruaich, Argyll, PA21 2EJ
Tel: 01700 811234

rt of Menteith, Perthshire Map Ref: 1H3

Renovated cottages with magnificent views over the Lake of Menteith. Peaceful yet convenient for many local attractions, including fishing on Lake of Menteith.

2 cottages, 1 pub rm, 1-2 bedrms (grd flr avail), sleeps 4-7, total sleeping capacity 11, £150.00-£275.00, Apr-Oct, bus 1/2 ml, rail 15 mls, airport 25 mls

Mrs E Forbes
Glenny, Port of Menteith, Perthshire, FK8 3RD
Tel: (Port of Menteith) 01877 385229

Farmhouse apartment with superb views over Lake of Menteith, on working sheep farm.

1 farmhouse extension, 1 pub rm, 1 bedrm (grd flr avail), sleeps 2, £190.00-£240.00, Jan-Dec, bus 1/2 ml, rail 15 mls, airport 30 mls

Mrs K MacPhail
Mondhui Farm, Port of Menteith, by Stirling, Perthshire, FK8 3RD
Tel: (Port of Menteith) 01877 385273

wardennan, Stirlingshire Map Ref: 1G3

Quality pine lodges on the shores of Loch Lomond.

2 chalets, 1 pub rm, 2-3 bedrms (grd flr avail), sleeps 4-6, total sleeping capacity 10, £500.00-£800.00, Jan-Dec, ferry on site

Rowardennan Hotel
Rowardennan by Drymen, Loch Lomond, G63 0AR
Tel: (Balmaha) 01360 870273 Fax: 01360 870251

VAT is shown at 17.5%: changes in this rate may affect prices.

Key to symbols is on back flap.

Rowardennan, Stirlingshire **Map Ref: 1G3**

ROWARDENNAN LODGE RENTALS

2 THE CROSS COURT, BISHOPBRIGGS, GLASGOW G64 2RD
Telephone: 0141 762 4828 Fax: 0141 762 1625

Situated at Rowardennan on the Bonnie Banks of Loch Lomond with Ben Lomond and the breathtaking Queen Elizabeth Forest Park as a backdrop. The development is only a short drive away from the spectacular scenery of the Scottish Highlands.

★★★★ SELF CATERING

SELF CATERING

Lodges on 10 acre site on the shore of Loch Lomond. Free mooring and landing facilities for the boaters.

6 pine lodges, 1 pub rm, 2-3 bedrms (grd flr avail), sleeps 4-6, total sleeping capacity 32, £250.00-£575.00, Jan-Dec, bus 6 mls, rail 15 mls, airport 30 mls

Rowardennan Lodge Rentals
2 The Cross Court, Bishopbriggs, Glasgow, G64 2RD
Tel: 0141 762 4828 Fax: 0141 762 1625

St Catherines, Argyll **Map Ref: 1F3**

Halftown Cottages, St Catherines

Two semi-detached historical cottages near Loch Fyne, Argyll opposite Inveraray and 54 miles from Glasgow. Each cottage is completely refurbished, sleeps four, TV, washing machine and is set in secluded woodland, on site of ancient township. Many interesting activities available in the surrounding area including golf, walking, fishing.

CONTACT: CROITACHONIE, CAIRNDOW, ARGYLL PA26 8BH
Tel/Fax: 01499 600239

SELF CATERING

Two semi detached cottages by Loch Fyne. Set in natural woodland on site of ancient township as described by author Neil Munro.

2 cottages, 1 pub rm, 2 bedrms (grd flr avail), sleeps 4, total sleeping capacity 8, £180.00-£400.00, Jan-Dec, bus 1/2 ml, rail 12 mls, ferry 20 mls, airport 45 mls

P J Dawson
Croitachonie, Cairndow, Argyll, PA26 8BH
Tel: 01499 600239 Fax: 01499 600239

SELF CATERING

Tastefully refurbished, traditional two-bedroomed cottage, in quiet position on old Shore Road with uninterrupted views of Loch Fyne. Secure parking.

1 cottage, 2 pub rms, 2 bedrms, sleeps 4, £210.00-£300.00, Jan-Dec, bus 1 ml, rail 16 mls, ferry 16 mls, airport 50 mls

Mrs C E Mactavish
Strathalmond, Clenches Farm Lane, Sevenoaks, Kent, TN13 2LX
Tel: (Sevenoaks) 01732 461318

Important: Prices stated are estimates and may be subject to amendments

kipness, Argyll — Map Ref: 1E6

★

SELF CATERING

Individual cottages in quiet seaside village with views over Kilbrannan Sound to Arran beyond. Open fires. Ideal for quiet relaxing holidays, dogs and children welcome.

1 house, 4 cottages, 1-3 pub rms, 2-4 bedrms, sleeps 4-10, total sleeping capacity 40, £100.00-£450.00, Jan-Dec, bus 1/2 ml, rail 60 mls, ferry 2 mls, airport 30 mls

Sophie James
Skipness Castle, nr Tarbert, Argyll, PA29 6XU
Tel: (Skipness) 01880 760207 Fax: 01880 760208

tirling — Map Ref: 2A4

✓✓✓

60

Auchenbowie Caravan Site

Auchenbowie, by Stirling, Stirlingshire, FK7 8HE Tel: (Denny) 01324 823999 Fax: 01324 822950
Booking Enquiries: Forsyth of Denny Ltd Easterton, Denny, Stirlingshire, FK6 6RF
Tel: (Denny) 01324 823999 Fax: 01324 822950

3 1/2 acres, mixed, Apr-Oct. Extra charge for electricity, awnings, showers.

60 tourers £8.00-9.00 or 60 motors £8.00-9.00 or 60 tents £8.00-9.00. Total Touring Pitches 60.

10 Holiday Caravans to let, sleep 6-8 £155.00-205.00, total sleeping capacity 62, min let 2 nights.

From junction 9 off M80 and M9 take A872 S towards Denny for 1/2 ml and turn right.

★★

SELF CATERING

Scandinavian type timber chalets in quiet location on University Campus. Access to sports and leisure facilities.

32 chalets, 80 flats, 71 apartments, 1 pub rm, 2-7 bedrms, sleeps 2-7, total sleeping capacity 1250, £140.00-£400.00, Jun-Sep, bus nearby, rail 1 1/2 mls, airport 33 mls

Conference and Vacation Campus
University of Stirling, Stirling, FK9 4LA
Tel: (Stirling) 01786 467141/467142 Fax: 01786 467143
Email: holidays@stir.ac.uk Web: www.stir.ac.uk/theuni/vacation

★★★★

SELF CATERING

Edwardian family villa with secluded garden on western outskirts of this historic town.

1 house, 3 pub rms, 4 bedrms, sleeps 6, min let weekend, £350.00-£550.00, Jan-Dec, bus nearby, rail 1 ml, airport 30 mls

Dr Andrew Jennings
Viewvale, 9 New Road, Bannockburn, Stirling, FK7 8LP
Tel: (Bannockburn) 01786 818456/813460 Fax: 01786 818456
Email: RagnarBlood-axe@MSN.com

VAT is shown at 17.5%: changes in this rate may affect prices.

Key to symbols is on back flap.

Strathyre, Perthshire

Map Ref: 1H3

SELF CATERING

Newly-renovated, traditional stone house in centre of village. Conveniently situated for walking and touring.

1 cottage, 1 pub rm, 3 bedrms (grd flr avail), sleeps 6-8, min let weekend, £150.00-£295.00, Jan-Dec, bus 100 yds

Mrs Beale
Newlands, 23 The Sands, Long Clawson, Melton Mowbray, Leicestershire, LE14 4PA
Tel: (Melton Mowbray) 01664 822247

SELF CATERING

Stonebuilt, traditional family house standing in own grounds within 5 minutes walk of harbour and shops. Views over Loch Fyne.

1 cottage, 3 pub rms, 3 bedrms, sleeps 7, £200.00-£500.00, Jan-Dec, bus nearby, rail 50 mls, ferry 1 ml, airport 33 mls

Mr Arnold
Holmes Farm, Long Bennington, Newark, Nottinghamshire, NG23 5EB
Tel: (Loveden) 01400 281282 Fax: 01400 281282

Tarbert, Loch Fyne, Argyll

Map Ref: 1E5

SELF CATERING

Victorian gate lodge and former Shepherd's cottage 6 miles (11kms) from Tarbert with fine panoramic views over the West Loch. Situated in quiet rural estate of 60 acres including natural oak woodland and extensive private shoreline, fishing and boat available.

2 cottages, 1 pub rm, 2 bedrms, sleeps 3-4, total sleeping capacity 7, min let weekend, £170.00-£320.00, Jan-Dec, bus nearby, rail 50 mls, ferry 8 mls, airport 40 mls

Shereen Gay
The Stables, Achaglachgach, by Tarbert, Argyll, PA29 6XX
Tel: (Tarbert) 01880 820892

SELF CATERING

First floor flat in conversion of Scottish baronial house in elevated position overlooking Loch Fyne. A central base for exploring the unspoilt landscape of Mid-Argyll.

1 flat, 1 pub rm, 3 bedrms, sleeps 5, £200.00-£350.00, Jan-Dec, bus nearby, rail 35 mls, airport 75 mls

Mrs Elizabeth Jessiman
75A Craigcrook Road, Edinburgh, EH4 3PH
Tel: (Blackhall) 0131 332 6678

SELF CATERING

Architect designed courtyard conversion of former steading. Secluded modern family villa on edge of loch with unrestricted views. Both properties on estate of over 1000 acres including large areas of natural oak woodland. Use of private harbour area suitable for day boats. Boats also available to hire.

1 house, 4 cottages, 2-3 pub rms, 2-5 bedrms (grd flr avail), sleeps 5-10, total sleeping capacity 43, £165.00-£750.00, Jan-Dec, bus 7 mls

Mrs Meg MacKinnon
Dunmore Home Farm, Dunmore, nr Tarbert, Argyll, PA29 6XZ
Tel: (Tarbert) 01880 820654

Important: Prices stated are estimates and may be subject to amendments

Tarbert, Loch Fyne, Argyll

Map Ref: 1E5

★★★ SELF CATERING

Recently renovated Listed farm steadings grouped around landscaped central courtyard. 1.5 miles (3kms) from Tarbert. Childrens play area. Horse-riding, mountain bike hire, boat trips and clay pigeon shooting all available by arrangement.

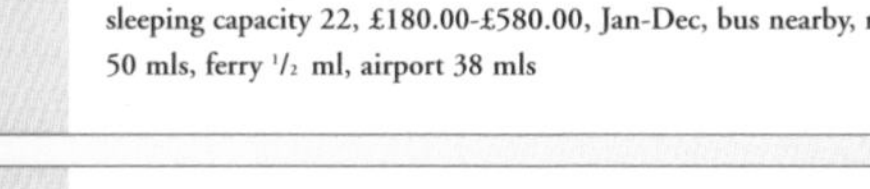

2 flats, 4 cottages, 1-2 pub rms, 1-2 bedrms, sleeps 4-6, total sleeping capacity 22, £180.00-£580.00, Jan-Dec, bus nearby, rail 50 mls, ferry 1/2 ml, airport 38 mls

Mr Scott
Barmore Farm, Tarbert, Argyll
Tel: (Tarbert) 01880 820222

★★★★ SELF CATERING

Two newly built pine lodges located within West Loch Holiday Caravan Park, situated 1.5 miles south from Tarbert village overlooking West Loch Tarbert. The Park is an excellent home for exploring Argyll and the Kintyre Peninsula. Good access to all ferries.

2 log cabins, 1 pub rm, 2 bedrms (grd flr avail), sleeps 4-6, total sleeping capacity 12, £90.00-£420.00, Apr-Oct, bus 1 1/2 mls, rail 45 mls, ferry 3 mls

West Loch Tarbert Holiday Park
West Loch, Tarbert, Argyll, PA29 6YF
Tel: 01880 820873

Tarbet, by Arrochar, Dunbartonshire

Map Ref: 1G3

★★★ SELF CATERING

Conversion of former blacksmith's cottage in its own enclosed garden with stream. 450 yards from Loch Lomond shore.

1 cottage, 1 pub rm, 2 bedrms, sleeps 6, £290.00-£360.00, Apr-Oct, bus nearby, rail 1 ml, airport 30 mls

Elizabeth McMillan
5a Bellevue Road, Kirkintilloch, Glasgow, G66 1AL
Tel: 0141 775 1432/578 1039

★★ UP TO ★★★★ SELF CATERING

Pine lodges and pair of semi-detached cottages in peaceful wooded area. Elevated site overlooking Loch Lomond with private jetty and slipway.

3 log cabins, 2 cottages, 1 pub rm, 2 bedrms, sleeps 6, total sleeping capacity 30, £300.00-£400.00, Jan-Dec, bus 1 ml, rail 2 mls, airport 25 mls

Mr & Mrs Tonks
Blairannaich, Tarbet, by Arrochar, Dunbartonshire, G83 7DN
Tel: (Arrochar) 01301 702257

Tayinloan, by Tarbert, Argyll

Map Ref: 1D6

★★ UP TO ★★★ SELF CATERING

Romantic period cottages and larger house beside 12c church and Pictish Fort with beach facing Donegal and Southern Hebrides. Wonderful exploring holidays.

1 house, 5 flats, 4 cottages, 1-3 pub rms, 1-5 bedrms (grd flr avail), sleeps 2-10, total sleeping capacity 46, from £200.00, Apr-Dec, bus 1 ml, rail 65 mls, ferry 1 ml, airport 17 mls

Mrs Jillian Miller
Killean Estate, Tayinloan, by Tarbert, Loch Fyne, PA29 6XF
Tel: (Tayinloan) 01583 441238 Fax: 01583 441307
Email: KilleanEst@aol.com

VAT is shown at 17.5%: changes in this rate may affect prices.

Key to symbols is on back flap.

Taynuilt, Argyll **Map Ref: 1F2**

SELF CATERING

Newly-built timber chalet and brick cottage in peaceful rural environment. Spectacular mountain scenery.

1 chalet, 1 cottage, 1 pub rm, 1-2 bedrms (grd flr avail), sleeps 2-4, total sleeping capacity 6, £130.00-£310.00, Jan-Dec, bus 1/4 ml, rail 1/2 ml

Mr & Mrs F Beaton
Dalry, Kirkton, Taynuilt, Argyll, PA35 1HW
Tel: (Taynuilt) 01866 822657

SELF CATERING

Flats in converted 18th century country house set amidst parkland about 1 mile (2kms) from Taynuilt village and shops. Bonawe Iron Furnace under the care of Historic Scotland is close by.

1 house, 3 flats, 6 cottages, 1 pub rm, 1-3 bedrms (grd flr avail), sleeps 2-6, total sleeping capacity 37, min let 2 nights (low season), £110.00-£320.00, Jan-Dec, bus 3/4 ml, rail 1/2 ml

Bonawe House
1 Springkerse Road, Stirling, FK7 7SN
Tel: (Stirling) 01786 462519 Fax: 01786 471872

SELF CATERING

Detached cottage and attached cottages in country house. Convenient for touring the west coast. 12 miles (19 kms) from Oban.

2 flats, 1 cottage, 2 pub rms, 2-3 bedrms (grd flr avail), sleeps 2-7, total sleeping capacity 16, £150.00-£325.00, Jan-Dec, bus 2 mls, rail 2 mls, airport 80 mls

Mrs R Campbell-Preston
Inverawe House, Taynuilt, Argyll, PA35 1HU
Tel: (Taynuilt) 01866 822446 Fax: 01866 822274

SELF CATERING

Semi-detached bungalow with enclosed back garden in small hamlet, 14 miles (22kms) from Oban. Ideal centre for touring, walking and fishing.

1 cottage, 1 pub rm, 2 bedrms (grd flr avail), sleeps 4-6, min let 3 nights not Fri/Sat incl, £130.00-£290.00, Apr-Oct, bus nearby, rail 2 mls, ferry 12 mls, airport 100 mls

John Garvie
Sliabh, Bridge of Awe, Taynuilt, Argyll, PA35 1HU
Tel: (Taynuilt) 01866 822637
Email: jgarvie@aol.com

Important: Prices stated are estimates and may be subject to amendments

aynuilt, Argyll

Map Ref: 1F2

★★★ SELF CATERING

Spacious first floor flat in a rural position 1 mile (2kms) from Taynuilt with panoramic views towards Ben Cruachan, Loch Etive and Glen Lonan.

1 flat, 1 pub rm, 2 bedrms, sleeps 5, £125.00-£275.00, Jan-Dec, rail 1 ml

Mrs McGougan
Brackendale, Taynuilt, Argyll, PA35 1JQ
Tel: (Taynuilt) 01866 822365 Fax: 01866 822548

★★★ SELF CATERING

Wooden chalets in peaceful rural setting. Fine views to mountains and close to village shops and Oban.

4 chalets, 1 pub rm, 2 bedrms, sleeps 4, total sleeping capacity 16, £165.00-£320.00, Mar-Nov, bus 1 ml, rail 1 ml

Mrs Olsen
Airdeny Chalets, Airdeny, Taynuilt, Argyll, PA35 1HY
Tel: (Taynuilt) 01866 822648 Fax: 01866 822665

yvallich, Argyll

Map Ref: 1E4

★★ SELF CATERING

Modernised cottage in superb setting overlooking the bay towards the hills beyond. Rear garden.

1 cottage, 2 pub rms, 4 bedrms (grd flr avail), sleeps 8, £250.00-£450.00, Jan-Dec, bus 10 mls

Mrs E Hume
Auchendoon House, Hollybush, by Ayr, KA6 7EB
Tel: (Dalrymple) 01292 560222

ott Bay, Isle of Tiree, Argyll

Map Ref: 1A1

★ SELF CATERING

Flat adjoining the hotel. Beach for wind surfing and other water sports facilities available nearby.

1 flat, 2 pub rms, 2 bedrms (grd flr avail), sleeps 7, £125.00-£300.00, Jan-Dec, ferry 2 mls, airport 7 mls

Tiree Lodge Hotel
Gott Bay, Isle of Tiree, PA77 1TN
Tel: 01879 220368 Fax: 01879 220884

e of Tiree, Isle of Tiree, Argyll

Map Ref: 1A2

★★★ SELF CATERING

Recently converted croft house with large kitchen/dining extension and garden area. Centrally situated 1 mile from shop and many beaches.

1 house, 2 pub rms, 4 bedrms (grd flr avail), sleeps 8, min let weekend, £200.00-£350.00, Jan-Dec, ferry 4 mls, airport 1 ml

Mrs Rosemary M Omand
Scarinish Villa, Scarinish, Isle of Tiree, Argyll, PA77 6UH
Tel: (Scarinish) 01879 220307 Fax: 01879 220607

Scarinish, Isle of Tiree, Argyll — **Map Ref: 1A1**

Traditional croft house with kitchen extension in centre of island, 4 miles (7 km) to ferry. Ideal base for families. Short stroll to sandy beach.

1 house, 1 pub rm, 4 bedrms (grd flr avail), sleeps 7, £140.00-£170.00, Jan-Dec, ferry 3 1/2 mls, airport 1 3/4 mls

Mrs Janet Paterson
6 Crossapol, Isle of Tiree, Argyll, PA77 6UP
Tel: 01879 220429

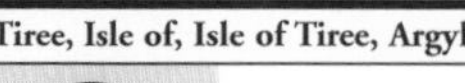

Tiree, Isle of, Isle of Tiree, Argyll — **Map Ref: 1A1**

★★
SELF CATERING

Traditional Hebridean thatched cottage within walking distance of beach at Sandaig and the magnificent Kenavara.

1 cottage, 1 pub rm, 1 bedrm (grd flr avail), sleeps 2, £115.00-£160.00, Jan-Dec, ferry 8 mls, airport 6 mls

Mrs Susan Atkins
Bloxham House, Highbridge Road, Wappenham, Towcester, Northants, NN12 8SL
Tel: (Blakesly) 01327 860102 Fax: 01327 860102

South facing property with all rooms on ground floor. Open views to neighbouring islands. 2 miles from ferry and airport.

1 cottage, 1 pub rm, 1 bedrm, sleeps 2, £160.00-£180.00, Apr-Oct, bus nearby, ferry 2 mls, airport 2 mls

Mrs G Latham
Baugh, Isle of Tiree, Argyll, PA77 6UN
Tel: (Scarnish) 01879 220538

Tyndrum, by Crianlarich, Perthshire — **Map Ref: 1G2**

The West Highland Way passes close to this chalet which has magnificent views, being set above the A82. Evening meals provided by prior arrangement.

1 chalet, 1 pub rm, 2 bedrms, sleeps 4, £200.00-£220.00, Jan-Oct, bus 1/4 ml, rail 1/4 ml, ferry 38 mls, airport 45 mls

Mrs E Cunningham
Glengarry House, by Tyndrum, Perthshire, FK20 8RY
Tel: (Tyndrum) 01838 400224

Cosy traditional stone built cottage in a small terrace. On West Highland Way. Near junction for Oban and Fort William roads.

1 cottage, 2 pub rms, 4 bedrms (grd flr avail), sleeps 6, £160.00-£295.00, Jan-Dec, bus nearby, rail 1/2 ml

Christina Honeybone
11 Park Lane, Roundhay, Leeds, LS8 2EX
Tel: (Leeds) 0113 2668456

Important: Prices stated are estimates and may be subject to amendments

Perthshire, Angus & Dundee and the Kingdom of Fife

This is an area offering plenty of contrasts: from the white-walled harbourfront houses of the East Neuk of Fife fishing villages to the windy silences of the edge of Rannoch Moor; from the pubs and upbeat nightlife of the city of Dundee to the upland tranquillity of the Angus glens. It makes a good choice if your Scottish break should have a little of everything.

That is something you will find in Perthshire itself, straddling the Highland-Lowland edge, with Perth as an important historic and commercial centre for an attractive hinterland. Here you will find excellent shopping and plenty of places nearby. Another Perthshire speciality are the little resort towns like Pitlochry or Aberfeldy, attractive places with a long tradition of catering for visitors in a Highland setting. These locations and others such as Dunkeld or Blairgowrie, make good touring centres. All of these places are especially good in autumn when the woodland colours at their best.

The old Kingdom of Fife has plenty of character. St Andrews' unique story includes its life as an academic centre (Scotland's oldest university is here), and as an important religious centre, though its cathedral is now only a ruin. To St Andrews' layers of history must be added its claim as the home of golf. Fife's story is certainly bound up with the sea, which is why the East Neuk villages, facing the Forth estuary are popular: Crail, Anstruther and their neighbours rate as some of Scotland's most attractive 'townscapes', while Anstruther's Scottish Fisheries Museum is well worth discovering.

Road and rail bridges across the Tay lead from Fife into Dundee, the 'City of Discovery'. This refers both to the many attractions here and, literally, the home of the RRS Discovery, the ship used by Captain Scott on his Antarctic expeditions.

Road and rail bridges across the Tay lead from Fife into Dundee, the 'City of Discovery'. This refers both to the many attractions here and, literally, the home of the RRS Discovery, the ship used by Captain Scott on his Antarctic expeditions. Discovery Point is one of the top attractions in Scotland and should not be missed. The city has plenty of other places of interest, including the McManus Galleries. As well as fine paintings, the history collection here tells the full story of the city's heritage of textiles, whaling and shipbuilding, journalism and jam making.

Glens such as Isla, Prosen, Clova or Esk run far into the mountains, with motorable roads to take you truly away from it all – great places to recharge the batteries. Visit in spring when the high tops are still snow covered. Meanwhile, across the other side of the wide valley called Strathmore with its woods and farms, the sea coast has its own charms. Discover red sandstone cliffs and fine beaches, as well as fishing ports such as Arbroath, home of the local delicacy, the Arbroath smokie. (Try this fishy delight when you get here!)

Angus looks both to the hills and the sea. The Angus Glens are one of Scotland's best-kept secrets.

Between the mountains and the sea are attractions such as Glamis Castle, associated with HM Queen Elizabeth the Queen Mother, or Edzell Castle with its unique garden. These, in turn, are reminders of more of the attractions scattered throughout the area: Blair Castle or Castle Menzies, the superb Deep Sea World at North Queensferry or the, perhaps unexpected, attraction of Scotland's Secret Bunker, a Cold War relic, tucked innocently into the rural surroundings of Fife. Many attractions open throughout the year. Surprises are guaranteed anywhere in this area.

Events

Perthshire, Angus & Dundee and The Kingdom of Fife

May 10 – 15

Dundee Jazz Festival

Week-long festival with emphasis on contemporary and modern jazz with local and international artists.
Dundee Rep Theatre, Dundee.
Tel: 0131 467 5200.

May 20 – 30

Perth Festival of the Arts

Various venues in Perth. Classical concerts, theatre, jazz, blues, comedy.
Tel: 01738 475295.

July 3 – 4

The Game Conservancy Fair

A full programme of falconry, fishing, working dog trials and pipe bands. Perth.
Tel: 01620 850577 Fax: 01856 871170.

Aug 22

Crieff Highland Games

Traditional Highland Games.
Tel: 01764 652578.

Sep 11

Battle of Britain International Air Show – Leuchars

International air show with over 100 aircraft on display plus simulators, exhibitions and fair.
Tel: 01334 839000.

Nov 24 – 30

Saint Andrews Week

Various events in different venues, St Andrews. A week of festivities celebrating St Andrews day.
Tel: 01334 477872.

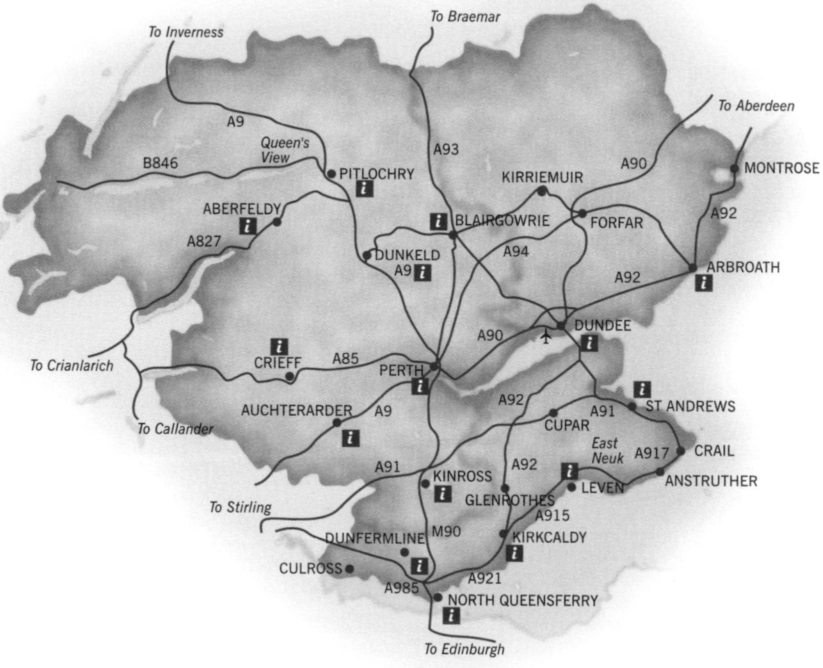

Area Tourist Board Addresses

1 **Angus and City of Dundee Tourist Board**
7-12 Castle Street
DUNDEE
DD1 3AA
Tel: 01382 527527
Fax: 01382 527500
e.mail:
arbroath@sol.uk
website:
www.angusanddundee.co.uk

2 **Kingdom of Fife Tourist Board**
St Andrews Tourist Information Centre
70 Market Street
ST ANDREWS
KY16 9NU
Tel: 01334 472021
Fax: 01334 478422

3 **Perthshire Tourist Board**
Administrative Headquarters
Lower City Mills
West Mill Street
PERTH PH1 5QP
Tel: 01738 627958
01738 861186 (Activity Line)
01738 449292 (Convention Bureau)
Fax: 01738 630416
e.mail:
perthtouristb@perthshire.co.uk

Perthshire, Angus & Dundee and the Kingdom of Fife

Tourist Information Centres in Scotland

ANGUS & CITY OF DUNDEE TOURIST BOARD

ARBROATH
Market Place
DD11 1HR
Tel: (01241) 872609
Jan-Dec

BRECHIN
St Ninians Place
Tel: (01356) 623050
April-Sept

CARNOUSTIE
1B High Street
Tel: (01241) 852258
April-Sept

DUNDEE
4 City Square
DD1 3BA
Tel: (01382) 434664

FORFAR
40 East High Street
Tel: (01307) 467876
April-Sept

KIRRIEMUIR
Cumberland Close
Tel: (01575) 574097
April-Sept

MONTROSE
Bridge Street
Tel: (01674) 672000
April-Sept

KINGDOM OF FIFE TOURIST BOARD

ANSTRUTHER
Scottish Fisheries Museum
Tel: (01333) 311073
April-Sept

CRAIL
Museum & Heritage Centre
Marketgate
Tel: (01333) 450869
Easter-Sept

DUNFERMLINE
13/15 Maygate
Tel: (01383) 720999
Jan-Dec

FORTH ROAD BRIDGE
by North Queensferry
Tel: (01383) 417759
Easter-Oct
Nov-Mar unmanned

KIRKCALDY
19 Whytescauseway
Tel: (01592) 267775
Jan-Dec

ST ANDREWS
70 Market Street,
KY16 9NU
Tel: (01334) 472021
Jan-Dec

PERTHSHIRE TOURIST BOARD

ABERFELDY
The Square
Tel: (01887) 820276
Jan-Dec

AUCHTERARDER
90 High Street
Tel: (01764) 663450
Jan-Dec

BLAIRGOWRIE
26 Wellmeadow
Tel: (01250) 872960
Jan-Dec

CRIEFF
Town Hall, High Street
Tel: (01764) 652578
Jan-Dec

DUNKELD
The Cross
Tel: (01350) 727688
Mar-Dec

KINROSS
Kinross Service Area
off Junction 6, M90
Tel: (01577) 863680
Jan-Dec

PERTH
45 High Street, PH1 5TJ
Tel: (01738) 638353
Jan-Dec

PERTH, INVERALMOND
(A9 Western City Bypass)
Tel: (01738) 638481
Jan-Dec

PITLOCHRY
22 Atholl Road
Tel; (01796) 472215/472751
Jan-Dec

 Accept written enquiries
Disabled access

erdour, Fife

Map Ref: 2C4

★★★★
SELF
ATERING

This unique seaside studio cottage has been built and equipped to exceptionally high standard. Located within a conservation village, overlooking the harbour and Inchcolm Abbey. Within easy reach of Edinburgh and St Andrews.

1 studio cottage, 1 pub rm, 1 bedrm, sleeps 2, £280.00-£330.00, Jan-Dec, bus 3/4 ml, rail 3/4 ml, airport 14 mls

Mrs W Henderson
6 Campbell Avenue, Edinburgh, EH12 6DS
Tel: 0131 337 5844 Fax: 0131 313 1464

★★★★
SELF
ATERING

Peacefully located on working dairy farm with panoramic views to Firth of Forth. The centre of Edinburgh is only 25 minutes by car or train.

1 cottage, 2 pub rms, 3 bedrms (grd flr avail), sleeps 6, min let 3 nights, £225.00-£375.00, Jan-Dec, bus 2 mls, rail 2 mls, airport 14 mls

Mrs June Weatherup
Parkend Farm, Crossgates, Cowdenbeath, KY4 8EX
Tel: (Aberdour) 01383 860277 Fax: 01383 860277

erfeldy, Perthshire

Map Ref: 2A1

★★★
SELF
ATERING

Aberfeldy is the geographical centre of Scotland and is surrounded by spectacular scenery. Hillview is a restored 18th Century cottage in a quiet location opposite the local park but within easy walking distance of the town's amenities. Several golf courses within 15 minutes drive.

1 house, 2 pub rms, 3 bedrms (grd flr avail), sleeps 6, £220.00-£520.00, Jan-Dec, bus 1/4 ml, rail 12 mls

Mrs M Clark
74 Forest Lane, Kirklevington, Yarm, TS15 9ND
Tel: 01642 782111/0410 280652 Fax: 01642 782111

★★★★
SELF
ATERING

Picturesque victorian cottage refurbished to a high standard. Large traditional country kitchen with a wood burning pot-belly stove and open fire in sitting room. Woodland garden with patio and garden furniture.

1 cottage, 3 bedrms (grd flr avail), sleeps 6, £245.00-£430.00, Jan-Dec

Angela Delph
Distillery Cottage, The Lagg, Aberfeldy, Perthshire, PH15 2ED
Tel: 01887 820754 Fax: 01887 829116

★★★★
SELF
ATERING

Cottage, tastefully renovated, conveniently situated near the town centre and adjacent to the Birks of Aberfeldy.

1 cottage, 2 pub rms, 1 bedrm, sleeps 2-4, min let 3 nights, £160.00-£275.00, Jan-Dec, bus nearby, rail 15 mls, airport 75 mls

Mrs Isobel S Kerr
17 Buchanan Drive, Cambuslang, Glasgow, G72 8BD
Tel: 0141 641 2856

Aberfeldy, Perthshire Map Ref: 2A1

DUNOLLY HOUSE

Taybridge Drive, Aberfeldy, Perthshire PH15 2BL
Telephone: 01887 820298

A superb group accommodation venue at the edge of Aberfeldy, next to the River Tay. This facility will suit family, youth and adult parties from eight to 60 persons. Take it catered or self-catered with or without activities provided. Two day minimum booking. Come and enjoy.

Large house with cottage annexe in grounds on outskirts of town, beside the Tay. Variety of activities arranged.

1 house, 1 cottage, 3 pub rms, 3-16 bedrms (grd flr avail), sleeps 8-60, total sleeping capacity 60, £6.00-£7.50, Jan-Dec, bus 400 yds, rail 15 mls, airport 80 mls

Dunolly House
Taybridge Drive, Aberfeldy, Perthshire, PH15 2BL
Tel: (Aberfeldy) 01887 820298

The ten minute drive up 1.5 miles of rough access road is well worth it for the spectacular view that greets you at Shenavail, a converted hill farmhouse situated high above Strath Tay. The house is set in 7 acres of farm land with a small fenced garden and south facing terrace.

1 house, 1 pub rm, 6 bedrms (grd flr avail), sleeps 9-10, £300.00-£575.00, Jan-Nov, bus 2 mls

Mrs I Macdonald
Ashmount, 8 Milligs Street, Helensburgh, G84 9LB
Tel: 01436 679204

On working farm, 2 miles (3kms) from the town centre in quiet and peaceful situation, two cottages adjacent to farm steading.

2 cottages, 1 pub rm, 2 bedrms (grd flr avail), sleeps 3-6, total sleeping capacity 10, £160.00-£300.00, Jan-Dec, bus 1 ml, rail 14 mls

Mrs J McDiarmid
Mains of Murthly, Aberfeldy, Perthshire, PH15 2EA
Tel: (Aberfeldy) 01887 820427 Fax: 01887 820427

Two stone built, well equipped cottages. All located separately on farm. 2 miles (3 kms) west of Aberfeldy.

2 houses, 1-2 pub rms, 2-3 bedrms (grd flr avail), sleeps 4-6, total sleeping capacity 10, min let weekend (low season), £150.00-£550.00, Jan-Dec, bus 2 mls, rail 15 mls

Mrs D D McDiarmid
Castle Menzies Home Farm, Aberfeldy, Perthshire, PH15 2LY
Tel: (Aberfeldy) 01887 820260 Fax: 01887 829666

Important: Prices stated are estimates and may be subject to amendments

erfeldy, Perthshire

Map Ref: 2A1

★★

SELF ATERING

Self-contained apartments on upper floors of 17th century inn situated in the delightful Tay Valley in a peaceful tranquil setting.

1 flat, 1 pub rm, 2 bedrms, sleeps 5, £203.00-£525.00, Jan-Dec, bus 3/4 ml, rail 13 mls, airport 60 mls

T G Wise & J M Hardaker
"The Weem", Weem, by Aberfeldy, Perthshire, PH15 2LD
Tel: (Aberfeldy) 01887 820381 Fax: 01887 820187

arn, by Kenmore, Perthshire

Map Ref: 2A1

★★★★

SELF ATERING

Converted Listed stone buildings in quiet picturesque Highland village. Sailing, fishing, bird watching and many lovely country walks.

4 houses, 2 flats, 1 pub rm, 2-3 bedrms (grd flr avail), sleeps 2-8, total sleeping capacity 32, min let weekend, £175.00-£460.00, Jan-Dec, bus 7 1/2 mls, rail 21 mls, airport 80 mls

A & J Duncan Millar
Loch Tay Lodges, Remony, Aberfeldy, Perthshire, PH15 2HR
Tel: (Kenmore) 01887 830209 Fax: 01887 830802
Email: remony@btinternet.com
Web: www.sunsys.com/lochtay-lodges/index.html

th, Perthshire

Map Ref: 2C1

★★

SELF ATERING

Traditional stone-built cottage in rural setting on a working farm. Peaceful, but convenient for touring and all outdoor activities.

1 cottage, 1 pub rm, 2 bedrms (grd flr avail), sleeps 4, £180.00-£220.00, Jan-Dec, bus 2 mls, rail 20 mls

Mr & Mrs Brian Groom
East Tullyfergus Farm, Alyth, Perthshire, PH11 8JY
Tel: (Alyth) 01828 633251

★★

SELF ATERING

Cottage with own garden on 90 acre arable farm situated close to River Isle. Free fishing. Near historic ruins of Inverquiech Castle.

1 cottage, 1 pub rm, 2 bedrms (grd flr avail), sleeps 4, min let weekend, £140.00-£190.00, Jan-Dec, bus 3 mls, rail 20 mls, airport 20 mls

Mrs K A L Saddler
Inverquiech, Alyth,by Blairgowrie, Perthshire, PH11 8JR
Tel: (Alyth) 01828 632463

Anstruther, Fife

Map Ref: 2D3

SELF CATERING

16th Century restored town house featuring four large bedrooms and top floor open plan lounge with uninterrupted seaviews. Separate garden flat would suit couples, with double bedroom and bed settee in living room.

1 house, 1 flat, 1-3 pub rms, 1-4 bedrms (grd flr avail), sleeps 2-8, total sleeping capacity 10, £130.00-£450.00, Jan-Dec, bus 1/2 ml, rail 15 mls, airport 50 mls

Paul Capaldi
The Great Lodging, 21 High Street, Anstruther, Fife, KY10 3DJ
Tel: (Anstruther) 01333 312389 Fax: 01333 312389

SELF CATERING

Semi-detached granite house recently renovated and refurbished to a high standard, 9 miles (14kms) south of St Andrews, close to beach.

1 house, 1 pub rm, 3 bedrms, sleeps 6, £200.00-£450.00, Jan-Dec, bus nearby, rail 9 mls, airport 50 mls

Mrs I Taylor
17 Glenbridge Court, Dunfermline, Fife, KY12 8DL
Tel: (Dunfermline) 01383 732416

Arbroath, Angus

Map Ref: 2D1

SELF CATERING

Second floor flat situated in quiet location yet only 5 minutes walk from town centre. Ideal family accommodation.

1 flat, 1 pub rm, 3 bedrms, sleeps 6, £160.00-£260.00, Jan-Dec

Mr Ian Kemp
32 Ernest Street, Arbroath, Angus, DD11 1UB
Tel: (Arbroath) 01241 879845/0411 346719

SELF CATERING

Cosy detached cottage adjacent to owners house offering excellent accommodation. 2 minutes from town centre on bus route. An ideal base for golfers and tourists in the Angus area.

1 cottage, 1. pub rm, 2 bedrms (grd flr avail), sleeps 4, £200.00-£250.00, Jan-Dec, bus 1/4 ml, rail 3 mls

I Moyse
Woodfield House, Forfar Road, Arbroath, DD11 3RB
Tel: (Arbroath) 01241 874788

Auchterarder, Perthshire

Map Ref: 2B3

SELF CATERING

Apartments in tastefully renovated cottage dating back to 1709. Convenient for town, shops and park. Ideal for golfers.

2 apartments, 2 pub rms, 2 bedrms (grd flr avail), sleeps 4-6, total sleeping capacity 12, £185.00-£310.00, Jan-Dec, bus 50 yds, rail 1 ml, airport 60 mls

Mrs Hazel Morrison
Ben Lawers, Townhead Dairy, Auchterarder, Perthshire, PH3 1JG
Tel: (Auchterarder) 01764 662369 Fax: 01764 662369

Important: Prices stated are estimates and may be subject to amendments

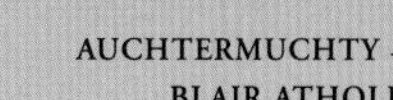

htermuchty, Fife — Map Ref: 2C3

★★ UP TO ★★★ SELF ATERING

Warm comfortable traditional style houses with private gardens. In a friendly rural town. Ground floor accommodation available.

3 houses, 1-2 pub rms, 3 bedrms, sleeps 5-6, total sleeping capacity 16, £240.00-£540.00, Jan-Dec, bus nearby, rail 5 mls, airport 40 mls

Auchtermuchty Holiday Homes
6 Gladgate, Auchtermuchty, Fife, KY14 7AY
Tel: (Auchtermuchty) 01337 828496

★★ UP TO ★★★★ SELF ATERING

Properties within 150 acre country estate of woodlands, stream, parklands and ornamental lake. Heated indoor pool. Four apartments in large wing of 16c mansion. Refurbished to high standard. Parklands grazed by highland cattle, rare breed sheep, horses, ponies, donkeys and peacocks.

4 flats, 1 cottage, 1 pub rm, 2-3 bedrms (grd flr avail), sleeps 2-6, total sleeping capacity 21, £240.00-£705.00, Jan-Dec, bus nearby, rail 4 mls, airport 35 mls

Heather McLay
Pitcairlie House, Auchtermuchty, Fife, KY14 6EU
Tel: (Auchtermuchty) 01337 827418 Fax: 01337 828464

kfoot, Perthshire — Map Ref: 2B2

★★ SELF ATERING

Stone built period cottage with modern interior. Spacious tiled and pine lined kitchen. Off street parking, and garden to rear. At centre of small village with hotels, restaurants, shops and hairdresser in walking distance. 10 miles N of Perth.

1 cottage, 1 pub rm, 2 bedrms (grd flr avail), sleeps 5, from £200.00, Jan-Dec, bus 500 yds, rail 8 mls

Mrs C McKay
Blair House, Main Street, Bankfoot, Perth, Perthshire, PH1 4AB
Tel: (Bankfoot) 01738 787338 Fax: 01738 787338

r Atholl, Perthshire — Map Ref: 4C12

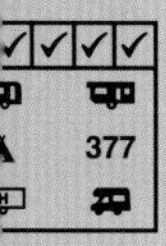

✓✓✓✓ 377

Blair Castle Caravan Park
Blair Atholl, Perthshire, PH18 5SR
Tel: (Blair Atholl) 01796 481263 Fax: 01796 481587

32 acres, mixed, Apr-Oct, prior booking in peak periods, latest time of arrival 2130, overnight holding area. Extra charge for electricity, awnings.

178 tourers £8.50-10.00 and 35 motors £8.50-10.00 and 70 tents £8.50-10.00. Total Touring Pitches 283.

28 Holiday Caravans to let, sleep 2-6 £160.00-350.00, total sleeping capacity 144, min let 3 nights.

Leisure facilities:

Take A9 N from Pitlochry. Turn off for Blair Atholl after 6 mls.

VAT is shown at 17.5%: changes in this rate may affect prices.

Key to symbols is on back flap.

Blair Atholl, Perthshire **Map Ref: 4C12**

The Firs Lodge

The Firs, St Andrews Crescent, Blair Atholl, Perthshire PH18 5TA
Telephone: 01796 481256 Fax: 01796 481661

This top quality fully equipped timber lodge provides outstanding year-round accommodation with secluded garden/patio area and verandah. Ideal touring base. Private off-street parking. Sleeps 4/5 in two bedrooms. *Sorry, no pets.*

★★★

SELF CATERING

Lodge set in its own garden with off street parking.

1 log cabin, 1 pub rm, 2 bedrms (grd flr avail), sleeps 4, £170.00-£375.00, Jan-Dec, bus nearby, rail 500 yds

Mrs Helen Crerar
The Firs, St Andrews Crescent, Blair Atholl, Perthshire, PH18 5TA
Tel: (Blair Atholl) 01796 481256

★★

SELF CATERING

Attractively furnished traditional stone cottage in Georgian stable block. Set amidst extensive grounds and beautiful scenery.

1 cottage, 2 pub rms, 3 bedrms (grd flr avail), sleeps 5-6, £275.00-£350.00, Jan-Dec, bus 5 mls, rail 8 mls

Mrs M MacDonald
Auchleeks, Trinafour, Pitlochry, Perthshire, PH18 5UF
Tel: 01796 483263 Fax: 01796 483337

★★

SELF CATERING

Traditional stone built farm house set in open hill ground. Spectacular views. Convenient for fishing and all outdoor activities.

1 house, 1 pub rm, 3 bedrms (grd flr avail), sleeps 6, £180.00-£260.00, Jan-Dec, bus 2 mls, rail 2 mls, airport 90 mls

Mrs Sandy Smith
Kincraigie Farm, Glen Fender, Blair Atholl, Perthshire, PH18 5TU
Tel: (Blair Atholl) 01796 481286

★★★

SELF CATERING

Modernised stone built cottages situated by leisure park with use of well heated indoor pool, multi gym, short tennis court.

5 cottages, 1 pub rm, 1-3 bedrms, sleeps 2-8, total sleeping capacity 26, £200.00-£490.00, Jan-Dec, bus nearby, rail 1 ml, ferry 75 mls, airport 75 mls

Vale of Atholl Country Cottages
Blair Atholl, by Pitlochry, Perthshire, PH18 5TE
Tel: (Blair Atholl) 01796 481467 Fax: 01796 481511

Important: Prices stated are estimates and may be subject to amendments

rgowrie, Perthshire

Map Ref: 2B1

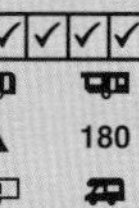

Blairgowrie Holiday Park
Rattray, Blairgowrie, Perthshire, PH10 7AL Tel: (Blairgowrie) 01250 872941 Fax: 01250 874535

180

15 acres, mixed, Jan-Dec, prior booking in peak periods, latest time of arrival 2000. Extra charge for electricity, awnings.

30 tourers £8.00-11.00 or 5 motors £8.00-11.00 or 15 tents £8.00-11.00. Total Touring Pitches 30.

10 Holiday Caravans to let, sleep 4-8 £185.00-360.00, total sleeping capacity 60, min let 3 nights.

Leisure facilities:

1/2 ml N of Blairgowrie town centre off A93 Braemar road, turn right at signpost.

★★★ SELF CATERING

Pine lodges with high level of insulation and feature pine decoration situated in 15 acre holiday park with own supermarket, laundry facility, putting green and children's play area.

9 pine lodges, 1 pub rm, 2-3 bedrms, sleeps 4-6, total sleeping capacity 48, min let 3 nights, £215.00-£530.00, Jan-Dec, bus 1/2 ml, rail 14 mls, airport 50 mls

Blairgowrie Holiday Park
Rattray, Blairgowrie, Perthshire, PH10 7AL
Tel: (Blairgowrie) 01250 872941 Fax: 01250 874535

★★ SELF CATERING

Conversion of former lodge in 2.5 acres of gardens and woodland of Glenshieling House Hotel. Town centre within easy reach.

1 house, 2 bedrms, sleeps 5, min let weekend, £150.00-£295.00, Jan-Dec, bus 1/2 ml, rail 30 mls

Mr Bradley
Glensheiling Lodge, Hatton Road, Rattray, Blairgowrie, PH10 7HZ
Tel: 01250 874605

UP TO ★★ SELF CATERING

Stone cottage and timber chalet on small holding situated on outskirts of Blairgowrie. Open views to beautiful countryside, ample space for children to play.

1 chalet, 1 cottage, 1 pub rm, 1 bedrm, sleeps 3-5, total sleeping capacity 8, min let 2 nights, £100.00-£220.00, Apr-Oct, bus 140 yds, rail 16 mls, airport 19 mls

Mrs P J Elder
Pondfauld, Alyth Road, Blairgowrie, Perthshire, PH10 7HF
Tel: (Blairgowrie) 01250 873284

Blairgowrie, Perthshire | **Map Ref: 2B1**

SELF CATERING

Spacious modernised conversion of an old flax mill situated on the banks of the River Ericht. 1 mile (2kms) from the town. Owners live adjacent.

1 house, 2 pub rms, 4 bedrms, sleeps 8, £300.00-£515.00, Jan-Dec, bus 1 ml, rail 18 mls, airport 40 mls

Mrs Catharine Jones
Brooklinn Mill, Blairgowrie, Perthshire, PH10 6TB
Tel: (Blairgowrie) 01250 873090

SELF CATERING

Cosy single storey cottage near centre of town. Sunny, enclosed patio to rear.

1 cottage, 1 pub rm, 3 bedrms, sleeps 5, £120.00-£280.00, Jan-Dec, bus nearby

Jean L Paterson
Kilbowie, 1 Westhill Road, Northmuir, Kirriemuir, Perthshire DD8 4
Tel: (Kirriemuir) 01575 572506 Fax: 01575 572506

★★ UP TO ★★★

SELF CATERING

Lodges in quiet location 10 minutes walk from town centre and its amenities. Ideal base for touring Perthshire, hillwalking and skiing.

6 chalets, 1 pub rm, 2 bedrms, sleeps 4-6, total sleeping capacity 30, £190.00-£405.00, Jan-Dec, bus 500 yds

Mrs Catherine Peebles
Ericht Holiday Lodges, Balmoral Road, Blairgowrie, PH10 7AN
Tel: (Blairgowrie) 01250 874686 Fax: 01250 875616
Email: ericht@compuserve.com

SELF CATERING

Spacious apartments of individual character in large Edwardian house. Set in private gardens near the small market town of Blairgowrie.

1 house, 4 flats, 1 pub rm, 2-9 bedrms (grd flr avail), sleeps 2-18, total sleeping capacity 27, min let weekend, £145.00-£1400.00, Jan-Dec, bus nearby, rail 18 mls, airport 20 mls

Mr Peter Russell
Eastfield House, New Road, Rattray, Blairgowrie, Perthshire, PH10 7DJ
Tel: (Blairgowrie) 01250 872105 Fax: 01250 872105
Email: efield@globalnet.co.uk

SELF CATERING

Stone built terraced cottage with private garden in quiet location close to town centre.

1 cottage, 1 pub rm, 2 bedrms, sleeps 4, min let weekend, £200.00-£389.00, Jan-Dec, bus nearby, rail 18 mls, airport 20 mls

Mr P A Russell
Eastfield House, New Road, Rattray, Blairgowrie, Perthshire, PH10 7DJ
Tel: (Blairgowrie) 01250 872105 Fax: 01250 872105
Email: efield@globalnet.co.uk
Web: www.users.globalnet.co.uk/~efield

Important: Prices stated are estimates and may be subject to amendments

irgowrie, Perthshire

Map Ref: 2B1

★★★

SELF ATERING

Well equipped modern bungalow in quiet residential area yet only 5 minutes walk from town centre. Ideal for touring Perthshire.

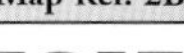

1 bungalow, 1 pub rm, 3 bedrms (grd flr avail), sleeps 7, £295.00-£425.00, Jan-Dec, bus 300 yds, rail 15 mls, ferry 50 mls, airport 15 mls

Mrs Wendy Thomson
Beech Cottage, Meikleour, Perth, Perthshire, PH2 6DZ
Tel: (Meikleour) 01250 883379

★

SELF ATERING

Scandinavian style chalets with own gardens in grounds of hotel. Peaceful setting 1 mile (2kms) from town centre, close to golf course.

2 chalets, 1 pub rm, 3 bedrms (grd flr avail), sleeps 6, total sleeping capacity 12, min let 3 nights, £195.00-£395.00, Jan-Dec, bus nearby, rail 16 mls

E M Walker
The Rosemount Golf Hotel, Golf Course Rd, Blairgowrie, Perthshire, PH10 6LJ
Tel: (Blairgowrie) 01250 872604 Fax: 01250 874496

dge of Cally, Perthshire

Map Ref: 2B1

★★★★

SELF ATERING

Apartments with south facing views set apart from caravan site. Games room and patio overlooking river.

4 flats, 1 pub rm, 1-2 bedrms, sleeps 2-6, total sleeping capacity 16, min let 2 nights, £140.00-£270.00, Dec-Oct, bus 6 mls, rail 23 mls

Corriefodly Holiday Park
Bridge of Cally, Perthshire, PH10 7JG
Tel: (Bridge of Cally) 01250 886236

★★

SELF ATERING

Three cottages in picturesque countryside on a mixed livestock hill farm. Superb views down glen, 3 miles (5kms) north of Bridge of Cally.

3 cottages, 1 pub rm, 2-3 bedrms (grd flr avail), sleeps 4, total sleeping capacity 15, £185.00-£350.00, Jan-Dec, bus 9 mls, rail 23 mls, airport 68 mls

Mrs D Farmer
Patrick Dean Ltd, Persie Mains, Bridge of Cally, Blairgowrie, Perthshire, PH10 7LQ
Tel: (Bridge of Cally) 01250 886250

rnside, By Forfar, Angus

Map Ref: 2D1

★★★★

SELF ATERING

Recently renovated small farm house on working farm. Rural location yet only 3 miles from Forfar. Loch fishing and golfing nearby. Woodland walks within the farm. Games room with pool table, darts and table tennis, adjacent to property. Ideal for family holidays.

1 house, 1 pub rm, 3 bedrms (grd flr avail), sleeps 6, £200.00-£350.00, Jan-Dec, bus 1 1/2 mls, rail 12 mls, airport 70 mls

Mrs E Jane C Skea
Dykehead, Burnside, by Forfar, Angus, DD8 2RY
Tel: (Letham) 01307 818900 Fax: 01307 818149

Bridge of Earn, Perthshire

Map Ref: 2B2

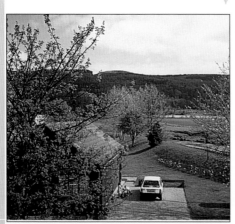

Comfortably furnished cedar lodges overlooking the River Earn and set in the scenic splendour of Perthshire. Easy access to Perth and Edinburgh via M90. Situated in secluded grounds with outdoor pursuits such as salmon fishing, tennis and bowling nearby.

11 log cabins, 1-2 pub rms, 1-3 bedrms, sleeps 2-8, total sleeping capacity 66, £155.00-£400.00, Jan-Dec, bus nearby, rail 4 mls, airport 40 mls

Mary & John Tulloch
River Edge Lodges, Bridge of Earn, Perth, Perthshire, PH2 9AB
Tel: (Bridge of Earn) 01738 812370 Fax: 01738 813161

Calvine, Perthshire

Map Ref: 4B12

Detached former shepherd's cottage, surrounded by grazing land and very close to River Errochty. Peaceful secluded setting, yet only 14 miles (22kms) from Pitlochry.

1 cottage, 2 pub rms, 2 bedrms, sleeps 5, £190.00-£290.00, Mar-Oct, bus 2 mls, rail 7 mls

Wendy Stewart
Clachan of Struan, Calvine, Perthshire, PH18 5UB
Tel: (Calvine) 01796 483207 Fax: 01796 483207

Carnoustie, Angus

Map Ref: 2D2

Recently refurbished semi-detached cottages, five minutes walk from town centre and all amenities. Ideal for many golf courses.

1 cottage, 1 pub rm, 2 bedrms (grd flr avail), sleeps 4, min let weekend, £180.00-£320.00, Jan-Dec, bus 200 yds, rail 1/2 ml, airport 16 mls

Mrs McLean
45 Taymouth Street, Carnoustie
Tel: (Carnoustie) 01241 854546 Fax: 01241 410480

Important: Prices stated are estimates and may be subject to amendments

rnoustie, Angus Map Ref: 2D2

★★★★ SELF ATERING

Spacious bright new ground floor apartment with private parking, situated adjacent to the golf course. Spectacular views, overlooking 18th green, and first tee of Carnoustie Championship Course.

1 flat, 1 pub rm, 2 bedrms (grd flr avail), sleeps 4, £175.00-£300.00, Jan-Dec, bus nearby, rail 1/4 ml

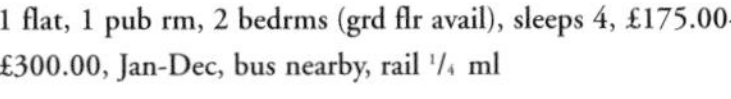

Mr D Milne
11 Little Carron Gardens, St Andrews, Fife, KY16 8QL
Tel: (St Andrews) 01334 479821

★★★ SELF ATERING

Attractive cottage in restored Manor House. Rural location convenient for town centre, golf and beach. Very well equipped with plenty extras. Ideal base for Tayside and the beautiful Angus Glens. Large garden and patio area with parking.

1 cottage, 1 pub rm, 2 bedrms (grd flr avail), sleeps 4-6, min let 1 night, £175.00-£400.00, Jan-Dec, bus 1/4 ml, rail 1 ml

Mr & Mrs S Pape
The Old Manor, Panbride, Carnoustie, Angus, DD7 6JP
Tel: (Carnoustie) 01241 854804

★ SELF ATERING

Comfortable family accommodation in cottage or flat, next to owner's property. Pleasant situation, with garden leading onto sandy beach. Close to shops trains etc. Ideal for golf, fishing and walking. Breakfast available.

1 flat, 1 cottage, 1 pub rm, 1-2 bedrms (grd flr avail), sleeps 4-6, total sleeping capacity 10, £120.00-£300.00, Jan-Dec, bus 1/4 ml, rail 1/2 ml, airport 15 mls

Mr & Mrs J Shearer
10 East Row, Westhaven, Carnoustie, Angus, DD7 6BG
Tel: (Carnoustie) 01241 855203 Fax: 01241 855203
Email: carnoustie@taynet.co.uk

★★ UP TO ★★★ SELF ATERING

Stone built detached adjacent farm cottages with small enclosed gardens situated on working farm 0.5 mile (1km) off main Dundee - Arbroath road. Panoramic views, good touring base. Ideal for golfing, peaceful location.

2 cottages, 1 pub rm, 2 bedrms (grd flr avail), sleeps 5, total sleeping capacity 5, from £170.00

Mrs E Watson
Balhousie Farm, Carnoustie, Angus, DD7 6LG
Tel: (Carnoustie) 01241 853533 Fax: 01241 857533
Email: balhousie@msn.co.uk

mrie, Perthshire Map Ref: 2A2

★★★★ SELF ATERING

Recently modernised and attractively furnished east wing of Comrie House. Situated beside the River Lednock and over the Lade stream which was used to generate electricity in earlier days. Access to garden, own entrance and completely self contained.

1 self-contained wing of house, 2 pub rms, 2 bedrms, sleeps 4, min let 3 days, £190.00-£320.00, Jan-Dec, bus 1/4 ml, rail 18 mls, airport 60 mls

Mrs Rosemary Dundas
Comrie House, Comrie, Crieff, Perthshire, PH6 2LR
Tel: (Comrie) 01764 670640 Fax: 01764 670640

VAT is shown at 17.5%: changes in this rate may affect prices.

Key to symbols is on back flap.

Coupar Angus, Perthshire

Map Ref: 2C1

SELF CATERING

Self contained wing of country house in peaceful rural area, access to grounds, including walled garden, listed mill and burn.

1 wing of mansion house, 3 pub rms, 2 bedrms, sleeps 4-5, £160.00-£320.00, Jan-Dec, bus 3/4 ml, rail 13 mls, airport 50 mls

Mrs Riddell-Webster
Lintrose, Coupar Angus, Perthshire, PH13 9JQ
Tel: (Coupar Angus) 01828 627472

Cowdenbeath, Fife

Map Ref: 2B4

SELF CATERING

Comfortable cottage with enclosed garden on working mixed farm. Historic sites, sport, nature and eating out all within 6 mile radius. Centrally located, only 45 minutes drive to Edinburgh, St. Andrews and Stirling.

1 cottage, 1 pub rm, 3 bedrms (grd flr avail), sleeps 6, £200.00-£300.00, Jan-Dec, bus 1/2 ml, rail 2 mls, airport 20 mls

Mrs Isobel Wilson
Lumphinnans Farm, Cowdenbeath, Fife, KY4 8HN
Tel: (Lochgelly) 01592 780279 Fax: 01592 780279

Craigrothie, by Cupar, Fife

Map Ref: 2C3

SELF CATERING

Well equipped modern cottage in quiet village, 8 miles (13 kms) from St Andrews and close to the quaint harbours of East Fife.

1 cottage, 1 pub rm, 2 bedrms (grd flr avail), sleeps 4-5, £200.00-£250.00, Jan-Dec, bus 600 yds, rail 2 3/4 mls, airport 40 mls

Mr and Mrs A Oliphant
Shillinghill, Old Mill Road, Craigrothie, Fife, KY15 5PZ
Tel: (Ceres) 01334 828361

Crail, Fife

Map Ref: 2D3

SELF CATERING

Charming country cottage with sea views and large garden. Convenient for village, golf and beaches. Easy access to Kingdom of Fife's coastal port walk and cycle routes. Child friendly garden and children's playhouse.

1 cottage, 2 pub rms, 2 bedrms (grd flr avail), sleeps 2-5, £200.00-£450.00, Mar-Nov, bus 1 ml, rail 10 mls

Mrs A Duffy
35 Rose Street, Dunfermline, Fife, KY12 0QT
Tel: (Dunfermline) 01383 723366

SELF CATERING

Peaceful location in the picturesque fishing village of Crail in the East Neuk. Traditional and spacious house with large, enclosed garden.

1 house, 3 pub rms, 3 bedrms, sleeps 6, min let weekend, £290.00-£400.00, Jan-Dec, bus nearby, rail 12 mls, airport 50 mls

Mrs Emma Fursman
27 Bellevue Place, Edinburgh, EH7 4BS,
Tel: 0131 556 4667 Fax: 0131 557 4456
Email: mail@dunpark-pm.demon.co.uk

Important: Prices stated are estimates and may be subject to amendments

il, Fife Map Ref: 2D3

SELF
ATERING

Attractive new, semi-detached villa in quality development, adjacent to open countryside and looking towards the sea, at edge of fishing village.

1 house, 2 pub rms, 3 bedrms, sleeps 6, min let 3 nights, £210.00-£410.00, Jan-Dec, bus 3/4 ml, rail 15 mls, airport 50 mls

Mrs Margaret Muir
7 Lyle Green, Livingston, West Lothian, EH54 8QE
Tel: (Livingston) 01506 441149 Fax: 01506 441149

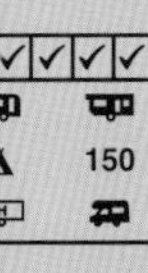

150

Sauchope Links Caravan Park
Crail, Fife, KY10 3XL Tel: (Crail) 01333 450460 Fax: 01337 870441
Email: largolp@aol.com Web: http://members.aol.com/largolp

12 acres, mixed, Mar-Oct, prior booking in peak periods, latest time of arrival 2000. Extra charge for electricity, awnings.

50 tourers or 50 motors or 50 tents. Total Touring Pitches 50. Charges on application.

4 Holiday Caravans to let, sleep 4-6, total sleeping capacity 22, min let 3 nights.

Leisure facilities:

1 ml E of Crail off A917.

SELF
ATERING

Modern, centrally heated bungalow with small enclosed private garden. Quiet position in picturesque fishing village. All rooms on ground floor.

1 bungalow, 2 pub rms, 2 bedrms (grd flr avail), sleeps 4, min let 2 nights, £140.00-£295.00, Jan-Dec, bus nearby, rail 15 mls, airport 50 mls

Mrs P L Taylor
20A Langhouse Green, Crail, Fife, KY10 3UD
Tel: (Crail) 01333 450845

---

eff, Perthshire Map Ref: 2A2

Loch Monzievaird Norwegian Chalets

Crieff, Perthshire PH7 4JR Tel: 01764 652586 Fax: 01764 652555
e.mail: monchalets@aol.com

The beautiful mature grounds at Loch Monzievaird are hidden away just two miles from the highland town of Crieff. Our Norwegian chalets are laid out amongst ancient oak, beech and scots pine. The chalets are private and well spread out, and all take advantage of differing elevated positions to enjoy the magnificent views over the loch. Walks right from your door, space and privacy.

Weekly rates from £225 (low season) to £575 (high season).

★★★★ SELF CATERING

SELF
ATERING

Quiet relaxation or an active holiday are both assured on this magnificent setting of 40 acres of parkland overlooking Loch Monzievaird. A mature wooded site offering seclusion to a range of pine chalets, all with open plan kitchen/living/dining area and covered deck. Tennis court, fishing, childrens play area on site and wide range of activities in area.

23 chalets, 2 pub rms, 2-3 bedrms (grd flr avail), sleeps 2-8, total sleeping capacity 136, min let 2 nights, £225.00-£575.00, Jan-Dec, bus 500 yds, rail 10 mls, airport 30 mls

Mr S J S & Mrs DS Brown
Loch Monzievaird Chalets, Ochtertyre, Crieff, Perthshire, PH7 4JR
Tel: (Crieff) 01764 652586 Fax: 01764 652555
Email: monchalets@aol.com

VAT is shown at 17.5%: changes in this rate may affect prices.

Key to symbols is on back flap.

Crieff, Perthshire — **Map Ref: 2A2**

Crieff Holiday Village

Turret Bank, Crieff, Perthshire, PH7 4JN Tel: (Crieff) 01764 653513 Fax: 01764 655028

4 acres, mixed, Jan-Dec, prior booking in peak periods, latest time of arrival 2400, overnight holding area. Extra charge for electricity, awnings.

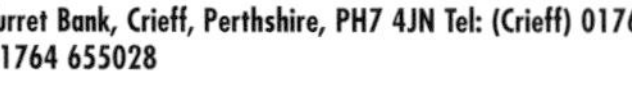

36 tourers £7.00-9.50 or 36 motors £7.00-9.50 or 10 tents £6.00-9.00. Total Touring Pitches 36.

5 Holiday Caravans to let, sleep 4-6 £145.00-310.00, total sleeping capacity 30, min let 2 nights.

Leisure facilities:

Follow A85 Crieff-Comrie road, turn left 1/2 ml from Crieff at first crossroads Site 300 yds on left.

★★★ UP TO ★★★★★ SELF CATERING

Chalets and cottages in hillside woodland setting in grounds of hotel. Sporting and leisure facilities of hotel available free to occupants.

15 chalets, 7 cottages, 1-2 pub rms, 2-3 bedrms (grd flr avail), sleeps 1-6, total sleeping capacity 142, min let 2 nights, from £100.00, Jan-Dec, bus 1 ml, rail 17 mls, airport 60 mls

Crieff Hydro Ltd

Crieff, Perthshire, PH7 3LQ
Tel: (Crieff) 01764 655555 Fax: 01764 653087

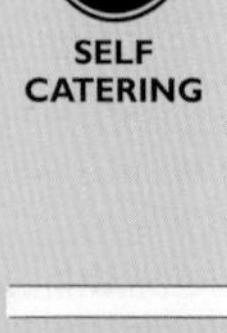

★★★ SELF CATERING

First floor flat located above cycle shop. Southerly open views to rear.

1 flat, 1 pub rm, 4 bedrms, sleeps 6, £160.00-£280.00, Jan-Dec, bus 1/4 ml, rail 17 mls, airport 60 mls

R & C Finnie

Arcachon, Ramsay Street, Crieff, Perthshire, PH7 3JF
Tel: (Crieff) 01764 652599 Fax: 01764 652599

★ SELF CATERING

Fifty year old cottage on working farm. Peaceful setting. 2 miles (3kms) out of Crieff. Ideal for touring, golfing, walking, and fishing.

1 cottage, 2 pub rms, 2 bedrms, sleeps 4, £130.00-£170.00, Apr-Oct, bus 800 yds, rail 9 mls, airport 50 mls

Mrs R E MacAskill

Kaimknowe, Glendevon,by Dollar, Clackmannanshire, FK14 7JZ
Tel: (Muckart) 01259 781331

★★★★ SELF CATERING

Attractive semi-detached cottage with enclosed garden on working farm. Excellent views over surrounding farmland to Ochil Hills.

1 cottage, 1 pub rm, 2 bedrms, sleeps 4, £140.00-£280.00, Mar-Oct, bus 1 ml, rail 7 mls, airport 40 mls

Mrs C Strang

Kintocher, by Crieff, Perthshire, PH7 3NQ
Tel: (Madderty) 01764 683258

Important: Prices stated are estimates and may be subject to amendments

par, Fife Map Ref: 2C3

SELF
ATERING

Clinkmill Cottage is tastefully modernised, situated in a grade B listed building on a working farm near the market town of Cupar.

3 cottages, 2 pub rms, 2-3 bedrms, sleeps 4-6, total sleeping capacity 14, £200.00-£450.00, Jan-Dec, bus 1 ml, rail 1 1/2 mls

C B Addison-Scott
Kirkton House, Houston, Renfrewshire, PA6 7HU
Tel: (Bridge of Weir) 01505 872900 Fax: 01505 613304

SELF
ATERING

On working farm in the beautiful Kingdom of Fife. Within easy reach of small picturesque fishing villages and the historic home of golf. 1 mile from Scottish Deer Centre.

1 cottage, 1 bungalow, 1-2 pub rms, 3 bedrms (grd flr avail), sleeps 6, total sleeping capacity 12, £220.00-£480.00, Jan-Dec, bus 1/2 ml, rail 2 mls, airport 40 mls

J G Lang & Son
Hilton of Carslogie, Cupar, Fife, KY15 4NG
Tel: (Cupar) 01334 652113 Fax: 01334 656710

★★ UP TO ★★★★

SELF
ATERING

A choice selection of quality properties in St Andrews or on our private country estate nearby. Real country living for country lovers. A home for all seasons.

3 houses, 3 flats, 6 cottages, 1-2 pub rms, 2-5 bedrms (grd flr avail), sleeps 4-10, total sleeping capacity 72, £235.00-£855.00, Jan-Dec, bus 2 mls, rail 5 mls, airport 45 mls

Mrs Andrew Wedderburn
Mountquhanie Holiday Homes, Cupar, nr St Andrews, Fife, KY15 4QJ
Tel: (Gauldry) 01382 330252 Fax: 01382 330480

Cupar, Fife Map Ref: 2C3

★★

SELF
ATERING

Set in beautiful scenery, a working farm by 16th century Scotstarvit Tower. Well placed for golfing etc. All ground floor rooms.

1 cottage, 1 pub rm, 3 bedrms (grd flr avail), sleeps 4-5, £160.00-£290.00, Jan-Dec, bus 1/2 ml, rail 2 mls, airport 40 mls

Morna Chrisp
Scotstarvit Farm, by Cupar, Fife, KY15 5PA
Tel: (Cupar) 01334 653591 Fax: 01334 653591

Dundee, Angus

Map Ref: 2C2

SELF CATERING

Centrally located accommodation in the University Residences. Ideal for St. Andrews, Perth and Forfar. Both sites easily accessible by public transport. Private parking at Alloway site. Both sites within walking distance of shops.

30 flats, 1 pub rm, 2-9 bedrms (grd flr avail), sleeps 2-9, total sleeping capacity 350, min let 1 night, from £80.50, Jun-Aug, bus 500 yds, rail 3 mls, airport 4 mls

Accommodation Office
University of Abertay Dundee, Bell Street, Dundee, DD1 1HG
Tel: 01382 308059 Fax: 01382 308877
Email: accommo@tay.ac.uk

SELF CATERING

New lodges, equipped to a high standard, in 12 acre woodland setting, overlooking idyllic trout fishing lochs. One lodge kitted out for disabled use.

3 chalets, 4-5 pub rms, 2-3 bedrms (grd flr avail), sleeps 6-8, total sleeping capacity 20, £200.00-£470.00, Jan-Dec, bus 1/2 ml, rail 6 mls, airport 7 mls

Mr Neil Anderson
Kingennie Fishings, Kingennie, Broughty Ferry, Dundee, DD5 3PJ
Tel: (Dundee) 01382 350777 Fax: 01382 350400

SELF CATERING

Secluded log house on working farm. 9 miles (14kms) north west of Dundee. Panoramic views to Sidlaw Hills, sheltered south facing garden.

1 log cabin, 1 pub rm, 3 bedrms (grd flr avail), sleeps 6, £155.00-£290.00, Jan-Dec, bus 2 mls, rail 10 mls, airport 9 mls

Mrs S E Baird
Scotston, Auchterhouse, Dundee, Angus, DD3 0QT
Tel: (Auchterhouse) 01382 320286

Dunkeld, Perthshire

Map Ref: 2B1

SELF CATERING

Former 19c shooting lodge in a remote situation with stunning views. Very comfortable. Shooting, fishing, squash available. Dunkeld 6 miles (10kms).

1 house, 3 pub rms, 4 bedrms, sleeps 8, £380.00-£568.00, Jan-Dec, bus 1 1/2 mls, rail 6 mls, airport 70 mls

W & W I Bruges
Laighwood, Dunkeld, Perthshire, PH8 0HB
Tel: (Butterstone) 01350 724241 Fax: 01350 724259

Important: Prices stated are estimates and may be subject to amendments

nkeld, Perthshire

Map Ref: 2B1

★

SELF
ATERING

Log cabin on secluded wooded site close to small village of Butterstone. 4 miles (6kms) from Dunkeld. Ideal for fishing, shooting and walking.

1 log cabin, 1 pub rm, 3 bedrms, sleeps 6, £200.00-£395.00, Jan-Dec, bus 4 mls, rail 4 mls, airport 60 mls

Country Retreats
135 Grahamsdyke Street, Laurieston, Falkirk, Stirlingshire, FK2 9LP
Tel: (Falkirk) 01324 625019

★★★★

SELF
ATERING

Former coach house, now a Listed building with sheltered patio and south facing garden, on edge of small village.

1 cottage, 1 pub rm, 2 bedrms, sleeps 4, £195.00-£320.00, Jan-Dec, bus 1/4 ml, rail 1/2 ml

Mrs Court
51 Bennochy Road, Kirkcaldy, Fife, KY2 5QZ
Tel: (Kirkcaldy) 01592 264369 Fax: 01592 592072

★★★

SELF
ATERING

Two flats adjoining Butterglen House and two houses, all in idyllic tranquil settings. Central for touring. Ideal for walking and fishing.

2 flats, 2 cottages, 1-2 pub rms, 2-3 bedrms (grd flr avail), sleeps 3-4, total sleeping capacity 15, £110.00-£235.00, Apr-Oct, bus 4 mls, rail 5 mls

Laighwood Self-Catering
Laighwood, Dunkeld, Perthshire, PH8 0HB
Tel: (Butterstone) 01350 724241 Fax: 01350 724259

★★★

SELF
ATERING

Renovated cottage, a mixture of old and new, in 1 acre of garden opening out onto extensive woodland walks. Open log fires in the lounge.

1 cottage, 2 pub rms, 3 bedrms, sleeps 6, £240.00-£350.00, Jan-Dec, bus 2 mls, rail 2 mls

Mrs Scott
Craig View, 17 West Shore, St Monans, Fife, KY10 2BT
Tel: 01333 730893

nning, Perthshire

Map Ref: 2B3

★★ UP TO ★★★★

SELF
ATERING

Selection of family run properties set in parklands and farm in rural Perthshire. Indoor facilities on site. Country sports by arrangement. Golf nearby. 2 unique properties form part of a unique 19th century listed chapel.

3 houses, 1 cottage, 1-2 pub rms, 1-3 bedrms (grd flr avail), sleeps 2-6, total sleeping capacity 16, min let 2 nights, £120.00-£480.00, Jan-Dec, bus 1/2 ml, rail 10 mls, airport 40 mls

Duncrub Holidays
Dalreoch, Dunning, Perthshire, PH2 0QJ
Tel: 01764 684368 Fax: 01764 684633
Email: dalreoch@globalnet.co.uk
Web: www.duncrub-holidays.com

Dunshalt, Fife

Map Ref: 2C3

SELF CATERING

Recently converted stable adjacent to owner's house. Pleasant private garden and gazebo. Easy access to East Neuk villages and many golf courses and M90 to Perth. Tay Bridge 20 minutes and Forth Road Bridge 35 mins drive. Shop 500 yards, pub 1 mile.

1 cottage, 1 pub rm, 1 bedrm (grd flr avail), sleeps 2, £160.00-£322.00, Jan-Dec, bus nearby, rail 2 mls, airport 30 mls

Frieda Watson
Homelands, Auchtermuchty Road, Dunshalt, Fife, KY14 7ET
Tel: (Auchtermuchty) 01337 828874

Dykehead, Cortachy, Angus

Map Ref: 4E12

SELF CATERING

Traditional cottages, now tastefully modernised, in a rural setting. Centrally located for touring the castles of Angus and Deeside.

3 cottages, 1 pub rm, 2-4 bedrms (grd flr avail), sleeps 4-6, total sleeping capacity 14, £240.00-£465.00, Apr-Oct, bus nearby, rail 20 mls, airport 20 mls

Mr R MacAlister
Dykehead Cottages, St Kessogs Rectory, High Street, Auchterarder, Perthshire, PH3 1AD
Tel: (Auchterarder) 01764 662525 Fax: 01764 662525

Edzell, Angus

Map Ref: 4F12

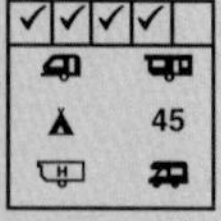

Glenesk Caravan Park
Edzell, by Brechin, DD9 7YP Tel: 01356 648565

8 acres, hard-standing, level, sheltered, Apr-Oct. Extra charge for electricity.

45 tourers £8.00-10.00 or 45 motors £8.00-10.00 or 15 tents £5.00-6.00. Total Touring Pitches 45.

2 Holiday Caravans to let, sleep 4-6 £176.26-211.50, total sleeping capacity 12, min let 3 nights.

Leisure facilities:

From A90 take B966 Edzell to Fettercairn. 1 ml N of Edzell, turn N signed Glenesk. Park is 1ml on right.

SELF CATERING

Whitewashed bungalows on working farm 100 yds from River North Esk. 2.5 miles from Edzell. Peaceful location with own garden. Rural but not isolated. Day rods available June-August.

1 bungalow, 2 pub rms, 3 bedrms (grd flr avail), sleeps 6, £245.00-£300.00, Nov-Jan, Jun-Aug, bus 1/2 ml, rail 12 mls, airport 35 mls

Mrs H Gray
Neuk Cottage, Burn Estate, Edzell, Angus, DD9 7XU
Tel: (Edzell) 01356 648523

Elie, Fife

Map Ref: 2D3

SELF CATERING

Converted stable overlooking golf course with garden. Off street parking and small courtyard. Access to Fife Coastal path and cycleway.

1 cottage, 2 pub rms, 3 bedrms, sleeps 6, £100.00-£440.00, Jan-Dec, bus 1/2 mile, rail 16 miles, airport 45 miles

Mrs S Pattullo
Elie Letting, The Park, Bank Street, Elie, Fife, KY9 1BW
Tel: (Elie) 01333 330219

ie, Fife

Map Ref: 2D3

★★ SELF CATERING

Comfortably furnished with own garden. Off street parking available. Excellent location, 50 metres from beach. Close to golf course and other sports facilities.

1 cottage, 2 pub rms, 2 bedrms, sleeps 5, min let weekend, £150.00-£320.00, Apr-Oct, bus 200 yds, rail 15 mls, airport 40 mls

Mr T Reekie
22 Carlton Place, Aberdeen, AB15 4BQ
Tel: (Denburn) 01224 642263 Fax: 01224 639773

arnan, by Kenmore, Perthshire

Map Ref: 2A1

★★★ SELF CATERING

Early 19c cottage situated on edge of scenic Fearnan on Loch Tayside. Ideal location for all outdoor pursuits. Coal or wood fire.

1 cottage, 2 pub rms, 2 bedrms, sleeps 4, £150.00-£300.00, Jan-Dec, rail 25 mls, airport 75 mls

Mr MacLean
Clach an Tuirc, Fearnan, Aberfeldy, Perthshire, PH15 2PG
Tel: (Aberfeldy) 01887 830615

rfar, Angus

Map Ref: 2D1

★★★ SELF CATERING

Comfortable and spacious single storey cottage enjoying 13 acres of pasture and woodland in lovely Angus countryside. Ideal base for touring, recreation or just relaxing.

1 cottage, 1 pub rm, 3 bedrms (grd flr avail), sleeps 6, £150.00-£280.00, Jan-Dec, bus ½ ml, rail 10 mls, airport 20 mls

Mrs P Gandy
Castle Cottage, Balgavies, Forfar, Angus, DD8 2TH
Tel: (Letham) 01307 818535 Fax: 01334 838899
Email: it.depmt@curtisfinepapers.btinternet.com

★★★ SELF CATERING

Red cedar cabins, situated in a meadow overlooking River South Esk, with panoramic view of the Angus Glens.

3 chalets, 1 pub rm, 2-3 bedrms (grd flr avail), sleeps 6-8, total sleeping capacity 22, £180.00-£390.00, Jan-Dec, bus 2 mls, rail 15 mls, airport 15 mls

Mr & Mrs Bruce Hunter
Hunters Cabins, Restenneth, Forfar, Angus, DD8 2SZ
Tel: (Forfar) 01307 463101
Email: hunter@spero.demon.co.uk

rgandenny, Perthshire

Map Ref: 2B2

★★ UP TO ★★★ SELF CATERING

Three individual cottages in farm setting. Tranquil location, yet only 9 miles from Perth. Centrally located for travel to Stirling, St Andrews, and Edinburgh. Walks with outstanding views over the Ochil Hills.

3 cottages, 2 pub rms, 2 bedrms (grd flr avail), sleeps 4-6, total sleeping capacity 16, £140.00-£345.00, Jan-Dec, bus 2 mls, rail 9 mls, airport 40 mls

Mr & Mrs Bywater
Ardargie Mains Estate, Forgandenny, Perthshire, PH2 9DQ
Tel: (Bridge of Earn) 01738 812748

Fortingall, Perthshire

Map Ref: 2A1

SELF CATERING

Thatched cottage with quiet enclosed garden situated in historic village at the foot of Glen Lyon. Loch Tay 2 miles (3kms).

1 cottage, 2 pub rms, 2 bedrms, sleeps 4-5, £150.00-£350.00, Jan-Dec, bus 10 mls, rail 20 mls

Mrs G D Stark
Craigard, Aberfeldy, Perthshire, PH15 2LB
Tel: 01887 829767

Foss, by Pitlochry, Perthshire

Map Ref: 4C12

★★★★

SELF CATERING

An early 18c stone built farmhouse of interesting character, lovingly restored. In isolated position with superb views.

1 house, 2 pub rms, 4 bedrms (grd flr avail), sleeps 8, £540.00-£790.00, Apr-Oct, bus 2 mls, rail 11 mls, airport 75 mls

Dr A Forsyth
Drumnakyle, Foss, Pitlochry, Perthshire, PH16 5NJ
Tel: 01882 634281
Web: http://come.to/drumnakyle

Glamis, Angus

Map Ref: 2C1

SELF CATERING

Old stone slated cottage within the historic village of Glamis. Compact interior refurbished to a very high standard. Private parking.

1 cottage, 1 pub rm, 1 bedrm (grd flr avail), sleeps 2, £165.00-£180.00, Jan-Dec, bus 200 yds, rail 12 mls, airport 12 mls

Mrs G Jarron
Hatton of Ogilvy Farm, Glamis, Angus, DD8 1UH
Tel: (Glamis) 01307 840229 Fax: 01307 840229

Glenesk, by Edzell, Angus

Map Ref: 4F12

SELF CATERING

A selection of cottages, rural locations in scenic Glenesk. Plenty of walks, fauna, wildlife and boat fishing on Loch Lee. Summer events include sheep dog trials and ceilidhs.

3 cottages, 1 pub rm, 2-4 bedrms, sleeps 3-6, total sleeping capacity 13, £190.00-£470.00, Jan-Dec, bus 19 mls, rail 30 mls, airport 90 mls

Blakes Cottages (Ref SM16)
Stoneybank Road, Earby, Colme, Lancashire, BB8 6PR
Tel: (Earby) 01282 445544 Fax: 01356 623725

lenfarg, Perthshire | **Map Ref: 2B3**

★★★ SELF CATERING

Comfortable cottage with full central heating set on working farm amidst scenic countryside. Good location for touring. 10 miles (16kms) south of Perth and under an hours drive to the centre of Edinburgh. Secluded garden with picnic table.

1 cottage, 1 pub rm, 2 bedrms (grd flr avail), sleeps 4, £150.00-£380.00, Jan-Dec, bus 3/4 ml, rail 10 mls, airport 25 mls

Mrs J D S Baillie
Colliston, Glenfarg, Perthshire, PH2 9PE
Tel: (Glenfarg) 01577 830434

★★ UP TO ★★★★ SELF CATERING

Beautifully restored, Scottish country house and courtyard development, with extensive grounds. Spectacular views over the surrounding area. Perth 8 miles, Edinburgh 40 miles. St Andrews 30 miles.

2 cottages, 1 east wing of house, 1-3 pub rms, 2-5 bedrms (grd flr avail), sleeps 4-10, total sleeping capacity 18, £275.00-£650.00, Jan-Dec, bus 1/2 ml, rail 6 mls, airport 30 mls

Mrs P Biddlecombe
Glenfarg Properties Ltd, Glenfarg House, Glenfarg, Perthshire, PH2 9PT
Tel: (Abernethy) 01738 850708 Fax: 01738 850661

★★ SELF CATERING

Traditional semi-detached cottage, centrally situated. Ideal for touring an hours drive from Edinburgh, St Andrews, Stirling & Glasgow. One bedroom, sleeps 2/3. Quiet outlook, 1 mile from Glenfarg village. Small enclosed gravelled area with garden furniture. Garage included.

1 cottage, 1 pub rm, 1 bedrm (grd flr avail), sleeps 3, £90.00-£200.00, Jan-Dec, bus 1/2 ml, rail 10 mls, airport 30 mls

Mrs M MacLean
Arngask House, Glenfarg, Perth, PH2 9QA
Tel: (Glenfarg) 01577 830311 Fax: 01577 830311

Glenisla, Angus

Map Ref: 4D12

SELF CATERING

Log chalet and bungalow, on mixed farm at the foot of Glen Isla, close to Lintrathen Loch. Ideal base for touring and all outdoor pursuits. Many golf courses within easy reach. 7 miles from Kirriemuir - home of J M Barrie (Peter Pan).

1 log cabin, 1 bungalow, 1 pub rm, 2-3 bedrms (grd flr avail), sleeps 4-6, total sleeping capacity 12, £200.00-£400.00, Jan-Dec, bus 7 mls, rail 23 mls, airport 23 mls

Mrs M Clark
Purgavie Farm, Glenisla, Kirriemuir, Angus, DD8 5HZ
Tel: (Lintrathen) 01575 560213/0860 392794 (mobile) Fax: 01575 560213

Glenlyon, Perthshire

Map Ref: 1H1

SELF CATERING

Former gardener's cottage on privately owned sporting estate, set amidst rugged scenery of Glen Lyon, 12 miles (19kms) from Aberfeldy.

1 cottage, 1 pub rm, 2 bedrms, sleeps 4, £175.00-£225.00, Jan-Dec, bus 11 mls, rail 28 mls

S Chesthill Est, per Mrs Pirie
Keepers Cottage, Chesthill, Glenlyon, Perthshire, PH15 2NH
Tel: (Glenlyon) 01887 877233

SELF CATERING

Stone built cottages and farmhouse with open fires, situated in a national scenic area. Peaceful but not isolated.

1 house, 2 cottages, 1-2 pub rms, 2-3 bedrms (grd flr avail), sleeps 4-6, total sleeping capacity 16, £150.00-£400.00, Jan-Dec, bus 18 mls, rail 33 mls, airport 95 mls

Mrs M Marshall
Garden Flat, Innerwick, Glenlyon, Aberfeldy, Perthshire, PH15 2PP
Tel: 01887 866222 Fax: 01887 866301

Glenshee, Perthshire

Map Ref: 4D12

SELF CATERING

East wing of baronial style castle set amidst beautiful scenery of Glenshee.

1 east wing of castle, 2 pub rms, 11 bedrms, sleeps 20, min let 2 nights, from £2100.00, Jan-Dec, bus 14 mls, rail 30 mls, airport 70 mls

Mrs Burke
Dalnaglar Castle, Glenshee, Blairgowrie, Perthshire, PH10 7LP
Tel: (Glenshee) 01250 882232 Fax: 01250 882277
Email: dalnaglar@zetnet.co.uk
Web: www.castles-scotland.com

SELF CATERING

Refurbished 19c former coach house set in 14 acres of Highland estate. Wide range of indoor and outdoor sporting activities.

1 flat, 3 bed sitting rooms, 1-2 bedrms (grd flr avail), sleeps 2-5, total sleeping capacity 14, £56.00-£280.00, Jan-Dec, bus 17 mls, rail 35 mls

The Compass Christian Centre
Glenshee Lodge, Glenshee, Blairgowrie, Perthshire, PH10 7QD
Tel: (Glenshee) 01250 885209 Fax: 01250 885309

Important: Prices stated are estimates and may be subject to amendments

lenshee, Perthshire Map Ref: 4D12

Dalmunzie Highland Cottages

Spittal o' Glenshee, Blairgowrie, Perthshire PH10 7QG
Telephone: 01250 885226 Fax: 01250 885225

Seven traditional stonebuilt cottages set on 6,000-acre sporting estate with log fires, well-equipped kitchens, bed linen included. Ideal base for touring the Highlands or for shooting, fishing, tennis, walking, with our 9-hole golf course on the doorstep. Excellent catering at nearby Dalmunzie House Hotel.

★★ SELF CATERING

Stone built cottages of individual style and character on 6000 acre shooting estate. 9 hole golf course, shooting, fishing, tennis and hill walking.

7 cottages, 1-2 pub rms, 1-3 bedrms (grd flr avail), sleeps 2-6, total sleeping capacity 30, £150.00-£430.00, Jan-Dec, bus 22 mls, rail 36 mls, airport 80 mls

Mr S N Winton
Dalmunzie Highland Cottages, Box 2, Spittal of Glenshee, Blairgowrie, PH10 7QG
Tel: (Glenshee) 01250 885226 Fax: 01250 885225

uthrie, by Forfar, Angus Map Ref: 2D1

★★★★ SELF CATERING

Newly renovated traditional cottage with modern facilities. Set in open farmland, with superb views across Angus. Easy access to coast and North.

1 cottage, 2 pub rms, 2 bedrms (grd flr avail), sleeps 4, £175.00-£300.00, Jan-Dec, bus nearby, rail 8 mls

Mrs C Shand
Crosshill, Guthrie, Forfar, Angus, DD8 2TL
Tel: (Friockheim) 01241 828548

elty, Fife Map Ref: 2B4

★★ SELF CATERING

Steading cottage on farm. Peaceful woodland setting in country park. Fishing, golf, gliding, water sports, riding and adventure playground all close by. Convenient for travel to Dundee, Edinburgh, Stirling, Perth and St. Andrews.

1 cottage, 1 pub rm, 3 bedrms (grd flr avail), sleeps 6, £175.00-£300.00, Jan-Dec, bus 1 1/2 mls, rail 6 mls, airport 20 mls

Mr & Mrs Constable
Benarty House, Kelty, Fife, KY4 0HT
Tel: (Dunfermline) 01383 830235

enmore, Perthshire Map Ref: 2A1

★ UP TO ★★★ SELF CATERING

Chalet, Austrian style 2-4 berth or detached 6 berth overlooking Loch Tay. All are adjacent to licensed hotel & have full central heating & colour TV

12 chalets, 5 log cabins, 1 pub rm, 1-3 bedrms (grd flr avail), sleeps 2-6, total sleeping capacity 78, min let 2 days, £210.00-£840.00, Jan-Dec, bus 7 mls, rail 20 mls, airport 85 mls

Hotel, Chalets & Activities Centre
Croft-na-Caber, Kenmore, Perthshire, PH15 2HW
Tel: (Kenmore) 01887 830236 Fax: 01887 830649

Kenmore, Perthshire

Map Ref: 2A1

Stone built cottages in courtyard setting close to loch/village. Own golf course, bowling and putting greens. Bistro Bar with games room.

4 cottages, 1-3 pub rms, 2-4 bedrms (grd flr avail), sleeps 3-8, total sleeping capacity 27, £300.00-£900.00, Jan-Dec, bus 6 mls, rail 30 mls, airport 80 mls

D Menzies and Partners
Mains of Taymouth, Kenmore, Aberfeldy, Perthshire, PH15 2HN
Tel: (Kenmore) 01887 830226 Fax: 01887 830211

Three traditional stonebuilt cottages in peaceful setting, close to lochside. Fishing by arrangement, ideal hill walking - Ben Lawers.

3 cottages, 1-2 pub rms, 2-3 bedrms (grd flr avail), sleeps 4-7, total sleeping capacity 16, £160.00-£450.00, Jan-Dec, bus 8 1/2 mls, rail 21 mls

Mr & Mrs J H Webb
Machuim Farm, Lawers, Aberfeldy, Perthshire, PH15 2PA
Tel: (Killin) 01567 820670

Killiecrankie, Perthshire

Map Ref: 4C12

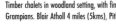

Timber chalets in woodland setting, with fine views to Blair Atholl and the Grampians. Blair Atholl 4 miles (5kms), Pitlochry 4 miles (6kms).

5 chalets, 1 pub rm, 2 bedrms (grd flr avail), sleeps 4, total sleeping capacity 20, £230.00-£340.00, Jan-Dec, bus 4 mls, rail 4 mls, airport 75 mls

Mr & Mrs Seath
The Lodge, Old Faskally, Killiecrankie, Pitlochry, Perthshire, PH16 5L
Tel: (Pitlochry) 01796 473436 Fax: 01796 473436

Kingsbarns, Fife

Map Ref: 2D3

Small award winning complex of converted farm buildings in courtyard setting. Heated indoor pool, sauna, gym, tennis court and children's play areas.

10 houses, 1 pub rm, 1-4 bedrms, sleeps 2-10, total sleeping capacity 60, £265.00-£1010.00, Jan-Dec, bus 1/2 ml, rail 9 mls, airport 55 mls

John Parker
Morton of Pitmilly, Kingsbarns, St Andrews, Fife, KY16 8QF
Tel: (Boarhills) 01334 880466 Fax: 01334 880437
Email: mop@sol.co.uk
Web: www.pitmilly.co.uk

Kingsbarns, by St Andrews, Fife

Map Ref: 2D3

Flats in Victorian mansion and cottages in grounds of wooded, lowland coastal estate. Extensive gardens, activities and walks to sandy beaches.

4 flats, 2 cottages, 1-2 pub rms, 1-4 bedrms (grd flr avail), sleeps 2-8, total sleeping capacity 42, £190.00-£645.00, Jan-Dec, bus 3/4 ml, rail 13 mls, airport 60 mls

Mr Peter Erskine
Cambo House, Kingsbarns, by St Andrews, Fife KY16 8QD
Tel: (Crail) 01333 450313 Fax: 01333 450987

Important: Prices stated are estimates and may be subject to amendments

Kinloch Rannoch, Perthshire

Map Ref: 1H1

★★★ SELF CATERING

Traditional cosy stone-built cottage, on quiet road in attractive village. Sheltered, sunny south facing garden with fine views to Schiehallion.

1 cottage, 1 pub rm, 2 bedrms (grd flr avail), sleeps 6, £200.00-£260.00, Apr-Oct, bus nearby, rail 17 miles

Dr Hazel Campbell
Drumashie Lodge, Dores, Inverness-shire, IV2 6TR
Tel: (Dores) 01463 751202

★★ SELF CATERING

Totally refurbished apartment in centre of quiet Highland village. Within walking distance of all local amenities.

1 flat, 1 pub rm, 3 bedrms, sleeps 10, £210.00-£450.00, Jan-Dec, bus nearby, rail 18 mls

James Stewart
2 Ashton Villas, Edinburgh, EH15 2QP
Tel: 0131 657 1718 Fax: 0131 657 1718
Email: stewart@sol.co.uk

Kinloch Rannoch, by Pitlochry, Perthshire

Map Ref: 1H1

★★ UP TO ★★★ SELF CATERING

Stone built cottages of unique charm and character, individually sited on Highland estate with excellent views. Free trout fishing and boats available. Tennis court.

8 cottages, 1-2 pub rms, 1-4 bedrms (grd flr avail), sleeps 2-8, total sleeping capacity 39, min let weekend, £163.00-£530.00, Jan-Dec, bus up to 3 mls, rail 18 mls, airport 80 mls

Mrs M A MacIntyre
Dunalastair Holiday Houses, Dunalastair Estate, Kinloch Rannoch, Perthshire, PH16 5PD
Tel: (Kinloch Rannoch) 01882 632491 Fax: 01882 632469
Email: dunalastair@sol.co.uk
Web: www.dunalastair.com

Kinross, Perthshire

Map Ref: 2B3

★★ SELF CATERING

Situated at the foot of the Lomond Hills, overlooking Loch Leven, you'll really enjoy a holiday in this quiet and unspoilt area. Ideally positioned for Scotland's main tourist attractions, Edinburgh, Stirling, Perth, St Andrews and Fife are within easy reach. Dundee, Crieff and Pitlochry are all within a relaxed hours drive.

18 chalets, 1 pub rm, 2-3 bedrms, sleeps 4-6, total sleeping capacity 86, min let 3 nights, £140.00-£360.00, Jan-Dec, bus 3 mls, rail 12 mls, airport 28 mls

Loch Leven Chalets
Stan-ma-Lane, Balgedie, Kinross, KY13 7HE
Tel: (Scotlandwell) 01592 840257

VAT is shown at 17.5%: changes in this rate may affect prices.

Key to symbols is on back flap.

Kirkmichael, Perthshire

Map Ref: 4D12

SELF CATERING

Detached modern house with own garden and private parking. In peaceful location overlooking Bannerfield, with easy access to village and facilities.

1 bungalow, 2 pub rms, 3 bedrms (grd flr avail), sleeps 5, £240.00-£360.00, Apr-Oct, bus nearby, rail 12 mls, airport 45 mls

Mrs Cynthia Hilton
18 The Glen, Endcliffe Vale Road, Sheffield, S10 3FN
Tel: (Sheffield) 01142 663188 Fax: 01142 687088

SELF CATERING

Cottages of individual character and style, situated in centre of small Perthshire village, close to shops and village amenities.

1 house, 2 cottages, 1-2 pub rms, 2-3 bedrms (grd flr avail), sleeps 4-6, total sleeping capacity 14, min let 2 nights, £144.00-£390.00, Jan-Dec, bus nearby, rail 12 mls, airport 60 mls

J & I Milne, Kirkmichael Village Cottages
Main Street, Kirkmichael, Blairgowrie, Perthshire, PH10 7NT
Tel: (Strathardle) 01250 881385 Fax: 01250 881385
Web: www.accomodata.co.uk/020496.htm

SELF CATERING

Individually sited properties on a Highland Estate in a rural setting. Open air swimming pool, tennis court and fishing. Shooting by arrangement. Riding nearby.

4 log cabins, 2 houses, 2 cottages, 1-3 pub rms, 2-3 bedrms (grd flr avail), sleeps 2-7, total sleeping capacity 50, £140.00-£440.00, Jan-Dec, bus ½ ml, rail 12 mls, airport 28 mls

Mrs Helen Reid
Balnakilly, Kirkmichael, Blairgowrie, Perthshire, PH10 7NB
Tel: 01250 881281 Fax: 01250 881281

Kirriemuir, Angus

Map Ref: 2C1

SELF CATERING

Terraced former weavers cottages with own gardens. In quiet residential area on south side of town centre. Ideal base for touring Angus glens. Both properties have private parking and open fires, for which a starter pack of coal and logs will be provided.

2 cottages, 1-2 pub rms, 2 bedrms (grd flr avail), sleeps 4-5, total sleeping capacity 9, min let weekend, £156.00-£250.00, Jan-Dec, bus nearby, rail 15 mls, airport 60 mls

Mr & Mrs H G McCrum
92 Glamis Road, Kirriemuir, Angus, DD8 5DF
Tel: (Kirriemuir) 01575 572085

By Kirriemuir, Angus

Map Ref: 2C1

SELF CATERING

Flat, cottage and ranch style house on working hill and arable farm, situated in an Angus glen with panoramic views. Access to local hills. Ideally situated for shooting, fishing, hill walking, golfing and ski-ing.

1 flat, 1 cottage, 1 colt house, 1 pub rm, 2 bedrms (grd flr avail), sleeps 2-4, total sleeping capacity 10, min let weekend, £145.00-£320.00, Jan-Dec, bus 6 mls, rail 22 mls, airport 25 mls

Mrs M Marchant
The Welton of Kingoldrum, by Kirriemuir, Angus, DD8 5HY
Tel: (Kirriemuir) 01575 574743 Fax: 01575 574743
Web: www.yell.co.uk/sites/welton-of-kingoldrum

euchars, Fife Map Ref: 2D2

★★ SELF CATERING

Situated on a small promentory between the Tay and the Eden Estuaries, with easy access to forest and beaches. Modernised farm cottages 15 minutes drive from St Andrews. Just a stepping stone to the historic East Neuk fishing villages and over the Tay to Dundee and Perth.

5 cottages, 1 pub rm, 2-4 bedrms (grd flr avail), sleeps 4-8, total sleeping capacity 29, £205.00-£385.00, Jun-Oct, bus 2 mls, rail 3 mls, airport 45 mls

J L W Foster & Co (Estate Office)
Craigie Farm, Leuchars, Fife, KY16 0DT
Tel: (Leuchars) 01334 839218 Fax: 01334 839503

eigle, Perthshire Map Ref: 2C1

★★ SELF CATERING

Traditional log cabins set within the grounds of Georgian mansion. Peaceful location, yet only 14 miles from Dundee and Perth. Fishing permit can be arranged and advice given. Shooting and golf courses nearby. Ski-ing within 40 minutes drive.

5 chalets, 1 pub rm, 2 bedrms (grd flr avail), sleeps 4-6, total sleeping capacity 30, min let 1/2 week, £245.00-£295.00, Apr-Sep, bus 1 ml, rail 14 mls, airport 44 mls

Mr & Mrs Herrald
Kings of Kinloch, Meigle, Blairgowrie, Perthshire, PH12 8QX
Tel: 01828 640273/640799 Fax: 01828 640273
Web: www.yell.co.uk/sites/herrald-antiques/

★★ SELF CATERING

Comfortable accommodation in traditional cottage. Attractive garden 0.5ml from Meigle. Ideal for golfing, fishing, touring and skiing. Pets welcome.

1 cottage, 1 pub rm, 2 bedrms (grd flr avail), sleeps 4, £180.00-£250.00, Jan-Dec, bus ³/₄ ml, rail 12 mls, airport 12 mls

Mrs M J Scott
Broomend, Ardler Road, Meigle, Perthshire, PH12 8TE
Tel: (Meigle) 01828 640596

ethven, by Perth, Perthshire Map Ref: 2B2

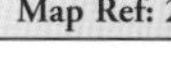

★★★★ SELF CATERING

Traditional farm cottages on 700 acre mixed arable farm in Strathearn. Golf, shooting, fishing and riding available. Open all year.

3 cottages, 1 pub rm, 1-2 bedrms (grd flr avail), sleeps 2-6, total sleeping capacity 14, £145.00-£295.00, Jan-Dec, bus ¹/₂ ml, rail 6 mls, airport 40 mls

Mr Howard England
Strathearn Holidays Ltd, Kilda Way, North Muirton Ind Est, Perth, PH1 3XS
Tel: (Perth) 01738 633322/(office hours only) Fax: 01738 621177

VAT is shown at 17.5%: changes in this rate may affect prices.

Key to symbols is on back flap.

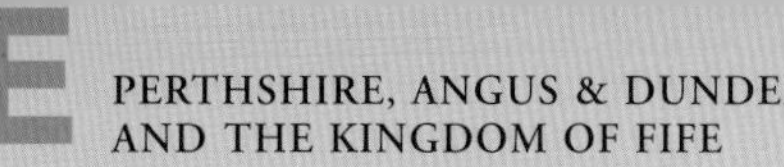

Methven, by Perth, Perthshire

Map Ref: 2B2

SELF CATERING

Cottages with extensive southerly views over Perthshire and beyond. Open fires. Ideal base for touring Perthshire. Shooting and fishing available.

3 cottages, 1 pub rm, 2 bedrms (grd flr avail), sleeps 4, total sleeping capacity 12, £200.00-£255.00, Jan-Dec, bus 1/3 ml, rail 8 mls, airport 30-50 mls

Mr David M A Smythe
Cloag Farm, Methven, Perthshire, PH1 3RR
Tel: (Methven) 01738 840239 Fax: 01738 840156
Email: cloagfarm@compuserve.com
Web: www.destination-scotland.com/cloagfarm

Newport-on-Tay, Fife

Map Ref: 2D2

SELF CATERING

Self-contained wing of large Listed house, standing in its own grounds in Newport-on-Tay. 3 miles (5kms) from Dundee and 10 miles (16kms) from St Andrews.

1 house, 3 pub rms, 3 bedrms (grd flr avail), sleeps 5-6, £170.00-£350.00, Jan-Dec, bus 200 yds, rail 3 mls, airport 5 mls

Mr & Mrs A Ramsay
Balmore, 3 West Road, Newport-on-Tay, DD6 8HH
Tel: (Newport-on-Tay) 01382 542274 Fax: 01382 542927

North Queensferry, Fife

Map Ref: 2B4

SELF CATERING

Secluded, centrally located 19c mansion house with superb view of the River Forth and its famous bridges. Within easy reach of Edinburgh and Glasgow. Perth, the gateway to the Highlands is less than 30 minutes away by road.

6 flats, 2 cottages, 1 pub rm, 1-3 bedrms (grd flr avail), sleeps 2-6, total sleeping capacity 33, £160.00-£400.00, Jan-Dec, bus nearby, rail nearby, ferry nearby, airport 7 mls

Mrs E Anderson
1 Inverkeithing Road, Crossgates, Fife, KY4 8AL
Tel: (Cowdenbeath) 01383 510666 Fax: 01383 510666

Perth

Map Ref: 2B2

SELF CATERING

Spacious first floor flat in the centre of the city. Short distance from bus and train stations and easy access to shops, theatre, cinema, many leisure activities and many restaurants.

1 flat, 1 pub rm, 3 bedrms, sleeps 5, min let weekend, £155.00-£350.00, Jan-Dec, bus nearby, rail 1/2 ml

Anderson
48 Victoria Street, Perth, Perthshire, PH2 8JY
Tel: (Perth) 01738 622272

SELF CATERING

Listed building in side street with easy walking access to city centre and all amenities. Main rooms on upper floor. A house of character, yet offering modern day comfort.

1 cottage, 1 bedrm (grd flr avail), sleeps 4, £150.00-£250.00, Jan-Dec, bus nearby, rail 1/2 ml, ferry 150 mls, airport 45 mls

Mrs Morritt
Balhousie Bank, 15 Hay Street, Perth, PH1 5HS
Tel: (Perth) 01738 638867

Important: Prices stated are estimates and may be subject to amendments

rth | **Map Ref: 2B2**

★★★ SELF CATERING

Nicely furnished lodge house within 3 acres of grounds on the banks of the River Tay, conveniently situated for all city centre amenities (10 minute walk), Trout fishing from the bank. Scone Palace close by. Many other activities are available.

1 house, 1 pub rm, 2 bedrms, sleeps 4, £200.00-£450.00, May-Oct, bus nearby, rail 2 mls

Queens Hotel
Leonard Street, Perth, PH2 8HB
Tel: (Perth) 01738 442222 Fax: 01738 638496
Email: email@lovat.co.uk

★★ SELF CATERING

Top floor flat accessed by communal stairway, conveniently situated in town centre near main shopping areas.

1 flat, 2 pub rms, 1 bedrm, sleeps 2, £150.00-£180.00, Jan-Dec, bus nearby, rail 1 ml, airport 15 mls

Mrs A E Roberts
Jessamine House, Hamsterley, Bishop Auckland,
Co. Durham, DL13 3QF
Tel: (Bishop Auckland) 01388 488630

★★★★ SELF CATERING

Very comfortably appointed garden flat located close to Perth City centre, directly oppsite South Inch Park. Several very good restaurants and hotels within easy walking distance. Ideally situated for exploring all of Central Scotland. Front and back gardens. Garage parking. No smoking. No pets. Brochure available.

1 flat, 1 pub rm, 2 bedrms (grd flr avail), sleeps 4, min let 3 days, £190.00-£420.00, Jan-Dec, bus 600 yds, rail 500 yds, airport 45 mls

Tricia Stiell
5 Marshall Place, Perth, PH2 8AH
Tel: (Perth) 01738 447524 Fax: 01738 444056

Perth | **Map Ref: 2B2**

★★★ SELF CATERING

Lovely smiddy cottage with charm and character, also two studio flats in former stables. 10 miles from Perth. Beautiful countryside. Large garden. Parking.

1 cottage, 2 studio flats, 1-3 pub rms, 1-3 bedrms (grd flr avail), sleeps 2-6, total sleeping capacity 10, £175.00-£600.00, Jan-Dec, bus 3 mls, rail 10 mls, airport 60 mls

Mrs Chapman
The Old Smiddy, Kinclaven, by Stanley, Perthshire, PH1 4QJ
Tel: 0131 440 0089/0403 540932 (mobile) Fax: 0131 440 0089
Email: vchapman1@aol.com

★★★ SELF CATERING

Spacious well furnished cottage with a large secluded lawned garden and putting green. Panoramic views from Strathmore valley

1 cottage, 1 pub rm, 3 bedrms (grd flr avail), sleeps 5-6, £225.00-£375.00, Jan-Dec, bus 1 1/2 mls

Mrs Christine Jeffrey
Airntully, Stanley, by Perth, PH1 4PH
Tel: 01738 828463

By Perth

Map Ref: 2B2

SELF CATERING

Tastefully renovated former post office dating from 1820, situated in quiet village midway between Perth and Blairgowrie.

1 cottage, 1 pub rm, 1 bedrm (grd flr avail), sleeps 4, from £170.00, Jan-Dec, bus 50 yds, rail 8 mls

Mrs Leadbitter
The Old Post Office, Caroline Place, Wolfhill, by Perth, Perthshire, PH2 6DA
Tel: (Balbeggie) 01821 650468

SELF CATERING

Beautifully constructed, comfortable cottage overlooking River Tay. Set in nicely maintained gardens. Private parking. Close to Perth and some of Scotland's tourist attractions.

1 cottage, 2 pub rms, 2 bedrms (grd flr avail), sleeps 4, £330.00-£450.00, Mar-Nov, bus 1/2 ml, rail 7 mls, airport 40 mls

A C Miller & MacKay
63 Scott Street, Perth, PH2 8JN
Tel: (Perth) 01738 620087

SELF CATERING

Two traditional, stone built semi-detached cottages on working farm. On an elevated site overlooking the Rivers Tay and Earn and the Ochil Hills. 5 miles south east of Perth in a peaceful haven of Perthshire.

2 cottages, 1 pub rm, 1-2 bedrms (grd flr avail), sleeps 2-6, total sleeping capacity 8, min let weekend, £120.00-£290.00, Jan-Dec, bus 3 mls, rail 5 mls, airport 38 mls

Mrs E Stirrat
Fingask Farm, Rhynd, by Perth, Perthshire, PH2 8QF
Tel: (Perth) 01738 812220 Fax: 01738 813325

Pitlochry, Perthshire

Map Ref: 2A1

SELF CATERING

Modern house, of individual style and character with own secluded gardens. Only a few minutes walk from town centre, park and Pitlochry Theatre.

1 house, 2 pub rms, 3 bedrms (grd flr avail), sleeps 5, £295.00-£475.00, Jan-Dec, bus 1/4 ml, rail 1/4 ml, airport 60 mls

Mrs V M M Beresford-Green
Tighnabruaich, Bruach Lane, Pitlochry, Perthshire, PH16 5DG
Tel: (Pitlochry) 01796 472556

★★★★

SERVICED APARTMENTS

Modern and comfortable apartments with a self catering and serviced element. Central quiet location. Taste of Scotland coffee shop open 10.00 - 19.00.

2 cottages, 9 serviced apartments, 1 pub rm, 1-2 bedrms (grd flr avail), sleeps 2-6, total sleeping capacity 34, £225.00-£435.00, Jan-Dec, bus 1/4 ml, rail 1/4 ml, airport 65 mls

Burnside Apartment Hotel
19 West Moulin Road, Pitlochry, Perthshire, PH16 5EA
Tel: (Pitlochry) 01796 472203 Fax: 01796 473586
Email: burnsideapts@sol.co.uk

Important: Prices stated are estimates and may be subject to amendments

tlochry, Perthshire | **Map Ref: 2A1**

★★★★
SELF CATERING

New detached bungalow with own garden, in quiet residential area with open south facing views. Ideal touring base.

1 bungalow, 2 pub rms, 3 bedrms (grd flr avail), sleeps 6, min let 4 days (low season), £190.00-£375.00, Jan-Dec, bus nearby, rail 5 mls, airport 80 mls

Mr and Mrs R D Chadwick
Whinrigg, Aldour, Perth Road, Pitlochry, Perthshire, PH16 5LY
Tel: (Pitlochry) 01796 472330

★★★
SELF CATERING

Spacious self catering apartments of a high standard, set at the centre of this renowned Highland town. Pitlochry Theatre 10 mins walk away.

2 flats, 1 cottage, 1-2 pub rms, 2-3 bedrms (grd flr avail), sleeps 4-6, total sleeping capacity 16, £250.00-£350.00, Jan-Dec, bus nearby, rail nearby, airport 60 mls

Mrs Crowe
Strathgarry Apartments, 113 Atholl Road, Pitlochry, Perthshire, PH16 5AG
Tel: (Pitlochry) 01796 472469

★★
SELF CATERING

Self contained garden flat, quietly situated a mile (1.5 kms) from the centre of Pitlochry. Owners are keen gardeners, with colourful summer flower beds.

1 flat, 1 pub rm, 1 bedrm, sleeps 2, £145.00-£190.00, Apr-Oct, bus 1/4 ml, rail 1 ml, airport 70 mls

Mrs P A David
St Leonard's, Moulin, Pitlochry, Perthshire, PH16 5QZ
Tel: (Pitlochry) 01796 472678

★★★
SELF CATERING

Self contained flat with conservatory, on ground floor of traditional, fully modernised Victorian villa, 150 metres from town centre (no gradients).

1 flat, 1 bedrm (grd flr avail), sleeps 2-4, £205.00-£250.00, Apr-Oct, bus nearby, rail nearby

Mr I Hendry
Vrackie View, Burnside Road, Pitlochry, Perthshire, PH16 5BP
Tel: (Pitlochry) 01796 472080/0411 580127 Fax: 01796 473502

★★★★
SELF CATERING

Modern flat in new residential area, overlooking surrounding hills. 10 minutes walk from the town centre.

1 flat, 1 pub rm, 2 bedrms, sleeps 4, £210.00-£320.00, Jan-Dec, bus 1/2 ml, rail 1/2 ml

Mrs Hohman
Balrobin Hotel, Higher Oakfield, Pitlochry, Perthshire, PH16 5HT
Tel: (Pitlochry) 01796 472901 Fax: 01796 474200

Pitlochry, Perthshire Map Ref: 2A1

★★
SELF CATERING

Traditional stone built cottage of unique charm and character, situated across courtyard from main farmhouse. 15 minutes walk to Pitlochry.

1 cottage, 2 pub rms, 2 bedrms, sleeps 5, £180.00-£355.00, Jan-Dec, bus 1/2 ml, rail 1 ml, airport 40 mls

Mrs Howman
Auchnahyle, Pitlochry, Perthshire, PH16 5JA
Tel: (Pitlochry) 01796 472318 Fax: 01796 473657
Email: howmana@aol.com

★★★★
SELF CATERING

Three bedroomed modern house with private garden. Situated within walking distance of Pitlochry town centre. Refurbished to provide facilities for both able bodied and disabled. One ground floor bedroom and shower room.

1 house, 2 pub rms, 3 bedrms (grd flr avail), sleeps 6, £120.00-£350.00, Jan-Dec, bus nearby, rail 1/2 ml, airport 80 mls

Mrs Leaman
Well House Hotel, 11 Toberargan Road, Pitlochry, Perthshire, PH16 5HG
Tel: 01796 472239

★★★
SELF CATERING

Bungalow situated on outskirts of Pitlochry. Open view to hills and golf course to front. Easy access to town centre and ideal for day trips within Perthshire.

1 bungalow, 2 pub rms, sleeps 8, £325.00-£525.00, Jan-Dec, bus 200 yds

Mr & Mrs Mackay
Buttonboss Lodge, 25 Atholl Road, Pitlochry, PH16 5BX
Tel: (Pitlochry) 01796 472065

★★★
SELF CATERING

Restored cottage with own small garden situated in grounds of Craigroyston Guest House. South facing views over the town to the hills beyond.

1 cottage, 2 pub rms, 2 bedrms, sleeps 4, £150.00-£390.00, Jan-Dec, bus 1/4 ml, rail 1/4 ml, airport 65 mls

Mrs G Maxwell
Craigroyston Lodge, 2 Lower Oakfield, Pitlochry, Perthshire, PH16 5HQ
Tel: (Pitlochry) 01796 472053 Fax: 01796 472053

★★★★
SELF CATERING

Luxury two bedroomed ground floor apartment on exclusive new development. Quietly set within walking distance of town centre.

1 flat, 1 pub rm, 2 bedrms (grd flr avail), sleeps 4, £200.00-£340.00, Jan-Dec, bus 1/2 ml, rail 1/2 ml

Mr & Mrs R Mitchell
7 Commander's Grove, Braco, Perthshire, FK15 9PL
Tel: (Braco) 01786 880574 Fax: 01786 880574

lochry, Perthshire **Map Ref: 2A1**

SELF
ATERING

Stonebuilt house, totally rebuilt with three apartments situated in quiet location in elevated position, close to the town centre with fine views of hills and Tummel Valley.

3 flats, 1 pub rm, 2 bedrms (grd flr avail), sleeps 4, total sleeping capacity 12, min let 1 night, £150.00-£400.00, Jan-Dec, bus 500 yds, rail 1/2 ml, airport 63 mls

Mrs Stephenson
Derrybeg Guest House, 18 Lower Oakfield, Pitlochry, Perthshire, PH16 5DS
Tel: (Pitlochry) 01796 472070

SELF
ATERING

Comfortable cottage attached to main house, in quiet location, yet convenient for town centre. Private parking.

1 cottage, 1 pub rm, 1 bedrm (grd flr avail), sleeps 2, £190.00-£235.00, Apr-Oct, bus 400 yds, rail 500 yds, airport 60 mls

Mrs Y Stewart
Elnagar, 2 Knockard Road, Pitlochry, Perthshire, PH16 5HJ
Tel: (Pitlochry) 01796 472871

Pitlochry, Perthshire **Map Ref: 2A1**

SCOTTISH TOURIST BOARD INSPECTED

Booking Enquiries: Mr & Mrs Malcolm Carr, Dalshian Holidays, Dalshian House, Old Perth Road, Pitlochry, Perthshire, PH16 5JS
Tel: (Pitlochry) 01796 472173

8 Holiday Caravans to let, sleep 4-6 £160.00-270.00, total sleeping capacity 46, min let 2 days, Apr-Oct.

Leisure facilities:

From Perth turn right approx. 1ml before Pitlochry, signed Dalshian. From Pitlochry turn left before A9 at sign Dalshian.

SELF
ATERING

Attractive stone built cottage with views over the River Tay. Five miles south of Pitlochry off the A827 Aberfeldy road. Garden with lovely views.

1 cottage, 2 pub rms, 2 bedrms (grd flr avail), sleeps 4, £225.00-£275.00, Jan-Dec, bus nearby, rail 6 mls

Mrs F Davidson
Tigh-na-Cnoc, Logierait, Pitlochry, Perthshire, PH9 0LH
Tel: (Pitlochry) 01796 482240 Fax: 01796 482240

By Pitlochry, Perthshire **Map Ref: 2A1**

Logierait Pine Lodges

Logierait, by Pitlochry, Perthshire PH9 OLH
Telephone: 01796 482253 Fax: 01796 48225

★★ SELF CATERING
Resident Proprietors: Mr & Mrs E Brodie

So peaceful with wonderful views, these chalets are beautifully situated on the banks of the River Tay. Fitted out to the highest standard for self-catering comfort and open all year. Extremely wa with double glazing and electric heating.
All have colour TV, refrigerators, full-sized cooke quality beds and fitted carpets. Bath and shower. Ideal centre for touring, golfing, birdwatching or j relaxing. River Tay coarse fishing free to residen Salmon fishing, shooting and stalking by arrangement.

Colour brochure by return. Stamp appreciated.

★★ SELF CATERING

Lodges located in a beautiful riverside setting, yet only a few minutes drive from Pitlochry.

15 chalets, 1 pub rm, 1-3 bedrms, sleeps 2-8, total sleeping capacity 82, £160.00-£500.00, Jan-Dec, bus nearby, rail 5 mls, airport 60 mls

Mr & Mrs E Brodie
Logierait Pine Lodges, Logierait, by Pitlochry, Perthshire, PH9 OLH
Tel: (Ballinluig) 01796 482253 Fax: 01796 482253

★★ SELF CATERING

Situated on working sheep farm, set back from A924, affording scenic views over Strathardle, 6 miles (10kms) from Pitlochry.

1 house, 1 pub rm, 3 bedrms, sleeps 4-6, £175.00-£325.00, Jan-Dec, bus 6 mls, rail 6 mls

Mrs Catherine J Michie
Clunskea Farmhouse, Enochdhu, by Blairgowrie, Perthshire, PH10 7
Tel: (Strathardle) 01250 881358/881361

★★★ SELF CATERING

Semi-detached Victorian stone built cottage retaining some period features. Garden centre, food stop and hotel bar nearby, with Pitlochry only 4 miles distance. White water rafting at Grantully and other outdoor activities.

1 cottage, 2 pub rms, 2 bedrms, sleeps 4, £190.00-£300.00, Jan-Dec, bus nearby, rail 5 mls

Kathleen Yates
Cherry Cottage, Ballinluig, by Pitlochry, Perthshire, PH9 OLG
Tel: (Ballinluig) 01796 482409 Fax: 01796 482409

tenweem, Fife Map Ref: 2D3

SELF ATERING

19c semi-detached house in East Neuk village centre, with large south facing garden. Quality garden furniture. Fine views over Firth of Forth. Easy access to the new Fife Coastal Path Walk.

1 house, 2 pub rms, 2 bedrms, sleeps 5-7, £190.00-£320.00, Jan-Dec, bus nearby

Mrs N I Sneddon
Glenlusset, 21 Redwood Crescent, Bishopton, Renfrewshire, PA7 5DJ
Tel: (Bishopton) 01505 862398/0141 887 9866 Fax: 0141 887 9993

nnoch Station, Perthshire Map Ref: 1G1

SELF ATERING

Cottages individual in character, on a 25 acre estate, with direct access to lochside. Boats for hire.

2 houses, 1 cottage, 1-2 pub rms, 2 bedrms, sleeps 4, total sleeping capacity 12, min let 2 nights, £165.00-£300.00, Jan-Dec, bus 200 yds, rail 5 mls

Mrs Jacqueline Murphy
The Factor's Office, Rannoch Lodge, Bridge of Gaur, by Pitlochry, Perthshire, PH17 2QD
Tel: (Bridge of Gaur) 01882 633204 Fax: 01882 633204

Andrews, Fife Map Ref: 2D2

SELF ATERING

A variety of properties in the St Andrews area. Ideal location for golfing and touring. Blue pendant award for beach. Some properties STB inspected.

Eve Brown Properties
23 Argyle Street, St Andrews, Fife, KY16 9BX
Tel: (ST Andrews) 01334 479900 Fax: 01334 478855

St Andrews, Fife | **Map Ref: 2D2**

SELF CATERING

Ground floor flat of a detached villa, south facing with conservatory and garden complete with garden furniture. Newly refurbished throughout. Modern kitchen and bathroom with bath and shower. All linen and towels supplied. Ideal for families young and old or golfers. Only 7 mins walk from the beach and the 1st tee of the R. &A. golf course and 2 mins. walk from all the towns amenities, yet in a quiet secluded spot with car parking facilities.

1 flat, 1 pub rm, 2 bedrms, sleeps 4, £200.00-£375.00, JAN-DEC, bus 5 mls, rail 5 mls, airport 40 mls

Mrs V Browning
2 Sinclair Avenue, Bearsden, Glasgow G61 3BT
Tel: 0141 9427498 Fax: 0141 563 9946

SELF CATERING

Terraced town house, central close to shops, restaurants, beach and golf course. Ideal for families or golfers.

1 house, 1 pub rm, 3 bedrms, sleeps 5, £320.00-£370.00, Jun-Aug, bus nearby, rail 5 mls

Mrs Cheng
31 Langham Way, Ely, Cambridgeshire, CB6 1DZ
Tel: (Ely) 01353 662723

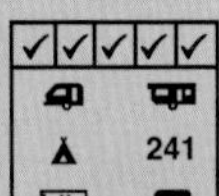

Craigtoun Meadows Holiday Park
Mount Melville, St Andrews, Fife, KY16 8PQ Tel: (St Andrews) 01334 475959 Fax: 01334 476424 Email: craigtoun@aol.com Web:

32 acres, mixed, Mar-Oct, prior booking in peak periods, latest time of arrival 2100, overnight holding area. Extra charge for awnings.

95 tourers £12.50-13.50 or 95 motors £12.50-13.50 or 98 tents £12.50-13.50. Total Touring Pitches 98.

32 Holiday Caravans to let, sleep 4-6 £170.00-425.00, total sleeping capacity 202, min let 3 days (low season).

Leisure facilities:

From M90 (Jct 8) take A91 to St Andrews turn right 400 yds after Guardbridge, signposted Strathkinness. Turn left at second crossroads after Strathkinness.

SELF CATERING

Victorian school, tastefully converted and set in two thirds of an acre of attractive, peaceful garden. Country setting, yet only 4 miles (6 kms) from St Andrews.

1 house, 3 pub rms, 3 bedrms, sleeps 6, £350.00-£650.00, Jan-Dec, bus 1 ml, rail 4 mls, airport 15 mls

Mr Graham Drummond
17 St Ronan's Circle, Peterculter, Aberdeen, AB14 0NE
Tel: (Aberdeen) 01224 732874 Fax: 01224 732874
Email: drummond@mcmail.com

SELF CATERING

Self-contained cottage, forming part of Law Park House. 1 mile from the centre of St Andrews, with it's beautiful beaches and famous golf courses. South facing sun terrace. Private parking.

1 house, 1 pub rm, 5 bedrms (grd flr avail), sleeps 7, £350.00-£550.00, Jan-Dec, bus at door, rail 5 mls

Mr S Fleming
Law Park House, 120 Hepburn Gardens, St Andrews, Fife, KY16 9
Tel: (St Andrews) 01334 477991

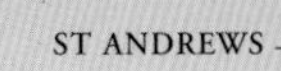

★★

SELF CATERING

Semi-detached modern villa on private estate 1 mile from town centre - small well stocked gardens. Telephone for incoming calls. Walking distance to Safeways - open till 10pm. Edinburgh/Dundee bus passes end of road.

1 house, 2 pub rms, 3 bedrms (grd flr avail), sleeps 5, £200.00-£240.00, Jun-Sep, bus nearby, rail 5 mls

Mrs M Hill
6 Ventnor Terrace, Edinburgh, EH9 2BL
Tel: 0131 667 4360
Email: hill@ednet.co.uk

★★ UP TO ★★★

SELF CATERING

Attractive Victorian town house on the cliff above St Andrews bay and overlooking the old course. Peaceful setting and private parking in large secluded garden.

1 house, 1 flat, 1 cottage, 1 pub rm, 2-5 bedrms (grd flr avail), sleeps 5-10, total sleeping capacity 21, £240.00-£950.00, Jun-Sep, bus 1/4 ml, rail 4 mls

Mrs A R Hippisley
Rockview, The Scores, St Andrews, Fife, KY16 9AR
Tel: (St Andrews) 01334 475844

★★★★

SELF CATERING

A Listed, terraced house of character in the centre of St. Andrews. Restored period features. Gardens. Only 3 minutes from the beach, golf and all town's amenities.

1 house, 2 pub rms, 4 bedrms (grd flr avail), sleeps 7-9, £500.00-£600.00, Jun-Sep, bus nearby, rail 5 mls, airport 40 mls

Lady Hirst
Glentirran, Kippen, Stirlingshire, FK8 3JA
Tel: 01786 870283 Fax: 01786 870679

★★

SELF CATERING

The cottage is a wing of the Hirsel 19th century house, but is totally self contained with a pleasant side garden. Car parking and direct access to St Andrews foreshore, close to old course and sealife centre, families and dogs welcome.

1 flat, 1 cottage, 1-2 pub rms, 4 bedrms (grd flr avail), sleeps 6, total sleeping capacity 12, £350.00-£400.00, Jun-Sep, bus 1/4 ml, rail 5 mls, airport 50 mls

Mrs L Kinsley
The Hirsel, 50 The Scores, St Andrews, KY16 9AS
Tel: 01334 472578

★★★★

SELF CATERING

Newly built ground floor flat in centre of St. Andrews. Very high standard throughout. Own parking.

2 flats, 1 pub rm, 2 bedrms, sleeps 4, total sleeping capacity 8, £306.00-£765.00, Jan-Dec, bus 300 yds, rail 3 mls, airport 55 mls

John G Parker
Morton of Pitmilly, Kingsbarns, St Andrews, Fife, KY16 8QF
Tel: (Boarhills) 01334 880466
Email: mop@sol.co.uk
Web: www.pitmilly,co.uk

VAT is shown at 17.5%: changes in this rate may affect prices.

Key to symbols is on back flap.

St Andrews, Fife **Map Ref: 2D2**

SELF CATERING

Central well equipped three bedroomed flat overlooking St Andrews market place and with secure city centre parking. Within walking distance of all amenities including shops, restaurants, churches, golf courses, beaches and leisure centre.

1 flat, £250.00-£330.00, Jun-Sep

Dr & Mrs Prudhoe
29 L'Arbre Cres, Whickham, Newcastle-upon-Tyne, NE16 5YQ
Tel: (Newcastle-upon-Tyne) 0191 4886273

SELF CATERING

Quietly located town house with south facing walled garden. Only minutes from Byre Theatre, cinemas and shops. In free parking zone. Available all year. Pets by arrangement.

1 house, 1 pub rm, 3 bedrms, sleeps 5, £250.00-£430.00, Jan-Dec, bus 1/2 ml, rail 6 mls

Struan Robertson
Carslogie House, Carslogie Road, Cupar
Tel: 01334 657856/7 Fax: 01334 657856/7

SELF CATERING

Town house close to Old Course, beach, University and all Amenities.

1 house, 1 pub rm, 5 bedrms (grd flr avail), sleeps 9, £400.00-£450.00, Jun-Sep, bus 500 yds, rail 4 mls, airport 14 mls

Susan Sinclair
The Thistles, 7 Albany Place, St Andrews, Fife KY16 9HH
Tel: (St Andrews) 01334 479823 Fax: 01334 479823

★★★★

SELF CATERING

Spacious farmhouse situated on working farm, recently refurbished to high standard with fine views over surrounding countryside. Approx 2 miles (3kms) from St Andrews.

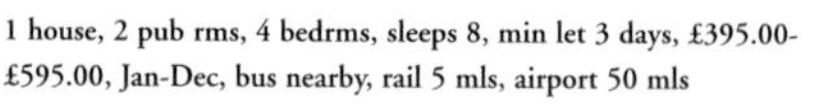

1 house, 2 pub rms, 4 bedrms, sleeps 8, min let 3 days, £395.00-£595.00, Jan-Dec, bus nearby, rail 5 mls, airport 50 mls

Mrs G Stephen
Inchdairnie Properties, 9 Bell Street, St Andrews, Fife, KY16 9UR
Tel: (St Andrews) 01334 477011 Fax: 01334 478643

SELF CATERING

Tastefully modernised and refurbished terraced cottage in quiet residential street. Close to the town centre with enclosed rear garden. Parking space in grounds.

1 house, 1 pub rm, 2 bedrms, sleeps 4, £275.00-£375.00, Jan-Dec, bus 1 ml, rail 10 mls

Mrs E M Thomson
Ravenswood, Tighnabruaich, Argyll, PA21 2EE
Tel: (Tighnabruaich) 01700 811603

Important: Prices stated are estimates and may be subject to amendments

★★

SELF CATERING

Comfortable sunny flat forming part of large family house. Quiet residential area 1 mile (2kms) from town centre. Private entrance with direct access to large sunny garden and open country beyond.

1 flat, 1 pub rm, 1 bedrm (grd flr avail), sleeps 3, £160.00-£170.00, Apr-Oct, bus 1 ml, rail 6 mls, airport 60 mls

Dr & Mrs D P Tunstall
4 West Acres, St Andrews, Fife, KY16 9UD
Tel: (St Andrews) 01334 473507

★★

SELF CATERING

Pine lodges of similar style, situated on private site, amidst rolling countryside with fine views. 3 miles (5kms) from St Andrews.

9 log cabins, 1 pub rm, 2 bedrms, sleeps 4, total sleeping capacity 36, £200.00-£415.00, Jan-Dec, bus 1/2 ml, rail 2 mls, airport 40 mls

Miss Pamela Smith, Woodland Holidays
Kincaple Lodge, Kincaple, St Andrews, Fife, KY16 9SH
Tel: (Strathkinness) 01334 850217 Fax: 01334 850217

★★★★

SELF CATERING

A choice selection of quality properties in St Andrews or on our private country estate nearby. Real country living for country lovers. A home for all seasons. Doo'cote Cottage is equipped for guests with disabilities and has wheelchair facilities.

4 houses, 6 cottages, 1-2 pub rms, 2-6 bedrms, sleeps 4-12, total sleeping capacity 65, £235.00-£855.00, Jan-Dec, bus 2 mls, rail 5 mls, airport 50 mls.

Mrs Andrew Wedderburn
Mountquhanie Holiday Homes, Cupar, by St Andrews, Fife, KY15 4QJ
Tel: (Gauldry) 01382 330252 Fax: 01382 330480

St Andrews, Fife

Map Ref: 2D2

★★★

SELF CATERING

19th century mansion house and stone built cottages in 30 acres of peaceful grounds. Nature walks, trout streams, riding, badmington, putting etc. St Andrews 3 miles (5kms). Easy access to Fife's signed cycle routes and new coastal path walks.

7 houses, 8 flats, 1 pub rm, 1-4 bedrms (grd flr avail), sleeps 2-7, total sleeping capacity 80, £195.00-£420.00, Jan-Dec, bus nearby, rail 7 mls, airport 14 mls

Mr & Mrs Chalmers
Stravithie Country Estate, Stravithie,by St Andrews, Fife, KY16 8LT
Tel: (Boarhills) 01334 880251 Fax: 01334 880297

VAT is shown at 17.5%: changes in this rate may affect prices.

Key to symbols is on back flap.

By St Andrews, Fife

Map Ref: 2D2

SELF CATERING

Stone-built cottage on working farm in peaceful, rural location. Close to forest walks. Sandy beach only 1.5 miles (2.5 kms). Close to St Andrews and main line railway station to Edinburgh-Aberdeen.

2 cottages, 1 pub rm, 2 bedrms, sleeps 4, total sleeping capacity 4, £180.00-£235.00, Jun-Sep, bus 1 1/2 mls, rail 2 mls, airport 12 mls

Mr A Clark
Cast Farm, Leuchars, Fife, KY16 0DP
Tel: (Leuchars) 01334 839524

SELF CATERING

Converted farmhouse and steadings in natural stone, each of individual character and design, situated around landscaped courtyard.

3 houses, 2 cottages, 1-2 pub rms, 2-4 bedrms (grd flr avail), sleeps 4-8, total sleeping capacity 29, min let 2 nights, £185.00-£525.00, Jan-Dec, bus nearby, rail 3 mls

Mrs Joan Inglis
Dron Court Holidays, 8 Dunure Place, Newton Mearns, Glasgow, G77 5SZ
Tel: 0141 616 3491 Fax: 0141 616 3491

SELF CATERING

Traditional farm cottages and old large farmhouse refurbished to a high standard, many with open fireplace. Rural location yet ideal for St Andrews, Crail and Fife coast.

1 house, 9 cottages, 2-3 pub rms, Sypsies Farm House,Crail bedrms (grd flr avail), sleeps 2-12, total sleeping capacity 57, min let 3 nights, £250.00-£1300.00, Jan-Dec, bus 1 ml, rail 15 mls

Mrs L Logan
Kingask House, St Andrews, Fife, KY16 8PN
Tel: (St Andrews) 01334 472011 Fax: 01334 473264
Email: kcc@easynet.co.uk
Web: www.calling-scotland/kingas/index.htm

★★

SELF CATERING

Terraced farm cottage in rural position, 4 miles (6kms) from St Andrews with easy access to East Neuk villages and beaches. Enclosed rear garden and ample car parking.

1 cottage, 1 pub rm, 3 bedrms, sleeps 5, £190.00-£300.00, Jan-Dec, bus nearby, rail 9 mls, airport 20 mls

Mrs S Paterson
Carloonan, Mawcarse, Milnathort, Kinross-shire, KY13 7SQ
Tel: (Kinross) 01577 862816 Fax: 01577 862816

St Fillans, Perthshire

Map Ref: 1H2

SELF CATERING

Modernnised self-catering apartments located in the village of St Fillans on Loch Earn side. Peaceful setting. Good base for exploring all of Perthshire, Tayside, Stirlingshire and the Trossachs. Boat, bike hire available locally. Excellent countryside for the outdoor enthusiast. Horseriding in nearby Comrie, 3 miles.

2 flats, 2 pub rms, 1 bedrm (grd flr avail), sleeps 2-4, total sleeping capacity 8, £120.00-£240.00, Jan-Dec, bus nearby, rail 28 mls, airport 60 mls

Mr John Murray
Achray House Hotel, St Fillans, Crieff, PH6 2NF
Tel: 01764 685231 Fax: 01764 685320

Important: Prices stated are estimates and may be subject to amendments

Monans, Fife — **Map Ref: 2D3**

★

SELF CATERING

Late 19th century fisherman's house in quiet location in village. Enclosed back garden opening onto playing field, bowling green and children's play park. Near coastal path, harbour and public transport.

1 house, £280.00-£350.00, Jun-Sep, bus nearby

Mrs Fyall Boyter
Holmwood,123 Steynton Road, Milford Haven, Dyfed, Wales, SA73 1AH
Tel: (Milford Haven) 01646 692936

★★★

SELF CATERING

Fisherman's cottage with garden gate onto the village green. Quiet position in picturesque fishing village. 100 yards from Fife Coastal Path Walk.

1 house, 2 pub rms, 3 bedrms, sleeps 6, £250.00-£375.00, Jan-Dec, bus 200 yds, rail 16 mls, airport 45 mls

Mrs B Wallace
16 Inglis Road, Colchester, Essex, CO3 3HU
Tel: (Colchester) 01206 547835
Email: wallace@anglia.net.co.uk

---

ne, by Perth, Perthshire — **Map Ref: 2B2**

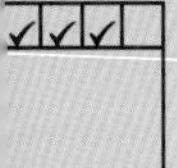

Scone Palace Holiday Caravans
Booking Enquiries: Balformo Enterprises Ltd Estate Office, Scone Palace, Scone, Perth, PH2 6BD
Tel: (Perth) 01738 552308 Fax: 01738 552588

20 Holiday Caravans to let, sleep 4-8 £140.00-400.00, total sleeping capacity 160, min let 2 nights.

Leisure facilities:

From Perth take A93. Turn onto Stormontfield road then onto drive to racecourse.

★★★

SELF CATERING

Newly renovated semi-detached stone cottage, comfortable and centrally located in village of New Scone. 2 miles (3km) from centre of Perth. Off-street parking available.

1 cottage, 1 pub rm, 2 bedrms, sleeps 4, £200.00-£325.00, May-Oct, bus 300 yds, rail 2 mls, airport 50 mls

Mrs Averill Fraser
27 Newmills Crescent, Balerno, Midlothian, EH14 5SX
Tel: 0131 449 3535 Fax: 0131 467 6055

Strathyre, Perthshire

Map Ref: 1H3

Tigh Na Carraig House. Log fires. Magnificent mountain views in extensive wooded garden grounds. Exclusive parking. Laundry facilities. Cosy home with real comfort.

1 log cabin, 1 house, 1-2 pub rms, 1-2 bedrms (grd flr avail), sleeps 2-6, total sleeping capacity 10, £120.00-£400.00, Jan-Dec.

Lisa & Colin Beattie
Hareswith Holt, Storrington, West Sussex, RH20 3EY
Tel: 01903 741000 Fax: 01903 741000

Spittal of Glenshee, Perthshire

Map Ref: 4D12

Modern log cabins with magnificent all round views of the glen. Very quiet situation. Ideal for skiing, walking, birdwatching or touring.

3 chalets, 2 log cabins, 1 pub rm, 2-3 bedrms, sleeps 2-6, total sleeping capacity 24, £175.00-£395.00, Jan-Dec, bus 19 mls, rail 36 mls, airport 80 mls

Mr D Stewart
Glenbeag Mountain Lodges, Spittal of Glenshee, Blairgowrie, Perthshire, PH10 7QE
Tel: (Glenshee) 01250 885204 Fax: 01250 885261

Tayport, Fife

Map Ref: 2D2

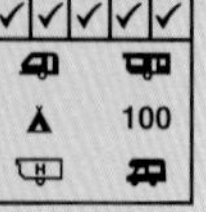

100

Tayport Caravan Park

East Common, Tayport, Fife, DD6 9ES Tel: (Tayport) 01382 552334 Fax: 01337 870441 Email: largolp@aol.com
Web: http://members.aol.com/largolp

4 acres, grassy, sandy, hard-standing, Mar-Oct, prior booking in peak periods, latest time of arrival 2000. Extra charge for electricity, awnings.

30 tourers or 30 motors or 30 tents. Total Touring Pitches 30. Charges on application

Holiday Caravan to let, sleeps 6, min let 3 nights.

Leisure facilities:

B945 to town centre. Signposted to Park.

Tummel Bridge, Perthshire

Map Ref: 2A1

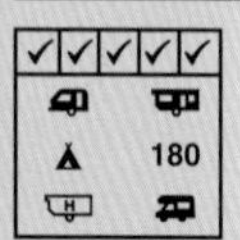

180

Tummel Valley Holiday Park

Tummel Bridge, Perthshire, PH16 5SA Tel: (Tummel Bridge) 01882 634221 Fax: 01882 634302
Booking Enquiries: Haven Reservations PO Box 218, 1 Park Lane, Hemel Hempstead, Herts, HP2 4GL
Tel: 0990 233111

55 acres, level, sloping, Apr-Oct, prior booking in peak periods, latest time of arrival 2100, overnight holding area. Extra charge for electricity, awnings.

40 tourers £10.00-17.00 or 40 motors £10.00-17.00. Total Touring Pitches 40. No tents.

82 Holiday Caravans to let, sleep 4-8 £162.00-520.00, total sleeping capacity 420, min let 2 nights.

Leisure facilities:

Take B8019 to Tummel Bridge, by leaving A9 1 1/2 mls N of Pitlochry. The park is 1 mls on left.

Wormit, Fife

Map Ref: 2C2

Ground floor property of a substantial stone building with views across the Tay to Dundee. Small garden and lockable shed providing cycle storage. Centrally heated throughout the year therefore suitable for off season breaks. Coastal walk from the front door.

1 Ground floor of substantial stone , 1 pub rm, 1 bedrm (grd flr avail), sleeps 2, min let 3 nights, £250.00, Jan-Dec, bus nearby, rail 6 mls, airport 35 mls

Mrs Martha Simpson
118 Munro Road, Jordanhill, Glasgow, G13 1SE
Tel: (Jordanhill) 0141 959 1037/950 1142 Fax: 0141 950 1142

Important: Prices stated are estimates and may be subject to amendments

Grampian Highlands, Aberdeen and the North East Coast

This is one of the most characterful areas in all of Scotland. It runs down from the high granites of the Cairngorm mountains down to a superb coastline. Between are high hills and wooded farmlands, river valleys and little towns, as well as Aberdeen, Scotland's third largest city, lying between the mouths of the Rivers Dee and Don.

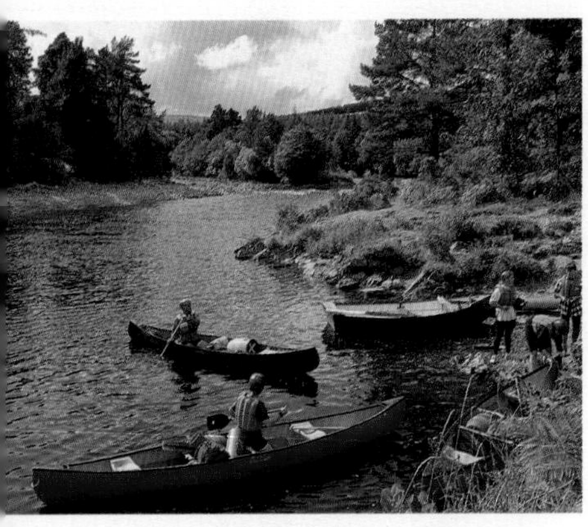

As a major Scottish centre, Aberdeen offers plenty for visitors: museums, art gallery, leisure centres, theatre, arts centre and, given the city's preoccupation with flowers, splendid parks, including Europe's largest glasshouse, the Winter Gardens in the Duthie Park. Children are also very well catered for with one of Scotland's largest funfairs and also the Satrosphere, a hands-on science discovery centre, among the many attractions. There is also a superb choice of accommodation and places to eat and drink.

Aberdeen is the gateway to Royal Deeside. This attractive area gained its fame through association with the royal family and their holiday home at Balmoral. However, there is plenty more to enjoy along the valley of the River Dee, including walking, climbing and nature interest, as well as castles and a distillery, the Royal Lochnagar.

All rivers lead to the sea – and no visit here is complete without sampling the coastline.

Malt whisky distilling is most strongly associated with the valley of the River Spey, within easy reach over the hills from the Dee. On Speyside, signposts guide you round the unique Malt Whisky Trail – more distilleries (and the Speyside Cooperage) to visit, as well as very attractive scenery of river-valley birch and pine, with high moors as a backdrop. (Most of the distilleries are open to visitors all year.) Yet another river valley is also worth discovering: the River Don also has many enthusiasts and leads past places like Kildrummy Castle, one of the finest of Scotland's mediaeval ruins, and also Kildrummy Castle Gardens. The birchwoods of the Dee, Don and the lower Spey in particular are a photographer's delight in autumn.

All rivers lead to the sea – and no visit here is complete without sampling the coastline. Find long empty beaches at places like Cruden Bay (superb golf as well) or Lossiemouth or awesome rocks and cliffs at the Bullers of Buchan near Peterhead or at many points on the Moray Firth coast. (Look for puffins, too.) There is also wildlife interest in plenty at the Loch of Strathbeg, a wintering ground of international importance for geese. Or discover photogenic little villages tucked below the cliffs at places like Pennan or Gardenstown. Birdwatchers will enjoy the seabird colonies in late spring, as well as the geese in winter.

Some more of the area's major attractions outside Aberdeen include Duff House, set within parkland in the attractive little coastal town of Banff.

This country house gallery is an outstation of the National Gallery of Scotland. Scotland's Lighthouse Museum at Kinnaird Head in Fraserburgh should also not be missed. It features not only a fascinating portrait of the traditions of two centuries of lighthouse keeping but also a tour of Kinnaird Lighthouse itself, on top of a 16th century castle. Both places open all year.

There is lots more to see, notably another local speciality – castles. The best of them are on the Castle Trail which takes in everything from ancient fortresses evolving into grand homes through the centuries, such as Fyvie, to elegant mansions like Haddo House. Lots of variety in city, countryside or coast.

Events

Grampian Highlands, Aberdeen and The North-east

Apr 16– 19

The Speyside Scotch Whisky Festival
Various venues in Speyside. Festival celebrating malt whisky.
Contact: Aberdeen & Grampian Tourist Board.
Tel: 01343 542666.

July 3 – 4

Portsoy Traditional Boat Festival
Features racing, traditional craft demonstrations, art, music, dance and drama. Portsoy.
Contact: Richard Leith.
Tel: 01261 813218.

July 16 – 18

Stonehaven Folk Festival
Contact: Charlie West .
Tel: 01569 765063.

Aug 4 – 14

Aberdeen International Youth Festival
Various venues in Aberdeen.
Contact: Nicola Wallis.
Tel: 0181 946 2995.

Sep 4

Braemar Highland Gathering
Princess Royal and Duke of Fife Memorial Park, Braemar.
Contact: W A Meston
Tel: 01339 755377.

Sep 10 – 19

Techfest
Annual Science Festival. Various venues in Aberdeen.
Contact: Vivienne Shute.
Tel: 01224 273161.

Oct 14 – 23

Aberdeen Alternative Festival
Mixture of music, dance and drama.
Contact: Paul Massey.
Tel: 01224 635822.

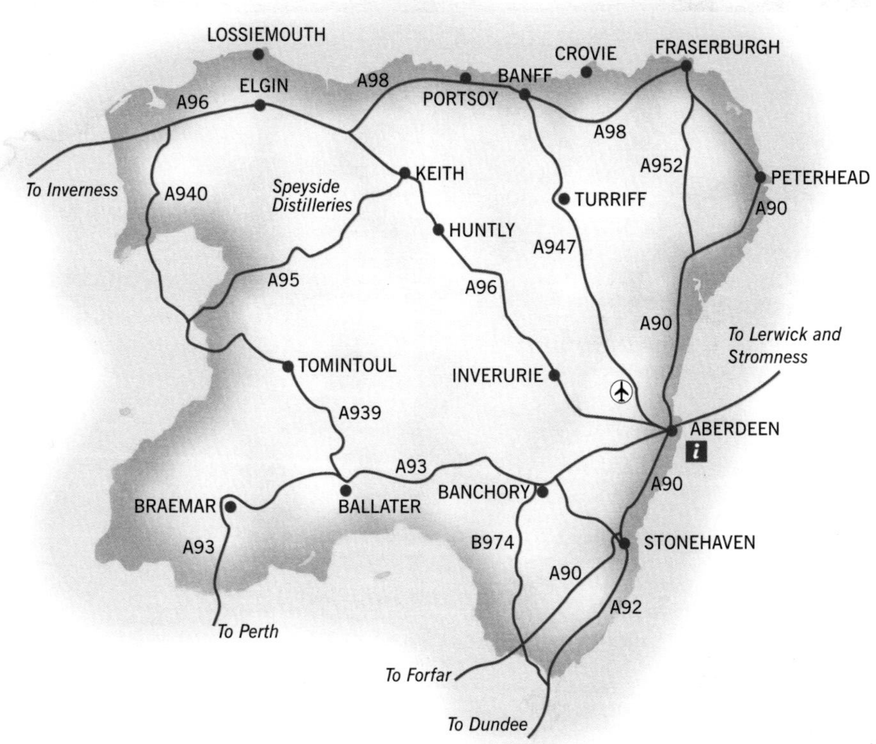

Area Tourist Board Addresses

Aberdeen and Grampian Tourist Board
27 Albyn Place
ABERDEEN
AB10 1YL
Tel: 01224 632727
Tel: 01330 825917
(Advance Accommodation Reservations)
Fax: 01224 581367
e.mail: tourism@agtb.org
website: www.agtb.org

Grampian Highlands, Aberdeen and the North East Coast

Tourist Information Centres in Scotland

ABERDEEN AND GRAMPIAN TOURIST BOARD

ABERDEEN ♿ ✉
St Nicholas House
Broad Street
AB9 1DE
Tel: (01224) 632727
Jan-Dec

ALFORD ♿
Railway Museum
Station Yard
Tel: (019755) 62052
April-Oct

BALLATER
Station Square
Tel: (013397) 55306
Easter-end Oct

BANCHORY ♿ ✉
Bridge Street
AB31 3SX
Tel: (01330) 822000
Jan-Dec

BANFF ✉
Collie Lodge
AB45 1AU
Tel: (01261) 812419
April-Oct

BRAEMAR ♿
The Mews
Mar Road
Tel: (013397) 41600
Jan-Dec

CRATHIE
Car Park
Balmoral Castle
Tel: (013397) 42414
Easter-Oct

DUFFTOWN
Clock Tower
The Square
Tel: (01340) 820501
April-Oct

ELGIN ✉
17 High Street
IV30 1EG
Tel: (01343) 542666
Jan-Dec

FORRES
116 High Street
Tel: (01309) 672938
April-Oct

FRASERBURGH
Saltoun Square
Tel: (01346) 518315
April-Oct

HUNTLY ♿
9a The Square
Tel: (01466) 792255
April-Oct

INVERURIE ♿
18 High Street
Tel: (01467) 625800
Jan-Dec

STONEHAVEN
66 Allardice Street
Tel: (01569) 762806
Easter-End Oct

TOMINTOUL
The Square
Tel: (01807) 580285
April-Oct

✉ Accept written enquiries
♿ Disabled access

Aberchirder, by Huntly, Banffshire

Map Ref: 4F8

Extensively refurbished holiday house on working farm. Centrally heated and double glazed. Plenty local interests including distilleries and castles.

1 house, 2 pub rms, 3 bedrms, sleeps 6-8, £160.00-£250.00, Feb-Nov, bus nearby, rail 10 mls, airport 40 mls

Mrs A Hay
Mill of Auchintoul, Aberchirder,by Huntly, Aberdeenshire, AB54 5RE
Tel: (Aberchirder) 01466 780349

Aberdeen

Map Ref: 4G10

★★★
SELF CATERING

A small charming cottage in a unique spot beside the River Don and Brig O' Balgonie. Quiet tranquility and wildlife right on your doorstep. Seals, geese, ducks and birdlife in abundance, this area is designated number one conservation area. 2 miles to city centre, 5 miles to airport.

1 cottage, 1 pub rm, 2 bedrms (grd flr avail), sleeps 2-4, £200.00-£290.00, Jan-Dec, bus 1/4 ml, rail 2 mls, ferry 2 mls, airport 5 mls

Mr Abraham
Nether Don, Don Street, Old Aberdeen, Aberdeen, AB24 1XP
Tel: (Aberdeen) 01224 488321 Fax: 01224 488650

An innovative new development of executive accommodation. Ideally situated in the west end of Aberdeen. On main bus route to city centre. Extensive private parking.

49 flats, 1 pub rm, 2 bedrms, sleeps 4-5, total sleeping capacity 245, min let 1 night, £430.00-£500.00, Jan-Dec, bus nearby, rail 2 mls, airport 6 mls

Burnhaven Properties Ltd
The Spires, 505 Great Western Road, Aberdeen, AB10 6WD
Tel: (Aberdeen) 01224 209991 Fax: 01224 310092

An attractive lodge bungalow with lovely views of woods and fields. Warm, comfortable and charmingly decorated it is a cosy hideaway for two. Within the half acre of fenced garden is a paved picnic spot with table and benches. A multitude of activities with golf, quad driving, horse riding and castle trails in easy driving distance. Aberdeen 9 miles, Dyce Airport 3 miles.

1 cottage, 1 pub rm, 1 bedrm (grd flr avail), sleeps 2, min let 4 days, £175.00-£265.00, Jan-Dec, bus 3 mls, rail 3 mls, ferry 12 mls, airport 4 mls

Mrs I Clarke
Paddockhurst, Kemnay, Inverurie, AB51 5LN
Tel: (Kemnay) 01467 642425

Aberdeen

Map Ref: 4G10

★UP TO ★★

SELF CATERING

Student flats at separate locations, all on or near to main bus routes for city centre. Use of sports facilities.

64 flats, 1 pub rm, 6-8 bedrms (grd flr avail), sleeps 1-8, total sleeping capacity 400, £215.00-£425.00, end May-Aug, bus nearby, rail 2 mls, ferry 2 mls, airport 5 mls

Peggy McInnes

Business & Vacation Accommodation Service, The Robert Gordon University, Schoolhill, Aberdeen, AB10 1FR
Tel: (Aberdeen) 01224 262134 Fax: 01224 262144
Email: accommodation@rgu.ac.uk
Web: www.calling-scotland.co.uk/rgu

✓✓✓✓ 75

Lower Deeside Holiday Park

Maryculter, Aberdeen, AB12 5FX Tel: (Aberdeen) 01224 733860 Fax: 01224 732490

14 acres, grassy, hard-standing, level, Jan-Dec, prior booking in peak periods, overnight holding area. Extra charge for electricity, awnings.

45 tourers £7.00-9.00 or 45 motors £7.00-9.00 or 45 tents £5.00-7.00. Total Touring Pitches 45.

10 Holiday Caravans to let, sleep 6 £165.00-285.00, total sleeping capacity 60, min let 2 nights.

Leisure facilities:

Take B9077 from Aberdeen for 6 mls, or B976 from Stonehaven for 10 mls, or B9077 from Banchory for 10 mls. Park is behind hotel.

★★

SELF CATERING

Spacious modern flat with landscaped gardens in quiet residential area. Centrally situated for all amenities.

1 flat, 1 pub rm, 2 bedrms, sleeps 4, £250.00, Jan-Dec, bus nearby, rail 1 ml, airport 8 mls

Mr D MacRae

8 Whitehill Place, Stirling, FK8 2JL
Tel: (Stirling) 01786 474837 Fax: 01786 474837

Aberlour, Banffshire

Map Ref: 4D8

★★★UP TO ★★★★

SELF CATERING

Fully modernised house and newly built cabin on two floors in 90 acres of farmland on the banks of the River Spey. Free fishing on trout pond. Cabin in secluded location.

1 log cabin, 1 house, 2 pub rms, 4 bedrms (grd flr avail), sleeps 6-8, total sleeping capacity 16, min let 3 days, £250.00-£530.00, Jan-Dec

Mr D Styles

10 Crichelmount Road, Poole, Dorset, BH14 8LT
Tel: (Poole) 01202 709435 Fax: 01202 707472

Aboyne, Aberdeenshire

Map Ref: 4F11

★★ UP TO ★★★★
SELF CATERING

Tastefully refurbished cottages, individual in character, on Highland estate. Wide range of leisure activities available on site and nearby.

2 houses, 2 cottages, 1-2 pub rms, 1-6 bedrms, sleeps 2-12, total sleeping capacity 30, £150.00-£820.00, Feb-Dec, bus 5 mls, rail 35 mls, airport 40 mls

Glen Tanar Estate
Brooks House, Glen Tanar, Aboyne, Aberdeenshire, AB34 5EU
Tel: (Aboyne) 013398 86451/86305 Fax: 013398 86047

★★★
SELF CATERING

Comfortable garden flat, located within easy walking distance of village centre. Convenient for walking, fishing, golf and tourist attractions.

1 house, 1 pub rm, 3 bedrms, sleeps 4-6, £250.00-£300.00, Apr-Oct, bus 1/2 ml, rail 30 mls, airport 30 mls

Mary Levie
Gordon Lodge, Aboyne, Aberdeenshire, AB34 5EL
Tel: (Aboyne) 013398 86466

by Aboyne, Aberdeenshire

Map Ref: 4F11

★★
SELF CATERING

Cosy cottage set in quiet hamlet with surrounding farmland. Two miles to Aboyne. Local adventure centre with wide range of activities.

1 cottage, 3 pub rms, 2 bedrms, sleeps 4, £280.00-£320.00, Jan-Dec, bus 1 ml, rail 30 mls, ferry 30 mls, airport 30 mls

Jonelle Collins
Clashinruich, Glen Gairn, Ballater, AB35 5UR
Tel: (Ballater) 013397 55587 Fax: 013397 55507
Email: admin@stuckpipe.co.uk

★★★
SELF CATERING

Converted steading in rural Deeside, original farmhouse just beside. Ideal area for outdoor pursuits, hills and rivers, bring yer boots.

1 cottage, 1 pub rm, 1 bedrm, sleeps 2, £100.00-£200.00, Jan-Dec, bus nearby, rail 30 mls, airport 30 mls

Donald & Anne Silcock
Oldyleiper Farmhouse, Birse, Aboyne, Aberdeenshire, AB34 5BY
Tel: (Aboyne) 013398 86332 Fax: 013398 87261
Email: 101526.2537@compuserve.com

By Aboyne, Aberdeenshire Map Ref: 4F11

★★★★
SELF CATERING

A cosy east wing of a large granite-built house with extensive landscaped and wooded garden. Lovely scenic views over Aboyne to hills beyond.

1 wing of house, 1 pub rm, 1 bedrm, sleeps 2, min let 3 nights, £138.00-£240.00, Jan-Dec, bus 1 1/2 mls, rail 30 mls, airport 30 mls

Mrs I Strachan
Dorevay, Birse, Aboyne, Aberdeenshire, AB34 5BT
Tel: (Aboyne) 013398 86232

By Alford, Aberdeenshire Map Ref: 4F10

★★★
SELF CATERING

16c Baronial Castle, restored 1968. Modern comforts, with some service. Open fire, grand piano. Set in quiet rural setting with hill views.

1 castle, 3 pub rms, 5 bedrms, sleeps 9, £650.00-£750.00, Jan-Dec, bus 1 ml, rail 12 mls, airport 27 mls

Mr Mark Tennant
30 Abbey Gardens, London, NW8 9AT
Tel: 0171 624 3200

Archiestown, Moray Map Ref: 4D8

★★
SELF CATERING

Traditional cottage with pleasant garden in quiet village. On Whisky Trail and central for Speyside area. Short stroll to Post Office and Hotel.

1 cottage, 1 pub rm, 3 bedrms (grd flr avail), sleeps 4, £90.00-£225.00, Jan-Dec, bus nearby, rail 18 mls, airport 45 mls

Mrs Marian B Mansfield
3A Resaurie, Smithton, Inverness, IV1 2NH
Tel: (Inverness) 01463 791714

Ballater, Aberdeenshire Map Ref: 4E11

★★★
SELF CATERING

Surprisingly spacious traditional stone built cottage set at the heart of this peaceful Royal Deeside village. A fine holiday home and base for a wide range of leisure and sporting activities available in the area.

1 cottage, 1 pub rm, 4 bedrms (grd flr avail), sleeps 8, £250.00-£580.00, Jan-Dec, bus nearby

Dr Paul Chadwick
70 Cluny Gardens, Edinburgh, EH10 6BR
Tel: (Edinburgh) 0131 447 1055

Important: Prices stated are estimates and may be subject to amendments

llater, Aberdeenshire

Map Ref: 4E11

SELF CATERING

Traditional, stone built cottage renovated to a very high standard. One of four in this secluded sunny, south facing spot. Balmoral Castle 7 miles away, Ballater 2 miles. An ideal holiday home set in a wonderfully peaceful situation yet with a wide range of sporting activities including golf, gliding and hillwalking.

1 cottage, 1 pub rm, 3 bedrms (grd flr avail), sleeps 6, £300.00-£450.00, Jan-Dec, bus 1 1/2 mls

Dr C W Gosden
Catbells, Orestan Lane, Effingham, Leatherhead, Surrey, KT24 5SN
Tel: (Bookham) 01372 459123 Fax: 01372 456784

SELF CATERING

Stone built house on outer edge of village, large garden and spectacular views over 15th fairway to the hills.

1 house, 3 pub rms, 3 bedrms (grd flr avail), sleeps 6, £375.00-£500.00, Apr-Oct, bus 1/2 ml, rail 35 mls, airport 35 mls

Mrs Harrison
P.O. Box 24, Inchbroom, Nigg, Aberdeen, AB12 3GF
Tel: (Aberdeen) 01224 897278 Fax: 01224 896954

SELF CATERING

Cosy bungalow cottage set in garden of owners house. Peaceful situation overlooking golf course with club house only 100 meters distance. Easy walking distance of village centre. Numerous leisure activities available in area.

1 bungalow, 2 bedrms (grd flr avail), sleeps 6, £225.00-£275.00, Jan-Dec, bus 300 yds

Ian A Hepburn
67 Golf Road, Ballater, Aberdeenshire, AB35 5RU
Tel: (Ballater) 013397 56025

SELF CATERING

A stylish conversion to a traditional georgian cottage with many artistic touches in centre of Ballater with views of River Dee. Sauna and jacuzzi, sun terrace and private garden.

1 house, 2-3 pub rms, 4-5 bedrms, sleeps 7-8, £450.00-£750.00, Jan-Dec, bus nearby, rail 42 mls, airport 40 mls

Mairi MacLeod
1 Bridge Square, Ballater, Aberdeenshire, AB35 5QJ
Tel: (Ballater) 013397 55056

SELF CATERING

Cosy terraced cottage in picturesque Highland town. Ideal for touring and walking, in Royal Deeside.

1 cottage, 2 pub rms, 2 bedrms, sleeps 4-6, £150.00-£350.00, Jan-Dec, bus nearby, rail 40 mls, airport 40 mls

Mr and Mrs Middleton
255 Holburn Street, Aberdeen, AB10 7FL,
Tel: (Aberdeen) 01224 315607 Fax: 591787

VAT is shown at 17.5%: changes in this rate may affect prices.

Key to symbols is on back flap.

Ballater, Aberdeenshire Map Ref: 4E11

SELF CATERING

Comfort and privacy of your own comfortable furnished lodge with full outdoor activity facilities and an indoor swimming pool, squash court and pool room. A spectacular estate of time share lodges within a peaceful woodland setting with fine views over the valley towards towering Lochnagar.

92 lodges, 1 pub rm, 1-3 bedrms, sleeps 2-8, total sleeping capacity 558, £295.00-£1995.00, Jan-Dec, rail 42 mls, airport 42 mls

Stakis Craigendarroch Resort
Braemar Road, Ballater, AB35 5XA
Tel: (Ballater) 013397 55858 Fax: 013397 56077

SELF CATERING

Traditional Victorian cottage lovingly restored to a bright stylish and comfortable holiday home with safe, sunny enclosed garden.

1 house, 3 pub rms, 3 bedrms (grd flr avail), sleeps 5-6, min let long weekend, £211.00-£520.00, Jan-Dec, bus 1/4 ml, airport 40 mls

Mr J R Wimpenny
Quarmby Farm, Blackmoorfoot, Linthwaite, Huddersfield, Yorkshire, HD7 5TR
Tel: (Huddersfield) 01484 847233 Fax: 01484 846969
Email: jwimpenny@aol.com

By Ballater, Aberdeenshire Map Ref: 4E11

SELF CATERING

A listed former kirk, with spacious family accommodation, tastefully converted into a holiday home in a secluded pine wood setting in beautiful Royal Deeside. An open plan kitchen, sitting room and dining area lead to the galleried bedrooms. Heated by a log burning stove and with tall church windows.

1 cottage, 2 bedrms, sleeps 4-5, £245.00-£385.00, Jan-Dec, rail 35 mls, airport 35 mls

Mrs Ronson
The Manse of the Braes of Cromar, Dinnet,by Ballater, Aberdeenshire AB34 5PS
Tel: (Tarland) 013398 81221/87311 Fax: 013398 87301

Ballindalloch, Banffshire Map Ref: 4D9

SELF CATERING

Surrounded by spectacular scenery and offering many sporting opportunities. Ideal for skiing, fishing, touring or just resting.

1 lodge, 1 pub rm, 3 bedrms (grd flr avail), sleeps 8, £250.00-£650.00, Jan-Dec, bus 1 ml, rail 20 mls, airport 50 mls

Mr Pottinger
Baille Farm, Bridge of Westfield, Thurso, Caithness, KW14 7QW
Tel: (Bridge of Westfield) 01847 871200 Fax: 01847 871222

Banchory, Aberdeenshire Map Ref: 4F11

SELF CATERING

Recently converted cottage and mews studio apartment situated in Banchory centre. Attractively finished and fully equipped.

1 cottage, 1 studio apartment, 1 pub rm, 1 bedrm (grd flr avail), sleeps 2-3, total sleeping capacity 6, £185.00-£220.00, Jan-Dec, bus nearby, rail 20 mls, airport 20 mls

Mrs Kathleen Balsamo
Towerbank House, 93 High Street, Banchory, AB31 5XT
Tel: (Banchory) 01330 824798/822657 Fax: 01330 823443

Important: Prices stated are estimates and may be subject to amendments

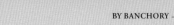

anchory, Aberdeenshire

Map Ref: 4F11

★★

SELF CATERING

Comfortable flat adjoining owners Victorian house in peaceful situation with large garden. Within 200 meters of the centre of Banchory with shops, bars and restaurants in easy walking distance.

1 flat, 3 pub rms, 2 bedrms, sleeps 4-6, £290.00-£400.00, Jan-Dec, bus nearby, rail 17 mls, airport 17 mls

Mrs M Bolland
Arbeadie House, Station Road, Banchory, Kincardineshire, AB31 5YA
Tel: (Banchory) 01330 825898

★★★★

SELF CATERING

Listed cottage, situated within heart of Royal Deeside village, offering charm and comfort. Ideal for fishing and Castle Trail.

1 cottage, 1 pub rm, 2 bedrms (grd flr avail), sleeps 4-5, £225.00-£425.00, Jan-Dec, bus nearby, rail 17 mls, airport 17 mls

Rosalind Holmes
Village Guest House, 83 High Street, Banchory, Kincardineshire, AB31 5TJ
Tel: (Banchory) 01330 823307 Fax: 01330 823307

y Banchory, Aberdeenshire

Map Ref: 4F11

★★

SELF CATERING

Former coach house in grounds of large private house, with own secluded area. Steep stairs to charming first floor flat. 0.5 mile to village.

1 flat, 1 pub rm, 3 bedrms, sleeps 5, £175.00-£250.00, Mar-Oct, bus 1/4 ml, rail 20 mls, airport 20 mls

Mrs J Hutton
Borrowstone House, Kincardine O'Neil, Aboyne, Aberdeenshire, AB34 5AP
Tel: (Kincardine O'Neil) 013398 84264 Fax: 013398 84264

★★

SELF CATERING

A selection of timber cabins set in a peaceful woodland setting with views across fields to hills beyond. A beautiful part of the Royal Deeside region with forest walks, castles and gardens. A wide range of outdoor activities available in the area.

7 chalets, 1 pub rm, 1-2 bedrms (grd flr avail), sleeps 3-5, total sleeping capacity 32, £99.00-£268.00, Jan-Dec, bus on route, rail 20 mls, airport 20 mls

Mr & Mrs A Kostulin
Woodend Chalet Holidays, Rose Cottage, Glassel, by Banchory, Kincardineshire, AB31 4DD
Tel: (Torphins) 013398 82562

By Banchory, Aberdeenshire

Map Ref: 4F11

★★★★ SELF CATERING

Detached Victorian garden cottage renovated to a high standard. Situated in owners garden in a peaceful secluded spot. The centre of Torphins village is within easy strolling distance. All accommodation is on the ground floor.

1 cottage, 2 pub rms, 1 bedrm (grd flr avail), sleeps 2, £150.00-£250.00, Jan-Dec, bus nearby, rail 22 mls, airport 22 mls

Mrs M Watson
3 William Street, Torphins, by Banchory, Kincardineshire, AB31 4FR
Tel: 013398 82277

Banff

Map Ref: 4F7

★★★★ SELF CATERING

Spacious cottage in rural location. Convenient for towns of Banff and Macduff, with their golfing and leisure amenities.

1 cottage, 2 pub rms, 4 bedrms (grd flr avail), sleeps 5, £150.00-£300.00, Jan-Dec, bus 3 mls, rail 20 mls, airport 40 mls

Ms M McDonald
55 Cecil Road, Lancing, West Sussex, BN15 8HP
Tel: (Lancing) 01903 767273

By Banff

Map Ref: 4F7

★★ SELF CATERING

Traditional farm cottage. Recently refurbished in quiet location. Trout fishing and clay pigeon shooting available. 7 miles from Banff and 4 miles from Turiff. Ideal for castle and whisky trails. Many golf courses within easy reach.

1 cottage, 1 pub rm, 2 bedrms, sleeps 4, £150.00-£280.00, Jan-Dec, bus 1/4 ml, rail 40 mls, airport 40 mls

Mrs W M Anderson
Strocherie Farm, King Edward, by Banff, Aberdeenshire, AB45 3PL
Tel: (King Edward) 01888 551220

★★ SELF CATERING

Lovely cottage peacefully situated among lawns and woodland beside River Deveron. Ideal for country lovers, fishermen, artists and for retreats.

1 cottage, 2 pub rms, 2 bedrms (grd flr avail), sleeps 4, £190.00-£280.00, Jan-Dec, bus 5 mls, rail 18 mls, airport 40 mls

Mrs M Kitchen
Wood of Shaws, Alvah, Banff, AB45 3UL
Tel: (Eden) 01261 821223 Fax: 01261 821223

Braemar, Aberdeenshire

Map Ref: 4D11

★★ UP TO ★★★ SELF CATERING

Stone built house with attached cottage and large garden in quiet location on edge of village. Plenty of car parking.

1 house, 1 cottage, min let weekend, £300.00-£475.00, Jan-Dec, bus 1/2 ml, rail 60 mls, airport 60 mls

Mrs A M Cheyne
Fife Cottages, Braemar, AB35 5YT
Tel: 013397 41608

Important: Prices stated are estimates and may be subject to amendments

raemar, Aberdeenshire

Map Ref: 4D11

★★★

SELF CATERING

Cottage and chalet in grounds of Callater Lodge Hotel. On the outskirts of the village close to Nature Reserves, Balmoral and ski slopes.

1 chalet, 1 cottage, 1 pub rm, 1-2 bedrms (grd flr avail), sleeps 2-4, total sleeping capacity 6, min let weekend (low season), £180.00-£330.00, Jan-Dec, bus $^1/_2$ ml, rail 49 mls, airport 58 mls

Mrs Maria Franklin, Callater Lodge Hotel
9 Glenshee Road, Braemar, Aberdeenshire, AB35 5YQ
Tel: (Braemar) 013397 41275 Fax: 013397 41275

★★★

SELF CATERING

Compact log cabin in hotel grounds, within easy walking distance of village and its Royal connections. Excellent base for touring, walking and winter activities.

4 log cabins, 1 pub rm, sleeps 6, total sleeping capacity 24, £200.00-£450.00, Jan-Dec, bus $^1/_4$ mile, rail 49 miles, airport 59 miles

Mr Moore
Braemar Lodge, Glenshee Road, Braemar, Aberdeenshire, AB35 5YQ
Tel: (Braemar) 013397 41627 Fax: 013397 41627

y Braemar, Aberdeenshire

Map Ref: 4D11

★★

SELF CATERING

Country cottage in small hamlet 4 miles from Ballater. Quiet, rural position. A good base for exploring Royal Deeside and surrounding countryside.

1 cottage, 1 pub rm, 3 bedrms (grd flr avail), sleeps 6, £250.00-£270.00, Jan-Dec, bus 5 mls, rail 60 mls, airport 60 mls

Helen Stuart
8 Hilltop Crescent, Westhill, Aberdeen
Tel: (Aberdeen) 01224 741787

uckie, Banffshire

Map Ref: 4E7

★★

SELF CATERING

Ground floor flat with south facing garden in quiet location close to sea in picturesque village of Portessie. Ideal for golf courses and beaches.

1 flat, 1 pub rm, 1 bedrm (grd flr avail), sleeps 2, min let weekend, £160.00-£190.00, Jan-Dec, bus nearby, rail 14 mls, airport 60 mls

Mr James Merson Grant
8 Great Eastern Road, Portessie, Buckie, Banffshire, AB56 1SL
Tel: (Buckie) 01542 831277

y Buckie, Banffshire

Map Ref: 4E7

★★

SELF CATERING

Finnish log cabins in peaceful rural setting, close to stock farm with magnificent views over the Moray Firth.

2 log cabins, 1-2 pub rms, 2 bedrms, sleeps 2-6, total sleeping capacity 10, £121.00-£305.00, Jan-Dec, bus 4 mls, rail 12 mls, airport 55 mls

Mr J Forbes
Maryhill Farm, Drybridge, Buckie, Banffshire, AB56 2JB
Tel: (Buckie) 01542 831284

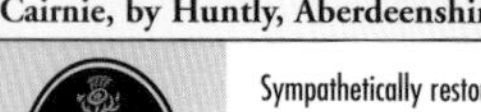

Cairnie, by Huntly, Aberdeenshire

Map Ref: 4E8

SELF CATERING

Sympathetically restored cottage set amidst mature trees. Quiet rural location yet only 7 miles from Huntly. Ideal location for castle trail and whisky trail. Many golf courses within 1 hours drive.

1 cottage, 2 pub rms, 3 bedrms, sleeps 6, £200.00-£375.00, Jan-Dec, bus 3/4 ml, rail 5 mls, airport 50 mls

Andrews
Glenhead, Coachford, Cairnie, Huntly, Aberdeenshire, AB54 4TU
Tel: 01466 760381 Fax: 01466 760222
Email: 113000.720@compuserve.com

Carron, Moray

Map Ref: 4D9

SELF CATERING

Semi-detached cottage in peaceful countryside, by River Spey and Speyside walkway. Ideal for touring Elgin, Grantown and Cairngorms area.

1 cottage, 1 pub rm, 3 bedrms (grd flr avail), sleeps 6, £140.00-£210.00, Easter-Oct, rail 18 mls, airport 42 mls

Mrs Patricia K Grieve
30 Provost Smith Crescent, Inverness, IV2 3TG
Tel: (Inverness) 01463 222565

Colpy, Aberdeenshire

Map Ref: 4F9

SELF CATERING

Rebuilt farmhouse providing compact holiday cottage of a high standard. Quiet location, with panoramic views.

1 cottage, 2 pub rms, 2 bedrms (grd flr avail), sleeps 4, min let 3 days, £175.00-£350.00, Jan-Dec, bus 1 ml, rail 4 mls, airport 26 mls

G Manning
Snipefield, Culsalmond, Insch, Aberdeenshire
Tel: (Colpy) 01464 841394

By Craigellachie, Banffshire

Map Ref: 4D8

SELF CATERING

Modern non-smoking bungalow in open country on picturesque Speyside. Lovely views all round. Enclosed garden available.

1 bungalow, 1 pub rm, 2 bedrms, sleeps 4, £150.00-£200.00, Jan-Dec, bus 2 mls, rail 14 mls, airport 40 mls

Mrs B W MacKintosh
Sandyhillock Farm, Craigellachie, Moray, AB38 9SP
Tel: (Carron) 01340 810272

Cullen, Banffshire

Map Ref: 4E7

SELF CATERING

Refurbished fisherman's cottage, situated in the Seatown area of the conservation village of Cullen. 200 yards from the beach. Non-smokers only.

1 cottage, 1 pub rm, 2 bedrms, sleeps 4, £100.00-£300.00, Jan-Dec, bus 100 yds, rail 12 mls, airport 65 mls

Mr & Mrs A W Clark
Carleatheran, Blantyre, Cullen, Banffshire, AB56 4UF
Tel: (Cullen) 01542 840391

Important: Prices stated are estimates and may be subject to amendments

llen, Banffshire

Map Ref: 4E7

★★

SELF ATERING

Traditional fisherman's houses in conservation village close to beach, harbour and golf courses. Watch bottle-nose dolphins at play.

2 houses, 1-2 pub rms, 2-3 bedrms (grd flr avail), sleeps 5-6, total sleeping capacity 11, £150.00-£330.00, Jan-Dec, bus nearby, rail 12 mls, airport 55 mls

Mrs Sarah J Grant
St Trewel, Kennethmont, Insch, Aberdeenshire, AB52 6YQ
Tel: (Kennethmont) 01464 831207

★★★

SELF ATERING

Modernised fisherman's cottage in coastal village close to sandy beaches.

1 cottage, 1 pub rm, 1 bedrm (grd flr avail), sleeps 4, £120.00-£240.00, Jan-Dec, bus nearby, rail 16 mls, airport 60 mls

Mrs Evelyn Taylor
Buschweide, Pitkeathly Wells Road, Bridge of Earn, Perthshire, PH2 9HA
Tel: (Perth) 01738 812862

nnet, by Aboyne, Aberdeenshire

Map Ref: 4E11

★★ UP TO ★★★★

SELF ATERING

Set in the heart of Royal Deeside this former victorian shooting lodge has been refurbished with attention to detail emphasising the unique character and ambience of this large and spacious holiday home. Standing in it's own extensive 7 acres of woodland. The house overlooks Loch Davan, a bird sanctuary settled at times by greylag geese, whooper swans, mallards, moorhens and a family of otters.

1 house, 1 cottage, 2-3 pub rms, 2-8 bedrms, sleeps 3-10, total sleeping capacity 14, min let weekend, £250.00-£900.00, Jan-Dec, bus 1/2 ml, rail 37 mls, airport 42 mls

Dr Milne
North Cookney Croft, Muchalls, Stonehaven, Kincardineshire, AB39 3SB
Tel: (Newtonhill) 01569 730613

VAT is shown at 17.5%: changes in this rate may affect prices.

Key to symbols is on back flap.

Dufftown, Banffshire

Map Ref: 4E9

★★★★ SELF CATERING

Cottages converted from farm buildings built around courtyard in scenic location 1 mile (2 km) east of Dufftown.

4 cottages, 1-2 pub rms, 2-4 bedrms (grd flr avail), sleeps 4-8, total sleeping capacity 23, min let 3 nights, £190.00-£495.00, Jan-Dec, bus 400 yds, rail 10 mls, airport 50 mls

Helen Trussell
Parkmore Farm, Dufftown, Keith, Banffshire, AB55 4DN
Tel: (Dufftown) 01340 820072 Fax: 01340 820072

Elgin, Moray

Map Ref: 4D8

★★ SELF CATERING

Recently converted old steading building, to provide facilities for two persons in secluded grounds and gardens, 3 miles (5km) from Hopeman. Ideal base for family holidays.

1 cottage, 1 pub rm, 4 bedrms (grd flr avail), sleeps 1-3, total sleeping capacity 14, £175.00-£250.00, Jan-Dec, bus 1 ml, rail 6 mls, airport 25 mls

Mr Graham Broad
Windmill Lodge, Gordonstoun School, Elgin, Moray, IV30 2RS
Tel: (Elgin) 01343 837880/830250 Fax: 01343 837879

★★★ SELF CATERING

Stone built semi-detached cottages with enclosed garden in rural setting overlooking open farmland. Elgin 5 miles, coast 1 mile.

2 cottages, 1 pub rm, 2 bedrms (grd flr avail), sleeps 4, total sleeping capacity 8, £170.00-£270.00, Jan-Dec, bus 1 ml, rail 5 mls, airport 30 mls

Mr & Mrs F Duncan
Westbank House, College of Roseisle, Elgin, Morayshire, IV30 2YD
Tel: (Burghead) 01343 835604

129

Station Caravan Park

West Beach, Harbour Street, Hopeman, Elgin, Moray, IV30 2RU Tel: (Hopeman) 01343 830880 Fax: 01343 830880

13 1/2 acres, mixed, Apr-Oct, prior booking in peak periods, latest time of arrival 1900, overnight holding area. Extra charge for electricity, awnings, showers.

E T SP W

37 tourers £7.50-9.95 or 37 motors £7.50-9.95 or 37 tents £5.50-9.95. Total Touring Pitches 37.

5 Holiday Caravans to let, sleep 6 £135.00-295.00, total sleeping capacity 30, min let 2 nights.

TV E WC P

Leisure facilities:

From Elgin take B9012 for 6 mls to Hopeman. Turn right down Harbour Street to Harbour, take last left turn to beach, second left into Site.

By Elgin, Moray

Map Ref: 4D8

★★ SELF CATERING

Detached modern house in rural farmland setting convenient for all local amenities.

1 house, 1 pub rm, 3 bedrms (grd flr avail), sleeps 6, £200.00-£250.00, Jan-Dec, bus 7 mls, rail 7 mls, airport 32 mls

Mrs E Albiston
Little Buinach, Kellas, Elgin, Moray, IV30 3TW
Tel: (Dallas) 01343 890233

Important: Prices stated are estimates and may be subject to amendments

By Elgin, Moray — Map Ref: 4D8

★★★ SELF CATERING

Well-appointed houses in magnificent woodland water garden on private estate with own tennis court. Secluded walks in exquisite natural surroundings.

5 cottages, 1-2 pub rms, 2-4 bedrms (grd flr avail), sleeps 3-8, total sleeping capacity 26, £160.00-£500.00, Jan-Dec, bus 1 ml, rail 6 mls, airport 40 mls

Mr John A Christie
Blackhills House, Elgin, Moray, IV30 3QU
Tel: (Lhanbryde) 01343 842223 Fax: 01343 842223
Email: holcots@aol.com
Web: www.blackhills.co.uk

Both cabins on secluded sites. Spectacular views. Private loch for fishing. Ideal for Whisky Trail, Castles and Touring.

2 log cabins, 1 pub rm, 2 bedrms, sleeps 4, total sleeping capacity 4, £160.00-£280.00, Mar-Jan, bus 1/2 ml, rail 3 1/2 mls, airport 36 mls

Mrs Mellis
Springburn, Miltonduff, Elgin, Moray, IV30 3TL
Tel: (Elgin) 01343 541939 Fax: 01343 548863

Findhorn, Moray — Map Ref: 4C7

208

Findhorn Bay Caravan Park

22 acres, mixed, Apr-Oct, prior booking in peak periods, latest time of arrival 2100. Extra charge for electricity, awnings.

75 tourers £7.00-9.50 or 75 motors £7.00-9.50 or 50 tents £5.50-6.50. Total Touring Pitches 75.

17 Holiday Caravans to let, sleep 6 £125.00-255.00, total sleeping capacity 102, min let 2 days.

From A96 in Forres take B9011 to Kinloss, then turn left for Findhorn. Site entrance 2 mls on right.

Traditionally furnished cottage, overlooking Findhorn Bay. Safe, sandy beaches nearby.

1 house, 2 pub rms, 3 bedrms, sleeps 6, £230.00-£470.00, Jan-Dec, bus nearby, rail 5 mls, airport 40 mls

Mr D M Sinclair
Balmalcolm, Kinrossie, Perth, Perthshire, PH2 6JA
Tel: (Kinrossie) 01821 650233

Findochty, Banffshire — Map Ref: 4E7

Traditional home in fishing village of Findochty, recently modernised giving a comfortable base for exploring this area of the Moray Firth coast line. Walking, cycling, golfing and many other activities available. Castle and whisky trail within reasonable distance.

1 house, 2 pub rms, 4 bedrms (grd flr avail), sleeps 8, £395.00-£575.00, Apr-Oct

Mrs Margaret S Reid
68 Craiglieth View, Edinburgh, EH4 3JY, ,
Tel: (Dalry) 0131 337 6192

By Fochabers, Moray Map Ref: 4E8

★★ SELF CATERING

Modern, self-contained ground floor flat attached to country bungalow. Panoramic views up Spey Valley to Ben Rinnes. Fishing boats and numerous golf courses available nearby.

1 flat, 1 pub rm, 1 bedrm, sleeps 4, £150.00-£190.00, Jan-Dec, bus 2 1/2 mls, rail 11 mls, airport 60 mls

Mr A A Mitchell
2 South March, Bogmoor, Spey Bay, Fochabers, Moray, IV32 7PU
Tel: (Fochabers) 01343 820459

Forres, Moray Map Ref: 4C8

★★★★ SELF CATERING

Traditional cottage in quiet location which has been sympathetically renovated and refurbished. View over river Findhorn and tree lined valley. Forres 9 miles.

1 cottage, 2 pub rms, 4 bedrms (grd flr avail), sleeps 7, min let weekend (off season), £450.00-£550.00, Jan-Dec, bus 7 mls, rail 7 mls, airport 20 mls

Anthony Laing
14 Saxe Coburg Place, Edinburgh, EH3 5BR
Tel: 0131 315 2775 Fax: 0131 552 0027

★★★ SELF CATERING

Recently converted stone built farmhouse, 4 miles (7 km) from Forres. Ideal base for group/family holidays.

1 house, 2 pub rms, 4 bedrms, sleeps 6-8, £323.00-£622.00, Jan-Dec, bus 2 mls, rail 2 mls, airport 20 mls

Mrs C Middleton
Earnhill Farm, Kincorth Estate, Forres, Moray, IV36 0SP
Tel: 01309 674132 Fax: 01309 674132

By Forres, Moray Map Ref: 4C8

★ SELF CATERING

Country cottage in its own large grounds near pleasant woodland walks. Castles, fishing, golf, beaches, hill-walking, distilleries and beautiful gardens also within easy reach. Ideal for family holidays.

1 cottage, 1 pub rm, 3 bedrms (grd flr avail), sleeps 6, £180.00-£240.00, Apr-Oct, bus 3/4 ml, rail 5 mls, airport 15 mls

Mrs Jean M Taylor
Wellhill Farm, Dyke, Forres, Moray, IV36 0TL
Tel: (Brodie) 01309 641205

Fraserburgh, Aberdeenshire Map Ref: 4G7

★★★ SELF CATERING

Self-contained flat on two floors, close to town amenities and beach areas. Ideal base for touring. Come and see the lighthouse museum. Car parking available.

1 flat, 1 bedrm, sleeps 4-5, £150.00-£250.00, Jan-Dec, bus nearby, rail 42 mls, airport 40 mls

Mr & Mrs E Simpson
89 Saltoun Place, Fraserburgh
Tel: (Fraserburgh) 01346 518626 Fax: 01346 518626

ardenstown, Banffshire

Map Ref: 4G7

★★ SELF CATERING

Comfortable cottages in picturesque fishing village. Steep access to attic rooms. Convenient for golf courses, fishing, bird watching and touring the spectacular rugged North East coast. Beautiful panoramic sea views across the Moray Firth from all lounges and bedrooms.

5 houses, 1 pub rm, 3 bedrms (grd flr avail), sleeps 4-6, total sleeping capacity 26, min let 3 days, £115.00-£350.00, Jan-Dec, bus nearby, rail 30 mls, ferry 45 mls, airport 40 mls

Charles & Lorna Davidson
Havenlee, 2 Markethill Road, Turriff, AB53 4AZ
Tel: 01888 563827 Fax: 01888 563827

★★★ SELF CATERING

Traditional 2 storey cottage, completely renovated, in heart of village. Superb views from secluded rear terrace over Gamrie Bay.

1 house, 5 pub rms, 2 bedrms, sleeps 4, £165.00-£335.00, Jan-Dec, bus nearby, rail 30 mls, ferry 40 mls, airport 40 mls

Mr M French
Old Mill Inn, South Deeside Road, Maryculter, Aberdeen, Aberdeenshire, AB12 5FX
Tel: (Aberdeen) 01224 733212 Fax: 01224 732884

★★ SELF CATERING

Two-storey fisherman's cottage situated close to the sea in this spectacular cliffside village.

1 cottage, 2 pub rms, 3 bedrms, sleeps 5, £160.00-£300.00, Jan-Dec, bus nearby

R L Morris
White Horse, Briningham, Melton Constable, Norfolk
Tel: (Melton) 01263 860514

★★ SELF CATERING

Luxury 3-bed house in elevated position in traditional fishing village. Spectacular seaviews. Beach, Pub, Cafe and shops nearby. Private Parking. 8 miles east from Banff on the B9031.

1 house, 2 pub rms, 3 bedrms, sleeps 6, £140.00-£340.00, Jan-Dec, bus nearby, rail 30 mls, airport 40 mls

Mrs Sainsbury
1 Newland Avenue, Great Bardfield, Essex, CM7 4RU
Tel: (Great Bardfield) 01371 810482 Fax: 01371 810340
Email: dsainsbury@aol.com.

Booking Enquiries: Mrs Smith, Bankhead Croft, Gamrie, Banffshire, AB45 3HN
Tel: (Gardenstown) 01261 851584 Fax: 01261 851584

Holiday Caravan to let, sleeps 6 £60.00-120.00, min let 1 night, Jan-Dec.

From Banff take A98 to Fraserburgh for 6 mls. Turn L at 3rd Gardenstown sign on left. Caravan is 2mls on at Bankhead Croft.

Glenlivet, Banffshire Map Ref: 4D9

The Croft Inn

Booking Enquiries: Tony & Joyce Andrews, The Croft Inn, Glenlivet, Ballindalloch, Baffshire, AB37 9DP
Tel: 01807 590361

2 Holiday Caravans to let, sleep 4-6 £120.00-160.00, total sleeping capacity 10, Apr-Oct.

From Dufftown take B9009 south-west for 9 mls, site on left.

Cosy semi-detached bungalow with Rayburn stove and open fire in sitting room. Pub/Restaurant 1(2km) mile away and others within 5 miles.

1 bungalow, 1 pub rm, 3 bedrms, sleeps 8, £270.00-£370.00, Jan-Dec

Mrs Jo R Durno
Deepdale, Glenlivet, Ballindalloch, Banffshire, AB37 9EJ
Tel: (Glenlivet) 01807 590364 Fax: 01807 590364

Situated in the peaceful, scenic countryside of the secluded Braes of Glenlivet, a modern double glazed bungalow in enclosed garden.

1 bungalow, 1 pub rm, 2 bedrms, sleeps 5, £180.00-£230.00, Jan-Dec, bus 2 1/2 mls, rail 30 mls, airport 50 mls

Mr & Mrs C G McGillivray
Auchnascraw, Chapeltown, Braes of Glenlivet, Ballindalloch, Banffshire, AB37 9JT
Tel: (Glenlivet) 01807 590256

Lodges and a cottage recently completely refurbished, situated amidst rolling upland scenery, with spectacular views. Bar/Restaurant and laundry on site, also open to non-residents.

10 chalets, 1 cottage, 1 pub rm, 2-3 bedrms, sleeps 2-8, total sleeping capacity 72, £200.00-£450.00, Dec-Oct, bus 8 mls, rail 17 mls, airport 53 mls

Mr Terry
Glenlivet Holiday Lodges, Glenlivet, Ballindalloch, AB37 9DR
Tel: (Ballindalloch) 01807 590209 Fax: 01807 590401

Converted cottages in contrasting situations. One secluded, near river, and with fenced garden, other in village centre, annexed to owners' house. Others in own grounds close to village.

1 cottage, 2 pub rms, 1 bedrm (grd flr avail), sleeps 2, £240.00-£260.00, Jan-Dec, bus on bus route, rail 25 mls, airport 60 mls

Jaquie White
The Post Office, Tomnavoulin, Ballindalloch, AB37 9JA
Tel: 01807 590220 Fax: 01807 590220

Important: Prices stated are estimates and may be subject to amendments

Glenlivet, Banffshire

Map Ref: 4D9

★★ UP TO ★★★ SELF CATERING

Converted farm cottages on working farm. Fine views of the surrounding hills. Situated right on the Speyside Way. 8 miles (14km) to Lecht ski area.

1 cottage, 1 annex, 1 pub rm, 2 bedrms, sleeps 4-6, total sleeping capacity 10, £220.00, Jan-Dec, rail 24 mls, airport 55 mls

Mrs Innes
Deskie Farm, Glenlivet, Ballindalloch, Banffshire, AB37 9BX
Tel: (Glenlivet) 01807 590207

Hopeman, Moray

Map Ref: 4D7

★ SELF CATERING

Flats on top floor of Listed building. Sited on a sandstone ridge adjacent to sandy beach and golf courses.

3 flats, 1 pub rm, 1-2 bedrms, sleeps 4-6, total sleeping capacity 14, £110.00-£210.00, Apr-Oct, bus 1/2 ml, rail 6 mls, airport 40 mls

Mr & Mrs Keith McKerron
Hopeman Lodge, Hopeman, Elgin, Moray, IV30 2YA
Tel: (Hopeman) 01343 830245

Huntly, Aberdeenshire

Map Ref: 4F9

★★★ SELF CATERING

Converted from a traditional, stone built farm steading our cottages stand beside 'Drumdelgie' our historic old farmhouse. Comfortable and very well equipped, in beautiful countryside. Just right for exploring castle and whisky trails, cliffs, beaches and mountains. Play golf, fish or just relax and enjoy the view. Evening meals available. All bed linen and towels provided. Welcome guaranteed.

3 cottages, 1 pub rm, 2-3 bedrms (grd flr avail), sleeps 3-5, total sleeping capacity 12, min let 3 nights, £160.00-£335.00, Jan-Dec, bus 2 mls, rail 3 mls, airport 40 mls

Drumdelgie House
Cairnie,by Huntly, Aberdeenshire, AB54 4TH
Tel: (Cairnie) 01466 760368

★ SELF CATERING

Modern cottage beside farm in beautiful wooded surroundings. Ideal base for touring the North East. Very near to fishing. 6 miles from Huntly.

1 bungalow, 1 pub rm, 3 bedrms, sleeps 6, £170.00-£300.00, Apr-Nov, bus 2 1/2 mls, rail 6 mls, airport 40 mls

Mrs Gordon
Rowanbrae Cottage, Tillyminate, Gartly,by Huntly, Aberdeenshire, AB54 4QS
Tel: (Gartly) 01466720 207

★★ SELF CATERING

Stone built cottage with own garden, situated on B9022 only 3 miles (5kms) from Huntly and on Castle and Whisky Trails.

1 cottage, 1 pub rm, 3 bedrms (grd flr avail), sleeps 6, £100.00-£250.00, Jan-Dec, bus 3 mls, rail 3 mls, airport 40 mls

Mrs A J Morrison
Haddoch Farm, Huntly, Aberdeenshire, AB54 4SL
Tel: (Rothiemay) 01466711 217

VAT is shown at 17.5%: changes in this rate may affect prices.

Key to symbols is on back flap.

Inverurie, Aberdeenshire

Map Ref: 4G9

Converted cart shed in rural setting. Magnificent views to Mither Tap, and close to area's stone circles and Maiden Stone. Walking country. Pets and children welcome.

1 flat, 1 pub rm, 1 bedrm (grd flr avail), sleeps 2-4, min let 1 day, £140.00-£220.00, Jan-Dec, rail 5 mls, airport 25 mls

Mrs Prentice
Old Blair, Chapel of Garioch, Inverurie, Aberdeenshire
Tel: (Pitcaple) 01467 681552

Keith, Banffshire

Map Ref: 4E8

A traditional stone built farmhouse with own garden, on owners' farm. 3 miles (5kms) from Keith just off the A96.

1 house, 2 pub rms, 3 bedrms (grd flr avail), sleeps 7, £150.00-£230.00, May-Oct, bus nearby, rail 4 mls, airport 45 mls

Mrs Milne
Whitehillock, Keith, Banffshire, AB55 3PH
Tel: (Huntly) 01466 760221

Kemnay, Aberdeenshire

Map Ref: 4F10

Modern chalets situated on working farm with views of open countryside and River Don. Access to Castle and Whisky Trail. Beautiful area for walking. Yet only 16 miles from Aberdeen.

2 chalets, sleeps 2-6, total sleeping capacity 12, £290.00-£500.00, Jan-Dec, bus 1/2 ml, rail 6 mls, airport 12 mls

Susan McNeil
Boatleys Farm, Kemnay, by Inverurie, Aberdeenshire, AB51 9NA
Tel: (Kemnay) 01467 643 141

Self-contained flat in wing of stone built farmhouse on mixed farm. Own garden with riverside location and superb views of surrounding countryside, rural, yet only 17 miles from Aberdeen. Ideally situated for the Castle Trail, The Whisky Trail and Stone Circle Trail.

1 flat, 1 pub rm, 1-2 bedrms (grd flr avail), sleeps 2-4, £150.00-£200.00, Jan-Dec, bus 2 mls, rail 7 mls, airport 12 mls

Mrs E C Riddell
Nether Coullie, Kemnay, Inverurie, Aberdeenshire, AB51 5LU
Tel: (Kemnay) 01467 642203 Fax: 01467 642203

Kingston-on-Spey, by Elgin, Moray

Map Ref: 4D7

Traditional fisherman's cottage built around 1910, which has been renovated and upgraded providing a comfortable cottage with a wide range of facilities. Seaside location, ideally suited to family and couples alike. Abundance of wildlife and birds in the nature reserves close by. Close to the whisky and Castle Trails. 15 minute drive to Elgin and all its amenities.

1 cottage, 2 pub rms, 3 bedrms (grd flr avail), sleeps 6, min let 3 nights, £160.00-£350.00, Jan-Dec, bus nearby, rail 10 mls, airport 40 mls

Mrs Helen Cruickshank
Drummuir, Duff Avenue, Elgin, Moray, IV30 1QS
Tel: (Elgin) 01343 541611

Important: Prices stated are estimates and may be subject to amendments

ntore, Aberdeenshire — **Map Ref: 4G10**

★★★
SELF
ATERING

Comfortable restored cottage on outskirts of village. Ideal touring base for castles, golf, fishing, walking and archaelogical sites. Tranquil location within 1/2 hour drive to Aberdeen and 10 minutes to Dyce Airport.

1 cottage, 2 pub rms, 2 bedrms (grd flr avail), sleeps 4, £225.00-£325.00, Feb-Nov, bus 1/2 ml, rail 4 mls, airport 12 mls

Mrs J T Lumsden
Kingsfield House,, Kingsfield Road, Kintore, Aberdeenshire, AB51 OUD
Tel: (Kintore) 01467 632366 Fax: 01467 632366

gie Coldstone, by Aboyne, Aberdeenshire — **Map Ref: 4E10**

★★★
SELF
ATERING

Rebuilt and modernised traditional cottage with own patio area. Peacefully situated in woodland clearing a short distance from the village.

1 cottage, 1 pub rm, 2 bedrms (grd flr avail), sleeps 4, £215.00-£295.00, Mar-Nov, bus post bus, rail 37 mls, airport 37 mls

Mrs M J Booth
9 Viewfield Gardens, Aberdeen, AB15 7XN
Tel: (Aberdeen) 01224 315008

★★
SELF
ATERING

Traditional 300-year-old stone cottage with small cosy bedrooms in 2 acres of ground. Modern facilities, with many original features retained. A quiet peaceful location on edge of pine forest with Ballater and Aboyne approximately 9 miles equidistant. A lovely rural part of Royal Deeside.

1 cottage, 1 pub rm, 2 bedrms, sleeps 4, £170.00-£220.00, Apr-Nov, bus 2 mls, rail 30 mls

Mrs Craigmile
40 The Chase, Marshalls Park, Romford, Essex, RM1 4BE
Tel: (Romford) 01708 726043 Fax: 01708 724284
Email: jcraigmile@compuserve.com

ssiemouth, Moray — **Map Ref: 4D7**

★
SELF
ATERING

Small semi-detached cottage with character, near to owner's property. Close to beaches and golf course. 0.5 mile to town centre.

1 cottage, 1 pub rm, 1 bedrm, sleeps 2-4, £95.00-£120.00, Jan-Dec, bus nearby, rail 6 mls, airport 40 mls

Mrs Lesley Leiper
Rowan Brae, Paradise Lane, Lossiemouth, Moray, IV31 6QW
Tel: (Lossiemouth) 01343 813000

VAT is shown at 17.5%: changes in this rate may affect prices.

Key to symbols is on back flap.

Lossiemouth, Moray

Map Ref: 4D7

BEACHVIEW HOLIDAY FLATS

STOTFIELD ROAD, LOSSIEMOUTH, MORAY. TEL: 0141 942 4135

Situated on the beautiful Moray Firth, these two spacious flats sleep 6 people. Overlooking golf course, yachting station and west beach. Ideal for golfing holiday and touring Scottish Highlands

Open April-October

For a brochure and details contact

Mrs A Reedie, 33 Henderland Road, Bearsden, Glasgow G61 1JF

★★

SELF CATERING

Apartments enjoying panoramic views of Moray Firth towards the hills of Sutherland. Ideal for seaside holiday and touring Highlands.

2 flats, 1 pub rm, 3 bedrms, sleeps 6, total sleeping capacity 12, £320.00-£380.00, Apr-Oct, bus nearby, rail 6 mls, airport 35 mls

Mrs Agnes J Reedie
33 Henderland Road, Bearsden, Glasgow, G61 1JF
Tel: 0141 942 4135

Memsie, by Fraserburgh, Aberdeenshire

Map Ref: 4G7

★

SELF CATERING

Sympathetically restored farmhouse a "charmer". Walled garden. Peaceful rural working farm location. Duck lake. Many local outdoor pursuits. Fraserburgh 5 miles, Aberdeen 40 miles, Dyce airport 35 miles.

1 house, 1 pub rm, 1 bedrm, sleeps 3, £80.00-£160.00, Jan-Dec, bus 1/2 ml, rail 40 mls, ferry 40 mls, airport 34 mls

J C K Neish
Sandhole Farm, Memsie, Fraserburgh, Aberdeenshire, AB43 4BA
Tel: (Memsie) 01346 541257 Fax: 01346 541257

Monymusk, Aberdeenshire

Map Ref: 4F10

★★★★

SELF CATERING

Newly modernised country cottage with superb views over Donside. Rural location with woods nearby.

1 cottage, 2 bedrms, sleeps 4, £294.00-£370.00, Jan-Dec, bus 3 mls, rail 20 mls, airport 20 mls

A Grant
Estate Office, Monymusk, Inverurie, AB51 7HS
Tel: (Monymusk) 01467 651250 Fax: 01467 651250

Important: Prices stated are estimates and may be subject to amendments

ymusk, Aberdeenshire

Map Ref: 4F10

The Lodge, PLACE OF TILLIEFOURE

Contact: Mr J M Uren, Priory Farmhouse, Appledore Road, Tenterden TN30 7DD
Tel: 01580 765799 or 01883 331071 Fax: 01580 766157 or 01883 331072

A charming recently modernised lodge on a small private estate known as the Place of Tilliefoure, which lies on the north bank of the river Don in Aberdeenshire, about three miles upstream of Monymusk on the road to Kieg. Salmon/ trout fishing is available on the estate.

★★ SELF CATERING

Entrance lodge with open fire in glorious wooded surroundings by the River Don. Salmon fishing available.

1 bungalow, 1 pub rm, 3 bedrms (grd flr avail), sleeps 6, £211.50-£300.00, Jan-Dec, bus 3 1/2 mls, rail 10 mls, airport 22 mls

Mr J M Uren
Priory Farmhouse, Appledore Road, Tenterden, Kent, TN30 7DD
Tel: (Tenterden) 01580 765799/01883 331071
Fax: 01580 766157/ 01883 331072

meldrum, Aberdeenshire

Map Ref: 4G9

★★★ SELF CATERING

Totally renovated former mill in market town of Old Meldrum. Ideally situated for touring the area, fishing and golfing, plenty NTS properties and whisky and castle trails. Only seventeen miles to Aberdeen centre and twelve miles to Dyce airport.

1 apartment, 1 pub rm, 1 bedrm, sleeps 4-5, min let 2 nights, £210.00-£260.00, Jan-Dec, bus 1/4 ml, rail 5 mls, ferry 17 mls, airport 15 mls

Mrs A E Duguid
Mill of Cromlet, Mill Road, Oldmeldrum, Aberdeenshire, AB51 0BD
Tel: (Oldmeldrum) 01651 872535 Fax: 01651 872933

meldrum, Aberdeenshire

Map Ref: 4G9

★ UP TO ★★★ SELF CATERING

Stone built farmhouses and spacious cottage on working stock and arable farm, 2 miles (3kms) from village. 40 miles (64kms) from Lecht ski slopes.

2 houses, 1 cottage, 1-2 pub rms, 3-4 bedrms (grd flr avail), sleeps 6-8, total sleeping capacity 22, £175.00-£360.00, Jan-Dec, bus 5ml, rail 10mls, airport 15mls

Mrs Simmers
Ardmedden, Oldmeldrum, Aberdeenshire, AB51 0AG
Tel: (Oldmeldrum) 01651 872261 Fax: 01651 872202

nan, Aberdeenshire

Map Ref: 4G7

★★★ SELF CATERING

Traditional fisherman's cottage in idyllic location. Modern comforts with lots of character. Awaken to the sounds of the sea. No problem with parking nearby. One dog welcome.

1 cottage, 1 pub rm, 2 bedrms, sleeps 3-4, min let weekend, £180.00-£300.00, Apr-Oct, bus 1/4 ml, rail 50 mls, airport 45 mls

Mrs A Anderson
40 East Barnton Avenue, Edinburgh, EH4 6AQ
Tel: 0131 336 3524

VAT is shown at 17.5%: changes in this rate may affect prices.

Key to symbols is on back flap.

Peterhead, Aberdeenshire — **Map Ref: 4H8**

SELF CATERING

Two houses adjacent in central location. Well equipped. Available on nightly, weekly or long term lets. Very reasonable rates.

2 houses, 1 pub rm, 6-7 bedrms (grd flr avail), sleeps 11-12, total sleeping capacity 23, min let 1 day, £12.00 per person per night, Jan-Dec, bus 200 yds, rail 32 mls, ferry 32 mls, airport 30 mls

Brown's Guest House
11 Merchant Street, Peterhead
Tel: 01779 838343

Portknockie, Banffshire — **Map Ref: 4E7**

SELF CATERING

Modernised cottages situated in Moray coast fishing village. Close to golf courses, fishing, sandy beaches and Whisky Trail.

4 cottages, 1-2 pub rms, 3-4 bedrms (grd flr avail), sleeps 6-8, total sleeping capacity 26, £160.00-£380.00, Jan-Dec, bus nearby, rail 15 mls, airport 55 mls

Scott Holiday Homes
8 Markethill Road, Turriff, AB53 4AZ
Tel: (Turriff) 01888 563524 Fax: 01888 563524

Portsoy, Aberdeenshire — **Map Ref: 4F7**

SELF CATERING

Two restored houses, over 200 years old, right on picturesque harbour, in peaceful setting, yet near amenities of area.

2 houses, 1-2 pub rms, 1-3 bedrms, sleeps 2-6, total sleeping capacity 8, £140.00-£365.00, Jan-Dec, bus nearby, rail 17 mls, airport 55 mls

Mr T Burnett-Stuart
Portsoy Marble, Portsoy, Banffshire, AB45 2PB
Tel: (Portsoy) 01261 842404 (day)/842220 (eve) Fax: 01261 842404

Portsoy, Aberdeenshire — **Map Ref: 4F7**

SELF CATERING

Fully refurbished and attractive property on elevated site, overlooking harbour. Private garden and patio area. Ideal base for touring. Private parking. Beautiful views.

1 house, 2 pub rms, 3 bedrms, sleeps 5, £150.00-£300.00, Jan-Dec, bus nearby, rail 17 mls, airport 50 mls

Mrs Elizabeth Goodyear
3 Almond Close, Barby, Rugby, Warwickshire, CV23 8TL
Tel: (Rugby) 01788 890606 Fax: 01788 891864

By Portsoy, Aberdeenshire — **Map Ref: 4F7**

SELF CATERING

Refurbished wing of farmhouse, with large enclosed garden set amidst rolling farmland, 2.5 miles (4kms) west of Portsoy, 15 miles from MacDuff House, home of the new aquarium. Plenty of golf courses - a golfers paradise.

1 house, 2 pub rms, 2 bedrms, sleeps 4, £140.00-£240.00, Jan-Nov, bus nearby, rail 14 mls, airport 60 mls

Mrs S Clements
Dytach Farm, Sandend, by Portsoy, Aberdeenshire, AB45 2UJ
Tel: (Cullen) 01542 840305

Important: Prices stated are estimates and may be subject to amendments

Portsoy, Aberdeenshire — Map Ref: 4F7

★★ SELF ATERING

Stone built cottage in residential area of Portsoy with large garden to rear, close to harbour, beach and town centre.

1 cottage, 2 pub rms, 2 bedrms, sleeps 4, £70.00-£300.00, Jan-Dec, bus nearby, rail 17 mls, airport 60 mls

Mr & Mrs M Vaughan
36 Prospect Road, Sevenoaks, Kent, TN13 3UA
Tel: (Sevenoaks) 01732 456442

berdeenshire — Map Ref: 4E9

★★★★ SELF ATERING

Comfortable ground floor apartment in detached house, close to Rhynie village and the Tap O'Noth. On the whisky and castle trail, fishing and golfing locally plus a variety of other sporting activities.

1 apartment, 2 pub rms, 1 bedrm (grd flr avail), sleeps 2-4, £170.00-£250.00, Jan-Dec, bus 600 yds, rail 9 mls, ferry 36 mls, airport 34 mls

Mains O'Noth
Rhynie, by Huntly, Aberdeenshire, AB54 4LJ
Tel: (Rhynie) 01464 861415

★ SELF ATERING

Traditional stonebuilt country cottage retaining many original features. Ideally located for walking, castle trail, and whisky trail. Huntly 12 miles.

1 cottage, 2 pub rms, 2 bedrms, sleeps 4, £150.00-£220.00, Jan-Dec, bus 3 mls, rail 13 mls, airport 30 mls

Mrs M Thomson
Belhinny Farm, Rhynie, AB54 4HN
Tel: (Rhynie) 01464 861238

hes, Moray — Map Ref: 4D8

★★★ SELF ATERING

Listed and modernised Victorian stable block with courtyard. Quietly situated near main Elgin-Rothes road, with access to River Spey, mountain and coast.

2 cottages, 3 pub rms, 2-3 bedrms (grd flr avail), sleeps 5-7, total sleeping capacity 12, £180.00-£320.00, Jan-Dec, bus nearby, rail 6 mls, airport 30 mls

Mrs Barbara O'Brien
Brylach, Rothes Glen, Rothes, Aberlour, Banffshire, AB38 7AQ
Tel: (Rothes) 01340 831355

y Bay, Moray — Map Ref: 4E7

★★★ SELF ATERING

Modern bungalow, well equipped, one mile from the sea, near golf courses and River Spey. 4 miles (7 km) from Fochabers.

1 bungalow, 1 pub rm, 3 bedrms (grd flr avail), sleeps 5, £200.00-£400.00, Jan-Dec, bus 1 ml, rail 15 mls, airport 45 mls

Miss Jill Wilshaw
Resthivet, Pitcaple, Inverurie, Aberdeenshire, AB51 5DT
Tel: (Inverurie) 01467 681702

VAT is shown at 17.5%: changes in this rate may affect prices.

Key to symbols is on back flap.

Stonehaven, Kincardineshire Map Ref: 4G11

Old School, Arbuthnott

★★★★ SELF CATERING

Estate Office, Arbuthnott, Laurencekirk AB30 1PA
Telephone: 01561 320417 Fax: 01561 320476
e.mail: keith@arbuth.u-net.com

Luxury holiday accommodation 25 miles south of Aberdeen in beautiful unspoilt area. Furnished to a very high standard of comfort and convenience. 3 bedrooms, bathroom, sitting room, kitchen, downstairs loo, drying facilities. Good road network enables easy access to coast, hills and Royal Deeside.

Excellent base for touring Scotland.

★★★★ SELF CATERING

Conversion of village school into three very comfortable self contained houses, in quiet rural location. Sandy beaches, hillwalks and golf courses nearby.

1 house, 3 pub rms, 3 bedrms (grd flr avail), sleeps 6, min let weekend, £190.00-£390.00, Jan-Dec, bus 3 mls, rail 10 mls, airport 28 mls

Mr Keith Arbuthnott
The Estate Office, Arbuthnott, Laurencekirk, AB30 1PA
Tel: (Auchenblae) 01561 320417 Fax: 01561 320476
Email: keith@arbuth.u-net.com
Web: www.arbuth.u-net.com

Strathdon, Aberdeenshire Map Ref: 4E10

★★ SELF CATERING

Modernised farm properties with fishing on River Don. Set amidst quiet scenic countryside, ideal for touring, hill walking and skiing. Indoor sports and putting green available June to September.

1 house, 2 cottages, 2 pub rms, 2-4 bedrms (grd flr avail), sleeps 6-8, total sleeping capacity 22, £200.00-£300.00, Jan-Dec, bus 500 yds, rail 20 mls, airport 45 mls

Buchaam Holiday Properties,
Mrs E Ogg
Buchaam Farm, Strathdon, Aberdeenshire, AB36 8TN
Tel: (Strathdon) 019756 51238 Fax: 019756 51238

Tarland, Aberdeenshire Map Ref: 4E10

★★★★★ SELF CATERING

Detached traditional stone built cottage with large south facing garden, in secluded Donside valley.

1 cottage, 3 pub rms, 3 bedrms, sleeps 6, £250.00-£475.00, Jan-Dec, bus 1 ml, rail 20 mls, airport 40 mls

Mr Tom Hanna
Kildrummy Castle Hotel, Kildrummy,by Alford, Aberdeenshire
Tel: (Kildrummy) 019755 71288 Fax: 019755 71345

Tarland, Aberdeenshire Map Ref: 4E10

★★★ SELF CATERING

Modern looking bungalow set in a quiet residential area with lovely views across this peaceful highland village to fields, woods and dark hills beyond. A gentle stroll to the village shops and restaurant approximately 1/2 mile distance. This picturesque region supports a wide range of outdoor and sporting activities.

1 house, 1 pub rm, 3 bedrms (grd flr avail), £150.00, Apr-Oct, bus nearby, rail 31 mls, airport 31 mls

Mrs E Smith
Mill Cottage, Logie Coldstone, Aboyne, Aberdeenshire, AB34 5PQ
Tel: (Tarland) 013398 81401

Important: Prices stated are estimates and may be subject to amendments

land, Aberdeenshire

Map Ref: 4E10

SELF ATERING

A substantial detached cottage situated on the extensive Tillypronie Estate in Upper Deeside. A magnificent panoramic vista over the farmland and wooded countryside to distant hills. Loch and river fishing.

1 house, 3 pub rms, 4 bedrms (grd flr avail), sleeps 8, £310.00-£740.00, Jan-Dec, bus 4 mls, rail 45 mls, airport 40 mls

Tillypronie Estate
c/o Strutt & Parker, 68 Station Road, Banchory, Kincardineshire, AB31 5YJ
Tel: (Banchory) 01330 824888 Fax: 01330 825577
Email: banchory@struttandparker.co.uk

aintoul, Banffshire

Map Ref: 4D10

SELF ATERING

Cosy semi-detached cottage with Rayburn and open fire. Situated in village centre with private parking.

1 cottage, 1 pub rm, 3 bedrms (grd flr avail), sleeps 6-8, £250.00-£280.00, Jan-Dec

Mrs Michele Birnie
Livet House, 34 Main Street, Tomintoul, Ballindalloch, Banffshire, AB37 9EX
Tel: (Tomintoul) 01807 580205

★★

SELF ATERING

Modern cottage 7 miles (11km) from Tomintoul. Superb views towards Ben Rinnes. 1 mile (2km) to nearest shop and telephone box.

1 cottage, 2 pub rms, 4 bedrms (grd flr avail), sleeps 8, £195.00, Jan-Dec, rail 14 mls

Alexander Turner
56 Main Street, Tomintoul, Ballindalloch, AB37 9HA
Tel: 01807 580293 Fax: 01387 580341

Turriff, Aberdeenshire

Map Ref: 4F8

SELF ATERING

Traditional cottages set individually in beautiful private 1000 acre estate. Centrally situated in an interesting area to explore.

8 cottages, 2 bungalows, 1-2 pub rms, 3-5 bedrms (grd flr avail), sleeps 6-9, total sleeping capacity 65, min let weekend, £106.00-£420.00, Jan-Dec, bus 3 mls, rail 35 mls, airport 35 mls

Forglen Estate (Hong Kong) Ltd
Home Farm Office, Forglen Estate, Turriff, Aberdeenshire, AB53 4JP
Tel: (Turriff) 01888 562918 Fax: 01888 562252

itehills, by Banff, Banffshire

Map Ref: 4F7

SELF ATERING

Very well equipped spacious house with enclosed garden at the centre of this typical fishing village. Sandy beaches, golf courses and historic Duff House nearby. On the whisky and castle trails. Garage with parking space.

1 house, 2 pub rms, 3 bedrms (grd flr avail), sleeps 6, min let 2 days, £210.00-£420.00, Jan-Dec, bus nearby, rail 45 mls, airport 45 mls

Lorna Dickson
Dounepark Farm, by Banff, AB45 3QP
Tel: (Banff) 01261 812121 Fax: 01261 812161

VAT is shown at 17.5%: changes in this rate may affect prices.

Key to symbols is on back flap.

Welcome to...

The Highlands and Skye

The largest loch by water volume (Loch Ness), the highest mountain (Ben Nevis), the most westerly place on mainland Britain (Ardnamurchan Point), the most spectacular mountain range (the Cuillins of Skye): superlatives abound in the Highlands and Skye.

Though the scenery is grand and wild, the sense of remoteness is tempered by excellent communications and transport links by road, rail and air. (Inverness Airport, for example, has direct London flights, while Skye now has its own bridge.) This in turn means that distance is no deterrent for that early spring break or autumn holiday, when the landscapes have that special sparkle. Besides, the Highlands' increasing resident population, as more and more escape to the unspoilt northlands, means an even better choice of accommodation and more places to eat than ever before.

The area is also big enough to have its own scenic variety, from the soaring crags of Glen Coe, looming over the main road, to the wide-open rolling moors of Caithness in the north, where the sense of space and sky is inspiring. Then there are the old pinewoods of upper Speyside, with the Cairngorms in the background; the long reaches of the Great Glen, whose most famous loch hides a monster mystery; the sunny shores of the inner Moray Firth around the resort of Nairn with its fine golf courses, and the glorious vistas to the Small Isles from the 'Road to the Isles' between Fort William and Mallaig (even better by rail). From the big glens such as Cannich and Affric on the backbone of Scotland, to the ancient sandstones from which the Torridon mountains are shaped, the north and west offer unmatched scenic spectacle, dramatic at every season.

Though the scenery is grand, there are also substantial towns with everything for the visitor. Inverness is often called the capital of the Highlands and is a natural gateway and route centre to the north.

Though the scenery is grand, there are also substantial towns with everything for the visitor. Inverness is often called the capital of the Highlands and is a natural gateway and route centre to the north. At the other end of the Great Glen, Fort William, in the shadow of Ben Nevis, is another busy location with an excellent range of tourist facilities. The eastern seaboard has a string of attractive towns, for example, picturesque Dornoch with its cathedral and famous golf course, while, further north, Wick and Thurso are other major centres.

You can ride a steam railway from Aviemore to Boat of Garten, or walk a treetop trail at the Landmark Centre at Carrbridge. You can explore the Norse connection at the Northlands Viking Centre beyond Wick, pan for gold near Helmsdale, or discover the life of the crofters on Skye.

In these towns and in other places there is plenty to entertain the visitor.

There are boat trips to see dolphins, four-wheel drive safaris in Speyside, self-guided tape tours of the attractive little burgh of Cromarty in Easter Ross, and a glorious garden at Inverewe which is in the same latitude as Leningrad – but a lot milder thanks to the Gulf Stream. All this and mountains, too! The Highlands and Skye are nearer than you think.

Events
The Highlands & Skye

Feb 20 – 27

Inverness Music Festival
Inverness.
Contact: Elizabeth Davis.
Tel: 01463 233902.

Mar 15 – 19

Badenoch & Strathspey Music Festival
Various venues throughout Badenoch and Strathspey.
Contact: Mrs Graham.
Tel: 01540 661349.

May 7 – 16

Highland Walking Festival
Walking and events throughout the Highlands
Tel: 0990 143070.

May 21 – June 5

4th Annual Highland Festival
Various venues in the Highlands & Islands. Theatre, dance and traditional music.
Tel: 01463 719000.

July 26 – Aug 1

Skye Folk Festival
Isle of Skye.
Tel: 01470 582224.

Sep 11 – 12

GOLF: Walker Cup
Nairn Golf Club, Nairn, Inverness. The 37th international amateur tournament played between teams from the USA, UK and Ireland.
Tel: 01667 453208.

Oct 8 – 15

Royal National Mod
Various venues in Lochaber.
Contact: Callum McDonald.
Tel: 01463 231226.

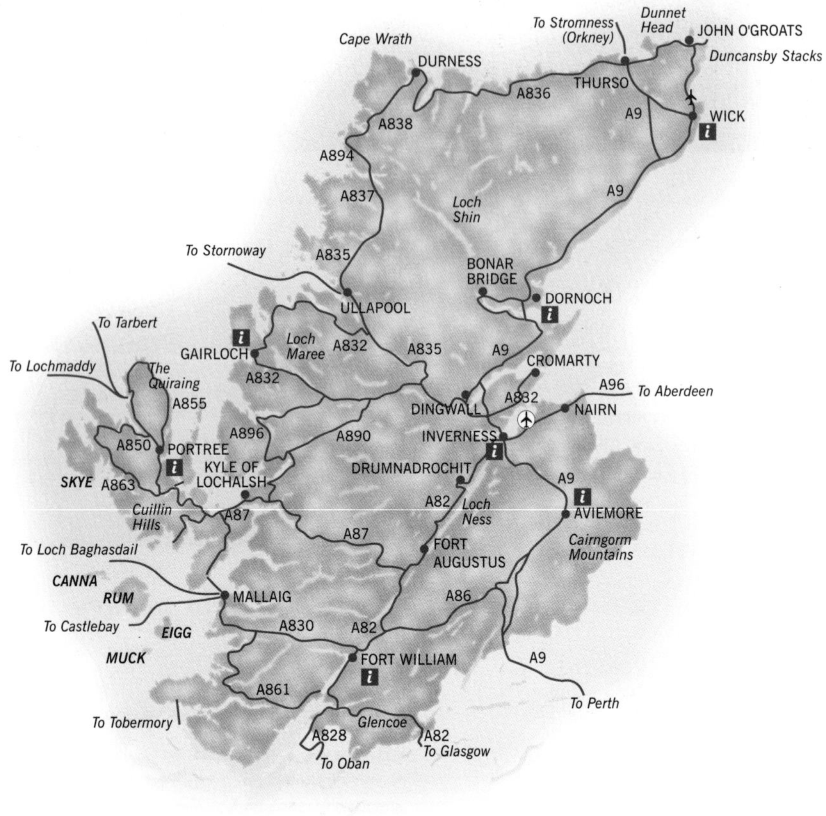

Area Tourist Board Address

The Highlands of Scotland Tourist Board
Peffery House
Strathpeffer
ROSS-SHIRE
IV 14 9HA
Tel: 0870 5143070
Fax: 01997 421168
e.mail: info@host.co.uk
website: www.host.co.uk

The Highlands and Skye

Tourist Information Centres in Scotland

THE HIGHLANDS OF SCOTLAND TOURIST BOARD

AVIEMORE ♿ ✉
Grampian Road
Inverness-shire
PH22 1PP
Tel: (01479) 810363
Jan-Dec

BALLACHULISH
Argyll
Tel: (01855) 811296
April-Oct

BETTYHILL ♿
Clachan
Sutherland
Tel: (01641) 521342
April-end Sept

BROADFORD
Isle of Skye
Tel: (01471) 822361
April-Oct

CARRBRIDGE
Main Street
Inverness-shire
Tel: (01479) 841630
May-Sept

DAVIOT WOOD
A9 by Inverness
Tel: (01463) 772203
April-Oct

DORNOCH ✉
The Square
Sutherland
IV25 3SD
Tel: (01862) 810400
Jan-Dec

DUNVEGAN
Isle of Skye
Tel: (01470) 521581
April-Sept

DURNESS ♿
Sango
Sutherland
Tel: (01971) 511259
April-end Oct

FORT AUGUSTUS
Car Park
Inverness-shire
Tel: (01320) 366367
April-Oct

FORT WILLIAM ♿ ✉
Cameron Square
Inverness-shire
PH33 6AJ
Tel: (01397) 703781
Jan-Dec

GAIRLOCH ♿ ✉
Auchtercairn
Ross-shire
Tel: (01445) 712130
Jan-Dec

GLENSHIEL
Shiel Bridge
Ross-shire
Tel: (01599) 511264
April-Oct

GRANTOWN ON SPEY
High Street
Morayshire
Tel: (01479) 872773
April-Oct

HELMSDALE
Coupar Park
Sutherland
Tel (01431) 821640
Apr-end Sep

INVERNESS ✉
Castle Wynd
IV2 3BJ
Tel: (01463) 234353
Jan-Dec

JOHN O'GROATS
County Road
Caithness
Tel: (01955) 611373
April-Oct

KINGUSSIE
King Street
Inverness-shire
Tel: (01540) 661297
May-Sept

KYLE OF LOCHALSH
Car Park
Inverness-shire
Tel: (01599) 534276
April-Oct

LAIRG ♿
Sutherland
Tel: (01549) 402160
April-Oct

LOCHCARRON ♿
Main Street
Ross-shire
Tel: (01520) 722357
Easter-Oct

LOCHINVER ♿
Main Street
Sutherland
Tel: (01571) 844330
April-Oct

MALLAIG
Inverness-shire
Tel: (01687) 462170
April-Oct

NAIRN
62 King Street
Nairnshire
Tel: (01667) 452753
April-Oct

NORTH KESSOCK ♿ ✉
Ross-shire
Tel: (01463) 731505
Jan-Dec

PORTREE ✉
Bayfield House
Isle of Skye
IV51 9EL
Tel: (01478) 612137
Jan-Dec

RALIA
A9 North by Newtonmore
Inverness-shire
Tel: (01540) 673253
Jan-Dec

SPEAN BRIDGE
Inverness-shire
Tel: (01397) 712576
April-Oct

STRATHPEFFER ♿
The Square
Ross-shire
Tel: (01997) 421415
April-Nov

STRONTIAN
Argyll
Tel: (01967) 402131
April-Oct

THURSO
Riverside
Tel: (01847) 892371
April-Oct

UIG
Ferry Terminal
Isle of Skye
Tel: (01470) 542404
April-Oct

ULLAPOOL
Argyle Street
Ross-shire
Tel: (01854) 612135
April-Nov

WICK ✉
Whitechapel Road
Caithness
KW1 4EA
Tel: (01955) 602596
Jan-Dec

✉ Accept written enquiries
♿ Disabled access

Abriachan, Inverness-shire

Map Ref: 4A9

Two storey house in remote situation high above Loch Ness. Superb views. Roughish road for 0.5 miles (1km), owner's working croft nearby.

1 house, 2 pub rms, 3 bedrms (grd flr avail), sleeps 6, £200.00-£375.00, Apr-Oct, bus 2 mls, rail 12 mls, airport 16 mls

Achabuie Holidays
Abriachan, Inverness, IV3 6LE
Tel: (Dochgarroch) 01463 861285

Sympathetically refurbished corn mill built around 1830. Quiet location, set in own grounds. Many walks from your own doorstep. Fishing available from lochside on Loch Ness. Central location for exploring the Highlands.

1 cottage, 2 pub rms, 3 bedrms, sleeps 6, min let 3 nights, £215.00-£450.00, Jan-Dec, bus 1 ml, rail 12 mls, airport 25 mls

Mrs Claire Wilson
Denwick House, Denwick Village, Alnwick, Northumberland, NE66 3RE
Tel: (Alnwick) 01665 605865

Acharacle, Argyll

Map Ref: 3F12

Elmbank is a modern three bedroomed bungalow standing in its own grounds in the scenic and peaceful village of Acharacle on the west edge of Ardnamurchan. Sandy beaches 4 miles away at Dorlin. Views of Loch Shiel, Moidart Hills and the Isles of Rhum and Eigg.

1 bungalow, 3 bedrms (grd flr avail), sleeps 2-7, £300.00-£400.00, Jan-Dec, bus nearby

Mrs Christine Cain
Utopia, Acharacle, Argyll, PH36 4SL
Tel: 01967 431717

Recently completely refurbished house with garden. 5 miles (8km) from Acharacle and all amenities including shop and pub. Ideal Family base.

1 cottage, 1 pub rm, 3 bedrms (grd flr avail), sleeps 7, £250.00-£475.00, Apr-Oct

Mrs Sharon Powell
Cala Darach, Glenmore, by Glenborrodale, Acharacle
Tel: (Glenborrodale) 01972 500204

Achiltibuie, Ross-shire

Map Ref: 3G6

A croft cottage, with magnificent view towards the summer isles, ideal for couples who enjoy a quiet relaxed holiday. Located in a small crofting and fishing community with shop close by. Ideal area for bird watching, hillwalking and touring the West Highlands. Some steps down to the cottage.

1 cottage, 2 bedrms (grd flr avail), sleeps 1-4, £150.00-£350.00, Jan-Dec, bus nearby, rail 75 mls, ferry 25 mls, airport 75 mls

Ian & Eva-Maria Campbell Whittle
88 Leathwaite Road, London, SW11 6RT
Tel: 0171 228 3423 Fax: 0171 228 3423
Email: ian@worldski.demon.co.uk
Web: http://members.aol.com/hpsourier/bothan.htm

Important: Prices stated are estimates and may be subject to amendments

iltibuie, Ross-shire **Map Ref: 3G6**

★★★ SELF CATERING

Douglas Fir log cabin, detached croft house and stone turf roofed house, with mountain views in close proximity to beach.

1 log cabin, 1 house, 1 turf house, 1-2 pub rms, 2-3 bedrms (grd flr avail), sleeps 4-6, total sleeping capacity 16, £210.00-£400.00, Jan-Dec, bus nearby, rail 75 mls, ferry 22 mls, airport 90 mls

†

Mr D & Mrs S Green
Stac Pollaidh Self Catering, Achnahaird, Achiltibuie, by Ullapool, Ross-shire, IV26 2YT
Tel: (Achiltibuie) 01854 622340 Fax: 01854 622352

★★★ SELF CATERING

Modern bungalows on working croft, in secluded location with beautiful views of Summer Isles.

2 houses, 1 pub rm, 2 bedrms, sleeps 4, total sleeping capacity 4, £200.00-£400.00, Jan-Dec, bus nearby

Mrs S MacLeod, Braeside Holiday Cottages
Roangorm, Badenscallie, Achiltibuie, Ross-shire
Tel: (Achiltibuie) 01854 622285 Fax: 01854 622285

★★★ SELF CATERING

Detached modern house built to a traditional style in a peaceful setting overlooking the Summer Isles.

1 house, 2 pub rms, 3 bedrms (grd flr avail), sleeps 6, min let weekend, £200.00-£450.00, Jan-Dec, bus nearby, rail 80 mls, airport 80 mls

Dr & Mrs Muir
Summer Isles Self Catering, West Polbain, Achiltibuie by Ullapool, Ross-shire
Tel: 01854 622494 Fax: 01854 622259
Email: andrew.muir@masoncom.co.uk
Web: www.muirco.u.net.com

★★★ SELF CATERING

Modernised house in elevated and peaceful position. Magnificent views to Summer Isles and Dundonnell mountains.

1 house, 2 pub rms, 3 bedrms (grd flr avail), sleeps 6, £160.00-£360.00, Mar-Nov, bus 22 mls

Mrs Strachan
Dorevay, Birse, Aboyne, Aberdeenshire, AB34 5BT
Tel: (Aboyne) 013398 86232

Achiltibuie, Ross-shire

Map Ref: 3G6

★★ SELF CATERING

Modern chalet on high isolated site with superb views over sea to Summer Isles. Village 1 mile (2kms).

1 chalet, 1 pub rm, 2 bedrms, sleeps 4, £185.00-£350.00, Jan-Dec, bus nearby, rail 50 mls, ferry 26 mls, airport 50 mls

Mrs M Thornton
3 Baberton Mains Cottages, Juniper Green, Edinburgh, EH14 5AB
Tel: 0131 442 2324
Email: christhornton@msn.com

Achmore, Ross-shire

Map Ref: 3F9

★★★ SELF CATERING

Comfortable modern bungalow adjacent to owners house in quiet crofting township of Achmore, 15 mins drive from Plockton. Peaceful location, children welcome.

1 chalet, 1 pub rm, 3 bedrms, sleeps 4-6, £250.00-£350.00, Apr-Oct

Dennis Fife
Birchwood, Achmore, Stromeferry, IV53 8UT
Tel: 01599 577211

Ardelve, by Dornie, Ross-shire

Map Ref: 3F9

CONCHRA FARM COTTAGES

Ardelve, Kyle of Lochalsh, Ross-shire IV40 8DZ
Tel: 01599 555233 Fax: 01599 555433
e.mail: conchra@aol.com

Quiet, comfortable, fully modernised farm cottages adjacent Loch Long and Eilean Donan Castle, 7 miles from Skye. Wonderful area for touring and walking. Centrally heated and fully equipped with all linen etc included in the rent together with colour TV, microwave, fridge/freezer, automatic washing machine and drying facilities.

★★ SELF CATERING

★★ SELF CATERING

Traditional farm buildings on working farm, in secluded and tranquil lochside setting. Ideal for families, walking and activity holidays. Close to proprietors hotel with full restaurant facility.

3 cottages, 1 pub rm, 2-4 bedrms (grd flr avail), sleeps 5-6, total sleeping capacity 17, min let weekend (low season), £150.00-£395.00, Jan-Dec, bus 1 ml, rail 8 mls, airport 80 mls

Mr Deans
Conchra House, Ardelve, by Kyle, Ross-shire
Tel: (Dornie) 01599 555233 Fax: 01599 555433

★ SELF CATERING

Situated overlooking Loch Duich, towards the Five Sisters of Kintail. Within easy reach of Skye, Wester Ross and Torridon.

2 cottages, 1 pub rm, 2 bedrms, sleeps 4-5, total sleeping capacity 9, £135.00-£225.00, Jan-Dec, bus 1 ml, rail 8 mls

Mrs C Silvester
Heatherbank, Ardelve, Kyle of Lochalsh, Ross-shire,
Tel: (Dornie) 01599 555285

Important: Prices stated are estimates and may be subject to amendments

dgay, Sutherland

Map Ref: 4A6

★★★★ SELF CATERING

A unique Victorian cottage set alone in 200 acres of unspoilt secluded wooded grounds surrounding a traditional hunting lodge. Magnificent scenery of lochs and mountains. A wildlife haven. Well situated for N, W and E coasts. Full modern domestic facilities. Wired for remote working. Itself a small snug highland lodge with wood panelling, drying room and log fire. 2 rods salmon/trout fishing incl. Stalking available. An ideal base for walking.

1 cottage, 4 pub rms, 2 bedrms, sleeps 4, £500.00, Jan-Dec, bus 10 mls, rail 4 mls, airport 55 mls

Mr & Mrs Head
Strathkyle Lodge, by Ardgay, Sutherland, IV24 3DP
Tel: (Invershin) 01549 421203 Fax: 01549 421238
Email: strayhkyle@aol.com

★★★★ SELF CATERING

Modernised and secluded 19c cottage with splendid views over Kyle of Sutherland. 5 miles (8kms) from Ardgay.

1 cottage, 2 pub rms, 3 bedrms (grd flr avail), sleeps 6, £185.00-£220.00, Jan-Dec, bus 5 mls, rail 1 ml, airport 60 mls

Mrs M Matheson
Ruie An Taoir, Strathkyle, Ardgay, Sutherland, IV24 3DP
Tel: (Invershin) 01549 421327

★★★★ SELF CATERING

Mid 19c watermill, sympathetically converted still retaining many of the original mill workings as features in most rooms. Peaceful location on the banks of the River Carron.

1 house, 1 pub rm, 3 bedrms, sleeps 6, £300.00-£700.00, Jan-Dec, bus 1/2 ml, rail 1/2 ml, airport 40 mls

Mr Smellie
Billy Hall Farm, Crook, Co Durham, DL15 9AF
Tel: (Crook) 01388 765809 Fax: 01388 767871
Email: gsmellie@compuserve.com

namurchan, Argyll

Map Ref: 3E12

★ SELF CATERING

Secluded, cedar-clad bungalow on elevated site, with large conservatory overlooking Loch Sunart. Extensive natural garden. A peaceful location, popular with hillwalkers, fishermen, cyclists and generally everyone wishing to enjoy the great outdoors. Birdlife and wildlife regularly seen.

1 bungalow, 3 pub rms, 3 bedrms, sleeps 7, £250.00-£450.00, May-Apr

Mrs S Mildenhall
Raineach, Laga Bay, Acharacle, Argyll, PH36 4JW
Tel: (Glenborrodale) 01972 500218
Email: sulayacht@msn.com

★★ SELF CATERING

In a uniquely remote, isolated situation, this comfortable country house offers a peaceful haven amongst some of Scotland's most dramatic scenery. The stunning location will reward the keenest of hillwalkers, anglers, ornithologists and wildlife enthusiasts. Six miles of forestry track have to be driven carefully.

1 house, 5 pub rms, 4 bedrms, sleeps 9-12, min let weekend (low season), £450.00-£775.00, Jan-Dec, bus 12 mls, rail 35 mls, ferry 24 mls

Mrs B Neish
Barbreck Farm, Kilchrenan, Taynuilt, PA35 1HF
Tel: 01866 833292 Fax: 01866 833292

Ardnamurchan, Argyll

Map Ref: 3E12

★UP TO ★★
SELF CATERING

Come to the Ardnamurchan Peninsula, Britain's most westerly point, from the heights of Ben Hiant to Sanna Sands, a place for the individual and nature lover. Islands, ferries, local nature centre, RSPB reserve and Ardnamurchan Lighthouse nearby, but above all peace and tranquility. To quote one of our many regular visitors "A safe and friendly environment for children". Our cottages are comfortable and welcoming with sea views.

3 cottages, 1 pub rm, 1-3 bedrms, sleeps 2-6, total sleeping capacity 16, £166.00-£567.00, Jan-Dec

Mrs J Chapple
Steading Holidays, Kilchoan, Acharacle, Argyll, PH36 4LH
Tel: (Kilchoan) 01972 510262 Fax: 01972 510337
Email: info@steading.co.uk
Web: www.steading.co.uk

★★★
SELF CATERING

Deltalodge chalets in Resipole Farm Caravan and Camping Park on the Shores of beautiful Loch Sunart. Modern detached cottage adjacent to farm. Bar and recreation facilities available on site. Centrally situated for touring all of Moidart and the Ardnamurchan Peninsula. Brochure available.

1 chalet, 1 cottage, 1 pub rm, 2 bedrms, sleeps 4-6, total sleeping capacity 16, min let 3 nights, £240.00-£405.00, Jan-Dec, bus nearby, rail 30 mls

Mr Sinclair
Resipole Farm, by Acharacle, Argyll, PH36 4HX
Tel: (Salen) 01967 431235 Fax: 01967 431777

★★
SELF CATERING

Edwardian house in a commanding position at the head of Salen Bay giving matchless views over Loch Sunart. Spacious and comfortable family living. Forestry walks, sailing,rocky beachcombing, cycling, bird watching from the house. Swimming from shell sand beaches nearby. Seals and dolphins in the loch. Highland magic in the air.

1 house, 2 pub rms, 4 bedrms, sleeps 10, £295.00-£490.00, Apr-Oct, bus nearby, rail 12 mls, ferry 22 mls

Mrs Tweed
Hob Hill, Tilston, nr Malpas, Cheshire, SY14 7DU
Tel: (Tilston) 01829 250301

Ardross, Ross-shire

Map Ref: 4B7

★
SELF CATERING

Tiny traditional cottage at edge of small hill village in lovely countryside. Located 26 miles from Inverness, 10 miles from Invergordon. Ideal centre for touring, walking, golf or watching birds, dolphins and seals.

1 cottage, 1 pub rm, 2 bedrms, sleeps 3, £80.00-£185.00, Jan-Dec, bus 5 mls, rail 5 mls, airport 35 mls

Miss J Robertson
The Old House of Ardross, by Alness, Ross-shire, IV17 0YE
Tel: (Alness) 01349 882906 Fax: 01349 882906

Important: Prices stated are estimates and may be subject to amendments

saig, Inverness-shire Map Ref: 3F11

Two cottages attractively sited on an elevated position at Kinloid Farm commanding magnificent views overlooking Arisaig to the sea and the islands of Skye, Eigg and Rhum. 5 minutes car journey to wonderful white sands. On site launderette. Good base for walking and touring.

2 chalets, 1 pub rm, 2 bedrms, sleeps 6, total sleeping capacity 12, £240.00-£360.00, Apr-Oct, bus 1 ml, rail 1 ml, ferry 4 mls

Mr A Gillies
Kinloid Farm, Arisaig, Inverness-shire, PH39 4NS
Tel: (Arisaig) 01687 450366 Fax: 01687 450611

Holiday accommodation in unspoilt countryside with superb views of Skye, Rhum and Eigg. 3 miles (5km) from Arisaig.

2 chalets, 1 flat, 1 pub rm, 2 bedrms, sleeps 4-5, total sleeping capacity 13, £160.00-£380.00, Jan-Dec, rail 4 mls, ferry 7 mls

Mr Henderson
Traigh Farm, Arisaig, Inverness-shire, PH39 4NT
Tel: (Arisaig) 01687 450645

Three chalets and one semi detached cottage set in own grounds with spectacular views towards Eigg, Rhum and Skye. 7 miles (11km) from Mallaig and ferry to Skye.

3 chalets, 1 cottage, 1-3 pub rms, 2 bedrms (grd flr avail), sleeps 4-5, total sleeping capacity 19, £170.00-£360.00, Jan-Dec, bus 100 yds, rail 1 ml, ferry 1-7 mls

S B Kingswood
Achnaskia Croft, Achnaskia, Arisaig, Inverness-shire, PH39 4NS
Tel: (Arisaig) 01687 450606 Fax: 01687 450606
Email: achnaskia@hotmail.com

1 bungalow and 1 cedar chalet with views to Isle of Skye and beaches of Arisaig. 5 minutes walk to first beach.

1 chalet, 1 house, 1 pub rm, 2-3 bedrms, sleeps 4-6, total sleeping capacity 11, £150.00-£400.00, Jan-Dec, bus nearby, rail 1 ml, ferry 1 ml, airport 100 mls

Brigid Moynihan
Derryfad, Back of Keppoch, Arisaig, Inverness-shire, PH39 4NS
Tel: (Arisaig) 01687 450667

★★ UP TO ★★★ SELF ATERING

Traditional stone built workers houses of traditional character in peaceful surroundings. Abundant wildlife.

2 flats, 1 cottage, 1-3 pub rms, 2-3 bedrms (grd flr avail), sleeps 4-8, total sleeping capacity 20, £200.00-£375.00, Jan-Dec, rail 4 mls, ferry 4 mls, airport 140 mls

A Simpson
Camusdarach, Arisaig, PH39 4NT
Tel: (Arisaig) 01687 450221 Fax: 01687 450221
Email: camdarach@aol.com

VAT is shown at 17.5%: changes in this rate may affect prices.

Key to symbols is on back flap.

Assynt, Sutherland

Map Ref: E

SELF CATERING

Modernised chalets situated at edge of Lochanoigael in peaceful setting close to sandy beach at Stoer Bay. Ideal for those who enjoy birdwatching, wildlife and walking.

3 chalets, 1 pub rm, 2 bedrms (grd flr avail), sleeps 4, total sleeping capacity 12, £160.00-£380.00, Jan-Dec, bus 7 mls, rail 50 mls, ferry 40 mls, airport 100 mls

Mrs M Watson
Baddidarroch, Lochinver, Assynt, Sutherland
Tel: (Lochinver) 01571 844446 Fax: 01571 844446

Auldearn, by Nairn, Inverness-shire

Map Ref: 4C8

SELF CATERING

A recently refurbished 2 storey property situated in the historic hamlet of Auldearn. In the heart of the Highlands, the village is 17 miles from Inverness and only 2 miles from the spa town of Nairn with its sandy beaches, swimming pool and championship golf courses.

1 house, 1 pub rm, 4 bedrms (grd flr avail), sleeps 6, £200.00-£375.00, Jan-Dec, bus 1/4 ml, rail 2 mls, airport 7 mls

Mrs V Mackinnon
Ardo House, High Street, Auldearn, Inverness-shire, IV12 5TG
Tel: (Nairn) 01667 455673

Aultbea, Ross-shire

Map Ref: 3F6

SELF CATERING

Flats peacefully situated with impressive views over Loch Ewe. 6 miles (10kms) from Inverewe Gardens. Good bird watching and walking area.

2 flats, 1 pub rm, 1 bedrm, sleeps 2-4, total sleeping capacity 8, £90.00-£230.00, Jan-Dec, bus 1/4 ml, rail 42 mls, ferry 44 mls, airport 85 mls

Joan & Peter Deakin
Oran na Mara, Drumchork, Aultbea, Ross-shire, IV22 2HU
Tel: (Aultbea) 01445 731394

SELF CATERING

Stone built modernised cottage with beamed lounge. Situated in village, with excellent views over Loch Ewe.

1 cottage, 1 pub rm, 3 bedrms (grd flr avail), sleeps 6, £175.00-£300.00, Jan-Dec, bus nearby, rail 45 mls, airport 90 mls

Mrs I Donald
Kerrisdale, 4 Muirfield Road, Inverness, IV2 4AY
Tel: (Inverness) 01463 235489 Fax: 01463 235489

SELF CATERING

Spacious modern luxury house. All bedrooms are ensuite. Restaurant, bistro and bars available for guests at Aultbea Hotel. Fishing also available.

124 houses, 1 bungalow, 3 pub rms, 3 bedrms (grd flr avail), sleeps 6-8, total sleeping capacity 6-8, £300.00-£550.00, Jan-Dec, bus nearby, rail 40 mls, ferry 45 mls, airport 90 mls

Loch Ewe Lodge
c/o Aultbea Hotel, Aultbea, Rossshire, IV22 2HX
Tel: (Aultbea) 01445 731201 Fax: 01445 731214
Email: aultea.hotel@btinternet.com

Important: Prices stated are estimates and may be subject to amendments

ltbea, Ross-shire

Map Ref: 3F6

★★★★ SELF ATERING

Two modern properties situated in a quiet spot overlooking Loch Ewe and Torridon mountains. Furnished and equipped with comfort in mind. Ideal for all outdoor pursuits. Safe sandy beaches close by.

1 flat, 1 bungalow, 1 pub rm, 2 bedrms (grd flr avail), sleeps 4, total sleeping capacity 8, £100.00-£290.00, Jan-Dec, bus 1 ml, rail 45 mls, ferry 40 mls, airport 80 mls

Mrs C MacLennan
Eilean View, 1 Mellon Charles, Aultbea, Ross-shire, IV22 2JN
Tel: (Gairloch) 01445 731546

★★★★ SELF ATERING

Two modern bungalows fully equipped to a high standard with panoramic sea views, in friendly crofting community.

2 bungalows, 1 pub rm, 2 bedrms (grd flr avail), sleeps 4, total sleeping capacity 8, £180.00-£380.00, Jan-Dec, bus 3 mls, rail 40 mls, airport 85 mls

Mrs A MacRae
47 Mellon Charles, Aultbea, Ross-shire, IV22 2JL
Tel: (Aultbea) 01445 731326 Fax: 01445 731326

Small group of lodges, situated within extensive grounds, occupying 4 peaceful acres. Unique rural setting on hillside overlooking Aultbea.

3 lodges, 1 pub rm, 2 bedrms (grd flr avail), sleeps 1-5, total sleeping capacity 15, £120.00-£490.00, Jan-Dec, bus nearby, rail 37 mls, airport 85 mls

Mrs N Smith
Aultbea Lodges, Aultbea, Ross-shire, IV22 2HU
Tel: 01445 731268 Fax: 01445 731268

iemore, Inverness-shire

Map Ref: 4C10

Comfortable detached holiday cottage is well located within 5 minutes walking distance of village centre and only minutes from Dalfaber Leisure Complex. With excellent views to Cairngorms, this well equipped property also has golf, fishing and watersports nearby.

1 bungalow, 2 bedrms (grd flr avail), sleeps 4, min let weekend, £195.00-£395.00, Jan-Dec, bus 3/4 ml, rail 1/2 ml, airport 35 mls

J Armour
Station Square, Grampian Road, Aviemore
Tel: (Aviemore) 01479 811463/810020 Fax: 01479 811577
Email: s-catering@hh-homes.co.uk
Web: www.hh-homes.co.uk

Cottages and apartments of individual style and character, peacefully situated on private Highland estate, yet only 1 mile (2kms) from Aviemore.

3 flats, 2 cottages, 1 bungalow, 1-2 pub rms, 2-5 bedrms (grd flr avail), sleeps 2-11, total sleeping capacity 37, min let weekend, £150.00-£695.00, Jan-Dec, bus 1 ml, rail 1 ml, airport 35 mls

Mrs R Birnie
Inverdruie House, Aviemore, Inverness-shire, PH22 1QH
Tel: (Aviemore) 01479 810889

VAT is shown at 17.5%: changes in this rate may affect prices.

Key to symbols is on back flap.

Aviemore, Inverness-shire | **Map Ref: 4C10**

★★★

SELF CATERING

Terrace house in quiet close on ski road to Cairngorms. Ideal base for wide range of activities in area.

1 house, 2 pub rms, 3 bedrms, sleeps 6, £350.00-£950.00, Jan-Dec, bus nearby, rail 1 ml, airport 35 mls

Bobsport (Scotland) Ltd
Ord-View House, 7 Dellmore, Rothiemurchus, Aviemore, PH22 1QW
Tel: 0131 332 6607 Fax: 0131 447 3500

★★★

SELF CATERING

Modern bungalows on secluded estate. Close to all amenities.

3 bungalows, 1 pub rm, 2 bedrms, sleeps 2-7, total sleeping capacity 14, £150.00-£580.00, Jan-Dec, bus 300 yds, rail 1 ml, airport 30 mls

Mr D Murray, Cairngorm Holiday Bungalows
Glen Einich, 29 Grampian View, Aviemore, Inverness-shire, PH22 1T
Tel: (Aviemore) 01479 810653 Fax: 01479 810262

★★ UP TO ★★★

SELF CATERING

Two comfortable well equipped Victorian cottages with character at end of cul de sac and easy walk to all village amenities and public transport. Both have three bedrooms, pleasant gardens with picnic tables and fine outlook over young birch trees to the Cairngorms. Large enough for families, yet cosy for couples, they are ideal bases for relaxing, walking, cycling or touring. Please phone for illustrated brochure.

2 cottages, 1 pub rm, 3 bedrms (grd flr avail), sleeps 6, total sleeping capacity 12, £120.00-£345.00, Jan-Dec, bus 1/4 ml, rail 1/2 ml

Mrs G Clark
21 Walton Street, Oxford, OX1 2HQ,
Tel: (Oxford) 01865 516414

✓✓✓✓

140

Dalraddy Holiday Park

Aviemore, Inverness-shire, PH22 1QB Tel: (Aviemore) 01479 810330
Fax: 01540 651380

25 acres, mixed, Jan-Dec, prior booking in peak periods, latest time of arrival 1900. Extra charge for electricity, awnings, showers.

28 tourers £7.00-9.00 or 28 motors £7.00-9.00 or 50 tents £7.00-9.00. Total Touring Pitches 28.

22 Holiday Caravans to let, sleep 4-6, total sleeping capacity 110, min let 2 nights.

3 1/2 mls S of Aviemore on B9152 (old A9).

★★★

SELF CATERING

Modern bungalow in quiet residential area. Ideal base for touring.

1 bungalow, 1 pub rm, 2 bedrms, sleeps 5, min let weekend, from £180.00, Jan-Dec

Mrs Fenton
15 Oakdene Court, Culloden, Inverness-shire, IV1 2XL
Tel: 01463 794647

Important: Prices stated are estimates and may be subject to amendments

Aviemore, Inverness-shire

Map Ref: 4C10

★★ SELF CATERING

Situated on a working farm. Superb views across the loch towards the Cairngorm Mountains.

1 house, 2 pub rms, 3 bedrms (grd flr avail), sleeps 7, min let 1 night, £300.00-£480.00, Jan-Dec, bus 3 mls, rail 3 mls, airport 35 mls

Fiona Grant
Avielochan Farm, Aviemore, Inverness-shire, PH22 1QD
Tel: (Aviemore) 01479 810846

★★★★ SELF CATERING

The chalets are part of a small complex run by the Vastano family for 21 years. Where standards and style have been influenced by continuity and continental flair.

7 chalets, 1 pub rm, 1-3 bedrms (grd flr avail), sleeps 2-6, total sleeping capacity 34, min let weekend, £200.00-£500.00, Jan-Dec, bus 500 yds, rail 500 yds, airport 40 mls

High Range Self Catering Chalets
Grampian Road, Aviemore, Inverness-shire, PH22 1PT
Tel: (Aviemore) 01479 810636 Fax: 01479 811322
Email: highrange@enterprise.net
Web: www.aviemore,co,uk.highrange.html

★★★ SELF CATERING

Modern detached bungalow in quiet cul de sac on outskirts of town. Well placed for access to Aviemore's many activities.

1 bungalow, 1 pub rm, 2 bedrms (grd flr avail), sleeps 4, min let weekend, £190.00-£400.00, Jan-Dec, bus nearby, rail 1 ml, airport 35 mls

Mrs Vyvienne Hosie
17 Ashburnham Gardens, South Queensferry, West Lothian
Tel: 0131 331 4941

★★★ SELF CATERING

Semi-detached house at end of cul-de-sac on northern edge of Aviemore, in town centre. A quiet residential area, bordered by wooded countryside, with some lovely walks and access to River Spey.

1 house, 1 pub rm, 2 bedrms, sleeps 4, £160.00-£300.00, Jan-Dec, bus 200 yds, rail 1 1/2 mls, airport 35 mls

Mrs M E Lambert
48 McIntosh Drive, Elgin, Moray, IV30 3AW
Tel: (Elgin) 01343 547701 Fax: 01343 547701

★★★ SELF CATERING

Modern bungalow in residential area on the outskirts of town. Pleasant walkway to town centre (10 minutes).

1 bungalow, 1 pub rm, 2 bedrms (grd flr avail), sleeps 4, min let 3 nights, £220.00-£400.00, Apr-Oct, bus 3/4 ml, rail 3/4 ml

Mrs E M Miller
Mambeag, Lochiepots Road, Miltonduff, Elgin, IV30 3WL
Tel: (Elgin) 01343 540608

VAT is shown at 17.5%: changes in this rate may affect prices.

Key to symbols is on back flap.

Aviemore, Inverness-shire | **Map Ref: 4C10**

89

Rothiemurchus Camping & Caravan Park

Coylumbridge, Aviemore, Inverness-shire, PA22 1QU Tel: (Aviemore) 01479 812800 Fax: 01479 812800

9 acres, mixed, Jan-Dec, prior booking in peak periods, latest time of arrival 2300. Extra charge for electricity, awnings.

17 tourers £9.00-11.00 or 17 motors £9.00-11.00 or 22 tents £6.00-10.00. Total Touring Pitches 39.

10 Holiday Caravans to let, sleep 4-6 £275.00-400.00, total sleeping capacity 56, min let 3 nights.

From Aviemore take B970 (Cairngorm skiroad) for 1 1/2 mls, Park on right at Coylumbridge beside Lairig footpath.

SELF CATERING

Scandinavian themes throughout in quiet private landscaped grounds yet close to all amenities.

5 houses, 5 flats, 1 pub rm, 1-2 bedrms, sleeps 4-6, total sleeping capacity 50, from £185.00, 18 Dec-9 Nov, bus 800 yds, rail 800 yds, airport 42 mls

Scandinavian Village

Aviemore Mountain Resort, Aviemore, Inverness-shire, PH22 1PF
Tel: (Aviemore) 01479 810500 Fax: 01479 811604
Email: rentals@scandinavian-village.co.uk

SELF CATERING

Situated in the heart of the Highlands and a perfect base from which to explore all that the Spey Valley and magnificent Cairngorm Mountains have to offer. Comfortable family accommodation in quiet cul-de-sac.

1 bungalow, 1 pub rm, sleeps 6, min let weekend, £300.00-£500.00, Jun-Nov, bus 1/2 ml, rail 1/2 ml, airport 38 mls

Mrs V Turnbull

66 Scandinavian Village, Aviemore Centre, Aviemore, Inverness-shire PH22 1PF
Tel: 01479 810265

SELF CATERING

Four bedrooms and two public rooms with open fires all look to the Cairngorms across the large garden. Comfortable, centrally heated. Games room, sauna and steam bath.

1 house, 2 pub rms, 4 bedrms, sleeps 8, min let 2 nights, £550.00-£800.00, Jan-Dec, bus nearby, rail nearby

Mrs Sheila Walls

40 Ibis Lane, Grove Park, Chiswick, London, W4 3UP
Tel: 0181 747 1855 Fax: 0181 747 1855
Email: suzy_walls@msn.com

Important: Prices stated are estimates and may be subject to amendments

iemore, Inverness-shire **Map Ref: 4C10**

SELF ATERING

Self catering bungalows of a high standard in this popular holiday village complex. 1 mile (3 kms) to village centre and all amenities.

41 bungalows, 1-3 pub rms, 1-4 bedrms (grd flr avail), sleeps 4-10, total sleeping capacity 256, min let 3 nights, £195.00-£1095.00, Jan-Dec, bus 1/4 ml, rail 1/4 ml, airport 30 mls

Silverglades
Dalnabay, Aviemore, Inverness-shire
Tel: 01479 810165 Fax: 01479 811246

SELF ATERING

Compact, cosy, pine lined chalet with two bedrooms, bathroom, sitting room with fully equipped kitchen area. Quiet location, close to all amenities.

1 chalet, 1 pub rm, 2 bedrms (grd flr avail), sleeps 4, min let 2 nights, £220.00-£260.00, Jan-Dec, bus nearby, rail nearby

Mrs Sheila Walls
40 Ibis Lane, Grove Park, Chiswick, London, W4 3UP
Tel: 0181 747 1855 Fax: 0181 747 1855
Email: suzy_walls@msn.com

SELF ATERING

Comfortable, spacious period house with five double bedrooms, three bathrooms, sauna, large lounge and separate dining room. Large garden, BBQ, close to River Spey.

1 house, 2 pub rms, 5 bedrms (grd flr avail), sleeps 12, £530.00-£820.00, Jan-Dec, bus nearby, rail nearby

Mrs Sheila Walls
40 Ibis Lane, Grove Park, Chiswick, London, W4 3UP
Tel: 0181 747 1855 Fax: 0181 747 1855

Aviemore, Inverness-shire Map Ref: 4C10

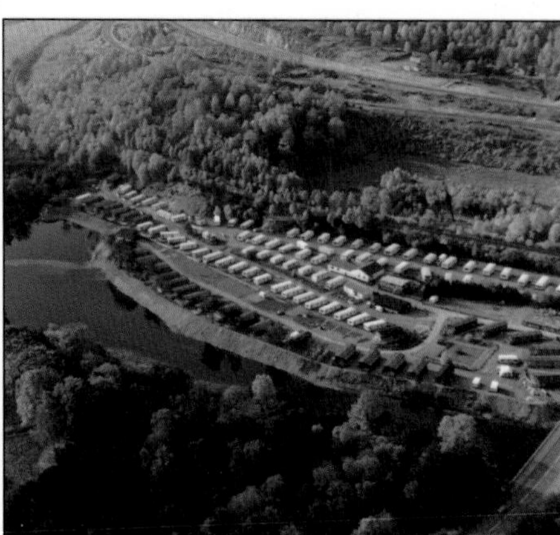

Speyside Leisure Par

Dalfaber Road, Aviemore, Inverness-shire PH22 1
Telephone: 01479 810236 Fax: 01479 811688

A range of self-catering chalets, cabins and caravans including 1998 model modified for disabled users, situated on a bank of the river Sp with views of the Cairngorm mountains. Colour T cooker, fridge, well-equipped kitchen, heated bedrooms, WC, shower, linen and towels. Electric and gas included. Free use of heated indoor pool sauna and gym. Launderette, childrens' play area 10 minutes from centre of Aviemore and ideally placed for a wide range of outdoor activities and attractions including; golf, fishing, Cairngorm reindeer herd, RSPB reserves, steam railway and whisky trail. Open all year, short breaks, discoun for couples.

SELF CATERING

A range of log cabins beside the Spey in this Highland Leisure Park. A small gymnasium and pool with sauna.

10 chalets, 9 -, 1 pub rm, 2-3 bedrms (grd flr avail), sleeps 4-6, total sleeping capacity 56, min let 3 days, £130.00-£650.00, Dec-Nov, bus 1 ml, rail 1 ml, airport 35 mls

Speyside Leisure Park
Dalfaber Road, Aviemore, Inverness-shire, PH22 1PX
Tel: (Aviemore) 01479 810236 Fax: 01479 811688

SELF CATERING

Well equipped house in small development. 5 minutes walk from town centre. In quiet cul de sac with views to Cairngorms.

1 bungalow, 1 pub rm, 2 bedrms (grd flr avail), sleeps 4, £240.00-£350.00, Jan-Dec

Mr H Weir
5 Langside Road, Bothwell, Glasgow, G71 8NG
Tel: (Bothwell) 01698 852322

Avoch, by Fortrose, Ross-shire Map Ref: 4B8

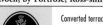

SELF CATERING

Converted terraced fisherman's cottage in historic part of Avoch. Close to sea. Dolphins and varied birdlife to be seen in the area. Ideal base for exploring the Black Isle and East Sutherland - Cromarty, Dornoch and beyond.

1 cottage, 1 pub rm, 2 bedrms, sleeps 4, £190.00-£315.00, Mar-Oct, bus nearby

Mrs J Gatcombe
16 Ness Bank, Inverness, IV2 4SF
Tel: (Inverness) 01463 231151 Fax: 01463 231151

Important: Prices stated are estimates and may be subject to amendments

dachro, Ross-shire Map Ref: 3F7

★★ UP TO ★★★ SELF ATERING

Traditional cottages, each with its own enclosed garden and garden furniture on working croft. Breathtaking views over the Minch to the Outer Isles. Sandy beach 0.5m (1km). Sailing, fishing, golfing and walking all close by.

1 house, 1 cottage, 2 pub rms, 2-4 bedrms, sleeps 4, total sleeping capacity 8, £170.00-£360.00, Apr-Oct, bus nearby, rail 27 mls, airport 80 mls

Caberfeidh Self Catering
c/o Mrs E Taylor, Philorth, Port Henderson, Gairloch
Tel: (Badachro) 01445 741244

★★★★ SELF ATERING

Renovated crofters cottage, refurbished to a high standard. Close to shore and overlooking Gairloch bay.

1 house, 1 pub rm, 3 bedrms (grd flr avail), sleeps 6, from £195.00, Jan-Dec, bus 1/4 ml, rail 30 mls, airport 80 mls

Mrs Carcas
Yarne Cottage, Tower Hill, Horsham, West Sussex, RH13 7JT
Tel: (Horsham) 01403 263591 Fax: 01403 211014

★★★ SELF ATERING

Old school converted to form large comfortable holiday accommodation. Peaceful location and lovely views to sea.

1 house, 2 pub rms, 3 bedrms, sleeps 6, £175.00-£360.00, Jan-Dec, bus 7 mls, rail 30 mls, airport 80 mls

Mr & Mrs S A Garrioch
Old School Road, Opinan, Gairloch, Ross-shire, IV21 2AT
Tel: (Badachro) 01445 741206

★ SELF ATERING

Semi-detached houses standing in small grassed garden at water's edge and overlooking the bay.

2 houses, 2-3 pub rms, 3 bedrms, sleeps 5-6, total sleeping capacity 11, £200.00-£500.00, Jan-Dec, bus 3 mls, rail 30 mls, airport 80 mls

Mr H Lawrie
The Moorings, Badachro, Gairloch, Ross-shire, IV21 2AA
Tel: (Badachro) 01445 741274

★★★★ SELF ATERING

Situated in a peaceful and secluded setting on the shores of Loch Sheildaig. A traditional stone house charmingly restored and decorated with superb views of the loch.

1 house, 3 pub rms, 4 bedrms (grd flr avail), sleeps 8, £340.00-£780.00, Jan-Dec, bus 5 mls, rail 30 mls, airport 90 mls

John MacDonald
Tigh Eibhinn, Easterton, Dalcross, Inverness, IV1 2JE
Tel: (Ardersier) 01667 462792

VAT is shown at 17.5%: changes in this rate may affect prices.

Key to symbols is on back flap.

Badachro, Ross-shire — **Map Ref: 3F7**

ARROWDALE and INNIS-BHEATHA

For brochure contact: John MacDonald, Tigh-Eibhinn, Easterton, Dalcross, Inverness IV1 2JE
Telephone: 01667 462792 Fax: 01463 713744

Two outstanding properties – restored and extended traditional stone cottages, each secluded in their own extensive private grounds and gardens. Arrowdale, pictured here, having spectacular views across Loch Shieldaig and Innis-Bheatha with views of the surrounding hills. Both offer spacious tasteful accommodation. Open fires and Agas, imaginative decor and many personal touches.

House, refurbished to a high standard of individual character and charm. Peacefully situated with superb views and large garden.

1 house, 3 pub rms, 4 bedrms, sleeps 7, £340.00-£780.00, Jan-Dec, bus 5 mls, rail 30 mls, airport 90 mls

J MacDonald
Tigh Eibhinn, Easterton, Dalcross, Inverness, IV1 2JE
Tel: (Ardersier) 01667 462792

Comfortable, well equipped bungalow 8 miles from Gairloch. Views to Skye and Torridon Hills. Ideal for a relaxing holiday.

1 bungalow, 1 pub rm, 3 bedrms, sleeps 7, £250.00-£320.00, May-Sep, bus 8 mls, rail 30 mls

Mrs Alice MacKenzie
18 Port Henderson, Gairloch, Ross-shire, IV21 2AS
Tel: (Badachro) 01445 741239

Booking Enquiries: Mrs A Tallagh 12 Porthenderson, Gairloch, Ross-shire

Tel: 01445 741270

Holiday Caravan to let, sleeps 6 £150.00-170.00, Mar-Oct.

1 ml before Gairloch turn left over bridge onto B8056 for 5mls. Caravan first right p Porthenderson sign.

Detached house sitting in approx. 0.5 acre. Superb views over Badachro Bay. Ample parking. Comfortable centrally heated house. Close to local facilities.

1 bungalow, 1 pub rm, 2 bedrms (grd flr avail), sleeps 5, Jan-Dec, bus 5 mls, rail 28 mls, airport 70 mls

Mr A J Tallach
The Old Garage, Port Henderson, Gairloch, Ross-shire
Tel: 01445 741361/741278

Important: Prices stated are estimates and may be subject to amendments

lachro, Ross-shire

Map Ref: 3F7

★★ SELF CATERING

Spacious flat with panoramic views to Skye and Torridon Hills. Use of garden. Beach nearby.

1 flat, 1 pub rm, 2 bedrms, sleeps 4, £100.00-£200.00, Apr-Oct, bus 7 mls, rail 30 mls, airport 85 mls

Mrs C Thomson
18 South Erradale, Gairloch, Ross-shire, IV21 2AU
Tel: (Badachro) 01445 741202

uly, Inverness-shire

Map Ref: 4A8

★★★ SELF CATERING

Scandinavian wooden chalets within wooded grounds with view to Beauly Firth and Strathglass. 3 miles (5km) from Beauly.

2 chalets, 1 pub rm, 2 bedrms (grd flr avail), sleeps 4, total sleeping capacity 8, £125.00-£260.00, Mar-Oct, bus ½ ml, rail 14 mls, airport 18 mls

Jean Fraser
Woodland Chalet, Cruachan Kilmorack, Beauly, Inverness-shire, IV4 7AQ
Tel: (Beauly) 01463 782467

★ SELF CATERING

Croft cottage in isolated position with magnificent views of Glen Affric and Strathglass. 4 miles (6kms) from Beauly. Former red deer hunting lodge, in isolated position etc. Hilltop position with rough road access.

1 cottage, 2 pub rms, 2 bedrms (grd flr avail), sleeps 4, £150.00-£200.00, Apr-Oct, bus 4 mls, rail 16 mls

Mrs C Guthrie
41 Barrow Point Avenue, Pinner, Middlesex, HA5 3HD
Tel: 0181 866 5026

★★★★ SELF CATERING

Attractive chalet bungalows built and equipped to a high standard. Privacy and comfort in well spaced wooded setting on hillside. Ideal base, for relaxing or touring in the heart of the Highlands.

9 chalets, 1 pub rm, 2-3 bedrms, sleeps 4-6, total sleeping capacity 40, £175.00-£545.00, Jan-Dec, bus 3 mls, rail 7 mls, airport 23 mls

Mrs Pauline Inghammar
Dunsmore Lodges, by Beauly, Inverness-shire, IV4 7EY
Tel: (Beauly) 01463 782424 Fax: 01463 782839
Email: inghammar@cali.co.uk
Web: www.cali.co.uk/dunsmore

★★ UP TO ★★★★ SELF CATERING

Coach house and cottages in a courtyard setting, and a detached 19th century farm cottage overlooking the beautiful scenery of Strathglass. Situated on working farm (beef) and adjacent to 9 hole golf course. Inverness 16 miles (26 kms).

1 house, 1 cottage, 3 apartments, 1-2 pub rms, 2-3 bedrms (grd flr avail), sleeps 4-6, total sleeping capacity 25, £165.00-£420.00, Feb-Nov, bus 5 mls, rail 14 mls, airport 27 mls

Mrs J A Masheter
Mains of Aigas, Beauly, Inverness-shire, IV4 7AD
Tel: (Beauly) 01463 782423/782942 Fax: 01463 782423

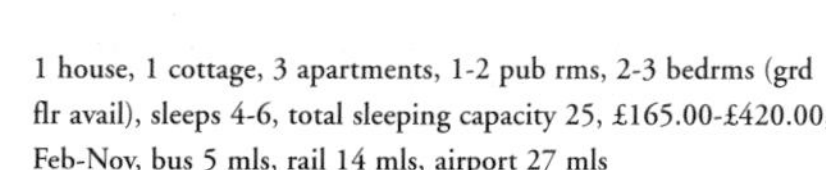

VAT is shown at 17.5%: changes in this rate may affect prices.

Key to symbols is on back flap.

Beauly, Inverness-shire

Map Ref: 4A8

Two detached chalets on working farm in elevated position overlooking Beauly and the Firth beyond.

2 chalets, 1 pub rm, 2 bedrms (grd flr avail), sleeps 4-6, total sleeping capacity 12, £130.00-£220.00, Mar-Nov, bus 1 ml, rail 1 1/2 mls, airport 16 mls

Mrs M M Ritchie
Rheindown Farm, by Beauly, Inverness-shire, IV4 7AB
Tel: (Beauly) 01463 782461

Bettyhill, Sutherland

Map Ref: 4B3

Modernised croft house in remote elevated position. Overlooks Torrisdale Sands and the River Naver. 0.5 mile (1km) from village.

1 house, 2 pub rms, 3 bedrms (grd flr avail), sleeps 6, min let weekend, £200.00-£300.00, Jan-Dec, bus 3/4 ml, rail 32 mls, ferry 32 mls, airport 55 mls

Mrs A Todd
Hoy Farm, Halkirk, Caithness, KW12 6UU
Tel: (Halkirk) 01847 831544

Boat of Garten, Inverness-shire

Map Ref: 4C10

'A' Frame Lodges on working farm. Rural situation with fine views. Boat of Garten two miles distance.

5 chalets, 1 pub rm, 3 bedrms (grd flr avail), sleeps 6, total sleeping capacity 30, £100.00-£375.00, Jan-Dec, bus nearby, rail 8 mls, airport 32 mls

Beechgrove Mountain Lodges
Mains of Garten Farm, Boat of Garten, Inverness-shire, PH24 3BY
Tel: (Boat of Garten) 01479 831551 Fax: 01479 831445

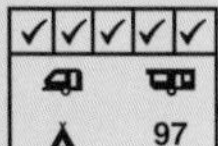

Boat of Garten Caravan Park

Boat of Garten, Inverness-shire, PH24 3BN Tel: (Boat of Garten) 01479 831652 Fax: 01479 831652

6 acres, mixed, Jan-Dec, prior booking in peak periods, latest time of arrival 2200, overnight holding area. Extra charge for electricity, awnings.

37 tourers or 37 motors or 37 tents. Total Touring Pitches 37. Charges on applicatio

5 Holiday Caravans to let, sleep 4-6 £180.00-390.00, total sleeping capacity 28, min let 2 nights.

Leisure facilities:

In village of Boat of Garten, 5 mls N of Aviemore.

Comfortable chalet, ideally situated for all this beautiful area has to offer. Perfect for bird watching, walking, fishing etc. Shops close by, non smoking.

1 chalet, 3 bedrms, sleeps 4, £195.00-£210.00, Jan-Oct

Chalet Morlich
Moorfield House, Deshar Road, Boat of Garten
Tel: 01479 831646 Fax: 01479 831646
Email: moorfieldhouse@msn.com

Important: Prices stated are estimates and may be subject to amendments

...t of Garten, Inverness-shire Map Ref: 4C10

★ SELF ...TERING

Upstairs flat in centre of village near to River Spey. Golf, tennis and Strathspey steam railway nearby.

1 flat, 2 pub rms, 3 bedrms, sleeps 7, £160.00-£250.00, Mar-Dec, bus nearby, rail 6 mls

Mrs J Crawford
10 Gailes Park, Bothwell, Glasgow, G71 8TS
Tel: (Bothwell) 01698 852901

30

Croft Na Carn Caravan Park/Holiday Homes

Loch Garten Road, Boat of Garten, Inverness-shire, PH24 3BY Tel: 01343 830880 Fax: 01343 830880

Booking Enquiries: Phoenix House Harbour Street, Hopeman, nr Elgin, IV30 2RU

Tel: 01343 830880 Fax: 01343 830880

3 acres, grassy, level, sheltered, Jan-Dec, prior booking in peak periods, latest time of arrival 1900. Extra charge for electricity, awnings.

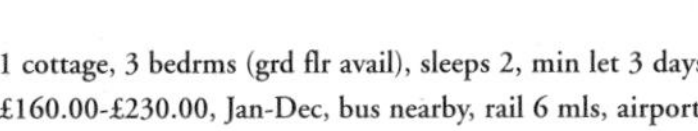

5 tourers £6.50-8.50 or 5 motors £6.50-8.50 or 5 tents £3.50-8.50. Total Touring Pitches 5.

2 Holiday Caravans to let, sleep 6 £95.00-250.00, total sleeping capacity 18, min let 2 nights (low season).

1 ml from Boat of Garten on Loch Garten road.

★ SELF ...TERING

Traditional timber built Highland cottage in grounds of owner's guest house situated in centre of village.

1 cottage, 3 bedrms (grd flr avail), sleeps 2, min let 3 days, £160.00-£230.00, Jan-Dec, bus nearby, rail 6 mls, airport 30 mls

Mrs Dixon
Firhill Cottage, Granlea Guest House, Deshar Road, Boat of Garten
Tel: 01479 831601 Fax: 01479 831601

★ SELF ...TERING

Detached, stone built house in famous "Osprey" village. Enclosed gardens and plenty of private parking space.

1 house, 2 pub rms, 3 bedrms (grd flr avail), sleeps 8, £280.00-£350.00, Dec-Oct, bus nearby, rail 6 mls, airport 30 mls

Hilary MacRae
5 Brockwood Avenue, Penicuik, Midlothian, EH26 9AJ
Tel: (Penicuik) 01968 673194
Email: h_macrae@compuserve.com

★★ SELF ...TERING

Stone built, ground floor flat situated in quiet part of village. 5 minutes walk from golf course, local shops etc.

1 flat, 1 pub rm, 2 bedrms (grd flr avail), sleeps 4, £125.00-£145.00, Mar-Oct, bus nearby, rail 6 1/2 mls

Mr G Keir
4 High Terrace, Boat of Garten, Inverness-shire, PH24 3BW
Tel: (Boat of Garten) 01479 831262

VAT is shown at 17.5%: changes in this rate may affect prices.

Key to symbols is on back flap.

Boat of Garten, Inverness-shire — Map Ref: 4C10

Tastefully appointed Highland cottages of character, with large enclosed garden, in rural setting.

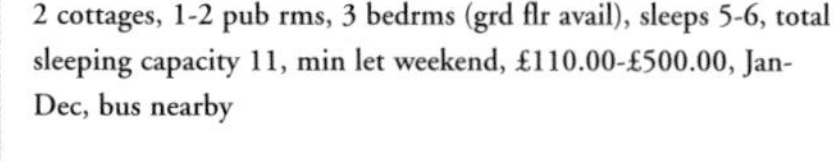

2 cottages, 1-2 pub rms, 3 bedrms (grd flr avail), sleeps 5-6, total sleeping capacity 11, min let weekend, £110.00-£500.00, Jan-Dec, bus nearby

Dr J Weir
Glenlora Cottage, Lochwinnoch, PA12 4DN
Tel: 01505 842062

Recently refurbished traditional croft house with some original features retained, set beside River Spey. Fishing, golfing, walking and winter sports.

1 cottage, 1 pub rm, 3 bedrms (grd flr avail), sleeps 6, £190.00-£440.00, Jan-Dec, bus 1 ml, rail 6 mls, airport 30 mls

Mrs C Wells
10 Maclardy Court, Uphall, West Lothian, EH52 5SL
Tel: (Livingston) 01506 854686

Brora, Sutherland — Map Ref: 4C6

Spacious modern detached house adjacent to the 12th tee of the golf course, and well equipped apartments within the grounds of the Links Hotel, also overlooking Brora golf course. Sandy beaches close by. Hotel services and a range of leisure facilities available at the Links and Royal Marine Hotels. Maid service available.

3 houses, 3 apartments, 2 pub rms, 2-4 bedrms (grd flr avail), sleeps 2-7, total sleeping capacity 26, £350.00-£700.00, Jan-Dec, bus nearby, rail 2 mls, airport 70 mls

Highland Escape Ltd
Royal Marine Hotel, Golf Road, Brora, Sutherland, KW9 6QS
Tel: (Brora) 01408 621225 Fax: 01408 621383

Traditional fisherman's cottage with open sea views, close to safe sandy beaches and golf course. Fishing nearby. Ideal touring base.

1 house, 2 pub rms, 3 bedrms, sleeps 7, min let weekend, £275.00-£320.00, Jan-Dec, bus 1/2 ml, rail 1 ml

Mrs M Mackay
12 Fulmar Crescent, Ardersier, Inverness-shire, IV1 2SY
Tel: (Nairn) 01667 462047

Cannich, Inverness-shire — Map Ref: 3H9

A warm Highland welcome awaits at this family run park. Fully equipped, comfortably furnished, three bedroom timber Lodges. Situated on the banks of the River Glass, enjoying some of Scotland's most spectacular mountains & glens. Ideal base for exploring north-west Scotland. With Games Room, Playground, Laundry. Barbecue area.

12 chalets, 2 pub rms, 3 bedrms (grd flr avail), sleeps 6, total sleeping capacity 72, £165.00-£475.00, Jan-Dec, bus nearby, rail 27 mls, airport 27 mls

Glen Affric Chalet Park
Cannich, Beauly, IV4 7LT
Tel: (Cannich) 01456 415369

Important: Prices stated are estimates and may be subject to amendments

nich, Inverness-shire **Map Ref: 3H9**

★ SELF CATERING

A detached cottage, quietly situated on private estate amidst rugged scenery of Strathglass. Fishing available.

1 cottage, 1 pub rm, 3 bedrms, sleeps 5, £145.00-£360.00, Mar-Nov, rail 30 mls, airport 40 mls

Mrs J Grove
34 Stevenage Road, London, SW6 6ET
Tel: 0171 736 1533 Fax: 0171 731 4159

★★★ SELF CATERING

Two cottages, two chalets and self-contained wing of house, all of individual style and character, set amidst beautiful scenery of Strathglass.

2 log cabins, 1 house, 2 cottages, 1-2 pub rms, 1-4 bedrms (grd flr avail), sleeps 2-10, total sleeping capacity 35, min let weekend, £200.00-£495.00, Jan-Dec, bus 2 mls, rail 26 mls,

Ms Gillian Kirkpatrick
Kerrow House, Cannich, Strathglass, Inverness-shire, IV4 7NA
Tel: (Cannich) 01456 415243 Fax: 01456 415425
Email: sab@kerrow-house.demon.co.uk

★ SELF CATERING

Spacious house situated amidst spectacular scenery at the eastern end of Loch Mullardoch. Fishing available, ideal hill-walking area.

1 flat, 1 pub rm, 2 bedrms (grd flr avail), sleeps 4, £175.00, Jan-Aug, bus 9 mls, rail 35 mls, airport 40 mls

Ninon Lawaetz
Benula Estate, Glen Cannich, IV4 7LX
Tel: (Cannich) 01456 415347

★★★ SELF CATERING

Well equipped ground floor accommodation attached to owners house and home farm - open views to Strathglass. Situated on the fringe of Glen Affric, 1 mile away. Loch Ness is 12.5 miles. Easy access to Munros for hillwalkers. Fishing and shooting by arrangement. Mountain bikes available in the area for hire. Post Office and local shop 2 miles.

2 apartments, 1 bedrm (grd flr avail), sleeps 4, total sleeping capacity 8, £290.00-£390.00, Easter-Oct, bus 2 mls, rail 28 mls, airport 38 mls

Mrs Christine Allen Noble
Hill House, Kerrow Farm, Cannich, Inverness-shire, IV4 7NA
Tel: (Cannich) 01456 415300

Cannich, Inverness-shire

Map Ref: 3H9

A modern family bungalow in a fenced garden on the edge of a village at the entrance of the famously beautiful Glen Affric and three other glens. Large sitting room, open fire, full gas central heating, airing cupboard, bathroom, separate shower room, telephone, washer drier, freezer, microwave, tv, video. Marked walks in the Caledonian Forest, lochs, waterfalls, mountains, birds of prey centre close by.

1 bungalow, 1 pub rm, 3 bedrms, sleeps 5, £210.00-£400.00, Jan-Dec, bus nearby, rail 27 mls, airport 27 mls

The Revd. & Mrs A M Roff
Rowan Glen, Culbokie, Dingwall, IV7 8JY
Tel: (Culbokie) 01349 877762
Email: 106770.3175@compuserve.com

Carrbridge, Inverness-shire

Map Ref: 4C9

Modern log cabin peacefully situated on the outskirts of the village, overlooking trekking centre.

1 log cabin, 1 pub rm, 3 bedrms (grd flr avail), sleeps 6, £180.00-£260.00, Apr-Oct, bus 400 yds, rail 400 yds

Mr & Mrs G Carnegie
Ravendean, West Linton, Peeblesshire, EH46 7EN
Tel: (West Linton) 01968 660687 Fax: 01968 660687
Email: 100566.2036@compuserve.com

Wooden chalets in hotel grounds surrounded by mature pinewoods and overlooking small lochan, in 7 acres of parkland near village. Ski slopes 13 miles (21kms).

6 chalets, 1 flat, 1 pub rm, 1-3 bedrms (grd flr avail), sleeps 2-6, total sleeping capacity 32, min let 2 days, £140.00-£400.00, Dec-Oct, bus nearby, rail 1/2 ml, airport 20 mls

Fairwinds Chalets
Carrbridge, Inverness-shire, PH23 3AA
Tel: (Carrbridge) 01479 841240 Fax: 01479 841240

Cawdor, Nairnshire

Map Ref: 4C8

Cottage situated at end of sheltered valley on edge of the Cawdor Estate grouse moors. Peaceful, idyllic location with fine views.

1 cottage, 2 pub rms, 2 bedrms, sleeps 6, £200.00-£380.00, Jan-Dec

Mr & Mrs J P Rochford
The Cose, Clunas, Nairn, Inverness-shire, IV12 5UT
Tel: 01667 404703/01309 651276

Cottage tucked away on the banks of the River Findhorn. Perfect for a holiday of relaxation, scenic beauty, fishing and walking.

1 cottage, 2 pub rms, 3 bedrms (grd flr avail), sleeps 6-7, £423.00-£550.00, Mar-Oct, bus 13 mls, rail 13 mls, airport 18 mls

Mrs A Tennant
Holiday Cottages, Cawdor Estate Office, Cawdor, IV12 5RE
Tel: (Cawdor) 01667 404666 Fax: 01667 404787
Email: office@cawdor-est.demon.co.uk

Important: Prices stated are estimates and may be subject to amendments

ᵧdor, Nairnshire

Map Ref: 4C8

★★

SELF ᴀTERING

A schoolhouse until 1950's, now a comfortable cottage of interesting design. Situated with own grounds, in woodland area. 4 miles (6kms) to Cawdor.

1 house, 1 pub rm, 4 bedrms (grd flr avail), sleeps 7, £185.00-£435.00, Apr-Nov, bus 3 mls, rail 9 mls, airport 8 mls

Mr & Mrs C R Thompson
18 Howard Place, Edinburgh, EH3 5JZ
Tel: 0131 556 4092 Fax: 0131 556 4092

ıtin, Ross-shire

Map Ref: 4A8

★★★

SELF ᴀTERING

Two purpose built lodges, total heating throughout, on edge of forest area with fields and wooded hills around.

2 chalets, 1 pub rm, 3 bedrms (grd flr avail), sleeps 6, total sleeping capacity 12, £185.00-£350.00, Jan-Dec, bus 250 yds, rail 7 mls, airport 24 mls

Mr L Melvin
Linsmore, Torview, Contin, by Strathpeffer, Ross-shire, IV14 9EE
Tel: (Strathpeffer) 01997 421551

pach, by Fort William, Inverness-shire

Map Ref: 3H12

★★

SELF ᴀTERING

Two cedar bungalows on small privately owned site in quiet residential area. 4 miles (6 kms) from Fort William, on Mallaig Road. Ideal base for touring.

2 chalets, 1 pub rm, 2 bedrms, sleeps 4, total sleeping capacity 8, £220.00-£320.00, Apr-Oct, bus nearby, rail ½ ml

Mr H Campbell
Rowanlea Holiday Chalets, Corpach, Inverness-shire, PH33 7LX
Tel: (Corpach) 01397 772586

marty, Ross-shire

Map Ref: 4B7

★★

SELF ᴀTERING

Charming pine chalet adjacent to owners house, a short walk from the centre of this historic village. Good sized private garden with patios; gate opening onto beach. A relaxed and tranquil setting. Dogs welcome.

1 chalet, 1 pub rm, 1 bedrm (grd flr avail), sleeps 2, £200.00, Apr-Sep, bus ¼ ml, rail 23 mls, ferry ¼ ml, airport 35 mls

Mrs J Campbell
Clunes House, Miller Road, Cromarty, IV11 8XH
Tel: (Cromarty) 01381 600503

VAT is shown at 17.5%: changes in this rate may affect prices.

Key to symbols is on back flap.

Culbokie, Ross-shire Map Ref: 4B8

WESTER BRAE HIGHLAND LODGES

CULBOKIE, BY DINGWALL IV7 8JU
TELEPHONE: 01349 877609 FAX: 01349 877221

5 LODGES IN ELEVATED POSITION WITH PANORAMIC VIEWS OF THE HILLS OF ROSS-SHIRE. IDEAL BASE FOR TOURING, WALKING, DOLPHIN WATCHING OR SIMPLY RELAXING IN A QUIET PEACEFUL SETTING. EQUIPPED AND FURNISHED TO A VERY HIGH STANDARD, CENTRAL HEATING, DISHWASHERS, WASHING MACHINES AND DRYERS IN EACH UNIT, ALL LINEN. COLOUR BROCHURE.

★★★★ SELF CATERING

★★★★ SELF CATERING

Five lodges on a small privately owned site with superb views over Cromarty Firth and Ben Wyvis. Approx 5 miles (8 kms) from Culbokie.

5 lodges, 1-2 pub rms, 2-3 bedrms (grd flr avail), sleeps 4-5, total sleeping capacity 26, £150.00-£350.00, Jan-Dec, bus 2 mls, rail 9 mls, airport 20 mls

Mrs Phillips
Wester Brae Highland Lodges, Culbokie, by Dingwall, Ross-shire, IV7 8JU
Tel: (Culbokie) 01349 877609 Fax: 01349 877221

Culkein, Sutherland Map Ref: 3G4

★ SELF CATERING

Three well equipped chalets situated in an area of outstanding natural beauty. Thirty yds (27m) from a safe sandy beach.

3 chalets, 3 pub rms, 2-3 bedrms, sleeps 4-6, total sleeping capacity 15, £155.00-£310.00, Apr-Oct, bus 10 mls, rail 50 mls

Mrs V MacLeod
7 Mount Stuart Road, Largs, Ayrshire, KA30 9ES
Tel: (Largs) 01475 672931 Fax: 01475 674655

★★★ SELF CATERING

Modern bungalow set back from the shore. Superb views across Culkein Bay to the hills beyond. Hill walking, mountain climbing, birds and wildlife in abundance. Ideal base for exploring North West Sutherland.

1 bungalow, 1 pub rm, 3 bedrms, sleeps 6, £120.00-£240.00, Mar-Oct, bus 10 mls, rail 55 mls, airport 100 mls

Mrs C MacLeod
Cherry Lodge, Kilmichael Glassary, Lochgilphead, Argyll, PA31 8QA
Tel: (Lochgilphead) 01546 605204

Dalcross, by Inverness, Inverness-shire Map Ref: 4B8

★★★ UP TO ★★★★ SELF CATERING

Tastefully decorated Victorian cottages in peaceful setting on working farm near Inverness. Short drive to Culloden, Fort George and Cawdor. 30 minutes to Aviemore. Woodland walks and open views.

3 cottages, 1 pub rm, 3 bedrms (grd flr avail), sleeps 4-6, total sleeping capacity 16, £120.00-£410.00, Jan-Dec, bus 1 ml, rail 8 mls, airport 1 ml

Bob & Margaret Pottie
Easter Dalziel Farm, Dalcross,by Inverness, Inverness-shire, IV1 2J
Tel: (Ardersier) 01667 462213 Fax: 01667 462213

Important: Prices stated are estimates and may be subject to amendments

iot, Inverness-shire — Map Ref: 4B9

100

Auchnahillin Caravan & Camping Park

Daviot East, Inverness-shire Tel: 01463 772286 Fax: 01463 772282
Email: auch@zetnet.co.uk Web: http:users.zetnet.co.uk/auch/

10 acres, grassy, hard-standing, level, Apr-Oct, prior booking in peak periods, latest time of arrival 2200, overnight holding area. Extra charge for electricity, awnings,

T SP

65 tourers from £7.50 or 65 motors £7.00-9.00 or 20 tents £5.50-8.00. Total Touring Pitches 65.

18 Holiday Caravans to let, sleep 4-6 £135.00-300.00, total sleeping capacity 104, min let 2 nights.

TV E

Leisure facilities:

Situated 7 mls sth of Inverness on B9154 off A9

aig, Ross-shire — Map Ref: 3F8

★★ SELF TERING

Traditional croft beside the road to Diabaig. Superb views over Diabaig Bay, surrounding hills and on a clear day over to Skye. Sleeping six, it is ideal for a family holiday and also well suited for climbers, walkers and nature watchers.

1 house, 3 bedrms (grd flr avail), sleeps 6, £160.00-£220.00, Mar-Dec, bus ½ ml, rail 30 mls, airport 80 mls

TV

M

Mrs C Duncan
13 Diabaig, Torridon, by Achnasheen, Ross-shire, IV22 2HE
Tel: (Diabaig) 01445 790259

★★ SELF TERING

Period cottage with original pine cladding in tranquil setting adjoining the village pier.

1 house, 1 pub rm, 4 bedrms (grd flr avail), sleeps 4-7, £250.00-£350.00, Jan-Dec, bus post bus, rail 36 mls

TV

M

Mr R Steward
The Forge, Upottery,by Honiton, Devon, EX14 9PL
Tel: (Upottery) 01404 861420

wall, Ross-shire — Map Ref: 4A8

★★ SELF TERING

Large T shaped bungalow with garden, split into two self contained units, quiet rural area 2 miles from Dingwall and Strathpeffer. Numerous golf courses and local walks in the area. Central for exploring the West Highlands and the far north, as well as the towns and villages of Easter Ross and East Sutherland.

2 cottages, 1-2 pub rms, 2-3 bedrms (grd flr avail), sleeps 3-5, total sleeping capacity 8, £100.00-£270.00, Apr-Oct, bus 150 yds, rail 3 mls, airport 25 mls

TV

Mrs C Manson
Inchvannie House, Strathpeffer, Ross-shire
Tel: (Strathpeffer) 01997 421436

★★ SELF TERING

Restored cottages on 4000 acres of richly wooded farmland. The estate offers free trout and pike fishing, garden and forest walks, shooting and stalking. Riding centre, bicycle hire. As well as local activities and attractions, the estate's location makes it an ideal base for exploring the rest of the far north and the West Highlands.

2 houses, 8 cottages, 1-3 pub rms, 2-7 bedrms (grd flr avail), sleeps 4-13, total sleeping capacity 60, £150.00-£690.00, Jan-Dec, bus ½ ml, rail 1 ml, airport 20 mls

TV

M T SP

Seaforth Highland Country Estate
Dingwall, Ross-shire, IV7 8EE
Tel: (Dingwall) 01349 865505/861150 Fax: 01349 861745
Email: seaforth@enterprise.net

VAT is shown at 17.5%: changes in this rate may affect prices.

Key to symbols is on back flap.

Dores, Inverness-shire

Map Ref: 4B9

SELF CATERING

Secluded site with three log cabins on farm above Loch Ness. Horse riding facilities available.

3 log cabins, 2 pub rms, 2 bedrms (grd flr avail), sleeps 4-6, total sleeping capacity 18, £175.00-£370.00, Jan-Dec, bus 2 mls, rail 10 mls, airport 15 mls

Mr & Mrs A I Cameron
Drummond Farm, Dores, Inverness-shire, IV1 2TX
Tel: (Dores) 01463 751251 Fax: 01463 751240

Dornie, by Kyle of Lochalsh, Ross-shire

Map Ref: 3G9

SELF CATERING

Traditional detached cottage in peaceful location on loch side with distant views of Eilean Donan Castle. 7 miles (11kms) from Isle of Skye bridge.

2 cottages, 1-2 pub rms, 2-3 bedrms, sleeps 4-6, total sleeping capacity 10, £250.00-£350.00, Jan-Dec, bus 1/4 ml, rail 7 mls, ferry 7 mls, airport 83 mls

Zoe Macleod
Tigh-na-Fasgadh, 23 Cumuslongart, Ardelve, Dornie,by Kyle of Lochalsh, Ross-shire , IV40 8EX
Tel: (Dornie) 01599 555 357/0468 428242 (mobile)

Dornoch, Sutherland

Map Ref: 4B6

SELF CATERING

Spacious detached house set in large garden, close to Royal Dornoch golf course and safe sandy beaches.

1 house, 3-4 pub rms, 3-4 bedrms (grd flr avail), sleeps 6, £300.00-£395.00, Apr-Oct, bus nearby, rail 10 mls, airport 40 mls

Mrs L Hartwell
Dall, Rannoch, Perthshire, PH17 2QH
Tel: (Kinloch Rannoch) 01882 632228 Fax: 01882 632228
Email: 106167.1152@compuserve.com

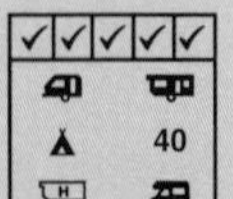

40

Pitgrudy Caravan Park

Poles Road, Dornoch, Sutherland, IV25 3HY Tel: (Edderton) 01862 821253 Fax: 01862 821382
Booking Enquiries: GNR Sutherland Caravan Sales Edderton, Tain, Ross-shire, IV19 1JY
Tel: (Dornoch) 01862 821253 Fax: 01862 821382

7 acres, grassy, hard-standing, sloping, May-Sep, prior booking in peak periods, latest time of arrival 2000. Extra charge for electricity, awnings.

35 tourers £7.50-9.50 or 35 motors £9.50 or 5 tents £7.00-8.50. Total Touring P 40.

8 Holiday Caravans to let, sleep 2-5 £100.00-285.00, total sleeping capacity 45, min let 3 nights.

Leisure facilities:

From Dornoch take B9168 N at war memorial. Site approx. 3/4 ml on right.

Drumnadrochit, Inverness-shire

Map Ref: 4A9

SELF CATERING

Cottage in row of three on working farm in rural setting near Urquhart Castle and Loch Ness. Riding available.

1 cottage, 1 pub rm, 3 bedrms (grd flr avail), sleeps 6, Jan-Dec, bus nearby, rail 15 mls, airport 25 mls

Borlum Farm Country Holidays
Reservations, Borlum Farm, Drumnadrochit, Inverness-shire, IV3
Tel: (Drumnadrochit) 01456 450358 Fax: 01456 450358

Important: Prices stated are estimates and may be subject to amendments

nnadrochit, Inverness-shire **Map Ref: 4A9**

★★ SELF TERING

Comfortable apartment, with own private entrance, adjoining owners' house in this small Highland village. Loch Ness nearby.

1 house, 1 flat, 1 pub rm, 2 bedrms (grd flr avail), sleeps 4-6, total sleeping capacity 10, £150.00-£350.00, Apr-Sep, bus nearby, rail 15 mls, airport 20 mls

Mrs M Campbell
Glen of Ferness, Lewiston, Drumnadrochit, Inverness-shire, IV3 6UW
Tel: (Drumnadrochit) 01456450 564

★★★ SELF TERING

Delightful cottage, sleeping 2/5 in 3 bedrooms, in Highland village amidst beautiful scenery near Loch Ness. High quality furniture and fittings – dish washer, washer/dryer, microwave, freezer, TV, hi-fi, open fire. Linen, heating inc., garden and parking. Visit Inverness, Glen Affric, day trips to Skye, Fort William, castles and distilleries. Non-smokers only. No pets. Visitors book comment: "Best cottage we've ever had".

1 cottage, 2 pub rms, 3 bedrms, sleeps 5, £195.00-£400.00, Jan-Dec, bus 1/2 ml, rail 16 mls, airport 22 mls

Mr & Mrs J Elmslie
Clach Mhuilinn, 7 Harris Road, Inverness, IV2 3LS
Tel: (Inverness) 01463 237059 Fax: 01463 242092
Email: elmslie@globalnet.co.uk

Booking Enquiries: Mrs J Fraser Lower Milton Farm, Drumnadrochit, Loch Ness, IV3 6TZ
Tel: (Drumnadrochit) 01456 450554 Fax: 01456 450554

2 Holiday Caravans to let, sleep 6 £120.00-165.00, total sleeping capacity 12, min let 3 nights, May-Sep.

From Drumnadrochit take A831 for 3/4 ml. Caravans on left immediately after Shell petrol station.

Drumnadrochit, Inverness-shire Map Ref: 4A9

House and lodges of individual style and character in a 70 acre woodland setting high above the village. Magnificent views of surrounding area and towards Loch Ness. Privacy and comfort.

10 chalets, 1 pub rm, 3 bedrms (grd flr avail), sleeps 2-6, total sleeping capacity 60, £195.00-£510.00, Mar-Nov, bus 1/2 ml, rail 16 mls, airport 23 mls

Mrs Elizabeth Mackintosh
Achmony Holidays, Drumnadrochit, by Loch Ness, IV3 6UX
Tel: (Drumnadrochit) 01456 450357 Fax: 01456 450830

Dulnain Bridge, by Grantown-on-Spey, Inverness-shire Map Ref: 4C9

Set in a peaceful rural location, and recently built, The Cabrach lies at the very heart of beautiful Strathspey, famous worldwide for its magnificient scenery. Abundance of wildlife, fishing, its malt whisky distilleries and winter sports facilities.

1 house, 2 pub rms, 4 bedrms (grd flr avail), sleeps 8, £200.00-£400.00, Jan-Dec, bus 1 ml, rail 10 mls, ferry 30 mls, airport 30 mls

Mrs Elizabeth Grant
Woodside, Skye of Curr, Dulnain Bridge, Inverness-shire, PH26 3F
Tel: (Dulnain Bridge) 01479 851229

Warm cosy cottage in a quiet, peaceful situation high up overlooking Cairngorms. With it's own garden and patio. Close to local amenities.

1 cottage, 1-2 pub rms, 1-2 bedrms, sleeps 4-5, £135.00-£210.00, Jan-Dec, bus 1/2 ml, rail 7 mls, airport 35 mls

Peter Strother
Upper Finlarig, Dulnain Bridge, Inverness-shire, PH26 3NU
Tel: (Dulnain Bridge) 01479 851209
Email: finlarig@enterprise.net

Important: Prices stated are estimates and may be subject to amendments

nain Bridge, by Grantown-on-Spey, Inverness-shire Map Ref: 4C9

★★★ SELF ATERING

Restored castle dating from 16c standing in its own grounds with fine views towards Cairngorms.

1 castle, 1 pub rm, 4 bedrms, sleeps 8, £590.00-£1030.00, Jan-Dec, bus 1/2 ml, rail 12 mls, airport 35 mls

Strutt & Parker
St Nicholas House, 68 Station Road, Banchory, Kincardineshire, AB31 5YJ
Tel: (Banchory) 01330 824888 Fax: 01330 825577

ıbeath, Caithness Map Ref: 4D4

★★★ SELF ATERING

Charming stone built terraced cottage in this quiet East coast village. Restaurant and bar meals nearby. Wick 20 miles (34 kms) and Thurso 25 miles (40 Kms).

1 cottage, 1 pub rm, 2 bedrms, sleeps 6, £105.00-£275.00, Jan-Dec exc Xmas/New Year, rail 16 mls, airport 20 mls

Mrs H Lindsay
Tigh A Mhuilinn, Dunbeath, Caithness, KW6 6EG
Tel: (Dunbeath) 01593 731259

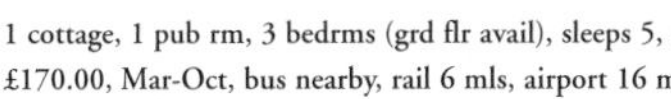

ıcanston, Ross-shire Map Ref: 4B8

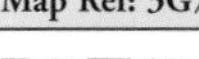

★★ SELF ATERING

Comfortable farm cottage on working farm with delightful views over the Cromarty Firth and surrounding hills. Central for touring.

1 cottage, 1 pub rm, 3 bedrms (grd flr avail), sleeps 5, £130.00-£170.00, Mar-Oct, bus nearby, rail 6 mls, airport 16 mls

Mrs A Hannan
Shalom, Dunvournie , Culbokie,by Dingwall, Ross-shire, IV7 8JB
Tel: (Culbokie) 01349 877246

ıdonnell, Ross-shire Map Ref: 3G7

★★★ SELF ATERING

Situated on shore of Little Loch Broom. Ideal for walkers being close to An Teallach Mountain Range.

2 chalets, 1 pub rm, 2 bedrms (grd flr avail), sleeps 4-6, total sleeping capacity 12, from £200.00, Jan-Dec, rail 34 mls, ferry 26 mls, airport 60 mls

Mrs A Ross
4 Camusnagaul, Dundonnell, Ross-shire, IV23 2QT
Tel: (Dundonnell) 01854 633237

★★★ SELF ATERING

A tranquil lochshore croft overlooking the mighty Anteallach with gas lighting, peat fires and crisp linen sheets. Watch otters, porpoises, red deer, pine martins, golden eagles, seals, mountain goats and ptarmigans (in white plumage in winter). Walk in Scotland's last great wilderness or just relax with a dram in our uniquely designed warm and cosy cottage and enjoy the view. Bliss!

1 cottage, 1-2 pub rms, 1-3 bedrms, sleeps 4, min let weekend, £120.00-£250.00, Jan-Dec, bus 7 mls, rail 30 mls, ferry 3 mls, airport 60 mls

Mrs A Stott
Croft 9, Badrallach, Dundonnell, by Garve, Ross-shire, IV23 2QP
Tel: (Dundonnell) 01854 633281

VAT is shown at 17.5%: changes in this rate may affect prices.

Key to symbols is on back flap.

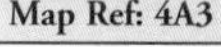

Durness, Sutherland

Map Ref: 4A3

★★ UP TO ★★★ SELF CATERING

Semi-detached stone cottages refurbished to a high standard with comfort and warmth a priority.

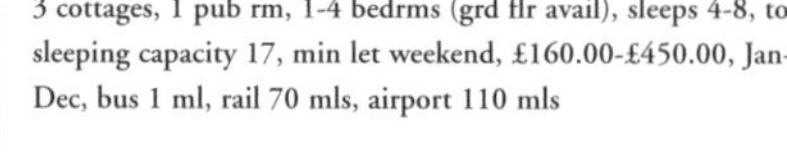

3 cottages, 1 pub rm, 1-4 bedrms (grd flr avail), sleeps 4-8, total sleeping capacity 17, min let weekend, £160.00-£450.00, Jan-Dec, bus 1 ml, rail 70 mls, airport 110 mls

Mr R Norman
Oldbury House, Ightham, Sevenoaks, Kent, TN15 9DE
Tel: (Borough Green) 01732 882320

★★ SELF CATERING

Traditional small cottage adjoining local village shop and some caravan parking. Partially converted with steep, narrow staircase, modern shower room and large conservatory with sea views.

1 cottage, 2 pub rms, 2 bedrms, sleeps 4-5, £140.00-£260.00, Apr-Sep, bus nearby, rail 55 mls, airport 100 mls

M Patience
1 Doric Drive, Kingswood, Surrey, KT20 6HH
Tel: (Tadworth) 01737 355740 Fax: 01737 270820

Eigg, Isle of, Inverness-shire

Map Ref: 3E11

★★ SELF CATERING

Sue and Alistair have renovated one of their two adjoining croft cottages to provide comfortable self contained accommodation. The nearby "Singing Sands" beach and magnificent views across the sea to Isle of Rum are all part of the unique Eigg experience.

2 cottages, 2 pub rms, 3 bedrms (grd flr avail), sleeps 6, total sleeping capacity 12, £180.00-£380.00, Jan-Dec, ferry 3 mls

Sue Kirk
Lageorna, Isle of Eigg, Inverness-shire, PH42 4RL
Tel: (Mallaig) 01687 482405

Embo, by Dornoch, Sutherland

Map Ref: 4B6

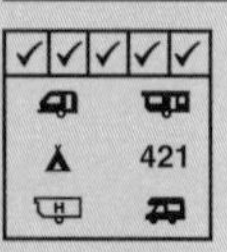

✓✓✓✓✓ 421

Grannies Heilan Hame Holiday Park

Embo, Dornoch, Sutherland, IV25 3QP Tel: (Dornoch) 01862 810383 Fax: 01862 810368

Booking Enquiries: Haven Reservations Po Box 218, 1 Park Lane, Hemel Hempstead, HP2 4GL

Tel: 0990 233111

32 acres, grassy, sandy, level, Mar-Oct, prior booking in peak periods, latest time of arrival 2300, overnight holding area. Extra charge for electricity, awnings.

224 tourers or 224 motors or 100 tents. Total Touring Pitches 324. Charges on application.

104 Holiday Caravans to let, sleep 6-8, total sleeping capacity 540, m let 2 nights.

Leisure facilities:

A9 from Inverness via Kessock Bridge to Dornoch. Then left at Main Square to Emb mls) beside Grannies Heilan Hame park.

Evanton, Ross-shire

Map Ref: 4B7

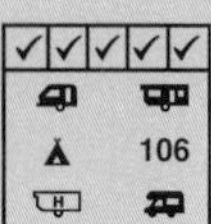

✓✓✓✓✓ 106

Black Rock Caravan & Camping Park

Evanton, Ross-shire, IV16 9UN Tel: (Evanton) 01349 830917
Fax: 01349 830321

4 1/2 acres, grassy, level, sheltered, Apr-Oct, prior booking in peak periods, latest time of arrival 2200, overnight holding area. Extra charge for electricity, awnings.

55 tourers £8.00-10.00 or 55 motors £8.00-10.00 or 12 tents £6.00-8.00. Total Touring Pitches 67.

6 Holiday Caravans to let, sleep 4-6 £175.00-265.00, total sleeping capacity 34, min let 3 nights.

Leisure facilities:

A9 N from Inverness for 15 mls, turn left for Evanton B817 proceed for 3/4 ml.

Important: Prices stated are estimates and may be subject to amendments

ton, Ross-shire Map Ref: 4B7

★★★ SELF TERING

Luxury apartment within Foulis Castle, home of the Chiefs of Clan Munro, who have lived here since at least the 12th century. Part of the pavillion dates from the early 16th century, the rest from the 1750s. Magnificent courtyard garden. Approx 18 miles (29kms) north of Inverness.

1 house, 2 pub rms, 2 bedrms, sleeps 4, min let 3 nights, £280.00-£420.00, Jan-Dec, bus 1 1/2 mls, rail 4 mls, airport 30 mls

Mrs Munro
Foulis Castle, Evanton, Ross-shire, IV16 9UX
Tel: (Evanton) 01349 830212

★★ SELF TERING

'A'-Framed chalet, one of three, situated near to local pub and restaurant. Close to railway line and main A9.

1 chalet, 1 pub rm, 2 bedrms, sleeps 4-6, £250.00, Jan-Dec, bus nearby, rail 3 mls, airport 20 mls

Wheel Inn
Novar Toll, Evanton, Ross-shire, IV16 9XH
Tel: (Evanton) 01349 830763

---

ie Bridge, by Kincraig, Inverness-shire Map Ref: 4C10

★★ SELF TERING

Modern cottage, in quiet setting by River Feshie. Within 8 miles (13kms) of Aviemore and 1 mile (2kms) of Loch Insh.

1 bungalow, 2 pub rms, 3 bedrms, sleeps 5, £260.00-£290.00, Apr-Oct, bus 8 mls, rail 8 mls

W Adam
Blinkbonny, Milnathort, Kinross-shire, KY13 7SD
Tel: (Milnathort) 01577 865083

★★★ SELF TERING

Two interconnecting, Scandinavian-style, pine chalets, nestling at edge of Cairngorm Nature Reserve, enjoying superb views of mountains and Glen Feshie.

2 chalets, 1-2 pub rms, 1-3 bedrms (grd flr avail), sleeps 2-5, total sleeping capacity 9, min let 5 days, £200.00-£380.00, Jan-Dec, bus 2 mls, rail 2 mls

Mr & Mrs W J Lornie
43 Dalmahoy Crescent, Balerno, Edinburgh, EH14 7BZ
Tel: 0131 449 3981 Fax: 0131 449 3981

Augustus, Inverness-shire Map Ref: 4A10

★ SELF TERING

Traditional cottage situated in its own grounds with burn. Views overlooking Fort Augustus village towards the Caledonian Canal.

1 cottage, 1 pub rm, 3 bedrms (grd flr avail), sleeps 6, min let 3 nights (low season), £150.00-£300.00, Jan-Dec, bus nearby, rail 23 mls, airport 38 mls

Mrs Cath Cameron
2 Balmaglaster, by Spean Bridge, Inverness-shire, PH34 4EB
Tel: (Invergarry) 01809 501289

VAT is shown at 17.5%: changes in this rate may affect prices.

Key to symbols is on back flap.

Fortrose, Ross-shire

Map Ref: 4B8

★★★
SELF CATERING

Spacious detached farm cottage, with large garden area, situated on the edge of Fortrose village. Close to the golf course and to Chanonry Point, an excellent spot for looking for the famous Moray Firth Dolphins. Good base for exploring the Black Isle, Easter Ross and beyond.

1 cottage, 1 pub rm, 3 bedrms (grd flr avail), sleeps 6, £120.00-£380.00, Mar-Nov, bus 1/2 ml, rail 14 mls, airport 21 mls

Mrs Grant
Fasgadh, Ness Road, Fortrose, Ross-shire, IV10 8SD
Tel: (Fortrose) 01381 620367

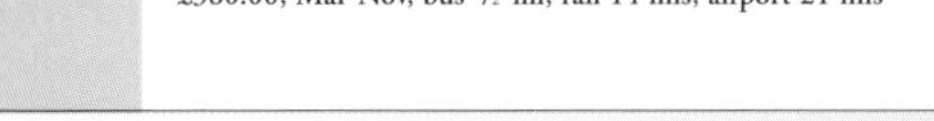

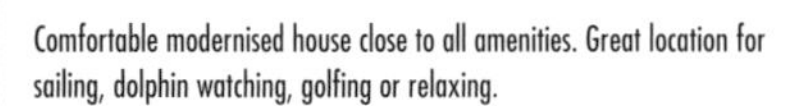

★★★
SELF CATERING

Comfortable modernised house close to all amenities. Great location for sailing, dolphin watching, golfing or relaxing.

1 cottage, 2 pub rms, 2 bedrms, sleeps 1-4, £180.00-£320.00, Apr-Oct, bus nearby, rail 15 mls, airport 20 mls

Middleton Ross & Arnot
Mansefield House, Dingwall, Ross-shire, IV15 9HJ
Tel: (Invergordon) 01349 862214/865125 Fax: 01349 863819

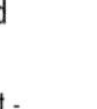

★★
SELF CATERING

Comfortable and well appointed house, with labour saving dishwasher and microwave provided, situated in quiet residential area of Fortrose. Safe secluded garden. Fine views over the Moray Firth, close to Chanonry Point - an excellent location for dolphin watching.

1 house, 1 pub rm, 4 bedrms (grd flr avail), sleeps 8, £195.00-£305.00, Apr-Oct, bus 1/2 ml, rail 12 mls, airport 15 mls

Mr M Strachan
332 Blackness Road, Dundee, DD2 1SD
Tel: (Dundee) 01382 660804

Fort William, Inverness-shire

Map Ref: 3H12

★★
SELF CATERING

Small ground floor flat of split level house in an elevated position overlooking Fort William and surrounding hills. Situated in a quiet cul-de-sac, private parking. Small patio area with garden furniture provided within a quiet garden. Use of laundry facilities. On bus route.

1 flat, 1 pub rm, 1 bedrm, sleeps 2-4, £160.00-£220.00, Jan-Dec, bus nearby, rail 1 ml

Abrach House
4 Caithness Place, Fort William, Inverness-shire, PH33 6JP
Tel: (Fort William) 01397 702535 Fax: 01397 702535
Email: cmoore3050@aol.com

★★
SELF CATERING

Modern compact flat attached to family home in quiet residential area 1 mile (2kms) from town centre. On main bus route. Walkers and climbers welcome. 5 miles from ski slope, 15 minutes walk from Fort William town centre. Own small patio area to rear. Brochure available on request.

1 flat, 1 pub rm, 1 bedrm, sleeps 4, £120.00-£185.00, Jan-Dec, bus 1/4 ml, rail 1 ml

Mrs E Clark
14 Perth Place, Fort William, PH33 6UL
Tel: 01397 702444 Fax: 01397 702141

Important: Prices stated are estimates and may be subject to amendments

t William, Inverness-shire **Map Ref: 3H12**

SELF CATERING

Lodge situated at the head of its own Glen, commanding spectacular views of the surrounding mountains. Solidly built and maintained as a family home, it is warm and snug in all weathers. Ideal for those seeking peace and solitude and for the active, there is Glen and hill-walking and trout fishing.

1 lodge, 3 pub rms, 4 bedrms, sleeps 8, £650.00-£750.00, Jan-Dec, bus 3 mls, rail 3 mls, ferry 31 mls, airport 80 mls

Mrs Fiona Gibson
Glenfinnan Estate, Fort William, Inverness-shire, PH37 4LT
Tel: (Fort William) 01397 722203

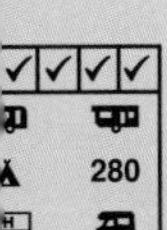

SELF CATERING

Modern semi-detached house, with own garden, at gable-end of terrace, in residential area above the town centre.

1 house, 2 pub rms, 3 bedrms, sleeps 6, £200.00-£305.00, Jan-Dec, bus nearby, rail 1 ml, airport 70 mls

Mrs A Gillies
West Highland Hotel, Mallaig, Inverness-shire, PH41 4QZ
Tel: (Mallaig) 01687 462210 Fax: 01687 462130

✓✓✓✓ 280

Glen Nevis Holiday Caravans
Glen Nevis, Fort William, Inverness-shire, PH33 6SX Tel: (Fort William) 01397 702191 Fax: 01397 703904 Email: holidays@glen-

4 acres, grassy, hard-standing, level, Easter-mid Oct, prior booking in peak periods.

29 Holiday Caravans to let, sleep 2-6 £200.00-375.00, total sleeping capacity 154, min let 3 nights, Easter-mid Oct.

From A82 at r/about N of Fort William, turn E signed Glen Nevis. Park 2.5 mls on right signposted Glen Nevis Holiday Caravans/Holiday Cottages.

SELF CATERING

Magnificent holiday lodges offering the utmost in comfort for up to 6 persons. 3 bedrooms (1 double and 2 twin) and two bath/shower rooms. Fully equipped kitchens. Non smokers only and regret no pets. Also modern purpose built cottages all in the midst of the best of highland scenery in famous Glen Nevis. Enjoy peaceful surroundings with lots to see and do nearby, only 4 kms from Fort William. Colour brochure available.

12 cottages, 1 pub rm, 2 bedrms (grd flr avail), sleeps 4-5, total sleeping capacity 60, £300.00-£480.00, Feb-mid Nov, mid Dec-Jan, bus 2 mls, rail 2 1/2 mls

Glen Nevis Holiday Cottages
Glen Nevis, Fort William, Inverness-shire, PH33 6SX
Tel: (Fort William) 01397 702191 Fax: 01397 703904
Email: holidays@glen-nevis.demon.co.uk
Web: www.lochaber.co.uk/glenevis/

SELF CATERING

Calluna enjoys fine elevated views across Loch Linnhe to the Ardgour Hills. Close to town (10mins walk) yet in a quiet area of Fort William. Ideal for families touring. (Inverness-Oban-Mallaig-Aviemore-Skye are within two hours drive) or mountaineers exploring Ben-Nevis and Glen-Coe. Walkers, canoeists welcome and can have use of the best drying rooms available. Ideal for sharing families or groups of outdoor folk.

1 flat, 2 apartment, 1 pub rm, 2-3 bedrms (grd flr avail), sleeps 6-8, total sleeping capacity 22, min let 1 night, £220.00-£425.00, Jan-Dec, bus nearby, rail nearby, airport 100 mls

Mr & Mrs A W Kimber
Calluna, Heather Croft, Fort William, Inverness-shire, PH33 6RE
Tel: (Fort William) 01397 700451 Fax: 01397 700489
Email: mountain@guide.u-net.com
Web: www.guide.u-net.com

Fort William, Inverness-shire **Map Ref: 3H12**

SELF CATERING

These apartments have been designed, built and furnished to ensure a most enjoyable holiday experience and they are maintained and serviced to ensure a relaxing holiday. Only 1.5 miles from Fort William and overlooking Loch Linnhe to the mountains. Cleanliness is the watchword of the management and staff. Adjoining hotel facilities available April/October.

1 bungalow, 6 apartments, 1 pub rm, 1-2 bedrms (grd flr avail), sleeps 4, total sleeping capacity 28, £175.00-£395.00, Jan-Dec, bus nearby, rail 1 ½ mls, airport 65 mls

Highland Holidays Scotland Ltd
Innseagan House, Achintore Road, Fort William, Inverness-shire, PH33 6RW
Tel: (Fort William) 01397 702452 Fax: 01397 702606

SELF CATERING

Cottage situated within the grounds of our home shielded from view by a mature terraced garden. Tastefully decorated and fully equipped with extra touches to give a 'home from home' feel. Only 1 mile from centre of Fort William. Bus stop 150 yards.

1 bungalow, 1 pub rm, 2 bedrms (grd flr avail), sleeps 4, £195.00-£400.00, Jan-Dec, bus nearby, rail 1 ¼ mls, ferry 8 mls, airport 76 mls

M E Levingston
Whinbrae, 6 Perth Place, Fort William, Inverness-shire, PH33 6UL
Tel: (Fort William) 01397 703743

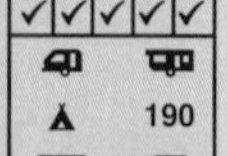

Linnhe Caravan & Chalet Park
Corpach, Fort William, Inverness-shire, PH33 7NL Tel: (Corpach) 01397 772376 Fax: 01397 772007

15 ½ acres, hard-standing, sheltered, mid Dec-Oct, prior booking in peak periods, latest time of arrival 2100, overnight holding area. Extra charge for awnings.

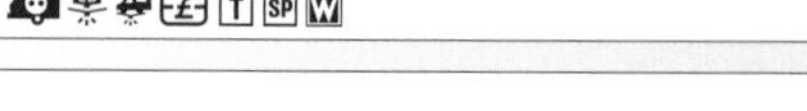

63 tourers £10.00-12.00 or 63 motors £10.00-12.00 or 10 tents £7.50-9.00. Total Touring Pitches 73.

73 Holiday Caravans to let, sleep 1-8 £150.00-415.00, total sleeping capacity 388, min let 2 nights.

Leisure facilities:

On A830, 1 ½ mls W of Corpach village.

SELF CATERING

Two self-contained studio apartments, situated 1 mile (1.5 kms) from town centre. 1 mile (1.5 kms) to foot of Ben Nevis.

2 studio apartments, 1 pub rm, 1 bedrm (grd flr avail), sleeps 2-4, total sleeping capacity 6, £150.00-£315.00, Jan-Dec, bus nearby, rail ½ ml, ferry 8-46 mls, airport 66 mls

Mr & Mrs MacBeth
Glenlochy Apartments, Nevis Bridge, Fort William, Inverness-shire, PH33 6PF
Tel: (Fort William) 01397 702909

Important: Prices stated are estimates and may be subject to amendments

rt William, Inverness-shire Map Ref: 3H12

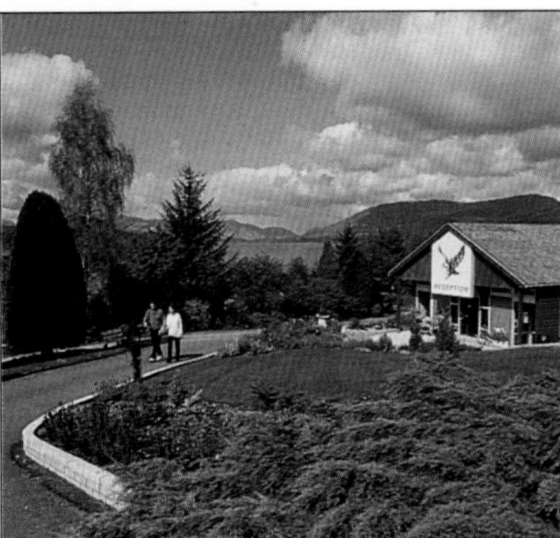

Linnhe Caravan & Chalet Park

Corpach, Fort William, Inverness-shire PH33 7NL
Tel: 01397 772376 Fax: 01397 772007

One of the most beautifully landscaped parks in Scotland with magnificent views over Loch Eil. Ideally situated for many outdoor adventures or for simply relaxing in tranquil, well-tended surroundings. Thistle Award winning HOLIDAY CARAVANS and luxury centrally heated PINE CHALETS offer all home comforts. Graded EXCELLENT, our facilities include a licensed shop, launderette, drying room, toddlers' playroom, playgrounds, private beach, slipway and free fishing. Pet welcome.

Caravans sleeping 1-8 from **£170-£425** per week.
Chalets sleeping 1-5 from **£360-£535** per week.
Breaks from £85.

★★★★ SELF CATERING

Open: 15 December-31 October.

Colour brochure on request.

Comfortable Alpine chalets on beautifully landscaped lochside park. Use of all amenities. Private beach.

6 chalets, 1 pub rm, 2 bedrms (grd flr avail), sleeps 4-5, total sleeping capacity 30, min let 3 nights, £325.00-£525.00, 15 Dec-31 Oct, bus 1 ml, rail 1 ml

Linnhe Caravan & Chalet Park
Corpach, Fort William, Inverness-shire, PH33 7NL
Tel: (Corpach) 01397 772376 Fax: 01397 772007

Purpose built flats in small village on the shores of Loch Linnhe. 3 miles (5kms) from Fort William. Ideal for touring Lochaber.

7 flats, 1 pub rm, 1-2 bedrms (grd flr avail), sleeps 2-4, total sleeping capacity 20, £165.00-£300.00, Jan-Dec, bus nearby, rail 3 mls, airport 60 mls

Mossfield Apartments
Lochyside, Fort William, Inverness-shire, PH33 7NY
Tel: (Fort William) 01397 703087/706061 Fax: 01397 703087

Flat on ground-floor of modern house, on upper outskirts of town, with excellent views across Loch Linnhe.

1 flat, 2 pub rms, 1 bedrm, sleeps 4, £110.00, Jan-Dec, bus nearby, rail 1 1/2 mls

Mrs M Wardle
16 Perth Place, Upper Achintore, Fort William, Inverness-shire, PH33 6UL
Tel: (Fort William) 01397 704392

Fort William, Inverness-shire

Map Ref: 3H12

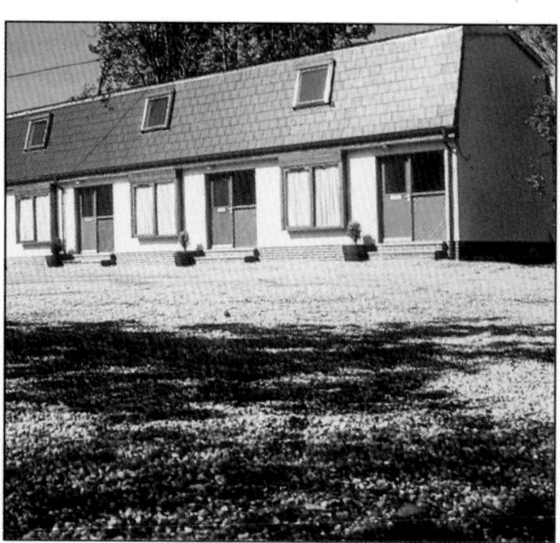

Nevis Bank Apartments

BELFORD ROAD · FORT WILLIAM
Tel: 01397 705721 Fax: 01397 706275

Situated to the rear of our apartments sleeping 2-4 persons is a terrace of 5 new cottages sleeping persons with occasional double bed settee in Loung Fully equipped with linen, central heating and colour TV. They are situated near the approach to Britain's highest mountain, Ben Nevis, and 4½ miles to the s slopes yet only 10 minutes' walk from town centre.

Adequate parking. Open all year. Pets welcome.

- ★ **Ladies/Gents Hairdressing**
- ★ **Childrens' creche on site**

Terms from £225-£425 per unit per week.

For brochure and tariff, please contact Florence Mackay.

★UP TO ★★ SELF CATERING

Terraced cottages with ample parking, 10 minutes walk from town centre. Creche facilities available.

5 cottages, 1-2 pub rms, 2 bedrms, sleeps 4, total sleeping capacity 20, £235.00-£425.00, Jan-Dec, bus nearby, rail 800 yds, airport 70 mls

Nevis Bank Apartments
Belford Road, Fort William, Inverness-shire, PH33 6BY
Tel: (Fort William) 01397 705721 Fax: 01397 706275

Foyers, Inverness-shire

Map Ref: 4A10

★★ SELF CATERING

6 chalets situated in 4 acres of grounds at Foyers Bay House overlooking Loch Ness and 20 miles (32kms) south of Inverness.

6 chalets, 1 pub rm, 3 bedrms (grd flr avail), sleeps 6, total sleeping capacity 36, £200.00-£450.00, Jan-Dec, bus ¼ ml, rail 20 mls, airport 25 mls

Mr & Mrs Panciroli
Foyers Bay House, Lower Foyers, Inverness-shire, IV1 2YB
Tel: (Gorthleck) 01456 486624 Fax: 01456 486337

Gairloch, Ross-shire

Map Ref: 3F7

★★ SELF CATERING

Comfortable self-catering apartments, quietly located a short walk from the sandy beach at Opinan. Other beaches at nearby Red Point. Excellent views of the Torridon hills and over towards Skye. Lounge bar on the premises.

5 flats, 1-2 bedrms, total sleeping capacity 17, £120.00-£275.00, Jan-Dec

Mrs Julia Alexander
Glendale House, South Erradale, Gairloch, Wester Ross
Tel: (Gairloch) 01445 741741 Fax: 01445 741741

Important: Prices stated are estimates and may be subject to amendments

[Gai]rloch, Ross-shire

Map Ref: 3F7

★★★ SELF [C]ATERING

Modern bungalow set in elevated peaceful position on southern edge of village, close to Creag Mor Hotel, sandy beaches and golf course.

2 bungalows, 2 pub rms, 2 bedrms, sleeps 4, total sleeping capacity 8, £150.00-£335.00, Jan-Dec, bus nearby, rail 28 mls, airport 80 mls

Mrs M Bone
Creag Beag, Gairloch, Ross-shire, IV21 2AH
Tel: (Gairloch) 01445 712322 Fax: 01445 712310

★★ SELF [C]ATERING

Original crofters cottage 70 yards up steep grassy hill set in 1 acre of fenced ground. Magnificent views of Gairloch and sandy bay.

1 house, 2 pub rms, 2 bedrms, sleeps 4, from £90.00, Jan-Dec, bus 500 yds, rail 30 mls, airport 76 mls

Mr A Duvill
Apronhill, Primrose Cottage, Badachro, by Gairloch, Ross-shire, IV21 2AB
Tel: (Badachro) 01445 741317 Fax: 01445 741377

★★★★ SELF [C]ATERING

Large fully equipped house in extensive secluded grounds. An idyllic location only minutes from the shops, golf course and beautiful beach. Easy access to open countryside, Inverewe Gardens and many attractive walks and drives.

1 house, 1 pub rm, 4 bedrms (grd flr avail), sleeps 7, £300.00-£550.00, Apr-Oct, bus 1 ml, rail 70 mls, ferry 60 mls, airport 75 mls

Mrs Elizabeth Jessiman
75a Craigcrook Road, Edinburgh, EH4 3PH
Tel: 0131 332 6678

★★★ SELF [C]ATERING

Specially designed bungalow, with disabled in mind, in a crofting township, overlooking Longa Island and Loch Gairloch to Skye and the Torridons.

1 bungalow, 2 pub rms, 3 bedrms (grd flr avail), sleeps 6, £170.00-£410.00, Jan-Dec, bus 5 mls, rail 35 mls, airport 75 mls

Mrs B Leslie
40 Big Sand, Gairloch, Ross-shire, IV21 2DD
Tel: (Gairloch) 01445 712448

★★★ SELF [C]ATERING

Well secluded cottage situated in hotel grounds. Use of hotel facilities, including restaurant, buttery, pool room and bars available.

1 chalet, 2 pub rms, 2 bedrms, sleeps 4, £260.00-£430.00, Jan-Dec, bus nearby, rail 28 mls, airport 80 mls

Mr & Mrs Nieto
Creag Mor Hotel, Gairloch, Ross-shire, IV21 2AH
Tel: (Gairloch) 01445 712068 Fax: 01445 712044
Email: 106505.1440@compuserve.com

VAT is shown at 17.5%: changes in this rate may affect prices.

Key to symbols is on back flap.

Gairloch, Ross-shire

Map Ref: 3F7

★★ SELF CATERING

Self contained ground floor flat adjacent to owners house. Quiet location just a short walk from Gairloch shops, hotels and restaurants. Stunning sea and mountain views. Totally non-smoking.

1 flat, sleeps 2-3, £175.00-£195.00, Mar-Oct, bus 1/4 ml

Mr J. S. Smith
26 Strath, Gairloch, Ross-shire, IV21 2DA
Tel: (Gairloch) 01445 712064 Fax: 01445 712256

Glencoe, Argyll

Map Ref: 1F1

★★★★ SELF CATERING

A choice of accommodation on the outskirts of this Highland village of either brand new lodges or refurbished two storey cottages. Built on the site of the house of MacIain, clan chief of the Macdonalds of Glencoe.

3 chalets, 3 cottages, 2-3 bedrms (grd flr avail), sleeps 2-6, total sleeping capacity 33, £200.00-£460.00, Jan-Dec, bus 1/4 ml, rail 15 mls, airport 100 mls

Mrs Lynn Brown
Invercoe Highland Holidays, Invercoe, Glencoe, Argyll, PA39 4HP
Tel: (Ballachulish) 01855 811210 Fax: 01855 811210

★★ SELF CATERING

Cosy, newly-built house in traditional cottage style with small fenced garden to rear. Superb uninterrupted panoramic views across Loch Leven to Mamores and Ardgour hills. 12 miles (19 kms) from Fort William. Ideal centre for sailing, hillwalking, skiing, fishing and touring the Glencoe area.

1 house, 1 pub rm, 3 bedrms, sleeps 5, £220.00-£320.00, Apr-Aug, bus nearby, rail 14 mls

Mrs C Dawson
49 Braid Farm Road, Edinburgh, EH10 6LE
Tel: 0131 447 7689

★★ SELF CATERING

Modern detached bungalow in a large garden overlooking the Loch. Near Glen Coe with skiing in winter and only 18 miles (29kms) from Fort William.

1 bungalow, 2 pub rms, 3 bedrms (grd flr avail), sleeps 6, £350.00-£425.00, Jan-Dec, bus 1/4 ml, rail 15 mls

Mrs C M Irvine
3 Enderby Drive, Highford Park, Hexham, Northumberland, NE46 2
Tel: (Hexham) 01434 606512

Glenelg, Ross-shire

Map Ref: 3F10

★ SELF CATERING

Homely cottage situated adjacent to the Glenelg Ferry road in a beautiful, remote part of the country. The summer ferry to Skye is only 2 miles away. Excellent base for those wishing to enjoy the great outdoors in peace and quiet.

1 cottage, 1 pub rm, 3 bedrms (grd flr avail), sleeps 6, min let weekend, £250.00, Jan-Dec, bus 7 mls, rail 30 mls, ferry 1/2 ml, airport 70 mls

Mrs Haywood
96 Viewforth (2F2), Edinburgh, Midlothian, EH10 4LG
Tel: (Fountainbridge) 0131 228 8399

Important: Prices stated are estimates and may be subject to amendments

Glenelg, Ross-shire

Map Ref: 3F10

★★★ SELF CATERING

Bungalow on working croft set amidst magnificent scenery. 3 miles (5kms) from summer ferry to Skye. Pets welcome.

5 chalets, 1 bungalow, 1 pub rm, 2-3 bedrms (grd flr avail), sleeps 4-6, total sleeping capacity 34, £110.00-£330.00, Jan-Dec, bus 8 mls, rail 25 mls, ferry 3 mls, airport 80 mls

Mr & Mrs M J Lamont
Creagmhor, Glenelg,by Kyle, Ross-shire
Tel: (Glenelg) 01599 522231 Fax: 01599 522231

★★ SELF CATERING

Large comfortable bungalow, pleasantly situated in elevated position in Glenelg. An ideal base for exploring much of the North West Highlands.

1 bungalow, 5 pub rms, 5 bedrms, sleeps 10, min let 2 nights, £200.00-£475.00, Jan-Dec, bus nearby, rail 23 mls, ferry 1 ml, airport 50 mls

P J Maughan Holiday Homes
24 Whaggs Lane, Whickham, Newcastle-upon-Tyne, NE16 4PF
Tel: (Newcastle) 0191 488 6218 Fax: 0191 4885571
Email: janet@pmaughan.demon.co.uk

Glenferness, Inverness-shire

Map Ref: 4C8

★ SELF CATERING

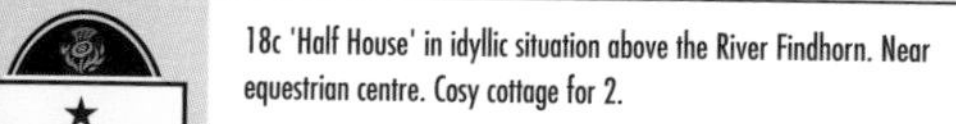

18c 'Half House' in idyllic situation above the River Findhorn. Near equestrian centre. Cosy cottage for 2.

1 cottage, 1 pub rm, 1 bedrm, sleeps 2-3, £125.00-£350.00, Jan-Dec, bus 10 mls, rail 10 mls, airport 15 mls

Mrs A S D Hilleary
Logie Farm, Glenferness, Nairn, IV12 5XA
Tel: (Glenferness) 01309 651226

Glenmore, Ardnamurchan, Argyll

Map Ref: 1A1

★★★★ UP TO ★★★★★ SELF CATERING

Centrally located on the Ardnamurchan Peninsula overlooking Loch Sunart, our houses and cottage offer comfort and a good touring base.

2 houses, 1 cottage, 1-3 pub rms, 2-4 bedrms (grd flr avail), sleeps 4-8, total sleeping capacity 18, £250.00-£1000.00, Jan-Dec, bus nearby, rail 40 mls, airport 120 mls

Mrs K MacGregor
Glenborrodale, Acharacle, Ardnamurchan, Argyll, PH36 4JP
Tel: (Glenborrodale) 01972 500263/500254 Fax: 01972 500203
Email: info@michael-macgregor.co.uk
Web: www.michael-macgregor.co.uk

Glen Strathfarrar, by Beauly, Inverness-shire

Map Ref: 3H9

★★ UP TO ★★★ SELF CATERING

Choice of cottage or Norwegian chalets. Situated in a National Nature Reserve. Guided tours of deer farm. Bikes for hire. Salmon and trout fishing.

4 chalets, 1 cottage, 1-2 pub rms, 2-3 bedrms (grd flr avail), sleeps 5-7, total sleeping capacity 29, £99.00-£399.00, late Mar-mid Nov, bus 11 mls, rail 13 mls, airport 27 mls

Frank & Juliet Spencer-Nairn
Culligran Cottages, Glen Strathfarrar, Struy, by Beauly, Inverness-shire, IV4 7JX
Tel: (Struy) 01463 761285 Fax: 01463 761285

VAT is shown at 17.5%: changes in this rate may affect prices.

Key to symbols is on back flap.

Glen Urquhart, Inverness-shire

Map Ref: 4A9

Traditional stone built cottage situated in a secluded, hillside position above the village of Balnain. Outstanding views to Loch Meiklie.

1 cottage, 2 pub rms, 4 bedrms, sleeps 7, £230.00-£450.00, Jan-Dec, airport 25 mls

Mrs D Beattie
Appleton House, Errol, Perth, PH2 7QE
Tel: (Errol) 01821 642412 Fax: 01821 642412

Situated in country hotel grounds (barn restaurant nearby). Local attractions include Loch Ness and Caledonian Canal for watersports and Glen Affric for hillwalking and pony trekking.

5 chalets, 1 pub rm, 3 bedrms (grd flr avail), sleeps 6, total sleeping capacity 30, min let 3 days, £150.00-£400.00, Jan-Dec, bus nearby, rail 20 mls, airport 25 mls

Glenurquart Lodges
Glenurquart, by Drumnadrochit, Loch Ness, Inverness-shire
Tel: (Glenurquhart) 01456 476234 Fax: 01456 476286

Golspie, Sutherland

Map Ref: 4B6

Semi-detached traditional cottage. Peaceful seafront location in quiet, friendly Highland seaside resort of Golspie.

1 house, 2 pub rms, 3 bedrms, sleeps 5, £120.00-£250.00, Jan-Dec, bus nearby, rail 400 yds

Mrs O A MacKenzie
59 Sandy Lane South, Wallington, Surrey, SM6 9RF
Tel: 0181 395 7048

Traditional style timber bungalow in woodland setting behind village. Superb views over sea and hills.

1 cottage, 1 pub rm, 3 bedrms, sleeps 5, £150.00-£250.00, Apr-Dec, bus 1 1/2 mls, rail 2 mls, airport 60 mls

Mr J M L Scott
The Old School, Ann Street, Gatehouse of Fleet, Castle Douglas, Kirkcudbrightshire, DG7 2HU
Tel: (Gatehouse of Fleet) 01557 814058

Grantown-on-Spey, Moray

Map Ref: 4C9

Well equipped bungalow on working farm. 2 miles from Grantown situated in beautiful Strathspey, offering panoramic views.

1 bungalow, 1 pub rm, 3 bedrms, sleeps 6, £250.00-£350.00, Jan-Dec, bus 1 1/2 mls, rail 15 mls, airport 28 mls

Elizabeth Grant
Toperfettle Farm, Grantown-on-Spey, PH26 3NN
Tel: (Grantown-on-Spey) 01479 872710

antown-on-Spey, Moray Map Ref: 4C9

CRAIGLEA

BREDHURST, THE STREET, THAKEHAM, WEST SUSSEX RH20 3EP
Telephone: 01798 813056
Spacious comfortable bungalow in quiet cul-de-sac close to excellent shopping centre. Secluded garden with summer house at rear. Well-equipped kitchen. Linen and oil heating included. Telephone and electricity on meter. Ideal for all activities or inactivity. Beautiful location with easy access. Good base for family holidays.

★★ SELF ATERING

Modern bungalow with sunny rear garden in quiet residential area only a few minutes walk from town centre. Many outdoor activities within easy reach. Private parking.

1 bungalow, 2 pub rms, 3 bedrms (grd flr avail), sleeps 6, £210.00-£350.00, Jan-Dec, bus nearby, rail 12 mls, airport 25 mls

Gillian Bird
Bredhurst, The Street, Thakeham, West Sussex, RH20 3EP
Tel: (West Chiltington) 01798 813056

★★ SELF ATERING

Comfortable cottage in excellent situation for many activities, ideal for families.

1 cottage, 2 pub rms, 2 bedrms, sleeps 5, min let weekend, £100.00-£300.00, Jan-Dec, bus nearby, rail 15 mls, airport 30 mls

Mrs Daphne Green
3 Cobden Crescent, Edinburgh, EH9 2BG
Tel: 0131 667 6447
Email: crb@dial.pipex.com

★★ SELF ATERING

Traditional refurbished cottage in peaceful country setting, with open views to Cairngorms. Ideal base for touring, hill walking, fishing etc.

1 cottage, 1 pub rm, 2 bedrms (grd flr avail), sleeps 4, £180.00-£200.00, Apr-Oct, bus 1 ml

R P McKenzie
9 Leys Drive, Inverness, IV2 3JB
Tel: (Inverness) 01463 712244

★★ SELF ATERING

Cottage attached to, but independent of main house, situated 1 mile (2kms)from town, overlooking the River Spey to the hills beyond.

1 cottage, 1 pub rm, 3 bedrms, sleeps 6, min let weekend, £200.00-£275.00, Jan-Dec, bus 1 ml, rail 13 mls, airport 30 mls

Miss Fenella Palmer
Fearna House, Old Spey Bridge, Grantown-on-Spey, Moray, PH26 3NQ
Tel: (Grantown on Spey) 01479 872016

Grantown-on-Spey, Moray

Map Ref: 4C9

★★★ UP TO ★★★★
SELF CATERING

Recently built spacious bungalow, on outskirts of Grantown, set amid quiet countryside with birch and pine trees. Excellent views. Farmhouse also avaliable.

1 house + 1 farmhouse, 2 pub rms, 3 bedrms, sleeps 6, from £250.00, Mar-Oct, bus 500 yds, rail 15 mls, airport 35 mls

E A Smith
Auchernack, Grantown-on-Spey, Moray, PH26 3NH
Tel: (Grantown-on-Spey) 01479 872093 Fax: 01479 872093

★★
SELF CATERING

A former shepherd's cottage in remote location, with superb views to Cairngorms. Own garden area and access by farm track.

1 cottage, 2 pub rms, 2 bedrms, sleeps 4, £225.00-£240.00, May-Sep, bus 5 mls, rail 12 mls

Mrs M Steedman
Muir of Blebo, Blebocraigs, by Cupar, Fife, KY15 5TZ
Tel: 01334 850781 Fax: 01334 850781

★★★
SELF CATERING

Modern bungalow in quiet residential area with off road parking. Enclosed rear garden area. Ideal base for touring, walking, fishing and golfing.

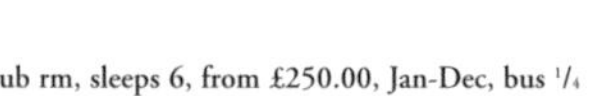

1 bungalow, 1 pub rm, sleeps 6, from £250.00, Jan-Dec, bus 1/4 ml, rail 13 mls, airport 29 mls

Mrs Bridget Thomson
33 Medina Road, Grays, Essex, RM17 6AQ
Tel: (Grays) 01375 370274

★★★★
SELF CATERING

Charming cottage tastefully refurbished with a modern farmhouse kitchen and log fire. Attractive surroundings and panoramic views of the Spey Valley.

1 cottage, 2 pub rms, 4 bedrms (grd flr avail), sleeps 8, £295.00-£595.00, Jan-Dec, bus 4 mls, rail 25 mls, airport 45 mls

Mrs C Wright
Begbie Farmhouse, Begbie, nr Haddington, East Lothian, EH41 4HQ
Tel: 01620 829488/7

By Grantown-on-Spey, Moray

Map Ref: 4C9

★★
SELF CATERING

A substantial, spacious, traditional farmhouse with magnificent views over Grantown to the Cairngorms and Cromdale Hills. Ideal touring base.

1 house, 2 pub rms, 4 bedrms (grd flr avail), sleeps 7, £280.00-£500.00, Feb-Dec, bus 1 ml, rail 12 mls, airport 30 mls

Mrs P M Laing
Craggan, Grantown-on-Spey, Moray, PH26 3NT
Tel: (Grantown-on-Spey) 01479 872120 Fax: 01479 872325

...inard Bay, Ross-shire

Map Ref: 3G6

★★★★ SELF CATERING

Quality holiday cottage on working croft, overlooking Gruinard Bay towards the mountains of Sutherland.

1 cottage, 1 pub rm, 3 bedrms (grd flr avail), sleeps 5, min let weekend (low season), £180.00-£495.00, Jan-Dec, bus nearby, rail 40 mls, ferry 40 mls, airport 80 mls

Mrs MacKenzie
Fraoch Eilean Mor , 1 Second Coast, Laide, Ross-shire, IV22 2NF
Tel: (Aultbea) 01445 731228

Helmsdale, Sutherland

Map Ref: 4C5

★★ SELF CATERING

Modernised cottage conveniently situated between Brora and Helmsdale. Set back from A9, overlooking fields to the sea.

1 cottage, 1 pub rm, 3 bedrms, sleeps 6, £150.00-£285.00, Jan-Dec, bus nearby, rail 6 mls, airport 60 mls

Mrs M Dudgeon
Crakaig, Loth,by Helmsdale, Sutherland, KW8 6HP
Tel: (Brora) 01408 621260

★★ SELF CATERING

Quietly situated former shepherds cottage, with views to the hills and the Helmsdale River. Accessible along an 'A' class road. Ideal base for birdwatching, fishing and gold panning!

1 cottage, 1 pub rm, 3 bedrms (grd flr avail), sleeps 6, £180.00-£280.00, Jan-Dec, rail 5 mls

Sally MacKinnon
Deible, Suisgill Estate, Sutherland, KW8 6HY
Tel: (Kinbrace) 01431 831246

...hnadamph, Sutherland

Map Ref: 3H5

★★★ SELF CATERING

Modernised shepherd's cottage in remote location, near Loch Assynt. Access via unsurfaced road, rough in places.

1 cottage, 1 pub rm, 3 bedrms (grd flr avail), sleeps 6, £230.00-£300.00, Apr-Oct, bus 1 ml, rail 40 mls, ferry 23 mls, airport 80 mls

Mrs E A Miles
8 Longfield Drive, West Parley, Ferndown, Dorset, BH22 8TY
Tel: (Bournemouth) 01202 571739

...h, Inverness-shire

Map Ref: 4C10

★★ SELF CATERING

Chalet in peaceful location beside the Insh Marshes Reserve. 8 miles (13kms) from Aviemore.

1 chalet, 1 pub rm, 2 bedrms, sleeps 4-6, £140.00-£220.00, Jan-Dec, bus 2 mls, rail 5 mls, airport 45 mls

Mrs A MacKintosh
Annandale, Gordon Hall, Kingussie, Inverness-shire, PH21 1NR
Tel: (Kingussie) 01540 661560

VAT is shown at 17.5%: changes in this rate may affect prices.

Key to symbols is on back flap.

Insh, Inverness-shire

Map Ref: 4C10

SELF CATERING

Timber cabin set in natural birch setting. Quiet location in excellent walking, wildlife, ski-ing area. Close to Loch Insh.

1 timber clad cabin, 1 pub rm, 2 bedrms (grd flr avail), sleeps 4, £180.00-£260.00, Jan-Dec, bus 3 mls, rail 5 mls, airport 40 mls

Mrs K Toynbee
Little Birch Cabin, Insh, by Kingussie, Inverness-shire, PH21 1NU
Tel: (Kingussie) 01540 661829

Inver, by Tain, Ross-shire

Map Ref: 4C7

SELF CATERING

Very well equipped comfortable holiday home. Within easy walking distance of beaches. Ideal centre for golf and touring.

1 house, 1 pub rm, 3 bedrms (grd flr avail), sleeps 6, £170.00-£285.00, Jan-Dec, bus 1/2 ml, rail 5 mls, airport 50 mls

Graeme Moyes
16 Cowden Way, Eaglesfield, Comrie, Perthshire, PH6 2NW
Tel: 01764 679811 Fax: 01764 679811
Email: 100410.2510@compuserve.com

Invergarry, Inverness-shire

Map Ref: 3H11

SELF CATERING

Small wooden chalet in elevated position, adjacent to owners' B and B cottage. On A82 at edge of Invergarry. Mini coach tours and taxi available.

1 chalet, 1 pub rm, 2 bedrms (grd flr avail), sleeps 4, £75.00-£275.00, Jan-Dec, bus nearby, rail 15 mls, airport 50 mls

Mrs A Buswell
Nursery Cottages, Invergarry, Inverness-shire, PH35 4HL
Tel: (Invergarry) 01809 501297

★★★

SELF CATERING

Modern bungalow in a peaceful setting in the Great Glen between Loch Lochy and Loch Oich. The cottage is situated on a 16 acre croft and looking on to the Glen Garry hills, 300 yrds from the A82. There are a host of activities in the area, water sports, hill-walking, climbing, forest walks, golf, fishing and skiing. Local hotels provide good meals and there are restaurants nearby.

1 chalet, 1 pub rm, 2 bedrms (grd flr avail), sleeps 4, £180.00-£360.00, Jan-Dec, bus 300 yds, rail 9 mls, airport 45 mls

Mrs Fraser
Allt-na-Sithean, South Laggan, by Spean Bridge, Inverness-shire, PH34 4EA
Tel: (Invergarry) 01809 501311

SELF CATERING

Four chalets situated out of sight of each other all with wonderful views. In a peaceful quiet corner of a working hill farm, ideally situated for walking, bird watching and fishing. A good central base for touring the Western Highlands. Brochure available.

4 chalets, 3 bedrms (grd flr avail), sleeps 4-6, total sleeping capacity 24, £125.00-£270.00, Apr-Oct, bus 2 mls, rail 25 mls, airport 45 mls

A & D Grant
Faichemard Farm, Invergarry, Inverness-shire, PH35 4HG
Tel: (Invergarry) 01809 501314

Important: Prices stated are estimates and may be subject to amendments

vergarry, Inverness-shire — **Map Ref: 3H11**

★★ UP TO ★★★★ SELF CATERING

Renovated, traditional stone cottage and lodges. Farm environment. Ideal base for touring. Open all year. 30 mins. drive from Nevis Range ski slopes. Wide range of farm animals and exotic birds, children particularly welcome to participate at feeding time.

4 log cabins, 1 cottage, 1 pub rm, 3 bedrms, sleeps 4-6, total sleeping capacity 28, £190.00-£430.00, Jan-Dec, bus 1/2 ml, rail 20 mls

Roy Wilson
Ardgarry Farm, High Garry Lodges, Faichem, Invergarry, Inverness-shire, PH35 4HG
Tel: (Invergarry) 01809 501226

Invergarry, Inverness-shire — **Map Ref: 3H11**

★★ SELF CATERING

In peaceful countryside overlooking the Caledonian Canal and Loch Oich. Ideal for hill walking. One hour's drive to Skye. Good base for touring.

1 self contained wing of farmhouse, 1 pub rm, 2 bedrms (grd flr avail), sleeps 6, £125.00-£325.00, Jan-Dec, bus 1 ml, rail 12 mls

Mrs Waugh
North Laggan Farmhouse, by Invergarry, Inverness-shire, PH34 4EB
Tel: (Invergarry) 01809 501335
Email: bw001@post.almac.co.uk

verinate, by Kyle of Lochalsh, Ross-shire — **Map Ref: 3G10**

★★★ SELF CATERING

Fully modernised traditional stone built cottage with scenic views of the Five Sisters of Kintail and Loch Duich.

1 house, 3 pub rms, 3 bedrms (grd flr avail), sleeps 5, £130.00-£320.00, Jan-Dec, bus nearby

Mrs Christine Dodds
Fernfield, Nostie, by Kyle, Ross-shire
Tel: (Dornie) 01599 555368

★★★★ SELF CATERING

Modern bungalows situated on the shores of Loch Duich. Ideal for boating, touring; Kyle of Lochalsh 10 miles (16kms). Very well equipped to a high standard. Breathtaking views over Loch and Kintail Mountains. Private slipway.

1 cottage, 1 pub rm, 2 bedrms (grd flr avail), sleeps 4, £250.00-£450.00, Jan-Dec, bus nearby, rail 12 mls, ferry 12 mls, airport 65 mls

Mrs H MacLean
Mullardoch, Inverinate, Glenshiel, by Kyle of Lochalsh, Ross-shire, IV40 8HB
Tel: (Glenshiel) 01599 511227 Fax: 01599 511227

★★★ SELF CATERING

Traditional stone built croft cottage, tastefully modernised and well equipped. On shore of Loch Duich beneath Five Sisters of Kintail.

1 cottage, 2 pub rms, 4 bedrms (grd flr avail), sleeps 6, £130.00-£330.00, Jan-Dec, bus 1 ml, rail 14 mls

Rev. Roger Whitehead
116 High Street, Harrold, Bedford, MK43 7BJ
Tel: (Bedford) 01234 721127 Fax: 01234 721127
Email: cottage@harrold.demon.co.uk

Invermoriston, Inverness-shire

Map Ref: 4A10

★ UP TO ★★ SELF CATERING

Chalets and lodges on Highland estate 3 miles (5kms) from Invermoriston on Skye road. Trout fishing available on River Moriston.

3 chalets, 1 cottage, 1-2 pub rms, 1-3 bedrms, sleeps 4-6, total sleeping capacity 20, £110.00-£320.00, Jan-Dec, bus 1/2 ml, rail 27 mls, airport 32 mls

Glenmoriston Estates Limited
Glenmoriston, by Inverness, Inverness-shire, IV3 6YA
Tel: (Glenmoriston) 01320 351202 Fax: 01320 351209

Inverness

Map Ref: 4B8

★★ SELF CATERING

Modern house with all amenities and open views to golf course.

1 house, 1 pub rm, 4 bedrms, sleeps 8, £500.00, Mar-Oct, bus nearby, rail 1 1/2 mls, airport 8 mls

G Blackhurst
Highgrove, Easter Muckovie, by Inverness, IV1 2BN
Tel: (Inverness) 01463 792551

✓✓✓✓ 100

Bunchrew Caravan Park
Bunchrew, Inverness, IV3 6TD Tel: 01463 237802 Fax: 01463 225803

20 acres, grassy, level, sheltered, 21 Mar-13 Dec. Extra charge for electricity, awnings.

125 tourers from £7.50 or 125 motors from £7.50 or 125 tents from £7.00. Total Touring Pitches 125.

14 Holiday Caravans to let, sleep 6 £145.00-235.00, total sleeping capacity 84, min let 1 night.

3 mls W of Inverness on A862 Beauly road.

★★ SELF CATERING

Comfortable flats/maisonettes beside River Ness. Town centre and all amenities within walking distance. Parking available. Linen, laundry, payphones.

6 flats, 1-3 pub rms, 1-3 bedrms (grd flr avail), sleeps 2-8, total sleeping capacity 25, min let 3 nights, £210.00-£360.00, Jan-Dec, bus 500 yds, rail 500 yds, airport 11 mls

Mrs K Burton
Hythe Quay, Dunain, Inverness, IV3 6JN
Tel: (Inverness) 01463 233230/0836 571315 Fax: 01463 23323

★★★★ SELF CATERING

Modern apartment (1989) with video entryphone. In residential area, central for all amenities. Panoramic views over city and Firth.

1 flat, 1 pub rm, 2 bedrms, sleeps 4, £200.00-£365.00, Jan-Dec, bus nearby, rail nearby, airport 5 mls

Mrs A Duncan
3 Connel Court, Ardconnel Street, Inverness
Tel: (Inverness) 01463 243363/237086

Important: Prices stated are estimates and may be subject to amendments

:rness | Map Ref: 4B8

★★★★ SELF CATERING

A small cottage in the style characteristic of recent highland developments. Just 20 minutes level walk from the town centre. In a quiet, sunny position and with a small garden. Close to the Moray Firth with beautiful walks for viewing dolphins and seals. Snug in winter. Full domestic facilities. Off road parking. An ideal touring base whilst allowing the enjoyment of the life of the highland capital. Fitted with facilities for remote working.

1 cottage, 1 pub rm, 1 bedrm, sleeps 2, from £250.00, Jan-Dec, bus nearby, rail 1 ml, airport 5 mls

Mr & Mrs Head
Strathkyle Lodge, by Ardgay, IV24 3DP
Tel: (Invershin) 01549 421203 Fax: 01549 421238
Email: strathkyle@aol.com

★★★★ SELF CATERING

Modern, self-contained and extremely well appointed holiday apartment located on the north wing of Westview House. Tastefully decorated and quality assured accommodation. Featuring elevated panoramic views over Inverness, The Moray Firth and mountain ranges beyond. We are situated in an outstanding location to enjoy the Scottish countryside and wildlife. Near the Culloden Battlefield and close to all the facilities of Inverness.

1 apartment, 1 pub rm, 1 bedrm (grd flr avail), sleeps 4, £200.00-£250.00, Jan-Dec, bus 1/2 ml, rail 3 1/2 mls, airport 5 mls

Mrs S Ireland
Westview House, Upper Myrtlefield, Nairnside, Inverness, IV1 2BP
Tel: (Inverness) 01463 794228 Fax: 01463 794228

★★★ SELF CATERING

A modern bungalow on the edge of Inverness, with panoramic views over the town towards Culloden Moor and the Moray Firth. Excellent facilities within easy reach e.g. golf, dolphin watching, walking, gardens and of course Loch Ness.

1 bungalow, 1 pub rm, 2 bedrms (grd flr avail), sleeps 4, £260.00-£320.00, Jan-Dec, bus nearby, rail 2 mls, airport 10 mls

Mrs P R Lyon
Camalaig, Dunvegan, Isle of Skye, Inverness-shire, IV55 8WA
Tel: (Dunvegan) 01470 521355 Fax: 01470 521355

★★ SELF CATERING

Semi-detached bungalow with own garden, in quiet residential area on outskirts of Inverness. Off road parking. Centrally located for touring the Highlands.

1 bungalow, 1 pub rm, 3 bedrms (grd flr avail), sleeps 5, £110.00-£300.00, Jan-Dec, bus nearby, rail 2 mls, airport 9 mls

Mrs A MacKenzie
6A Green Drive, Inverness, IV2 4EX
Tel: (Inverness) 01463 236763

★★ UP TO ★★★ SELF CATERING

Two well appointed flats in a small modern purpose built block in a quiet corner of the centre of Inverness, looking to the Castle. Station, shops, restaurants, riverside walks immediately to hand. Off street private parking. Linen included. Both with two bedrooms, telephone, TV, freezer, washer drier, bath and shower. One has balcony, one has microwave, hi-fi, dishwasher, penthouse lounge.

2 flats, 1-2 pub rms, 2 bedrms, sleeps 4, total sleeping capacity 8, from £210.00, Jan-Dec, bus nearby, rail nearby, airport 1 ml

The Revd and Mrs A M Roff
Rowan Glen, Culbokie, Dingwall, IV7 8JY
Tel: (Culbokie) 01349 877762
Email: 106770.3175@compuserve.com

VAT is shown at 17.5%: changes in this rate may affect prices.

Key to symbols is on back flap.

Inverness Map Ref: 4B8

Torvean Caravan Park

Glenurquhart Road, Inverness, IV3 6JL Tel: (Inverness) 01463 220582
Fax: 01862 821382

2 acres, grassy, level, sheltered, Easter-Oct, prior booking in peak periods, latest time of arrival 2000. Extra charge for electricity, awnings, showers.

50 tourers £8.50-9.50 or 50 motors £8.50-9.50. Total Touring Pitches 50. No tents.

10 Holiday Caravans to let, sleep 2-5 £160.00-295.00, total sleeping capacity 45, min let 3 nights.

Leisure facilities:

From town centre take A82 signposted Fort William. Site is on outskirts of town, first right at canal bridge.

By Inverness Map Ref: 4B8

★★ SELF CATERING

Stable block cottages, chalets and cozy apartments in grounds of country house. Private fishing on River Nairn, a peaceful countryside location.

2 chalets, 1 log cabin, 4 flats, 5 cottages, 1-2 pub rms, 1-3 bedrms (grd flr avail), sleeps 2-5, total sleeping capacity 34, £130.00-£395.00, Jan-Dec, bus 1 ml, rail 7 mls, airport 10 mls

Clava Lodge Holiday Homes

Culloden Moor,by Inverness, Inverness-shire
Tel: (Inverness) 01463 790228 Fax: 01463 790228

John O'Groats, Caithness Map Ref: 4E2

★★ UP TO ★★★ SELF CATERING

Renovated former mill building, and modernised cottage, both situated a short distance from John O' Groats. Great base to explore Caithness and the far north coast of Sutherland, or for day trips to Orkney.

1 house, 1 pub rm, 3 bedrms, sleeps 6, £140.00-£190.00, Apr-Oct, bus nearby, rail 18 mls, ferry 1 ml, airport 17 mls

Mrs Houston

Mill House, John O'Groats, Caithness, KW1 4YR
Tel: (John O'Groats) 01955611 239

Kentallen, by Appin, Argyll Map Ref: 1F1

★★ SELF CATERING

On private site, situated at waters edge with spectacular views over Loch Linnhe and to the mountains beyond.

8 chalets, 1 pub rm, 2 bedrms, sleeps 4, total sleeping capacity 32, £200.00-£400.00, Jan-Dec, bus nearby, rail 15 mls

Loch Linnhe Chalets

Moorpark, Foulden, Berwick upon Tweed, TD15 1UH
Tel: (Ayton) 01890 781255 Fax: 01890 781255

ntallen, by Appin, Argyll — Map Ref: 1F1

★

SELF CATERING

Detached cottage in secluded setting yet close to the A828. Convenient base for touring and walking.

1 cottage, 2 pub rms, 3 bedrms (grd flr avail), sleeps 6-9, £300.00-£500.00, Jan-Dec

Mrs A R Murray
39 Hesketh Road, Southport, Lancs, PR9 9PB
Tel: 01704 542360 Fax: 01695 622041

choan, Ardnamurchan, Argyll — Map Ref: 3E12

★★

SELF CATERING

Cottage on seashore at south side of Sanna Bay. 1.5 miles (2kms) from most westerly point of British Isles, overlooking Eigg, Muck and Rhum.

1 cottage, 1 pub rm, 3 bedrms, sleeps 6, £250.00-£400.00, Jan-Dec, bus 5 mls, rail 30 mls, ferry 5 mls

Mrs C G Cameron
Mo Dhachaidh, Portuairk, Kilchoan,by Acharacle, Argyll, PH36 4LN
Tel: (Kilchoan) 01972 510285

★★ UP TO ★★★

SELF CATERING

Bungalow and renovated cottages enjoying a remote setting with dramatic views of Eigg and the small Isles. Farm nearby, roughish track for 150 metres.

1 house, 1 cottage, 1 bungalow, 1-3 pub rms, 2-3 bedrms (grd flr avail), sleeps 4-6, total sleeping capacity 14, min let weekend, £170.00-£570.00, Jan-Dec, bus 4 mls, rail 53 mls, ferry 9 mls, airport 130 mls

Mrs Sue Cameron
3 Pier Road, Kilchoan, Argyll, PH36 4LJ
Tel: 01972 510321 Fax: 01972 510321

lundine, Argyll — Map Ref: 1D1

UP TO ★★

SELF CATERING

Lodge and farm cottages in isolated setting with superb views over Sound of Mull and to Mull. Ideal for touring Mull and for walking and birdwatching.

3 cottages, 1 pub rm, 2-3 bedrms (grd flr avail), sleeps 4-6, total sleeping capacity 14, £88.00-£220.00, Jan-Dec, bus 40 mls, rail 50 mls, ferry 7 mls

Mr W Lauder
Atherton House, Atherton Lane, Totnes, Devon, TQ9 5RT
Tel: (Totnes) 01803 863059

ncraig, by Kingussie, Inverness-shire — Map Ref: 4C10

★★

SELF CATERING

Cottages situated in the grounds of Invereshie Estate with small private golf course free for guests' use. 1/2 mile from Loch Insh.

4 cottages, 1 pub rm, 2-3 bedrms (grd flr avail), sleeps 4-6, total sleeping capacity 19, £195.00-£415.00, Jan-Dec, bus 1 ml, rail 6 mls, airport 30 mls

Roger Bruce, Invereshie Est Hol Cottages
Kincraig,by Kingussie, Inverness-shire, PH21 1NU, PH21 1NF
Tel: (Kincraig) 01540 651332 Fax: 01540 651332

VAT is shown at 17.5%: changes in this rate may affect prices.

Key to symbols is on back flap.

Kincraig, by Kingussie, Inverness-shire — **Map Ref: 4C10**

SELF CATERING

Traditional farm cottages and cedar-clad bungalow individually sited on working and sporting estate, 4 miles (6kms) south of Aviemore.

2 flats, 4 cottages, 2-3 pub rms, 2-5 bedrms, sleeps 4-10, total sleeping capacity 40, £160.00-£510.00, Jan-Dec, bus 4 1/2 mls, rail 4 1/2 mls, airport 40 mls

Alvie Estate Office
Kincraig, by Kingussie, Inverness-shire, PH21 1NE
Tel: (Kincraig) 01540 651255/651249 Fax: 01540 651380

SELF CATERING

Self catering chalet and lodge accommodation set apart from main outdoor centre, situated in remote Glen Feshie. Nestling in the edge of the Cairngorm Mountains yet easily accessible from main routes.

6 chalets, total sleeping capacity 53, £175.00-£525.00, Jan-Dec, bus 3 mls, rail 9 mls, airport 45 mls

Lagganlia Outdoor Centre
Kincraig, Kingussie, PH21 1NG
Tel: (Kincraig) 01540 651265 Fax: 01540 651240
Email: lagganlia@dial_pipex.com

SELF CATERING

Log chalets with fine views of Loch Insh and mountains beyond. Watersports, skiing, cycling and walking. 150 metres to lochside restaurant.

4 log cabins, 1 pub rm, 2-3 bedrms (grd flr avail), sleeps 4-7, total sleeping capacity 25, min let 2 nights, £294.00-£850.00, Jan-Dec, bus 1 ml, rail 6 mls, airport 35 mls

Loch Insh Chalets
Insh Hall, Kincraig,by Kingussie, Inverness-shire, PH21 1NU
Tel: (Kincraig) 01540 651272 Fax: 01540 651208
Email: user@lochinsh.dial.netmedia.co.uk

SELF CATERING

A Scots Pine log house, situated in a quiet, secluded position, amongst birch trees on the approach to Glen Feshie.

1 bungalow, 1 pub rm, 4 bedrms (grd flr avail), sleeps 8, £310.00-£485.00, Mar-Dec, bus 2 mls, rail 8 mls, airport 45 mls

Mrs C MacGregor
The Dairy House, Corton Denham, Sherborne, Dorset, DT9 4LX
Tel: (Corton Denham) 01963 220250 Fax: 01963 220613

Kincraig, by Kingussie, Inverness-shire

Map Ref: 4C10

★★★★ SELF CATERING

Recently built bungalow in woodland setting on edge of quiet village. Approximately 6 miles (12kms) from Aviemore.

1 house, 2 pub rms, 3 bedrms (grd flr avail), sleeps 6, £275.00-£375.00, May-Oct, bus 1/2 ml, rail 6 mls

Roy Smart
6 Ancrum Bank, Dalkeith, EH22 3AY
Tel: 0131 654 2291

★★ SELF CATERING

Attractive timber lodges within spacious grounds of Insh House, in good walking country. Skiing, watersports, riding, gliding and birdwatching nearby.

2 cottages, 1 pub rm, 2 bedrms (grd flr avail), sleeps 4, total sleeping capacity 8, min let 3 days, £150.00-£300.00, Jan-Dec, bus 2 mls, rail 7 mls, airport 40 mls

Nick and Patsy Thompson
Fraser & Telford Cottages, Insh House, Kincraig,by Kingussie, Inverness-shire, PH21 1NU
Tel: (Kincraig) 01540 651377
Email: inshhouse@btinternet.com

ingussie, Inverness-shire

Map Ref: 4B11

★★ SELF CATERING

Delightful end-terrace property beside scenic railway line. Small sheltered patio.

1 cottage, 1 pub rm, 3 bedrms (grd flr avail), sleeps 6, min let 4 days, £170.00-£350.00, Jan-Dec, bus 1/4 ml, rail nearby

Mr Drummond
15 Heriot Road, Lenzie, Glasgow, G66 5AX
Tel: 0141 776 6867
Email: mike2drummond@compuserve.com

inlocheil, by Fort William, Inverness-shire

Map Ref: 3G12

★★★ UP TO ★★★★ SELF CATERING

A timber lodge and a semi-detached cottage, set above Loch Eil, with panoramic views.

2 houses, 1-2 pub rms, 2-3 bedrms, sleeps 4-7, total sleeping capacity 11, £275.00-£500.00, Jan-Dec, bus nearby, rail 1 ml, ferry 40 mls, airport 100 mls

A G MacLeod
Altdarroch Farm, Kinlocheil, by Fort William, Inverness-shire, PH40 4PA
Tel: (Mallaig) 01687 462346 Fax: 01687 462212

nlochewe, Ross-shire

Map Ref: 3G8

★★★★ SELF CATERING

A detached modern bungalow superbly equipped standing by itself within the Beinn Eighe Nature Reserve and overlooking 2 of Scotland's greatest mountains, Slioch and Beinn Eighe. The area is a haven for walking, fishing, bird watching and wildlife. Cearn Shiel is just a short distance from Torridon, Loch Maree and some of the many sandy beaches and bays around Gairloch and Redpoint.

1 bungalow, 1 pub rm, 3 bedrms, sleeps 6, from £195.00, Jan-Dec, bus 1/2 ml, rail 8 mls, ferry 86 mls, airport 60 mls

F M Buckley
The Croft, Melvaig,by Gairloch, Ross-shire, IV21 2EA
Tel: (North Erradale) 01445 771225

VAT is shown at 17.5%: changes in this rate may affect prices.

Key to symbols is on back flap.

Kinlochewe, Ross-shire Map Ref: 3G8

SELF CATERING

Two comfortable, well equipped semi-detached cottages with scenic views towards Torridon hills. Ideal base for hill walking and climbing.

2 cottages, 1 pub rm, 2 bedrms (grd flr avail), sleeps 4, total sleeping capacity 8, £140.00-£300.00, Jan-Dec, bus nearby, rail 10 mls, ferry 50 mls, airport 60 mls

Mrs S MacLean
Duart, Kinlochewe, by Achnasheen, Ross-shire, IV22 2PB
Tel: (Gairloch) 01445 760230 Fax: 01445 760230
Email: emac@cali.co.uk

Kinlochlaggan, by Newtonmore, Inverness-shire Map Ref: 4A11

ARDVERIKIE ESTATE LTD

Jenny Sargent, Highland Hideaways
c/o Finlayson Hughes, 45 Church Street, Inverness IV1 1DR
Telephone: 01463 224707 Fax: 01463 243234

Enjoy the variety of this large Highland estate, magnificent mountains, wild red deer, rivers, lochs. Sandy beach, woods, farmland, climbing, hill walking, ski-ing (Aonach Mor). Central for touring. Four comfortable stone-built houses including quaint Victorian gate lodge and large farm houses. Log fires. Open all year. Sleeps 3-16, please enquire.

SELF CATERING

Five houses, of different character, each individually sited, on large privately owned Highland estate. Forest walks, sheep, deer, sandy beach.

2 houses, 2 cottages, 1-3 pub rms, 2-6 bedrms (grd flr avail), sleeps 3-16, total sleeping capacity 35, £230.00-£800.00, Jan-Dec, rail 15 mls

Highland Hideaways
C/O Finlayson Hughes, 45 Church Street, Inverness, IV1 1DR
Tel: (Laggan) 01463 224707 Fax: 01528 544304

Kirkhill, by Inverness, Inverness-shire Map Ref: 4A8

KINGILLIE COTTAGES

Kingillie House, Kirkhill, Inverness IV5 7PU
Tel: 01463 831275 Fax: 01463 831550

★★

Two charming country cottages eight miles apart. All conveniences. Secluded but not isolated. Near glens and lochs but within easy reach of Inverness and villages with shops and restaurants.

SELF CATERING

Enjoy the best of both worlds. Relax in a comfortable traditional Highland cottage in beautiful surroundings; secluded but not isolated. Restaurants and shops are within easy reach but so are spectacular lochs and glens. Two cottages 8 miles apart are comfortably furnished with the personal attention of the owners. Private tennis court for the use of guests. Both have sheltered gardens for sitting out of children's play.

2 cottages, 1 pub rm, 2-4 bedrms (grd flr avail), sleeps 4-6, total sleeping capacity 10, £170.00-£325.00, Apr-Sep, bus 1/4 mls, rail 8 mls, airport 15 mls

Mr & Mrs E Fraser
Kingillie House, Kirkhill, Inverness-shire, IV5 7PU
Tel: (Drumchardine) 01463 831275 Fax: 01463 831550

horn, Ross-shire Map Ref: 3F9

★★ SELF ATERING

Two harled wooden chalets in a slightly elevated position, at rear of Craigellachie B&B. Overlooking Loch Kishorn and the Applecross mountains beyond. Car parking alongside chalets.

2 chalets, 1 pub rm, 2 bedrms (grd flr avail), sleeps 4, total sleeping capacity 8, £120.00-£220.00, Mar-Oct, bus 1 ml, rail 8 mls

Mrs P Van Hinsbergh
Craigellachie, Achintraid, Kishorn, Ross-shire, IV54 8XB
Tel: (Kishorn) 01520 733253 Fax: 01520 733253

e of Lochalsh, Inverness-shire Map Ref: 3F9

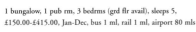

★★ SELF ATERING

Pleasant modern bungalow beautifully situated in secluded grounds on the outskirts of Kyle of Lochalsh. Overlooking woodland to Raasay and Skye. A very rural setting but only two minutes walk to all facilities in village centre.

1 bungalow, 1 pub rm, 3 bedrms (grd flr avail), sleeps 5, £150.00-£415.00, Jan-Dec, bus 1 ml, rail 1 ml, airport 80 mls

Colin Deans
Conchra House, Ardelve, Kyle of Lochalsh, Ross-shire IV40 8DZ
Tel: (Dornie) 01599 555233 Fax: 01599 555433

★★★ SELF ATERING

Very comfortable first floor apartment in centre of village, close to all amenities and Skye Bridge. Ideal for larger groups.

1 flat, 1 pub rm, 3 bedrms, sleeps 8, min let weekend, £90.00-£375.00, Jan-Dec, bus nearby, rail nearby, ferry nearby, airport 85 mls

M J Gardiner
Kyle Pharmacy, Station Road, Kyle of Lochalsh, Ross-shire, IV40 8AG
Tel: (Kyle) 01599 534206 Fax: 01599 534206

★ SELF ATERING

Bungalow situated in large, secluded garden, overlooking Kyle of Lochalsh. Near Kyle shops, swimming pool, play-park and station. Ideal centre for touring NW mainland and Skye. Photograph available on application.

1 bungalow, 1 pub rm, 3 bedrms (grd flr avail), sleeps 6, £280.00-£350.00, Apr-Oct, bus 500 yds, rail 500 yds

M R Wright
16 Duntrune Terrace, West Ferry, Dundee, Angus, DD5 ILF
Tel: (Dundee) 01382 477462

Kylesku, Sutherland

Map Ref: 3H4

★★★

SELF CATERING

Purpose-built, comfortable cottages in magnificent setting on sea loch. Ideal for Assynt wilderness, walking, climbing, bird watching and fishing.

3 cottages, 1 pub rm, 1-2 bedrms (grd flr avail), sleeps 2-5, total sleeping capacity 10, £160.00-£330.00, Jan-Dec, bus nearby, rail 40 mls, airport 90 mls

Mr D Daffron
Unapool House, Kylesku, Sutherland, IV27 4HW
Tel: (Scourie) 01971 502344 Fax: 01971 502344

Modernised croft house. Accessible by footpath 50 yards from road. South of Kylesku bridge and 100 yards from rocky shore.

1 cottage, 2 pub rms, 2 bedrms, sleeps 4, £100.00-£285.00, Jan-Dec, bus nearby, rail 45 mls, ferry 32 mls, airport 100 mls

Mrs F J MacAulay
Linne Mhuirich, Unapool Croft Road, Kylesku,by Lairg, Sutherland, IV27 4HW
Tel: (Scourie) 01971 502227

Laggan, by Newtonmore, Inverness-shire

Map Ref: 4B11

★

SELF CATERING

Well equipped new bungalow with breathtaking views to Lochaber hills, beyond River Spey. Ideal for bird-watchers.

1 cottage, 1 pub rm, 3 bedrms (grd flr avail), sleeps 5, £130.00-£350.00, Jan-Dec, rail 9 mls, airport 55 mls

Mrs Wilson
Blaragie, Inverness-shire, PH20 1AJ
Tel: (Laggan) 01528 544229

Laggan Bridge, by Newtonmore, Inverness-shire

Map Ref: 4B11

Cosy detached cottage furnished in traditional style. Ideally situated for summer and winter pursuits.

1 cottage, 2 pub rms, 4 bedrms, sleeps 6, £180.00-£290.00, Jan-Dec, rail 11 mls

S M B Fleming
Saxon House, Molly Hurst Lane, Woolley, Wakefield, West Yorkshi
WF4 2JY
Tel: (Barnsley) 01226 383258

Laide, Ross-shire

Map Ref: 3F6

Hillside crofters cottage and 5 chalets overlooking sandy beach, with spectacular views towards the Summer Isles and mountains of Sutherland.

5 chalets, 1 cottage, 1-2 pub rms, 3 bedrms, sleeps 2-6, total sleeping capacity 36, £180.00-£380.00, Mar-Oct, bus 3 mls, rail 40 mls, airport 75 mls

Arran Properties Ltd
P O Box 624, St Helier, Jersey, Channel Islands, JE4 5YJ
Tel: (Jersey) 01534 27264

le, Ross-shire

Map Ref: 3F6

★ UP TO ★★★ SELF CATERING

Two detached houses in their own grounds. One a traditional croft house, fully equipped to today's standards and extended, in an elevated position with a superb outlook northwards over Gruinard Bay to the Summer Isles and beyond. The other, a log constructed house built in 1992 in a uniquely beautiful situation above the shore line to Gruinard Bay with direct access to the sandy beaches and with canoes provided for tenants.

2 cottages, 1 pub rm, 3 bedrms (grd flr avail), sleeps 6, min let weekend, £220.00-£360.00, Jan-Dec, bus nearby, rail 73 mls, airport 80 mls

Mr & Mrs A Gilchrist
Grassvalley Cottage, 12 Woodhall Road, Colinton, Edinburgh, EH13 ODX
Tel: 0131 441 6053 Fax: 0131 441 4849

★★★ SELF CATERING

Traditional Highland cottage retaining many original features. In centre of small crofting settlement on main Dundonnell to Gairloch road.

1 cottage, 1 pub rm, 3 bedrms (grd flr avail), sleeps 3, £190.00-£250.00, Jan-Dec, bus nearby, rail 40 mls, ferry 20 mls, airport 80 mls

Mrs R Graham
66 Eshe Road North, Liverpool, Merseyside, L23 8UF
Tel: (Liverpool) 0151 924 5589

✓✓✓ 47

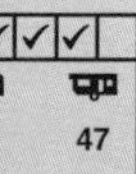

Gruinard Bay Caravan & Camping Park

Laide, Ross-shire, IV22 2ND Tel: (Aultbea) 01445 731225 Fax: 01445 731225

3 ¼ acres, mixed, Apr-Oct, prior booking in peak periods, latest time of arrival 2200. Extra charge for electricity.

18 tourers £8.50 or 18 motors £8.50 or 16 tents £8.50. Total Touring Pitches 34.

7 Holiday Caravans to let, sleep 4-6 £140.00-225.00, total sleeping capacity 37, min let 3 nights (low season).

On the seafront at Laide on A832.

★★★ SELF CATERING

Superior, comfortable, spacious, well equipped cottages. Peaceful private location beside forest. Glorious views to sea and hills. Fishing arranged.

2 cottages, 1 pub rm, 2-3 bedrms (grd flr avail), sleeps 4-6, total sleeping capacity 10, £200.00-£500.00, Jan-Dec, bus 300 yds, rail 40 mls, ferry 45 mls, airport 84 mls

Mrs Catherine Macdonald
Old Smiddy Self Catering, Laide, Ross-shire, IV22 2NB
Tel: (Aultbea) 01445 731425 Fax: 01445 731425

★★★ SELF CATERING

Self-contained cottage adjoining owner's house. Excellently placed for visiting Inverewe Gardens, Lochinver, Ullapool and many other beautiful areas. Watch the seals, otters and a myriad of birds closeby.

1 cottage, 1 pub rm, 1 bedrm (grd flr avail), sleeps 2, £120.00-£260.00, Jan-Dec

Mrs A MacIver
The Sheiling, Achgarve, Laide, Ross-shire, IV22 2NS
Tel: (Aultbea) 01445731 487

VAT is shown at 17.5%: changes in this rate may affect prices.

Key to symbols is on back flap.

Laide, Ross-shire

Map Ref: 3F6

SELF CATERING

Situated on the sea front - yards from the sea shore and a small sandy beach, Gruinard Bay with panoramic views of the Dundonnel mountains, An Tealach Range & Ben Ghablach. The cottage is located at Udrigle, 1.5 miles from the small village of Laide.

1 house, 2 pub rms, 4 bedrms (grd flr avail), sleeps 7, min let weekend, £150.00-£250.00, Mar-Nov, bus 1 1/2 mls

C & J Ross
Udrigle, Laide, by Achnasheen, Ross-shire
Tel: (Aultbea) 01445 731277

Lairg, Sutherland

Map Ref: 4A6

SELF CATERING

Detached villa with own gardens and sun lounge. Walking distance of shops and small town. Ideal touring base.

1 house, 1 pub rm, 4 bedrms (grd flr avail), sleeps 6, £160.00-£320.00, Apr-Oct, bus nearby, rail 1 ml, airport 60 mls

Mrs J Reid
Upper Grange Farm, Peterhead, Aberdeenshire, AB42 1HX
Tel: (Peterhead) 01779 473116

Lentran, Inverness-shire

Map Ref: 4A9

★★
SELF CATERING

3 courtyard cottages situated on a working farm under 1 mile (2kms) from main A862, 6 miles (10kms) from Inverness.

3 cottages, 1 pub rm, 2-3 bedrms, sleeps 4-6, total sleeping capacity 16, £145.00-£350.00, May-Oct, bus 1/4 ml, rail 6 mls, airport 12 mls

MacKays Agency
30 Frederick Street, Edinburgh, EH2 2JR
Tel: 0131 225 3539 Fax: 0131 2265284

Lochcarron, Ross-shire

Map Ref: 3G9

SELF CATERING

Croft house and three cottages a mile from the sea on unspoilt 32000 acre Highland estate. Deer, pine-martins and 75 species of birds. Hill walking, climbing and fishing hill lochs. Boat hire. Ideal base for exploring the West Coast and Skye.

1 house, 2 cottages, 1 bungalow, 1-2 pub rms, 2-4 bedrms (grd flr avail), sleeps 4-8, total sleeping capacity 23, £230.00-£400.00, Mar-Nov, rail 1 ml

Attadale Holiday Cottages
by Strathcarron, Ross-shire, IV54 8YX
Tel: (Lochcarron) 01520 722396 Fax: 01520 722396

ıcarron, Ross-shire Map Ref: 3G9

★★★

SELF TERING

Traditional cottage at waters edge with views across to Plockton and Skye. Lovely peaceful area. Lochcarron 5 miles.

1 cottage, 2 pub rms, 2 bedrms, sleeps 4-5, min let weekend, £120.00-£310.00, Jan-Dec

Mr M F Dennett
5 Hargate Close, Bury, Lancs, BL9 5NU
Tel: (Rossendale) 01706 826590

★★

SELF TERING

Modernised croft set in spectacular scenery near the West Coast in the Scottish Highlands about 4 miles (6.5kms) east of Loch Carron.

1 house, 1 pub rm, 3 bedrms, sleeps 6, to £425.00, Apr-Oct, bus nearby, rail 2 mls, airport 55 mls

Mrs Fooks
Woodgate House, Beckley, Rye, East Sussex, TN31 6UH
Tel: (Beckley) 01797 260472 Fax: 01797 260334

★★★

SELF TERING

A traditional Highland cottage fully modernised and located within easy walking distance of the shore of Loch Carron. Ideal for activity or relaxing holiday.

1 house, 2 pub rms, 3 bedrms, sleeps 5, £190.00-£395.00, Jan-Dec

Mrs Linda Gillespie
120 Findhorn, Forres, Moray, IV36 0YJ
Tel: (Findhorn) 01309 690227

★

SELF TERING

Lodge attached to period house in own grounds. Beautiful Highland setting 3 miles (5kms) from village. Older style of rooms and furnishings.

1 cottage, 2 pub rms, 4 bedrms (grd flr avail), sleeps 8, £255.00-£425.00, Jan-Dec, bus 1/2 ml, rail 1/2 ml, airport 60 mls

Mr M J Knatchbull
Kelso Hotels Ltd, Newhouse, Mersham, Ashford, Kent, TN25 6NQ
Tel: (Ashford) 01233 503636 Fax: 01233 502244

P TO ★★

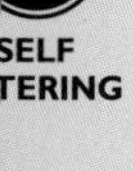

SELF TERING

Two individual cottages of character on shores of Loch Carron. Magnificent views. Ideal for walkers and nature lovers.

1 cottage, 1 bungalow, 1 pub rm, 2-3 bedrms (grd flr avail), sleeps 4-6, total sleeping capacity 10, £100.00-£300.00, Jan-Dec, rail 10 mls, airport 70 mls

Mrs MacKay
Oakdale, Ardaneaskan, Lochcarron, Ross-shire, IV54 8YL
Tel: (Lochcarron) 01520 722281

VAT is shown at 17.5%: changes in this rate may affect prices.

Key to symbols is on back flap.

Lochcarron, Ross-shire

Map Ref: 3G9

SELF CATERING

Cosy detached cottage in centre of village, overlooking Loch Carron. Ideal base for touring Wester Ross and Torridon Hills.

1 cottage, 2 pub rms, 2 bedrms, sleeps 4, £160.00-£340.00, Jan-Dec, rail 3 mls, airport 65 mls

Dr D Murray
The Surgery, Lochcarron, Ross-shire, IV54 8YD
Tel: (Lochcarron) 01520 722221 Fax: 01520 722230

SELF CATERING

Modern, well equipped bungalow overlooking Loch Carron. Private parking. Ideal centre for walking, fishing and touring.

1 bungalow, 1 pub rm, 1 bedrm (grd flr avail), sleeps 2, £80.00-£250.00, Jan-Dec, rail 3 mls

Mrs M Neilson
Ardach, Allt a Chuirn, Lochcarron, Ross-shire, IV54 8YD
Tel: (Lochcarron) 01520 722511

Lochinver, Sutherland

Map Ref: 3G5

SELF CATERING

Admire beautiful sunrises and sunsets. Panoramic views of mountains and sea. Watch fishing boats steaming to Lochinver and The Minch. The bungalow is modern, very comfortable and equipped to a high standard. It is situated $1^1/_2$ miles south of Lochinver on a private road against a backdrop of heather clad hills and a lochan where deer can often be seen.

1 bungalow, 1 pub rm, 2 bedrms, sleeps 4, £195.00-£415.00, Jan-Dec, bus 30 mls, rail 70 mls, ferry 30 mls, airport 90 mls

Mr & Mrs N Lloyd-Jenkins
Creigard, Badnaban, Lochinver, Sutherland, IV27 4LR
Tel: (Lochinver) 01571 844448

SELF CATERING

Nestling in a secluded glen with glorious views of the mountains of Assynt and Wester Ross, Glendarroch House offers the perfect setting for a peaceful and relaxing holiday. Enjoy a traditional Highland home sympathetically modernised to high standards. Price includes all electricity, full central heating, electric blankets and a well stocked library. 15 acre grounds with nature all around yet less than a mile from shops.

1 house, 2 pub rms, 4 bedrms, sleeps 6, £350.00-£650.00, Mar-Nov, bus 1 ml, rail 45 mls, airport 100 mls

Mrs M MacKenzie
Braeside, Navidale Road, Helmsdale, Sutherland, KW8 6JS
Tel: (Helmsdale) 01431 821207

SELF CATERING

Pine chalets set in beautiful, peaceful situation on the shores of Kirkaig Bay. Overlooking a nature reserve the area is abundant with wildlife, seals, otters, ducks and other seabirds.

2 chalets, 2 flats, 1 pub rm, 2 bedrms (grd flr avail), sleeps 2-6, total sleeping capacity 18, £210.00-£360.00, Jan-Dec, bus 1 ml, rail 40 mls, ferry 40 mls, airport 100 mls

Mrs MacLeod
Apt 1, The Wheelhouse, Culag, Lochinver, Sutherland
Tel: 01571 844270 Fax: 01571 844483

Important: Prices stated are estimates and may be subject to amendments

inver, Sutherland Map Ref: 3G5

Cathair Dhubh Estate

LOCHINVER, SUTHERLAND IV27 4JB
Telephone/Fax: 01571 855277

4 miles north of Lochinver on 80 acres coastal estate. 5 modern comfortable cottages with jacuzzi bath. Panoramic views over Achmelvich Bay as far as Cuillins of Skye and the Outer Hebrides. An ideal base for hillwalking, angling and climbing with abundant wildlife. Close to sandy beaches.

★★★ SELF CATERING

Secluded coastal estate, modern comfortable cottages all with jacuzzi baths. Near sandy beaches, an ideal base for walking, angling, hillclimbing and abundant wildlife.

5 cottages, 1 pub rm, 2-3 bedrms (grd flr avail), sleeps 4-6, total sleeping capacity 22, min let 2 nights, £210.00-£640.00, Jan-Dec, bus 4 mls, rail 65 mls, ferry 37 mls, airport 97 mls

Mr & Mrs M MacLaurin
Cathair Dhubh Estate, Lochinver, Sutherland, IV27 4JB
Tel: (Lochinver) 01571 855277 Fax: 01571 855277

★★★ SELF CATERING

Wooden chalets of a good overall standard set away from the shore overlooking Lochinver Bay. 2 miles (3 kms) to Lochinver.

3 chalets, 1 pub rm, 2 bedrms, sleeps 4, total sleeping capacity 12, min let 2 nights, £160.00-£430.00, Jan-Dec, bus ½ ml, rail 50 mls, ferry 40 mls, airport 100 mls

Mrs J C MacLeod
Caisteal Liath Chalets, Baddidarrach, Lochinver, Sutherland, IV27 4LP
Tel: (Lochinver) 01571 844457 Fax: 01571 844457

★★★ SELF CATERING

Modern bungalow on a private site with garden and car parking area. In a peaceful location 1 mile from Lochinver. Ideal base for walking, fishing and bird-watching. Sandy beaches within easy reach. Suilven is in close proximity to the bungalow.

1 bungalow, 1 pub rm, 2 bedrms (grd flr avail), sleeps 4, £195.00-£375.00, Apr-Oct, bus 1 ml, rail 45 mls, ferry 40 mls, airport 100 mls

Mr K J MacLeod
37 Strathan, Lochinver, Sutherland, IV27 4LF
Tel: (Lochinver) 01571 844631

★★★ SELF CATERING

Modern chalet on working croft. Lochinver 1.5 miles (3kms) away with shops and restaurants. Renowned sandy beach at Achmelvich 1.5 miles (3 kms).

1 chalet, 1 pub rm, 3 bedrms, sleeps 5, £200.00-£400.00, Jan-Dec, bus 1 ½ mls, rail 45 mls, airport 110 mls

Mrs S MacLeod
Ardmore, Torbreck, Lochinver, Sutherland IV27 4JB
Tel: (Lochinver) 01571 844310

VAT is shown at 17.5%: changes in this rate may affect prices.

Key to symbols is on back flap.

Lochinver, Sutherland **Map Ref: 3G5**

SELF CATERING

Secluded, extensively modernised croft house with picture windows and magnificent views across Lochinver Bay to the mountains of Assynt and Coigach. Fenced garden, private parking, some steps up to cottage, village 15 minute walk.

1 cottage, 1 pub rm, 2 bedrms (grd flr avail), sleeps 2-4, min let 2 nights, £150.00-£330.00, Jan-Dec, bus 1 ml, rail 46 mls, airport 100 mls

Mrs F J McClelland
Tigh-Mo-Chridhe, Baddidarrach, Lochinver, Sutherland, IV27 4LP
Tel: (Lochinver) 01571 844377 (eve) Fax: 01571 844766

SELF CATERING

Traditional cottage attractively situated in centre of village with fine harbour views.

1 house, 2 pub rms, 3 bedrms, sleeps 6, £90.00-£360.00, Jan-Dec, bus nearby, rail 45 mls, airport 100 mls

Dr P McMichael
12 Craigleith Gardens, Edinburgh, EH4 3JW
Tel: 0131 332 1100 Fax: 0131 332 1100

SELF CATERING

Log cabin and cottage situated close to the water's edge, near the picturesque fishing village of Lochinver in the heart of the magnificent Scottish Highlands.

2 log cabins, 1 cottage, 1-3 pub rms, 1-3 bedrms (grd flr avail), sleeps 2-6, total sleeping capacity 12, £150.00-£495.00, Jan-Dec, bus 1 ml, rail 46 mls, ferry 40 mls, airport 100 mls

Mountview Self Catering
70 Baddidarroch, Lochinver, Sutherland, IV27 4LP
Tel: (Lochinver) 01571 844648 Fax 01571 844648

SELF CATERING

Modern A line chalet with own enclosed garden. Excellent position overlooking Inverkirkaig Bay, 30 yards from shore. Birds, otters and seals.

1 chalet, 1 pub rm, 2 bedrms (grd flr avail), sleeps 4, £225.00-£350.00, Mar-Nov, bus 3 mls, rail 50 mls, ferry 37 mls, airport 110 mls

Mrs Mary C Ross
Tighnuilt, Inverkirkaig, Lochinver, Sutherland, IV27 4LR
Tel: (Lochinver) 01571 844233

SELF CATERING

Large family house, set in peaceful rural location. Ideal base for touring the West Coast.

1 house, 1 pub rm, 4 bedrms (grd flr avail), sleeps 8, £250.00-£320.00, Jan-Dec

Moira Stramentov
Gurrington House, Woodland, Ashburton, Devon TQ13 7JS
Tel: (Ashburton) 01364 652246 Fax: 01364 654370

Important: Prices stated are estimates and may be subject to amendments

hinver, Sutherland — Map Ref: 3G5

★★★★ SELF ATERING

Extensively modernised and refurbished former Cottar's Cottage. Privately situated, with garden and 1/4 acre fenced ground in hillside position. Overlooking Loch Inver with views of surrounding mountains and bay. Own drive and parking, car to door, village 10 minute walk.

1 cottage, 1 pub rm, 1 bedrm (grd flr avail), sleeps 2, £120.00-£320.00, JAN-DEC, bus 1/4 ml, rail 45 mls, airport 100 mls

Mr & Mrs Stuart & Fiona McClelland
Baddidarroch, Lochinver, Sutherland, IV27 4LP
Tel: (Lochinver) 01571 844377

★★ SELF ATERING

Comfortable croft with open fire, excellent south-facing sheltered wooded area. Courses available in stone-cutting, photography and painting. Walks from the house. River and Loch at the back of the croft. Ideal location for touring the West Coast. 1.5 miles from safe sandy beach at Achmelvich. 1.5 miles from Lochinver.

1 cottage, 2 pub rms, 3 bedrms (grd flr avail), sleeps 6, £200.00-£400.00, Jan-Dec, rail 40 mls, airport 100 mls

Mr & Mrs I Yates
114 Achmelvich, Lochinver, Sutherland, IV27 4JB
Tel: 01571 844312 Fax: 01571 844521
Email: gemsy@aol.com

h Maree, Ross-shire — Map Ref: 3F7

★★ SELF ATERING

Timber built chalet close to shore of Loch Maree. Halfway between Kinlochewe and Gairloch. Ideal for resting, walking and sightseeing.

1 bungalow, 1 pub rm, 3 bedrms (grd flr avail), sleeps 5, £180.00-£320.00, Jan-Dec, bus nearby, rail 20 mls, airport 60 mls

A & M Allan
Torguish, Daviot, Inverness-shire, IV1 2XQ
Tel: (Inverness) 01463 772208 Fax: 01463 772308
Email: the.shieling@torguish.com
Web: www.torguish.com

laig, Inverness-shire — Map Ref: 3F11

★★★★ SELF ATERING

Nevis Bank is situated in a secluded position at the mouth of Loch Nevis in the delightful, unspoilt country at the end of the "Road to the Isles" and the ferry to the romantic Isle of Skye. We overlook a quiet beach where otters and seals are frequently seen. Unlimited space for walking, climbing and exploring with an abundant variety of wild flora, fauna and birds.

1 cottage, 1 pub rm, 3 bedrms, sleeps 6, £283.00-£510.00, Jan-Dec, bus 1/2 ml, rail 1 1/2 mls, ferry 1 1/2 mls, airport 100 miles

Mrs MacPhie
Aranmore, Mallaig, Inverness-shire, PH41 4QN
Tel: (Mallaig) 01687 462051 Fax: 01687 462051
Email: emacphie@zetnet.co.uk

Mallaig, Inverness-shire

Map Ref: 3F11

ESSAN COTTAGE

Essan Cottage, Morar, Mallaig PH40 4PA
Telephone: 01687 462346 Fax: 01687 462212

Trout fishing, hill climbing, boating, sailing, canoeing, bird-watching and golfing. Twice daily rail connections from London, Glasgow and Edinburgh. One double, one twin, lounge, kitchen, bathroom, small garden, double glazing. Hotel and pub 100 yards. Railway and bus station 50 yards. Cruises to Skye.

★★

SELF CATERING

Detached cottage with enclosed garden in centre of village. Ideal base for hillwalking and birdwatching. Close to owners hotel (across the road) which offers bar, meals and telephone facilities.

1 house, 1 pub rm, 2 bedrms (grd flr avail), sleeps 5, £250.00-£300.00, Jan-Dec, bus nearby, rail 10 yds, ferry 2 mls, airport 130 mls

Mrs M M MacLeod
Essan House, Morar Hotel, Morar, Mallaig, Inverness-shire, PH40 4PA
Tel: (Mallaig) 01687 462346 Fax: 01687 462212

Melvich, Sutherland

Map Ref: 4C3

Halladale Inn Chalet Park

Melvich, Sutherland KW14 7YJ
Telephone/Fax: 01641 541282

Open April to October. Chalet accommodation to suit all ages. Clean beaches and golf course nearby. Salmon and trout fishing available. Bird watching and diving are recommended. Licensed bar and restaurant next to chalet park on A836, 17 miles west of Thurso, Orkney ferry 20 minutes away.

★

SELF CATERING

Two semi-detached sets of chalets, overlooking the sea and standing in their own ground, near a restaurant and pub. Ideal base for touring north coast.

3 chalets, 1 pub rm, 2 bedrms (grd flr avail), sleeps 4-6, total sleeping capacity 18, £100.00-£205.00, Apr-Oct, bus nearby, rail 13 mls, ferry 18 mls, airport 40 mls

Mr Jack Paterson
Dallangwell Farmhouse, Strathy West, Sutherland, KW14 7RZ
Tel: 01641 541282 Fax: 01641 541282

Nairn

Map Ref: 4C8

★★

SELF CATERING

Comfortable, spacious 1920's bungalow near swimming pool, leisure park, beach and golf course, with views over the Moray Firth. Secluded garden. Only 15 miles from Inverness, Nairn is ideal centre for touring the Moray coast, Speyside, the Cairngorms, the Great Glen, Skye and the inspiring scenery of the north-west Highlands. Golf deals are available in Moray and Grampian.

1 bungalow, 1 pub rm, 5 bedrms (grd flr avail), sleeps 6, £225.00-£375.00, Apr-Oct, bus 1/2 ml, rail 3/4 ml, airport 10 mls

Mr & Mrs A L MacKinlay
21 Braidburn Crescent, Edinburgh, EH10 6EL
Tel: (Edinburgh) 0131 4475294

Important: Prices stated are estimates and may be subject to amendments

n Map Ref: 4C8

✓✓✓✓ 279

Nairn Lochloy Holiday Park

East Beach, Nairn, IV12 4PH Tel: (Nairn) 01667 453764 Fax: 01667 454721
Booking Enquiries: Haven Reservations PO Box 218, 1 Park Lane, Hemel Hempstead, HP2 4GL
Tel: 01442 233111

6 1/2 acres, grassy, sandy, mid Mar-Oct, prior booking in peak periods, latest time of arrival 2200, overnight holding area. Extra charge for electricity, awnings.

45 tourers £10.00-16.00 or 45 motors £10.00-16.00 or 8 tents £8.00-14.00. Total Touring Pitches 45.

81 Holiday Caravans to let, sleep 4-8 £100.00-480.00, total sleeping capacity 405, min let 2 nights.

Leisure facilities:

From either Inverness or Aberdeen take A96. East Beach in town of Nairn adjacent Dunbar Golf course.

★★★ SELF CATERING

Unique, circular luxury flat with balcony overlooking salmon smokehouse, harbour, river and golf course. Dolphin boat trips available

1 flat, 1 pub rm, 2 bedrms, sleeps 4, £295.00-£350.00, Jan-Dec, bus 7 mls, rail 1 ml, airport 7 mls

Mrs M Stewart
Round House Flat 154, The Harbour, Nairn, IV12 4PH
Tel: 01667 455198

★★★ SELF CATERING

Nairn is a small coastal town with beautiful beaches and two championship golf courses. The Moorings is a modern development on the banks of the River Nairn with one of the town's golf courses beyond. A short walk to the marina.

1 house, 2 pub rms, 2 bedrms, sleeps 5, £150.00-£350.00, Jan-Dec, bus 200 yds, rail 1/4 ml, airport 5 mls

Mr E S Walker
1 Findhorn Road, Kinloss, Forres, Moray, IV36 0TT
Tel: (Findhorn) 01309 691266

ny Bridge, Inverness-shire Map Ref: 4C10

★★ UP TO ★★★ SELF CATERING

Comfortable stone built cottage accommodation, each of individual character and style, in attractive rural setting on edge of Nethy Bridge.

3 cottages, 1 pub rm, 1-2 bedrms (grd flr avail), sleeps 1-6, total sleeping capacity 10, £120.00-£400.00, Jan-Dec, bus 1/2 ml, rail 10 mls, airport 39 mls

Mr & Mrs M T Collins
Birchfield Cottages, Birchfield, Nethy Bridge, Inverness-shire, PH25 3DD
Tel: (Nethy Bridge) 01479 821613 Fax: 01479 821613

Nethy Bridge, Inverness-shire | **Map Ref: 4C10**

Large timber bungalow at the centre of this delightful Highland village.

1 bungalow, 1 pub rm, 3 bedrms (grd flr avail), sleeps 6, min let weekend, £180.00-£410.00, Jan-Dec, bus nearby, rail 12 mls, airport 30 mls

Mr & Mrs John Craib
3 Albert Drive, Bearsden, East Dunbartonshire, G61 2NT
Tel: 0141 563 7830

Two separately located traditional cottages, with enclosed gardens, seclusion and exceptional individual character and charm. Pets by arrangement, non-smokers preferred.

2 cottages, 1 pub rm, 3 bedrms (grd flr avail), sleeps 5, total sleeping capacity 10, min let weekend, £250.00-£425.00, Jan-Dec, bus 1/2 ml, rail 10 mls, airport 40 mls

Fhuarain Forest Cottages
Badanfhuarain, Nethy Bridge, Inverness-shire, PH25 3ED
Tel: (Nethy Bridge) 01479 821642
Email: dv.dean@virgin.net
Web: http://freespace.virgin.net/dv.dean/

★★★
SELF CATERING

Warm comfortable stone built cottages of individual character set in large garden of lawns and mature woodland, marked "Dell Lodge" on most maps.

3 cottages, 3 bungalows, 1 pub rm, 2-3 bedrms (grd flr avail), sleeps 3-7, total sleeping capacity 34, £150.00-£410.00, Jan-Dec, bus 1 ml, rail 10 mls, airport 35 mls

Mr J Fleming
Dell of Abernethy, Nethy Bridge, Inverness-shire, PH25 3DL
Tel: (Nethy Bridge) 01463 224358 Fax: 01479 821643

Modern detached bungalows situated on outskirts of Nethy Bridge, affording excellent views of Cairngorm range.

1 house, 2 bungalows, sleeps 6-8, total sleeping capacity 20, £150.00-£380.00, Jan-Dec, bus 1/2 ml, rail 12 mls, airport 34 mls

A R Fraser
36 Lynstock Crescent, Nethy Bridge, PH25 3DX
Tel: 01479 821312

Quiet, sheltered site on banks of River Nethy. Well kept, fenced garden. Near village and golf course.

1 bungalow, 1 pub rm, 3 bedrms (grd flr avail), sleeps 5, £200.00-£300.00, Mar-Nov, bus 500 yds, rail 9 mls, airport 40 mls

Miss K M Grant
West Cullachie, Boat of Garten, Inverness-shire, PH24 3BY
Tel: (Nethy Bridge) 01479 821226

Important: Prices stated are estimates and may be subject to amendments

thy Bridge, Inverness-shire

Map Ref: 4C10

★★★★ SELF CATERING

Innis Bhroc (Badgers Meadow) is set in a peaceful rural location in the Abernethy Forest Reserve, a paradise for bird watchers and naturalists.

1 house, 2 pub rms, 3 bedrms (grd flr avail), sleeps 6, min let 2/3 nights, £225.00-£400.00, Jan-Dec, bus 3 mls, rail 12 mls, airport 36 mls

Mr & Mrs Grant
Easter Gallovie, Dulnain Bridge, by Grantown-on-Spey, Moray, PH26 3LZ
Tel: (Dulnain Bridge) 01479 851342

★★★ SELF CATERING

Cosy, well equipped bungalow in small private development on edge of picturesque village.

1 house, 2 pub rms, 3 bedrms (grd flr avail), sleeps 5, £190.00-£400.00, Jan-Dec, bus 1 1/2 mls, rail 12 mls, airport 30 mls

Mrs I E G Hamilton
Tullochgribban Mains, Dulnain Bridge, Grantown-on-Spey, PH26 3NE
Tel: (Dulnain Bridge) 01479 851333

★★★ SELF CATERING

Stone built cottage, in grounds of owner's house, recently converted and modernised to a high standard, superb views to Cairngorms.

1 cottage, 1 pub rm, 2 bedrms (grd flr avail), sleeps 5, £135.00-£285.00, Jan-Dec

Mr & Mrs R Kunz
Ailanbeg Lodge, Nethy Bridge, Inverness-shire, PH25 3DY
Tel: (Nethy Bridge) 01479 821363 Fax: 01479 821841
Email: cottage@schottland.com
Web: www.schottland.com

★★★ SELF CATERING

Traditional Highland croft with own garden, in rural situation on edge of Abernethy Forest.

1 cottage, 2 pub rms, 4 bedrms (grd flr avail), sleeps 8, £200.00-£400.00, Jan-Dec, bus 300 yds, rail 8 mls, airport 30 mls

Mr W. G. MacDonald
Redwood, Nethy Bridge, Inverness-shire, PH25 3DH
Tel: (Nethy Bridge) 01479 821437

★★★★ SELF CATERING

Converted, stone built steading of original style and character, retaining some original features. Large garden. Near centre of village.

1 house, 1 pub rm, 3 bedrms, sleeps 7, £275.00-£440.00, Jan-Dec, bus nearby, rail 11 mls, airport 42 mls

Mrs G Mitchell
Skerryvore, Seaview Terrace, Johnshaven, by Montrose, Angus, DD10 0HF
Tel: (Laurencekirk) 01561 362203 Fax: 01674 840705

Nethy Bridge, Inverness-shire

Map Ref: 4C10

Cottages and converted smithy, separately sited in Highland village, each with its own character and enclosed gardens.

2 cottages, 3 bungalows, 1 converted smithy, 1 pub rm, 1-4 bedrms (grd flr avail), sleeps 2-9, total sleeping capacity 29, min let 2 nights, £120.00-£680.00, Jan-Dec, bus nearby, rail 9 mls, airport 30 mls

Mr & Mrs J B Patrick
IE Chapelton Place, Forres, Moray, IV36 0NL
Tel: (Forres) 01309 672505 Fax: 01309 672505

Newtonmore, Inverness-shire

Map Ref: 4B11

One cottage and lodge wing recently refurbished and a former shooting lodge on private estate.

2 houses, 1 bungalow, 1-3 pub rms, 3-7 bedrms (grd flr avail), sleeps 6-18, total sleeping capacity 23, £181.00-£1009.00, Jan-Dec, bus 1-15 mls, rail 1-15 mls, ferry 65 mls, airport 48-56 mls

Mrs E Drysdale
Ralia Sporting Enterprises, Ralia Lodge, Ralia Estate, Newtonmore, Inverness-shire, PH20 1BE
Tel: (Newtonmore) 01540 673500

Ideal holiday retreat, secluded beautiful peaceful surroundings, on outskirts of lovely highland village. Refurbished cottage includes: upstairs; 2 twin bedrooms, bathroom, drying room; downstairs, ensuite bedroom; living room, open fire, TV; well-equipped kitchen, microwave, fridge freezer, washing machine. Tariff, incl. central heating and electricity. Many local activities and attractions, central for touring, short breaks, pets welcome.

2 cottages, 1 pub rm, 1-3 bedrms (grd flr avail), sleeps 4-6, total sleeping capacity 10, min let 2 days, from £180.00, Jan-Dec, bus $^1/_2$ ml, rail 1 ml

Mrs D MacKenzie
Croft Holidays, Newtonmore, Inverness-shire, PH20 1BA
Tel: (Newtonmore) 01540 673504

Small complex of cosy cottages in sympathetically converted 18c steading in the heart of the Highlands. Sauna, solarium and games/fitness room.

7 cottages, 1 pub rm, 1-2 bedrms, sleeps 2-5, total sleeping capacity 24, £200.00-£360.00, Jan-Dec, bus 5 mls, rail 5 mls, airport 50 mls

Miss Miggi Meier/Jennifer Graham
Crubenbeg Farm Steading, Newtonmore, Inverness-shire, PH20 1BE
Tel: (Newtonmore) 01540 673566 Fax: 01540 673509

Modern bungalow, with own garden. In quiet part of village, within easy reach of shops, amenities and public transport.

1 bungalow, 2 pub rms, 3 bedrms, sleeps 2-6, £170.00-£380.00, Jan-Dec, bus 800 yds, rail 400 yds, airport 45 mls

Alistair and Peggy Troup
29 Muswell Close, Solihull, West Midlands, B91 2QS
Tel: 0121 705 4249

Important: Prices stated are estimates and may be subject to amendments

ewtonmore, Inverness-shire

Map Ref: 4B11

★ SELF CATERING

Situated in the heart of small village, modern detached bungalow with large enclosed gardens and garage.

1 bungalow, 1 pub rm, 2 bedrms, sleeps 4, £125.00-£210.00, Jan-Dec, bus nearby, rail 1 1/2 mls

Mrs D J M Whymant
The Gardens, Redstone, Darnaway, by Forres, Moray, IV36 0ST
Tel: (Brodie) 01309 641512

orth Ballachulish, Inverness-shire

Map Ref: 1F1

★★★★ SELF CATERING

In a quiet village setting close to the Ballachulish Bridge this semi-detached former ferryman's cottage has been recently refurbished to offer holiday accommodation of a high standard. Bright spacious and tastefully furnished, the house sits in its own garden with spectacular views of the surrounding hills and lochs.

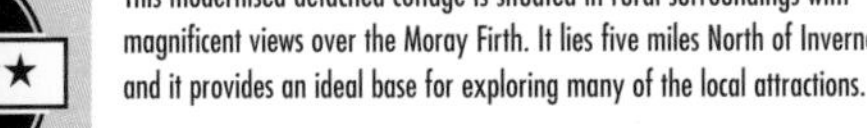

1 house, 1 pub rm, 3 bedrms, sleeps 7, £245.00-£395.00, Jan-Dec

Mrs J Morrison
Islanders, 10 Achnalea, Onich, Fort William, PH33 6SA
Tel: 01855 821403

orth Kessock, Ross-shire

Map Ref: 4B8

★★★★ SELF CATERING

This modernised detached cottage is situated in rural surroundings with magnificent views over the Moray Firth. It lies five miles North of Inverness, and it provides an ideal base for exploring many of the local attractions.

1 cottage, 2 pub rms, 2 bedrms (grd flr avail), sleeps 4, £270.00-£330.00, Jan-Dec, bus 2 mls, rail 5 mls, airport 11 mls

Mrs D Lawlor
Woodside, Kilmuir, North Kessock, Ross-shire, IV1 1XG
Tel: (Kessock) 01463 731425

y North Kessock, Ross-shire

Map Ref: 4B8

★★★ SELF CATERING

Modern terraced cottage in village of North Kessock, just 3 miles from Inverness. Ideal location for exploring the north Highlands.

1 cottage, 1 pub rm, 2 bedrms (grd flr avail), sleeps 4, £165.00-£285.00, Apr-Sep, bus nearby, rail 3 mls, airport 10 mls

P A Saunders
Whin Brae, Craigton Point, North Kessock, by Inverness, Ross-shire IV1 1YB
Tel: (Kessock) 01463 731786

★★★ SELF CATERING

Modernised stone cottage with large private garden and driveway. Patio with BBQ. Spectacular sea views. Convenient to A9 and Inverness. Comfortable sun lounge and modern luxury kitchen. Ideal touring base.

1 cottage, 1 pub rm, 3 bedrms (grd flr avail), sleeps 5-6, £195.00-£485.00, Apr-Oct, bus 1/4 ml, rail 4 mls, airport 12 mls

Mr W J MacKay
Fern Villa, Hale Bank Road, Widnes, Cheshire, WA8 8NP
Tel: (Liverpool) 0151 425 2129

VAT is shown at 17.5%: changes in this rate may affect prices.

Key to symbols is on back flap.

Onich, by Fort William, Inverness-shire Map Ref: 3G12

INCHREE CHALETS

ONICH, FORT WILLIAM, HIGHLAND PH33 6SD
Telephone/Fax: 01855 821287

The ideal centre, 8 miles south of Fort William, midway between Ben Nevis and Glencoe, for touring, walking or relaxing. Comfortable, fully equipped chalets with loch and mountain views, sleeps up to 4 or 6 persons. Licensed restaurant and pub, launderette, children's play area etc. Information pack provided. Open all year. Pets welcome. Reduced rates for couples. Short breaks. For information please write or phone. **Rates from £179 per week.**

★★ SELF CATERING

Chalets on hillside in natural surroundings with views of loch and hills. Ideal for touring and hillwalking. Pub-restaurant on site.

5 chalets, 1 pub rm, 2-3 bedrms (grd flr avail), sleeps 4-6, total sleeping capacity 46, min let 2 nights, £189.00-£379.00, Jan-Dec, bus nearby, rail 8 mls, airport 70 mls

Inchree Chalets
Onich, Fort William, Inverness-shire, PH33 6SD
Tel: (Onich) 01855 821287 Fax: 01855 821287

★★ UP TO ★★★ SELF CATERING

Ardrhu nestles by the shores of Loch Linnhe nine miles south of Fort William. 15 Self Catering properties accommodating four to ten persons with spectacular uninterrupted mountain scenery. Enjoy the splendour of the Highlands with a leisurely walk along the shoreline or for the more energetic hillwalking and climbing. Please telephone for a brochure and tariff which includes electricity and bed linen, in fact no extras at all.

14 cottages, 1 mansion, 1 pub rm, 2-4 bedrms (grd flr avail), sleeps 4-10, total sleeping capacity 80, min let 3 nights, £184.00-£894.00, Jan-Dec, bus 1/4 ml, rail 9 mls, ferry 1 1/2 mls, airport 76 mls

David & Helen King
Ardrhu Holiday Cottages, Onich, by Fort William, PH33 6SD
Tel: (Onich) 01855 821418

★★★ SELF CATERING

Apartment with own access and two modern cottages. Bunree is situated on the outskirts of Onich which is ideally situated between fabulous Glencoe and Ben Nevis - 8 miles south of Fort William. We are a small croft on the shores of Loch Linnhe at Corran Narrows. Free fishing on loch.

2 cottages, 1 apartment, 1 pub rm, 2 bedrms, sleeps 4, total sleeping capacity 12, £205.00-£375.00, Jan-Dec, bus 8 mls, rail 8 mls, airport 100 mls

Mrs M MacLean
Janika, Bunree, Onich,by Fort William, Inverness-shire, PH33 6SE
Tel: (Onich) 01855 821359

★★★★ SELF CATERING

Modern Scandanavian style lodges set in woodland overlooking Corran Ferry on Loch Linnhe. 8 miles (13kms) from Fort William.

7 chalets, 1 pub rm, 3 bedrms (grd flr avail), sleeps 6, total sleeping capacity 42, £200.00-£490.00, Jan-Dec, bus nearby, rail 8 mls, ferry 1/2 ml, airport 70 mls

I D Graham Munro
Drumbrae, Onich, Fort William, Inverness-shire, PH33 6SE
Tel: (Onich) 01855 821261 Fax: 01855 821261

Important: Prices stated are estimates and may be subject to amendments

›ich, by Fort William, Inverness-shire

Map Ref: 3G12

★★

SELF CATERING

Four holiday cottages fully equipped and centrally heated. Sleep 4 to 6. Situated in 17 acres of private hillside with magnificent views across Loch Linnhe into the mountains of Argyllshire and Glencoe. Ideal location for all pursuits and relaxation.

4 cottages, 1-2 pub rms, 2-3 bedrms (grd flr avail), sleeps 4-6, total sleeping capacity 18, £180.00-£380.00, Jan-Dec, bus nearby, rail 10 mls, ferry 2 mls, airport 100 mls

Mr & Mrs William Murray
Springwell Holiday Homes, Onich, Fort William, Inverness-shire, PH33 6RY
Tel: (Onich) 01855 821257 Fax: 01855 821257

›ckton, Ross-shire

Map Ref: 3F9

★★★

SELF CATERING

Comfortable 3 bedroom cottage sleeping 7. In beautiful isolated location in the picturesque village of Plockton. The cottage has unspoilt views over Loch Carron to the Applecross hills. Ample garden space for children and one pet.

1 house, 2 pub rms, 3 bedrms (grd flr avail), sleeps 7, £250.00-£450.00, Jan-Dec, rail 1 ml

Mrs M A Byrne
27 Milner Road, Glasgow, G13 1QL
Tel: 0141 959 9439

★★★

SELF CATERING

Large modern detached family home set in unique elevated quiet location 2 minutes walk from village centre. 3/4 acre own grounds, full central heating, very comfortable holiday home, private parking.

1 house, 2 pub rms, 3 bedrms (grd flr avail), min let 3 days, £200.00-£500.00, Jan-Dec, bus 6 mls, rail 1 ml

Mrs Glasgow
Culcairn Mill, Evanton, Ross-shire, IV16 9XN
Tel: 01349 830110

★★

SELF CATERING

Large detached house in centre of Plockton and on the shore of Loch Carron. Superb views in all directions.

1 house, 3 pub rms, 5 bedrms (grd flr avail), sleeps 9, min let weekend (low season), £400.00-£700.00, bus 6 mls, rail 1 ml, ferry 6 mls, airport 80 mls

Mrs Ann B MacLaren
34 Westbourne Gardens, Glasgow, G12 9PF
Tel: 0141 357 5152 Fax: 0141 357 5152

Plockton, Ross-shire

Map Ref: 3F9

SELF CATERING

Secluded cottage set in its own extensive fenced grounds, 3 miles (4 kms) from Plockton, many good restaurants and shops locally.

1 cottage, 1 pub rm, 3 bedrms, sleeps 6, £160.00-£350.00, Jan-Dec

Mrs Nicholson
Claymoddie, Whithorn, Newton Stewart, Wigtonshire DG8 8LX
Tel: 01988 500422

Poolewe, Ross-shire

Map Ref: 3F7

SELF CATERING

Modern, purpose built bungalows in peaceful setting. Main bedrooms are ensuite. One bungalow suitable for disabled. Within walking distance of Inverewe Gardens.

6 bungalows, 1 pub rm, 3 bedrms (grd flr avail), sleeps 6, total sleeping capacity 36, min let 3 days, £170.00-£415.00, Jan-Dec, rail 36 mls, ferry 52 mls, airport 85 mls

Mr F Hughes
Innes-Maree Bungalows, Poolewe, Ross-shire, IV22 2JU
Tel: (Poolewe) 01445 781454 Fax: 01445 781454
Email: innes-maree@lineone.net
Web: www.destination-scotland.com/innes/

SELF CATERING

Modern semi-detached bungalows, furnished to a high standard. Set above a sandy beach with fine views across Loch Ewe.

2 bungalows, 1 pub rm, 2 bedrms, sleeps 4, total sleeping capacity 8, £170.00-£320.00, Jan-Dec, bus 7 mls

Mr M MacDonald
6 Pier Road, Aultbea, Ross-shire
Tel: (Aultbea) 01445 731251

SELF CATERING

Two recently modernised croft houses overlooking Loch Ewe. Magnificent scenery, walks, bird watching and fishing.

2 cottages, 2 pub rms, 2-3 bedrms (grd flr avail), sleeps 4-6, total sleeping capacity 10, £150.00-£340.00, Jan-Dec, bus 4 mls, rail 40 mls, ferry 54 mls, airport 90 mls

Mrs H MacLeod
3 Braes, Inverasdale, Poolewe, Ross-shire, IV22 2LN
Tel: (Poolewe) 01445 781434

SELF CATERING

New secluded cottage on the banks of the River Ewe. Close to Inverewe Gardens. Ideal for hillwalking and climbing in Wester Ross.

1 chalet, 1 pub rm, 2 bedrms (grd flr avail), sleeps 4, from £200.00, Jan-Dec, bus 1/2 ml, rail 35 mls, ferry 50 mls, airport 90 mls

Kenneth Mitchell
14 Croft, Poolewe, Ross-shire, IV22 2JY
Tel: (Poolewe) 01445 781231

Important: Prices stated are estimates and may be subject to amendments

olewe, Ross-shire

Map Ref: 3F7

★★★★ SELF ATERING

Refurbished former croft house, with extensive enclosed safe garden. Superb views over Loch Ewe, and access to small beach area. Games room with dartboard, multi-gym, exercise bike and table football. Fishing rods and canoes available.

1 cottage, 1 pub rm, 3 bedrms (grd flr avail), sleeps 5, £150.00-£330.00, Jan-Dec, bus 3 mls

Mrs N Taylor
8 Naast, Poolewe, Achnasheen, Ross-shire, IV22 2LL
Tel: (Poolewe) 01445 781360 Fax: 01445 781408
Email: nicola.taylor@virgin.net
Web: http://freespace.virgin.net/nicola.taylor/anbothan.htm

★★ SELF ATERING

Semi detached stone built crofter's cottages, with fine views over River Ewe towards mountains and Loch Maree. Location precludes TV reception.

2 cottages, 2 pub rms, 2 bedrms, sleeps 4, total sleeping capacity 8, from £80.00, Jan-Dec, bus nearby, rail 25 mls, airport 84 mls

Mr A Urquhart
Torwood Croft, Poolewe, Ross-shire, IV22 2JY
Tel: (Poolewe) 01445 781268 Fax: 01445 781704

rtmahomack, Ross-shire

Map Ref: 4C7

★★★ SELF ATERING

Former lighthouse keeper's cottage. 3 miles (5kms) from Portmahomack. Exceptional views over Dornoch and Cromarty Firths.

1 cottage, 1 pub rm, 3 bedrms (grd flr avail), sleeps 6, £250.00-£450.00, Jan-Dec, bus 3 mls, rail 13 mls, airport 45 mls

Ecosse Unique
Thorncroft, Lilliesleaf, Melrose, Roxburghshire, TD6 9JD
Tel: (Melrose) 01835 870779

saay, Isle of

Map Ref: 3E9

★★ SELF ATERING

Traditional cottage by sea, looking out towards mountains of Skye. Explore this peaceful island, or just relax.

1 cottage, 1 pub rm, 4 bedrms (grd flr avail), sleeps 6, £180.00-£220.00, Jan-Dec, ferry 1 ml

Mr John MacLeod
Moorholme, 42 Buchanan Stret, Milngavie, Glasgow, G62 8AP

tagan, Ross-shire

Map Ref: 3G10

★★★ SELF ATERING

Cottage on shores of Loch Duich. Superb mountain views of Five Sisters. Great care taken over decor and furnishings. Open fire and oil fired stove.

1 cottage, 4 pub rms, 2 bedrms, sleeps 6, Jan-Dec, bus 1 1/4 mls, rail 17 mls, ferry 8 mls, airport 70 mls

Mr V R Vyner-Brooks
Middle Barrows Green, Kendal, Cumbria, LA8 0JG
Tel: (Sedgwick) 015395 60242/0151 526 9321/5451 Fax: 0151 526 1331

Reay, Caithness — Map Ref: 4C3

★★ SELF CATERING

Traditional, spacious stone house within walking distance of extensive sandy beach. Centrally situated for exploring the north coast.

1 house, 2 pub rms, 4 bedrms, sleeps 8, £150.00-£300.00, Apr-Sep, bus nearby, rail 10 mls, ferry 8 mls, airport 30 mls

Mrs J MacKay
West Greenland, Castletown, Caithness, KW14 8SX
Tel: (Castletown) 01847821 633 Fax: 01847 821633

Rogart, Sutherland — Map Ref: 4B6

★★★ SELF CATERING

Attractively restored traditional cottage, with solid fuel stores and full electric heating. Outstanding views down Little Rogart Glen.

1 cottage, 2 pub rms, 2 bedrms, sleeps 4, £90.00-£300.00, Jan-Dec, bus postbus, rail 1 ml, airport 63 mls

Robert Mills
St Callans Manse, Rogart, Sutherland
Tel: 01408 641363 Fax: 01408 641313

Rosemarkie, Ross-shire — Map Ref: 4B8

★★★ SERVICED APARTMENTS

Five self-contained cottages central to the Highlands. The traditional sandstone and windstone barn has been carefully and sensitively converted to provide warm, comfortable accommodation throughout the year. Stunning views over the Moray Firth, recreation facilities and the freedom to roam the 160 acres of SSSI wooded land, including access to a secluded beach, provides plenty to do on travel free days. www.hillock-head.co.uk

5 cottages, 1 ground floor sudio, 1-2 pub rms, 1-3 bedrms (grd flr avail), sleeps 2-6, total sleeping capacity 22, min let 3 nights, £100.00-£450.00, Jan-Dec, bus 3 mls, rail 13 mls, ferry 6 mls, airport 25 mls

Highland Heritage Holidays
Hillockhead Farm, Eathie Road, Rosemarkie, Ross-shire, IV10 8SL
Tel: 01381 621184 Fax: 01381 621537
Email: hillockhead@cali.co.uk
Web: http://www.hillock-head.co.uk

Roy Bridge, Inverness-shire — Map Ref: 3H12

★★★ UP TO ★★★★ SELF CATERING

In magnificent, quiet setting with beautiful views and grounds. Mountain bikes and golf equipment available.

4 cottages, 1 bungalow, 1-2 pub rms, 3 bedrms (grd flr avail), sleeps 6, total sleeping capacity 30, min let 3 days, £160.00-£350.00, Jan-Dec, bus 1/2 ml, rail 1/2 ml, airport 60 mls

Cottage Holidays
Guildford Heath Cottage, Haven Street, Isle of Wight, PO33 4DT
Tel: 01983 884886
Email: sims@holidays.force9.co.uk
Web: www.cottage-holidays.co.uk

★ SELF CATERING

Two hundred year old traditional stone built croft home in secluded setting amid majestic scenery with uninterrupted views of the Ben Nevis range. Central for touring, bird watching, walking, climbing, skiing or just for a relaxing holiday in peaceful surroundings. Spean Bridge/Roy Bridge 1.5 miles in both directions with selection of pubs and restaurants.

1 cottage, 2 pub rms, 4 bedrms (grd flr avail), sleeps 6, £200.00-£320.00, Jan-Dec, bus 1 1/2 mls, rail 1 1/2 mls, ferry 47 mls, airport 60 mls

Mrs A MacKintosh
Druimandonich, Roy Bridge, Inverness-shire, PH31 4AQ
Tel: (Spean Bridge) 01397 712443

Important: Prices stated are estimates and may be subject to amendments

y Bridge, Inverness-shire

Map Ref: 3H12

★★

SELF ATERING

A modern warm, double-glazed, comfortably furnished bungalow on main Spean Bridge to Newtonmore Road. Uninterupted views of the Ben Nevis range. Spean Bridge 3 miles, Fort William 13 miles. Only 1/4 mile from Roy Bridge village where the main London Line stops. The area is central for touring, walking and climbing. Aonach Mor ski slope only 9 miles away.

1 bungalow, 1 pub rm, 3 bedrms, sleeps 6, £270.00-£450.00, Jan-Dec, bus nearby, rail 1 ml, airport 70 mls

Mr John McDonald
March Cottage, Roy Bridge, Inverness-shire, PH31 4AE
Tel: (Spean Bridge) 01397 712240

rfskerry, Caithness

Map Ref: 4D2

★★★

SELF ATERING

Modern cottage with glorious views to the Orkney Isles. Sandy beaches and restaurant food are both within easy distance. Loch fishing available. Pets welcome. Ideal spot for relaxing and unwinding, or for exploring the far north coast of Caithness and Sutherland.

1 cottage, 1 pub rm, 2 bedrms (grd flr avail), sleeps 4, min let 3 days, £160.00-£240.00, Jan-Dec, bus nearby, rail 14 mls, ferry 8 mls, airport 20 mls

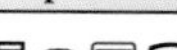

Ms Morrison
Brier Cottage, Scarfskerry, Caithness, KW14 8XN
Tel: (Barrock) 851244 Fax: 01847 851244

urie, Sutherland

Map Ref: 3H4

★★★★

SELF ATERING

Newly built modern house in elevated position with front views over Scourie to the bay. 2 ground floor bedrooms.

1 house, 1 pub rm, 4 bedrms (grd flr avail), sleeps 8, £200.00-£375.00, Jan-Dec, bus 300 yds

Mr & Mrs W J O Nicoll
3 The Logan, Liff, by Dundee, Angus, DD2 5PJ
Tel: 01382 580358

★★

SELF ATERING

Large modern, airy bungalow overlooking village with fine views over Scourie Bay, Handa Island (R.S.P.B. reserve) and beyond.

1 house, 2 pub rms, 3 bedrms, sleeps 6, £200.00-£300.00, Apr-Oct, bus nearby, rail 43 mls, airport 100 mls

Mr J M Williams
Deers Hill, Sutton Abinger,by Dorking, Surrey, RH5 6PS
Tel: (Dorking) 01306 730331 Fax: 01306 730913
Email: jmwqc@dial.pipex.com

ilbridge, Ross-shire

Map Ref: 3G10

★★★

SELF ATERING

Comfortable cottage, situated at foot of Five Sisters of Kintail. Good base for climbing, walking and exploring Wester Ross, Skye and Lochalsh.

1 house, 2 pub rms, 3 bedrms, sleeps 6, £150.00-£350.00, Jan-Dec, bus nearby, rail 16 mls, ferry 16 mls, airport 70 mls

Mr Lee
Carn Gorm, Invernate, by Kyle, Ross-shire, IV40 8HQ
Tel: (Glenshiel) 01599 511276

Shieldaig, Ross-shire

Map Ref: 3F8

Secluded position on south end of Loch Damph, excellent for walking, bird watching and fishing. No TV reception available, but video provided.

1 lodge, 2 pub rms, 3 bedrms (grd flr avail), sleeps 6, £250.00-£390.00, Feb-Oct, bus 1 ml, rail 14 mls, airport 75 mls

Mrs M Pattinson
Couldoran, Kishorn, Strathcarron, Ross-shire, IV54 8UY
Tel: (Kishorn) 01520 733227 Fax: 01520 733429

Ardvasar, Sleat, Isle of Skye, Inverness-shire

Map Ref: 3E11

Comfortable cottage situated 0.5 miles from Ardvasaar, 2 miles from the Mallaig/Armadale ferry. A peaceful location with sea views amidst the greenery of this area, Sleat, known as the "Garden of Skye".

1 cottage, 1 pub rm, 3 bedrms (grd flr avail), sleeps 6, £120.00-£220.00, Apr-Oct, bus 1/2 ml, ferry 1 1/2 mls, airport 18 mls

Mrs A Kennedy
32 Cedar Road, Cumbernauld, G67 3BH
Tel: (Cumbernauld) 012367 25499

Armadale, Sleat, Isle of Skye, Inverness-shire

Map Ref: 3E11

Spacious properties on a secluded site overlooking the Sound of Sleat. Convenient for ferry, village and nearby Visitors Centre.

6 log cottages, 1 pub rm, 2-3 bedrms (grd flr avail), sleeps 4-6, total sleeping capacity 31, min let 2 nights, £300.00-£550.00, Jan-Dec, bus nearby, rail 1/4-22 mls, ferry 1/4-22 mls, airport 100 mls

Clan Donald Visitor Centre
Armadale Castle, Sleat, Isle of Skye, Inverness-shire, IV45 8RS
Tel: (Ardvasar) 01471 844305/844227 Fax: 01471 844275

Bernisdale, by Portree, Isle of Skye, Inverness-shire

Map Ref: 3D8

Two modern bungalows in small crofting village with private access to secluded site on shore of Loch Snizort. Portree 7 miles (10kms).

1 house, 2 cottages, 1 pub rm, 2-3 bedrms, sleeps 4-5, total sleeping capacity 13, £140.00-£240.00, Jan-Dec, bus 800 yds, rail 40 mls, ferry 40 mls

Mrs K C MacKinnon
Daldon, Bernisdale,by Portree, Isle of Skye,
Inverness-shire, IV51 9NS
Tel: (Skeabost Bridge) 01470 532331 Fax: 01470 532331

Important: Prices stated are estimates and may be subject to amendments

ve, by Portree, Isle of Skye, Inverness-shire Map Ref: 3E8

★★★

SELF CATERING

Modern cottages on working croft with views of hills and surrounding countryside. 3.5 miles (7 kms) north of Portree.

2 houses, 2 pub rms, 2 bedrms, sleeps 6, total sleeping capacity 12, £150.00-£250.00, Jan-Dec, bus nearby, rail 45 mls, ferry 40 mls

Mrs M MacDonald
Moorside, Borve,by Portree, Isle of Skye, Inverness-shire, IV51 9PE
Tel: (Skeabost Bridge) 01470 532301

★★

SELF CATERING

Converted croft house with views to the west. Quiet location yet just off the main Portree to Dunvegan and Uig road.

1 house, 2 pub rms, 3 bedrms, sleeps 5, £160.00-£270.00, Jan-Dec, bus 800 yds

Mrs Mackenzie
24 Borve, Skeabost Bridge, Isle of Skye, Inverness-shire
Tel: (Skeabost Bridge) 01470 532391

★★

SELF CATERING

Modern bungalow on Highland croft. Ideal home base for exploring Skye. Portree 5 miles (8kms).

1 house, 2 pub rms, 3 bedrms (grd flr avail), sleeps 6, £290.00-£350.00, Mar-Dec, bus 1 ml

Mrs M MacLeod
Chalna, Daviot, Inverness, Inverness-shire, IV1 2XQ
Tel: (Daviot) 01463 772239

kish, Isle of Skye, Inverness-shire Map Ref: 3F10

UP TO ★★

SELF CATERING

Charming, traditional croft house recently renovated. Open fire, central heating and comfort in ideal base for visiting Skye. Price includes all bedlinen, electricity and coal. Flat also available.

1 cottage, 1 pub rm, 2 bedrms, sleeps 4, £200.00-£320.00, Jan-Dec, bus ½ ml, rail 7 mls, airport 100 mls

Mrs Pat Anderson
4 Heaste, by Broadford, Isle of Skye, Inverness-shire
Tel: (Broadford) 01471 822388

Broadford, Isle of Skye, Inverness-shire Map Ref: 3E10

SELF CATERING

Fully refurbished traditional Skye Cottage very comfortable and cosy with all modern facilities in quiet area of Broadford. Convenient for Skye and mainland touring, 10 minutes from Skye Bridge.

1 cottage, 1 pub rm, 3 bedrms, £150.00-£450.00, Jan-Dec, bus nearby, rail 8 mls, airport 80 mls

Mr Michael Davidson
Old Post Office House, Balmacara, Kyle, Ross-shire, IV40 8DH
Tel: 01599 566200 Fax: 01471 822477
Email: witts@globalnet.co.uk
Web: www.calling-scotland.co.uk

SELF CATERING

Spacious self contained apartment in quiet area of Broadford. Very well equipped to high standards and with full central heating. Ideal for touring, walking, climbing or cosy winter breaks. Sleeps 2 plus sofa bed available.

1 flat, 1 pub rm, 1 bedrm (grd flr avail), sleeps 4, min let weekend, £230.00-£250.00, Apr-Oct, bus nearby, rail 8 mls, ferry 18 mls, airport 98 mls

Mrs Humphrey
Corriegorm Beagg, Bayview Crescent, Broadford, Isle of Skye, IV49 9AB
Tel: (Broadford) 01471 822517

SELF CATERING

100 year old traditional croft house in peaceful location in Broadford. Open fires.

1 croft house, 2 pub rms, 2 bedrms, sleeps 4, £175.00-£250.00, Jan-Dec, bus ½ ml, ferry 5 mls

Mrs Fiona Kennedy
12 Station Road, Blanefield, G63 9HR
Tel: (Blanefield) 01360 770677/01879 230395

SELF CATERING

Timber built cottage, close to the shore which is rich in fossils and wildlife, looking out over Broadford Bay. A short distance from the village.

1 cottage, 1 pub rm, 2 bedrms (grd flr avail), sleeps 4-6, £150.00-£325.00, Jan-Dec, bus ½ ml, rail 9 mls, ferry 8 mls

Mrs MacHattie
10 Waterloo, Breakish, Broadford, Isle of Skye, Inverness-shire, IV42 8QE
Tel: (Broadford) 01471 822506

Important: Prices stated are estimates and may be subject to amendments

mus Croise, Isle Ornsay, Isle of Skye, Inverness-shire — **Map Ref: 3F10**

★★ SELF ATERING

Cottage overlooking the Sound of Sleat and the hills of Knoydart beyond.

1 cottage, 2 pub rms, 2 bedrms (grd flr avail), sleeps 3, £150.00-£200.00, Jan-Dec, bus nearby, rail 14 mls, ferry 7 mls

TV

Miss M M Fraser
Old Post Office House, Isle Ornsay, Isle of Skye, Inverness-shire, IV43 8QR
Tel: (Isle Ornsay) 01471 833201

rbost, by Portnalong, Isle of Skye, Inverness-shire — **Map Ref: 3D9**

★ SELF ATERING

New bungalow in elevated position with panoramic views over Loch Harport. 1 mile from Carbost and The Talisker Distillery.

1 cottage, 1 pub rm, 2 bedrms (grd flr avail), sleeps 6, £200.00-£250.00, May-Sep, bus nearby, rail 35 mls

TV

Mrs Brown
11 Laggan Road, Inverness, IV2 4EH
Tel: (Inverness) 01463 235793

★★★ SELF ATERING

Modern bungalow at side of quiet road. Magnificent views across Loch Harport to the Cuillin Hills beyond.

1 bungalow, 2 pub rms, 2 bedrms (grd flr avail), sleeps 4, £170.00-£260.00, Jan-Dec, bus nearby, ferry 40 mls

TV

Mrs Joan M Campbell
1 Carbost Beg, Carbost, Isle of Skye, Inverness-shire, IV47 8SH
Tel: (Carbost) 01478 640242

★★ SELF ATERING

Traditional cottage on edge of village of Carbost, overlooking Loch Harport. Close to Glenbrittle and Cuillins. Portree 18 miles (29kms).

1 house, 1 pub rm, 3 bedrms, sleeps 6, £180.00-£280.00, Jan-Dec, bus nearby, rail 28 mls, ferry 28 mls, airport 120 mls

TV

Mrs J MacCaskill
3 Carbost Mor, Carbost, Isle of Skye, Inverness-shire, IV47 8ST
Tel: (Carbost) 01478 640236

★★ SELF ATERING

Modern semi-detached cottage in an elevated position, at the head of Loch Harport. Ideal for walkers and climbers.

2 cottages, 1 pub rm, 2 bedrms (grd flr avail), sleeps 2-4, total sleeping capacity 8, min let weekend, £50.00-£200.00, Jan-Dec, bus 300 yds

TV

Dorothy Morrison
8 Satran, Carbost, Isle of Skye, Inverness-shire, IV47 8TU
Tel: (Carbost) 01478 640324 Fax: 01478 640324

Carbost, by Portnalong, Isle of Skye, Inverness-shire

Map Ref: 3D9

Very comfortable, traditional timber, semi-detached home in remote Skye Glen. Ideal base for walking/climbing and nature watching.

1 house, 2 pub rms, 3 bedrms (grd flr avail), sleeps 6, £230.00-£335.00, Jan-Dec, bus 10 mls, rail 40 mls, ferry 50 mls, airport 120 mls

Deirdre M Wright
Upper Feorlig, by Dunvegan, Isle of Skye, IV55 8ZL
Tel: 01478 521718 Fax: 01478 521718

Clachamish, by Portree, Isle of Skye, Inverness-shire

Map Ref: 3E9

Modern comfortable family cottage on working croft. A rural location and ideal base for all activities based in Skye.

1 house, 2 pub rms, 3 bedrms, sleeps 5, £100.00-£210.00, Jan-Dec, bus nearby, rail 40 mls, ferry 40 mls, airport 33 mls

Mrs Nicolson
Drumorel, Tayinloan, Clachamish,by Portree, Isle of Skye, Inverness-shire, IV51 9NY
Tel: (Edinbane) 01470 582215

Culnacnoc, by Portree, Isle of Skye, Inverness-shire

Map Ref: 3E8

Traditional stone-built croft house in rural location. Own enclosed garden with complete privacy. Fine views across the sea to Torridon Hills.

1 cottage, 2 pub rms, 3 bedrms, sleeps 5, £130.00-£350.00, Jan-Dec, bus 1 ml

D J Hudson
Lilacs, High Street, Coddenham, Suffolk, IP6 9PN
Tel: (Coddenham) 01449 760428

Dunvegan, Isle of Skye, Inverness-shire

Map Ref: 3D9

Newly renovated croft house with open fire. Superb views over Loch Dunvegan. Flight of steps leads to cottage.

1 cottage, 1 pub rm, 1 bedrm, sleeps 2, £170.00-£280.00, Jan-Dec, bus nearby, rail 50 mls, ferry 50 mls

Mrs A Gracie
Silverdale, 14 Skinidin, Dunvegan, Isle of Skye, Inverness-shire, IV55 8ZS
Tel: (Dunvegan) 01470 521251 Fax: 01470 521251

Comfortable former croft house built in traditional Skye style. Views to Harris and 1 mile from Coral Beach.

1 house, 3 pub rms, 3 bedrms (grd flr avail), sleeps 6, £150.00-£325.00, Jan-Dec

M MacInnes
3 Claigan, Dunvegan, Isle of Skye, IV55 8WF
Tel: (Dunvegan) 01470 521215

Important: Prices stated are estimates and may be subject to amendments

ıvegan, Isle of Skye, Inverness-shire Map Ref: 3D9

★★ SELF ATERING

Cottages, individual in character, close to Castle and gardens. Boat trips to seal colony available.

1 house, 2 pub rms, 3 bedrms (grd flr avail), sleeps 7, from £180.00, Jan-Dec, bus 1 ml, rail 50 mls, ferry 50 mls, airport 40 mls

MacLeod Estate Office
Dunvegan Castle, Dunvegan, Isle of Skye, Inverness-shire
Tel: (Dunvegan) 01470521 206 Fax: 01470521 205

ɔl, Isle of Skye, Inverness-shire Map Ref: 3E10

★★ SELF ATERING

Stone cottage with magnificent views. Beamed ceilings and stone walls creating the perfect cosy atmosphere. Boat trips to wilderness from beach a stones throw away.

1 cottage, 3 pub rms, 3 bedrms (grd flr avail), sleeps 6, from £260.00, Jan-Dec, bus nearby, rail 40 mls, airport 130 mls

Mr Dodds
The Moorings, 29 Banks Road, Westkirby, Wirral, Merseyside, L48 0RA
Tel: (Westkirby) 0151 6256137

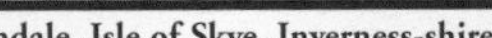

★ SELF ATERING

Secluded semi detached cottage to rear of main house. Views of Cuillins and use of extensive grounds. 10 miles (16kms) west of Broadford.

1 self sufficient annexe, 1 pub rm, 2 bedrms (grd flr avail), sleeps 4, £150.00-£230.00, Apr-Sep, bus nearby, rail 20 mls, ferry 20 mls, airport 100 mls

Mr & Mrs Kubale
Strathaird House, Strathaird, by Elgol, Isle of Skye, Inverness-shire, IV49 9AX
Tel: (Loch Scavaig) 01471 866269/01444 452990 (off season)
Email: 100405.2710@compuserve.com

ndale, Isle of Skye, Inverness-shire Map Ref: 3C8

★★ SELF ATERING

Modernised croft house in 8 acres of ground extending down to the river. Double-glazed picture windows and scenic views.

1 cottage, 2 pub rms, 3 bedrms (grd flr avail), sleeps 5, £180.00-£260.00, Jan-Dec, bus 1/2 ml, rail 60 mls, ferry 60 mls, airport 55 mls

Mrs Painting
376 Warwick Road, Banbury, Oxfordshire, OX16 7AY
Tel: (Banbury) 01295 252120

★★★ SELF ATERING

Former lighthouse keepers cottage in unique and isolated position. Fully refurbished to very comfortable and warm standards. 15 minutes walk from car park - real "get away from it all" holiday homes.

2 cottages, 1 bunkhouse, 1 pub rm, 2-3 bedrms (grd flr avail), sleeps 4-12, total sleeping capacity 22, £325.00-£495.00, Jan-Dec, bus 12 mls, rail 50 mls, ferry 50 mls, airport 50 mls

Roy Stoten
Neist Point Lighthouse, Glendale, Isle of Skye, Inverness-shire, IV55 8WU
Tel: (Glendale) 01470 511200

Kensaleyre, by Portree, Isle of Skye, Inverness-shire

Map Ref: 3D8

SELF CATERING

Detached recently built bungalow in a quiet rural area overlooking Loch Snizort to Waternish beyond. 8 miles (10kms) from Portree and Uig.

1 cottage, 1 pub rm, 2 bedrms, sleeps 4, £200.00-£260.00, Jan-Dec, bus nearby

Mrs C Lamont
Corran House, Kensaleyre,by Portree, Isle of Skye, Inverness-shire, IV51 9XE
Tel: (Kensalyre) 01470 532311

Kilmuir, Isle of Skye, Inverness-shire

Map Ref: 3D7

SELF CATERING

Skye Croft House in Historic Trotternish. Spectacular coastal location with magnificent sea views. Very comfortable with traditional furnishings.

1 house, 2 pub rms, 3 bedrms, sleeps 5, £175.00-£275.00, Jun-Sep

Mrs A MacDonald
2 Stanley Drive, Bishopbriggs, Glasgow, G64 2LA
Tel: 0141 772 5642

Kyleakin, Isle of Skye, Inverness-shire

Map Ref: 3F10

SELF CATERING

Semi-detached cottage in centre of Kyleakin and close to bridge. Good centre for touring all of Skye.

1 flat, 1 pub rm, 2 bedrms, sleeps 4, £160.00-£200.00, Jan-Dec, bus nearby

M MacAskill
Westhaven, Kyleakin, Skye, IV41 8PH
Tel: (Kyle) 01599 534476

Luib, by Broadford, Isle of Skye, Inverness-shire

Map Ref: 3E9

SELF CATERING

Attractive shore side location approximately 6 miles north of Broadford. Ideal for a wide range of activities.

1 cottage, 2 pub rms, 2 bedrms, sleeps 4, £100.00-£250.00, Jan-Dec, bus nearby

Mrs Wilkie
10 Mary Brown Walk, Garelochhead, Helensburgh, Dunbartonshire, G84
Tel: (Garelochhead) 01436 810632

Ord, Sleat, Isle of Skye, Inverness-shire

Map Ref: 3E10

SELF CATERING

Spacious, homely house in a quiet, picturesque setting with sea and mountain views. A perfect base for peace and relaxation in this secluded corner of Sleat, the "Garden of Skye".

1 house, 3 pub rms, 4 bedrms, sleeps 5-9, £180.00-£490.00, Jan-Dec, bus 4 mls

Mrs E White
66 Woodend Drive, Glasgow, G13 1TG
Tel: 0141 954 9013 Fax: 0141 954 9013

Important: Prices stated are estimates and may be subject to amendments

rtree, Isle of Skye, Inverness-shire **Map Ref: 3E9**

★★★★ SELF CATERING

On Portree waterfront with parking and garden to shore. Harbour facing double bedroom and lounge/diner (both with TVs) fully equipped kitchen, bathroom with spa bath, shower and sauna cabin.

1 apartment, 1 pub rm, 1 bedrm (grd flr avail), sleeps 2, £250.00-£350.00, Mar-Oct, bus nearby, rail 35 mls, ferry 35 mls, airport 125 mls

Mr Hugh Andrew
Beaumont House, Beaumont Crescent, Portree, Isle of Skye, Inverness-shire, IV51 9DF
Tel: (Portree) 01478 612219

★★★ SELF CATERING

Detached cottage in grounds of owner's house. Minutes walk to centre of Portree. Leisure centre and swimming pool nearby. Own parking.

1 cottage, 1 pub rm, 2 bedrms, sleeps 4, £170.00-£260.00, Apr-Oct, bus 1 ml, rail 35 mls, ferry 45 mls

Mrs M MacDonald
1 Woodpark, Dunvegan Road, Portree, Isle of Skye, Inverness-shire, IV51 9HQ
Tel: (Portree) 01478 612358

★★★ SELF CATERING

Very comfortably refurbished former stable block in extensive grounds of historic Viewfield House. Secluded location but only 10 minutes walk from Portree village centre, local restaurants and attractions.

1 cottage, 1 pub rm, 5 bedrms (grd flr avail), sleeps 7, £200.00-£500.00, Jan-Dec, bus 1/4 mile, rail 33 miles, ferry 33 miles, airport 30/120 miles

Mrs MacDonald
Viewfield House, Portree, Isle of Skye, IV51 9EU
Tel: (Portree) 01478 612217 Fax: 01478 613517

★★★ SELF CATERING

Semi-detached bungalows with panoramic views of Loch Greshornish and the hills beyond. 14 miles (22kms) to Portree. 9 miles (14kms) to Dunvegan.

2 houses, 1 pub rm, 3 bedrms (grd flr avail), sleeps 6, total sleeping capacity 12, £180.00-£300.00, Jan-Dec, bus 1/2 ml

Mr R R MacFarlane
Edinbane Holiday Homes, 15 Edinbane, by Portree, Isle of Skye, Inverness-shire, IV51 9PR
Tel: (Edinbane) 01470 582270 Fax: 01470 582270
Email: e-mailinfo@cortex.co.uk
Web: www.destination-scotland.com/scaview/

★★★★ SELF CATERING

Very well equipped and comfortable three storey Georgian house on the seafront, with magnificent views of harbour and over to Rasaay. Many personal touches, private parking, 2 minutes walk to Portree village centre.

1 house, 2 pub rms, 3 bedrms, sleeps 2-6, £250.00-£450.00, Jan-Dec, bus nearby, rail 30 mls

Mrs C R Salt
Cedar Mount, Water End, Brompton, North Allerton, N Yorks, DL6 2RN
Tel: (Northallerton) 01609 772433/01478 612048 Fax: 01478 612048

Portree, Isle of Skye, Inverness-shire

Map Ref: 3E9

Detached cottage and annexe to family house recently refurbished to high standard. Peaceful location, within walking distance of town centre.

1 house, 1 cottage, 1 pub rm, 2 bedrms (grd flr avail), sleeps 4, total sleeping capacity 6, £160.00-£300.00, Jan-Dec, bus 1/2 mls, rail 37 mls

Mrs Simmister
Kiltaraglen, Portree, Isle of Skye, Inverness-shire, IV51 9HR
Tel: (Portree) 01478 612435

Bungalow, with open outlook to Cuillin Hills, Portree 2.5 miles (4kms).

1 bungalow, 2 pub rms, 2 bedrms (grd flr avail), sleeps 2-5, £110.00-£260.00, Jan-Dec, bus 1 ml

Mrs Thorpe
5 Achachork, Portree, Isle of Skye, Inverness-shire, IV51 9HT
Tel: (Portree) 01478 612274

Staffin, Isle of Skye, Inverness-shire

Map Ref: 3E8

Booking Enquiries: Mr John Mackenzie Lynton, Staffin, Isle of Skye, Inverness-shire, IV51 9JS
Tel: (Staffin) 01470 562204/562214

Holiday Caravan to let, sleeps 8 £90.00-120.00, Apr-Oct.

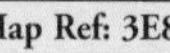

By shop and BP station, facing Staffin Bay and islands.

Struan, by Dunvegan, Isle of Skye, Inverness-shire

Map Ref: 3D9

Purpose built holiday cottages on a small croft overlooking Loch Beag. Beautiful views to Portnalong. Children welcome.

3 cottages, 1 pub rm, 3 bedrms, sleeps 6, total sleeping capacity 18, £170.00-£300.00, Jan-Dec, bus nearby

A Streeton
2 Balgown, Struan, Isle of Skye, Inverness-shire
Tel: (Struan) 01470 572231

Tarskavaig, Isle of Skye, Inverness-shire

Map Ref: 3E10

Modernised stone built cottage in quiet crofting community. 6 miles (10 kms) from Armadale ferry terminal.

1 house, 2 pub rms, 2 bedrms, sleeps 4, £150.00-£280.00, Jan-Dec, bus 6 mls, ferry 9 mls

Mrs J MacGregor
Kilbeg House, Ostaig, Sleat, Isle of Skye, IV44 8RQ
Tel: 01471 844331

rrin, by Broadford, Isle of Skye, Inverness-shire

Map Ref: 3E10

★★★★ SELF CATERING

Well equipped bungalow in peaceful crofting village. Magnificent views across Loch Slapin to Blaven. Ideal for nature lovers and climbers. Broadford 6 miles (10kms).

1 bungalow, 1 pub rm, 3 bedrms (grd flr avail), sleeps 6, £160.00-£395.00, Jan-Dec, bus nearby

Mrs E Bushnell
Rowanlea, 1/2 6 Torrin, by Broadford, Isle of Skye, Inverness-shire, IV49 9BA
Tel: (Broadford) 01471 822763

te, Skeabost Bridge, Isle of Skye, Inverness-shire

Map Ref: 3D8

★ SELF CATERING

Self contained flat for two people situated on working croft. Overlooking Snizort River and Loch Snizort. Portree 6 miles (10kms).

1 flat, 1 pub rm, 1 bedrm, sleeps 2, £140.00-£190.00, Jan-Dec, bus 1 ml, rail 40 mls, ferry 40 mls

Mrs E Dagless
Melton Croft, 5 Tote, Skeabost Bridge, Isle of Skye, Inverness-shire, IV51 9PQ
Tel: (Skeabost Bridge) 01470 532251

g, Isle of Skye, Inverness-shire

Map Ref: 3D8

★★ SELF CATERING

House converted to 3 modern apartments. Magnificent views of Loch Snizort and Uig Bay.

2 flats, 1-2 pub rms, 1-2 bedrms, sleeps 2-4, total sleeping capacity 6, £150.00-£250.00, Jan-Dec, bus nearby, rail 50 mls, ferry 1 ml

D C Taylor
The Hermitage, Spey Street, Kingussie
Tel: 01540 661691 Fax: 01540 662137

★★ SELF CATERING

Upper flat of crofthouse on working croft of 72 acres, at end of the Fairy Glen. Ideal for walkers, climbers and bird watchers.

1 flat, 1 pub rm, 2 bedrms, sleeps 4, £120.00-£185.00, Easter, Jun-Sep, bus 2 mls, rail 52 mls, ferry 3 mls, airport 140 mls

Mrs C Willoughby
3 Balnacnoc, Uig, Isle of Skye, Inverness-shire
Tel: (Uig) 01470 542249

aternish, Isle of Skye, Inverness-shire

Map Ref: 3D8

★★★ SELF CATERING

Unique former boathouse in beautiful shoreside location once owned by singer Donovan. Attractively furnished and spacious with open fire and gallery. Short walk from village with pub, seafood restaurant and yacht anchorage, discount offered for couples.

1 house, 3 pub rms, 3 bedrms (grd flr avail), sleeps 8, £300.00-£600.00, Jan-Dec, bus nearby

Mr & Mrs D Bell
Barr Cottage, Auchencairn, Castle Douglas
Tel: (Auchencairn) 01556 640245

Waternish, Isle of Skye, Inverness-shire

Map Ref: 3D8

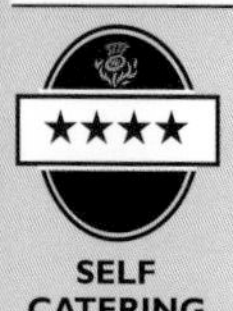

Stone cottage in elevated quiet location with outstanding views. Fully refurbished and equipped to high standards but retaining traditional charm.

1 cottage, 1 pub rm, 2 bedrms (grd flr avail), sleeps 4, £140.00-£400.00, Jan-Dec, rail 40 mls, ferry 50 mls, airport 100 mls

Mrs J L MacDonald

The Tables Hotel, Dunvegan, Isle of Skye, Inverness-shire, IV55 8W
Tel: (Dunvegan) 01470 521404 Fax: 01470 521404

Spean Bridge, Inverness-shire

Map Ref: 3H12

Attractive, timber-built chalet in elevated position with outstanding panoramic views towards Ben Nevis mountain range. Cosy lounge, dining area, well equipped kitchen and full central heating. Set in own grounds with small lawn and heather garden. Ample parking close to unit. 1 mile from centre of Spean Bridge. Ideal base for skiers (Aonach Mor 5 miles) open all year - even Christmas. Friendly welcome guaranteed.

1 chalet, 1 pub rm, 2 bedrms (grd flr avail), sleeps 4, £160.00-£315.00, Jan-Dec, bus nearby, rail 1 ml, ferry 52 mls, airport 68 mls

Mr & Mrs Baldon

Faegour,Tirindrish, Roybridge Road, Spean Bridge, Inverness-shire, PH34 4EU
Tel: (Spean Bridge) 01397 712903

SCOTTISH TOURIST BOARD INSPECTED

Mrs Catherine Cameron

Booking Enquiries: Mrs Catherine Cameron 2 Balmaglaster, Spean Bridge, Inverness-shire, PH34 4EB
Tel: (Invergarry) 01809 501289

Holiday Caravan to let, sleeps 6 £100.00-£165.00, min let weekend (lo season), Jan-Dec.

Take A82 22 mls N of Fort William. Turn left at Balmaglaster, Kilfinnan road sign. Caravan at fifth house. Approx 1 1/2 mls up this road.

Compact 2 bedroom chalet in quiet location, short walk from centre of Spean Bridge. Ideal base for walkers, climbers and skiers.

1 chalet, 1 pub rm, 2 bedrms, sleeps 4, £140.00-£200.00, Jan-Dec, bus 600 yds, rail 800 yds, airport 55 mls

Mrs J Ferguson

The Oaks, Spean Bridge, Inverness-shire, PH34 4DX
Tel: (Spean Bridge) 01397 712593

✓✓✓✓ 20

Gairlochy Holiday Park

Booking enquiries: Jackson Anderson
Spean Bridge, Inverness-shire, PH34 4EQ
Tel: (Spean Bridge) 01397 712711 Fax: 01397 712712

1 acre, grassy, hard-standing, level, Apr-Oct, prior booking in peak periods. Extra charge for electricity, awnings, showers.

10 tourers £6.50-£7.50 or 10 motors £6.00-£7.00 or 10 tents £6.00. Total Touring Pitches 10.

4 Holiday Caravans to let, sleep 4 £170.00-£360.00, total sleeping capacity 16, min let 3 nights.

Turn off A82 1/2 ml N of Spean Bridge on to B8004 at Commando Memorial, signposted Gairlochy. Site is 1 ml on left and signposted.

Important: Prices stated are estimates and may be subject to amendments

an Bridge, Inverness-shire

Map Ref: 3H12

★★ SELF ATERING

Cosy, traditional 125 year old Highland cottage with open fire. Overlooking beautiful Loch Lochy. Eat at owners' Taste of Scotland restaurant.

1 cottage, 1 pub rm, 2 bedrms, sleeps 4, £175.00-£370.00, Jan-Dec, bus nearby, rail 7 mls, ferry 65 mls, airport 52 mls

Mrs C Kerr
Corriegour Lodge Hotel, Loch Lochy,by Spean Bridge, Inverness-shire, PH34 4EB
Tel: (Spean Bridge) 01397 712685 Fax: 01397 712696

★★★★ SELF ATERING

Cosy, former steading in secluded Glen Gloy, 15 miles north of Fort William. The interior is bright and airy and is fully equipped to cater for all weather needs. Situated amongst mature trees, with the river Gloy close by. The garden provides a safe play area for children. The Glen is a haven for wildlife happily co-existing with our hill farm and sporting activities. Sorry no pets.

1 cottage, 2 pub rms, 2 bedrms (grd flr avail), sleeps 4, £230.00-£400.00, Jan-Dec, bus 500 yds, rail 5 mls, airport 60 mls

Mrs Kirsty MacLeod
Glen Gloy Estate, by Spean Bridge, Inverness-shire, PH34 4DZ
Tel: (Spean Bridge) 01397 712668 Fax: 01397 712655

★★★ SELF ATERING

A very peaceful wooded riverside site, yet within walking distance of village/restaurant. These attractive one bedroomed timber lodges are ideal for couples but 3 can sleep up to 4 on bed-settees, and are fully equipped and newly refurbished. Ideal touring base close to Nevis Range. Walking/fishing from site. Towels/microwave available on request. Drying room for walkers available.

12 chalets, 1 pub rm, 1 bedrm, sleeps 2-3, total sleeping capacity 24, min let 2 nights, £155.00-£295.00, Jan-Dec, bus 1/4 ml, rail 1/4 ml

Mrs Pickering
Burnbank House, Spean Bridge, Inverness-shire, PH34 4EU
Tel: (Spean Bridge) 01397 712520 Fax: 01397 712520

★★★★ SELF ATERING

Superbly equipped three bedroomed single storey house in grounds of historic house where Jacobite Rebellion started. Situated on outskirts of village, ten minutes drive from mountain gondolas and ideal base for touring area, many beauty spots. Terrace and major rooms including sun lounge overlook mountains.

1 house, 2 pub rms, 3 bedrms (grd flr avail), sleeps 6, £290.00-£510.00, Dec-Oct, bus 1/2 ml, rail 1/2 ml, airport 60 mls

Mr & Mrs P Wilson
Tirindrish House, Spean Bridge, Inverness-shire, PH34 4EU
Tel: (Spean Bridge) 01397 712398 Fax: 01397 712595

er, Sutherland

Map Ref: 3G4

★★★ SELF ATERING

Renovated croft cottages in rural setting close to Loch Clash and 3 miles (5kms) from nearest shop. Fishing and sea fishing available locally.

3 cottages, 1-2 pub rms, 1-3 bedrms, sleeps 2-5, total sleeping capacity 12, £160.00-£320.00, Jan-Dec, bus 10 mls, rail 50 mls

Mrs F MacKenzie
216 Clashmore, Stoer, Lochinver, Sutherland, IV27 4JQ
Tel: (Stoer) 01571 855226 Fax: 01571 855226

Strathconon, Ross-shire Map Ref: 4A8

★★ SELF CATERING

Detached timber cottage, with an open fire, situated in beautiful Strathconon. Ideal for a quiet holiday, walking, fishing, touring or wildlife watching. Very peaceful location.

1 bungalow, 1 pub rm, 3 bedrms, sleeps 7, £130.00-£270.00, Jan-Dec

Mrs Jacqueline Cameron
Inverchoran, Strathconon, By Muir of Ord, Ross-shire IV6 7QQ
Tel: (Muir of Ord) 01997 477252

★★★ SELF CATERING

Refurbished farm cottage, situated on a working farm within the Scatwell Estate, at the lower end of Strathconon. Loch fishing can be arranged. Extensive woodland and hill walks in the vicinity.

1 cottage, 3 bedrms (grd flr avail), sleeps 6, min let weekend, £190.00-£305.00, Jan-Dec, airport 30 mls

Mrs C Watt
Little Scatwell, by Strathpeffer, IV14 9EW
Tel: 01997 466221 Fax: 01997 466230

Strathpeffer, Ross-shire Map Ref: 4A8

★★★★ SELF CATERING

Detached Scandinavian style chalets situated in woodland setting about 1 mile from Highland village of Strathpeffer.

2 log cabins, 1 pub rm, 2 bedrms (grd flr avail), sleeps 4, total sleeping capacity 8, £195.00-£305.00, Apr-Oct, bus 1/3 ml, rail 5 mls, airport 20 mls

Mr & Mrs R Borrows
Fir Lodge, Blackmuir Wood, Strathpeffer, Ross-shire, IV14 9BT
Tel: (Strathpeffer) 01997 421682

★★★ SELF CATERING

Detached cottage with own garden, situated in the centre of this charming Victorian Spa village. Ideal base for exploring the Highlands, Wester Ross, the far north or even the islands. Sorry no pets.

1 cottage, 1 pub rm, 2 bedrms, sleeps 4, £275.00-£285.00, Jan-Dec, bus 500 yds, rail 6 mls, airport 23 mls

Mrs J Cameron
White Lodge, Strathpeffer, Ross-shire, IV14 9AL
Tel: (Strathpeffer) 01997 421730
Email: whitelodge@vacations-scotland.co.uk
Web: www.vacations-scotland.co.uk/whitelodge.html

Important: Prices stated are estimates and may be subject to amendments

‹hpeffer, Ross-shire

Map Ref: 4A8

★★★ SELF ‹TERING

Exceptionally well equipped, charming wing of Victorian country house sleeping four and offering many additional features for your enjoyment and comfort.

1 wing of country house, 1 pub rm, 2 bedrms, sleeps 4, £260.00-£295.00, Mar-Nov, bus nearby, rail nearby

Sally Gilbert-Smith
Nutwood House, Strathpeffer, Ross-shire, IV14 9DT
Tel: (Strathpeffer) 01997 421666 Fax: 01997 421796
Email: sally@gilsmith.demon.co.uk

★★ SELF ‹TERING

Spacious bungalow with ample off-road parking, quietly situated 2 miles (3km) from the delightful Victorian Spa village of Strathpeffer. Magnificent views from the sun lounge over Strathpeffer and the valley.

1 bungalow, 2 bedrms (grd flr avail), sleeps 4-5, £200.00-£295.00, Mar-Nov, bus 1 ml, rail 4 1/2 mls, airport 28 mls

Mrs E MacLean
Castle View, Ardival, Strathpeffer, Ross & Cromarty, IV14 9DS
Tel: (Strathpeffer) 01997 421506

‹meferry, Ross-shire

Map Ref: 3F9

★★★ SELF ‹TERING

Comfortable, semi-detached cottage on the shores of Loch Carron. Plockton 7 miles (11 kms).

1 cottage, 1 pub rm, 3 bedrms, sleeps 5, min let 4 days, £158.00-£310.00, Jan-Dec, bus 7 mls, rail 3 mls, airport 80 mls

Mr Charles R Begg
167 Portachullin, Stromeferry, Ross-shire, IV53 8UR
Tel: (Stromeferry) 01599 577267

‹ntian, Argyll

Map Ref: 1E1

★★ SELF ‹TERING

Timber chalet, with views of Loch Sunart. 1 mile (2kms) from village. Ideally situated for touring.

1 chalet, 1 pub rm, 2 bedrms (grd flr avail), sleeps 4-5, £190.00-£320.00, Apr-Oct, rail 24 mls, ferry 14 mls

Mr J Cunningham
14 St Quintin Park, Bathpool, Taunton, Somerset, TA2 8TB
Tel: (West Monkton) 01823 413840 Fax: 01823 413840

Strontian, Argyll — Map Ref: 1E1

✓✓✓✓

35

Glenview Caravan Park

Strontian, Argyll, PH36 4JD Tel: 01967 402123 Fax: 01967 402123

3 1/2 acres, mixed, Mar-Jan, prior booking in peak periods, latest time of arrival 2300. Extra charge for electricity.

14 tourers £8.50-10.00 or 14 motors £8.50-10.00 or 15 tents £7.00-8.00. Total Touring Pitches 29.

3 Holiday Caravans to let, sleep 6, £190.00-£310.00, total sleeping capacity 18, min let weekend.

On A82 Corran Ferry to Ardgour, follow signs to Strontian. Right at police station and follow road round green.

Tain, Ross-shire — Map Ref: 4B7

Split level house in its own grounds overlooking the villages of Hilton, Balintore and Shandwick with panoramic views across the Moray Firth. Beautiful clean beaches in all three villages, line fish from the harbour, explore the rock pools or take a trip out ot sea to fish or watch the seals and dolphins at play. Ideally situated for walks, bird watching and golf, as well as many Pictish sites in the area.

1 house, 2 pub rms, 3 bedrms, sleeps 6, £250.00-£415.00, Jan-Dec

Mrs Sheila Hall
Talisker, 25 Ness Bank, Inverness
Tel: 01463 236221 Fax: 01463 234173
Email: 106735.2241@compuserve.com

Talmine, Sutherland — Map Ref: 4A3

Modern detached bungalow with magnificent views towards Rabbit Island and Gilean Nan Ron Island. Sandy beaches in the local vicinity, craft shop and Post Office. Ideal location for touring the North Coast, or simply relaxing, enjoying the view, birds and wildlife.

1 bungalow, 2 pub rms, 3 bedrms (grd flr avail), sleeps 5, £160.00-£330.00, Apr-Oct

Mr & Mrs G Gunn
97 Kenneth Street, Inverness, IV3 5QQ
Tel: 01463 234420

Thurso, Caithness — Map Ref: 4D3

Comfortable bungalow, quietly situated close to the centre of the town of Thurso. Non-smoking house and all rooms on ground floor. Great base for exploring the far north coast, or for day trips to Orkney.

1 cottage, 1 pub rm, 2 bedrms (grd flr avail), sleeps 4, from £150.00, Jan-Dec, bus 1/2 ml, rail 1/2 ml, ferry 1 1/2 mls, airport 21 mls

Mrs E Fitzpatrick
13 Mill Road, Thurso, Caithness, KW14 8PT
Tel: (Thurso) 01847 892537

Delightful cottage with garden in peaceful country setting 4 miles from Thurso and 18 miles from John O' Groats. Warm, spacious and well-equipped with panoramic views - a superb centre for exploring the far north and for day trips to Orkney. Children welcome, cot provided, but regret no pets. Sandy beaches, puffins and peregrines, Scottish primroses, ancient cairns, flow country, 3 golf-courses, salmon and trout fishing - all nearby.

1 cottage, 2 pub rms, 2 bedrms (grd flr avail), sleeps 4, min let 3 nights, £185.00-£325.00, Jan-Dec, bus 5 mls, rail 5 mls, ferry 7 mls, airport 20 mls

Mrs C E MacGregor
Curlew Cottage, Hilliclay Mains, Weydale, by Thurso, Caithness, KW14 8YN
Tel: (Thurso) 01847 895638

macharrick, Inverness-shire

Map Ref: 3H12

SELF ATERING

Norwegian log house in peaceful rural setting 3 miles from Fort William. Magnificent views of Aonoch Mhor and Ben Nevis. Offering accommodation of a high standard for up to 10 people. Situated in a large, natural garden with garden shed with storage space for ski's etc.

1 log cabin, 3 pub rms, 6 bedrms (grd flr avail), sleeps 10, £350.00-£650.00, Jan-Dec

Mr Alistair Smyth
24 Zetland Avenue, Fort William, PH33 6LL
Tel: (Fort William) 01397 702532

matin, Inverness-shire

Map Ref: 4B9

SELF ATERING

Attractive croft cottage set amidst magnificent scenery in a quiet farm location. Good base for walking, wildlife and touring. Convenient village inn with bar food.

1 cottage, 1 pub rm, 2 bedrms (grd flr avail), sleeps 4, £141.00-£235.00, Apr-Oct, bus 2 mls, rail 15 mls, airport 20 mls

Mrs P H MacKintosh-Grant
Balvraid Lodge, Tomatin, Inverness-shire, IV13 7XY
Tel: (Tomatin) 01808 511204

ngue, Sutherland

Map Ref: 4A3

SELF ATERING

Traditional cottage, set in quiet country location, yet close to village amenities. Enclosed garden with seating area. Ideal location for touring the north coast of Scotland.

1 bungalow, 1 pub rm, 3 bedrms, sleeps 6, £160.00-£220.00, Apr-Oct, bus nearby, rail 40 mls, airport 65 mls

Mr C Burr
Ard Cruaidh, Tongue, Sutherland, IV27 4XJ
Tel: (Tongue) 01847 611328

rridon, Ross-shire

Map Ref: 3G8

SELF ATERING

A modern property in quiet location on the slopes of Ben Alligin with open views across Upper Loch Torridon to the mountains. Otters, eagles and deer seen. Open fires and full c.h. Bathroom, separate shower room, 3rd wc. Telephone, washer drier, freezer. In one acre of fenced grounds, including woodland hillside plantation to rear, with pines, rhododendrons, eucalyptus and retreat house. 4 mins footpath walk to beach.

1 bungalow, 1 pub rm, 3 bedrms, sleeps 5, from £220.00, Jan-Dec, bus nearby, rail 25 mls, airport 70 mls

The Revd. and Mrs A M Roff
Rowan Glen, Culbokie, Dingwall, IV7 8JY
Tel: (Culbokie) 01349 877762
Email: 016770.3175@compuserve.com

lapool, Ross-shire

Map Ref: 3G6

★★

SELF ATERING

Completely modernised, listed, sandstone houses in quiet conservation area of Ullapool. Each has its own small garden area and off road parking. Ullapool Golf Course near by.

1 house, 1 bungalow, 1-2 pub rms, 1-2 bedrms (grd flr avail), sleeps 4, total sleeping capacity 8, £180.00-£250.00, Apr-Oct, bus ¼ ml, rail 31 mls, ferry ¼ ml, airport 60 mls

Mrs P E Campbell
5 Custom House Street, Ullapool, Ross-shire, IV26 2XF
Tel: (Ullapool) 01854 612107

Ullapool, Ross-shire — **Map Ref: 3G6**

★★ SELF CATERING

Situated in a remote glen and reached by private road, the area is a haven for wild flowers, birds and red deer. Ullapool 6 miles (11 kms).

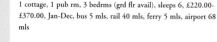

1 cottage, 1 pub rm, 3 bedrms (grd flr avail), sleeps 6, £220.00-£370.00, Jan-Dec, bus 5 mls, rail 40 mls, ferry 5 mls, airport 68 mls

Mr A Fenwick
The Granary, Eaton, Grantham, Lincolnshire, NG32 1ET
Tel: (Grantham) 01476 870243 Fax: 01476 870687

★★★★

SELF CATERING

Well designed and constructed timber chalets. Lochside location with picture windows giving excellent views over the bay and hills beyond.

2 chalets, 1 pub rm, 2-4 bedrms, sleeps 4-6, total sleeping capacity 10, £175.00-£400.00, Jan-Dec, bus nearby, rail 35 mls, airport 60 mls

P Fraser
Ardmair Point Chalets, Ullapool, Ross-shire, IV26 2TN
Tel: (Ullapool) 01854 612054 Fax: 01854 612757
Email: p.fraser@btinternet.com

★★★ SELF CATERING

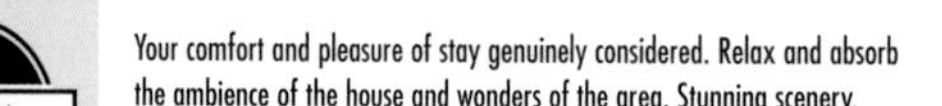

Your comfort and pleasure of stay genuinely considered. Relax and absorb the ambience of the house and wonders of the area. Stunning scenery, sunsets, wildlife and outdoor pursuits. Easy access to village and it's amenities, from Sports Centre, swimming pool, restaurants and entertainments or simply the pleasure of watching the activities of the harbour. Welcome aboard! - The Skipper.

1 house, 1 pub rm, 3 bedrms (grd flr avail), sleeps 6, £550.00, Jan-Dec, bus 1/4 ml, rail 20 mls, ferry 1/4 ml, airport 40 mls

Ms Margaret Gordon
Speyroy, Old Spey Bridge, Grantown on Spey, Morayshire, PH26 3NQ
Tel: 01479 872955/872979

★★

SELF CATERING

Centrally located, extensive modern detached house within its own garden. Covered garage available. Views towards Loch Broom.

1 cottage, 2 pub rms, 4 bedrms (grd flr avail), sleeps 8, £180.00-£375.00, Jan-Dec, bus nearby, rail 20 mls, ferry nearby, airport 60 mls

Mr B Hicks
16 Ely Gardens, Tonbridge, Kent, TN10 4NZ
Tel: (Tonbridge) 01732 367827

★★★ SELF CATERING

Modernised traditional stone cottage on main street in Ullapool. Small fenced garden. Open fire and central heating. Ideal base for touring or activity holiday.

2 cottages, 1-2 pub rms, 2-3 bedrms (grd flr avail), sleeps 4-5, total sleeping capacity 9, £180.00-£350.00, Jan-Dec, bus 1/2 ml, rail 30 mls, ferry 1/2 ml, airport 65 mls

Mrs A L MacKenzie
The Willows, Elphin, by Lairg, Sutherland, IV27 4HH
Tel: (Ullapool) 01854 666217

Important: Prices stated are estimates and may be subject to amendments

ıpool, Ross-shire **Map Ref: 3G6**

Leckmelm Holiday Cottages

Lochbroom, Ullapool, Ross-shire IV23 2RN Tel: 01854 612471

Well-equipped traditional stone cottages, lochside bungalows and timber chalets all in beautiful rural surroundings on Leckmelm Estate. An ideal base for exploring The Highlands or just enjoying the peace and quiet of this 7000 acre private estate.

★★

SELF ATERING

Compact timber chalets and cottages grouped on a hillside overlooking Loch Broom. 3 miles (5kms) from Ullapool.

9 chalets, 7 cottages, 4 bungalows, 1-2 pub rms, 1-4 bedrms (grd flr avail), sleeps 2-10, total sleeping capacity 76, £130.00-£360.00, Jan-Dec, bus 3 1/2 mls, rail 30 mls, airport 60 mls

Leckmelm Holiday Cottages
Lochbroom, Ullapool, Ross-shire, IV23 2RN
Tel: (Ullapool) 01854 612471 Fax: 01854 612471

★★

SELF ATERING

Modernised fisherman's cottage with views over Loch Broom. Ideal centre for touring and outdoor pursuits.

1 cottage, 2 pub rms, 3 bedrms (grd flr avail), sleeps 6, from £250.00, Jan-Dec, bus 300 yds, rail 35 mls, ferry 300 yds, airport 70 mls

Mrs S MacLeod
Ardengare, 2 Kidston Drive, Helensburgh, Dunbartonshire, G84 8QA
Tel: (Helensburgh) 01436 671807 Fax: 01436 674407

★★★

SELF ATERING

Traditional stone built villa in Conservation area of Ullapool. Close to all town amenites.

1 house, 2 pub rms, 4 bedrms, sleeps 10, £295.00-£365.00, Jan-Dec, bus 500 yds

Mr A J MacNab
13 Upper Bourtree Drive, Burnside, Rutherglen, Glasgow, G73 4EJ
Tel: 0141 634 1681 Fax: 0141 570 3901
Email: macnabaj@aol.com

★★

SELF ATERING

Cottage in centre of village. Ideal for all amenities, and as base for touring North West Highlands. Private parking available.

1 bungalow, 2 pub rms, sleeps 6, £130.00-£275.00, Jan-Dec, bus 1 ml, ferry 1 ml

Mr W MacRae
Creggan House, 18 Pulteney Street, Ullapool, IV26 2UP
Tel: 01854 612397/612296 Fax: 01854 613396

VAT is shown at 17.5%: changes in this rate may affect prices.

Key to symbols is on back flap.

Ullapool, Ross-shire

Map Ref: 3G6

Wonderful panoramic views from this compact cottage. Easy access to shoreline, through owners private sheep grazing land. Ullapool 12 miles (19kms).

1 bungalow, 1 pub rm, 2 bedrms (grd flr avail), sleeps 4, £190.00-£240.00, Jan-Dec, bus 4 mls, rail 28 mls, ferry 12 mls, airport 60 mls

Mrs C Mathieson
1a Rhiroy, Lochbroom, by Ullapool, Ross-shire, IV23 2SF
Tel: (Lochbroom) 01854 655229

House and apartment, set in peaceful picturesque location, with beautiful views over Loch Broom and easy access to the shore. Parking on-site. Short drive to Ullapool, ideal for touring Torridon and North West coast.

1 house, 1 flat, 1 pub rm, 2-3 bedrms (grd flr avail), sleeps 3-5, total sleeping capacity 8, £150.00-£325.00, Apr-Oct, bus 4 1/2 mls, rail 30 mls, ferry 12 mls, airport 68 mls

Mrs L Renwick
Spindrift, Keppoch Farm, Dundonnell, Ross-shire, IV23 2QR
Tel: (Dundonnell) 01854 633269 Fax: 01854 633269

Whitebridge, Inverness-shire

Map Ref: 4A10

Stone built house in quiet location on Knockie Estate, deer stalking and trout fishing can be arranged. 27 miles (43kms) from Inverness.

1 house, 2 pub rms, 3 bedrms, sleeps 6, £320.00-£380.00, Jan-Dec, bus 3 mls, rail 27 mls, airport 30 mls

Mrs I Ross
Knockie Estate, Whitebridge, Inverness-shire, IV1 2UP
Tel: (Gorthleck) 01456 486648

Situated south of Loch Ness, a small group of well-appointed Fyfestone and Cedar Lodges set along a wooded river bank in an unspoilt nature paradise.

10 chalets, 1-3 pub rms, 1-2 bedrms (grd flr avail), sleeps 1-6, total sleeping capacity 36, min let 1 night, £185.00-£550.00, Jan-Dec, bus nearby, rail 24 mls, airport 24 mls

Wildside Highland Lodges
Whitebridge, Inverness-shire, IV2 6UN
Tel: (Gorthleck) 01456 486373 Fax: 01456 486 371
Email: wildside@enterprise.net

Wick, Caithness

Map Ref: 4E3

Self-contained flat on elevated site overlooking Wick harbour. Conveniently situated a short distance from the town centre. 'Frosty' the pony is a friendly resident of the garden.

1 flat, 1 bedrm, sleeps 4, £120.00-£150.00, Jan-Dec, bus 3/4 ml, rail 3/4 ml, airport 1 1/2 mls

Mrs Banks
Gleneagles, 33 Whitehouse Park, Wick, Caithness, KW1 4NX
Tel: (Wick) 01955 602487

Important: Prices stated are estimates and may be subject to amendments

Outer Islands

The Outer Islands are for people looking for a totally different experience – for a sense of being outside Britain and seeing a different culture.

They are for discriminating visitors, for those who enjoy wild places and a glimpse of the past and who appreciate that distinct character and a strong heritage are precious in this modern age. They are also for those who enjoy adventure and fun. The three island groupings – the Western Isles, Orkney and Shetland differ from each other, though Orkney and Shetland share a common Norse heritage. All three have good links by ferry and by air. Late spring in the islands is a particular delight, with rare northern wild flowers and spectacular seabird colonies adding to the sense of being somewhere different.

The Western Isles are the stronghold of the Gael, though everyone speaks English as well. Some of the finest sandy beaches in Britain can be found here, mostly on the west side of the islands, along with the characteristic machair – shell-sand on which a rich sward of wild flowers grows. There are some spectacular ancient monuments as well, notably the famous Calanais (Callanish) Standing Stones – Scotland's Stonehenge. You can glimpse more recent ways of life at the Black House at Arnol, an old-style restored croft house and there are a variety of other visitor centres portraying the heritage of the Gael. However, it is the pace of life, set in a distinct landscape and culture which will make the deepest impression.

Older than Stonehenge, the Standing Stones of Callanish on Lewis in the Western Isles are one of the many ancient sites scattered throughout the Outer Islands.

Orkney is a scattering of green islands, relatively fertile, with a strong sense of community and also more prehistoric sites to the square mile than anywhere else in Britain. Skara Brae, a 5000 year old Stone Age village and Maes Howe, a unique burial chamber probably pillaged by the Vikings, are just two of them. There are wildlife sites galore, especially seabirds, notably on the rugged island of Hoy.

Orkney's strong naval tradition is portrayed in a brilliant museum at Lyness on Hoy, overlooking the former naval anchorage at Scapa Flow. The highest vertical sea-cliff in Britain is also on Hoy and is just another surprise, as is the superb Norman work in St Magnus Cathedral in Kirkwall. However, the friendliness of the people should not be surprising – that is common in these Outer Island communities.

Shetland is another cluster of islands, bound together like Orkney by an excellent network of inter-island ferries. Below the horizon, out of sight of the Scottish mainland, Shetland has the strongest sense of somewhere different.

Here the Scandinavian influence is strongest. Nowhere is more than 3 miles (5 km) from the sea. Magnificent seascapes and seabird colonies, from Sumburgh Head in the south to Hermaness in the north, are a speciality. There are brochs (circular defensive towers) and other early sites, as well as a croft museum, castles, and the main town of Lerwick to explore. June in these northern latitudes is a special time. This is the land of the 'simmer (summer) dim' – where the short night brings only twilight, leaving even more daylight hours to enjoy the stark beauty of the place.

Events

The Outer Islands

Throughout 1999

YEAR OF THE NORSE

Various venues throughout the whole of the Western Isles. A year long programme of events to celebrate the legacy of the Norse people in the Western Isles.
Contact: Western Isles Tourist Board
Tel: 01851 703088 Fax: 01851 705244.

Jan 1

NEW YEAR'S DAY MENS BA' GAME

Kirkwall, Orkney. Traditional game of mass street football between the 'Uppies' and the 'Doonies'.
Contact: J D M Robertson.
Tel: 01856 872961.

Jan 26

UP HELLY AA

Lerwick, Shetland. Traditional Viking Fire Festival.
Contact: Lerwick Tourist Information Centre.
Tel: 01595 693434.

June 1 – 19

ORKNEY HOMECOMING

Various venues in Orkney. An invitation to Orcadians in Canada and the USA to "come home".
Contact: Kirkwall Tourist Information Centre.
Tel: 01856 872856

June 18 – 23

ST MAGNUS FESTIVAL

Kirkwall, Orkney. Music, drama, dance and poetry.
Contact: Dorothy Rushbrook.
Tel: 01856 872669.

July

HEBRIDEAN CELTIC MUSIC FESTIVAL

Various venues, Stornoway, Isle of Lewis. Celtic music performed by national and international artists in the shadow of Lews Castle.
Tel: 01851 701818.

Aug 9 – 12

CUTTY SARK TALL SHIP RACE

Lerwick, Shetland.
Contact: Ruth Henderson, Sail Shetland Ltd.
Tel: 01595 694335 Fax: 01595 693588.

Welcome to...

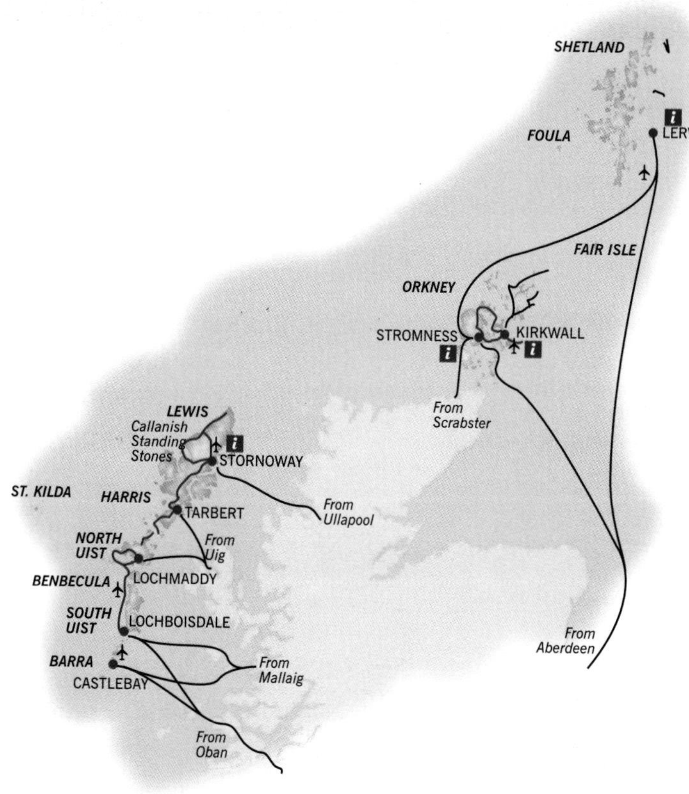

Area Tourist Board Addresses

1 **Orkney Tourist Board**
6 Broad Street
KIRKWALL
Orkney
KW15 1NX
Tel: 01856 872856
Fax: 01856 875056

2 **Western Isles Tourist Board**
4 South Beach Street
Stornoway
Isle of Lewis
HS1 2XY
Tel: 01851 701818
Fax: 01851 701828
e.mail:
witb@sol.co.uk
website:
www.witb.co.uk

3 **Shetland Tourist Board**
Market Cross
LERWICK
Shetland
ZE1 0LU
Tel: 01595 693434
Fax: 01595 695807

Tourist Information Centres in Scotland

ORKNEY TOURIST BOARD

KIRKWALL ✉
6 Broad Street, KW15 1DH
Tel: (01856) 872856
Jan-Dec

STROMNESS
Ferry Terminal Building
The Pier Head
Tel: (01856) 850716
Jan-Dec

WESTERN ISLES TOURIST BOARD

CASTLEBAY
Main Street
Isle of Barra
Tel: (01871) 810336
Easter-Oct

LOCHBOISDALE
Pier Road
Isle of South Uist
Tel: (01878) 700286
Easter-Oct

LOCHMADDY
Pier Road
Isle of North Uist
Tel: (01876) 500321
Easter-Oct

STORNOWAY ✉
26 Cromwell Street
Isle of Lewis
Tel: (01851) 703088
Jan-Dec

TARBERT
Pier Road
Isle of Harris
Tel: (01859) 502011
Easter-Oct

SHETLAND ISLANDS TOURISM

LERWICK ✉
The Market Cross
Shetland, ZE1 0LU
Tel: (01595) 693434
Jan-Dec

✉ Accept written enquiries
♿ Disabled access

...sary, Isle of Barra, Western Isles

Map Ref: 3B11

★ SELF ...TERING

Detached cottages in peaceful lochside setting on east coast of Barra, 3 miles (5 kms) from Castlebay.

2 cottages, 1-2 pub rms, 1-3 bedrms (grd flr avail), sleeps 4-8, total sleeping capacity 12, from £80.00, Jan-Dec, ferry 4 mls, airport 4 mls

Dr C Bartlett
1 The Green, Frimley Green, Camberley, Surrey, GU16 6HF
Tel: (Deepcut) 01252 835123/837522

...hasaig, Isle of Harris, Western Isles

Map Ref: 3C6

★★ SELF ...TERING

Modern detached cottage looking over Ardhasaig Bay to North Harris Hills.

1 chalet, 3 bedrms (grd flr avail), sleeps 7, £200.00-£250.00, Jan-Dec, ferry 3 mls, airport 36 mls

Mrs MacAskill
Clisham House, Ardhasaig, Harris, Western Isles
Tel: (Harris) 01859 502066 Fax: 01859 502077

...bay, Isle of Harris, Western Isles

Map Ref: 3C7

★★ SELF ...TERING

Pretty cottage. Peaceful, rocky inlet, seals, maybe otters, birdlife, mussel beds and walks. What else?

1 cottage, 5 pub rms, 3 bedrms (grd flr avail), sleeps 6, £135.00-£300.00, Jan-Dec, bus nearby, ferry 5 mls, airport 45 mls

Mrs MacIntyre
Struthmore, Finsbay, South Harris, HS3 3JD
Tel: (Manish) 01859 530255

...abay, Isle of Harris, Western Isles

Map Ref: 3B7

★★ SELF ...TERING

Traditional 150 year old crofter's restored cottage. Enjoy the Hebrides from this peaceful location.

1 cottage, 2 pub rms, 2 bedrms, sleeps 4, £220.00-£280.00, Jan-Dec, ferry 12 mls, airport 50 mls

John M MacAulay
Fernhaven, Flodabay, Harris, HS3 3HA
Tel: (Manish) 01859 530340

...bost, Isle of Harris, Western Isles

Map Ref: 3C6

★★★ SELF ...TERING

Two cottages looking over a dazzling white sandy bay to the mountains of North Harris. Comfortable and equipped to a high standard.

2 cottages, 1-2 pub rms, 3 bedrms (grd flr avail), sleeps 5-7, total sleeping capacity 12, £260.00-£330.00, Jan-Dec, bus nearby, ferry 10 mls, airport 47 mls

Mrs C Morrison
Beul na Mara Cottages, Seilebost, Harris, Western Isles, HS3 3HP
Tel: (Scarista) 01859 550205

VAT is shown at 17.5%: changes in this rate may affect prices.

Key to symbols is on back flap.

Tarbert, Isle of Harris, Western Isles

Map Ref: 3C6

Detached bungalow in elevated position above Tarbert. Quiet residential location. Ideal location for touring Harris & Lewis. Hillwalking, birdwatching, sandy beaches within easy reach.

1 bungalow, 2 pub rms, 3 bedrms (grd flr avail), sleeps 7-9, £230.00-£300.00, Mar-Oct, bus 150 yds, ferry 1/4 ml, airport 45 mls

I E Goodfellow
3 Barony Knoll, Jedburgh Road, Kelso, TD5 8JE
Tel: 01573 224751

Terrace of four cottages overlooking Tarbert. Close to ferry. Ideal for touring Harris and Lewis.

4 houses, 4 pub rms, 2 bedrms, sleeps 4, total sleeping capacity 16, £180.00-£290.00, Jan-Dec, bus 400 yds, ferry 600 yds, airport 36 mls

Angus J MacLeod
Kirklea Terrace Cottages, Pier Road, Tarbert, Harris, Western Isles, HS3 3DG
Tel: (Harris) 01859 502138 Fax: 01859 502578

Laxdale, Isle of Lewis, Western Isles

Map Ref: 3D4

Well equipped accommodation fitted out to high standard. Located only 1.5 miles from Stornoway. Pleasing views over croft land and to Broad Bay.

1 bungalow, 2 pub rms, 3 bedrms (grd flr avail), sleeps 6, £180.00-£290.00, Jan-Dec, bus nearby, ferry 1 1/2 mls, airport 4 mls

Mr G Macleod
Woodside, Laxdale Lane, Laxdale, Isle of Lewis, HS2 0DR
Tel: (Stornoway) 01851 706966/703234 Fax: 01851 706966
Email: gordon@laxdaleholidaypark.force9.co.uk

Lochs, Isle of Lewis, Western Isles

Map Ref: 3D4

Very comfortable semi-detached adjoining owners home. Excellent views over Loch Leurbost and surrounding area, 20 minutes drive from Stornoway. Good base for touring all of Lewis and Harris.

1 flat, 1 pub rm, 2 bedrms, sleeps 3, £70.00-£120.00, Mar-Nov, bus nearby, ferry 10 mls, airport 13 mls

Mrs K MacAskill
Flat, 32 Crossbost, Lochs, Isle of Lewis, HS2 9NP
Tel: 01851 860284

Important: Prices stated are estimates and may be subject to amendments

hs, Isle of Lewis, Western Isles | **Map Ref: 3D4**

★★★ SELF ATERING

Traditional, modernised croft cottage, sitting on hillside with superb views to the front. Ideal for walking and trout fishing.

1 cottage, 1 pub rm, 3 bedrms (grd flr avail), sleeps 4, £120.00-£170.00, Jan-Dec

Katie McLeod
6 Calbost, Lochs, Isle of Lewis
Tel: (Gravir) 01851 880406

nsay, Lochs, Isle of Lewis, Western Isles | **Map Ref: 3D5**

★★ SELF ATERING

Modern bungalow, situated on hillside overlooking Loch Shiant, with views of the Isle of Skye in the distance.

1 bungalow, 2 pub rms, 3 bedrms (grd flr avail), sleeps 6, £120.00-£195.00, Jan-Dec, bus nearby, ferry 30 mls, airport 33 mls

Mrs A M Kennedy
3 Orinsay, Lochs, Lewis, Western Isles
Tel: (Gravir) 01851 880375

nt, Isle of Lewis, Western Isles | **Map Ref: 3E4**

★★★ SELF ATERING

Modern spacious croft house on site affording open views to coastline and beyond to West Sutherland. Peace and quiet assured, yet near Stornoway.

1 house, 1 pub rm, 2 bedrms (grd flr avail), sleeps 4, £130.00-£250.00, Jan-Dec, bus nearby, ferry 10 mls, airport 5 mls

S Ferguson
1 Jamieson Drive, Stornoway, Isle of Lewis, Western Isles, HS1 2TG
Tel: (Stornoway) 01851 703025 Fax: 01851 706915

★★★ SELF ATERING

Purpose built modern bungalows in 'A' line style in rural position close to small village of Cnoc, 5 miles (8kms) from Stornoway.

4 chalets, 1 pub rm, 2 bedrms (grd flr avail), sleeps 4, total sleeping capacity 16, £125.00-£250.00, Jan-Dec, bus nearby, ferry 4 mls, airport 1 ½ mls

Mrs Mary MacLeod
Cnoc Cottages, 5a Knock, Point, Lewis, Western Isles, HS2 0BW
Tel: (Stornoway) 01851 703000/870537 Fax: 01851 706384

noway, Isle of Lewis, Western Isles | **Map Ref: 3D4**

★★★ SELF ATERING

Two adjacent properties, compact but comfortable and well equipped, quietly located on the outskirts of Stornoway. Excellent sandy beaches a short distance away. Well situated for exploring Lewis and Harris - much to see and do in the area.

2 houses, 1 pub rm, 3 bedrms (grd flr avail), sleeps 5, total sleeping capacity 10, £180.00-£225.00, Jan-Dec, ferry 2 mls, airport 4 mls

Murdo MacLeod
31 Urquhart Gardens, Stornoway, Lewis, Western Isles
Tel: (Stornoway) 01851 702458

Uig, Isle of Lewis, Western Isles

Map Ref: 3C5

★★
SELF CATERING

Situated in very scenic area near hills and beaches. Ideal for quiet restful holiday.

1 cottage, 1 pub rm, 4 bedrms (grd flr avail), sleeps 6, £150.00-£200.00, Jan-Dec, ferry 35 mls, airport 40 mls

Mrs MacKay
2 Melbost, Stornoway, Isle of Lewis, Western Isles, H52 0BG
Tel: (Stornoway) 01851 704594 (Mon-Sat)

Nibon, by Hillswick, Shetland

Map Ref: 5F4

SELF CATERING

Timber chalet in isolated location overlooking sea and Isles. Safe pebble beach nearby. Ideal for walking and birdwatching. Magnificent cliff scenery makes Nibon ideal for walking, bird watching, landscape painting or just relaxing and enjoying the view.

1 cottage, 1 pub rm, 2 bedrms, sleeps 4, £110.00-£160.00, Mar-Nov, bus 2 mls

Mrs Balfour
Busta, Brae, Shetland
Tel: (Brae) 01806 522230/01806 522589 (eve)

Berneray, Isle of North Uist, Western Isles

Map Ref: 3B7

SELF CATERING

On the peaceful island of Berneray, off North Uist. This recently refurbished stone house provides a comfortable and spacious holiday home.

1 house, 1 pub rm, 4 bedrms (grd flr avail), sleeps 8, £200.00-£280.00, Jan-Dec, bus 1 ml, ferry 1 ml, airport 28 mls

Mrs C MacAskill
Morven, Isle of Berneray, North Uist, HS6 5BJ
Tel: (Berneray) 01876 540230 Fax: 01876 540230

Claddach Kirkibost, Isle of North Uist, Western Isles

Map Ref: 3B8

SELF CATERING

Cottage built on sheep rearing croft overlooking the island of Baleshare. Tidal sandy beach.

1 cottage, 1 pub rm, 2 bedrms, sleeps 4, £190.00-£295.00, Jan-Dec, bus nearby, ferry 10 mls, airport 10 mls

Mrs Tosh
Seabreeze, Claddach Baleshare, North Uist, Western Isles
Tel: (Locheport) 01876 580644

Lochmaddy, Isle of North Uist, Western Isles

Map Ref: 3B8

SELF CATERING

Traditional thatched island cottage re-built to original design but incorporating all modern conveniences, comforts and a 4-poster bed. Situated in quiet location for romantic breaks away from it all.

1 cottage, 1 pub rm, 1 bedrm (grd flr avail), sleeps 2-4, £200.00-£330.00, Jan-Dec, bus 1/2 ml, ferry 2 mls, airport 20 mls

Mr Neil Nicholson
4 Clachan Sands, Lochmaddy, North Uist, Western Isles, HS6 5AY
Tel: (Lochmaddy) 01876 500409 Fax: 01876 500409

Important: Prices stated are estimates and may be subject to amendments

hportain, Isle of North Uist, Western Isles

Map Ref: 3B7

★★★ SELF ATERING

Semi-detached cottage, former manse attached to small church in fishing/crofting community 9 miles (14kms) from Lochmaddy. Fine views over bay.

1 house, 2 pub rms, 3 bedrms (grd flr avail), sleeps 6-7, £190.00-£325.00, Jan-Dec, bus nearby, ferry 9 mls, airport 30 mls

Alasdair Seale
Trinity Factoring Services Ltd, 209 Bruntsfield Place,
Edinburgh, EH10 4DH
Tel: 0131 447 9911 Fax: 0131 452 8303
Email: trifac@globalnet.co.uk
Web: www.trinityfactors.co.uk

ay, Orkney

Map Ref: 5B11

★★★ SELF ATERING

Cottage full of character in idyllic lochside setting. Peat fire, antique furniture, perfect peace. Close to RSPB reserve, trout lochs and within easy reach of the major archaeological sites. Excellent base for a relaxing stay.

1 cottage, 1 pub rm, 3 bedrms (grd flr avail), sleeps 6, £180.00-£380.00, Jan-Dec, ferry 17 mls, airport 22 mls

Mrs K Reid
Orkney Self Catering, Finstown, Orkney, KW17 2EH
Tel: (Finstown) 01856 761581 Fax: 01856 875361

erness, Orkney

Map Ref: 5C12

★★★ SELF ATERING

Traditional 2 storey stonebuilt house on working farm. Completely renovated to form a comfortable family home from home.

1 house, 4 bedrms (grd flr avail), sleeps 8, £150.00-£280.00, Apr-Oct, bus 10 mls, ferry 25 mls, airport 7 mls

Mrs M Eunson
Staye, Deerness, Orkney, KW17 2QH
Tel: (Deerness) 01856 741240

stown, Orkney

Map Ref: 5B12

★★★★ SELF ATERING

Self contained apartments at water's edge. Breathtaking views to North Isles. Wildlife to hand close by. Midway between Kirkwall and Stromness. Daily rates available.

13 lodges, 1 pub rm, 1-2 bedrms, sleeps 2-4, total sleeping capacity 36, £180.00-£380.00, Jan-Dec, bus nearby, ferry 7 mls, airport 10 mls

Mrs K Reid
Atlantis Lodges, Finstown, Orkney, KW17 2EH
Tel: (Finstown) 01856 761581 Fax: 01856 875361

★★★★ SELF ATERING

A novel "upside-down boat" house and 5 spacious chalets, siyuated right on the sea shore with lovely open views across the Bay of Firth towards Shapinsay.

1 house, 3 bungalows, 1-2 pub rms, 2-3 bedrms (grd flr avail), sleeps 4-6, total sleeping capacity 18, £180.00-£380.00, Jan-Dec, bus nearby, ferry 7 mls, airport 10 mls

Mrs K Reid
Orkney Self Catering, Finstown, Orkney, KW17 2EH
Tel: (Finstown) 01856 761 581 Fax: 01856 875361

VAT is shown at 17.5%: changes in this rate may affect prices.

Key to symbols is on back flap.

Firth, Orkney

Map Ref: 5B12

SELF CATERING

Purpose built semi-detatched cottages, adjacent to a burn and the shore. Lovely views across the bay. Set in quiet farming area 10 miles from Stromness and Kirkwall. Easy access to the major historical and archaeological sites. Good for bird watching, fishing, day trips to the Northern Isles, or just enjoying the peace and quiet.

2 cottages, 1 pub rm, 2 bedrms (grd flr avail), sleeps 5, total sleeping capacity 10, £80.00-£290.00, Jan-Dec, bus 1 1/2 mls, ferry 9 mls, airport 12 mls

Mrs A Stevenson
Burness, Firth, Orkney, KW17 2ET
Tel: (Finstown) 01856 761 442

Holm, Orkney

Map Ref: 5C12

SELF CATERING

Farmhouse with views to the Southern Isles and from the kitchen window views to Scapa Flow and Hoy.

1 house, 2 pub rms, 4 bedrms (grd flr avail), sleeps 7, min let weekend, £150.00-£320.00, Jan-Dec, bus 1 ml

M A Fox
Craebreck House, Holm, Orkney Isles, KW17 2RX
Tel: (Kirkwall) 01856 781220

Kirkwall, Orkney

Map Ref: 5B12

SELF CATERING

Six holiday homes on outskirts of Kirkwall with outstanding views towards the Northern Isles.

6 chalets, 1 pub rm, 2 bedrms (grd flr avail), sleeps 4, total sleeping capacity 24, min let 4 days, £100.00-£280.00, Jan-Dec, bus 1 ml, ferry 1 ml, airport 3 mls

Mrs I Gray
Bilmaris, Glaitness Road, Kirkwall, Orkney, KW15 1TW
Tel: (Kirkwall) 01856 874515 Fax: 01856 874515
Web: www.orkneyislands.com/bilmaris

Rendall, Orkney

Map Ref: 5B11

SELF CATERING

Modern spacious wing of owners house set in large garden area. Quiet farming area, 15 miles from Stromness and Kirkwall. A short walk down to the shoreline, where you may expect to see seals. Views across the bay to the Northern Isles.

1 house, 1 pub rm, 3 bedrms (grd flr avail), sleeps 6, £80.00-£230.00, Jan-Dec, bus 2mls, ferry 13mls, airport 16mls

Mrs H Balfour
Rennabreck, Rendall
Tel: (Finstown) 01856 761 479

St Margaret's Hope, Orkney

Map Ref: 4E1

SELF CATERING

Small traditional cottage with creature comforts. Superbly sited at water's edge overlooking St Margaret's Hope.

1 cottage, 1 pub rm, 1 bedrm, sleeps 4, £160.00-£180.00, Jan-Dec, bus nearby

John Holmes
42 Eglinton Road, Ardrossan, Strathclyde, KA22 8NQ
Tel: (Ardrossan) 01294 467642 Fax: 01294 467642
Email: misitu@globalnet.co.uk

Important: Prices stated are estimates and may be subject to amendments

Margaret's Hope, Orkney

Map Ref: 4E1

★★

SELF
ATERING

Cottage peacefully situated on its own jetty by rocky shore on the edge of picturesque fishing village. Comfortable, centrally heated accommodation in which to base yourselves, as you explore the area, and the rest of Orkney.

1 house, 2 pub rms, 2 bedrms, sleeps 3, £215.00, Jan-Dec, bus 1/4 ml, airport 12 mls

Mrs J Rose
The Priory, St Olaves, Great Yarmouth, Norfolk, NR31 9HE
Tel: (Great Yarmouth) 01493 488609 Fax: 01493 488265
Email: priory@netcomuk.co.uk

day, Orkney

Map Ref: 5D10

★★

SELF
ATERING

Comfortable recently modernised house, situated close to a large sandy bay on the delightful island of Sanday, with abundant wildlife, walks and tranquility.

1 bungalow, 2 pub rms, 3 bedrms (grd flr avail), sleeps 6, £100.00-£170.00, Jan-Dec, ferry 3 mls, airport 7 mls

Mrs S Towrie
West Brough Farm, Sanday, Orkney, KW17 2BN
Tel: (Sanday) 01857 600347 Fax: 01857 600347

omness, Orkney

Map Ref: 5B12

★★★

SELF
ATERING

Spacious house and unique split level apartment set above Stromness Harbour with views to Scapa Flow.

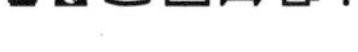

1 cottage, 2 pub rms, 1 bedrm, sleeps 1-2, £80.00-£150.00, Jan-Dec, bus 500 yds

Mrs Ishbel Borland
Bea House, Back Road, Stromness, Orkney, KW16 3AW
Tel: (Stromness) 01856 851043

★ UP TO ★★★

SELF
ATERING

Cottage wing and garden cottage on owners' property. Excellent views over Stromness harbour. Adjacent to golf course and yacht club. Explore the delights of this town with its sea-faring history, or visit the many important archaeological sites of Orkney. Whatever you choose to do, you will find this a peaceful and relaxing base.

1 flat, 1 cottage, 1 pub rm, 1-2 bedrms (grd flr avail), sleeps 2-4, total sleeping capacity 6, £100.00-£250.00, Jan-Dec, bus 1/2 ml, ferry 1/2 ml, airport 15 mls

Mrs Thomas
Stenigar, Ness Road, Stromness, Orkney, KW16 3DW
Tel: (Stromness) 01856 850438

stray, Orkney

Map Ref: 5B10

★★★★

SELF
ATERING

Refurbished to a high standard comfortable, centrally heated cottage is situated close to lovely white sandy beaches. Ideal for peaceful holiday. Birdwatching and seals nearby.

1 cottage, 1 pub rm, 3 bedrms (grd flr avail), sleeps 6, £100.00-£230.00, Jan-Dec, ferry 2 mls, airport 9 mls

Mrs M Bain
Twiness, Rapness, Westray, Orkney, KW17 2DE
Tel: (Westray) 01857 677319

VAT is shown at 17.5%: changes in this rate may affect prices.

Key to symbols is on back flap.

Lerwick, Shetland

Map Ref: 5G6

Modern flat in conservation area. Close to town centre, with view over Bressay Sound. Adjacent to children's play area. A couple of hotels within a 2 minutes walk.

1 flat, 2 pub rms, 2 bedrms (grd flr avail), sleeps 5, £180.00-£275.00, Jan-Dec, bus 250 yds, ferry 1/2 ml, airport 25 mls

Mrs I Rutherford
The North House, Gletness, South Nesting, Shetland, ZE2 9PS
Tel: (Skellister) 01595 890219

Ollaberry, Shetland

Map Ref: 5F4

Modern cottage and traditional croft house on a working croft, in the heart of the community of Bardister. The scenery is varied and makes good walking country.

1 house, 1 cottage, 1 pub rm, 3 bedrms (grd flr avail), sleeps 5, total sleeping capacity 5, £100.00-£250.00, Jan-Dec

Mr & Mrs Stephen
Sunnyside, Ollaberry, Shetland, ZE2 4RT
Tel: (Ollaberry) 01806 544277

Sumburgh, Shetland

Map Ref: 5F4

Historic keeper's house at working lighthouse, on spectacular headland. Superb views, seabird cliffs on all sides.

1 house, 2 pub rms, 4 bedrms (grd flr avail), sleeps 6, min let 3 days, £350.00, Apr-Oct, bus 2 mls, ferry 28 mls, airport 1 1/2 mls

Mr T Johnson-Ferguson
Solwaybank, Canonbie, Dumfries-shire, DG14 0XS
Tel: (Chapelknowe) 01387 372240

North Boisdale, Isle of South Uist, Western Isles

Map Ref: 3B10

Recently modernised croft house approx 7 miles from Lochboisdale. Very close to wonderful beaches and perfect for a peaceful holiday. Golf, hillwalking and birdwatching close by.

1 cottage, 2 pub rms, 3 bedrms, sleeps 6, min let weekend, from £160.00, Jan-Dec, bus nearby, ferry 6 mls, airport 25 mls

Roderick MacInnes
364 South Boisdale, Isle of South Uist, HS8 5TE
Tel: (Loch Boisdale) 01878 700371/347 Fax: 01878 700371

Important: Prices stated are estimates and may be subject to amendments

Hostel Accommodation

Aberdeen
Aberdeen Youth Hostel
8 Queens Road, Aberdeen AB15 4ZT
Tel: 01224 646988
Min Price: £7.10 Max Price: £9.60

Achnashellach
Achnashellach Hostel
Craig Achnashellach, Strathcarron
Wester Ross IV54 8YU
Tel: 01520 766232
Min Price: £8.00 Max Price: £9.00

Arden
Loch Lomond Youth Hostel
Arden, Alexandria, Dunbartonshire
G83 8RD
Tel: 01389 850226
Min Price: £7.10 Max Price: £9.60

Ardgartan, by Arrochar
Ardgartan Youth Hostel
Ardgartan, by Arrochar
Dunbartonshire G83 8AR
Tel: 01301 702362
Min Price: £6.50 Max Price: £7.75

Aviemore
Richard & Katherine Scarffe
Allt Na Criche Christian Holiday Centre
Aviemore, Inverness-shire PH22 1PZ
Tel: 01479 810237
Min Price: £10.25
Max Price £10.50

Ayr
Ayr Youth Hostel
5 Craigweil Road, Ayr KA7 2XJ
Tel: 01292 262322
Min Price: £6.50 Max Price: £7.75

Badachro
Mr Iain Thomson
Badachro Bunkhouse, Badachro
Gairloch, Ross-shire IV21 2AA
Tel: 01445 741291
Min Price: £8.50 Max Price £8.50

Breakish
Fiona Mandeville
13 Lower Breakish, Isle of Skye
Inverness-shire
Tel: 01471 822644
Min Price: £7.50

Cannich
Glen Affric Backpackers
Cannich, by Beauly, Inverness-shire
Tel: 01456 415263
Min Price: £5.00 Max Price: £5.00

Crianlarich
Crianlarich Youth Hostel
Station Road, Crianlarich FK20 8QN
Tel: 01838 300260
Min Price: £6.50 Max Price: £7.75

Crieff
St Ninian's Centre
Comrie Road, Crieff, Perthshire PH7
Tel: 01764 653766
Max Price Single £10.30

Drumnadrochit
Loch Ness Backpackers Lodge
Coiltie Farmhouse, East Lewiston
Drumnadrochit IV3 6UT
Tel: 01456 450807
Max Price: £8.50

Dundonnell
Sail Mhor Croft Hostel
Camsunagaul, Dundonnell
Ross-shire IV23 2QT
Tel: 01854 633224
Min Price: £8.00

Edinburgh
Backpackers, Princes Street West
3 Queensferry Street
Edinburgh EH2 4PA
Tel: 0131 226 2939
Min Price: £6.50
Max Price: £13.00

Backpackers Royal Mile
105a High Street, Edinburgh EH1 1SG
Tel: 0131 557 6120
Min Price: £9.90
Max Price £11.00

Belford Hostel
6 Douglas Gardens, Edinburgh EH4 3DA
Tel: 0131-225 6209
Min Price: £12.00
Max Price £22.50

Bruntsfield Youth Hostel
7/8 Bruntsfield Crescent
Edinburgh EH10 4EZ
Tel: 0131 447 2994
Min Price: £7.10 Max Price £9.60

Castle Rock Hostel
15 Johnston Terrace
Edinburgh EH1 2PW
Tel: 0131 225 9666
Min Price: £10.00
Max Price £12.00

Cowgate Tourist Hostel
112 The Cowgate, Edinburgh EH1 1JN
Tel: 0131 226 2153
Min Price: £12.50
Max Price £20.00

Edinburgh Backpackers Hostel
65 Cockburn Street, Edinburgh EH1 1BU
Tel: 0131 220 1717
Min Price: £12.50
Max Price £23.75

Eglinton Youth Hostel
18 Eglinton Crescent, Edinburgh EH12 5DD
Tel: 0131 337 1120
Min Price: £9.95 Max Price £12.50

High Street Hostel
8 Blackfriars Street
Edinburgh EH1 1NE
Tel: 0131 557 3984
Min Price: £9.90 Max Price £11.00

Elgin
Elgin Backpackers
Saltire Lodge, Pluscarden Road
Elgin, Moray IV30 3TE
Tel: 01343 551467
Min Price: £7.50 Max Price: £8.50

Hostel Accommodation

Gairloch

Achtercairn Hostel
Gairloch Sands Hotel, Achtercairn
Gairloch, Ross-shire IV21 2BH
Tel: 01445 712131
Min Price: £8.50 Max Price: £8.50

Fran Cree
Rua Reidh Lighthouse Hostel
Melvaig, Gairloch, Ross-shire IV21 2EA
Tel: 01445 771263
Min Price £11.00
Max Price £15.00

Glasgow

Apparthotel YMCA
David Naismith Court
33 Petershill Drive, Glasgow G21 4QQ
Tel: 0141 558 6166
Max Price Single £17.00

Grantown-on-Spey

Speyside Backpackers
16 The Square, Grantown-on-Spey
Moray PH26 3LG
Tel: 01479 873514
Min Price: £8.50
Max Price: £10.00

Inveraray

Inveraray Youth Hostel
Dalmally Road, Inveraray PA32 8XD
Tel: 01499 302454
Min Price: £4.95 Max Price: £6.10

Inverness

Backpackers Hotel
4 Culduthel Road, Inverness IV2 4AB
Tel: 01463 717663
Min Price: £7.50 Max Price: £9.00

Eastgate Backpackers Hostel
38 Eastgate, Inverness IV2 3NA
Tel: 01463 718756
Min Price Single £10.40
Min Price per room £8.90

Ho Ho Hostel
23a High Street, Inverness IV1 1HY
Tel: 01463 221225
Min Price: £8.50
Max Price: £10.50

Killin

Killin Youth Hostel
Killin, Perthshire FK21 8TN
Tel: 01567 820546
Min Price: £4.95 Max Price: £6.10

Kincraig by Kingussie

Sheila A Paisley
Kirkbeag, Kincraig, Kingussie PH2 1ND
Tel: 01540 651298
Min Price: £8.50 Max Price: £9.50

Kinlochleven

Mr Beard
Hostel Brae, Kinlochleven
Argyll PA40 4RT
Tel: 01855 831471
Min Price: £7.00
Max Price: £12.00

New Lanark, by Lanark

New Lanark Youth Hostel
Wee Row, New Lanark, by Lanark ML11 1DJ
Tel: 01555 666710
Min Price: £8.35 Max Price: £9.35

Newtonmore

Mr & Mrs P Main
Newtonmore Independent Hostel
Main Street, Newtonmore PH20 1DA
Tel: 01540 673360
Min Price: £8.50 Max Price: £8.50

North Ronaldsay

North Ronaldsay Bird Observatory Hostel
Orkney, KW17 2BE
Tel: 01857 633200
Min Price Single £10.00
Max Price Single £14.00

Oban

Jeremy Inglis Hostel & Budget Accommodation
21 Airds Crescent, Oban
Min Price Single £11.00
Max Price Single £12.00

Oban Youth Hostel
Esplanade, Oban PA34 5AF
Tel: 01631 562025
Min Price: £7.10 Max Price: £9.60

Onich by Fort William

Inchree Bunkhouse Hostel
Onich, Fort William
Inverness-shire PH33 6SD
Tel: 01855 821287
Min Price: £7.00 Max Price: £7.50

Perth

Perth Youth Hostel
Glasgow Road, Perth PH2 0NS
Tel: 01738 623658
Min Price £6.50 Max Price £7.75

Pitlochry

Pitlochry Youth Hostel
Braeknowe, Knockard Road, Pitlochry
Perthshire PH16 5HJ
Tel: 01796 472308
Min Price £6.50 Max Price £7.75

Port Charlotte

Islay Youth Hostel
Port Charlotte, Isle of Islay PA48 7TY
Tel: 01496 850385
Min Price: £4.95 Max Price: £6.10

Portnalong

Mr and Mrs Mann
Skyewalker Independent Hostel
The Old School, Portnalong
Isle of Skye, Inverness-shire IV47 8SL
Tel: 01478 640250
Min Price: £7.00 Max Price: £7.00

Mr Thomas
7 Portnalong, Portnalong, Isle of Skye
Inverness-shire
Tel: 01478 640254
Min Price: £6.50 Max Price: £8.00

ortree

Peter Gooch
9 Stormyhill Road, Portree
Isle of Skye IV51 9DY
Tel: 01478 613332
Min Price: £7.50 Max Price: £8.50

Portree Backpackers Hostel
Dunvegan Road, Portree IV51 9HQ
Tel: 01478 613644
Min Price: £7.50 Max Price: £9.00

Portree Independent Hostel
Old Post Office, Portree
Isle of Skye, Inverness-shire IV51 9BT
Tel: 01478 613731
Min Price: £7.50 Max Price: £9.50

ousay

Ms C Rae, Rousay Hostel
Trumland Farm, Rousay
Orkney KW17 2PU
Tel: 01856 821252
Min Price Single £6.00

owardennan

Rowardennan Youth Hostel, Rowardennan
by Drymen G63 0AR
Tel: 01360 870259
Min Price: £6.50 Max Price: £7.75

leat

Peter MacDonald
Sleat Independent Hostel
The Glebe, Kilmore, Isle of Skye
Tel: 01471 844272
Min Price Single £7.00

tirling

Stirling Tourist Hostel
Richard Lindsay, 1a Bayne Street
Stirling FK8 1PG
Tel: 01786 449123
Min Price: £11.00
Max Price: £15.00

Stirling Youth Hostel
St John Street, Stirling FK8 1DU
Tel: 01786 473442
Min Price: £9.95
Max Price: £12.50

Stromness

SYHA Youth Hostel
Hellihole Road, Stromness, Orkney
Tel: 01856 850589
Min Price £4.95 Max Price £6.10

Thurso

Thurso Youth Club Hostel
Old Mill, Millbank, Thurso
Caithness KW14 8PS
Tel: 01847 892964
Min Price £8.00 Max Price £8.00

Tighnabruaich

Tighnabruaich Youth Hostel
High Road, Tighnabruaich
Argyll PA21 2BU
Tel: 01700 811622
Min Price £4.95 Max Price £6.10

Uyeasound

Mrs W Jamieson
Musseburgh, Uyeasound, Unst
Shetland ZE2 9DW
Tel: 01957 755259
Min Price: £6.50 Max Price: £7.75

Whiting Bay

Scottish Youth Hostels Association
Shore Road, Whiting Bay, Isle of Arran
Argyll KA27 8QW
Tel: 01770 700339
Min Price: £4.95 Max Price: £6.10

Facilities
For Visitors with Disabilities

The Scottish Tourist Board, in conjunction with the English and Wales Tourist Boards, operates a national accessible scheme that identifies, acknowledges and promotes those accommodation establishments that meet the needs of visitors with disabilities.

The three categories of accessibility, drawn up in close consultation with specialist organisations concerned with the needs of people with disabilities, are:

CATEGORY 1

Unassisted wheelchair access for residents

CATEGORY 2

Assisted wheelchair access for residents

CATEGORY 3

Access for residents with mobility difficulties

Category 1

8 Ormiscaig
Aultbea, by Achnasheen
Ross-shire IV22 2JQ

Delgatie Castle
Turriff, Aberdeenshire AB5 7TD

Eildon Holiday Cottages
Dingleton Mains, Melrose
Roxburghshire TD6 9HS

Kingennie Lodges
Kingennie, Broughty Ferry
Tayside DD5 3RD

Miss M Brook
Lochletter Lodges
Balnain, Drumnadrochit
Inverness-shire

2A Laide
Laide, Ross-shire

Category 2

4 Halistra
Waternish, Isle of Skye
IV55 8GL

Appin House Apartments
Appin, Argyll
PA38 4BN

Arrochar
Well Brae, Pitlochry
Perthshire PH16 5HG

Avon Glen Chalets
Melons Place
Melons Place Farm
Maddiston

Badanfhuarain Cottage
and Flox Cottage, Nethybridge
Inverness-shire

Ballintean Bungalow
Ballintean
Glenfeshie, by Kincraig
Inverness-shire
PH21 1NX

Barncrosh Farm
Castle Douglas
Kirkcudbrightshire
DG7 1TX

Brewhouse Flat and Royal
Artillery Cottage, Culzean Castle
Maybole, Ayrshire
KA19 8JX

Brooklinn Mill
Blairgowrie, Perthshire
PH10 6TB

Burnside Apartments
19 West Moulin Road
Pitlochry, Perthshire
PH16 5EA

Cairncross House
20 Kelvinhaugh Place
Glasgow G3 8NH

Caledonian Court
Glasgow Caledonian University
Caledonian Court, Glasgow

Carden Self-catering
Alves, by Elgin
Moray IV30 3UP

Colony Lodge
Colony Wood, Cromarty
Ross-shire IV11 8XX

Craigadam Lodge
by Castle Douglas DG7 3HU

Crosswoodhill Farm
By West Calder, West Lothian
EH55 8LP

Crubenbeg Farm Steadings
Newtonmore, Inverness-shire
PH20 1BE

Drumdelgie House
Drumdelgie, by Huntly
Aberdeenshire AB54 4TH

Dunsmore Lodges
By Beauly, Inverness-shire
IV4 7EY

Glen Tanar Estate
Brooks HouseGlen Tanar
Aboyne, Aberdeenshire
AB34 5EU

Glenprosen Cottages
Balnaboth, Glenprosen, Kirriemuir
Angus DD8 4SA

Glenview
Achmore, Stromeferry
Ross-shire IV53 8UT

Gordon Holiday Cottages
Gartly, by Huntly
Aberdeenshire AB5 4QA

Hillhead Halls
University of Aberdeen
Aberdeen AB9 1FX

Ifferdale Farm Cottage
Saddell, by Campbeltown
Argyll PA28 6QZ

Inverawe Holiday Cottage
Inverawe House
Taynuilt, Argyll
PA35 1HU

Kilmardinny Estate
Milngavie Road, Bearsden
Glasgow G61 3DH

Lady Jean Fforde
Derneneach, Shiskine
Isle of Arran KA27 8JE

Little Seinton Cottages 2, 3 and 5
Little Swinton, Coldstream
Berwickshire TD12 4HH

Loch Tay Lodges
Remony, Aberfeldy
Perthshire PH15 2HR

Lochland Chalets
Dounby, Orkney KW17 2HR

Mar Lodge
Braemar, Ballater
Aberdeenshire AB35 5YJ

Mr A P Davis
Roskhill Barn Flats Roskhill
by Dunvegan, Isle of Skye
IV55 8ZD

Mr D M Buchanan
Mill Lodge and Burnside Lodge
Geddes, Nairn, Inverness-shire
IV12 55A

Mrs K Mitchell
Lochview Holidays Ormiscaig
Aultbea, Ross-shire

Mrs O C Lawrence
East Faldonside Lodge
Melrose TD6 9BG

Napier University
Wrights Houses, Bruntsfield
Edinburgh EH10 4HR

Nith Riverside Lodges
Blackaddie House Hotel
Sanquhar, Dumfriesshire
DG4 6JJ

Oakbank Farm
Lamlash, Isle of Arran KA27 8LH

Parkhead Croft
Drummuir, by Keith
Banffshire AB55 3PQ

Parkmore Farm
Dufftown, Keith, Banffshire
AB55 4DN

Pine Bank Chalets
Aviemore, Inverness-shire
PH22 1PX

Quality Street Ltd
Aviemore, Inverness-shire
PH22 1TD

Synton Mains Farm
The Davies Partnership
Ashkirk, Selkirk TD7 4PA

The Pierhouse
The Pier, Melfort, Kilmelford
by Oban, Argyll PA34 4XD

Tree Tops & Kestrels Nest
Laikenbuie, Grantown Road
Nairn IV12 5QN

University of Abertay Dundee
Bell Street, Dundee DD1 1HG

Willow Croft
Big Sand, Gairloch, Ross-shire
IV21 2DD

Woolman Hill & Kepplestone Flats
John Street & Queens Road
Aberdeen, Aberdeenshire

Facilities
For Visitors with Disabilities

Category 3

1/2 6 Valtos
Staffin, by Portree
Isle of Skye

2 Burnmouth Road
Little Dunkeld, Dunkeld
Perthshire

2,4,6,8 & 10 Garden Crescent
Gardenstown, Banffshire
AB4 3YN

32 Riddrie Knowes
Glasgow G33 2QH

Ailanbeg Cottage
Ailanbeg Lodge, Nethy Bridge
Inverness-shire PH25 3DR

Aithness
Fetlar, Shetland ZE2 9DJ

An Bothan
8 Naast, Poolewe
Ross-shire IV22 2LL

Ardgour House
Ardgour, Clovullin
by Fort William, Argyll
G11 7SH

Ardo House
High Street, Auldearn, Nairn
IV12 5TG

Benarty Steading Cottage
Benarty House, Kelty, Fife
KY4 0HT

Bridge Cottage
Killumpha, Port Logan
Stranraer, Wigtownshire
DG9 9NT

Caberfeidh
17 Highland Crescent, Crieff
Perthshire PH7 4LH

Cabhalan
1 Quidinish, Isle of Harris
Western Isles PA85 3JQ

Cauldside Farmhouse
St.Andrews, Fife
KY16 9TY

Coille nam Beithe
Dalnavert, Kincraig
by Aviemore PH

Cologin Homes Ltd
Lerags, by Oban
Argyll PA34 4SE

Corriegorm Beag
Bay View Crescent
Broadford, Isle of Skye
IV49 9AB

Craiglyn
50 West Moulin Road, Pitlochry
Perthshire PH16 5EQ

Craigmore
Upper Baila, Lerwick
Shetland ZE1 0SF

Craw's Nest Bungalow
Kilfillan, Glenluce
Dumfriesshire DG8 0JN

Croftnacarn
Loch Garten, Boat of Garten
Inverness-shire

Curlew Cottage
Hilliclay Mains Weydale
Thurso, Caithness
KW14 8YN

Duirinish Chalets
Duirinish, Ross-shire IV40 8BE

Egmont
Shore Road, Toward
by Dunoon, Glasgow PA23 7UA

Eleraig Highland Chalets
Kilninver, by Oban, Argyll
PA34 4UX

Enochdhu
5 Rosemount Park Gardens
Blairgowrie, Perthshire
PH10 6TW

Garden Cottage
Lyon Street, Killin, Perthshire
FK21 8UH

Glenview
Fowlis Wester, Crieff, Perthshire
PH7 3NL

Innes Maree
Poolewe, Ross-shire IV22 2JU

Kilcamb Cottage
Strontian, Argyll PH36 4HY

Kwathu
Blackwaterfoot, Isle of Arran

Laebrak
Gulberwick, by Lerwick
Shetland ZE1 ORJ

Lagganlia Outdoor Centre
Kincraig, Kingussie
Inverness-shire PH21 1NG

Little Woodside Cottage
Kilmuir, North Kessock
Ross-shire IV1 1XG

Loch Insh Chalets
Kincraig, Inverness-shire
PH21 1NU

Lochview, Ardach
Allt a Chuirn, Lochcarron
Ross-shire

Mossfield Holiday Apartments
Lochyside, Fort William
Inverness-shire PH33 7NY

Mountquhanie Holiday Homes
Cupar, Fife KY15 4QJ

Mr A C Oag
The Lodge, Dalmore, Alness
Ross-shire IV17 0UY

Mr M R Fraser
Reelig Glen Estate, Reelig House
Kirkhill, Inverness-shire
IV5 7PR

Mrs C H Grant
Logie, 16 Craig na Gower Ave
Aviemore, Inverness-shire
PH22 1RW

Mrs C H Struthers
Ardmaddy Castle Holiday Cottages
Ardmaddy, Argyll PA34 4QY

Mrs Haggart
Hillhead Cottages, Bodachra Farm
Dyce, Aberdeen, Aberdeenshire
AB2 0AQ

Mrs M E C Ferrier
Balvatin Cottages, Perth Road
Newtonmore, Inverness-shire
PH20 1BB

Mrs M Riach
Corronich, Boat of Garten
Inverness-shire PH24 3BN

Outlook
Avielochan Farm, Aviemore
Inverness-shire PH22 1QD

Scottish College of Textiles
Netherdale, Galashiels TD1 3HE

Seabraes Hall, Duncan House and Lodge,.Roseangle, Dundee
Angus

Sealladh-Ard-Innis
Rhiconich Hotel, Rhiconich
Sutherland IV27 4RN

Speyside Holiday Houses
Nethybridge, Inverness-shire
IV36 ONL

Stronchullin Holiday Cottages
Ardentinny, by Dunoon
Argyll PA23 8TP

Tanaree & Dykeside
Logie Newton, Huntly
Aberdeenshire AB5 6BB

Templar's Cottage
Kinermony Ltd, by Aberlour
Morayshire AB38 9NR

The Chalets
Gord, Cunningsburgh
Shetland

The Old School Cottage
Pouton Farm
Garlieston, Newton Stewart
Wigtownshire DG8 8HH

The Reed and The Toftin
Lairdie Lowes Steading
2 Losset Road, Alyth
Perthshire PH11 8BT

The Schoolhouse
Tombuie, Aberfeldy, Perthshire
PH15 2JS

The Shieling
Aberfeldy Road, Killin Perthshire
FK21 8TX

The Smiddy
Glasserton, by Whithorn
Galloway DG8 8NB

The Welton of Kingoldrum
Kingoldrum, by Kirriemuir
Angus DD8 5HY

The Willows
Cambus O'May, by Ballater
Aberdeenshire AB3 5SD

Thornielee Vale
Near Clovenfords, by Galashiels
Selkirkshire TD1 3LN

Tipperwhig & Brankam
Purgavie Farm, Glenisla
by Kirriemuir, Angus
DD8 5HZ

Tulloch Holiday Lodges
Rafford, Forres, Moray
IV36 0RU

Woodvale Cottage
Penifiler, Portree, Isle of Skye
IV51 9NF

Index
By Location

Area codes

2–40	A	South of Scotland
41–60	B	Edinburgh and Lothians
61–70	C	Greater Glasgow and Clyde Valley
71–126	D	West Highlands and Islands, Loch Lomond, Stirling and Trossachs
127–174	E	Perthshire, Angus and Dundee and the Kingdom of Fife
175–205	F	Grampian Highlands, Aberdeen and the North East Coast
206–302	G	The Highlands and Skye
303–316	H	Outer Islands

Location	Area code	Page no.
Abbey St Bathans by Duns	A	8
Aberchirder by Huntly	F	181
Aberdeen	F	181
Aberdour	E	133
Aberfeldy	E	133
Aberfoyle	D	77
Aberlady	B	47
Aberlour	F	182
Aboyne	F	183
Abriachan	G	212
Acharacle	G	212
Acharn by Kenmore	E	135
Achiltibuie	G	212
Achmore	G	214
Ae	A	8
Alford	F	184
Alloway	A	8
Alyth	E	135
Annbank	A	8
Anstruther	E	136
Appin	D	77
Arbroath	E	136
Archiestown	F	184
Ardelve by Dornie	G	214
Arden	D	78
Ardentinny by Dunoon	D	79
Ardfern	D	79
Ardgay	G	215
Ardhasaig	H	309
Ardnamurchan	G	215
Ardrishaig by Lochgilphead	D	79
Ardross	G	216
Arduaine	D	80
Ardvasar, Sleat	G	284
Arisaig	G	217
Armadale, Sleat	G	284
Arnprior by Kippen	D	80
Aros	D	109
Ashkirk	A	11
Assynt	G	218
Auchterarder	E	136
Auchtermuchty	E	137
Auldearn by Nairn	G	218
Aultbea	G	218
Aviemore	G	219
Avoch by Fortrose	G	224
Ayr	A	12
Badachro	G	225
Ballantrae	A	13
Ballater	F	184
Ballindalloch	F	186
Balloch	D	80
Ballygrant	D	95
Balquhidder	D	81
Balvicar	D	82
Banchory	F	186
Banff	F	188
Bankfoot	E	137
Barr by Girvan	A	13
Bearsden	C	67
Beauly	G	227
Benderloch by Oban	D	82
Berneray	H	312
Bernisdale by Portree	G	284
Bettyhill	G	228
Birsay	H	313
Blair Atholl	E	137
Blairgowrie	E	139
Boat of Garten	G	228
Borve by Portree	G	285
Bowden by Melrose	A	13
Bowmore	D	95
Braemar	F	188
Breakish	G	285
Bridge of Allan	D	82
Bridge of Cally	E	141
Bridge of Earn	E	142
Bridgend	D	96
Broadford	G	286
Brodick	A	8
Brora	G	230
Bruichladdich	D	96
Buchlyvie	D	82
Buckie	F	189
Bunessan	D	109
Burnside By Forfar	E	141
Cairndow	D	83
Cairnie by Huntly	F	190
Cairnryan	A	14
Calgary	D	110
Callander	D	83
Calvine	E	142
Cambuslang	C	67

Location	Area code	Page no.
Campbeltown	D	83
Camus Croise, Isleornsay	G	287
Cannich	G	230
Carbost by Portnalong	G	287
Carbost by Portree	G	291
Carmichael	C	67
Carnoustie	E	142
Carradale	D	83
Carrbridge	G	232
Carron	F	190
Carsphairn	A	14
Castle Douglas	A	14
Catrine	A	15
Cawdor	G	232
Clachamish by Portree	G	288
Claddach Kirkibost	H	312
Clovenfords by Galashiels	A	16
Clynder	D	86
Cockburnspath	A	16
Coldingham	A	16
Coldstream	A	17
Colmonell by Girvan	A	17
Colonsay Isle of	D	87
Colpy	F	190
Comrie	E	143
Contin	G	233
Corpach by Fort William	G	233
Corrie	A	9
Coupar Angus	E	144
Cowdenbeath	E	144
Craigellachie	F	190
Craigrothie by Cupar	E	144
Crail	E	144
Craobh Haven by Lochgilphead	D	87
Creetown	A	17
Crianlarich	D	88
Crieff	E	145
Crinan by Lochgilphead	D	89
Crocketford	A	18
Cromarty	G	233
Crossapol	D	89
Culbokie	G	234
Culkein	G	234
Cullen	F	190
Culnacnoc by Portree	G	288
Cupar	E	147
Dailly	A	19
Dalbeattie	A	19
Dalcross by Inverness	G	234
Dalkeith	B	47
Dalmally	D	89
Dalry by Castle Douglas	A	19
Daviot	G	234
Deerness	H	313
Dervaig	D	110
Diabaig	G	235
Dingwall	G	235
Dinnet by Aboyne	F	191
Dolphinton West Linton	A	20
Dores	G	236
Dornie by Kyle of Lochalsh	G	236
Dornoch	G	236
Drumnadrochit	G	236
Dufftown	F	192
Dulnain Bridge by Grantown-on-Spey	G	238
Dumfries	A	20
Dunbar	B	47
Dunbeath	G	239
Dunblane	D	90
Duncanston	G	239
Dundee	E	148
Dundonnell	G	239
Dunkeld	E	148
Dunning	E	149
Dunoon	D	90
Dunshalt	E	150
Dunure by Ayr	A	20
Dunvegan	G	288
Durness	G	240
Dykehead Cortachy	E	150
Earsary	H	309
Easdale by Oban	D	91
Edinburgh	B	48
Edzell	E	150
Eigg Isle of	G	240
Elgin	F	192
Elie	E	150
Embo	G	240
Ettrick Valley	A	21
Evanton	G	240
Fairlie	A	21
Falkirk	D	91
Fearnan by Kenmore	E	151
Feshie Bridge by Kincraig	G	241
Findhorn	F	193
Findochty	F	193
Finsbay	H	309
Finstown	H	313
Fintry	D	92
Fionnphort	D	111
Firth	H	314
Flodabay	H	309
Fochabers	F	194
Ford by Lochgilphead	D	92
Forfar	E	151
Forgandenny	E	151
Forres	F	194
Fort Augustus	G	241
Fort William	G	242
Fortingall	E	152
Fortrose	G	242
Foss by Pitlochry	E	152
Foulden	A	21
Foyers	G	246
Fraserburgh	F	194
Gairloch	G	246
Galashiels	A	22
Gardenstown	F	195

Index
By Location

Area codes

2–40	A	South of Scotland	127–174	E	Perthshire, Angus and Dundee and the Kingdom of Fife
41–60	B	Edinburgh and Lothians	175–205	F	Grampian Highlands, Aberdeen and the North East Coast
61–70	C	Greater Glasgow and Clyde Valley	206–302	G	The Highlands and Skye
71–126	D	West Highlands and Islands, Loch Lomond, Stirling and Trossachs	303–316	H	Outer Islands

Location	Area code	Page no.
Garlieston	A	22
Gartocharn	D	93
Gatehouse of Fleet	A	22
Girvan	A	23
Glamis	E	152
Glasgow	C	67
Glen Strathfarrar by Beauly	G	249
Glen Urquhart	G	250
Glencoe	G	248
Glendale	G	289
Glendaruel	D	93
Glenelg	G	248
Glenesk by Edzell	E	152
Glenfarg	E	153
Glenferness	G	249
Glenisla	E	154
Glenlivet	F	196
Glenlyon	E	154
Glenmore Ardnamurchan	G	249
Glenshee	E	154
Golspie	G	250
Gott Bay	D	125
Grantown-on-Spey	G	250
Greenock	C	69
Gretna	A	24
Gruinard Bay	G	253
Gruinart Bridgend	D	97
Gruline	D	111
Guthrie by Forfar	E	155
Haddington	A	58
Hamilton	C	69
Hawick	A	24
Helmsdale	G	253
Holm	H	314
Hopeman	F	197
Humbie	B	58
Huntly	F	197
Inchmurrin		
Island of, Loch Lomond	D	93
Inchnadamph	G	253
Innerwick by Dunbar	B	59
Insh	G	253
Inver by Tain	G	254
Inveraray	D	93
Inverbeg	D	95
Invergarry	G	254
Inverinate by Kyle of Lochalsh	G	255
Invermoriston	G	256
Inverness	G	256
Inveruglas	D	95
Inverurie	F	198
Isle of Seil	D	100
Isle of Tiree	D	125
Jedburgh	A	25
John O'Groats	G	258
Keith	F	198
Kelso	A	25
Kelty	E	155
Kemnay	F	198
Kenmore	E	155
Kensaleyre by Portree	G	290
Kentallen by Appin	G	258
Kilchoan Ardnamurchan	G	259
Kilchoman	D	97
Killiechronan	D	112
Killiecrankie	E	156
Killin	D	100
Killundine	G	259
Kilmarnock	A	27
Kilmartin by Lochgilphead	D	103
Kilmelford by Oban	D	103
Kilmichael Glen		
by Lochgilphead	D	105
Kilmuir	G	290
Kilmun by Dunoon	D	105
Kilninver by Oban	D	106
Kincraig by Kingussie	G	259
Kingsbarns	E	156
Kingston-on-Spey by Elgin	F	198
Kingussie	G	261
Kinloch Rannoch	E	157
Kinlocheil by Fort William	G	261
Kinlochewe	G	261
Kinlochlaggan		
by Newtonmore	G	262
Kinlochspelve	D	112
Kinross	E	157
Kintore	F	199
Kippford by Dalbeattie	A	28
Kirkcudbright	A	28

Location	Area code	Page no.
Kirkhill by Inverness	G	262
Kirkmichael	E	158
Kirkoswald	A	28
Kirkwall	H	314
Kirriemuir	E	158
Kishorn	G	263
Kyle of Lochalsh	G	263
Kyleakin	G	290
Kylesku	G	264
Laggan Bridge by Newtonmore	G	264
Laggan by Newtonmore	G	264
Laide	G	264
Lairg	G	266
Lamlash	A	10
Lanark	C	69
Largs	A	29
Laxdale	H	310
Lendalfoot by Girvan	A	30
Lentran	G	266
Lerags by Oban	D	106
Lerwick	H	316
Leuchars	E	159
Linlithgow	B	58
Loch Maree	G	271
Lochawe	D	106
Lochcarron	G	266
Lochdon	D	112
Lochearnhead	D	107
Lochgilphead	D	107
Lochgoilhead	D	107
Lochinver	G	268
Lochmaben	A	30
Lochmaddy	H	312
Lochportain	H	313
Lochs	H	310
Lochwinnoch	C	69
Lockerbie	A	30
Logie Coldstone by Aboyne	F	199
Longformacus	A	30
Lossiemouth	F	199
Luib by Broadford	G	290
Luss	D	107
Machrihanish	D	108
Maddiston	D	108
Mallaig	G	271
Maybole	A	31
Meigle	E	159
Melrose	A	31
Melvich	G	272
Memsie by Fraserburgh	F	200
Methven by Perth	E	159
Millport	A	18
Minard by Inveraray	D	108
Minto	A	32
Moffat	A	32
Moniaive	A	33
Monymusk	F	200
Mordington	A	33
Muckhart	D	109
Nairn	G	272
Nethy Bridge	G	273
New Galloway	A	33
New Lanark by Lanark	C	70
Newmilns	A	33
Newport-on-Tay	E	160
Newtonmore	G	276
Newton Stewart	A	33
Nibon by Hillswick	H	312
North Ballachulish	G	277
North Berwick	B	59
North Boisdale	H	316
North Connel	D	115
North Kessock	G	277
North Queensferry	E	160
Oban	D	115
Old Kilpatrick	C	70
Oldmeldrum	F	201
Ollaberry	H	316
Onich by Fort William	G	278
Ord Sleat	G	290
Orinsay Lochs	H	311
Otter Ferry	D	119
Parton by Castle Douglas	A	34
Peebles	A	34
Pennan	F	201
Pennyghael	D	113
Perth	E	160
Peterhead	F	202
Pirnmill	A	11
Pitlochry	E	162
Pittenweem	E	167
Plockton	G	279
Point	H	311
Poolewe	G	280
Port Bannatyne	D	83
Port Charlotte	D	97
Port Ellen	D	98
Port William	A	00
Port of Menteith	D	119
Portavadie	D	119
Portknockie	F	202
Portmahomack	G	281
Portpatrick	A	35
Portree	G	291
Portsoy	F	202
Port William	A	36
Prestwick	A	36
Raasay Isle of	G	281
Rannoch Station	E	167
Ratagan	G	281
Reay	G	282
Rendall	H	314
Rhynie	F	203
Ringford	A	36
Roag by Dunvegan	G	288
Rockcliffe by Dalbeattie	A	36
Rogart	G	282
Romanno Bridge	A	36
Rosemarkie	G	282

Index
By Location

Area codes

2–40	A	South of Scotland
41–60	B	Edinburgh and Lothians
61–70	C	Greater Glasgow and Clyde Valley
71–126	D	West Highlands and Islands, Loch Lomond, Stirling and Trossachs
127–174	E	Perthshire, Angus and Dundee and the Kingdom of Fife
175–205	F	Grampian Highlands, Aberdeen and the North East Coast
206–302	G	The Highlands and Skye
303–316	H	Outer Islands

Establishment	Location	Area code	Page no.
Rothes		F	203
Rothesay		D	83
Rowardennan		D	119
Roy Bridge		G	282
Salen Aros		D	113
Saltcoats		A	36
Sanday		H	315
Sandhead		A	36
Sandyhills by Dalbeattie		A	38
Scarfskerry		G	283
Scarinish		D	126
Scone by Perth		E	173
Scourie		G	283
Seamill		A	38
Seilebost		H	309
Shielbridge		G	283
Shieldaig		G	283
Shiskine		A	11
Skelmorlie		A	38
Skipness		D	121
South Queensferry		B	60
Southerness		A	38
Spean Bridge		G	294
Spey Bay		F	203
Spittal of Glenshee		E	174
St Andrews		E	167
St Catherines		D	120
St Fillans		E	172
St Margaret's Hope		H	315
St Monans		E	172
Stirling		D	121
Stoer		G	295
Stonehaven		F	204
Stornoway		H	311
Straiton by Maybole		A	38
Stranraer		A	39
Strathconon		G	296
Strathdon		F	204
Strathpeffer		G	296
Strathyre		D	122
Stromeferry		G	297
Stromness		H	315
Strontian		G	297
Struan by Dunvegan		G	292
Sumburgh		H	316
Tain		G	298
Talmine		G	298
Tarbert		H	310
Tarbert Loch Fyne		D	122
Tarbet by Arrochar		D	123
Tarland		F	204
Tarskavaig		G	292
Tayinloan by Tarbert		D	123
Taynuilt		D	124
Tayport		E	174
Tayvallich		D	125
Thurso		G	298
Tiree Isle of		D	126
Tobermory		D	114
Tomacharrick		G	299
Tomatin		G	299
Tomintoul		F	205
Tongue		G	299
Torridon		G	299
Torrin by Broadford		G	293
Tote Skeabost Bridge		G	293
Troon		A	39
Tummel Bridge		E	174
Turriff		F	205
Tyndrum by Crianlarich		D	126
Uig		G	293
Ullapool		G	293
Waternish		G	293
West Calder		B	60
West Linton		A	40
Westray		H	315
Westruther by Gordon		A	40
Whitebridge		G	302
Whitehills by Banff		F	205
Whiting Bay		A	8
Wick		G	302
Wiston		C	70
Wormit		E	174
Yetholm by Kelso		A	40

Books
To Help You

The Scottish Tourist Board produces a series of four accommodation guides to help you choose your holiday accommodation. The most comprehensive guides on the market, they give details of facilities, price, location and every establishment in them carries a quality assurance award from the Scottish Tourist Board.

SCOTLAND: HOTELS & GUEST HOUSES 1999 £9.50 (incl. p&p)

Over 1,400 entries, listing a variety of hotels and guest houses throughout Scotland. Also includes inns, lodges, restaurant with rooms, bed and breakfasts, campus accommodation, serviced apartments and international resort hotels. Comprehensive location maps. Completely revised each year. Full colour throughout.

SCOTLAND: BED & BREAKFAST 1999 £6.50 (incl. p&p)

Over 1,700 enties, listing a variety of bed and breakfast establishments throughout Scotland. Also incledes hotels, guest houses, inns, lodges, restaurant with rooms and campus accommodation. Comprehensive location maps. Completely revised each year.

SCOTLAND: CARAVAN & CAMPING PARKS 1999 £4.50 (incl. p&p)

Over 200 entries, listing caravan parks and individual caravan holiday homes for hire. Includes self-catering properties. Comprehensive location maps. Completely revised each year.

SCOTLAND: SELF CATERING 1999 £7.00 (incl. p&p)

Over 1,100 entries, listing cottages, flats, chalets, log cabins and serviced apartments to let. Many in scenic areas or bustling towns and cities. Caravan holiday homes included. Comprehensive location maps. Completely revised each year. Full colour throughout.

TOURING GUIDE TO SCOTLAND £6.00 (incl. p&p)

A new, fully revised edition of this popular guide which now lists over 1,500 things to do and places to visit in Scotland. Easy to use index and locator maps. Details of opening hours, admission charges, ageneral description and information on disabled access.

TOURING MAP OF SCOTLAND £4.00 (incl. p&p)

A new and up-to-date touring map of Scotland. Full colour with comprehensive motorway and road information, the map details over 20 categories of tourist information and names over 1,500 things to do and places to visit in Scotland

You can order any of the above by filling in the coupon or by telephone.

ORDER FORM ON NEXT PAGE

Publications
Order Form

Mail Order

Please tick the publications you would like, cut out this section and send it with your cheque, postal order (made payable to Scottish Tourist Board) or credit card details to:
Scottish Tourist Board, FREEPOST, Dunoon, Argyll PA23 8PQ

Scotland: Hotels & Guest Houses 1999 ______ **£9.50** (incl. P&P) ☐

Scotland: Bed & Breakfast 1999 ______ **£6.50** (incl. P&P) ☐

Scotland: Camping & Caravan Parks 1999 ______ **£4.50** (incl. P&P) ☐

Scotland: Self Catering 1999 ______ **£7.00** (incl. P&P) ☐

Touring Guide to Scotland ______ **£6.00** (incl. P&P) ☐

Touring Map of Scotland ______ **£4.00** (incl. P&P) ☐

BLOCK CAPITALS PLEASE:

NAME (Mr/Mrs/Ms) ______

ADDRESS ______

______

POST CODE ______ TELEPHONE NO. ______

TOTAL REMITTANCE ENCLOSED £ ______

PLEASE CHARGE MY *VISA/ACCESS ACCOUNT (*delete as appropriate)

Card No.																	Expiry Date				

Signature ______

Date ______

Telephone Orders

To order BY PHONE: simply call free 08705 511511 (national call rate) quoting the books you would like and give your credit card details.

Notes

Notes

Notes

Notes